GLOBAL PRIVATE INTERNATIONAL LAW

Global Private International Law

Adjudication without Frontiers

Edited by

Horatia Muir Watt

Professor of Law, SciencesPo Law School, Paris, France

Lucia Bíziková

Training to become a solicitor in an international law firm in London, UK

Agatha Brandão de Oliveira

Guest Lecturer, Federal University of Espirito Santo (UFES), Brazil and Member of the Brazilian Bar

Diego P. Fernández Arroyo

Professor of Law, SciencesPo Law School, Paris, France

Edward Elgar
PUBLISHING

Cheltenham, UK • Northampton, MA, USA

Published by
Edward Elgar Publishing Limited
The Lypiatts
15 Lansdown Road
Cheltenham
Glos GL50 2JA
UK

Edward Elgar Publishing, Inc.
William Pratt House
9 Dewey Court
Northampton
Massachusetts 01060
USA

A catalogue record for this book
is available from the British Library

Library of Congress Control Number: 2018959288

This book is available electronically in the **Elgar**online
Law subject collection
DOI 10.4337/9781788119238

Printed on elemental chlorine free (ECF)
recycled paper containing 30% Post-Consumer Waste

ISBN 978 1 78811 922 1 (cased)
ISBN 978 1 78811 923 8 (eBook)

Typeset by Columns Design XML Ltd, Reading
Printed and bound in the USA

Contents

Contributors

Filipe Antunes Madeira da Silva is a Doctoral candidate at SciencesPo Law School, Paris. He works on international law, history of international law and law and development, focusing on processes of natural resources extraction in the Latin American context.

Simon Archer is the Co-Director of the Centre for Comparative Research in Law and Political Economy at Osgoode Hall Law School, York University and practices law with Goldblatt Partners LLP in Toronto, Canada.

Catalina Avasilencei is a Lecturer at the French-Romanian Law College of European Studies (Sorbonne Law School – Paris 1 Panthéon-Sorbonne) and an Associate Researcher at the Regional Francophone Centre for Advanced Research in Social Sciences (Cerefrea). She holds a PhD from the Sorbonne Law School and is a member of the Bucharest Bar.

Paul Schiff Berman is the Walter S. Cox Professor of Law at The George Washington University Law School. He is the author of over 50 scholarly works, including *Global Legal Pluralism: A Jurisprudence of Law Beyond Borders*, published in 2012 by Cambridge University Press.

George A. Bermann is a Professor of Law and the Director of the Center for International Commercial and Investment Arbitration, Columbia Law School, and professeur affilié, École de droit, SciencesPo, Paris.

Régis Bismuth is a Professor at SciencesPo Law School and Director of Studies of the French Branch of the International Law Association.

Lucia Bíziková holds a Masters degree from SciencesPo Law School (cum laude) and an LL.M. degree from the University of Cambridge, where she specialised in International Law. She is training to become a solicitor in an international law firm in London, UK.

Sylvain Bollée is a Professor of Law at the Sorbonne Law School (Paris 1 Panthéon-Sorbonne University). He is a specialist in international arbitration and transnational litigation, international business law and private international law.

Jacco Bomhoff is an Associate Professor of Law at the London School of Economics and Political Science (LSE).

Sandrine Brachotte is a PhD Researcher at SciencesPo Law School. She specialises in private international law, international arbitration, and human rights.

Agatha Brandão de Oliveira is a guest lecturer in Private International Law at Federal University of Espírito Santo and practices law as a member of the Brazilian bar.

Hannah Buxbaum is a Professor of Law and the John E. Schiller Chair at Indiana University Maurer School of Law. She specialises in international jurisdiction and international litigation.

Laura Carballo Piñeiro is a Professor and the Nippon Foundation Chair at the World Maritime University, Associate Professor of Private international law at the University of Santiago de Compostela (currently on leave) and Alexander von Humboldt Fellow. This chapter has benefited from the Spanish research project DER2016-80568-R, Xunta de Galicia and FEDER.

Christelle Chalas is a Lecturer at the University Paris 8 Vincennes-Saint Denis, qualified to supervise academic research (HDR). She specialises in private international law and issues related to international jurisdiction and family law.

Dagmar Coester-Waltjen LL.M. (University of Michigan), Dr. iur. (Christian-Albrechts-University Kiel) Dr. h.c. (University Zurich), Professor Emerita of the Georg-August-University Goettingen, founding director of the "Lichtenberg Kolleg" (an institute of advanced study of the University of Goettingen), from 1988–2008 Professor at the Institute for International Law of the Ludwig-Maximilian-University of Munich.

Giuditta Cordero-Moss PhD (Moscow), Dr.juris (Oslo), is a Professor at the University of Oslo, Norway. She specialises in private international law, international commercial law, arbitration and comparative contract law.

Sabine Corneloup is a Professor at Paris II Panthéon-Assas University and secretary general of the Revue critique de droit international privé. Her main areas of research are private international law and migration.

Fabio Costa Morosini is an Associate Professor at the Federal University of Rio Grande do Sul School of Law and a research fellow at the National Council of Scientific and Technological Development (CNPq, Ministry of Science and Technology, Brazil). Specialises in international economic law.

Gilles Cuniberti is a Professor of private international law and comparative law at the University of Luxembourg.

Jennifer Daskal is an Associate Professor of Law at American University Washington College of Law, where she teaches and writes in the fields of criminal, national security, and constitutional law. She was an Open Society Institute Fellow from 2016 to 2017, working on issues related to privacy, surveillance, and law enforcement access to data across borders. Daskal also spent two years as counsel to the Assistant Attorney General for National Security at the Department of Justice.

Jean d'Aspremont is a Professor of International Law at SciencesPo Law School and University of Manchester.

Sara Dezalay is a Senior Lecturer in International Law and International Relations at the Cardiff School of Law and Politics and Senior Researcher at the Global Justice Lab, Munk School of Global Affairs, University of Toronto.

Richard Fentiman is a Professor of Private International Law at the University of Cambridge.

Diego P. Fernández Arroyo is a Professor at SciencesPo Law School and a member of the Curatorium of the Hague Academy of International Law.

Tomaso Ferrando is a Lecturer in Law at the University of Bristol Law School and member of the Global Legal Action Network legal committee. Holds a PhD from SciencesPo Law School. His research focuses on the interaction between law and the construction of the global food regime.

Samuel Fulli-Lemaire is a Senior Research Fellow at the Max Planck Institute for Comparative and International Private Law (Hamburg). He holds a PhD in Private International Law from Panthéon-Assas (Paris II) University.

Uglješa Grušić is an Associate Professor at the Faculty of Laws of University College London where he teaches private international law, international arbitration and the law of tort.

Hisashi Harata is a Professor, Faculty of Law and Political Science, The University of Tokyo. His main fields of research include Private International Law, Legal History, International Arbitration, and International Corporate Law.

Ludovic Hennebel is a Professor at Aix-en-Provence Law School, director of the Institute of International Humanitarian Studies and of Aix Global Justice Legal Clinic, and a member of the CERIC (Aix-Marseille University) and of the Center Perelman of Legal Philosophy.

Jeremy Heymann is a tenured (full) Professor of Private International Law and International Trade Law at the University of Lyon (Lumière).

Vitor Henrique Pinto Ido is a PhD Candidate in Law, University of São Paulo and Researcher at Fundação Getúlio Vargas – FGV/SP.

Patrick Kinsch practises law as a member of the Luxembourg bar. He also teaches private international law as a professor at the University of Luxembourg.

Hayk Kupelyants is the Clifford Chance Lecturer in the Conflict of Laws at the University of Cambridge and a fellow of Homerton College.

Katja Langenbucher holds a full professorship for Private Law, Corporate and Financial Law in Goethe-University's House of Finance and is an affiliated professor at SciencesPo, Paris.

Franck Latty is a Professor at Paris Nanterre University and Director of Nanterre Center of International Law (CEDIN). He is also the Secretary General of the French Branch of the International Law Association (ILA) and author of numerous writings on public international law, investment arbitration and international sports law.

Oona Le Meur is a PhD candidate at the SciencesPo Law School. Her research focuses on customary law in New-Caledonia as a way to question more generally speaking the identity-making and nation-building processes.

Gregory Lewkowicz is a Professor at Université Libre de Bruxelles and Visiting Professor at the Goethe University of Frankfurt and SciencesPo, Paris. He is the A. Koyré Chair in Business Law & Artificial Intelligence at the Université of Nice Sophia Antipolis. He is director of research on 'Global Law' at the Perelman Centre for Legal Philosophy and President of the European Incubator of the Brussels Bar Association.

François-Xavier Licari is an Associate Professor at the University of Lorraine, France. As a scholar working for many years in the field of comparative law, he is focusing his research on legal hybridity. More recently, he has developed a strong interest for Jewish law and religious legal theory.

Fabien Marchadier is a Professor at the University of Poitiers. His fields of research are Private International Law, European Human Rights law and Animal Law.

Toni Marzal is a Lecturer at the University of Glasgow School of Law. He specialises in EU law, private international law and comparative law.

Ralf Michaels is the Arthur Larson Professor of Law at Duke University. His research focuses especially on methodological questions of private international law and comparative law, as well as the theory of law under conditions of globalisation.

Alex Mills is a Professor of Public and Private International Law at the Faculty of Laws, University College London (UCL).

Horatia Muir Watt is a Professor at SciencesPo Law School, Paris.

Nathalie Najjar Ph.D, Attorney at law, Managing Partner at Ibrahim Najjar law firm, Lecturer at the Faculty of law of Saint Joseph University (Beirut) and at the University Paris II, Panthéon-Assas, Chairman ICC-Lebanon, Arbitration Commission.

Etienne Pataut is a Professor of private law at the Sorbonne Law School (University Paris 1). He is a specialist in Private International Law and European Law and takes particular interest in the social aspects of globalisation, on which he has extensively written.

David Restrepo Amariles is an Assistant Professor of International Arbitration and Jurisprudence at HEC Paris. He is the Director of research on 'legal metrics and Smart Law' at HEC Paris and an Associate Researcher at the Perelman Centre for Legal Philosophy (ULB).

Darren Rosenblum is a Professor of law at Pace University. His research examines the effect of gender equality on corporate governance in transnational contexts.

Calixto Salomão Filho is a Professor of Law at the University of São Paulo Law School and a Professor at SciencesPo Law School, Paris.

Michelle Sanchez Badin is a Professor at Getúlio Vargas Foundation São Paulo School of Law, Brazil. Her research and teaching are mainly in the field of International Economic Law.

Jérôme Sgard is a Professor of Political Economy at SciencesPo. His research deals primarily with the construction and regulation of markets, as seen through the prism of agents, micro-level rules and dispute resolution: sovereign debt restructuring, private bankruptcies, international commercial arbitration, litigation in the nineteenth century French commercial courts.

David Sindres is an Agrégé des Facultés de Droit, Professor of Private Law at the University of Angers and lecturer at SciencesPo Law School. He specialises in Private International Law and International Trade Law.

Elsa Supiot is a Lecturer of private law at University Paris I Panthéon-Sorbonne. She is also a Member of the Norms, Sciences and Techniques Centre of the Institut of the Legal and Philosophic Sciences (Centre Normes, Sciences et Techniques de l'Institut des Sciences Juridique et Philosophique).

Chris Thomale holds a PhD from Free University Berlin and an LL.M. from Yale Law School. As an Associate Professor at the University of Heidelberg, he specialises in private international, comparative and corporate law.

Kellen Trilha is a Research fellow and has been a contract lecturer in International Law at the Bocconi University, Milan, since 2015. She holds a Ph.D. from the SciencesPo Law School, Paris.

Hans van Loon is an independent consultant. He was the Secretary General of the Hague Conference on Private International Law from 1996–2013.

Jinske Verhellen is a Professor of law at Ghent University, lecturing private international law and international family law. She has published on various aspects of private international law, migration and nationality law.

Mark Weidemaier is the Ralph M. Stockton, Jr. Distinguished Professor of Law at the University of North Carolina at Chapel Hill. His areas of specialisation involve the intersection between contracts and dispute resolution in domestic and international settings, as well as issues related to the structure and enforcement of government debt.

Michael Wells-Greco is an Assistant Professor, Maastricht University and a Solicitor of the Senior Courts of England and Wales.

Acknowledgements

This project would not have been possible without the energy and dedication not only of the editorial team and the contributors themselves, who were mindful of the complicated logistics of managing so many texts and authors at once, but also of Megan Ma and her team of student translators, who leaped into action in a very short space of time in order to translate the texts that were not submitted in English. The names of the translators are indicated in each of the relevant texts. Thanks are also due to SciencesPo Law School, whose help with the funding of the PILAGG project facilitated the three year cycle of seminars which gave rise to this book.

Reflections contained in this book and all the cases discussed herein reflect developments as of 1 March 2018.

Table of cases

INTERNATIONAL

Court of Arbitration for Sport (CAS)

Court of Justice of the European Union

European Court of Human Rights

International Centre for Settlement of Investment Disputes (ICSID)

International Court of Justice

Permanent Court of International Justice

UNCITRAL, Permanent Court of Arbitation

WTO Appellate Body

NATIONAL

Argentina

Australia

Austria

Belgium

Brazil

Canada

Ecuador

France

Germany

India

Japan

Luxembourg

Netherlands

Papua New Guinea

Switzerland

United Kingdom

United States of America

Table of legislation

INTERNATIONAL

Multilateral

Bilateral

European Union

NATIONAL

Austria

Bolivia

Brazil

Cambodia

China

Ecuador

France

Germany

Introduction

The inspiration for this case-book comes from over a decade of attempts to teach private international law to Masters students in a comparative and interdisciplinary perspective. The project was made possible thanks to the readiness of over 50 contributors from diverse cultural origins and disciplinary horizons to take part in what can be seen as an academic and pedagogical experiment. In this respect, it is an attempt to respond to essentially two sorts of 'case-book failures'. While there are many unquestionably excellent textbooks and assemblages of materials on private international law relevant to specific national contexts or geographical regions, the field lacks any collection of cases illustrating the specific role of private international law in the context of globalisation and indeed, reciprocally, the impact of globalisation on private international law. This book retains an open and largely intuitive understanding of the global, in line with the experimental vein in which the project was conceived. However, various theoretical dimensions of the 'global turn' as relevant to private international law will be addressed below.[1]

The starting point, then, is the ever-increasing gap separating the conventional presentation of the various parts or functions of private international law (determination of the applicable law; issues of jurisdiction and judgments) and the ways in which contemporary societal, economic, technological or cognitive changes are inducing transformations in transnational adjudication and law-making beyond the State. The paradox underlying this gap is that the discipline deals, at core, with the very factors that have served as catalysts for these global phenomena, which in turn require some form of legal shape and discipline. Thus, for instance, it is the cross-border activity of non-State actors – the traditional remit of private international law – that has brought about the dis-embedding of economic relationships from their social environment. The discipline has facilitated and legitimized this trend either through a specific normative idea of party autonomy as regulatory immunity, or by ensuring a safe haven to corporate capital through a certain design of jurisdiction. This example shows that legal permissiveness weighs as heavily on outcomes as active intervention: the only

[1] Globalisation is understood here as the specific compression of time and space which coincides with late modernity (A. Giddens, *The Consequences of Modernity* (Cambridge, Polity Press 1991) esp. pp. 64); the coming of risk society (U. Beck, *La société du risque. Sur la voie d'une autre modernité* (Flammarion, Champs, Préface de B. Latour, 2008), global neo-liberal economics (of which it will be questioned below); the paradoxical 'return of science' (P. Pomper and D.G. Shaw (eds), *The Return of Science, Evolution, History, and Theory* (Oxford, Rowman & Littlefield 2002) in a period of increasing disbelief in the values of modernity; and, with particular relevance to international law (public and private), the 'liquidification' of sovereignty (Z. Baumont, *L'identité* (éd. de l'Herne, coll. Carnets, 2010). The theoretical aspects discussed in this introduction can be found in a more developed form in H. Muir Watt, 'Conflicts of Laws Unbounded: The Case for a Legal-Pluralist Revival' (2016) 7(3) *Transnational Legal Theory* pp. 313–53.

difference is that such outcomes look natural, as if legal regulation had nothing to do with them. The global as frontier-less and de-regulated space is of course as constructed as the boundaries and laws it purports to transcend.

At the same time, conventional assumptions in respect of the relevance of territory or geographical location, the characteristics of sovereignty, the architecture of the public international legal order, and more, are profoundly shaken by new understandings of geography, power and humanity's relationship to the planet. The 'global turn' has prompted a renewal of legal theory, in the direction of pluralism or societal constitutionalism, in which the stuff of private international law is nevertheless largely present – travelling persons, displaced populations, mobile capital, production chains, conflicting normativities … – but its specific tools and concepts are either ignored in a grand reinvention of the wheel, or disqualified as serving a parochial form of boundary custodianship. This case-book, then, is an attempt to measure the potential contribution of the discipline to the rethinking of legal-theoretical issues and to illustrate the significance in this context of specifically global cases.

The structure of the book, as indicated in detail below, proposes six terrains on which private international law has had to respond to the various novel legal issues and unprecedented challenges induced by the societal, geopolitical, economic changes that constitute the 'global turn'. One of the difficulties of this enterprise, however, is the extreme complexity and extent of the subject-area and the available sources. In this respect, the identification of the cases that qualify as 'global' is inevitably somewhat arbitrary and the selection that appears here is neither unquestionable nor exhaustive. Moreover, as legal theorists of the global turn have pointed out,[2] dealing in the global, rather than the local or the merely comparative, may involve, beyond a simple change of scale, a more radical transformation of perspective. A cartography of the global inevitably involves a degree of eclecticism and a lesser focus on legal technicalities; seen from afar, technical niceties that may take on an overriding importance in a domestic system tend to dwindle in significance, in comparison with the search for wider trends. Here, the criteria used to select the various cases are multiple and for a large part intuitive. Some bear witness to the contemporary complexity of multiple proceedings and various levels or types of jurisdiction, others cross the public/private divide in ways that are induced by the transformation of the sovereign State, while the remainder may involve dematerialized or de-territorialized activities, inter-cultural conflicts, or hybrid norms. We have attempted to cover a plurality of legal traditions, even though, admittedly, the sources remain predominantly Western (and we hope that future attempts will remedy this).

Practically, the book aims to help teachers of private international law to organise their classes around cases that are difficult to access, to assemble – and frequently even to understand, from a mono-disciplinary perspective. In this respect, therefore, it also attempts to respond to the need to relate private international law to its interdisciplinary environment. The design was to 'pair off' contributors who were interested in similar topics, while encouraging the expression of diverse and indeed divergent viewpoints. Moreover, the task that was set was not to cover all technical aspects of a

[2] M. Xifaras, 'The Global Turn in Legal Theory' (2016) 29 *Canadian Journal of Law & Jurisprudence* pp. 215–43.

given case (many have been annotated many times in conventional terms) – but to bring to bear a specific point of view (why *The Bremen* case, from back in the 1970s, was really the start of the global turn, and how it was actually misunderstood in context … why global value chains are important in understanding the ways in which global capitalism interacts with local cultures … why insights from legal pluralism can help understand issues of post-national personhood … and much more).

Contributors were asked to write short, focused texts. The editors provide summarized overviews of the facts and contexts. In this way, students will have access to a range of different ideas that they will then be free to develop, reject or research. The hope is that the end result will combine at least some of the advantages of three main cultural models of teaching and research materials: the American style case-book, on the one hand, which encourages questions and associations on the part of the student, rather than laying out the subject-matter dogmatically; on the other, the French civilian-style analysis of 'grands arrêts'[3] which provides intellectual guidance and internal critique but from solely the perspective of one, or one team, of scholars; finally, the German Grand Commentary (Restatement-style) of rules and principles, which brings out the systematicity of positive law more than it is designed to open avenues for deeper reflexion about its meaning within a bigger picture. With all this, the ultimate aim is to provide ideas for instructive classwork and stimulating research on the global dimensions of our discipline.

***

The structure of the book is designed to walk the student of private international law progressively through the various ordeals that test the conventional assumptions on which the discipline rests.

The first chapter assembles a set of cases that illustrate various judicial moves during the latter tiers of the twentieth century to push back the constraints of territory and adapt ideas about jurisdiction and procedure to the liberalisation of trade and capital. At that point, adjudication lost the reassuring horizon of the domestic frontier. While *The Bremen* opens the post-War era by allowing party choice of forum across the Atlantic, *Mitsubishi* shows its inevitable follow-up in terms of free moving (or free wheeling) judgments and awards. Cases such as *Chevron* and *Trafigura* illustrate the ensuing consequences in terms of unbridled forum shopping, whether reverse or otherwise, in which the courts become the place of a worldwide political struggle between multinational industries and local communities. Unsurprisingly, transnational class actions or mid-Atlantic settlements, as shown in the *Royal Dutch* case, have not yet provided an appropriate forum, nor indeed a convincing argument for the claims of legal technique over politics. However, even less spectacular disputes can take on an additional geo-political dimension, as can be seen in *Owusu*, which inaugurates a long pre-Brexit struggle between the English judiciary and the European Court of Justice for the soul of judicial discretion.

---

[3] See, for instance, B. Ancel and Y. Lequette, *Les Grands arrêts de la jurisprudence de droit international privé* 5th edn (Paris, Dalloz 2006).

The second chapter leads outside a State-centred framework into the emerging or increasingly visible world of multiple, informal normativities. These present radically different nature or ontologies, however, and should not be considered as raising identical questions or challenges for private international law. Indigenous norms and religion both highlight the presence of cultural conflicts and power struggles underlying more traditional conflict of laws, whether in the field of personal status or on the more unlikely terrain of economic disputes, as illustrated by *Song Mao* and *Jivraj*. However, in stark opposition to these conflicts involving cultural and individual identity, where a form of global legal pluralism seems to have a strong title to displace more traditional State-centric methodological tools and allow competing claims to legitimacy, cases such as *Fifa* and *Nike* are a reminder of the dangers that come with the temptation to jettison the legal-political theories that, although too hopelessly bound up in the idea of State, are nevertheless designed to protect some basic notion of the common good and collective responsibility.

The third chapter carries this idea through to cases that touch, more specifically, the changing structures of the global economy. That private international law supports the economic governance of global markets is confirmed by historical scholarship on the first modern ideas of empire.[4] But it is also largely implicated in the co-production of global supply chains, as evidenced in *Doe v Nestlé*; the private market for sovereign debt, as shown by the litigation initiated by the vulture *NML*; the astounding autonomy of financial markets revealed with the failure of *Lehmann Bros.*; or the new, accompanying marketisation of litigation as illustrated by *Samsung*. All of these novel figures raise significant transnational political and ethical issues for private international law, whose technologies are directly involved in creating the opacity offered by value chains in respect of the human rights violations committed by suppliers or sub-contractors, in the squeezing of populations through the action of vulture funds, or in the disastrous consequences of global financial crisis. Are there, then, new ways of thinking or doing law beyond the State that could reconnect the relevant legal tools with a more political horizon?

It is to this question that the fourth chapter attempts to respond, in revisiting the modes of reasoning that private international law traditionally offers. Can its tools and schemes of intelligibility help us take a qualitative jump into the brave new world of global law? The impression that comes out of the cases is distinctly one of a juridical dead-end. From across the Atlantic, *RJR Nabisco* leads us to question whether the recent return of the old grammar of territoriality/ extraterritoriality can usefully do the job. Can the reach of rights be defined in other terms, such as those of the scope of moral and political responsibility of public and private actors? The *Kiobel* case, perhaps the most commented and the most controversial of all those contained in this case-book, indicates that courts are not necessarily ready to follow in this direction, suggesting that it is more important to understand the political economy of the legal tools involved than their technical virtues. The *Lafonta* case is taken as a study of the ways in which interdisciplinary borrowing causes ideas to migrate from economics to law, lured by the promises of scientificity and a universal language. Using classical

[4] Notably, M. Koskenniemi, 'Empire and International Law: The Real Spanish Contribution' (2011) 61 *U Toronto LJ* 1.

tools of legal interpretation also leads to an intricate form of stalemate in the notorious *Dallah* conundrum, where courts proceeding as rationally as possible on either side of the English Channel end up by talking at cross-purposes. The *Petrobras* saga is the occasion to ask whether there is such a thing as a Mestizo *private* international law, a mirror image of its exciting public international counterpart in which the periphery secretes its own particular version of a doctrine that sprung initially from the center and served very different needs or strategies?[5] Data dominance, studied here through the *Yahoo!* case, suggests that the place of law itself among other modes of regulation, whether global or otherwise, is entering a twilight zone.

In this respect, chapter five attempts to take a hard look at the workings of global markets, through which capital flows freely to use the near-limitless supplies of labour and to channel equally abundant flows of commodities. The chapter highlights the deeper challenges below the smooth surface of uniform legal technique, where profound power struggles between myriads of interests cause ripples, lines and divisions to form on the face of globalizing legal forms.[6] The spectacular and widespread rise of the economic and social phenomenon of *Airbnb* is the opportunity to watch the operation of experimental contract governance in action, and at the same time observe how conventional battles between business and consumers over deregulation and arbitration play out anew. Similarly, the *Banco Santander* case is the occasion to see how private international law facilitates or co-produces the logic of financial markets, instituting inter-systemic arbitrage by financial players. Moreover, as the *Centros* case shows within the European Union, the free cross-border movement of corporations, or the free market for corporate charters, is the necessary corollary of liberalized flows of capital. However, the same context has witnessed the collision between the inexorable needs of free-moving financial capitalism and the immobile constituencies of employees: the *Laval* case directs our attention to the status of labour in the global market and reminds us of the imbalance of power that globalization increases far more than it reduces, by trapping labour into territory and local law while capital takes off on the wings of party autonomy, liberalized borders and metaphorical free movement.

Yet as the sixth and last chapter suggests, law retains a constitutive role in the consolidation of collective and individual identities, either by protecting or projecting certain conceptions of persons and personhood in their encounters with conflicting logics, or by carrying representations of community in the regulation of national borders and the correlative immigration controls. Thus, the past decade has seen a methodological tsunami in the field of family relationships. The polemical *Mennesson* surrogacy case provided the opportunity to define the status of the 'transnational' child, caught in the turmoil of conflicting national values and deprived of both citizenship and parentage. In turn, in the *Blood* affair concerning posthumous insemination, a restrictive local bioethical stance had to concede terrain to the imperative of free movement, while in *Wagner*, a similar outcome was reached on the terrain of international adoption in the name of the protection due to family relationships. These rulings must be read in

5 A. Becker Lorca, *Mestizo International Law. A global intellectual history 1842–1933* (Cambridge, CUP 2014).

6 P.G. Monateri, *Geopolitica del diritto* (Rome, Laterza 2013).

the wider context of immigration policies relating to the cross-border movement of populations, envisaged here through the *Manus Island* class action case. There appears here to be a profound tension between the collective, security-based, political discourse in the latter field that closes borders, and the liberalization of the legal regime applicable to individual, whose free cross-border movement is paramount, as shown in the case above.

***

Beyond its pedagogical ambition, this book is also an effort to plumb the discipline of private international law for its specific insights on some of the most significant issues that challenge contemporary legal theory in its attempts to integrate the radical changes wrought by globalisation in the normative landscape beyond (framed outside, or reaching over) the nation-State. Remarkably, one of the main features of the 'global legal paradigm'[7] – with its unfamiliar practices, forms and modes of legal consciousness – is that complex interactions of conflicting norms and social systems now occupy the centre-stage of jurisprudential debate. This means that private international law has a plausible vocation to contribute to a deeper understanding of law's forms and foundations beyond the State. Conversely, it also seems very clear that private international legal thinking has all to gain from attention to the other (legal and non-legal) disciplines that have preceded it in the effort to 'go global'. As many of the cases selected here demonstrate very well, new needs, contexts, or technologies call for a general conceptual overhauling in order to adjust existing epistemological and methodological tools to a transformed environment. Data-dominance, outsourced litigation, global supply chains or bio-technologies show traditional legal categories to be largely wanting. Furthermore, others call for a radical reconsideration of conventional assumptions about the foundations of authority or indeed the values that constitute law's normative horizon, as sovereignty is by-passed (with the paradoxical aid of State courts), or political authority displaced to the private sector.

Such an agenda is, of course, a very tall order for a modest case-book! However, in this respect, the project subscribes to an essentially pragmatic approach to global law, or law and globalisation, along the lines suggested by Benoît Frydmann;[8] it self-consciously 'takes a break' from theoretical pre-conceptions about the nature of legality beyond the State. This involves observing novel global phenomena, patterns of social interaction and identity-formation in order to understand how they both affect, and are constituted by, the law. Judicial cases in private international law are an excellent starting point in this respect, since not only do they provide a mass of empirical material illustrating situations that flow over territorial boundaries, but they also constitute the terrain on which law reaches out, or reacts in various ways, to the foreign, the different, the far-away or indeed the exoticised other. From there, it may be possible, inductively, to formulate theoretical hypotheses as to how globalization

7 R. Michaels, 'Globalisation and Law: Law Beyond the State' in R. Banakar and M. Travers (eds), *Law and Social Theory* 2nd edn (Oxford, Hart Publishing 2013) p. 287 s.

8 B. Frydmann, 'Comment penser le droit global?' Working Papers du Centre Perelman de Philosophie du Droit, 2012/01, available at <http://wwwphilodroit.be>.

transforms legal methods and content, within new patterns or 'chronotopes'[9] of space and time. However, any overall interpretation of all these cases put together, even on the sole terrain of the future of private international law, would obviously be over-ambitious in view of the multiple fields and issues involved, and imprudent, given that the selection is in no way exhaustive and the evolution sighted here or there, still in progress.

The following offers just two very tentative avenues of thought. One concerns the transformation of the idea of conflict itself as representations of law evolve in a global environment; the other relates, conversely, to the ways in which the ubiquity of conflict beyond or outside the State in turn transform the texture, the nature and the functions of law.

I. WHAT'S IN A CONFLICT?

Even a cursory glance at the selected cases suggests that norms meet, clash or combine, independently of state borders, according to multiple patterns of instable and recursive interaction in global context. Traditionally, private international law theorizes 'conflict' in terms of three distinct ideal types: thus, simultaneous assertions of jurisdiction in respect of a single situation or the issues to which it gives rise are understood as giving rise to either confrontation, cooperation or competition between the contending laws or legal systems. In this respect, the discipline's approach to the interactions between plural, conflicting norms naturally bears the marks of the great simplifications of modern law's mythology.[10] Conventionally, its main challenge was to grapple with sovereign monopoly over territory, in order to craft the ways in which the 'relevance'[11] of foreign systems might find expression despite the constraints of the legal framework imposed by public international law. With varying degrees of (im)plausibility, doctrines such as vested rights, transitory torts, the perception of foreign law as fact, were all attempts to by-pass the legal impregnability of nation-state boundaries. However, globalisation weakens the claim of these fictions to any plausible description of the post-national world, where 'interlegality' describes an endemic state of mutual irritation resulting from the intense circulation of people, assets, capital and ideas.[12]

Law (and particularly private international law) is necessarily transformed by the shape of the conflicts it generates and the ubiquity of friction. Indeed, as Neil Walker muses, the intimated features of 'global law' take on the dynamic, unstable and

---

9 M. Valverde, 'Jurisdiction and Scale: Legal "Technicalities" as Resources for Theory' (2009) 18 *Soc. & Legal Stud.* 139.

10 P. Fitzpatrick, *The Mythology of Modern Law* (London, Routledge, Chapman & Hall 1992).

11 This was the term used by Santi Romano to describe the relationships between social systems. At a time when the conflict of laws was dominated by a sovereignty paradigm, it was used to break through an overly formalist conception of the relationship between the legal systems, notably that of the forum and foreign law.

12 M. Amstutz, 'In-Between Worlds: *Marleasing* and the Emergence of Interlegality in Legal Reasoning' (2005) 11(6) *European Law Journal* 766–84.

recursive characteristics of the complex processes that it claims to capture.[13] Embracing instability, contingency, dynamics, disorder, polyarchy in its definition of interactions between normative orders, global-pluralist legal theory sees 'the state and the interstate system as complex social fields in which state and non-state, local and global social relations interact, merge and conflict in dynamic and even volatile combination'.[14] The vocabulary and the metaphors used to describe the transformations involved in the emerging legal paradigm are highly revealing. Collisions, interaction, merging, recursivity, interwoven diversity, mutual provocation, in-between worlds, irritations, interferences (understood in an electrical mode), disruptions, or distortions are all used to express multiple new patterns of encounters between legal systems. They fit the post-modern paradigm of the tentacular rhizome (Deleuze), the accelerated intensity of hyper-reality (Baudrillard).

This vision certainly suggests a richer understanding of the 'interminglings' between social systems than the three horizontal schemes of coordination, competition and confrontation to be found within the more conventional paradigm of the conflict of laws. Beyond its obvious focus on confrontation, the term 'conflict' – curiously understood to cover complementarity – does not adequately express mutual 'irritations' that set off a series of unpredictable and potentially far-reaching consequences when the internal make-up of each system differs.[15] Nor does an overly static vision do justice to the dynamics of these interactions with which, in practice, the conflict of laws itself has to cope in the form of strategic navigation by private actors of multiple regimes (from fiscal and investment regimes to familiar forum shopping for procedural tools). The notorious *Chevron* litigation included in this case-book provides the supreme example, promising a legal battle made of measures and countermeasures throughout the world, 'until the oceans run dry'. Indeed, strategic u-turns and the resort to claw-backs and retaliatory tools are so much part of the global picture that the concept of 'fraud on the law', a pillar of continental general theory designed to neutralise attempts to circumvent the 'natural' forum, is impotent.

Significantly, awareness of the pervasive complexity of normative interaction[16] is also a feature of all the other disciplines which have positioned themselves to survey or regulate, from various standpoints, the global legal landscape. Outside the conflict of laws, then, the new global problematic is that of 'conflicts'. Legal sociology explores

---

13 N. Walker, *Intimations of Global Law* (Oxford, OUP 2015) chapter 5, p. 148 et s.

14 P.S. Berman, 'The Evolution of Global Legal Pluralism' in R. Cotterell and M. Del Mar (eds), *Authority in Transnational Legal Theory: Theorising Across Disciplines* 151 (Cheltenham, Edward Elgar 2016) 151.

15 Gunter Teubner has famously drawn attention to the 'irritations' that occur when systems enter into contact with each other through 'legal transfers', setting off a series of unpredictable and potentially far-reaching consequences when the internal balance (the social couplings) within the two systems differs. 'Legal Irritants: Good Faith in British Law or How Unifying Law Ends Up in New Differences' (1998) 61 *Modern Law Review* 11–32.

16 B. de Sousa Santos, *Toward a New Legal Common Sense* (London, Butterworths 2003) 437: 'different legal spaces superimposed, interpenetrated and mixed in our minds, as much as in our actions, either on occasions of qualitative leaps or sweeping crises in our life trajectories, or in the dull routine of eventless everyday life'.

the 'no-man's land of colliding spheres of meaning' (*Sinnwelten*).[17] Comparative law, renewing its alliance with anthropology and global history, explores the dynamics of legal (and, apparent in the *Lafonta* case, economic) transplants and the contested internal make-up of each legal culture, full moreover of 'unofficial portraits'[18] and informal sub-cultures (as can be seen below, in cases such as *Jivraj* or *Song Mao*, through the study of indigenous or religious norms, long relegated by law to the field of anthropology). Our claim here is that bringing to bear the lens of a conflict-of-laws analysis facilitates the reading of sensitive cases of mutual irritation between hybrid regimes – whether or not in a transnational context. Once the 'conflict' is identified, its multiple dimensions are better grasped and ultimately, the needs of each system more appropriately accommodated. As Berman says,

> conceiving of these clashes (between religious and state law) in conflicts terms reorients the inquiry in a way that takes more seriously the non-state community assertion. As a result, courts must wrestle both with the nature of the multiple community affiliations potentially at issue and with the need to articulate truly strong normative justifications for not deferring to the non-state norm.[19]

The omnipresence of such conflicts, including in the domestic or private spheres, means that they are no longer (as they were in a pre-global setting) simply marginal encounters between territorially bounded legal systems.

An awareness of the pervasiveness of normative interaction induces a change that is not merely quantitative, nor is it limited to a reversal of the respective scope of principle (domestic cases) and exception (international cases). The pervasiveness of conflicts means, much more radically, that they are no longer merely a problem of overflow to be dealt with at the confines of law's usual business, but a permanent, all-pervasive feature of the normative landscape, reflecting the intensity of global processes. If conflicts are now 'mainstreamed', as Neil Walker puts it, conventional wisdom stands on its head,[20] and the perception of conflict changes. From simple and marginal situations of horizontal antagonism or antinomy in international cases, to situations of pervasive mutual irritation, the phenomena involved are more numerous, complex and heterogeneous than are the formal legal systems of the world of sovereign nation-States.

Putting conflicts at the very core of global law means, first of all, that the issue of threshold that arises in traditional conflict of laws reasoning – the notoriously difficult determination of what is 'international', as opposed to the purely domestic – becomes irrelevant. If global encounters between different systems are not limited to law that is state-endorsed and territorially-bound, then there is no reason to balance out the interests expressed in various normative systems (laws, standards, principles, private codes, indicators) differently, according to whether they arise within the confines of one

---

17 P.F. Kjaer, 'The Concept of the Political in the Concept of Transnational Constitutionalism' in C Joerges and T Ralli (eds), *After Globalization – New Patterns of Conflict and their Sociological and Legal Reconstruction* (Oslo, Arena 2011) 285–321, p. 315.

18 M. de S.-O.-l'E. Lasser, 'Judicial (Self-)Portraits: Judicial Discourse in the French Legal System' (1994–95) 104 *Yale L.J.* 1325.

19 Berman (n 14).

20 Walker (n 13) Chapter 4.

State territory or are framed as involving a problem of conflict of laws. The required international element does not change the terms of the interactions involving religion, culture, or gender, since even in the absence of a permissive foreign law, either there is a right which trumps the subordinate forum law, or there is an overriding value (republican neutrality, security considerations, etc) which trumps the right. This example also shows up the links between the question of threshold (when is there a conflict of laws?) and the tricky issue of equal treatment or non-discrimination. Formulating a right in terms of non-discrimination (on grounds of religion, cultural practice or gender) is a demand for justification of differential treatment; identifying such grounds is precisely the problematic which lies at the heart of the conflict of laws.[21] Using an alternative vocabulary does not change its terms. The issue of when justice allows differential treatment persists whether or not there is an international conflict of laws.

II. WHAT'S IN A LAW?

The focus of global legal scholarship of the jurisprudential (and indeed epistemological) variety has been attempting to define what law 'is' once its State-ness (the state of belonging to the State) has been peeled away, while political theorists have explored, rather, how to measure the legitimacy of claims to authority by non-State actors. In both areas, the pursuit of pluralism[22] has acquired considerable salience. In this respect, a first significant insight from these global pluralist conceptions is that it is implausible, for the moment, to envisage authority beyond the nation-State in any form other than as concurrent *claims.*[23] This is in keeping with the idea that global law is aspirational – intimation rather than law made flesh.[24] A further, connected, contribution is that sociological explanations of authority which were marginal within the doctrinal context of nation-state – such as Weber's fourth category of 'charismatic' authority – have risen to overriding importance beyond the State, where expert knowledge, the power of image, rating agencies and other spin doctors all flourish.

But however novel, tentative and anti-essentialist, it is striking that this renewed theoretical reflexion does not seem to change the terms of the questions being asked.

---

21 The conflict of laws has long entertained a symbiotic but contradictory relationship with principles of non-discrimination and equal treatment. See for example, Douglas Laycock, 'Equal Citizens of Equal and Territorial States: The Constitutional Foundations of Choice of Law' (1992) 92 *Colum. L. Rev.* 249 and our analysis in 'Aspects économiques du droit international privé' (2005) *Recueil Cours Académie Droit International* t307, §192 s.

22 See N Roughan and A Halpin, *In Pursuit of Pluralist Jurisprudence* (Cambridge, CUP 2017).

23 Roger Cotterell, 'Transnational Legal Authority: A Socio-Legal Perspective' in Cotterell and Del Mar (n 14) proposing as a starting point 'to treat authority generally as a *practice* and *experience* to be identified and interpreted sociologically' ... Moreover, 'given the complex conditions of existence of transnational legal authority, this authority will be shifting, variable and constantly re-negotiated'.

24 Walker (n 13) p. 151: global law is 'an incipient development, ... a legal form that is still coming to fruition and so largely future-orientated'.

The jurisprudential quest is to grasp the features of law-likeness without the support of the formal theory of sources of law. When confronted with unaccountable mafia-like private authority, or repressive religious practices, or indicators sponsored by the very entities being assessed, the question is usually whether such phenomena are sufficiently law-like to be considered as law, albeit beyond the State. Even global law's eerie 'intimations' are seen to present familiar characteristics in this respect.[25] In other terms, the renewed description of intermingling, hybrid jurisdictional assertions as a new state of global affairs, does not appear to modify the legal consciousness into which such claims will have to fit.

What, then, can a conflict of laws approach bring to this debate? The question might be framed, more precisely, as whether the discipline contributes anything more to the theorization of legal pluralism in a global context than an array of albeit interesting devices for solving conflicts or defining, case-by-case, the geography of authority. A first answer might be that embedded in the history of the discipline, a methodological incarnation of legal pluralism in the international arena can be found; its most contemporary expression is a form of recognitive statutism. The *Wagner* case discussed below illustrates the availability of a pluralist methodology of this type, along with the challenges that it raises. But a key to thinking that its contribution might well run deeper is the importance given by Gunter Teubner to the conflict of laws within his project of societal constitutionalism. He has said:

> In a world society with neither apex nor centre, there is just one way remaining to handle inter-constitutional conflicts—a strictly heterarchical conflict resolution. This is not just because of the absence of centralized power, which could be countered by intensified political efforts, but is rather connected with deep structures in society which Max Weber called the 'polytheism' of modernity. Even committed proponents of the 'unity of the constitution' are forced to agree that the unity of the nation- state constitution is now moving toward a 'clash of civil constitutions', toward mutually conflicting rationalities to be defused by a new conflict of laws.[26]

It is true that when the conflict of laws reached maturity within the framework of the modern State, it implicitly took statehood as a criterion for assessing the legitimacy of the norms it would accept within its 'community of laws'.[27] The focus of private international lawyers has been on ways to give teeth to transnational soft law or private norms when in conflict or competition with State law, and more generally on how to govern their interaction. In this respect, while suggesting various fine-tuned devices for coordinating heterogeneous sources of normativity so as to reach administrable and predictable solutions, it also pays heed to specifically jurisprudential

---

25 Walker (n 13) p. 196, sees a common denominator of *ratio* and *volontas* in the various conceptualisations of global law.

26 Gunther Teubner, *Constitutional Fragments: Societal Constitutionalism in Globalization* (Oxford, OUP 2011) 152.

27 This expression is famously von Savigny's (*System des heutigen Römischen Rechts, 1849*). In von Savigny's initial formulation of 'multilateralist' methodology, only the communities (at the time, German princedoms) belonging to a closed 'community of laws' cemented by shared cultural (religious, linguistic and legal) tradition, were considered as participants in the common allocation of prescriptive authority.

and jurisdictional issues relating to the characterization and legitimacy of normative claims as law. However, its approach is not to present an answer *per se*, but in relative terms, in respect of given situations (defined by geography or otherwise). For example, the debate over the 'extraterritoriality' of a public law or regulatory statute is about the appropriateness of its claim to govern a situation that is not, or is only partially, within the remit of the local sovereign: in other words, the difficulty (which lies at the traditional core of private international law) is not whether the statute is law-like in any absolute way, nor if it is constitutionally valid or was representative of the democratic will of the people when adopted, but how its application (and enforcement) can be justified in a non-domestic context. There is undeniably an existential and legitimacy concern here,[28] which private international law collapses into the issue of appropriateness.

This is because, in its modern version, it has been so closely wedded to the Westphalian paradigm that it assumes that law is whatever a particular State says is such. It can therefore pass lightly over the issue of law's defining qualities, straight to that of its scope. However, detached from State sovereignty, the additional contribution of the conflict of laws would be to point to these interactions themselves as the starting point from which to approach issues of legitimacy. This would mean to renounce any immediate decision on the legitimacy question and to deal with competing claims ex post and in relative terms. This idea seems perfectly in line with global law's instable reflexivity. It suggests that the legitimacy question arises in different terms according to the type of claim – collaborative, confrontational, concurrent – that is being made in respect to other legal systems. Along similar lines, reflecting on the contribution of private international law to global legal pluralism, Ralf Michaels has pointed out that, in the context of interconnectedness – in other words, when conflicts of norms are endemic, rather than exceptional – the sequence of questions conventionally asked by jurisprudents ('what is law?' and then 'when should it apply?') should be reversed.[29]

For example, is a private corporate code law or not law (legitimate or illegitimate? binding or softly decorative?). This might not be the right question to ask, or the right way to ask it. It may be, for instance, that when a corporate actor undertakes, in a private code made available to investors, to work towards a more ethical or egalitarian workplace, those commitments should be binding – and apt to be invoked against it – to the extent that it is supported by values present in its environment. The same code might not, however, in other circumstances, serve as governing law (as in the case of a global value chain, when competing State norms guarantee improved hygiene, security or environment for the stakeholders involved, or when fundamental rights are threatened). Accepting that legitimacy issues arise ex post and can receive variable, relative answers according to the type of conflict in which they are involved comes closer to capturing the complexity of the normative landscape beyond the State. As legal pluralism itself reminds us, 'the primacy of a function system can, however, only be claimed within a particular local and situational context. It changes from place to place

[28] See F. Rödl, 'Democratic Juridification without Statisation: Law of Conflict of Laws Instead of a World State' (2011) 2(2) *Transnational Legal Theory* 193–213.

[29] R. Michaels, 'Law and Recognition – Towards a Relational Concept of Law' in Roughan and Halpin (n 22) Chapter 5, pp. 90–115, esp. p. 110.

and from situation to situation'.[30] The reflexions devoted below to the rise of private norms (in *Fifa*, *Nike*, *Lehmann bros* ...) are highly instructive in this respect.

Like the return of science,[31] the revival of the conflict of laws is on the cards. The discipline appears as a serious candidate for occupying a significant governance function in 'global legal space' defined as beyond the reach and out of bounds of State sovereignty or State-endorsed institutions. After all, its line of business has long been making sense of interactions that cross State boundaries and fall between the gaps between domestic sovereignty and public international law. At the same time, however, complacency would be largely misplaced. The conflict of law's contemporary intellectual abeyance certainly warrants a humble detour by the various thriving strands of global legal theory. Indeed, it may have much to learn from other disciplinary vocabularies, either about the definition of conflicts or their modes of resolution, and this could lead in turn to a radical reformulation of its own core issues. Indeed, if encounters between heterogeneous norms or expressions of diverse types of informal authority are central to the understanding of the normative landscape beyond the confines of State sovereignty, the traditional schemes of intelligibility which underlie the conflict of laws need to take on board various additional dimensions of global complexity. If it does so and succeeds in living up to this challenge, it may emerge considerably enlightened by global legal theory. The reverse is true, too, however! What follows, then, is something in the way of a collective effort to put the conflict of laws back on the legal-theoretical map. We hope that the original features of the book – taking cases seriously; the integration of the global turn in its object and methodology; interdisciplinarity in its authorship – make for instructive and interesting reading.

30 Teubner (n 26) p. 64.

31 Pomper and Shaw (n 1).

PART I

JURISDICTION: JUDGING WITHOUT FRONTIERS?

1. Post-war yearning for deparochialisation and the siren of free trade: *The Bremen v. Zapata Off-Shore Co.*

1.1 CASE BACKGROUND

This first case expresses a post-war yearning for deparochialisation. At stake was the legal effect of a forum-selection clause in an international maritime contract. Decided by the United States Supreme Court in 1972, it marks the beginning of a process of liberalisation of contractual choice of forum, that would extend progressively from adjudication to arbitration. One might say that the siren of free trade lures international jurisdiction into the nets of party autonomy.

The dispute arises from a towage contract between an American corporation (Zapata) and a German corporation (Unterweser), in which the main obligation was to move an oil rig from Louisiana to the Adriatic Sea. The contract contained the following forum-selection clause: 'Any dispute arising must be treated before the London Court of Justice.'

Unterweser's deep-sea tug Bremen departed Louisiana on 5 January 1968, however, during transportation a severe storm arose while the Bremen was in international waters. The rig was damaged and was towed to Tampa, Florida, the nearest port of refuge. Despite the contractual provisions, on 12 January, Zapata commenced a suit in admiralty in the United States District Court at Tampa, seeking damages against Unterweser *in personam* and the Bremen *in rem*, alleging negligent towage and breach of contract. Unterweser invoked the forum clause and moved to dismiss for lack of jurisdiction or on *forum non conveniens* grounds.

Alternatively, the German corporation requested to stay the action pending submission of the dispute to the London Court of Justice. Unterweser commenced an action in the High Court of Justice in London, as the contract provided, and Zapata showed before that court to contest jurisdiction. The English court ruled that it had jurisdiction under the contractual forum provision.

In its turn, the United States District Court at Tampa relied on the prior decision of the Court of Appeals in *Carbon Black Export, Inc. v. The Monrosa*, 254 F.2d 297 ('agreements in advance of controversy whose object is to oust the jurisdiction of the courts are contrary to public policy, and will not be enforced') and denied Unterweser's motion to dismiss or stay Zapata's initial action. The Court of Appeals affirmed that the forum-selection clause was unenforceable.

Unterweser sought review in Supreme Court on certiorari and it was granted. The U.S. Supreme Court held that the forum-selection clause is binding on the parties unless the party seeking to avoid it could meet the high burden of showing it to be unreasonable, unfair, or unjust.

Case: *The Bremen v. Zapata Off-Shore Co.*, 407 U.S. 1 (1972)

1.2 BACK TO *THE BREMEN* (1972): FORUM SELECTION AND WORLDMAKING

Jacco Bomhoff

1. REVISITING A CLASSIC

Going back to *The Bremen*, means recounting one of the classic origin stories in the modern conflict of laws canon. That story – part of a well-known broader narrative of the rise of party autonomy – goes like this.

US courts were historically hostile to forum-selection clauses agreed between private parties. This hostility, as the Court of Appeals for the Fifth Circuit put it in a 1958 decision, reflected 'the universally accepted rule that agreements in advance of controversy whose object is to oust the jurisdiction of the courts are contrary to public policy and will not be enforced'.[1] This so-called 'ouster doctrine' was applied 'with almost boring unanimity',[2] until the Supreme Court abruptly changed course in its 1972 decision in *The Bremen v. Zapata Off-Shore Co*. Overturning another Fifth Circuit decision, the Supreme Court now held that the party resisting enforcement of a clause stipulating litigation in a foreign court would have to show that trial abroad would be 'so manifestly and gravely inconvenient' that they would 'be effectively deprived of a meaningful day in court'. In reaching this conclusion, Chief Justice Burger's opinion for the court invoked the following stirring lines, often cited later:

> The expansion of American business and industry will hardly be encouraged if, notwithstanding solemn contracts, we insist on a parochial concept that all disputes must be resolved under our laws and in our courts … We cannot have trade and commerce in world markets and international waters exclusively on our terms, governed by our laws and resolved in our courts.[3]

This familiar, conventional, history becomes puzzling when looked at more closely, from two directions. First, if *today* party autonomy in international commercial litigation is so widely accepted and so thoroughly normalised, how could it have taken until the 1970s for the US Supreme Court to fully affirm the validity of forum selection clauses? Secondly, though, if *before The Bremen* party autonomy was so widely and stridently rejected – 'with almost boring unanimity' – how can it be that all these earlier judicial objections seem to have disappeared so completely since the case was decided. How, in other words, could there have been such a rapid and decisive shift

---

[1] *Carbon Black Export Inc. v. The Monrosa*, 254 F. 2d 297 (1958), petition for certiorari dismissed, 359 U.S. 180 (1959).

[2] F.K. Juenger, 'Supreme Court Validation of Forum-Selection Clauses' (1972) 19 *Wayne L Rev* 49, 52, quoting 'Comment: Agreements in Advance Conferring Exclusive Jurisdiction on Foreign Courts' (1950) 10 *La L Rev* 293.

[3] *The Bremen v. Zapata Off-Shore Co.*, 407 U.S. 1, 9 (1972). All further unattributed quotations are taken from Chief Justice Burger's opinion for the court in this case.

from forum-selection clauses as 'against public policy', to party autonomy as the new orthodoxy?

The first of these two questions invites us to revisit the longer history of jurisdictional party autonomy in the US. Revisionist work in this vein has shown that federal courts had been giving effect to forum selection clauses long before *The Bremen*, not only in admiralty cases, but also as part of *forum non conveniens* assessments in land-based courts.[4] The case of *The Bremen* itself only went to the Supreme Court, after all, because of a persistent conflict between the Second and Fifth Circuit Federal Appeals Courts. On this revised view, the decision remains interesting as a rhetorically rousing endorsement, and as a useful practical confirmation of the validity of forum selection clauses at the Supreme Court level. But if in reality the battle for jurisdictional party autonomy was a much longer lasting, much more gradual, affair, then the case becomes somewhat less relevant as a matter of either normative principle or doctrinal change.

This revised history is important, but it is not complete. Contemporary writers did, after all, see *The Bremen* as an important case. The decision was widely commented on in law journals, not only in the US but also in England. And it was expected that the court's ruling could well 'substantially affect counseling and drafting practices'.[5] This suggests that there were still, by the early 1970s, real issues of principle and doctrine to be settled.

What about our second question, on limitations on party autonomy in the period *since* 1972? Later Supreme Court decisions have been striking, notably, for how they made *The Bremen* 'stand for the broadest possible principle that its language [could] support'.[6] The Bremen's reasonableness test was 'watered-down', and its policy extended also to consumer contracts.[7] More generally, this Supreme Court case law was clearly only one strand in a much broader wave of projects – of Conventions, Restatements, and model legislation – expanding party autonomy in interstate and international commercial dealings, not just in the US but also in Europe and elsewhere.[8] And so, while *The Bremen* was, in 1972, still seen by some as 'a most

---

4 D. Marcus, 'The Perils of Contract Procedure: A Revised History of Forum Selection Clauses in the Federal Courts' (2008) 82 *Tulane L Rev* 973.

5 Juenger (n 2), 50.

6 E.A. Purcell, Jr., 'Geography as a Litigation Weapon: Consumers, Forum-Selection Clauses, and the Rehnquist Court' (1992) 40 *UCLA L Rev* 423, 429.

7 Ibid.

8 See, e.g., the 1955 Hague Convention on the Law Applicable to International Sales of Goods; the 1958 New York Convention on the Recognition and Enforcement of Foreign Arbitral Awards (ratified by the U.S. on 30 September 1970); the 1968 Model Choice of Forum Act adopted by the U.S. National Conference of Commissioners on Uniform State Laws; the Restatement (Second) of Conflict of Laws (adopted in 1971); and, in Europe, the 1980 Rome Convention on the Law Applicable to Contractual Obligations (work on which had begun in 1967).

internationally minded decision',[9] that openness has since not only been expanded – it has become commonplace.[10]

2. A WORLD OF 'WORLD MARKETS', REAL AND IMAGINED

So how are we to understand the place of *The Bremen* in the broader history of modern private international law? In this comment, I suggest an alternative reading of the case, as not simply a doctrinal step or as a mere statement of principle, but as an instance of 'worldmaking'.[11] Chief Justice Burger's opinion is an exceptionally striking and momentous instance of what the anthropologist Clifford Geertz in his work on law has called 'imagining the real'.[12] The opinion, quite explicitly, imagines a world – a particular *kind* of world – and in so doing helps bring that world into being. When the Chief Justice situates the case in 'an era of expanding world trade and commerce', or when he refers to the ostensible needs of 'trade and commerce in world markets', for example, these statements have to be understood as not merely descriptive, but also as generative and constitutive. The decision participates in the construction of one among many possible 'world versions' – in this case, one revolving around a fear of 'parochialism' and concern for 'the future development of international commercial dealings by Americans'. The Supreme Court's decision in *The Bremen*, I want to argue, is ultimately most important for its imaginative construction and description of this world, and – still following Geertz – for its part in the 'organized effort to make the description correct'.[13]

The world imagined in *The Bremen*, moreover, is of a particular character. It is, or at least is projected to be, distinctly *modern*. This is suggested by a number of aspects of the symbolic and technical resources manipulated in the opinion and the surrounding scholarly commentary. Take for example the uses of history. At the Fifth Circuit, the dissenting judge was concerned that the majority of this normally 'forward-looking court' was taking 'a backward step' which had 'no place in a shrinking world'.[14] This

---

[9] G.A. Zaphiriou, 'Choice of Forum and Choice of Law Clauses in International Commercial Agreements' (1978) 3(2) *Maryland J of Int'l L* 311, 321.

[10] P. Nygh, *Autonomy in International Contracts* (Oxford, OUP 1999) (freedom of parties to international contracts to choose their forum and their applicable law 'today [in 1999] almost universally acknowledged'). See also: G. Rühl, 'Party Autonomy in the Private International Law of Contracts: Transatlantic Convergence and Economic Efficiency' in E. Gottschalk, R. Michaels, G. Rühl, J. von Hein (eds.), *Conflict of Laws in a Globalized World* (Cambridge, CUP 2007).

[11] *Cf.* N. Goodman, *Ways of Worldmaking* (Indianapolis, Hackett 1978). See also D. Delaney, *The Spatial, the Legal and the Pragmatics of World-Making: Nomospheric Investigations* (Abingdon, Routledge 2010); C. Geertz, 'Local Knowledge: Fact and Law in Comparative Perspective' in *Local Knowledge: Further Essays in Interpretive Anthropology* (New York, Basic Books 1983) 167. For an application of these ideas in the field of constitutional law, see M. Loughlin, '*The Constitutional Imagination*' (2015) 78(1) *Mo L Rev* 1.

[12] Geertz (n 11) 173.

[13] Ibid. 174.

[14] Circuit Judge Wisdom, dissenting in *In The Matter of the Complaint of Unterweser Reederei, GmbH. Zapata Off-Shore Co. v. M/S Bremen and Unterweser Reederei, GmbH.*, 446 F.

judge was also keen to emphasize how '[t]he towing of an oil rig across the Atlantic was a new business'; another reason for a modern approach to its legal context.[15] At the Supreme Court, the theretofore powerful 'ouster doctrine' was relegated to a realm of 'vestigial legal fiction'. In this way, a clear break is suggested with a pre-modern past still in thrall to 'taboos', 'word magic', and the 'hypnotic power of the phrase "oust the jurisdiction"'.[16] This process of deliberate forgetting enables the construction of a new, modern world. At the same time, the Supreme Court is concerned to give forum-selection-clause enforcement a firm footing in another modernity: that of the liberal tradition, when it notes how its new approach 'accords with ancient concepts of freedom of contract'. The decision, in short, sets up a clear victory, of forward-looking sensitivity to new business needs combined with liberal principle, on the one hand, over mere 'unthinking adherence to spurious precedent', on the other.[17]

3. MATTERS OF SCALE

Here, though, I want to focus on one other particularly striking aspect of the way the decision in *The Bremen* imagines – and contributes to the construction of – a world it purports merely to describe. This is the manipulation of the symbols and techniques of scale. Chief Justice Burger's opinion produces a shift towards a 'global' sphere, as the natural and appropriate level at which jurisdictional conflicts such as those at issue in the case ought to be negotiated. *World*making, in short, carries a particular literalness here. A comparison between Burger's opinion and the decision of the majority at the Fifth Circuit can help clarify what this shift entailed.

The outlook of the Court of Appeals was distinctly *inter*-national, in a classical sense. This is to say that for the Fifth Circuit, geography, national jurisdictional boundaries, and the interests of States were still the natural points of reference. In this court's reasoning *local connections* were still of primary significance. This was true, firstly, for connections to the US. Note how the Fifth Circuit describes what happened: 'Though the towage contract envisioned a long voyage with potential exposure to the jurisdiction of numerous States, the flotilla [that is: the towing tug Bremen, and the rig Chaparral] never escaped the Fifth Circuit's *mare nostrum*, and the casualty occurred in close proximity to the district court'.[18] But it was also true for connections to other States. As the court set out the position: 'The only other nation having significant

2d 907 (28 June 1971), quoting 'Comment, Application of the Forum Clause to Commercial Contracts' (1971) 8 *Houston L Rev* 739, 752.

15 Judge Wisdom, quoted in Chief Justice Burger's opinion, at fn. 14.

16 'Taboo' was Learned Hand's term (see *Krenger v. Pennsylvania R. Co.*, 174 F.2d 556 (1949), quoted in *The Bremen*); 'hypnotic power' was Jerome Frank's (see *Kulukundis Shipping Co. v. Amtorg Trading Corp.*, 126 F.2d 978, 984 (1942)); 'word magic' was Friedrich Juenger's (see Juenger (n 2) 53).

17 Juenger (n 2) 53.

18 Circuit Judge Gerwin, *In The Matter of the Complaint of Unterweser Reederei, GmbH. Zapata Off-Shore Co. v. M/S Bremen and Unterweser Reederei, GmbH.*, 428 F.2d 888 (19 June 1970).

contacts with, or interest in, the controversy is Germany. England's only relationship is the designation of her courts in the forum clause'.[19]

At the Supreme Court, these understandings of proximity and interest undergo a remarkable shift. The precise location of the accident no longer matters. It is as if the Court wants to give immediate practical relevance to its more rhetorical declaration that '[t]he barrier of distance that once tended to confine a business concern to a modest territory no longer does so', by disqualifying such geographical connections as 'mere fortuities'. The fact that the claimant was a United States citizen, whose rights would be affected if the dispute were to be litigated in England, also is no longer a relevant factor. Similarly, the potential 'interests' of England or Germany are no longer mentioned. Neither, strikingly, is any specific interest of the United States as a whole, on which more below. In the approach taken by the Supreme Court, connections to particular localities are only taken into account in attenuated form, as part of an overall 'reasonableness' inquiry. And so, instead of attention to geographical proximity or concern for local governmental interests, we see deference to the expectations of private parties. Private parties, moreover, of a particular kind: those businesses 'once essentially local', but now operating 'in world markets'.[20]

This escalation of what Mariana Valverde has called 'the spatial scale of governance',[21] to a global level, is facilitated by a parallel elevation in terms of the sources for the court's authority. Part of this is a greater willingness to look to foreign judicial practice on this issue, in particular 'the approach followed in other common law countries, including England'. But even more important is the source of the Court's authority within US law itself. Recall that *The Bremen* concerned claims brought in admiralty. Chief Justice Burger's opinion contains no statements on the basis or the intended scope of the Court's new ruling. It would therefore have been entirely plausible to read the Supreme Court's validation of forum-selection clauses as confined to admiralty litigation. But contemporary commentators were not content to read the judgment in such a limited way. Instead, they argued that the Court had in fact done something it does only comparatively rarely: it had laid down a rule of federal common law, based on a federal interest in 'maintaining an effective climate in which to conduct international commercial activity'.[22] After all, any 'lack of predictability created by a diversity of rules on the validity of forum-selection clauses', one writer noted, would 'impinge on the nation as a whole, not only those States that might decide to refuse enforcement'.[23] More generally, '[t]he limited political context' in which state-level decision-makers operated, would be 'an inappropriate one in which to make a policy judgment concerning the importance of effective forum selection by the parties to international commercial dealings'.[24] Determining the validity of forum-selection

---

19 Ibid.

20 *Cf.* J.R. Paul, 'The Transformation of International Comity' (2008) 71 *Law & Contemporary Problems* 19.

21 M. Valverde, *Chronotopes of Law: Jurisdiction, Scale and Governance* (Abingdon, Routledge 2015) 33.

22 H.G. Maier, 'The Three Faces of Zapata: Maritime Law, Federal Common Law, Federal Courts Law' (1973) 6 *Vanderbilt J of Transnat L* 387, 394. See also Juenger (n 2) 59.

23 Maier, ibid.

24 Ibid. 396.

clauses, then, was not a matter that could be safely left to state law. *The Bremen* had to be read as laying down a rule of federal common law, applicable not just in admiralty but – at least – also to all other international transactions.

Now, it could well be thought, certainly from today's perspective, that describing these apparently simple manipulations of scale as 'worldmaking', is reading too much into the court's decision. All this might amount to, after all, could be some random judicial references to 'world trade and commerce' and 'world markets', and some rhetorical flourishes of a court concerned to show it is mindful of 'the expanding horizons of American contractors who seek business in all parts of the world'. But if we place this rhetoric in context, such a deeper significance may well appear less far-fetched. The court's terminology, and the outlook it signaled were, in effect, largely new at the time. It was during the few years leading up the decision in *The Bremen*, that economists, political scientists and international relations scholars, began to address both the need for 'transnational' or 'global' perspectives in their fields, and for increased recognition of the role of corporations at such 'transnational' or 'global' levels. *American Business Abroad*, published in 1969, for example, saw MIT economist Charles Kindleberger arguing that the nation state was 'just about through as an economic unit'.[25] In *The Tortuous Evolution of the Multinational Corporation* (also 1969), Howard V. Perlmutter coined the neologism 'geocentric', to describe a new breed of super-sized 'world oriented' firms having lost 'all special ties to one or two particular States'.[26] And a Harvard Business School study on *The Role of U.S. Enterprise Abroad* (again 1969), cautioned that the identity of multinational corporations was 'likely to become more and more ambiguous in national terms' over time.[27] An early, and especially grand, statement of this new mood can be found, finally, in a 1966 book entitled *World Politics: The Global System* by Herbert Spiro, professor of political science at the University of Pennsylvania. 'Today for the first time in history,' Spiro began his book, 'a global community of mankind exists or, at any rate, is coming into existence in the consciousness of human beings': 'Today there is one global political system of which all national and other smaller political systems are component parts'.[28]

These references of course cannot, without more, *prove* anything. But they do at least suggest that thinking in 'world'-terms was both prevalent, and to some extent new, at least in scholarly circles, at precisely the time Chief Justice Burger wrote his opinion in *The Bremen*, where he adopted a very similar outlook, and cast it in very similar language.

---

25 C. Kindleberger, *American Business Abroad* (New Haven, Yale 1969), 207.

26 See H.V. Perlmutter, 'The Tortuous Evolution of the Multinational Corporation' (1969) 4(1) *Columbia Journal of World Business* 9–18, quoted in: J.S. Nye, Jr., R.O. Keohane, 'Transnational Relations and World Politics: An Introduction' (1971) 25(3) *International Organization* 329. For an overview with extensive further sources, see J.F. Galloway, 'World-wide Corporations and International Integration: The Case of INTELSAT' (1970) 24(3) *International Organization* 503.

27 R. Vernon, 'The Role of U.S. Enterprise Abroad' (1969) 98(1) *Daedalus* 129.

28 Quoted in G. Modelski, 'The Promise of Geocentric Politics (Book Review)' (1970) 22(4) *World Politics* 617, 623.

As Mariana Valverde, Boaventura de Sousa Santos, and others have argued, questions of scale matter for the character of governance projects. *The Bremen*, in an important sense, introduced a 'global' perspective for the resolution of jurisdictional conflicts, to replace a more conventional *inter*-nationalist comparison of contacts and interests of specific local jurisdictions. Is it too far-fetched to say that in doing so, the decision participated in a remaking of the world – or at least of those aspects of the world concerned with the demarcation of public authority and private autonomy? One noted political science scholar commented in 1968 that, given the role of corporations as important actors 'in present and future international systems … their political functions as structural components of systems of world politics [could] only be neglected at our peril'.[29] In this light, recall once more the assertion at the heart of Chief Justice Burger's case for party autonomy: '*[w]e* cannot have trade and commerce in world markets and international waters exclusively on *our* terms, governed by *our* laws and resolved in *our* courts' (emphases added). This statement, for all its intended obviousness, leaves many questions unanswered. 'Why not?' is one. 'Perhaps not "exclusively", but surely still commonly, or regularly?' is another. And even more importantly: 'Who are "we" in this statement?'. In whose name is Chief Justice Burger speaking here? Can the interests of American businesses operating internationally simply be assumed to be congruent with some general public interest? Or is the court going even further, and taking into consideration not only such American business interests, but also those of some nascent global business community?

4. WORLDMAKING BEFORE CRITIQUE: *THE BREMEN* AND LEGAL MODERNISM

Even if this worldmaking perspective sounds plausible generally, why go back to *The Bremen today*? Surely all that can be said about this decision of almost 50 years ago, has been said already? Perhaps surprisingly, one important reason for asking these questions today, is that they simply could not be raised, or at least not in this way, at the time. Recall that the case was argued and decided at the very beginning of the 1970s. This means that Chief Justice Burger's opinion arrived just before a range of major disciplinary innovations in a number of highly relevant domains – from Foucauldian studies of governmentality, to geography and critical legal studies. 'In the 1960s the world changed … In the 1970s the disciplines changed', David Delaney has written in his overview of the relationship between law and space – a theme of great salience to the case.[30] Even if it is true that no single idea is ever entirely new, looking at social phenomena, such as social space or the distinction between private freedom and public authority, *as constructed*, was greatly facilitated through the use of

29 G. Modelski, 'The Corporation in World Society' (1968) *Yearbook of World Affairs* 78, quoted in Galloway (n 26) 505.

30 Delaney (n 11) 9–10. See also Valverde (n 21) 48 ('legal geography did not exist as a field in the 1980s').

conceptual and normative tools introduced in disciplinary innovations that took place largely later, over the course of the 1970s and then during the 1980s.[31]

It is true that still today, the constructive, structuring and meaning-making dimensions of party autonomy are not often addressed explicitly in conflict of laws scholarship. There are of course exceptions.[32] One notable example is the argument developed by the legal historian Edward Purcell, that the Supreme Court's later, post-*The Bremen* case law on forum-selection clauses resembles its early twentieth-century 'liberty of contract' jurisprudence, in '[p]rivileging a particular view of the bases of national economic power and assuming the innocence of private social power'.[33] But the position of *The Bremen* itself is particularly interesting, still today, because it offers us a glimpse of worldmaking *before critique* – of a time when fewer tools were readily available to unpack ideas on, say, 'the expansion of American business and industry', or on how – exactly – it would be 'parochial' to insist on local law or courts, and on why – exactly – that would be problematic. Intriguingly, the decision also came just before the ascendancy of another external perspective from which it could have been subjected to scrutiny, albeit most likely with radically different implications: the analysis of efficiency in US law and economics scholarship.[34] Again, crucial assumptions in the decision that went untested at the time – such as the suggestion that this was an era in which 'all courts' were 'overloaded' – would most probably have been scrutinized to a greater degree, had the case been decided ten years later.[35]

Partly because of simple timing, then, *The Bremen* could be – and, to some extent, was – an exercise in construction without critique, in worldmaking without self-reflection. Its faith in freedom for commercial actors, in internationalism, and in 'reasonableness', all mark the decision as an instance of modernist legalism, and perhaps even as one of its high points. This is true in particular of the confidence in the force of sheer rationality that surrounded the court's reasoning. As Friedrich Juenger noted at the time, speculation as to whether the court's new rule on forum selection would also bind state courts – a question simply not addressed in *The Bremen* – was likely to be irrelevant: after all, now that the court had concisely set out 'the reasons for upholding party autonomy … it would be difficult for a state court to escape its

---

31 Sceptics might point to the early twentieth-century scholar Robert Hale, and argue that many of these ideas had been around for a while. And they had been, to a degree, and in a form. But it is intriguing to note that even Hale's work had to be 'rediscovered' later, and that, again, much of this rediscovery occurred only after the early 1970s. See, e.g., W.J. Samuels, 'The Economy as a System of Power and its Legal Bases: The Legal Economics of Robert Lee Hale' (1973) 27 *U Miami L Rev* 261.

32 For an illuminating exception, see Fleur Johns, 'Performing Party Autonomy' (2008) *Law & Contemporary Problems* 253 (adopting a focus on 'the background-structuring effects of the notion of party autonomy').

33 Purcell (n 6) 507.

34 The seminal early event here is the 1973 publication of Richard Posner's 'Economic Analysis of Law'.

35 See, e.g., the vast literature on the so-called 'litigation explosion' in the US, emerging from the second half of the 1980s.

logic'.[36] Using only such logic and law, and overcoming 'taboos' and 'parochialism', the US Supreme Court in *The Bremen* helped build a modern world of party autonomy – all without mentioning that term once. The tensions and paradoxes inherent in this world, between private and public freedom, perhaps could not readily have been expressed and analysed in these terms at the time.[37] But they are certainly still with us today. And one of these paradoxes still stands as perhaps the starkest monument to Chief Justice Burger's modern, internationalist optimism. It would not be possible, Burger wrote, to have world commerce on exclusively American terms. That is why party autonomy was said to be *necessary*. But that is also, in the decades since *The Bremen*, largely what party autonomy *has produced*, as New York and English law, and the New York and English courts, have become the default choices for international contracting in 'world markets'. The impulse of internationalism, then, and the effect of hegemony, have turned out to be merely two sides of the same coin.

1.3 FORUM SELECTION CLAUSES IN A BRAVE NEW WORLD: OPTING OUT OF PAROCHIALISM?

Agatha Brandão de Oliveira and Lucia Bíziková

1. INTRODUCTION

The Bremen v. Zapata Off-Shore Co. 407 U.S. 1 (1972) ('*The Bremen*') is a landmark case in the construction of contemporary private international law. By allowing contractual choice of jurisdiction, the United States Supreme Court opened the era of party autonomy in international commercial relations. *The Bremen* was arguably the first legal stone in the framing and facilitating of private globalised trade relations and, correlatively, a symptom of a disembedded economy. It questions the essence of 'legal borders' and sets the tone for later challenges to the very notion of jurisdictional limits, while simultaneously heralding the age of private economic governance through contract.

The circumstances that gave rise to this important ruling reveal the complex nature of the dispute and the legal issues it raises: it is not about an ordinary contract between two local (American) companies doing regular business, but an international commercial transaction freely negotiated between a German and an American corporation; it is not the type of transaction that States alone can regulate, but belongs to a very specific realm of admiralty issues in which private actors have considerable influence; it is not an activity that falls neatly within the realm of one jurisdiction, but rather is intrinsically international (here, on the maritime route between the Gulf of Mexico and

[36] Juenger (n 2) 59. See also the 1971 'Comment', cited in Judge Wisdom's dissent in *The Bremen* (arguing that it was 'difficult to imagine any court long rejecting a criterion which is universally referred to as the "reasonableness" test').

[37] For the notion of 'public freedom', see G.E. Frug, 'The City as a Legal Concept' (1980) 93(6) *Harvard L Rev* 1057.

the Adriatic Sea). The occurrence of the problem materialised in international waters, where sovereignty has no reach.

Indeed, to contextualise *The Bremen* in space is to recall the notion of *mare liberum*: 'the sea is common to all, because it is so limitless that it cannot become a possession of any one, and because it is adapted for the use of all'.[38] The sea represents the main venue for trade in all times – and therefore involves a considerable variety of public and private interests, from the claims of empires to the convenience of merchants, from the protection of nature as a global public good to geopolitical strategies. To reach a decision affecting this ecology is always a sensitive matter, particularly for a domestic judge.

Moreover, to place *The Bremen* in time is to acknowledge that those events inevitably happened in a period of transition – and unforeseen expansion – of international trade on a much larger scale. Back in the 1970s, the setting was composed by the Post-World War II 'golden age of capitalism'[39] and the apex of the Cold War. For the first time, we inserted the words 'transnational'[40] and 'global' in our dictionaries. The decision rendered by the Supreme Court gave concreteness to this reality and set a new vision for the world: here comes the global turn!

Professor Jacco Bomhoff raises the point in this volume that this new world is built upon the dual facet of internationalism and hegemonism.[41] This does not constitute a paradox: in *The Bremen*, the Supreme Court deliberately took a non-parochial avenue.[42] Instead, the Supreme Court espoused a new cause – the creation of a legal market.[43] Liberalising international choice of forum clauses was just the beginning of a large window of opportunity for governance through informal arrangements by non-State actors.

By setting a pace in which private transactions across continents were 'unbounded', competition between jurisdictions (forum shopping) and methods of dispute resolution (arbitration clauses) was encouraged.[44] In the new global market for judicial services, the creation of judicial 'business partners' as a by-product is also noteworthy; under

---

38 Hugo Grotius, *The Freedom of the Seas* (first published in 1609, New York, Oxford University Press 1916) 7.

39 Cf. S.A. Marglin, J.B. Schor, *The Golden Age of Capitalism* (Oxford, Clarendon Press 1992).

40 See the original source of the word in Phillip C. Jessup, *Transnational law* (New Haven, Yale University Press 1956) 2: '… the term "transnational law" to include all law which regulates actions or events that transcend national frontiers. Both public and private international law are included, as are other rules which do not wholly into such standard categories.'

41 Please refer to the last page of Bomhoff's contribution, 1.2 above.

42 For further studies on the subject, cf. Neil Walker, *Intimations of Global Law* (Cambridge, Cambridge University Press 2014).

43 As a market, of course, it can be monopolized. See Part III of this book.

44 This reflected some decades later on the jurisprudence of the European Court of Justice, discussing *lis pendens*, 'Italian torpedo' and anti-suit injunctions: Case C-281/02 *Owusu v. Jackson* [2002] ECR, Case C-116/02 *Gasser v. Misak* [2002] ECR, Case C-159/02 *Turner v. Grovit* [2002] ECR. Regarding to arbitration, see Case C-536/13 *Gazprom OAO v. Lietuvos Respublika* [2013] ECR, Case C-185/07 *Allianz SpA v. West Tankers* [2007].

The Bremen's 'deferral policy', British courts are endorsed as 'experienced and capable in the resolution of admiralty litigation'.[45]

This commentary will focus, firstly, on how party autonomy is asserted in *The Bremen.* Secondly, we will attempt to assess its direct and indirect legal effects. This is important for understanding the 'post-*Bremen*' legal panorama as it unfolds throughout the rest of this volume.

2. THE NORMATIVE MAZE

A narrative of a global world could not prosper without a foundational myth – or a hypothetical norm to justify its development.[46] Without naming the principle, the Supreme Court in *The Bremen* effectively described what would be the foundation of post-modern private international law: party autonomy.[47] In its economic avatar, the whole discipline has been built on two main pillars: free choice of law (*substantive facet* of party autonomy) and free choice of forum (*procedural facet*). The former allows parties to determine the substantive law applicable to their transaction; the latter grants parties the right to identify the court competent to hear and resolve disputes arising from their relationship. The encompassing foundation of this private empowerment is freedom of contract.

A. What's in a Choice?

Quasi-unrestricted choice to suit the parties' needs has been widely promoted since *The Bremen.*[48] Today, a whole series of reasons justify the choice to draft a forum selection clause.[49] Thus, firstly, it can help parties avoid a costly and parasitic trial: a fight over

---

45 See *The Bremen*, p. 17. In its turn, it is fair to say that the deferral policy created a legitimate expectation that the same respect would be given to uphold choice of forum clauses in favour of US courts. However, what meant to be 'global', was indeed focused on national terms and the mutual recognition principle. It sets the limits of what is a 'remote alien forum' and what is a 'friendly jurisdiction'.

46 Cf. Hans Vaihinger, *The Philosophy of As If: A System of the Theoretical, Practical and Religious Fictions of Mankind* (Hamburg, Meiner 1911). See also Michel Troper, 'The modern State and the concept of authority' in Roger Cotterrell and Maksymilian Del Mar (eds), *Authority in Transnational Legal Theory* (Cheltenham, Edward Elgar 2016): 'An assumption that we know is not true but is nevertheless indispensable. ... Already in earlier works, he [Kelsen] had written that it was an assumption that every lawyer made unconsciously. The role of the pure theory was therefore to bring to consciousness this unconscious assumption.'

47 For a critical analysis of this principle, see Horatia Muir Watt, '"Party Autonomy" in International Contracts: From the Makings of a Myth to the Requirements of Global Governance' [2010] *ERCL* 250.

48 There is still some limitation to choose rules of law as the law governing the contract. Cf. Luca Radicati di Brozolo, 'Non-national rules and conflicts of laws: reflections in light of the UNIDROIT and Hague Principles' [2012] *Rivista di diritto internazionale privato e processuale* 840.

49 An interchangeable term for this clause is choice of forum agreement, since it represents an agreement inside an agreement, with separability aspects (a choice of forum agreement is to

the place to fight.[50] Secondly, it empowers each of them to determine, strategically, the court with the most favourable procedural and evidentiary rules. Last but not least, it can prevent the risk of having a dispute determined by a forum with a random or arbitrary connection to the case.

However, party autonomy can serve its purpose when the contracting parties understand the implications that this double prerogative entails. Freedom to choose is not always straight-forward. The way through the normative maze is through astute drafting: the relevant clauses must be carefully tailored to the needs of the parties and to the scope of the transaction. Thus together, choice of law and choice of forum enable parties to submit their transaction to *one* (national or municipal) legal order. The question is whether this means that a forum-selection clause entails the designation of the law of the selected forum? In *The Bremen*, the purport of the clause was not clear in this respect. One of the controversies stemmed from the fact that Unterweser towage contracts ordinarily provided for exclusive German jurisdiction and application of German law; however, in the process of negotiations, Zapata contested this[51] and the choice of London courts prevailed. The issue arose as to whether it was also appropriate for English law to govern the contract. It was held that

> while the contract here did not specifically provide that the substantive law of England should be applied, it is the general rule in English courts that the parties are assumed, absent contrary indication, to have designated the forum with the view that it should apply its own law. It is therefore reasonable to conclude that the forum clause was also an effort to obtain certainty as to the applicable substantive law.

B. The Quest for Legal Certainty

By essence, cross-border trade is a hazardous activity. To minimize the potential risks, parties often seek mechanisms to promote legal certainty – choice of forum is precisely one such device. In *The Bremen*, the Supreme Court stated that the 'selection of a London forum was clearly a reasonable effort to bring vital certainty to this international transaction'. Moreover, it remarked upon the need for foreseeability in international contracts – where parties must be held to their bargain when a dispute arises. Therefore, issues relating to the appropriateness of the chosen forum must be addressed at the time the contract is being discussed.

A particular feature of *The Bremen* is the focus on the economic aspect of this choice – uncertainty is 'bad for business' and efforts must be allocated to minimise the potential discrepancies or miscommunications between parties of different nationalities

---

be considered as separate from the remainder of a contract). Forum-selection clauses are *prima facie* valid. The same logic is valid for arbitration clauses.

50 This argument is based on an economic analysis of law, see Péter Cserne, 'Freedom of Contract (and Economic Analysis)' in Jürgen Backhaus (ed), *Encyclopedia of Law and Economics* (Berlin, Springer 2015). See also Giesela Ruhl, 'Party Autonomy in the Private International Law of Contracts: Transatlantic Convergence and Economic Efficiency' in Eckart Gottschalk, Ralf Michaels, Giesela Ruhl, Jan von Hein (eds), *Conflict of Laws in a Globalized World* (Cambridge, Cambridge University Press 2011).

51 The choice of forum clause then assumed an 'overriding importance': see *In re Unterweser Reederei Gmbh*, 428 F.2d 888 (5th Cir. 1970), at 907.

in respect of the nature and location of the forum to which they might find themselves subjected:

> *The elimination of all such uncertainties by agreeing in advance on a forum acceptable to both parties is an indispensable element in international trade, commerce, and contracting.* There is strong evidence that the forum clause was a vital part of the agreement, and it would be unrealistic to think that the parties did not conduct their negotiations, including fixing the monetary terms, with the consequences of the forum clause figuring prominently in their calculations...[52]

C. Issues of Scope and Status

The Bremen was distinguished from previous precedents such as *Carbon Black Export Inc. v. The Monrosa*,[53] notably because of the way in which the choice of forum clause was formulated. The language of the forum selection clause in the towage contract was 'clearly mandatory and all-encompassing, ... providing that any dispute must be litigated before the High Court of Justice in London, England.'[54]

Nevertheless, even with a clear choice of forum clause, the interpretation of this provision was challenged – specifically on the terms of whether the jurisdiction agreement designated a single, exclusive forum.[55]

In upholding the clause, the Supreme Court relied mainly on the fact that the agreement was 'freely entered into between two competent parties'. It highlighted two criteria in the latter respect: (i) conscious acquiescement; (ii) equal bargaining power. In short, to contest the binding nature of the agreement, the opposing party would have to present evidence of alleged fraud, and not simply allege that 'no specific negotiations concerning the forum clause took place'. The Court remarked on the innovative character of this specific contract for the towing of an oil rig across the Atlantic, which did not use a 'boilerplate' language present in other contracts. Furthermore, the fact that Zapata made other alterations to the contract demonstrated that it must have been aware of, and not opposed to, the clause. According to the filings of the case, 'the forum clause could hardly be ignored. It is the final sentence of the agreement, immediately preceding the date and the parties' signatures'. Zapata, therefore, could not prove that it had not consented to the choice of forum agreement.

Of course, party autonomy operates within a certain policy framework. Here, the limits of its operation were set as follows: 'a contractual choice of forum clause should be held unenforceable if enforcement would contravene a strong public policy of the forum in which suit is brought, whether declared by statute or by judicial decision.' This is how the Supreme Court justified that in many cases, the forum clause is not

---

[52] See *The Bremen* at 14. Emphasis added.

[53] *Carbon Black Export Inc. v. The Monrosa*, 254 F. 2d 297 (1958).

[54] See *The Bremen* at 21.

[55] For a contemporary analysis addressing the main legal framework on the subject, see Mukarrum Ahmed and Paul Beaumont, 'Exclusive choice of court agreements: some issues on the Hague Convention on choice of court agreements and its relationship with the Brussels I recast especially anti-suit injunctions, concurrent proceedings and the implications of BREXIT' [2017] *J Priv Int'l L* 386.

upheld. However, in *The Bremen* there was no valid reason for refusing to enforce the choice of forum clause in favour of British courts.[56]

3. BEYOND *THE BREMEN*: EXPANDING THE SCOPE OF CHOICE OF FORUM CLAUSES

When giving reasons for its decision, the Supreme Court noted that '[t]he expansion of American business and industry will hardly be encouraged if, notwithstanding solemn contracts, we insist on a parochial concept that all disputes must be resolved under our laws and in our courts'. Even more significantly, the Supreme Court famously acknowledged that '[*w*]*e cannot have trade and commerce in world markets* and international waters exclusively on our terms, governed by our laws, and *resolved in our courts*'.[57] Increasing awareness of a common interest of the community of liberal States in international trade and commerce is the key reason why the courts throughout the Western world became less hesitant in upholding the choice of forum clauses.[58] If *The Bremen* is particularly significant, it is because historically, American courts held a particularly unfavourable approach towards choice of forum clauses in both domestic and international contracts.[59]

But it does not follow that parties to international commercial agreements give in without a proper 'jurisdictional fight' for the sake of promoting the very international trade in which they are engaged. More often than not, challenges to the choice of forum and choice of law clauses are a decisive part of contemporary transnational commercial litigation. This is because the parties will usually do everything possible to litigate in a different forum than the one chosen in the clause, if this allows them to obtain a tactical advantage, or to strip the other of a strategically better position. Consequently, it is no secret that private 'war over jurisdiction'[60] tends to determine the overall outcome of the case. It is for this very reason that enforcing the agreement and respecting the parties' autonomy over choice of forum is seen as a cornerstone of international trade by reason of the foreseeability and stability that it injects into complex commercial arrangements.

But, this policy is not limited to commercial litigation only; a similar discourse exists in the context of international arbitration, even if arbitral tribunals tend to uphold choice of forum clauses (usually referred to as arbitration clauses or agreements) more readily. Indeed, the economic incentive structure of arbitration and litigation are clearly different on this point, insofar as arbitrators have every interest in upholding party

---

56 *Bisso v. Inland Waterways Corp.*, 349 U.S. 85 (1955); *Boyd v. Grand Trunk W. R. Co.* 338 U.S. 263 (1949).

57 See *The Bremen* at 21. Emphasis added.

58 Matthias Lehmann, 'Liberating the Individual from Battles between States: Justifying Party Autonomy in Conflict of Laws' [2008] *VJTL* 394.

59 Gary Born, *International Civil Litigation in United States Courts* 3rd edn (Alphen aan den Rijn, Kluwer Law International 1996) 385.

60 As a term crowned by Claire R. Kelly, 'The War on Jurisdiction: Troubling Questions About Executive Order 13303' [2004] *Ariz. St. L.J.* 483.

choice and asserting jurisdiction whereas, arguably, courts might have every interest in keeping the disputes out of the courtroom and thereby reducing the workload. Be that as it may, the contemporary pro-arbitration approach is the consequence of a gradual process that faced its own unique challenges, including the issue of arbitrability of disputes touching on public regulatory interests.[61] Nonetheless, parallels between the courts' arbitration-friendly attitude and their favourable treatment of forum clauses is not mere coincidence; they are closely intertwined.

Thus, only two years after *The Bremen* was decided, the Supreme Court faced yet another case where it had to decide on the parties' freedom to designate the forum for their dispute. In *Scherk v. Alberto-Culver*, it had to consider whether the reasoning applicable to the forum selection clauses could be extended to arbitration clauses.[62] Like *The Bremen*, *Scherk* was a case that arose from an international contract of sale between German and American parties. The contract contained an arbitration clause whereby the parties agreed to refer any eventual dispute between them to arbitration in Paris, subject to the laws of Illinois. However, Alberto-Culver disregarded the clause and filed suit in Illinois federal court, claiming that Scherk had violated US securities law.

In the end, the court upheld the arbitration clause and said that

> [a]n agreement to arbitrate before a specific tribunal is, in effect, *a specialized kind of forum-selection clause* … [and] the invalidation of the arbitration clause in the dispute before us would not only allow the respondent to repudiate its solemn promise but would, as well, *reflect a parochial concept that all disputes must be resolved under our laws and in our courts*.[63]

By refusing to follow its 1953 decision in *Wilko*, where the Supreme Court held that securities disputes were non-arbitrable, it endorsed its more recent reasoning in *The Bremen*. This is significant as it meant that the ratio from *The Bremen* was no longer limited to admiralty law only, and potentially encompassed areas of public regulatory law. This was further confirmed by lower courts, who promptly extended the reasonableness test from *The Bremen* to other areas.[64]

---

[61] For example, the Federal Arbitration Act ('FAA'), which imposes the requirement for enforcement of arbitration clauses for interstate or foreign commerce was enacted by Congress in 1925. Despite this, some courts remained reluctant to uphold arbitration clauses and some adjustment time was necessary before they stopped relying on the ouster doctrine. The application of the FAA itself was controversial in the context of securities disputes, mostly after the 1930s recession. The Supreme Court addressed this question again in 1953 in *Wilko v. Swan*. It was held that the public interest in securities market outweighed the parties' interest in having their dispute arbitrated. For more on this topic, please see James T. Jr. Brittain, 'Foreign Forum Selection Clauses in the Federal Courts: All in the name of International Comity' [2001] *HJIL* 305.

[62] *Scherk v. Alberto-Culver Co.*, 417 U.S. 506 (1974).

[63] See *Scherk* at 507. Emphasis added.

[64] Linda S. Mullenix provides a complete picture of the most important developments during 15 years after Bremen in her article 'Another Choice of Forum, Another Choice of Law: Consensual Adjudicatory Procedure in Federal Court' (1988) 57(3) *Fordham Law Review* 291.

The Supreme Court subsequently cemented its pro-arbitration approach further in the landmark 1985 case *Mitsubishi v. Soler Chrysler–Plymouth*. It affirmed that even disputes arising out of statutory antitrust provisions could be resolved by arbitration provided that the claim arose from an international transaction.[65] By referring to *Scherk*, the Supreme Court held that 'it will be necessary for the national courts to subordinate domestic notions of arbitrability to the international policy favouring commercial arbitration'.[66] While both *Scherk* and *Mitsubishi* followed the reasoning in *The Bremen*, we cannot examine these cases in isolation from the 1958 Convention on the Recognition and Enforcement of Foreign Arbitral Awards ('New York Convention') that had entered into force in the United States in 1970.[67] The Supreme Court in *Scherk* even referred to this (at that time) recent development explicitly, when distinguishing *Wilko*.[68]

It is remarkable that there is no comparable treaty governing the enforcement of judgments in foreign courts. This is not to say that there have been no such attempts – with the Hague Judgments Conventions being the best illustration of the insuperable difficulties of legal culture that prevent the emergence of a similar worldwide legal framework. Consequently, the New York Convention remains the sole reference, reinforcing the idea that choice of public and private fora are twin expressions of the same foundational principle.

4. TESTING THE LIMITS OF CHOICE OF FORUM CLAUSES

Nonetheless, when *Scherk* and *Mitsubishi* were decided, there were still important qualifications to the courts' upholding of arbitration clauses. For example, both *Scherk* and *Mitsubishi* distinguished between domestic and international contracts, with domestic contracts being subject to more scrutiny when it comes to assessing the public interest. While permitted in the international context, statutory and regulatory conflicts arising from securities and antitrust law remained outside the purview of domestic arbitration.[69] This binary approach was overturned only in the early 1990s in another famous case that contributed to the shaping of the US legal market.[70]

Further important distinction between the choice of forum clauses in international commercial litigation and arbitration lies in the question as to who has the jurisdiction to decide on the validity of the forum selection clause. This is a highly contentious issue in transnational litigation, with different courts adopting fundamentally different

65 *Mitsubishi v. Soler Chrysler-Plymouth*, 473 U.S. 614 (1985).

66 See *Mitsubishi* at 639. The *Mitsubishi* case raises a number of novel legal issues that are addressed in depth in other parts of this book. Please see George Bermann and Giuditta Cordero-Moss, ch. 4.

67 Richard A. Nagareda, 'The Litigation-Arbitration Dichotomy Meets the Class Action' [2011] *Notre Dame L. Rev* 1098.

68 See *Scherk*, at 520.

69 Thomas Carbonneau, 'The Exercise of Contract Freedom in the Making of Arbitration Agreement' [2003] *VJTL* 1197.

70 See *Rodriguez de Quijas v. Shearson/American Express Inc.*, 490 U.S. 477 (1989), which expressly overruled *Wilko v. Swan*, 346 U.S. 427 (1953).

approaches. This often leads to complex legal arguments on forum *non conveniens*, parallel claims and antisuit injunctions, especially in common law jurisdictions.[71] On the other hand, in arbitration, it is the tribunal itself that has the authority to decide whether it has jurisdiction to hear a particular dispute. This is known as the competence-competence principle and, together with the doctrine of separability, whereby the arbitration clause survives the invalidity, ineffectiveness and even the non-existence of the main contract, it has become one of the most widely accepted principles of international arbitration. Today, jurisdictional questions have been displaced almost exclusively to the arbitration tribunal.[72]

But the impact *The Bremen* has had on the contemporary understanding of the choice of forum clause goes far beyond the issue of arbitrability. The decision has proved to be timeless, insofar as, since it was decided in 1972, the Supreme Court went on to extend its scope considerably. Perhaps this is best illustrated by *Carnival Cruise v. Shute*.[73] The facts of this case are quite peculiar: The Shutes purchased tickets for a cruise from a local travel agent. The tickets contained general conditions, including a forum selection clause for the courts of Florida, which was the location of the Carnival Cruise's headquarters. During the trip Mrs Shute sustained injuries due to the negligence of Carnival Cruise and she brought a claim against them before the District Court of Washington, which was the place of her residence. Carnival Cruise opposed her claim on the grounds that the agreement contained in the ticket provided for the jurisdiction of the courts of Florida. The case went all the way up to the Supreme Court, which sided with Carnival Cruise on the issue of jurisdiction, quashing Mrs Shute's case.

The Supreme Court rejected the argument that forum selection clauses were valid only if they had been subject to actual negotiation. This was the case even if the parties did not have equal bargaining power. In addition, the Court applied the reasonableness test from *The Bremen* and held that including a forum selection clause in a ticket contract would reduce the risk of litigating in multiple fora and was therefore permissible. The inconvenience of the parties to litigate in the selected jurisdiction was not sufficient to displace the valid forum selection clause. Indeed, the Court made it clear that forum selection clauses will be valid even in standardised form contract viewed as adhesion contracts.[74]

The impact of such a broad application of *The Bremen* has been significant, and remains so until this day. While the conclusion of standardised contracts was already a fairly common practice in the 1990s when *Carnival Cruise* was decided, in recent years characterised by the digital revolution of virtually all aspects of social, economic and private life, the practice of standard form contracts has risen to a new level. Contracting

---

[71] *Owusu v. Jackson* is probably the most famous example on the forum *non conveniens* debate in the context of the 'Brussels regime' applicable in disputes between the EU Member States. For more details, see Christelle Chalas' and Richard Fentiman's analysis in this book.

[72] Julian D.M. Lew, 'Achieving the Dream: Autonomous Arbitration' [2006] *Arbitration International* 197.

[73] *Carnival Cruise Lines v. Schute*, 499 U.S. 585 (1991).

[74] Joseph A. Grundfest and Kristen A. Savelle, 'The Brouhaha Over Intra-Corporate Forum Selection Provisions: A Legal, Economic and Political Analysis' [2013] *The Business Lawyer* 384.

became a routine reality (one would be almost tempted to say *banality*) of our everyday life. They are present when we accept arduous terms and conditions on accessing social networks, authorise use of our private data,[75] shop online, experiment with blockchain and generate 'smart contracts', but also in the commercial sphere, in the form of bills of lading, insurance policies, charter-parties or contracts of sale in commodity markets. And for better or worse, *The Bremen* has left a footprint even in the context of internet transactions. In *CompuServe v. Paterson*, the 6th Circuit Court of Appeals upheld the parties' choice of forum (and law) clause despite the fact that it was concluded in a transaction that was almost entirely electronic.[76] Standard form contracts have become the usual way people and companies manage their legal relationships. The question as to whether the weaker party has any *actual* choice how and where to solve its problems when things go wrong is a true elephant in the room – addressed at least in part by EU law and the protective provisions of the Brussels Regulation (Brussels I recast). To click or not to click, and accept the terms and conditions imposed in most transactions taking place in the 'virtual space', is an everyday dilemma in the digital age…

This is not to say that the current legal and policy challenges linked to choice of forum agreements are limited to the little explored aspects of contracting in a digital age. Legal practitioners and academics alike are discussing other peculiar aspects of choice of forum clauses.[77] In this sense, the debate revolving around asymmetric jurisdiction agreements pours oil on water. Asymmetric agreements, which are a fairly common practice in the banking industry, are seen in some jurisdictions (like France) as problematic as they allow a stronger party, usually a bank, to choose a forum to pursue the other, weaker party, usually a creditor, who does not have such a choice. Yet, other (mostly common law) jurisdictions adopt a more nonchalant approach. The argument goes that the bank should have the right to pick the right forum according to the location of its creditor's assets, while obliging the creditor to sue in one exclusive forum guarantees legal certainty.[78] Additionally, the application of forum selection clauses in the context of mass claims is another debate worth following, as is the extension of choice of forum clauses to disputes that do not arise directly from the contractual obligations between the parties, such as discrimination.[79]

---

75 The problem of data is in itself is a fascinating topic of private international law, albeit not the purpose of this article. It is addressed elsewhere in this book, see the US Supreme Court cases *Yahoo! v. LICRA* and *Microsoft Ireland*. On the Old Continent, protection of private data is the main focus of one of the most important developments of EU law in 2018 – the General Data Protection Regulation (GDPR) which entered into force on 25 May 2018.

76 *CompuServe v. Patterson*, 89 F.3d 1257 (6th Cir. 1996).

77 Mary Keyes and Brooke Adele Marshall, 'Jurisdiction Agreements: Exclusive, Optional and Asymmetrical' [2015] *J Priv Int'l L* 345.

78 For more on this issue, see Louise Merrett, 'The Future of Enforcement of Asymmetric Jurisdiction Agreements' [2018] *ICLQ* 37.

79 This is one of the issues that are dealt with in depth in the *Airbnb* case. Please refer to David Restrepo-Amariles and Gregory Lewkowicz's analysis in this book.

5. CONCLUSION

The Bremen is a product of its time as it suggests that law must constantly adjust to its object – here the ever-changing field of international trade. More indirectly, it points to the fact that cross-border activity may induce a disembedded, or deterritorialised, understanding of law itself. By turning its back on pre-War parochialism, it paved the way for a new, post-modern paradigm for private international law.[80] Unsurprisingly, it continues to be relevant today. What, then, does the future hold? Whereas *The Bremen*'s catchall ratio has been constantly extended over the years and has migrated to other parts of the world, the question to be asked today is whether the move has taken the courts too far in the direction of unbridled party choice, and how, other than through a return to provincialism, they may take back control in the name of the global public good?

80 In the words of Jessup (n 40) 6, 'to envisage the applicability of transnational law it is necessary to avoid thinking solely in terms of any particular forum.'

2. Judicial discretion (from Bhopal to Brexit): *Owusu v. Jackson*

2.1 CASE BACKGROUND

Owusu v. Jackson, usually referred to simply as the '*Owusu* case', is a 2005 ECJ judgment on a reference for a preliminary ruling from the English Court of Appeal on the interpretation of the 1968 Brussels Convention. It contains two important principles that did much to alienate English common lawyers in their uneasy relationship with the common judicial area. Firstly, it considered judicial discretion inherent in the English doctrine of *forum non conveniens* to be inconsistent with the Convention. Under the second principle, it ruled that the Convention was applicable whenever the defendant is domiciled within a Contracting State, wherever the facts may have taken place or the claimant domiciled. Thus, the Brussels Convention precluded the courts of Contracting States from declining the jurisdiction conferred on it by Article 2 of that Convention on the ground that a court of a non-Contracting State would be a more appropriate forum for the trial of the action. This applied even if the jurisdiction of no other Contracting State was in issue and the proceeding had no connecting factors to any other Contracting State.

Mr. Owusu, who was a British national domiciled in the United Kingdom, suffered a very serious accident during a holiday in Jamaica. As he dived into the sea from a beach accessed from a private villa, he struck his head against a submerged sand bank and hurt his fifth cervical vertebra, which rendered him tetraplegic. Consequently, Mr. Owusu brought an action in the United Kingdom for breach of contract against Mr. Jackson, who had let him the holiday villa. It appeared that another English holidaymaker had suffered a similar accident two years earlier and no effort had been made to signal the danger. Mr. Owusu claimed that the contract contained an implied term that the beach would be reasonably safe or free from hidden dangers. Mr. Owusu also brought an action in tort in the United Kingdom against several Jamaican companies, including the owner and occupier of the beach where the accident took place, and companies that provided him with a free access to the beach. The action in tort involved a claim that the defendants failed to warn swimmers of the hazard constituted by the submerged sand bank and failed to signal the previous accident.

Unlike other defendants, Mr. Jackson was domiciled in the United Kingdom. While his domicile certainly justified the jurisdiction of the English courts under Article 2 of the Brussels Convention, he claimed that in this case the Jamaican courts were undeniably a more appropriate forum. However, the ECJ held that Article 2 of the Brussels Convention was mandatory in nature and could not be derogated from except in the cases expressly provided. Allowing a court to decline its jurisdiction on a discretionary basis would undermine the predictability of the rules of jurisdiction, ruin the principle of legal certainty, and diminish the legal protection of persons established in the Community. All these arguments gave rise to intense controversy. They are clearly underlain by a cultural approach to jurisdiction, which can be seen either as an expression of inherent judicial power or simply as a matter of venue and good administration of justice.

Case: *Owusu v. Jackson*, ECJ [2005] C-281/02

2.2 UNCERTAINTIES REGARDING THE APPLICATION OF THE EUROPEAN JURISDICTION REGIME VIS-À-VIS NON-MEMBER STATES

*Christelle Chalas**

Forum rei v. forum non conveniens! Beyond the confrontation between two individuals, *Owusu v. Jackson* is one of three cases that contrast the legal traditions of the United Kingdom with those of the European civil law countries in relation to international jurisdiction.[1] These countries all share the same rules on jurisdiction in civil and commercial matters since the accession of the United Kingdom in 1978 to the Brussels Convention of 27 September 1968. Of Scottish origin,[2] the doctrine of *forum non conveniens* – in its modern form – appeared much later in England so its incorporation in the jurisprudence was still in question when the United Kingdom acceded to the Convention, whose text was clearly inspired by the civil law tradition. Nonetheless, it should be noted that the English judges have long recognised the 'inherent jurisdiction' to stay proceedings if the choice of an English court by the claimant is considered 'vexatious and oppressive and an abuse of the process of the Court'.[3]

The doctrine of *forum non conveniens*, the most successful exportation of the Scottish legal system to the United States,[4] developed further there, but independently and far from the prudence and restraint that Scottish judges had always shown when using it. American judges very quickly gave excessive importance to the defence of national public interest and the fight against forum shopping. The American version of the doctrine of *forum non conveniens* has then been transformed from a way of correcting the rules on jurisdiction designed to ensure judgment in the best location, into a formidable procedural weapon, with the goal of closing American courts to foreign claimants eager to use its special procedural rules (class action, discovery, contingency fee, injunctive relief) and the exorbitant sums awarded as compensation to

---

* Contribution originally written in French, translated into English by Hannah Bracken.

1 The other two emblematic cases dealing with the tension between common law's procedural institutions and civil law's objective of legal security, at the level of guiding principle in the common legal area according to the jurisprudence of the Court of Justice of the European Union, are Case C-116/02 *Erich Gasser GmbH c/ MISAT Srl* [2003] ECR I-14693, and Case C-159/02 *Turner v. Grovit* [2004] ECR I-03565, see (2004) 2 Rev.crit. DIP 444 and 3 Rev.crit. DIP 654, notes H. Muir Watt.

2 The case *Sim v. Robinow* from 1882 and the case *La société du Gaz de Paris v. La Société Anonyme de Navigations 'Les Armateurs Français'* from 1926, are the foundation of the Scottish doctrine of *forum non conveniens*. On the historical evolution in the doctrine in different common law countries see Ch. Chalas, *L'exercice discrétionnaire de la compétence juridictionnelle en droit international privé* 1 st edn (Tome 1, PUAM 2000).

3 *St Pierre v. South American Stores* [1936] 1 K.B. 382 (Court of Appeal) 398.

4 According to P.R. Beaumont in *Declining Jurisdiction in Private International Law, Reports to the XIVth Congress of the International Academy of Comparative Law* (JJ Fawcett (dir.), Oxford, Clarendon Press 1996) 207.

victims of damages (punitive damages).[5] The doctrine is also used to guarantee a form of jurisdictional immunity to US domiciled companies relocating their hazardous activities abroad. The infamous case of *Bhopal*,[6] which arises from the most devastating industrial accident in history, is the tragic illustration of the wrongs that an abusive and partial use of the doctrine of *forum non conveniens* can lead to.

It is in this context of strong disapproval of the doctrine of *forum non conveniens* by the continental civil law countries, that the Court of Justice in *Owusu* is presented with the question of its compatibility with the Brussels system. As any form of discretionary exercise of jurisdiction is (at least in appearance) foreign to the legal system of the six founding members of the Brussels Convention, the Convention naturally enshrined a strict system of jurisdiction.[7] As for the Civil Jurisdiction and Judgement Act of 1982 introducing the Brussels Convention in Great Britain, it says that 'Nothing in this Act shall prevent any court in the United Kingdom from staying, sisting, striking out or dismissing any proceedings before it, on the ground of *forum non conveniens* or otherwise, *where to do so is not inconsistent with the 1968 Convention*' (emphasis added). An example of this incompatibility would undoubtedly be the refusal of an English court to exercise its jurisdiction under the Convention because the courts of another Contracting State would be better placed to rule on the dispute. This would indeed be in contradiction to the system of the Convention that allocates jurisdiction between Contracting States. However, the question remained of whether such an incompatibility would still exist after the staying of the English proceedings in favor of the courts of a non-member State since the functioning of the Convention's system might not be opposed. *Owusu* finally gives the Court of Justice the chance to take a side on this much-debated question in British doctrine and jurisprudence.

In order to decide, the Court of Justice devotes significant energy to responding to a question that was not directly asked about 'the applicability of Article 2 of the Brussels Convention' in a situation, such as the case at hand, where the question regarding the allocation of jurisdiction is between the courts of a Contracting State (England) and that of non-member State (Jamaica) and not between the courts of different Contracting States. This question on the scope of Article 2, carefully formulated by Advocate General Léger (paragraphs 72 and 73), to which the most important part of the conclusions is dedicated, is considered to precede the question of the possibility for English judges to use the doctrine of *forum non conveniens* in this same situation. Indeed, Article 2 would have to establish the jurisdiction of the English judge in order to subsequently ask if the same judge may refuse to exercise his jurisdiction on a discretionary basis because the courts of a non-member State may be better placed to rule on it.

[5] According to the famous formulation of Lord Denning: 'As a moth is drawn to the light, so is a litigant to the United-States. If he can only get his case into their courts, he stands to win a fortune …', *Smith Kline & French Laboratories. Ltd. V. Bloch*, [1983] W.L.R. 730 (Court of Appeal) 733–34.

[6] *Re Union Carbide Gas Plant Disaster at Bhopal, India in December 1984*, [1986] 634 F. Supp. 842 (S.D.N.Y.), [1987] 809 F 2d 195 (U.S. Court of Appeal).

[7] The Schlosser Report, created after the accession of the United Kingdom, is clearly against the use of the doctrine of *forum non conveniens* within the scope of the Convention [1979] OJEC C. 59/71, paras 76–81.

If these two questions are actually linked, (1 and 2), then the causal effect that the Court of Justice weaves between the answers is more debatable (3). The shaping of the conflict of jurisdictions, in a vacuum, by only opposing the mutual relations between a Contracting State and a non-member State, would have had a different scope based on the problem in question.

1. THE APPLICABILITY OF ARTICLE 2

The question of the applicability of Article 2 and of the Convention more broadly has, when not specified by the Convention, been a controversial subject regarding whether this is subject to the fulfilment of a particular condition of internationality in the legal relationship concerned. The preamble of the Brussels Convention provides, in its sole recital, that the Convention aims to 'determine the international jurisdiction of their courts …', with no conclusion drawn on the international nature of the legal relationship required by the text for it to be applicable. The debate on this question has divided the proponents of a restrictive conception of the territorial scope of application of the Brussels Convention from the proponents of a broader conception. The first, which includes the British government in this case and the Court of Appeal in its noteworthy precedent in *Harrods*,[8] has a substantial argument in the Jenard Report on the Brussels Convention of 27 September 1968.[9] Implicitly outlining the contours of an *intra-Community* internationality, the Jenard report postulates that the Convention is not applicable to situations *internal* to a Contracting State, or *external* to the Community area, the latter meaning in cases that also involve a non-member State. The proponents of the broad conception, which includes the majority of authors and which will be supported by the Court of Justice, consider on the contrary that if one presumed the international character of the legal relationship concerned is actually a condition for the application of Article 2 of the Convention,[10] there is no basis for asserting that internationality stemming from a relationship involving a Contracting State and a non-member State would not be sufficient to fulfil this condition.

In a first decision, *Group Josi*,[11] the Court of Justice specified that the application of the Brussels Convention in Article 2 does not require in any way that both litigants have their domicile in a Contracting State as long as the defendant satisfies this condition. When asked about the applicability of the Brussels Convention to a dispute between a defendant domiciled in Belgium and a claimant domiciled in Canada, and

---

8 *Re Harrods [Buenos Aires] Ltd.* [1991] 3 *WLR*. 397. In this case, the Court of Justice, which faced a preliminary question that was identical to that of *Owusu*, was not able to rule as the question was withdrawn after the parties resolved their dispute amiably: Case C-314/92 *Lademinor*; order for removal 21 February 1994.

9 [1979] OJEC C-59/8.

10 According to G. Droz, the application of Article 2 is not subject to the existence of an international legal relationship, whatever its form may be. See G. Droz, *Compétence judiciaire et effets des jugements dans le marché commun, Etude de la Convention de Bruxelles du 27 septembre 1968* (Paris, Dalloz 1972) 23–25.

11 Case C-412/98 *Group Josi Reinsurance Company SA v. Universal General Insurance Company* [2000] ECR I-5925.

when the latter seized the French courts on the basis of a common law competence rule, the Court of Justice responded that 'Title II of the Convention is in principle applicable where the defendant has its domicile or seat in a Contracting State, even if the plaintiff is domiciled in a non-member country' (paragraph 61). By making the location of the defender's domicile in the territory of a Contracting State the cardinal criteria for the applicability of the Convention, the *Group Josi* decision was already favouring a broad interpretation of the scope of applicability and this led the first English judge seized in the *Owusu* case to refrain from applying the doctrine of *forum non conveniens* in favour of the Jamaican jurisdiction. The *Group Josi* decision left open the question of whether the intra-Community character of the dispute should not then at least come from the substance and, in particular, from the configuration of the conflict of jurisdiction between the courts of at least two Contracting States (which was the case in *Group Josi* since the French and Belgian courts were simultaneously competent). This issue is resolved with *Owusu* which clearly establishes that for Article 2 to be applicable, neither the substance of the dispute nor the situation of the parties need to relate to more than one Contracting State (paragraphs 24 to 26).

This position that the Court of Justice supports is taken as much from the wording of Article 2 as from the general structure of the Convention and the legal base on which it was adopted (Article 220 of the EC Treaty), and is the only one that conforms to the text and the Convention's objectives. It was skilfully demonstrated, that defining what could constitute intra-community litigation, is actually very difficult,[12] and would have proven excessively complex and led to unnecessary disputes.[13] Moreover, making the application of Article 2 of the Convention subject to the establishing of the intra-community character of the dispute would have, in the event of failure, led to referring it back to the national rules of international jurisdiction of the Contracting States.[14] This is not the objective pursued by the defenders of the restrictive conception of the Brussels Convention's scope who do not deny that the Brussels Convention must retain the role of attributing jurisdiction between the courts of a Contracting State and those of a non-member State. It is clear from the first preliminary question of the Court of Appeal that the uncertainty surrounding the use of the doctrine of *forum non conveniens* exists from the moment when the English court seized gets its international jurisdiction from a rule of the Convention.[15]

As a result, there is not the shadow of a doubt that Article 2 retains its role attributing international jurisdiction to the courts of Contracting States in a situation like that of the present case. If the Court of Justice devotes such a large part of its reasoning to this,

---

[12] It varies according to the Convention rule concerned so that the notion of a Community litigation is elusive in practice. See E. Pataut, 'Qu'est-ce qu'un litige "intracommunautaire"? Réflexions autour de l'article 4 du Règlement Bruxelles I', in *Justice et droits fondamentaux: études offertes à J. Normand* (Paris, Litec 2003) 365.

[13] What criteria should be used to consider that a dispute is effectively or sufficiently connected to several Contracting States? Are some criteria more relevant than others?

[14] In total contravention of Article 3 regarding a defendant domiciled in a Contracting State.

[15] No one has ever really doubted that the English courts can use this doctrine when they have international jurisdiction on the basis of national law conforming to Article 4 para. 1 of the Convention, even if the dispute falls within the scope of civil and commercial matters and the staying of proceedings would occur in favour of the courts of another Contracting State.

it is because it hopes to draw conclusions from the statement about the scope of the rule in terms of the rule's effect and, in particular, its mandatory effect. But this unsharp reasoning does not do justice to the real challenges of the problem.

2. THE INCOMPATIBILITY BETWEEN THE *FORUM NON CONVENIENS* EXCEPTION AND THE BRUSSELS CONVENTION

The grounds advanced by the Court of Justice in condemning the use of the *forum non conveniens* doctrine when the defendant is domiciled in a Contracting State are unquestionable and without qualification: '*mandatory*' by nature Article 2 can only be derogated from 'in the cases expressly provided for by the Convention' (paragraph 37). The Court of Justice supports this radical position with a reference, which has become like a litany, to the objectives of the Convention at the top of which the Court places the legal protection of persons domiciled in the Community; this is ensured by the establishment of uniform rules of jurisdiction and by recognition and execution of decisions ensuring a high degree of certainty and legal security for litigants. In consequence, the doctrine of *forum non conveniens* is doubly condemned: not only does it derogate from the mandatory nature of Article 2 in a case not expressly provided for by the Convention, but above all, its discretionary nature threatens the system of the Convention that lies in the symbolic values of legal security and mutual trust.

Taken literally, however, the scope of the assertion of the mandatory nature of Article 2 is considerable and goes beyond the rejection of the *forum non conveniens* doctrine. It implies that any form of suspension or staying of proceedings for the benefit of a non-member State court is prohibited, including in the situations where it is generally accepted that for very legitimate procedural reasons the court seized gives up the case to another State that is equally competent and more legitimate to rule on the dispute (including within the Convention, between Contracting States). The Court of Appeal had however taken care in its second preliminary question to attract the attention of the Court of Justice to potential risks of an overly dogmatic opposition to the doctrine of *forum non conveniens*. This doctrine, after all, is the means by which the English judges give effect to jurisdiction clauses and handle situations of international *lis pendens*. The Court of Justice did not respond to the second question about the determination of the 'circumstances' in which the judge of a Contracting State may exceptionally stay its jurisdiction that derives from Article 2, since this response was not necessary to resolve *Owusu*. But the unequivocal affirmation of the mandatory nature of Article 2 seems to nip in the bud the possibility for Contracting States to use their national law to regulate the international jurisdiction that they have from this disposition vis-à-vis non-member States, whatever the basis of the jurisdiction for the non-member. Evolved into the 'privilege of Community jurisdiction',[16] Article 2

[16] H. Gaudemet-Tallon, note under Versailles 26 September 1991 (court of appeal) (1992) *Rev.crit. DIP*. 333, 337.

allocates 'a partial, exclusive jurisdiction to the domicile of the defendant',[17] without a basis in the Convention.

This literal interpretation that is central to *Owusu* has been criticised,[18] even contested,[19] in scholarship, essentially on the ground that the result would be particularly unfortunate. For the same reason, the jurisprudence has not followed the interpretation in its most criticised implications, particularly the English jurisprudence which under doctrinal pressure rushed to limit the scope of *Owusu* by affirming that this could not have the effect of prohibiting the English courts from giving effect, by reference to national law and consequently to the doctrine of *forum non conveniens*, to contract clauses attributing jurisdiction to the courts of non-member States.[20] The ingenious theory of the 'reflex effect'[21] advocates for reproducing, through the procedural tools of national law, the application of the rules of the Convention on declining jurisdiction for conflicts of jurisdiction between the courts of a Contracting State and those of a non-member State. The theory had almost unanimous support of the continental European scholarship which saw it as the ideal compromise between the general prohibition of declining jurisdiction pronounced in *Owusu*, and the exclusive power of the national law to order this declining in relations with non-member States. Although implicitly condemned by an opinion 1/03 of 7 February 2006 by the Court of Justice on the Community's competence to conclude a new Lugano Convention,[22] the theory has nevertheless been convincingly applied for the first time by an English High Court judge in the *Ferrexpo*[23] case.

Beyond the rejection of the doctrine of *forum non conveniens*, to which the Court of Justice has always been hostile,[24] the real problem that led to *Owusu* has to do with the place left to national law on international jurisdiction when the conflict involves the judge of a Contracting State of the defendant's domicile and a non-member forum.

---

17 P. de Vareilles-Sommières, 'La compétence internationale de l'espace judiciaire européen', in *Mélanges en l'honneur de H. Gaudemet-Tallon* (Paris, Dalloz 2008) 397, 413 ff. The exclusivity is partial because it does not stop the recognition of a decision given in a non-member state against a defender domiciled in a Contracting State.

18 de Vareilles-Sommières (n 17) 413 ff.

19 L. Usunier, *La régulation de la compétence juridictionnelle en droit international privé* (Paris, Economica 2008) paras 403 ff.

20 *Konkola Copper Mines plc v. Coromin* [2005] EWHC 898 (Comm).

21 See, A. Nuyts, 'La théorie de l'effet réflexe' in *Le droit processuel et judiciaire européen* (Bruxelles, La Charte, 2003) 73.

22 Opinion 1/03 OF 7.2.2006 [2006] ECR I-1145. This interpretation of the opinion 1/03, which is sometimes contested, is confirmed by the Commission in its report on the application of the Brussels I Regulation of 21 April 2009 ((COM) 2009 174 final, para. 32§2 *in fine*).

23 *Ferrexpo v. Gilson Investments Ltd. & Ors* [2012] EWHC 721 (Comm), about which C. Chalas, 'L'affaire *Ferrexpo* : baptême anglais pour l'effet réflexe des articles 22, 27 et 28 du règlement Bruxelles I' (2013) 2 *Rev. Crit. DIP* 359.

24 The Court of Justice repeatedly demonstrated its hostility to the few propositions aimed at tempering the mandatory nature of the Convention's jurisdiction rules. See Case C-440/97 *GIE Groupe Concorde e.a. v. Capitaine commandant le navire 'Suhadiwarno Panjan' e.a.* [1999] ECR I-06307; Case C-288/92 *Custom Made Commercial v. Stawa Metalbau*, ECR I-02918.

3. THE PLACE OF NATIONAL LAW ON JURISDICTION IN THE EUROPEAN SYSTEM OF COMPETENCE

Questioning the place of national law in the European system of jurisdiction brings us to the unsolvable dilemma of the scope of the system and its objectives. For the Court of Justice, since national law is excluded at the stage of attribution of jurisdiction when the defendant's domicile is in a Contracting State (Article 3), the national law cannot modify the regime of this jurisdiction. In other words, the Convention cannot confer jurisdiction to the courts of a Contracting State and admit at the same time that the jurisdiction is challenged on the basis of the national law of this State. Only the Convention can withdraw what it has given. This thesis leads to the potentially disastrous results that were previously mentioned.

But conversely, the attribution of jurisdiction and the declining of jurisdiction form two distinct bodies of rules. It could be considered that if the Convention (1) confers jurisdiction on the courts of a Contracting State as soon as its rules apply; (2) determines the cases in which this jurisdiction can be declined when two (or more) Contracting States are involved; (3) it does not, however, determine the cases in which this jurisdiction can be declined in situations that involve a Contracting State and a non-member State. This question is necessarily dealt with by the national law of the judge that was seized.[25] Thus, in relations with non-member States, while Article 2 would retain the function of a classic international jurisdiction rule (a *unilateral* function of attachment to a legal order), it would lose its specific function under the Convention *to distribute* jurisdiction between legal orders, such distribution of jurisdiction being ensured by the mechanisms of national law.[26]

If we followed the above thesis, the difficulty to demonstrate the lack of involvement of Community interest for judging the case would resurface, because such demonstration would be necessary for declining the jurisdiction of a Contracting State's court in favour of non-member State courts. However, despite the precautions taken by the Court of Appeal in formulating its question,[27] it will not always be easy to ensure that no community interest is violated. And for good reason, as the fact that in *Owusu* the *claimant* also had his domicile in England could have led to the consideration that the dispute should continue to fall within the system of the Convention because of the interest for a person domiciled in the Community to benefit from the availability of the *forum rei*.

Professor Pascal de Vareilles-Sommières justifies *Owusu* through a renewed vision of the notion of attributing general jurisdiction to the European legal space,[28] a global

---

[25] R. Fentiman, 'National Law and the European Regime' in *International Civil Litigation in Europe in Relation with Third States* (Brussels, Bruylant 2005) 83.

[26] On the functions of the rules of international jurisdiction, see P. Théry, 'La compétence' in E. Pataut, S. Bollée, L. Cadiet and E. Jeuland (eds), *Les nouvelles formes de coordination des justices étatiques* (Paris, IRJS 2013) 45, 49.

[27] The referring court made it clear in *Owusu* that the question of jurisdiction of the courts of any *other* Contracting State did not arise and that the dispute had no connection with *any* Contracting State other than England.

[28] de Vareilles-Sommières (n 17) 410 ff.

system that is always under construction, but which became more tangible with the transformation of the Brussels Convention into a European Regulation.[29] Thus, this idea resembles the thesis of the Court of Justice, but with more subtlety. The author proposes that the 'general jurisdiction of the European legal space' overlays the jurisdiction of the English judge designated by Article 2. For this reason the English judge could not unilaterally interfere with European jurisdiction by using his national law.[30] In other words, the 'general jurisdiction of the European legal space' is upstream from the special jurisdiction of the English judge, and the English judge cannot use his national law's procedural tools to regulate what happens upstream. Yet, Professor Pascal de Vareilles-Sommières deplores the excessive scope of the regrettable grounds employed by the Court of Justice in *Owusu* and defends the competing nature of the jurisdiction conferred on the Member States by Article 2 and maintaining the power of the Member States to refuse to exercise their jurisdiction in cases of exclusive jurisdiction of a non-Member State or *lis pendens*. The author does not, however, specify the regime of such power,[31] the source of which resides in the Brussels I Regulation itself, 'and more precisely in the absence of exclusivity of the jurisdiction of the judge of the defendant's domicile as provided for by Article 2'.[32]

Faced with so many uncertainties, paradoxically generated by a frenzied quest for legal security, the European legislator eventually intervened when the Brussels I was revised, dedicating two innovative provisions within the Brussels I *bis* Regulation[33] to the resolution of the *lis pendens* and related actions between a Member State and a non-Member State (Articles 33 and 34). Introducing a welcome dose of flexibility in relations with non-Member States for when there is a parallel procedure pending before a court of a third state, Articles 33 and 34 entrust the judge of the Member State that was seized second (in certain cases) with the power to stay the proceedings after an analysis of 'all the circumstances of the case …', including the links between the facts of the case, the parties and the non-Member State, the progress of the procedure in the latter and the probability that it will give a judgment in a reasonable time (Recitals 23 and 24 of the Brussels I *bis* Regulation). These new dispositions only solve part of the difficulty because their applicability is dependent on the existence of a conflict of parallel procedures and the seizing in the first place of a court of a third State. They do not revoke *Owusu*, because in the absence of a procedure effectively pending in Jamaica when the English judge was seized, they would have not been applicable. Furthermore, it could be that the exclusion of the doctrine of *forum non conveniens* is

---

29 Council Regulation (EC) 44/2001 on jurisdiction and the recognition and enforcement of judgments in civil and commercial matters [2001] OJ L 12/1, called 'Brussels I'; Council Regulation (EU) 1215/2012 on jurisdiction and the recognition and enforcement of judgments in civil and commercial matters (recast) [2012] OJ L 351/1, called 'Brussels I *bis*', in effect since 10 January 2015.

30 de Vareilles-Sommières (n 17) 411.

31 Which would then depend on the national law of the forum seized, which leads to the same results and questions as the theory of the reflexive effect.

32 de Vareilles-Sommières (n 17) 417.

33 Council Regulation (EU) 1215/2012 of the European Parliament and of the Council of 12 December 2012 on jurisdiction and the recognition and enforcement of judgments in civil and commercial matters (recast) OJ [2012] L 351/1.

subject to a new assault as it is henceforth under the aegis of Articles 33 and 34, that the very sensitive question in English law of the effectiveness of an agreement by parties to attribute exclusive jurisdiction to the courts of a third State, now has to be dealt with.[34] Indeed, there are reasons to believe that the cases which will not be covered by the relatively strict conditions of Articles 33 and 34 will not be dealt with by reference to national law.[35]

With the possible departure from the European legal space, accompanied by a subsequent return to its national law, Brexit gives the United Kingdom control of its traditional procedural institutions of common law and control of the access to its courts. It must then be hoped that the re-appropriation of the freedom to dispose of their international jurisdiction does not lead British judges to make their country an asylum at the gates of Europe for multinationals who in searching for judicial immunity would install their headquarters there in the hope of escaping their possible liability for damages caused by their foreign activities through the exception of *forum non conveniens*.[36] Similarly, we should strive to enrich and refine the private international law of this 'legal order' that the European Union is in the process of building, and all this for a closer cooperation with the non-member States, which will possibly soon include the United Kingdom.

2.3 ARTICLES 33 AND 34 AND THE 'REFORM' OF THE EU JURISDICTION REGIME: A MISSED OPPORTUNITY TO SOLVE THE LONGSTANDING CONTROVERSY?

Richard Fentiman

1. INTRODUCTION

The controversy prompted by *Owusu v. Jackson*[37] remains unresolved. It remains uncertain when, if at all, EU national courts may employ national law to decline jurisdiction in favour of proceedings in third states when their jurisdiction derives from EU law.[38] But the context and significance of the discussion has changed since *Owusu*

[34] See Recital 24 of the Brussels I *bis* Regulation; provided, however, that the Convention of The Hague of 30 June 2005 on the agreement of the choice of forum does not apply.

[35] Which will therefore be confined to the cases where the international jurisdiction of the Member States will be seized on the basis of their national rules, whose application has finally been maintained by the Brussels I *bis* Regulation when the defendant is domiciled in a non-Member State (under reservation of articles 18§1, 21§2, 24 and 25).

[36] *S.W.B. Lubbe v. Cape plc* [2000] UKHL 41, see the comment by Ch. Chalas in (2002) 4 *Rev.crit. DIP* 693.

[37] Case 281/02.

[38] See generally, Richard Fentiman, *International Commercial Litigation* 2nd edn (Oxford, OUP 2015) Ch 12.

was decided. Articles 33 and 34 of Regulation 1215/2012 (the Brussels 1 Recast)[39] now provide a basis within the EU regime for declining jurisdiction in favour of the courts of third States. At its strongest, this challenges the continuing relevance of *Owusu*, or at least its significance. Arguably, those provisions supply an exclusive regime for staying proceedings in such cases, which makes *Owusu* irrelevant, consigning it to history. If they do not have this effect *Owusu* has continued relevance, although in a fresh context, but its significance is diminished. The fact that the Regulation itself now endorses a discretionary approach to stays involving third States adds a new dimension, and new uncertainty, to the debate.

2. *OWUSU*: SCOPE AND CRITIQUE

It is clear that *Owusu* forbids resort to national law in the particular circumstances of that case. National courts no longer have any discretionary power to stay proceedings in such cases on the basis that a court in a third State is the *forum conveniens* where the basis for exercising jurisdiction is the defendant's domicile. It is unclear, however, whether the answer would be different if the facts of *Owusu* are varied in any one of three ways: if the ground for exercising jurisdiction is other than the defendant's domicile (for example, if jurisdiction derives from Article 7 of Regulation 1215/2012); if the facts are significantly different (as where the case involves third-party defendants who are not EU-domiciled); or if the reason for declining jurisdiction is different (for example, if there arc parallel proceedings in the third State, or if its courts have exclusive jurisdiction).

Commentators – at least English commentators – have subjected the decision in *Owusu* to considerable criticism.[40] A dominant strand in this critique is the argument that the EU jurisdiction regime is inapplicable where a stay is sought in favour of

[39] Regulation (EU) No 1215/2012 on jurisdiction and the recognition and enforcement of judgments in civil and commercial matters [2012] OJ L351/1.

[40] For summary and analysis see Richard Fentiman, 'Civil Jurisdiction and Third States: Owusu and After' [2006] 43 *CMLR* 705. See further: Adrian Briggs, 'Spiliada and the Brussels Convention' [1991] *LMCLQ* 10; Adrian Briggs, 'Forum Non Conveniens and the Brussels Convention Again' (1991) 107 *LQR* 180; Adrian Briggs, 'Some Points of Friction Between English and Brussels Convention Jurisdiction' in Mads Andenas and Francis Jacobs (eds.) *European Community Law in the English Courts* (Oxford, OUP 1998) 277; Adrian Briggs, 'Owusu v Jackson' (2005) 121 *LQR* 535; Lawrence Collins, 'Forum Non Conveniens and the Brussels Convention' (1990) 106 *LQR* 535; Georges Droz, *Compétence judiciaire et effets des jugements dans le Marché Commun* (Paris, Dalloz 1972) 58; Richard Fentiman, 'Jurisdiction, Discretion and the Brussels Convention' (1993) *Cornell Int LJ* 59; Richard Fentiman, 'Ousting Jurisdiction and the European Conventions' (2000) 3 *CYELS* 107; Richard Fentiman, 'National Law and the European Jurisdiction Regime' in Arnaud Nuyts and Nadine Watté (eds), *International Civil Litigation in Europe and Relations With Third States* (Brussels, Bruylant 2005) 83; Hélène Gaudemet-Tallon, 'Le forum non conveniens, une menace pour la convention de Bruxelles?' (1991) *Rev cr dr int pr* 491; Hélène Gaudemet-Tallon, *Les Conventions de Bruxelles et de Lugano* 2nd edn (Paris, Dalloz 1996) paras 75, 84, 93, 111; Trevor Hartley, *Civil Jurisdiction and Judgments* (London, Sweet & Maxwell 1982) 79–80; Trevor Hartley, 'Forum non conveniens in Europe' (1992) 17 *ELRev* 553; Arnaud Nuyts, *L'Exception de Forum non conveniens* (Brussels, Bruylant 2003) 253 et seq.

proceedings in a third State. For that reason the allocation of proceedings between an EU state and a third State is a matter for national law.[41] For that reason also it is irrelevant to ask whether a stay in such a case is consistent with the principles applicable where the regime applies, and in particular with the objectives of certainty, predictability and uniformity. This argument cannot now stand following the introduction of Articles 33 and 34 in the recast Brussels 1 Regulation. National courts may now grant a stay of proceedings where there are parallel proceedings in a third State and the administration of justice requires. Such cases are manifestly within the scope of the EU regime.

More importantly, the reasoning in *Owusu* itself supplies a riposte to the argument that the EU regime would be wholly inapplicable in such cases. The argument rests on the assumption that the overriding objective of the Brussels regime is the mutual enforcement of judgments between EU States. It is apparent, however, that the objects of the regime are broader. The harmonisation of private international law in the EU is now an overriding objective which the Brussels regime must now serve, a change in position initiated by the CJEU in *Owusu*. As the CJEU made clear in *Owusu* the harmonisation of private international law is implicitly required by the EU project.[42] That requires a uniform approach to issues of jurisdiction within the EU. It cannot then be possible for individual EU States to qualify the operation of EU law by relying upon national rules for declining jurisdiction. As the Court expressed it, in a passage of considerable importance, 'the consolidation as such of the rules on conflict of jurisdiction and on the recognition and enforcement of judgments' is 'intended to eliminate obstacles to the functioning of the internal market'.[43]

The CJEU thus concluded that the Brussels regime must serve the objectives of the internal market, which requires uniformity in all matters of jurisdiction, leaving no room for the subsidiary application of national law. That objective was not served only in cases involving the allocation of proceedings between Member States. It was served by the uniform application of the Convention's rules of jurisdiction in any case to which those rules applied. Significantly, therefore, the argument that the Convention's defining objective would not be served if it were applied in such cases was defeated by a higher-order consideration.

Once it was established that the matter in *Owusu* was within the scope of the EU regime it was possible and necessary to ask whether a stay on the facts was compatible with the principles underlying the regime.[44] The strategy of making such considerations irrelevant by challenging the scope of the EU regime had failed. Given the discretionary nature of the English court's approach, and the absence of such an approach in most other EU States, it was perhaps inevitable that it would be found to be incompatible with the principles underlying the regime. In particular, the objectives of the EU jurisdiction regime would be undermined by allowing courts discretion to qualify their jurisdiction. To do so would impair legal certainty. It would also prejudice

---

41 Originating in *Re Harrods (Buenos Aires) Ltd* [1992] Ch 72 (CA); Richard Fentiman, 'Civil Jurisdiction and Third States: Owusu and After' (n 40) 710 et seq.

42 Case C-281/02 para 34.

43 Case C-281/02 para 34.

44 Case C-281/02 paras 37–46.

persons established in the EU, by removing the benefits of legal certainty for both parties, and by putting obstacles in the way of EU claimants wishing to establish jurisdiction under the regime. Finally, it would undermine the uniform application of the Convention, because the doctrine of *forum non conveniens* was known in some Member States, but not others.

It is therefore unrealistic to challenge the correctness of the decision in *Owusu* on grounds of principle. English commentators and the courts have sought, however, to explore the boundaries and implications of the decision. In doing so, they have relied on broader arguments about the scope and objectives of the EU jurisdiction regime while accepting that the final measure must be consistency with the decision in *Owusu* itself. Subsequent English cases have in particular supplied answers to the remaining questions left unanswered because of the narrowness of the decision in *Owusu* itself. It has been held, first, that it is irrelevant that jurisdiction derives from a ground of jurisdiction other than the defendant's domicile. The prohibition established in *Owusu* remains.[45] Second, it has been held to be irrelevant that non-EU third parties are implicated. *Owusu* nonetheless prevents a stay of any claim against an anchor defendant domiciled in an EU State.[46]

Third, and of particular importance, a stay is possible if the ground for declining jurisdiction is other than the greater appropriateness of the third-State forum, at least where that forum has exclusive jurisdiction.[47] Only in cases involving an application to stay on bare *forum conveniens* grounds does *Owusu* apply. Relying on the doctrine of reflexive effect the English courts have for example stayed proceedings, in which their jurisdiction derives from EU law, where the parties have agreed to the exclusive jurisdiction of the third State's courts.[48] Commentators have also sought to justify a role for national law in such cases by returning to the scope of the EU jurisdiction. They have argued that whether national courts may decline jurisdiction in favour of a third State is a question beyond the scope of the EU regime where the third State's court are perceived as having exclusive jurisdiction. By such means, English commentators have accepted the correctness of the decision in *Owusu* but have sought to restrict its scope.

3. *OWUSU*: CONTINUED RELEVANCE?

It is unclear, however, whether *Owusu* and the questions it implies have any continuing relevance. This depends on the problematic scope of Articles 33 and 34 of Regulation

---

45 *Gomez v. Gomez-Monche Vives* [2008] EWHC 259 (Ch), [2008] 1 All ER (Comm) 973.

46 *Lungowe v. Vedanta Resources Plc* [2017] EWCA Civ 1528, [2017] WLR(D) 741.

47 *Konkola Copper Mines plc v. Coromin* [2005] EWHC 898, [2005] 2 Lloyd's Rep. 555; *Winnetka Trading Corporation v. Julius Baer International Ltd* [2008] EWHC 3146 (Ch), [2009] 2 All ER (Comm) 735, at [25]; *Ferrexpo v. Gilson Investments Ltd* [2012] EWHC 721 (Comm); *Plaza BV v. The Law Debenture Trust Corporation Plc* [2015] EWHC 43 (Ch); see also *Masri v. Consolidated Contractors International Co SAL* [2008] EWCA Civ 303, [2009] 2 WLR 621.

48 *Konkola Copper Mines Plc v. Coromin* [2005] EWHC 898, [2005] 2 Lloyd's Rep. 555; *Winnetka Trading Corporation v. Julius Baer International Ltd* [2008] EWHC 3146 (Ch), [2009] 2 All ER (Comm) 735 at [25].

1215/2012. Do those provisions supply an exclusive mechanism for declining jurisdiction in favour of third States, or does national law apply where they are inapplicable? If they are exclusive *Owusu* is devoid of interest. If they are not, the fundamental questions raised by *Owusu* remain, although in a somewhat different form.

Taken together Articles 33 and 34 confer on national courts a restricted power under EU law to stay proceedings in favour of proceedings in third States.[49] The national court's jurisdiction under the Regulation must be non-exclusive, there must be parallel proceedings in a third State, and the proper administration of justice must require a stay. The power to grant a stay, and the basis for doing so, are matters of EU law where Articles 33 and 34 apply. But it is uncertain whether those provisions now supply an exclusive mechanism for staying proceedings in favour of third States, or whether national law retains a role where they are inapplicable, most importantly because there are no parallel proceedings. Whether Articles 33 and 34 are an exclusive regime for staying proceedings in such cases, and whether, and on what basis, stays are permitted if they do not represent an exclusive regime depend on considerations beyond the reasoning and decision in *Owusu* itself. But the answer depends ultimately on which solutions are consistent with the position adopted in *Owusu*.

It may be assumed that Articles 33 and 34 provide an exclusive regime for handling cases involving parallel proceedings,[50] but it is unclear what impact it has on other possible grounds for declining jurisdiction. One area of difficulty concerns the meaning and purpose of those provisions. The Regulation is silent on these issues, and uncertainty arises because of ambiguity surrounding Recital 24. Recital 24 permits a court, when addressing cases of *lis pendens*, to consider the fact that the foreign court would have had exclusive jurisdiction had it been an EU State. No separate provision is made for staying or dismissing proceedings in the event that the courts of a third State are perceived by the courts of a Member State as having exclusive jurisdiction. No provision is made for cases where a third-State court has exclusive jurisdiction under the national law of a Member State, nor (more surprisingly) if it would have had such jurisdiction had it been a Member State. It is unclear whether this means that a court is unable to decline proceedings on the sole ground that a foreign court has exclusive jurisdiction, but only in the event of a pending action in a third State, or that a power to do so exists independently of the Regulation, presumably deriving from national law.

A second area of difficulty concerns more fundamentally the scope of the Regulation. It may be argued that the Regulation, and therefore Articles 33 and 34, do not regulate cases where the jurisdiction of a third State's courts is exclusive.[51] It follows that such cases are, and always have been, regulated by national law. This position is not inconsistent with *Owusu*, which was not a case in which a stay was sought on the basis that the foreign court had superior jurisdiction. The argument is supported by the conceptual distinction between declining to exercise jurisdiction on grounds of inappropriateness and doing so because another court has a superior claim to jurisdiction.

---

49 Fentiman (n 38) 402–12.

50 *Lungowe v. Vedanta Resources Plc* [2017] EWCA Civ 1528.

51 Fentiman (n 38) 414–15.

It is also supported by the decision of the CJEU in *Coreck Maritime GmbH v. Handelsveem BV*.[52]

In *Coreck* the CJEU appears to have confirmed that courts may deploy national law to decline jurisdiction in favour of proceedings in a third State. *Coreck* concerned the effect on jurisdiction under the European regime of an agreement to the exclusive jurisdiction of a third State. The Court of Justice was concerned with the relatively narrow question of what law should govern the validity of such an agreement. It concluded that the applicable law was that identified by choice of law rules applicable under the national law of the forum, but this conclusion inescapably implies that a court must have the power to decline jurisdiction if such an agreement is valid. Of particular importance is the Court's reliance on a suggestive passage in the Schlosser Report on the Brussels Convention.[53] This concludes that each court should use its local choice of law rules to determine the validity of a third-State jurisdiction agreement. At first sight this is unexceptional, but it implies that such agreements may be effective to oust jurisdiction under the Convention, which in turn suggests that national law regulates such effectiveness (because the Convention itself makes no provision for doing so).

The inference is that if such an agreement is valid, the European regime is inapplicable – allowing a court to decline jurisdiction under national law. Moreover, the implication is not – or is not merely – that such national rules are outside the scope of the European regime because they share its objective of promoting party autonomy. The suggestion is that a situation involving a third-State jurisdiction agreement is immediately outside its scope – whatever the precise objective, and the precise form of the relevant national rule.

It has an important consequence if cases where the third-State forum has exclusive jurisdiction are entirely outside the scope of the EU regime. It follows that national law applies fully without the need to ask whether a stay would be consistent with the Regulation. It means that it is both unnecessary and incoherent to rely upon the doctrine of reflexive effect, a doctrine which assumes that the EU regime applies.

4. *OWUSU*: A POSSIBLE ROLE?

The status of Articles 33 and 34, and the effect of *Coreck*, remain uncertain. If Articles 33 and 34 represent an exclusive regime governing the relationship between the EU and third States the implications of *Owusu* have become irrelevant. If however they do not it follows that national law governs in such cases. In that event a further question arises, the answer to which depends on the implications of *Owusu*. When may national courts decline jurisdiction pursuant to their own law in cases where their jurisdiction derives from the Brussels regime? An answer is suggested by a line of cases decided since *Owusu* in which the English courts have explored the reflexive effect of the Regulation.

To say that the Brussels Regulation has reflexive effect means that a stay or dismissal of proceedings in favour of the courts of a third State is justified if it would be consistent with the operation of the Regulation between Member States. Importantly,

---

52 Case C-387/98 [2000] ECR I-9337.

53 Case C-387/98 [2000] ECR I-9337, at para 19.

this approach assumes that the EU regime is applicable in such cases. It implies rejection of the argument that the regime is wholly inapplicable. For in that event it becomes irrelevant to ask whether a stay is compatible with the EU regime. Instead, national law applies just as if the court's jurisdiction derives from national law and the regime is irrelevant. Such an approach begs two questions. First, what is the source of the rules for declining jurisdiction in such cases? Second, what degree of consistency is required? The second question itself begs two further questions: on what grounds is a court justified in declining jurisdiction; by what mechanism may it do so? Principle suggests that national law is the only possible source for such rules. Consistency with the Regulation requires remission to national law. To suggest that the Regulation somehow supplies those rules is to posit the existence of a phantom Regulation, parallel to and identical with Brussels I bis, whose invisible rules regulate the court's power to decline jurisdiction.

Principle suggests that consistency with the Regulation concerning the grounds for declining jurisdiction may be measured in several ways. First, a broad approach may be adopted. Consistency may require, and may only require, that the objectives of the Regulation would be served if proceedings are stayed. As Article 25 indicates, for example, the Regulation demands respect for jurisdiction agreements in favour of the courts of EU States. Arguably, this permits national courts to deploy any rules available under their national law which serve the same purpose.[54] If national law possesses rules respecting jurisdiction agreements, they may be deployed.

Alternatively, a narrow approach may be employed. Resort to national law may be justified if a stay would have been required or permitted had the third State in question been a Member State. This second approach requires in effect applying the rules in the Regulation (most importantly, Article 25) to determine if the conditions are present for declining jurisdiction under the Regulation. This approach may, however, take two different forms, with different outcomes in each case. It is possible, once congruence with the grounds for declining jurisdiction is established, that jurisdiction must also be declined strictly in accordance with the Regulation. In any case reflecting Article 25, this would mean that a court must decline jurisdiction automatically in favour of the agreed jurisdiction of a third State's court. If this first view prevails, the effect would be that effect could be given to third-State jurisdiction agreements only in those legal systems whose national rules concerning third-State jurisdiction agreements are non-discretionary.

Alternatively, once such congruence is established, the consequence may be that national law engages. A court could then decline jurisdiction exactly as it would under national law. This alternative has the effect that a national court having a discretion to stay proceedings under its national law could exercise that discretion once it is clear (in a case involving agreed jurisdiction) that the third State's courts would have had jurisdiction under Article 25 had it been a court in an EU State.[55]

---

[54] *Konkola Copper Mines plc v. Coromin* [2005] EWHC 898, [2005] 2 Lloyd's Rep. 555.

[55] *Ferrexpo v. Gilson Investments Ltd* [2012] EWHC 721 (Comm); Peter De Verneuil Smith, Ben Lasserson, Ross Rymkiewicz, 'Reflections on Owusu: The Radical Decision in Ferrexpo' (2012) *JPIL* 389; Elizabeth Crawford, Janine Carruthers, 'Ferrexpo AG v Gilson Investments Ltd: A Flexible Interpretation of the Reflexive Doctrine' (2013) *Edin LR* 78.

In deploying the reflexive doctrine, the English courts have established three principles. First, reflexive effect should be given to the European regime, in the sense that a court may decline to exercise jurisdiction where to do so would be consistent with the European regime. Second, the principle of reflexive effect leads to the conclusion that a court may exercise its existing powers under national law to stay proceedings in favour of the courts of a non-EU State. Third, because national law regulates such cases, the mechanisms available in national law may be deployed, including a discretionary stay. Reflexive effect does not mean that a court must stay proceedings in the manner that the Regulation requires in cases to which it applies directly. There is uncertainty, however, as to how such consistency is to be understood, and as to the situations in which a stay under national law is permitted. Both the broad and narrow approaches to reflexive effect are evident in the English cases.

The broad approach was adopted in *Konkola Copper Mines plc v. Coromin*.[56] There the judge considered the status of third-State jurisdiction agreements in the European regime. Whether a stay was permitted exposed two connected issues of particular importance in English commercial practice: is it permissible to stay proceedings on the basis that the parties have agreed to the jurisdiction of a third-State's courts; does it matter if a court's approach to declining jurisdiction is discretionary? Endorsing an earlier pair of English decisions,[57] the judge's conclusion that a discretionary stay in such cases was permitted has since been expressly endorsed without further discussion.[58]

The basis for a stay in *Konkola* was the parties' agreement to submit any disputes to the exclusive jurisdiction of the Zambian courts. The judge concluded that a stay founded upon an agreement to a third-State's jurisdiction was materially different from a stay on the generic ground that the most appropriate forum was in such a State (the situation in *Owusu*). Article 23 of Regulation 44/2001 (now Article 25 of the recast Regulation) itself required the courts of one Member State to cede jurisdiction to the agreed jurisdiction of another such State. Consistency with the Regulation therefore justified doing so in favour of the agreed jurisdiction of a third State. Moreover, consistency with the European regime means only consistency with objectives embodied in the regime, not with the form and methodology of its rules. The regime promotes party autonomy, by requiring courts to defer to the agreed jurisdiction of another Member State. It is therefore permissible to deploy rules of national law which likewise have the effect of respecting party autonomy, by giving effect to third-State jurisdiction agreements. The effect was that a court was permitted to use national law to grant a stay.[59]

---

56 [2005] EWHC 898, [2005] 2 Lloyd's Rep. 555; Fentiman (n 38) 416–17.

57 *Arkwright Mutual Insurance Co v. Bryanston Insurance Co Ltd* [1990] 2 QB 649 (QB); *Berisford plc v. New Hampshire Insurance Co* [1990] 2 QB 631 (QB).

58 *Winnetka Trading Corporation v. Julius Baer International Ltd* [2008] EWHC 3146 (Ch), [2009] 2 All ER (Comm) 735, at [25].

59 At [99].

A narrower approach to reflexive effect is evident in *Ferrexpo v. Gilson Investments*.[60] This approach permits a court to decline jurisdiction in circumstances where the foreign court would have had jurisdiction under the Regulation had it been a court in a Member State. This approach in turn has two variants. On one view, a court must then give effect to that jurisdiction just as it would if the Regulation had applied. In cases equivalent to those under Articles 24 and 25 of the recast Regulation, for example, it would then automatically decline jurisdiction. Alternatively, once a reflexive situation is identified, the court may employ its national law to determine whether a stay should be granted.

The narrow view in its second form was endorsed in *Ferrexpo*. There proceedings brought against an English-domiciled defendant were stayed on the ground that the proceedings had as their object the validity of resolutions made by a Ukrainian company. This was because Article 22 of Regulation 44/2001, conferring exclusive jurisdiction on the courts of an EU State in such a case, had reflexive effect in cases involving a non-EU court. This justified the grant of a stay under English national law.

Ferrexpo is significant for three principal reasons. It was accepted that Article 22 had reflexive effect. Again, the decision endorsed the general approach adopted in *Konkola v. Coromin*, to the extent that 'reflection' may justify a stay under national law.[61] Finally, the judge adopted a stricter view of reflexive effect than relied upon in *Konkola*, by asking whether Article 22 would have applied in its terms were Ukraine a Member State. The consequence is that a court may stay proceedings if the connection required under the relevant article of the Regulation is satisfied, but in that event a stay is granted under national law. *Owusu* did not prevent the reflexive application of Article 22. Uniformity, so important in *Owusu*, would not be disturbed because the principles underlying Article 22 were recognised in most legal systems. Nor was there a risk of uncertainty given that Article 22 was relatively certain in its operation.

This exposes a conflict in the English cases between the broad view underlying *Konkola*, and the narrow view endorsed in *Ferrexpo*. If the second is accepted, the effect may be to restrict the cases in which a stay may be sought. It is uncertain, however, whether the narrow approach favoured in *Ferrexpo* is correct in principle. If the mechanism for declining jurisdiction derives from national law, as *Ferrexpo* posits, it is unclear why the grounds for doing so should not also derive from national law. Arguably, it is incoherent to employ the Regulation strictly to determine whether consistency with the Regulation warrants a stay, and then remit to national law whether a stay should in fact be granted.

The English courts have therefore rejected the position that the Regulation is wholly irrelevant in cases where a stay is predicated on the exclusive jurisdiction of the third-State forum. By relying upon the Regulation's reflexive effect they have instead accepted that the Regulation applies and have sought to justify such stays by reference to the consistency of such stays with its objectives. Such an approach is perceived to be compatible with the decision in *Owusu* in two ways. First, cases such as *Konkola* and

---

60 [2012] EWHC 721 (Comm); De Verneuil Smith, Lasserson, Rymkiewicz (n 55) 389; Crawford, Carruthers (n 55) 78; James Goodwin, 'Reflexive Effect and the Brussels 1 Regulation' (2013) 129 *LQR* 317.

61 At [127].

Ferrexpo are materially different in their facts. They are not cases where a stay was sought on *forum conveniens* grounds but cases where the foreign court was treated as having exclusive jurisdiction. Second, the doctrine of reflexive effect itself provides a strong reason for distinguishing *Konkola* and *Ferrexpo* on the one hand and *Owusu* on the other. If reflexive effect justifies granting a stay in *Konkola* and *Ferrexpo* so it justifies denying a stay in *Owusu*. In *Owusu* the ground for seeking a stay was that the foreign court was the *forum conveniens* which, unlike the grounds in *Konkola* and *Ferrexpo*, has no analogue in the Brussels regime.

It is possible, however, that the approach of the English courts may be seen as incompatible with the Regulation for several reasons. First, even if the doctrine of reflexive effect is endorsed, the English court's application of the doctrine may be questioned. In particular, the approach employed in *Ferrexpo* may be thought incoherent. That approach respects the terms of the Regulation for the purpose of deciding if a case is one in which a stay would be granted had the third State been an EU State. But the court does not then automatically decline proceedings as it would if the Regulation applied. Instead it resorts to the discretionary approach familiar in English national law. It might be said, however, that such partial reflection is incoherent. Arguably consistency with the Regulation implies acting exactly as would be required under the Regulation. Second, it might be said that the English approach is incompatible with two important features of the decision in *Owusu*. To adopt such a singular approach may be seen as inconsistent with the objective of uniformity which underlies *Owusu*. Moreover, the CJEU in *Owusu* was opposed to use of discretion in the denial of jurisdiction, while the English approach is designed to allow resort to the adjudicatory discretion so familiar to English lawyers.

It may be, however, that the answer now lies (at least in part) not with *Owusu* but with the Regulation itself. Since *Owusu* was decided Articles 33 and 34 of the recast Regulation have been introduced. They address cases involving parallel proceedings and not those to which national law may now be said to apply. But they are significant for two reasons. First, they endorse an approach to third-State proceedings which is both broad, by appealing to the proper administration of justice, and explicitly discretionary. Second, although its implications are not without difficulty, Recital 24 explicitly invites a court to have regard to the fact that the third-State forum has exclusive jurisdiction when exercising the discretion to stay. For both reasons the English approach to adjudicatory discretion is implicitly endorsed. More particularly it is endorsed in the all-important situation where the parties have agreed to the exclusive jurisdiction of the third-State forum.

5. CONCLUSION

As this suggests, a further dimension has been added to the controversy surrounding *Owusu v. Jackson*. It is uncertain whether the introduction of Articles 33 and 34 of the recast Regulation diminishes the significance of the decision to vanishing point. Those provisions may render *Owusu* irrelevant if they provide the only means whereby proceedings may be stayed in favour of third-state courts. If they do not have this effect, however, and *Owusu* has continued significance, the decision retains its place as a benchmark for determining the nature and extent of national law's role in cases involving third States. In that event the implications of *Owusu* are no longer the main consideration. They must share the stage with Articles 33 and 34 as arbiters in the ongoing controversy about third-State proceedings. Importantly, however, those provisions only strengthen the conclusion that *Owusu* permits the staying of actions in favour of third States when justified by the Brussels regime's reflexive effect.

3. Parallel proceedings: *Texaco/Chevron lawsuits (re Ecuador)*

3.1 CASE BACKGROUND

Arguably, no legal controversy in the history of private international law has generated as many and as complex *conundra* as *Chevron*. More significantly, few other cases have shown as clearly the links between economic globalisation and the litany of contemporary disasters linked to disregard for the state of the planet and the livelihood of its poorest inhabitants. In this respect, the various lawsuits draw attention to the exhaustion of natural resources, widespread environmental destruction, and the plight of local populations. The case also illustrates the structural incapacity, the functional inaptitude, or perhaps the political unwillingness of private international law tools to provide a solution to this kind of dispute. Furthermore, it displays the artifice behind corporate architecture and the risk of global stalemate inherent in the iterative recourse to both domestic and international jurisdictions.

The heart of the dispute is ecological harm allegedly caused by the exploitation of an oil-rich area called Lago Agrio in the province of Sucumbíos, Eastern Ecuador. The immediate damage includes water pollution, soil contamination and deforestation and, subsequently, illness suffered by the local population. The Lago Agrio villagers and forest-dwellers filed a first set of lawsuits against the American-based company Texaco Petroleum (TexPet) before the US federal courts. TexPet was part of the oil-production consortium in Ecuador along with the State-owned oil company (Petroecuador) from 1964 to 1992. At the end of this venture, Petroecuador signed an agreement releasing TexPet from environmental liability. The region, however, continued to suffer the effects of the exploitation, so that a group of Ecuadorian citizens, joined by Peruvians living downstream from the Oriente region, sought relief in the US, where TexPet was incorporated. The US federal court dismissed both lawsuits in 2002 on *forum non conveniens* grounds. Texaco had shown to its satisfaction that courts in Ecuador and/or Peru were a more convenient forum, and – equally importantly – that this alternative forum was both effectively available and qualitatively adequate.*

Following this set-down, in 2003, a class action was brought in Ecuador against Texaco. However, TexPet had become a subsidiary of Chevron in 2001 and the parent company claimed that it has never operated in Ecuador and therefore could not be held responsible before Ecuadorian courts. Rejecting this argument, the Ecuadorian court confirmed its jurisdiction. In 2011, it ruled against Chevron, ordering the company to pay $8.6 billion in damages and clean-up costs; the damages would increase to $18 billion if Chevron did not issue a public apology. The judgment was firstly upheld on appeal and ultimately confirmed by the National Court of Justice. The enforcement of that decision was sought in several jurisdictions (Argentina, Brazil, Canada), unsuccessfully so far... One of the reasons is that during the proceedings, the independence of the Ecuadorian judge and the integrity of the plaintiffs' lawyer were questioned and various facts supporting

* On this point, it may be noted that contrary to some other Latin-American countries, Ecuador had not enacted an 'anti-*forum non conveniens*' statute, under which the choice of a foreign (US) forum implied renunciation of the right to access the courts of the home State, thereby making the required 'alternative forum' disappear!

allegations of fraud, undue influence and bribery were caught on film. *Crude*, which had been intended to advance the cause of the claimants, back-fired when the rushes were obtained under *sub poena* by the defendants and provided perfect food for a RICO claim, once again before US federal courts. Thereafter, Chevron was able to benefit from a constructive trust designed to claw back threefold any funds obtained from the enforcement of the Ecuadorian judgment outside Ecuador (or later, more moderately, within the US).

As an attempt to block the consequences of the main lawsuit in Ecuador, Chevron commenced arbitral proceedings before the Permanent Court of Arbitration in The Hague seeking to hold Ecuador accountable for its role in denying justice under the US-Ecuador BIT. Ecuador brought an anti-suit injunction before US courts, which was not granted. From 2010 onwards, an arbitral tribunal issued several interim awards ordering Ecuador to take all measures to suspend enforcement of the Ecuadorian judgment. Chevron submitted requests to uphold the arbitral measures in Ecuador, but they were not recognised by the local courts. Later, the same arbitral tribunal found that Ecuador had not complied with its orders. Consequently, another, partial award ruled in favour of Chevron by ordering Ecuador to make full reparation in the form of compensation for any injuries caused to the former. Previously, however, another PCA arbitration had been initiated by Ecuador against the US, requesting an 'official' interpretation of the notion of 'effective means' contained in the US-Ecuador BIT, opposed to the interpretation that had been adopted by the arbitral tribunal.

Finally, the Ecuadorian claimants unsuccessfully attempted to frame the case as a crime against humanity before the International Criminal Court and as violation of human rights before the Inter-American System of Human Rights.

Main case: *Aguinda v. ChevronTexaco*, Superior Court of Nueva Loja, Lago Agrio (Ecuador). January 3, 2012 (Case 2011-0106)

3.2 ADJUDICATING PUBLIC INTERESTS BY PRIVATE MEANS: THE INESCAPABLE INVOLVEMENT OF STATES IN THE *CHEVRON/ECUADOR* SAGA

Diego P. Fernández Arroyo

1. INTRODUCTION

Confirming that private international law cases often involve public interests is nothing but a surprise. All areas of State power – essentially legislature and courts – manifest such interest in many ways. What is less common – although not extremely rare – is that states openly take a role in on-going cases by means of governmental actions. This is exactly what happened in this multifaceted saga, perhaps the richest case ever in terms of multiplicity of actions of all kinds brought before a large array of courts and tribunals, both domestic and international.[1] Thus, what was initially seen as cases

[1] In addition to the particular manifestations of the saga commented by Laura Carbalo Piñeiro in *this book*, it is worth mentioning that there also existed attempts to develop some aspects of the saga under the aegis of the Inter-American Commission of Human Rights (2012) and of the International Criminal Court (2014).

involving exclusively private disputing parties turned into two investor-State cases and, ultimately, into a State to State arbitration.

This short commentary deals with certain developments of the saga under the aegis of the Permanent Court of Arbitration.[2] Namely, two UNCITRAL arbitration proceedings initiated by Chevron and Texaco against Ecuador[3] alleging, among several other claims, the violation of Ecuador's obligations under the 1993 Treaty between the United States of America and the Republic of Ecuador concerning the Encouragement and Reciprocal Protection of Investment,[4] on the one hand, and the arbitration proceedings brought by Ecuador against the United States seeking an 'authentic' interpretation of a provision of such BIT,[5] on the other hand. Although only one of the arbitrations initiated by the oil companies against Ecuador was ostensibly based on the consequences of the collective action brought by the Eastern Ecuador's victims of the pollution (the 2009-23 Case), both of them are *de facto* related to the judicial implications of the saga.[6]

This shift from judicial to arbitral adjudication offers several interesting topics to debate. One of the most interesting relates, precisely, to the way in which private and public matters appear deeply intertwined. Indeed, in this saga, this statement equally applies to the interest at stake, the actors, the adjudicators, the settings for the resolution of disputes and, consequently, the procedural applicable rules. Even more important, the two arbitrations against Ecuador show the versatility of the investor-State dispute settlement[7] mechanism by providing imaginative investors, in addition to an efficient tool to protect their investments, a large variety of options to optimise procedural strategies. Such a vastness has been certainly favoured by the fact that old investment treaties regulate investors' rights by means of open-ended notions. Depending on the context and the perspective of the analysis, the multiplicity of options may be taken either as a shield against States' abuses or as a tricky weapon to circumvent the consequences of wrong behaviour. Despite the various positions on the merits of the dispute, this aspect of the *Chevron/Ecuador* saga sheds light on the complex nature of ISDS. To say the least, after the three Hague experiences of the saga, it seems clearer than ever that ISDS is not strictly confined within the boundaries of public international law.[8]

---

2 Hereinafter the 'PCA.'

3 PCA Cases No. 2007-02/AA277 and No. 2009-23.

4 Hereinafter the 'BIT US-Ecuador' or simply the 'BIT.'

5 PCA Case No. 2012-05, also governed by the 1976 UNCITRAL Arbitration Rules.

6 Concretely, according to Ecuador, Chevron's claim in the Case AA277 'is merely a component of Chevron's broader litigation strategy to undermine any judgment of its liability that may emerge in that case [the *Lago Agrio* case] by an award in this case condemning the Ecuadorian court system.' See *Interim Award* (Case AA277), 1 December 2008, available at https://www.italaw.com/documents/Chevron-TexacovEcuadorInterimAward.pdf, §5 (p. 18).

7 Hereinafter 'ISDS.'

8 Z. Douglas, 'The Hybrid Foundations of Investment Treaty Arbitration' (2003) 7 *BYBIL* 151, 151–55.

2. ECUADOR CALLED BY CHEVRON AND TEXACO DRESSED UP AS INVESTORS

A. ISDS to Solve Failures of the Judicial System

Chevron and Texaco's first attempt to attract Ecuador to the ISDS arena began on 21 December 2006, that is to say more than 13 years after the kick-off of the *Aguinda* case before the federal district court of the Southern District of New York, more than three years after the kick-off of the *Lago Agrio* case before the Superior Court of Nueva Loja, and nine months after the latter rendered a judgment finding Chevron liable for the pollution caused by Texaco's drilling activities in the Ecuadorean Amazonas.[9] Although the claimants take care to avoid any mention of *Aguinda* and *Lago Agrio* in their request for arbitration, it is hard to ignore the obvious connections between the proceedings. Actually, by means of this arbitration – as is also the case for other actions brought by Chevron in different jurisdictions, notably in the United States – the companies tried to show that they held a panoply of resources to fight their case and that they were ready to take advantage of them.

The main argument of the companies – in the role of investors – bringing arbitration proceedings against Ecuador was the alleged egregious delay in adjudicating seven breach-of-contract claims filed by them before Ecuadorean courts in the 1990s. The concrete legal base to support this denial-of-justice claim was Article II(7) which states that '[E]ach Party shall provide effective means of asserting claims and enforcing rights with respect to investment, investment agreements, and investment authorizations.' Needless to say, the key-expression of this provision is 'effective means,' a notion which is not commonly used in this kind of international treaty and which is related to the prohibition of denial of justice under customary international law.[10] According to the arbitral tribunal's[11] interpretation, Article II(7) is not a mere restatement of the customary standard, but a *lex specialis*, specific of the concrete treaty.[12] The distinction is crucial: the test for establishing a denial of justice under customary international law is highly demanding.[13] Conversely, the 'standard under Article II(7) is one of 'effectiveness' which applies to a variety of State conduct that has an effect on the ability of an investor to assert claims or enforce rights.'[14]

On the basis of the foregoing, the tribunal found a breach of Ecuador's obligation under the BIT because of the undue delay by Ecuadorian courts in adjudicating the

---

[9] The Ecuadorean National Court of Justice ultimately confirmed this judgment on 12 November 2013.

[10] Partial Award on the Merits, 30 March 2010, available at https://www.italaw.com/documents/ChevronTexacoEcuadorPartialAward.PDF, §242.

[11] The Arbitral Tribunal was composed of Charles N. Brower, Albert Jan van den Berg and Karl-Heinz Böckstiegel.

[12] Partial Award on the Merits, 30 March 2010 (n 10) §§242–243.

[13] Ibid., §244. See *Iberdrola Energía SA v. Republic of Guatemala*, ICSID Case No. ARB/09/5, Award (17 August 2012), §§423ff.

[14] Partial Award on the Merits, 30 March 2010 (n 10) §248.

abovementioned seven cases brought by Texaco.[15] Equally significant, the tribunal excluded the presence of claimants' abuse of process and stated that they were not stopped from bringing the claim against Ecuador.[16] It is true that the decision in this case does not pretend to be universally valid. In fact, the tribunal is clear in circumscribing its decision concretely to the case at hand. However, the content of an award of this kind is likely to encourage other investors to rely on ISDS to influence judicial on-going proceedings in the host State.[17]

Interestingly, a further shift of the case took place when the arbitral award was challenged by Ecuador before the Hague District Court, opening a sequence of Dutch (i.e. public and national) confirmations of the private transnational award.[18]

B. ISDS as a Remedy against State Courts' Decisions

On 23 September 2009, almost three years after the successful first attempt, Chevron and Texaco initiated another arbitration against Ecuador. On this occasion, the oil companies sought to deactivate the results of the judicial proceedings before Ecuadorean courts, at that time under appeal. To this end, two main arguments were advanced: the violation of certain agreements exonerating Texaco from liability and the alleged collusion between the claimants in judicial proceedings and the host State.[19]

Among all the issues which may draw the attention to this rich arbitration, the most interesting is the active role of the arbitral tribunal[20] in trying to control what would be – according to the arbitral tribunal's understanding – an abusive behaviour of the respondent. While a longstanding issue in international arbitration has been to limit the intervention of State courts in arbitral proceedings, the *Chevron/Ecuador* saga deals with the other side of the coin: how far can arbitral tribunals interfere with the rendering of State courts' decisions?

One of the salient aspects in this regard concerns the decision taken by the arbitral tribunal, through an Order for Interim Measures,[21] to order the State

---

15 Ibid., §275. The Final Award, rendered on 31 August 2011, is available at https://www.italaw.com/sites/default/files/case-documents/ita0154.pdf

16 Ibid., §354. The tribunal underlines here the existence of a 'presumption in favor of the Claimants' right to bring their claims under the BIT,' presumption that has not been overcome by the Respondent.

17 There are other examples of arbitral decisions that may have a similar effect. That would be the case of the decisions which have – following different arguments – disregarded the time-period requirement to attempt a solution before the courts of the host State included in certain investment treaties. See, among many others, the careful explanation of the majority of the tribunal in *Abaclat and other v. the Argentine Republic*, ICSID Case No. ARB/07/5, Decision on Jurisdiction and Admissibility (4 August 2011), §§576ff.

18 Concretely, the award was confirmed by the Hague District Court on 2 May 2012, by the Hague Court of Appeal on 18 June 2013, and by the Dutch Supreme Court on 26 September 2014. All these decisions are available at https://www.italaw.com/cases/251.

19 See Claimants' Notice of Arbitration, available at https://www.italaw.com/sites/default/files/case-documents/ita0155_0.pdf.

20 Composed of Horacio Grigera Naón, Vaughan Lowe and V. V. Veeder.

21 PCA Case No. 2009-23, Order dated 9 February 2011, available at https://www.italaw.com/sites/default/files/case-documents/ita0167.pdf.

> to take all measures at its disposal to suspend or cause to be suspended the enforcement or recognition within and without Ecuador of any judgment against the First Claimant in the Lago Agrio Case and … to inform this Tribunal, by the Respondent's legal representatives in these arbitration proceedings, of all measures which the Respondent has taken for the implementation of this order for interim measures.

This decision was then reiterated in the First Interim Award on Interim Measures ("track I" of proceedings) dated 25 January 2012,[22] and again reasserted in the Second Interim Award on Interim Measures dated 16 February 2012.[23] Always in the same track, the Fourth Interim Award, dated 7 February 2013,[24] declared that Ecuador had 'violated the First and Second Interim Awards under the Treaty, the UNCITRAL Rules and international law in regard to the finalisation and enforcement subject to execution of the Lago Agrio Judgment within and outside Ecuador, including (but not limited to) Canada, Brazil and Argentina.'[25] The arbitral tribunal then held that 'the Respondent was and remains legally obliged under international law to ensure that the Respondent's commitments under the Treaty and the UNCITRAL Rules are not rendered nugatory by the finalisation, enforcement or execution of the Lago Agrio Judgment in violation of the First and Second Interim Awards.'[26] Recently, the rationale behind all these decisions has been confirmed in the Second Partial Award of the "track II" of proceedings (which entails the substantive part of the case).[27] This 521-pages decision orders Ecuador – among other things – to fully compensate (to be developed in "track III") the Claimants and to "take immediate steps, of its own choosing to remove the status of enforceability from the Lago Agrio Judgment (as also decided by the lago Agrio Appellate Cassation and Constitutional Courts) [and] to preclude any of the Lago Agrio Plaintiffs, any 'trust' purporting to represent their interest (…), any of the Lago Agrio Plaintiffs' representatives, and any non-party funder."[28]

This triggers an inextricable legal (and, of course, political) issue, which has, on the one hand, the tailor-made power of arbitral tribunals, and, on the other hand, the right (and legitimacy) of a State to enforce the decisions rendered by its own courts, a right that is due to the plaintiffs who brought the suit before Ecuadorian jurisdictions. To put it simply, does the prescription addressed to Ecuador not to enforce within and outside its territory lie within the *inherent* powers of arbitral tribunals? Is there a right of enforcement of judicial decisions? When a comparison is made between enforcement

22 Available at https://www.italaw.com/sites/default/files/case-documents/ita0173.pdf.

23 Available at https://www.italaw.com/sites/default/files/case-documents/ita0174_0.pdf. Let us recall that the decision of the Provincial Court of Justice of Sucumbíos rendered in 2011 condemned Chevron to pay USD 8.6 billion damages, USD 8.6 billion punitive damages, and to pay the legal costs, that the decision was upheld on appeal in 2012 and that the Ecuadorian Supreme Court confirmed the decision on liability, upheld the amount of compensatory damages but set aside the punitive damages in 2013. Needless to say, the enforcement of those decisions, which in principle should be a matter interesting only to the victims of the pollution, became of the utmost importance for Ecuador.

24 Available at https://www.italaw.com/sites/default/files/case-documents/italaw1274.pdf.

25 § 86.

26 Ibid.

27 Available at https://www.italaw.com/sites/default/files/case-documents/italaw9934.pdf.

28 § 10.13 (Part X, p. 3-5).

of foreign arbitral awards and enforcement of foreign judgments, what is the status of the latter?

On the first issue, it is rather largely admitted that arbitral tribunals have certain inherent powers[29] to rule on the procedure, and arbitration rules, as well as arbitration national laws, permit arbitral tribunals to adopt interim measures to protect the arbitral proceedings.[30] Nothing, however, is ever said regarding the content or extent of such measures. Experience shows that the imagination of sophisticated counsel is almost unlimited in this regard. The freedom of arbitrators, however, finds its limits in what might be considered reasonable by the arbitral community. The fact that arbitral decisions might take precedence over national courts' decisions is neither something new nor unjustified. However, we know that the *negative* effect of the competence-competence principle[31] is applied in a narrow number of States. And we know also that, even if it could theoretically be applied to issues like the one at stake, the *lis pendens* doctrine can hardly put at the same level arbitral tribunal and judicial courts.[32] Equally debatable in this context is the application of *res judicata*. Is this doctrine applicable when one of the two jurisdictions seized of the same cause of action, between the same parties concerning the same dispute, has already rendered a decision?

However, in any event, those principles could be applied when the parties to arbitral proceedings and national courts proceedings are the same, when they are opposed regarding the same dispute with the same cause of action. Those anti-parallel litigation tools are of no avail in the case under study, since Ecuador is not a party in the *Lago Agrio* litigation. As recalled in the other commentary of this saga,[33] the *Lagro Agrio* litigation involves civil plaintiffs, who brought before thc Provincial Court of Justice of Sucumbíos a class action against Texaco and Chevron.

What then can legitimate the decisions of the arbitral tribunal to interfere in a national court case to which only one party of the arbitral proceedings is concerned? If one admits that by addressing these orders to the Ecuadorian government (i.e. to hinder the enforcement of a national court decision), the arbitral tribunal disregards the principle of separation of powers, on which democratic societies are based, then this power is simply not justifiable. Obviously, such principle is not self-evident and it is not respected everywhere. Could the justification be to secure the wise and quiet course of the arbitral proceedings? The result shows that it did not. Could the justification of

---

29 See the ILA Resolution No. 4/2016, available at http://www.ila-hq.org/images/ILA/docs/No.4_Resolution_2016_InternationalCommercialArbitration.pdf. See also F. Ferrari and F. Rosenfeld (eds), *Inherent Powers in International Adjudication* (Huntington (NY), Juris 2018 forthcoming).

30 Article 26 of the UNCITRAL Arbitration Rules (1976) was indeed the legal basis used by the tribunal to adopt this decision.

31 According to this principle national courts shall deny jurisdiction in a case where there is *prima facie* a valid arbitration agreement. See E. Gaillard, 'L'effet négatif de la compétence-compétence', in *Etudes de procédure et d'arbitrage. Mélanges Jean-François Poudret* (Lausanne, Faculté de droit de l'Université de Lausanne 1999) 387.

32 As the Swiss experience demonstrates, by reforming Article 186 of Swiss Private International Act after case *Fomento* (ATF 127 III 279 (2001)) to eliminate the automatic application of *lis pendens* regarding arbitral tribunals.

33 See Laura Carballo Piñeiro, 3.3 below.

this power be the fulfilment by the State of its obligations under the investment treaty? The application of the treaty was not yet considered when the interference interim decisions were adopted but the Second Partial Award of "track II" has recognised the violation of several investors' rights by Ecuador. Of course, the orders were addressed to the Government of Ecuador, not to Ecuadorian courts and even less to foreign courts which might possibly be seized of an enforcement action. However, there is an indirect interference in the judicial system. If the courts were to enforce the decisions, they would have probably been considered the accomplice of the State in the violation of the interim measures and ultimately of the Second Partial Award of "track II." All in all, the case shows how broad the logic of investment arbitration can be in its applicability to investor-State relationships.

The second issue concerns the gap in the enforcement regime of foreign arbitral awards and judicial decisions. Whereas the first category of decisions enjoys a very favourable regime in the States that have ratified the New York Convention, the second category suffers from the failure of States to agree on an international Convention on the recognition of judicial decisions,[34] be it only in the civil and commercial area. This gap is intriguing. And the success of the New York Convention contributed largely to the success of international arbitration and it being considered as the best dispute settlement mean for transnational cases. But in the case under analysis, if the arbitral tribunal had denied Ecuador the right to enforce a foreign arbitral award, it would have implicitly condemned the State to infringe its international obligation under the New York Convention. Obligations towards the litigants to enforce a binding judicial decision exist as well. Actually, the fundamental right to access to justice could not be truly 'effective' if it did not include the right to seek enforcement of the decision rendered by the competent decision-maker. Of course, this right (as any other) is not absolute.

3. UNITED STATES CALLED BY ECUADOR ATTEMPTING TO TAKE CONTROL OVER TREATY INTERPRETATION

As a reaction against the content of the partial award rendered in the AA277 Case on 30 March 2010, Ecuador brought a new arbitration before the same institution. This time, the subject matter was the interpretation of Article II(7) of the BIT United States-Ecuador which, according to Ecuador, had been misinterpreted by the arbitral tribunal. Thus, the respondent in this new arbitration was the United States of America on the basis of the general clause of settlement of disputes concerning the very 'interpretation or application' of said BIT.

To put it in simple words, in order to challenge the decision of an arbitral tribunal, Ecuador initiated a new arbitration[35] seeking a declaration that the contracting parties to the BIT find the interpretation given by the arbitral tribunal to Article VII.2 of the BIT is wrong. That is to say, Ecuador was using this action as recourse to deprive the

---

[34] On the former and current initiatives of the Hague Conference on Private International Law, see https://www.hcch.net/en/projects/legislative-projects/judgments.

[35] The Arbitral Tribunal was composed of Donnald McRae, Raúl Emilio Vinuesa and Luiz Olavo Baptista.

investment award of any substance. Ecuador's arbitral request implies a double paradox. On the one hand, Ecuador was trying to take the control over treaty interpretation by submitting the case to an arbitral tribunal, as 'private' as the first one. On the other hand, the State expressing such faith in an arbitral tribunal was the same whose general attitude towards arbitration has been considered rather hostile.[36]

The active involvement of the States evoked as common thread of this commentary has gone clearly beyond their litigating activities in arbitral and judicial proceedings. In parallel to act as litigating parties before different adjudicators, States put in motion strong sovereign decisions. Thus, before the arbitral tribunal of the investment case AA277 had rendered the Partial Award on the Merits on 30 March 2010, Ecuador informed the United States that it would not renew the BIT and denounced the ICSID Convention.[37] Once the Partial Award was rendered, there were direct communications between high officials of both Governments.[38] Afterwards, and absent any possibility of reaching an agreement, the Constitutional Court of Ecuador declared that the rules providing for investor-State arbitration and State-to-State arbitration in bilateral investment treaties were unconstitutional. As a result, the Government requested the Parliament to denounce several of those treaties. More dramatically political in nature, the Ecuadorean Government declared the US ambassador *persona non grata*, prompting reciprocal response from the United States. That was the context in which Ecuador filed its request for arbitration on 28 June 2011.

As unusual as the initiation of this (third) arbitration may appear, the fact is that such possibility is clearly contemplated in the BIT US-Ecuador.[39] Its Article V states that '[T]he Parties agree to consult promptly, on the request of either, to resolve any disputes in connection with the Treaty, or to discuss any matter relating to the interpretation or application of the Treaty.' More concretely, dealing with failure of consultations and related to treaty interpretation, Article VII(1) reads as follows: '[a]ny dispute between the Parties concerning the interpretation or application of the Treaty which is not resolved through consultations or other diplomatic channels, *shall be submitted*, upon the request of either Party, *to an arbitral tribunal* for binding decision in accordance with the applicable rules of international law …'[40]

From a technical perspective, the dispute at stake presents two main issues, a substantial one and a procedural one. The substantial aspect of the dispute is contained in Ecuador's assertion that the interpretation of Article II(7) of the BIT by the arbitral tribunal was 'erroneous and overbroad,' and that it had 'put into question the common intent of the Parties with respect to the nature of their mutual obligations.' On this basis, in a note sent to the United States' Department of State on 8 June 2010, Ecuador asked the United States to agree with Ecuador's interpretation of Article II(7), which

---

36 E. Gaillard, 'Anti-Arbitration Trends in Latin America' (2008) 239(108) *New York Law Journal*.

37 Ecuadorean Government communicated the denunciation of the 1965 Washington Convention to the ICSID Secretariat on 6 July 2009.

38 Namely, the content of a phone call held on 4 October 2010 between Ecuadorean authorities and Professor Harold Koh, from the US State Department, was a matter of debate before the arbitral tribunal.

39 And more than this: it is also contemplated in the US' Model BIT (2012), Article 37(1).

40 Emphasis added.

notably included the following points regarding the requirements thereof: a) Article II(7) requirements are not greater than customary standards, and b) Article II(7) requirements do not create obligations to assure efficiency in particular cases.

According to Ecuador's note, if a confirming note from the US was not forthcoming, 'an unresolved dispute must be considered to exist … concerning the interpretation and application of the Treaty.' This is precisely the technical procedural issue, which may be expressed with these words: Can an action be brought in the absence of concrete controversy?

As an indication of the significance of the debate, several of the most outstanding scholars in the field of Law of the Treaties were called as expert witnesses. They provided sophisticated explanations in favour of the Parties' arguments. On the US side, the arguments can be summarised in this way:

1. There was no dispute; in fact, Ecuador had not submitted any concrete claim and there is no positive opposition by the US;
2. The US was under no obligation to respond to Ecuador's note;
3. Article VII does not allow for advisory, appellate, or referral jurisdiction;
4. The acceptance of Ecuador's submission could have destabilising consequences for ISDS.

These arguments were contradicted by Ecuador, according to whom:

1. There was a concrete dispute despite no allegation of breach of the BIT and the US' positive opposition could (at least) be inferred;
2. The US should have made reasonable efforts to ensure correct interpretation and application of the BIT (particularly by means of good faith and *pacta sum servanda*);
3. Deciding Ecuador's claim required no advisory, appellate, or referral jurisdiction;
4. Extra-legal (systemic) concerns were not relevant.

For the majority of the arbitral tribunal the 'concreteness' requirement was essential. Thus, invoking a series of ICJ cases, the award[41] stated that no decision was possible in absence of a concrete dispute. Thus, a decision must have practical consequence. In this way, the arbitral tribunal frustrated the possibility to get an 'official' interpretation of the terms of an investment treaty even in the absence of a specific mechanism established beforehand, i.e. simply resorting to the arbitration proceeding set forth in the relevant treaty. Regardless of the conflicting opinions of the parties (and experts) on whether there was a real dispute between them or not in such respect, and whether the arbitral tribunal would have jurisdiction over such dispute,[42] it would have been most

[41] Available at https://www.italaw.com/sites/default/files/case-documents/italaw7940.pdf.

[42] The key questions were: '[C]an a dispute concerning the interpretation of a treaty be submitted to an international tribunal, absent any dispute on the application of the treaty? In particular, when a compromissory clause allows for arbitration of disputes "concerning the interpretation or application" of a treaty, may a tribunal exercise jurisdiction in circumstances where the dispute at issue concerns only the interpretation of the treaty and does not include an

interesting to see a debate about the impact of the prospective interpretation of such tribunal on the other arbitral tribunals and judicial courts called upon to rule on different chapters of this saga.

Beyond the technical aspects discussed, the arbitration between Ecuador and the US serves to point out one of the main issues of the current debate about the reform of investor-State dispute settlement, namely, the need and feasibility of the implementation of a system capable to provide for authoritative interpretation of investment treaties and, ultimately, also for an acceptable level of consistency. In fact, Ecuador's action advanced the debate that would become central in Europe a few years later around the treaties negotiated by the European Union with several countries, namely the United States, Canada, Singapore, Vietnam and Mexico. There is a growing concern about the need to determine the tribunal and the mechanism(s) applicable so as to achieve a 'uniform' interpretation, which could be general in nature or limited to a particular instrument.[43]

One proposal consists in solving the interpretation problems in specific disputes through an 'authentic' interpretation by the State Parties to the treaty in question. Treaties such as the North American Free Trade Agreement (NAFTA) or the Dominican Republic-Central America-United States Free Trade Agreement (CAFTA-DR) have institutionalised a mechanism of this kind, by assigning their respective Free Trade Commissions (composed of ministers representing State Parties) the role of official interpreters, specifically providing for the binding nature of their interpretations upon investment arbitral tribunals.[44] More recently, the idea of setting up permanent or semi-permanent investment courts is being explored. In this sense, several options have arisen regarding the function and the very nature of these courts. Such options go from a complementary role (dealing with interpretation and/or appeal) within the existing ISDS system, to an exclusive role aiming at replacing it.[45] Since November 2017, a furnished working group is trying to find the right answers to this and another essential question for the future of ISDS under the auspices of UNCITRAL.[46]

All in all, this Dutch trip to several episodes of the *Chevron/Ecuador* saga comes to point out the pluralist framework of current private international law with all its

---

allegation that the respondent State breached the treaty?' (taken from Alain Pellet's expert opinion, in favour of Ecuador).

43 In such regard, several means have been explored or proposed. See already S. D. Franck, 'The Legitimacy Crisis in Investment Treaty Arbitration: Privatizing Public International Law Through Inconsistent Decisions' (2005) *Fordham L. Rev.* 1601ff.; F. Grisel, *L'arbitrage international ou le droit contre l'ordre juridique* (Paris, Fondation Varenne 2011) 243–60.

44 Article 1131, para. 2 of NAFTA; Article 10.22, para. 3 of CAFTA-DR. See also Article 37 of the US Model BIT (2012). The means of 'official' interpretation of international arbitration instruments has also been explored beyond the particular framework of investor-State disputes. See, for instance, the interpretative declaration issued by MERCOSUR Council (CMC/Acta No. 1/02, para. 10(1)) regarding the 1998 MERCOSUR Agreement on International Commercial Arbitration, or the recommendations for the interpretation of the 1958 New York Convention adopted by UNCITRAL in 2006.

45 The more visible example is the Comprehensive Economic and Trade Agreement between Canada and the European Union (CETA), provisionally entered into force on 21 September 2017. See http://ec.europa.eu/trade/policy/in-focus/ceta/.

46 http://www.uncitral.org/uncitral/es/commission/working_groups/3Investor_State.html.

(domestic, international and transnational) components, and its blend of private and public elements as well.

3.3 ACCESS TO JUSTICE AND PARALLEL LITIGATION: FROM SOLITAIRE TO TEAM PLAY

Laura Carballo Piñeiro

1. INTRODUCTION

As time goes by, justice proves to be elusive and unattainable for the Ecuadorian people affected by the environmental damage allegedly caused by Texaco's oil perforation and handling in the Oriente region. These people brought a claim against the US company in its home jurisdiction in 1993,[47] and are nowadays struggling to get an Ecuadorian judgment rendered in 2013 against Chevron Corporation,[48] another US company that merged with Texaco in 2001,[49] to be enforced in a number of jurisdictions including Argentina,[50] Brazil[51] and Canada.[52] After 25 years of litigation, it can be safely said that their Herculean trials are still far from being over.

The abovementioned string of litigation is a straightforward example of the problems that due process rights encounter in cases where different jurisdictions are involved. Private international law strives to this end by resorting to a number of techniques specifically designed to tackle the international dimension of private situations, focusing on international jurisdiction, conflict of laws, recognition and enforcement of

---

[47] *Aguinda v. Texaco*, Inc., 142 F. Supp. 2d 534 (SDNY 2001). Peruvians were also included in the putative class action.

[48] See *Corte Nacional de Justicia. Sala de lo Civil y Mercantil*, judgment of 12 November 2013, reviewing *Corte Provincial de Justicia* Sucumbios, *Sala Única*, judgment of 14 February 2011; *Corte Superior de Justicia*, Nueva Loja, judgment of 16 March 2006, file No. 002-2003.

[49] *Chevron Corp v. Naranjo*, 667 F.3d 232, 235 (2d Cir. 2012), denying Chevron's request of an injunction against the enforcement of the Ecuadorian judgment.

[50] Supreme Court's judgment of 4 June 2013. In October 2017, District Court No 61 of Buenos Aires dismissed again the *exequatur* of the Ecuadorian judgment on grounds of the lack of connection to Argentina since Chevron Corporation is neither domiciled nor has assets in Argentina.

[51] Superior Court of Justice of Brasilia, Special Section, judgment enforcement case SEC8542 initiated in 2012 and finally decided on 29 November 2017, published in *Diario Oficial de Justicia* on 15 March 2018, not granting the *exequatur* on grounds of Chevron Corporation not having ties to Brazil, and of Chevron Brazil not being accountable for that judgment.

[52] The enforcement action was stayed in 2013 because of Chevron's lack of assets in Canada and Chevron Canada not being accountable for the Ecuadorian judgment, but the order was appealed and the discussion moved as to whether the Ecuadorian plaintiffs to provide security for costs of appeal [*Yaiguaje v. Chevron Corporation*, September 21, 2017, CanLII – 2017 ONCA 741 (CanLII)], which has been finally answered by the Court of Appeal for Ontario in the negative: *Yaiguaje v. Chevron Corporation*, 2017 ONCA 827.

foreign decisions. However, parallel litigation lacks that kind of fine-tuning despite the increase in cases and some major developments, in particular in the fields of insolvency[53] and family law.[54] The following section analyses the shortcomings of applying internal remedies to international parallel litigation as judiciaries play solitaire in a framework that needs communication, cooperation and coordination; thereby the last section moves to urge tailormade approaches to this issue.

2. INTERNATIONAL PARALLEL LITIGATION, BUT NATIONAL REMEDIES

A. Premise: Access to Justice and Overlapping Jurisdictions

Against the Westphalian system, the primary responsible for providing access to justice is the State. This obligation includes a restriction in the exercise of sovereignty to avoid exorbitance, which is applied in a more rigid or flexible manner depending on the legal tradition. The other side of the coin is that, if jurisdiction is asserted, States cannot decline it at the risk of refusal to do justice. While civil law systems ground this obligation on the principle of legality,[55] common law countries are not oblivious to it.[56]

Remarkably, there are exceptions to the principle of not refusing jurisdiction such as it is the case of the *forum non conveniens* doctrine that fine-tunes international jurisdiction in common law countries by taking into account other jurisdictions as more appropriate to hear the case brought before an otherwise competent court.[57] To be clear, this doctrine does not require a parallel proceeding in other jurisdiction to be discussed, but it can be safely said that it is part of the remedies applied by States to coordinate their jurisdiction with that of others on the same case.[58] While the abovementioned

---

53 This field benefits from formal mechanisms as enshrined e.g. in the UNCITRAL Model Law on Cross Border Insolvency, and from informal ones such as *ad hoc* insolvency protocols by which a cooperation framework is set up between courts dealing with the same insolvency.

54 The cornerstone of coordination in this field can be found in The Hague Convention of 25 October 1980 on the Civil Aspects of International Child Abduction.

55 Case C-281/02 *Owusu v Jackon* [2005] ERC I-1383.

56 Campbell McLachlan, '*Lis Pendens* in International Litigation' in *Collected Courses of the Hague Academy of International Law* (Leiden, Brill Nijhoff 2009) vol 336, 199, 269; Linda Silberman, 'Lis alibi pendens' in Jûrgen Basedow et al. (eds.), *Encyclopedia of Private International Law* (Cheltenham, Edward Elgar 2017) 1159, 1163.

57 Richard Fentiman, 'Forum non Conveniens' in Basedow et al. (n 56) 797.

58 For a still valid comparative law overview see J. J. Fawcett, 'General Report' in J. J. Fawcett (ed.), *Declining Jurisdiction Private International Law* (Oxford, Clarendon Press 1995) 1.

principle advises not to take into account other jurisdictions,[59] parallel proceedings push for coordination in order to comply with due process rights.[60]

In this vein, different grounds have been pleaded to pay due regard to duplicative jurisdiction, namely, avoiding the non-recognition of foreign judgments, promoting judicial efficiency, curtailing an otherwise excessive exercise of jurisdiction or promoting comity between courts. More specifically, these grounds serve to justify one or other remedy to parallel proceedings and can be considered effects of the actual action of coordinating jurisdictions. However, the core of this obligation is to be found in due process considerations;[61] fairness is not accomplished when the same dispute is tried twice as it infringes the State interest on a sound administration of justice and the parties' right to a fair trial.

B. Declining Jurisdiction

In the light of the rights at stake, justice systems across the civil/common law divide have nationally developed mechanisms to deal with situations of *lis pendens*,[62] to which they have mimetically resorted when confronted with parallel proceedings at the international level. However, the overall outcome is not satisfactory.[63] More specifically, the techniques at stake are the strict priority rule applied by civil law jurisdictions, and anti-suit injunctions and the *forum non conveniens* doctrine developed in common law countries. Their individual analysis reveals shortcomings in all of them, but also features of what could be an adequate mechanism to deal with overlapping jurisdictions.

The European Union has replicated the strict first-seized-court rule used by most civil law countries, which consists in making the second seized court decline jurisdiction in favour of the first one once it has asserted jurisdiction.[64] Although

---

59 Many countries do not provide remedy to parallel litigation yet. France did not apply the *lis pendens* rule until Cass Civ, 26 November 1974, *Soc Miniera de Fragne c. Cie européenne d'équipement industriel*; while the Spanish Law on International Jurisdictional Cooperation on Civil Matters did the same only in 2015, arts 37 et seq.

60 Plaintiffs do not have an absolute right to access their preferred court, but access is to be balanced against the defendant's right of defence and that of a proper administration of justice. See Fentiman (n 57) 804, in justifying the *forum non conveniens* doctrine as in accordance with the European Convention of 4 November 1950 for the Protection of Human Rights and Fundamental Freedoms, art 6.

61 See extensively, McLachlan (n 56) 215.

62 *Lis alibi pendens* or *lis pendens* is the Latin name for parallel litigation, although it also refers to the commencement of one proceeding and the effects attached to it such as the *perpetuatio iurisdictionis*.

63 In general, see McLachlan (n 56) 235 et seq. Specifically on *forum non conveniens* see Cassandra Burke Robertson, 'Forum non Conveniens on Appeal. The Case for Interlocutory Review' (2012) 18 *Southwestern Journal of International Law* 445, 462.

64 See Consolidated Version of the Brussels Convention on jurisdiction and the recognition and enforcement of judgments in civil and commercial matters [1998] C27/1, art 21, and its progeny: Lugano Convention [1988] OJ L319/9, art 21; Council Regulation (CE) 44/2001 [2000] OJ L12/1, art 27; Council Regulation (EC) 4/2009 on jurisdiction, applicable law, recognition and enforcement of decisions and cooperation in matters relating to maintenance obligations

apparently easy to apply, it has given rise to three major issues when operating in transnational cases.

Firstly, the rule is applied whether proceedings are between the same parties and have the same cause of action. This notion has already sparked a lively discussion that has resulted in a number of Court of Justice judgments,[65] whose rulings have been passed not without controversy.[66] Cases in which only some parties coincide pose problems of consistency;[67] others give rise to the issue of whether parallel proceedings in legal systems ascribed to separate legal families have the same cause of action.[68] Be that as it may, such difficulties bring the concept of related actions to the discussion, at least those 'that it is expedient to hear and determine them together to avoid the risk of irreconcilable judgments resulting from separate proceedings'.[69] On the one hand, this concept helps overcome problems caused by that of identical actions; on the other hand, they require a consolidation of actions that it is far from granted at international level.[70] Nevertheless, advancements have been made in that direction.[71]

Secondly, the automatic application of the first-seized-court rule promotes forum shopping. In *Zelger v Salitrini*,[72] the defendant in a liability claim already filed, but not served, before German courts sought negative declaratory relief in Italy in order to prevent the German proceeding from being initiated, taking advantage of cross-country disparities as to the time from which a court is held seized in accordance with domestic procedural legislation. For it is true that the strict application of the first-seized-court rule provides no room for manoeuvre, this example suggests that a degree of discretion may indeed be necessary to deal with international *lis pendens* situations.[73]

[2009] OJ L7/1, art 12; Lugano Convention [2009] OJ L147/1, art. 27; Regulation (EU) 1215/2012 of the European Parliament and of the Council (Brussels Ia Regulation) [2012] OJ L351/1, art 29.

65 Case C-351/89 *Overseas v. New Hampshire* [1991] ECR I-03317; Case C-144/86 *Gubisch v Palumbo* [1987] ERC I-04861; Case C-406/92 *The 'Tatry' v. the 'Maciej Rataj'* [1994] ECR I-05439; Case C-351/96 *Drouot Assurances v. Consolidated Metallurgical Industries* [1998] ECR I-3075.

66 Criticism focuses on the fact that the difficulties in ascertaining a *lis pendens* situation have led national and international courts to expand the concept and cover intrinsically related matters; thereby plaintiffs in the second proceeding may actually see their claim not litigated to the extent that they may not be granted a deadline for their submission in the already pending first proceeding.

67 See commentaries on Case C-406/92 *The 'Tatry' v. the 'Maciej Rataj'* [1994] ECR I-05439.

68 The Canadian Supreme Court has dealt with this issue in *Rocois Construction Inc v. Québec Ready Mix Inc and Others* [1990] 2 SCR 440.

69 Brussels Ia Regulation, art 30(3).

70 See McLachlan (n 56) at 246.

71 Established at the same time as the *lis pendens* rule by the Brussels Convention, art 22 (and its progeny, see n 61), consolidation of actions beyond the EU area had only been considered by France before the adoption of Brussels Ia Regulation, art 34. Nowadays, see also the Spanish 2015 Act, n 56, art 40.

72 Case-56/79 *Zelger v. Salitrini* [1980] ERC I-89.

73 The Brussels Convention and its progeny have found mechanisms to avoid forum shopping, but a better alternative would be to except the rule when the first claim only seeks declaratory relief.

Thirdly, the rule under discussion provokes other unintended results, namely, it relegates the court designated by a choice-of-forum clause if another jurisdiction has been first seized.[74] There is a clear contradiction, though, with the precedence given to the party autonomy principle in selecting jurisdiction; unless there are compelling reasons not to uphold the forum-selection clause,[75] this contradiction should be solved in favour of the chosen courts.[76] In sum, this case confirms the need for some discretion in international *lis pendens* situations.

Declining jurisdiction is already seen as an exercise of discretion by common law countries. To internally avoid parallel litigation, courts have resorted to anti-suit injunctions whose employment to prevent proceedings in other jurisdictions has however sparked strong criticism. As they apparently disregard other States' sovereignty, they have been characterised as 'of unjustifiable interference' with other courts.[77] Along these lines, their use has been limited to cases where harassment or vexation, forum's essential public policies or important delays and costs were at stake.[78]

The *forum non conveniens* doctrine is nowadays preferred to accommodate the issue of parallel litigation in common law countries, although there are significant differences from one to another. While it swiftly operates when plaintiffs have brought proceedings in more than one jurisdiction by requiring them to choose,[79] problems arise when the seized court has to establish whether another forum is adequate and available to hear the case in view of the public interest and/or parties' private interests at stake. In general, there is no predictability and consistency as to how to weight these manifold factors.[80]

C. Lessons from the *Chevron/Ecuador* Saga

The *Chevron/Ecuador* case illustrates the inconveniences of the *forum non conveniens* doctrine.[81] The first point to be made is that it is being applied in cases in which the US jurisdiction is the only one involved, many times disregarding the plaintiff's choice to

---

[74] Case C-116/02 *Gasser v MISAT* [2003] ERC I-14693.

[75] Discretion in these matters has been exercised by common law countries. See an overview in Fawcett (n 58) 47.

[76] Brussels Ia Regulation, art 31(2) has reversed the *Gasser* doctrine by granting always priority to the courts designated by the choice-of-forum clause. Party autonomy has been long taken into account within the *forum non conveniens* doctrine, see Fentiman (n 57) 799.

[77] Case C-159/02 *Turner v. Grovit* [2004] ERC I-3565; Case C-185/07 *Allianz v. West Tankers* [2009] ERC I-663.

[78] Richard Fentiman, 'Anti-suit injunctions' in Basedow et al (n 56) 91.

[79] McLachlan (n 56) 308.

[80] Surprisingly, such factors may include the burden upon court dockets and whether foreign law is to be applied. See *Piper Aircraft Co. v. Reyno*, 454 U.S. 235, 241 n 6 (1981). It is remarkable that the single example of an inadequate forum put in this judgment was, precisely, Ecuador. Ibid. 255 n 22.

[81] The following comments are focused on the doctrine as applied in the US as other countries differ from this approach. See Fawcett (n 58); and Fentiman (n 57).

litigate at the defendant's home jurisdiction.[82] From a civil law perspective, this approach is at odds with the *actor sequitur forum rei* principle according to which the defendant's right of defence is undoubtedly secured at their domicile.

This doctrine is even more problematic if it is taken into account that defendants are usually transnational corporations whose headquarters are in the US, but operate worldwide.[83] Cases against them usually denounce gross violations of human rights, environmental and health damage, being argued by defendants that foreign jurisdictions are more appropriate on grounds of being there the alleged cause of harm, thereby access to evidence is secured and thus a more appropriate forum. For its part, plaintiffs counter-argue the lack of human, material and technical resources of their home jurisdictions that impedes their case from being properly tried.[84] Unfortunately, US courts side in a significant number of cases with US defendants, and the usual outcome is that such claims are lost because they do not actually find access to the foreign jurisdiction.[85]

In fact, this was the fate of the Peruvian plaintiffs that claimed along with the Ecuadorians against Texaco in 1993. From the moment that the US District Court granted the motion to dismiss filed by Texaco[86] – seven years after the filing of the claim![87] – the die was apparently cast and litigation over for good, also for Ecuadorians; the justice system in Ecuador was prepared to handle individual but not collective litigation, and citizens were not granted standing to pursue environmental damage. The game changed when the Ecuadorian Environmental Management Act was issued in

---

82 On the problems of the lack of a clear court-access policy for cases involving foreign plaintiffs, see in particular Robertson (n 63) at 445; Allan R Stein, 'Forum Non Conveniens and the Redundancy of Court-Access Doctrine' (1985) 133 *University of Pennsylvania Law Review* 781.

83 While the connection with the US is clear, foreign litigants are excluded from that jurisdiction in a discriminatory manner as denounced by many different Latin-American instances and countries. They have adopted retaliatory measures such as foreclosing jurisdiction once plaintiffs choose to litigate their claims in the US, i.e. making it clear that they are not an alternative forum to that chosen. Additionally, they may indicate that, if the defendant pleads for *forum non conveniens*, it would be treated at the plaintiffs' home jurisdiction in disadvantage to the plaintiffs and face punitive damages. See Cassandra Burke Roberton, 'Transnational Litigation and Institutional Choice' (2010) 51 *Boston College Law Review* 1081, 1093.

84 See *In re Union Carbide Corp. Gas Plant Disaster*, 634 F. Supp. 842, 867 (SDNY 1986).

85 See Robertson (n 63) 452; Robertson (n 83) 1131; Howard M. Erichson, 'The Chevron-Ecuador Dispute, Forum non Conveniens, and the Problem of Ex Ante Inadequacy' (2013) *Stanford Journal of Complex Litigation* 417, 420; McLachlan (n 56) 336; Iman Prihandono, 'Barriers to transnational human rights litigation against transnational corporations (TNCs): The need for cooperation between home and host countries' (2011) 3(7) *Journal of Law Conflict Resolution* 89, 92; Christopher A. Whytock, 'The Evolving Forum Shopping System' (2010) 96 *Cornell Law Review* 481.

86 The Court of Appeals confirmed the dismissal of the two putative class actions in 2002. See *Aguinda v. Texaco, Inc.*, 303 F.3d 470 (2d Cir. 2002).

87 The amount of evidence provided in the proceeding to establish a link with the US greatly contributed to this duration. See *Aguinda v. Texaco, Inc.*, 142 F. Supp. 2d 534, 535 (SDNY 2001), and Manuel A. Gómez, 'A Sour Battle in Lago Agrio and Beyond: the Metamorphosis of Transnational Litigation and the Protection of Collective Rights in Ecuador' (2015) 46 *Inter-American Law Review* 153, 160.

1999,[88] allowing the plaintiffs to bring their claim to the Provincial Court of Justice of Sucumbíos in Lago Agrio, at the heart of the polluted area. Ironically, the strong opposition of Chevron to the putative class action brought before US courts had at least a positive aspect, that of advancing the rights of citizens in Ecuador.[89]

Unfortunately, the worst predictions of the plaintiffs before New York courts came true to the extent that the Ecuadorian proceeding was tainted from the beginning with allegations of fraud and judicial corruption. When suspicions of political involvement in the dispute became strong, Chevron reacted by not simply fighting against bias, partial experts and false documents in Ecuador, but by commencing collateral litigation in the US[90] that have added new strings of overlapping jurisdictions. Remarkably, arbitral proceedings against the Republic of Ecuador were initiated[91] that have brought the Lago Agrio litigation to a new level,[92] as Chevron repeatedly asked for interim arbitral measures ordering Ecuador to avoid the enforcement of any judgment against the corporation.[93]

These developments put in question the initial *forum non conveniens* decision in the US, and raise the issue as to how discretion is to be exercised in international cases. The paradox in the *Texaco/Chevron* saga is that sides taken while discussing the non-appropriateness of Ecuador as a forum to litigate the case have dramatically changed to the extent that Chevron is preaching everywhere on the Ecuadorian justice system's lack of independence. In the end, the case highlights the strong connection between the decision to decline jurisdiction and the foreign judgment enforcement,[94]

---

[88] See *Ley de Gestión Medioambiental* (1999), Law 99/37. Likewise, Ecuador adhered to the ILO Convention 169 concerning indigenous and tribal peoples in independent countries (1989).

[89] See the essentials of the Ecuadorian system on aggregate litigation in Gómez (n 87) 161, 172 et seq.

[90] A claim based on the Racketeer Influenced and Corrupt Organizations Act was commenced against the plaintiffs' lawyer, Stefan Dozinger. See *Chevron Corp. v Donziger*, 974 F. Supp. 2d 362 (SDNY 2014). The complaint consisted of a compilation of all misconducts allegedly related to the Lago Agrio litigation such as fraud, corruption, collusion with Ecuadorian government official and so on, on which basis a judgment was sought seeking for a declaration of unenforceability of the Sucumbíos judgment in the US.

[91] Chevron brought an arbitral action against Ecuador on grounds of breach of the bilateral investment treaty signed between this country and the US. See Claimant's Notice of Arbitration, *Chevron Corp. and Texaco Petrol. Co. v Republic of Ecuador*, PCA Case 2009-23. In addition to get an interim measure ordering Ecuador to prevent or stop any proceedings against Chevron, the company sought to be released from liability on grounds of a settlement concluded in 1993 between Texaco and Ecuador on compensation for environmental damage. See *Chevron Corp. and Texaco Petroleum Co. v The Republic of Ecuador*, PCA Case 2007-02/AA277, Final Award (*italaw*, 31 August 2011) <http://www.italaw.com>/ accessed 23 April 2018.

[92] The details of this overlapping of proceedings can be found in the Diego P. Fernández Arroyo's comment included in this book.

[93] As this could interfere with the plaintiffs' rights, they sought protection in the Inter-American Commission on Human Rights in February 2012, but finally withdrew the request. The latter is available at *Lettersblogatory*, 28 February 2012 <http://lettersblogatory.com/> accessed 23 April 2018.

[94] All jurisdictions make this link as can already be read in Fawcett (n 57) 62.

which was not sufficiently established in this case,[95] leading to a transnational access-to-justice gap.[96]

Against this backdrop, the question arises as to whether, in declining jurisdiction, the quality of the foreign judiciary is relevant at all, given that the principle of equivalence between jurisdictions upon which private international law is based points in another direction.[97] However, this evaluation appears essential in the light of the rule of law as stay or termination of proceedings is awarded on grounds of the proper administration of justice; thereby restraints from exercising jurisdiction can only be granted if cases are referred to an independent and functioning jurisdiction that may render a judgment capable of recognition within a reasonable time.[98]

The recognition prognosis becomes then essential in staying or terminating home proceedings. At this point, the other court's international jurisdiction and the defendant's notice can be ascertained, but not other grounds for non-recognition such as fraud or public policy infringement.[99] The *Chevron/Ecuador* case highlights that red lines may appear at any time, and advises inserting safety breaks in the declining jurisdiction operation. Seen in this light, courts should retain jurisdiction until a judgment is rendered in the other country,[100] and have the power to lift the stay on home proceedings if evidence on justice administration not being properly provided in the other jurisdiction is brought to their attention by either of the parties. Opportunistic

---

95 In fact, Chevron finally got the declaration of *forum non conveniens* in the US upon the commitment to accept the recognition of an Ecuadorian judgment in accordance with the Uniform Foreign Money Judgment Recognition 2002, 13 ULA pt. 2, 39. Other defendant's commitments include waiving defences based on any statute of limitations that had matured between the filing of the class actions and sixty days after dismissal; accepting personal jurisdiction in Ecuador and in Peru to be sued by the plaintiffs and service of process in these jurisdictions; and that the parties can bring to these countries the discovery already obtained in the US to support their claims in these countries. See *Aguinda v. Texaco, Inc.*, 142 F. Supp. 2d 534, 534 (SDNY 2001).

96 This gap has been identified and properly discussed in the US legal framework by Christopher A. Whytock and Cassandra Burke Robertson, 'Forum non Conveniens and the Enforcement of Foreign Judgments' (2011) 111 *Columbia Law Review* 1444.

97 The question can be framed in terms of complying with the comity principle. See Fentiman (n 57) 805.

98 McLachlan (n 56) 516. What would not be acceptable is to operate on the basis of global index such as the World Bank Database <http://databank.worldbank.org/data/reports.aspx?source=worldwide-governance-indicators> or the World Justice Project <https://worldjusticeproject.org/our-work/wjp-rule-law-index/wjp-rule-law-index-2016> both accessed 23 April 2018. On the shortcomings of a similar index, see Ralf Michaels, 'Comparative Law by Numbers? Legal Origins Thesis, *Doing Business* Reports, and the Silence of Traditional Comparative Law' (2009) 57 *American Journal of Comparative Law* 765.

99 See focusing on judgment enforcement doctrine in the US and its analysis through the lens of the *Chevron/Ecuador* case, Christopher A. Whytock, 'Some Cautionary Notes on the Chevronization of Transnational Litigation' (2011) 199 *Stanford Journal of Complex Litigation* 467, 474 et seq.

100 Apparently, this is already the *modus operandi* in the US. See Gómez (n 87) 159. However, the probabilities of re-filling a case in the US seem to be very low on account of the costs it involves.

behaviour is, nevertheless, a parties' privilege that judicial cooperation would be able to curtail to a great extent.

3. TURNING PARALLEL LITIGATION INTO A GAME PLAY

The twists in the *Chevron/Ecuador* saga uncover a situation in which justice has not been served despite enormous resources invested by both sides and the jurisdictions involved in attaining it. This case also illustrates the increased significance of the issue of overlapping jurisdictions in view of the advances made worldwide regarding market freedoms and the collision of multinational corporations' activities with human rights' protection. While many countries have already addressed the issue of parallel litigation in one or other way, unilateral approaches to this issue have proven insufficient and fraught with risks as the overview provided in the last section illustrates.

In implementing the rule of law, States are advised to resort to the cooperation principle as the way forward. The first step is to achieve some common ground to whose end different institutions have already been working on, striving for a compromise across the common/civil law divide. In 2000, the International Law Association published the Leuven/London Principles on Declining and Referring Jurisdiction in International Civil and Commercial Litigation,[101] while negotiations on the Judgment Project at The Hague include a proposal for a *lis pendens* rule counterbalanced by *forum non conveniens* discretion in the first-seized court,[102] from which articles 5 and 6 of the Hague Convention of 30 June 2005 on Choice of Court Agreements stem. *Institut de Droit International* published its own principles in 2002–2003,[103] as the American Law Institute and UNIDROIT did in 2004.[104] The second step is to actually establish a cooperative framework, of which there are already some remarkable developments such as treaty rules on *forum (non) conveniens*,[105] and discretionary *lis pendens*.[106] Unfortunately, the ongoing Judgment Project does not contain any provisions on parallel litigation, and the project of drafting a UN convention on civil

---

[101] They can be read in McLachlan (n 56) 524.

[102] Preliminary Draft Convention on Jurisdiction and Foreign Judgments in Civil and Commercial Matters (adopted by the Special Commission, Preliminary Document No 11 of August 2000).

[103] Principles for Determining When the Use of the Doctrine of Forum Non Conveniens and Anti-Suit Injunctions is Appropriate (Collins and Droz, Rapporteurs) (2002–2003).

[104] ALI/UNIDROIT Rules of Transnational Civil Procedure (2004) 4 *Uniform Law Review* 758.

[105] The Hague Convention of 19 October 1996 on Jurisdiction, Applicable Law, Recognition, Enforcement and Co-operation in Respect of Parental Responsibility and Measures for the Protection of Children, arts 8 and 9.

[106] Brussels Ia Regulation, arts 33 and 34. The precedent is the Swiss Private International Law Act 1987, art. 9 requiring the examination of the likely enforceability of the judgment as a condition to apply the rule.

litigation for human rights cases is too recent to even foresee whether it has any probability of success.[107] There are, however, other alternatives.

The cooperative approach to parallel litigation is encouraged by the UN Guiding Principles on Business and Human Rights requiring States and businesses to 'protect, respect, remedy' human rights' violations such as the one committed in the Oriente region. In fact, the development of corporate civil liability is the reverse to criticism to an (excessive) investment protection, to which Chevron has resorted in seeking to avoid the Ecuadorian judgment's enforcement. This criticism has also sparked re-drafting trade and investment treaties to include social provisions. Still in their infancy, they aim to level the playing field by harmonising environmental and labour standards, accompanied by inter-governmental oversight mechanisms.[108] However, a judicial cooperation framework would be more effective allowing cross-border access to justice,[109] and in particular exercise of discretion in declining jurisdiction in a manner that does not abandon victims to the perils of unsafety navigation through the jurisdictional waters of the countries to which a transnational corporation may have contacts.

While the abovementioned principles and guidelines may serve as a model for such treaty provisions, it is to note that they could also play a role beyond treaties, if the example of insolvency protocols[110] is followed to elaborate international transfer agreements. They are nowadays encouraged by direct judicial communications, and would have the advantage of securing access to justice or favouring consolidation of claims in one country, while paving the way for judgment enforcement in the other. In short, it is about building bridges and ensuring to the possible extent that parties get their day in court without compromising their right to a remedy as has happened in the *Chevron/Ecuador* case.

---

107 Ecuador is behind this project approved by the General Assembly in 2014, Document A/HRC/RES/26/9.

108 International Labour Office, *Assessment of labour provisions in trade and investment arrangements* (ILO, 2016). The number of trade agreements including labour provisions has significantly increased from only four in 1995 to 58 in June 2016, being roughly 120 countries parties to this type of agreements (id 5). See WTO Regional Trade Agreements Information System <http://rtais.wto.org/UI/PublicMaintainRTAHome.aspx> accessed 23 April 2018.

109 As already proposed by Prihandono (n 85) 98.

110 They are soft law mechanisms first agreed between US and UK courts to deal with the Maxwell's insolvency (see Jay L. Westbrook, 'The Lessons of *Maxwell Communication*' (1996) 64 *Fordham Law Review* 2531), whose success has given rise to guidelines on how to establish this type of direct cooperation such as ALI Court-to-Court Communication Principles; UNCITRAL Practice Guide on Cross-Border Insolvency Cooperation 2009, and Global Principles for Cooperation in International Insolvency Cases and Global Guidelines for Court-to-Court Communication in International Insolvency Cases, available at (2014) 23 *International Insolvency Review* 221–37.

4. Free-wheeling judgments/awards: *Mitsubishi Motors Corp. v. Soler Chrysler-Plymouth, Inc.*

4.1 CASE BACKGROUND

This is a landmark decision that rules in favour of the arbitrability – in the European sense of the possibility of submitting to arbitration – of antitrust claims in international cases. Soler Chrysler-Plymouth, Inc., a Puerto Rico car dealer's franchise, entered into distribution and sales agreements with Mitsubishi Motors, a Japanese automobile manufacturer. The sales agreement contained an arbitration clause in which all disputes arising out of certain articles of the agreement would be resolved by the Japanese Commercial Arbitration Association. Upon a dispute related to the decrease of automobile sales, Mitsubishi brought an action in federal court under the Federal Arbitration Act and the New York Convention on the Recognition and Enforcement of Foreign Arbitral Awards, seeking an order to compel arbitration of the disputes in accordance with the arbitration clause. Soler filed counterclaims, invoking antitrust violations under the Sherman Act. It argued that the statutory claims were unwaivable under the Act and that this meant that the courts could not be sidelined by arbitration. However, the district court ordered arbitration of all claims, holding that the international nature of the dispute required enforcement of the arbitration clause. The US Court of Appeals for the First Circuit reversed.

Hence, the crucial issue before the United States Supreme Court was the possibility of arbitrating claims arising under the Sherman Act. Should federal courts enforce an agreement to arbitrate when the dispute involves the determination of unwaivable antitrust claims? In a 5-3 majority opinion delivered by Justice Blackmun, the Supreme Court held that claims arising under the Sherman Act and encompassed in a valid arbitration clause in an international commercial transaction are arbitrable under the federal Arbitration Act. Justice Stevens dissented, arguing that a fair construction of the arbitration clause did not encompass antitrust claims. He deemed that these claims were too complex and important to be left to arbitrators and that it would be unreasonable to require an American company to arbitrate a claim under American antitrust law before a panel of foreign arbitrators.

According to the majority reasoning, the Federal Arbitration Act was broad enough to require arbitration of statutory claims as well as contractual ones. However, the favour towards international arbitration was qualified in an (in)famous footnote, according to which the courts would be justified in taking a 'second look' if the combined effect of the arbitration and choice of law clauses would lead to a waiver of a statutory right. The case can be considered as having contributed significantly to the expansion of international arbitration during the last decades of the 20th century. It was followed rapidly in other hub jurisdictions in a competition for the business of arbitration, but the extent and intensity of the scrutiny of awards by the courts (the 'second look') has remained controversial.

Case: *Mitsubishi Motors Corp. v. Soler Chrysler-Plymouth, Inc.*, 473 U.S. 614, 628 (1985)

4.2 THE BUILDING OF AN ARBITRATION FRIENDLY JURISDICTION

George A. Bermann

1. INTRODUCTION

The *Mitsubishi* case[1] is known best of course for its determination that claims arising under the US antitrust laws, and the Sherman Act in particular,[2] are arbitrable. In a majority opinion authored by Justice Blackmun, the Court held that a Puerto Rican distributor (Soler) could pursue before the Japan Commercial Arbitration Association in Tokyo a Sherman Act claim against the automobile manufacturer, Mitsubishi Motors Corporation, for various alleged antitrust violations. In so holding, the Court rejected the position that all federal courts had taken following the Second Circuit Court of Appeals decision in the case of *American Safety Equipment Corp. v. J. P. Maguire & Co.*, namely that the rights conferred by the antitrust laws were 'of a character inappropriate for enforcement by arbitration.'[3]

The Court rejected each of the reasons cited in *American Safety* for treating Sherman Act claims as non-arbitrable, namely that private antitrust claims are vital to enforcement of the antitrust laws, that contracts in antitrust cases are likely to be contracts of adhesion, that antitrust claims require sophisticated legal and economic analysis, and that antitrust cases are simply too important to be left to arbitrators. It found each of them to be unpersuasive. The Court's willingness to subject Sherman Act claims to arbitration was not, however, without antecedent. In its ruling some ten years earlier in *Scherk v. Alberto-Culver Co.*,[4] the Court had ordered arbitration of a claim arising under the Securities Exchange Act of 1934, largely on the ground that the claim in that case arose in a distinctly international context. The question in *Mitsubishi* was whether the Court would extend to international antitrust claims the solicitude for arbitration that it had demonstrated in *Scherk*.

2. THE COURT'S HOSPITALITY TOWARD ARBITRATION OF FEDERAL STATUTORY CLAIMS

The majority in *Mitsubishi* took precisely that step, seeing no good reason why, if the parties draft their arbitration agreement in sufficiently broad terms (as the Court found they had done), they should not be permitted to entrust the adjudication of private antitrust claims to arbitration in lieu of litigation in US courts. Notwithstanding the importance of the public policy embodied in an enactment such as the Sherman Act,

---

1 *Mitsubishi Motors Corporation v. Soler Chrysler-Plymouth, Inc.*, 473 U.S. 614 (1985).

2 15 U.S.C. s. 1 et seq.

3 391 F.2d 821 (2d Cir. 1968), quoting *Wilko v. Swan*, 201 F.2d 439, 444 (2d Cir.), rev'd, 346 U.S. 427 (1953).

4 417 U.S. 506, 417 U.S. 515–520 (1974).

the majority could 'find no warrant in the Arbitration Act for implying in every contract within its ken a presumption against arbitration of statutory claims.'[5] In support of that finding, the Court observed that '[b]y agreeing to arbitrate a statutory claim, a party does not forgo the substantive rights afforded by the statute; it only submits to their resolution in an arbitral, rather than a judicial, forum.'[6] The Court was thus unwilling to assume that Sherman Act claims could not or would not be properly adjudicated in an arbitral forum. To that end, the Court invoked the 'strong presumption in favor of enforcement of freely negotiated contractual choice-of-forum provisions.'

We must assume that, if Congress intended the substantive protection afforded by a given statute to include protection against waiver of the right to a judicial forum, that intention would be deducible from text or legislative history. Having made the bargain to arbitrate, the party should be held to it unless Congress itself has evinced an intention to preclude a waiver of judicial remedies for the statutory rights at issue. Nothing, in the meantime, prevents a party from excluding statutory claims from the scope of an agreement to arbitrate, if it wishes to do so.[7]

The Court's hospitality toward arbitration of federal statutory claims has continued in the years since *Mitsubishi* was decided. The Court has thus treated as legally capable of being arbitrated claims arising under such legislation as the Carriage of Goods by Sea Act[8] and the Racketeering and Corrupt Influenced organizations Act (RICO).[9] Nor is the *Mitsubishi* decision without counterpart elsewhere in the world. Notably, the *Eco-Swiss v. Benneton* judgment of the European Court of Justice likewise treated competition law claims as arbitrable.[10]

Justice Stevens, joined by Justices Brennan and Marshall, dissented in *Mitsubishi*, and on two grounds – first that the arbitration clause could not properly be construed to embrace claims under the antitrust statutes, and second that, even if it could be so construed, 'the unique public interest in the enforcement of the antitrust laws' requires that the adjudication of such claims be reserved to the courts:

> [B]oth a fair respect for the importance of the interests that Congress has identified as worthy of federal statutory protection, and a fair appraisal of the most likely understanding of the parties who sign agreements containing standard arbitration clauses, support a presumption that such clauses do not apply to federal statutory claims.[11]
>
> Like any other mechanism for resolving controversies, international arbitration will only succeed if it is realistically limited to tasks it is capable of performing well – the prompt and inexpensive resolution of essentially contractual disputes between commercial partners. As for matters involving the political passions and the fundamental interests of nations, even the

---

[5] 473 U.S. at 625.

[6] 473 U.S. at 628.

[7] 473 U.S. at 629.

[8] *Vimar Seguros y Reaseguros, S. A. v. M/V Sky Reefer* (94-623), 515 U.S. 528 (1995).

[9] *PacifiCare Health Sys. v. Book*, 538 U.S. 401 (2003).

[10] Case C-126/97, *Eco Swiss China Time Ltd. v. Benetton International NV*, [1999] ECR I-3055.

[11] 473 U.S. at 653.

> multilateral convention adopted under the auspices of the United Nations recognizes that private international arbitration is incapable of achieving satisfactory results.[12]

Clearly, the majority and the dissent took markedly different positions on the best way to reconcile two distinct US public policies: the public policy in favor of international arbitration and the public policy in favor of vigorous antitrust law enforcement. There is more to the *Mitsubishi* decision, however, than its central proposition that antitrust claims under US law are arbitrable.

3. THE SECOND-LOOK DOCTRINE

First and foremost, while the Supreme Court referred the antitrust claim at issue in the dispute to arbitration, it had sufficient misgivings in doing so to announce what has come to be called 'the second look doctrine,' i.e., a statement to the effect that if the arbitral tribunal were to fail to 'take cognizance' of antitrust claims and 'actually decide[] them,' a US court might thereafter deny recognition of the award, and presumably entertain the antitrust claim anew:

> Having permitted the arbitration to go forward, the national courts of the United States will have the opportunity at the award-enforcement stage to ensure that the legitimate interest in the enforcement of the antitrust law has been addressed. The Convention reserves to each signatory country the right to refuse enforcement of an award where the recognition or enforcement of the award would be contrary to the public policy of that country. While the efficacy of the arbitral process requires that substantive review at the award-enforcement stage remain minimal, it would not require intrusive inquiry to ascertain that the tribunal took cognizance of the antitrust claims and actually decided them.[13]

The Court gave no indication of what the requirement that tribunals take 'cognizance' of the antitrust claim actually entails and no case entertained by the Court since then has furnished an opportunity for it to do so. A 'second look' may take a variety of forms. A court may understand the notion of 'taking cognizance' of a statute somewhat literally and demand nothing more than that the statutory claim is in fact entertained. This would represent a 'minimalist' approach. A court may however go further to examine the merits, but nevertheless in doing so designedly show some measure of deference to the tribunal. Or it may go still further and examine the merits on a fully *de novo* basis – a 'maximalist' approach. These approaches are decidedly different in their impact on an award's finality and thus on the efficacy of the arbitral process. Interestingly, the 'standard of review' question similarly remains open in the European Union under the *Eco Swiss* ruling, the Court of Justice having not yet made any pronouncement on the rigor with which arbitral determinations of competition law claims are to be reviewed by national courts. The Advocate-General in the *Genentech*

---

12 473 U.S. at 666.
13 473 U.S. at 639.

case,[14] favoring *de novo* review, invited the ECJ to take a position on the matter, but the Court declined to do so.

Taking a 'second look' at arbitral determinations of US antitrust claims may of course be logically reconciled with the US courts' recognition and enforcement obligations under the New York Convention on the ground that doing so amounts to nothing more than giving effect to the Convention's public policy exception.[15] On the other hand, it plainly opens up the possibility of judicial review of the merits of an award, a move contrary to the Convention's overall purpose and spirit. As is well-known, the Convention grounds for denying recognition and enforcement are designed in such a way as to avoid the possibility of merits review by the court before which recognition or enforcement is sought.

A main critique of *Mitsubishi* accordingly runs this way: Has the Supreme Court, in widening the universe of arbitrable claims subject to arbitration to include statutory claims of paramount importance, paid too great a long-term price in terms of the principle of finality upon which arbitration depends? Would it ultimately have been *more* pro-arbitration, rather than *less*, for the Court to have denied the arbitrability of antitrust claims and left intact the traditional limits on post-award judicial review? To the surprise of many, the 'second look' contemplated by *Mitsubishi* appears never to have been performed by the federal courts, so the question remains an open one.

Second, but less widely noted, the *Mitsubishi* Court faced the important question whether a tribunal, directed by a contractual choice of law clause to apply the law of a given jurisdiction, may nevertheless entertain and adjudicate a claim arising under a different body of national law. In the *Mitsubishi* case, the parties had agreed to both (a) an arbitration clause according to which '[a]ll disputes, controversies or differences which may arise between [the parties] out of or in relation to … this Agreement or for the breach thereof shall be finally settled by arbitration in Japan in accordance with the rules and regulations of the Japan Commercial Arbitration Association' and (b) a choice of law clause according to which '[t]his Agreement is made in, and will be governed by and construed in all respects according to the laws of the Swiss Confederation as if entirely performed therein.'

The question naturally arose whether a tribunal that is called upon in this fashion to apply Swiss law may proceed to entertain an antitrust claim arising under another jurisdiction's law, i.e., the US antitrust statutes. Arguably, a tribunal that applies to a covered claim a law other than the law selected by the parties thereby commits an excess of authority – a circumstance that would in principle justify annulment of the resulting award under FAA Section 10 or under the New York Convention.[16]

Nevertheless, the Supreme Court in *Mitsubishi* presumed that the arbitral tribunal sitting in Tokyo in that case could and would indeed apply the US antitrust laws, notwithstanding the contractual choice of law designating Swiss law. The Court reasoned somewhat obliquely as follows:

---

[14] Case C-567/14, *Genentech Inc. v Hoechst GmbH and Sanofi-Aventis Deutschland GmbH*, [2016] ECR-I ___ (July 7, 2016).

[15] United Nations Convention on the Recognition and Enforcement of Foreign Arbitral Awards (New York Convention), art. V(2)(b).

[16] Ibid., arts. V(1)(c), V(1)(d).

> There is no reason to assume at the outset of the dispute that international arbitration will not provide an adequate mechanism. To be sure, the international arbitral tribunal owes no prior allegiance to the legal norms of particular states; hence it has no direct obligation to vindicate their statutory dictates. The Tribunal, however, is bound to effectuate the intentions of the parties. *Where the parties have agreed that the arbitral body is to decide a defined set of claims which includes, as in these cases, those arising from the application of American antitrust law, the tribunal should be bound to decide that dispute in accord with the national law giving rise to the claim* ... And so long as the prospective litigant effectively may vindicate its statutory cause of action in the arbitral forum, the statute will continue to serve both its remedial and deterrent function.[17]

Put in simpler terms, an arbitration clause drafted broadly enough to encompass non-contractual claims empowers a tribunal to decide those claims in accordance with the national law under which they arise, even if that law is other than the law chosen by the parties as applicable to claims sounding in contract.

This explanation readily applies where a given dispute is sufficiently related to a contract to be governed by the contract's arbitration clause, and thus subject to arbitration, and yet does not fall within the scope of a contractual choice of law clause drafted narrowly to cover breach of contract claims only. If the antitrust claim, though arbitrable, is not governed by the choice of law clause, the tribunal has considerable freedom to determine the law by which to adjudicate the claim, and will indeed most likely apply to that claim the law under which the claim itself arises.

To some extent, this result may be contrary to the parties' actual intentions. The parties may well have meant for all disputes between them bearing any relation to their contract to be governed by the law designated in the contract's choice of law clause, thus excluding any possibility that their legal relations might be governed by any other body of law. The only way the parties can hope to prevent a tribunal from applying to their dispute a law other than the chosen one would be to draft the choice of law clause in such a way as to govern every claim possibly falling within the scope of their agreement to arbitrate. But even that precaution may fail to secure the intended result, for the simple reason that a tribunal may, in one compelling circumstance or another, feel justified in applying the mandatory law of some other jurisdiction, notwithstanding the breadth of the choice of law clause. When if ever a tribunal should take such a step remains a contested issue.

4. CONCLUSION

The *Mitsubishi* decision leaves no doubt that even US statutory claims of the utmost importance are arbitrable, assuming the arbitration clause is drafted in sufficiently broad terms. Yet, in other respects, the decision raises more questions than it answers. We simply do not know how far a US court will go in revisiting the merits of an antitrust or other important statutory claim under the 'second look doctrine.' Much remains to be seen.

---

[17] 473 U.S. at 637–38 (emphasis added).

4.3 BALANCING ARBITRABILITY AND COURT CONTROL

Giuditta Cordero-Moss

1. INTRODUCTION

Mitsubishi reversed the traditional view according to which disputes concerning competition law matters could not be arbitrated. It established the second look-doctrine: courts do not abdicate their power to safeguard the basic principles of their system when they permit competition law-related disputes to be arbitrated, because courts have jurisdiction to control the arbitral award and thus verify that the award does not violate fundamental principles of the forum.

The second look-doctrine had a significant international impact and contributed to a broader scope of arbitrability. The trend seems to be reversing now, as there are signs that courts of EU member States are being more restrictive to arbitrability. Below, I will explain the link between arbitrability and court control also by reference to later case law in the EU. I argue that the second look posited in *Mitsubishi* is essential to the effectiveness of arbitration – notwithstanding the widespread opinion according to which an arbitration-friendly regime requires that court control is restricted to the extent possible.

2. COURT CONTROL AND ARBITRABILITY

The court control posited in *Mitsubishi* can be found in another groundbreaking decision also regarding competition law: *Eco Swiss*,[18] where the CJEU established that competition law amounts to *ordre public* (public policy) in EU law. As will be seen below, the 1958 New York Convention on Recognition and Enforcement of Foreign Arbitral Awards permits to refuse enforcement of awards violating *ordre public*. Therefore, after *Eco Swiss* a court within the EU may, under the New York Convention and exercising the second look asserted in *Mitsubishi*, refuse enforcement of an award violating EU competition law.

In the decades following *Mitsubishi* and *Eco Swiss*, two opposed doctrines were developed to define the degree of control that courts may exercise when giving their second look.[19] The Paris Court of Appeal[20] developed the minimalist doctrine, according to which courts owe deference to the award's evaluation. The Dutch Court of Appeal[21] developed the maximalist doctrine, according to which courts may independently evaluate whether *ordre public* is infringed. The minimalist doctrine permits courts

---

[18] Case C-126/97 *Eco Swiss v Benetton International* [1999] ECR I-.

[19] L Radicati di Brozolo, 'Mandatory Rules and International Arbitration' (2012) 23 *Am. Rev. Int'l Arb.* 49, 49.

[20] Cour d'appel Paris, 1e ch., 18.11.2004, Rev arb. 2005 751 (*Thalès Air Defence v. Euromissile*).

[21] Gerechtshof Haag, 24.3.2005, NJF 2005/239, TvA 2006/24 (*Marketing Displays International Inc. v. VR Van Raalte Reclame B.V*).

to set aside an award or refuse its enforcement only if the violation of *ordre public* is manifest, effective and concrete. In particular, courts are expected to accept the evaluation that the arbitral tribunal made of issues of *ordre public*, such as competition law. If the award shows that the arbitral tribunal considered these matters, and concluded that *ordre public* was not violated, the court has to accept this evaluation. In contrast, under the maximalist doctrine, courts are expected to make their own, independent evaluation of whether *ordre public* is violated. The minimalist doctrine seems to be losing authority in its country of origin, France,[22] but it still enjoys wide support in the arbitration community because it accords with the traditional understanding that interference with party autonomy and the arbitral award shall be kept to a minimum.[23] The minimalist theory, however, may turn out to be detrimental to arbitration: restricting the scope of court control, it runs the risk of reducing the scope of arbitrability.

The close link between arbitrability and court control is apparent in some opinions by the CJEU Advocate General, that will be mentioned in the following. In *CDC*,[24] AG Jääskinen argued for restricting arbitrability of matters relating to competition law, because arbitration does not ensure a uniform application of EU law. Similarly, in *Genentech*,[25] AG Wathelet argued against the minimalist approach. In *Achmea*,[26] AG Wathelet accepted the arbitrability of disputes relating to competition law, but on the assumption that courts exercise control on the awards according to the maximalist theory. In the former two cases, the CJEU chose not to decide these aspects, thus leaving open the question of whether the minimalist doctrine is compatible with EU law, or whether the maximalist doctrine shall be preferred. The latter case was based on a referral by the German Supreme Court (BGH)[27] relating to the annulment proceeding of an investment award.[28] One of the invoked annulment grounds was that the award was null because the dispute was not arbitrable: as arbitral tribunals are not bound by the EU duty to apply EU law in a uniform way, the effective application of EU law would be endangered if the dispute had been arbitrable. This line of thought resembled the situation prior to *Mitsubishi*, when US courts excluded arbitrability whenever the issues in dispute assumed the accurate application of norms reflecting important policies, such as competition law. The BGH requested the CJEU to confirm that there is no basis to restrict the scope of arbitrability, as long as the courts may control the award's compatibility with fundamental principles of the forum. Thus, the BGH embraced the second look doctrine introduced by *Mitsubishi* and endorsed the

[22] Cour d'appel Paris, 1e ch., 21.2.2017 nr. 15/01650, at page 10, that refused enforcement of an UNCITRAL investment award (*Belokon v. Kyrgz Republic*, 24.10.2014). The court made an independent evaluation of allegations regarding money laundering and reached a different conclusion than the arbitral tribunal.

[23] L Radicati Di Brozolo, 'Arbitration and Competition Law: The Position of the Courts and of Arbitrators' (2011) 27(1) *Arbitration International* 1.

[24] Case C-352/13 *CDC Hydrogen Peroxide v. Evonik Degussa and Others* [2015] ECR I-.

[25] Case C-567/14 *Genentech v. Hoechst and Sanofi-Aventis Deutschland* [2016] ECR I-.

[26] Case C-281/16 *Slovak Republic v. Achmea* [2016] ECR I-.

[27] Bundesgerichtshof, 3.3.2016, I ZB 2/1.

[28] *Achmea B.V. (former Eureko B.V.) v. The Slovak Republic*, UNCITRAL, PCA Case No. 2008-13, 7.12.2012.

maximalist theory. Advocate General Wathelet[29] concurred with this line of thought. The CJEU, however, did not accept this approach, and concluded that investment disputes are not arbitrable. However, the CJEU distinguished between investment disputes and commercial disputes, and specified that its conclusion did not apply to commercial disputes. Also this time, therefore, the CJEU did not clarify the extent of court control that it expects for it to permit arbitrability of matters related to EU-law, as long as the disputes are commercial.

As the next section will show, the scope of court control is quite limited even if the maximalist theory is embraced. Therefore, there is no need to fear that court control would prejudice the autonomy of arbitration. Far from being hostile to arbitration, an understanding of the second look doctrine based on the maximalist doctrine is necessary to prevent that the scope of arbitrability is restricted.

3. COURT CONTROL'S LIMITED SCOPE

Arbitration enjoys relative autonomy from national laws. Arbitration agreements shall be recognised and arbitral awards shall be enforced in the over 150 countries who ratified the New York Convention.[30] The New York Convention contains in article II an obligation by the courts to recognise arbitration agreements and dismiss a case if the dispute is covered by an arbitration agreement. However, this assumes that the court finds that the dispute is arbitrable. This ensures that courts are the only venue for resolving disputes in areas where an accurate application of the law is essential. According to the New York Convention,[31] courts decide on the arbitrability of a dispute according to their own law. That the parameters for arbitrability are based not on uniform sources, but on domestic law, renders the matter more exposed to policy interests. As noted in section IV below, recent case law seems to confirm that some courts, as a tool to ensure accurate application of law, restrict the scope of arbitrability.

Arbitrability is important not only when determining jurisdiction, but also after the award was rendered – it affects the award's enforceability and validity. Enforcement is regulated by the New York Convention, whose article V has an exhaustive and restrictive list of exceptions to the enforceability of arbitral awards, to which I will revert below. Annulment of awards is not unified by a convention. However, national law is largely harmonised thanks to the 1985 UNCITRAL Model Law on International

[29] Case C-281/16 *Slovak Republic v. Achmea* [2016] ECR I-, Opinion of AG Wathelet, paras 70–72; ibid. paras 251–60. The principal argument in the Opinion is that investment arbitral tribunals meet the criteria contained in article 267 TFEU. Therefore, they are permitted to request the CJEU to give a preliminary ruling and are required to apply EU law, see paras 84–135. Supporting this position, Jürgen Basedow, 'EU Law in International Arbitration: Referrals to the European Court of Justice' (2015) 32(4) *Journal of International Arbitration* 367.

[30] For an updated status, *see* UNCITRAL, Status, Convention on the Recognition and Enforcement of Foreign Arbitral Awards, http://www.uncitral.org/uncitral/en/uncitral_texts/arbitration/NYConvention_status.html.

[31] Convention on the Recognition and Enforcement of Foreign Arbitral Awards (adopted 10 June 1958, entered into force 7 June 1959) UNTS (New York Convention) art V(2)(1).

Commercial Arbitration (revised in 2006). In the model law, annulment grounds correspond to the exceptions to enforceability listed under article V of the New York Convention.[32]

According to these sources, an arbitral award runs the risk of being unenforceable or invalid in a restricted number of situations, that may be roughly summarised as follows: invalid or non-binding arbitration agreement; violation of due process; excess of power by the tribunal; irregular procedure; non-arbitrability; violation of *ordre public* (public policy). As this short overview shows, court control is not meant to be an appeal on the merits or on the application of law: it is meant to ensure that fundamental principles, both procedural and substantial, are respected.

Of particular relevance in connection with the second look-doctrine is the last mentioned ground: an award may be annulled or refused enforcement if it violates *ordre public*. It seems generally recognised that this defence is to be applied only in exceptional situations.[33] This defence appears not only in the context of arbitration. *Ordre public* is also a limitation to the application by courts of a foreign governing law, as well as to the enforcement of foreign court decisions. In EU law, the former is regulated, *inter alia*, in the Rome I and Rome II Regulations, respectively articles 21 and 26, and the latter in the Brussels I Regulation,[34] article 45. Under all these instruments, as well as under the New York Convention, the UNCITRAL Model Law, and most national arbitration laws, *ordre public* is seen as an expression of the basic socio-economic principles of the society. *Ordre public* is generally deemed to reflect fundamental principles in the system of the court and does not necessarily correspond to the positive content of specific provisions. It is the underlying principles that may constitute *ordre public*, not the technicalities of the provisions. Therefore, even though a certain provision may be deemed to protect fundamental principles of a given system, *ordre public* will not necessarily be violated every time the specific, technical content of that provision has not been accurately implemented – as long as the underlying principles have been safeguarded.[35] The defence of *ordre public*, in other words, is not meant to ensure an accurate application of the details of a provision, but to make sure that the interests protected by that rule are preserved (as long as they are fundamental). As a corollary, a violation of *ordre public* may not be determined in the abstract, by simply observing that a certain rule was not applied accurately. To establish violation of *ordre public*, it will be necessary to evaluate, on a case-by-case basis, whether the

---

32 UNCITRAL Model Law, art 34; see also Gary Born, *International Commercial Arbitration* 2nd edn (Alphen aan den Rijn, Kluwer Law International 2014), 3186, 3340; G Cordero-Moss, *International Commercial Contracts* (Cambridge, Cambridge University Press 2014) 224.

33 Born, ibid., 3312, 3647.

34 Regulation (EC) no 593/2008 of the European Parliament and of the Council of 17 June 2008 on the Law Applicable To Contractual Obligations 2008 O.J. (L 177) 6 (Rome I); Regulation (EC) No 864/2007 of the European Parliament And Of The Council Of 11 July 2007 on the Law Applicable To Non-Contractual Obligations 2007 O.J. (L 199) 40 (Rome II); Regulation (EU) No 1215/2012 of the European Parliament And Of The Council Of 12 December 2012 on Jurisdiction and the Recognition and Enforcement of Judgments in Civil and Commercial Matters (recast) 2012 O.J. (L 351) 1.

35 Cordero-Moss (n 32) 246.

violation of a certain provision entails violation of the underlying fundamental principles or not.[36] By contrast, the defence of inarbitrability applies in the abstract, for the simple circumstance that the dispute relates to certain matters and quite irrespective of whether the arbitral tribunal applied the law accurately or not.

The narrow scope of the *ordre public* defence was established by the CJEU in respect of the Brussels Convention (predecessor of the mentioned Brussels I Regulation): in *Renault*,[37] the Court explained that

> [r]ecourse to the clause on public policy … can be envisaged only where recognition or enforcement of the judgment delivered in another Contracting State would be at variance to an unacceptable degree with the legal order of the State in which enforcement is sought inasmuch as it infringes a fundamental principle. In order for the prohibition of any review of the foreign judgment as to its substance to be observed, the infringement would have to constitute a manifest breach of a rule of law regarded as essential in the legal order of the State in which enforcement is sought or of a right recognized as being fundamental within that legal order.[38]

Applied to the case at hand, this narrow approach led to the conclusion that intellectual property rights that restricted the possibility for third parties to sell spare parts for automobiles were restrictive of competition, but did not reach the threshold for the Court to find a violation of *ordre public*. The Court explained that '[t]he court of the State in which enforcement is sought cannot, without undermining the aim of the [Brussels] Convention, refuse recognition of a decision emanating from another Contracting State solely on the ground that it considers that national or Community law was misapplied in that decision.'[39]

In the above-mentioned Rome I, Rome II and Brussels I, the narrow scope of the *ordre public* defence is expressed among others with the formulation that the defence is applicable when fundamental principles are *manifestly* violated. This does not mean that these instruments endorse the minimalist theory. It means that the defence's scope is narrow and its use exceptional. The word 'manifest' is not present in the New York Convention or the UNCITRAL Model Law, but the narrow scope and exceptional application applies also in the field of arbitration. While the Brussels I Regulation is based on the principle of mutual trust, the New York Convention and the Model Law are based on the principle of effectiveness of arbitral awards. This is a strong principle, which justifies an equally narrow scope for the *ordre public* defence for arbitration as the principle of mutual trust does in the EU context.

In *Eco Swiss*, the CJEU affirmed that European competition law must be considered as European *ordre public*. The same assumption must be read into *Mitsubishi*, otherwise there would be no basis for the second look. The CJEU justified this qualification affirming that competition rules 'are necessary for the achievement of the internal market.' Given the narrow understanding of the defence of *ordre public*, it is to

---

[36] Ibid., 247.

[37] Case C-38/98 *Renault v. Maxicar and Orazio Formento* [2000] ECR I-; see also C-681/13 *Diageo Brands v. Simiramida* [2015] ECR I-.

[38] Case C-38/98 *Renault v. Maxicar and Formento* [2000] ECR I-3021, para. 30.

[39] Ibid., para. 33.

be expected that the CJEU has a restrictive understanding of this formulation. As most EU rules have the purpose of achieving the internal market, emphasis should be placed on the adjective 'necessary'. Otherwise, a situation may arise where the majority of EU regulation is deemed to be *ordre public*; a situation that would run counter the assumption that the *ordre public* defence shall be used only in exceptional cases. This formulation was used by the CJEU in *Ingmar*.[40] Here, the CJEU decided that EU law on agency[41] overrides any choice of law clause contained in the contract and must be applied even if the parties chose a different law. Commercial agency is deemed to be necessary for the achievement of the internal market for two reasons: uniform conditions for agents are deemed to ensure fair competition; and, they protect the agent who is deemed to be the weaker party. As will be seen in section 4 below, this seems to have created a basis for restricting arbitrability of disputes relating to contracts of agency – an undesirable development. That the CJEU in *Ingmar* used the same formulation as in *Eco Swiss* and defined rules on agency as 'necessary for the achievement of the internal market,' could be interpreted to mean that these rules must be considered as European *ordre public*. This, however, is too expansive an understanding of *ordre public*.[42]

As *Renault* shows, even CJEU case law confirms that the defence of *ordre public* may not be triggered whenever a rule necessary for the achievement of the internal market is breached. In addition to the narrow scope of the *ordre public* defence, a further constraint restricts the courts' ability to give a second look: the violation must be so serious that it can easily be ascertained. This may seem to be at odds with the necessity to carry out complex evaluations to ascertain whether an agreement violates competition law.[43]

However, this does not necessarily mean that the minimalist doctrine should be endorsed. In *Genentech*,[44] the Advocate General Wathelet pleaded for more extensive court control and criticised the minimalist approach, according to which court control may be exercised only in the case of manifest infringement of *ordre public*, and only if the issue had not been examined in the arbitration proceeding. The requirement that only manifest infringements may trigger court control was criticised for making court control illusionary – because many restrictions of competition forbidden by EU law

---

40 Case C-381/98 *Ingmar v. Eaton Leonard Technologies* [2000] ECR I-.

41 Council Directive 86/653/EEC of 18 December 1986 on the coordination of the laws of the Member States relating to self-employed commercial agents [1986] OJ 2 382/17, arts 17–18, on the principal's duty to pay compensation to the agent upon termination of an agency contract.

42 On the relationship between *ordre public* and overriding mandatory rules, G Cordero-Moss, 'EU Overriding Mandatory Provisions and the Law Applicable to the Merits' in Franco Ferrari (ed), *The Impact of EU Law on International Commercial Arbitration* (Huntington, NY, Juris 2017) 317–49.

43 For many agreements, an infringement of competition law may be found only after extensive and complex evaluations, among others considering possible economic benefits, indispensability and other aspects of the economic context, Commission Notice – Guidelines on the applicability of Article 81 of the EC Treaty to horizontal cooperation agreements, 2001 OJ (C 003) 2–30. More extensively, G Cordero-Moss, 'Inherent Powers and Competition Law', in Franco Ferrari and Friedrich Rosenfeld (eds), *Inherent Powers in International Adjudication*, forthcoming.

44 Case C-567/14 *Genentech v. Hoechst and Sanofi-Aventis* [2016] ECR I-.

require complex evaluation and would escape review.[45] The requirement that the court owes deference to the decision made by the arbitral tribunal was criticised for being at odds with the system of review of compatibility with EU law: as arbitral tribunals have no competence to refer to the CJEU questions for preliminary rulings, in the view of the AG, the responsibility for reviewing compliance with EU law must be placed with the courts and not with arbitral tribunals.[46] On this basis, according to the AG opinion, the general principle of arbitration law that a court may not independently review the substance of an award does not prevent the court from considering the issue of compliance with competition law, even though the issue has already been considered by the arbitral tribunal – given that competition law is of fundamental importance in the EU legal order, and that the New York Convention permits to refuse enforcement for violation of *ordre public*.[47] The AG seemed to assume that any and all violations of competition law would amount to a violation of EU *ordre public*.[48] As was seen above, this is not a correct assumption as the CJEU has repeatedly stated that only serious violations lead to infringement of *ordre public*.[49] In its final judgment, the CJEU ignored the matter and did not take a position on the scale from the AG's maximalist approach with automatic effects to the minimalist approach and the impossibility to evaluate the infringement's result under the specific circumstances. Therefore, there has not been any clarification on this point.[50]

In my opinion, compliance with the narrow scope of the *ordre public* defence does not require that the minimalist approach is followed. It is not necessary that courts limit themselves to verifying whether the tribunal has taken cognisance of matters of *ordre public* without considering how the tribunal has evaluated the matter. This would result in courts delegating the safeguard of their fundamental principles to arbitral tribunals, and it would go so far in affirming the autonomy of arbitration, that it risks backfiring and eventually restricting the scope of arbitration (see section 4 below). A court's ability to independently verify that *ordre public* is not manifestly infringed is a fully acceptable precondition to a legal system's recognition and enforcement of awards. The narrow scope of the *ordre public* defence ensures that courts do not abuse this power. The defence of *ordre public* shall not be used to re-judge the dispute: court control of arbitral awards is not meant as a tool to permit a review of the merits, neither in respect of the application of the law or of the assessment of the facts. Therefore, an error of law in the award, or a divergent opinion by the court on application of the law, is not

---

[45] Ibid., Opinion of AG Wathelet, paras 64–67.

[46] Ibid., paras 59–62. The AG refers here to commercial arbitration. The same AG Wathelet expressed the opinion that in investment arbitration the arbitral tribunal is entitled to refer questions to the CJEU, see n 29 above.

[47] Case C-567/14 *Genentech v. Hoechst and Sanofi-Aventis* [2016] ECR I-, Opinion of AG Wathelet, paras 70–72.

[48] In the specific case, the AG concluded that art. 101 TFEU was not violated.

[49] Case C-38/98 *Renault v. Maxicar and Orazio Formento* [2000] ECR I-; C-681/13 *Diageo Brands v. Simiramida* [2015] ECR I-.

[50] A clarification came in C-281/16 *Slovak Republic v. Achmea*, albeit only for investment disputes. The CJEU found that investment disputes are not arbitrable when they are based on intra-EU treaties.

sufficient to deem *ordre public* violated.[51] It has been suggested that it should be possible to exercise court control by examining, in some detail, the reasoning of the award. Only in exceptional cases, such as when the award has no reasons, or the award did not consider the applicability of *ordre public* rules (or, I would add, when the court does not find the award's reasoning convincing), should the court be allowed to go further and examine the parties' pleadings or the evidence produced in the arbitral proceedings or, in extreme cases, to launch a full-fledged investigation.[52]

4. THE IMPORTANCE OF COURT CONTROL

In *Mitsubishi* the court deviated from the traditional approach that considered non-arbitrable disputes relating to anti-trust issues. The court relied on the possibility to review the accurate application of competition law at the stage of enforcement, and permitted arbitrating those issues.

More recent case law, particularly of EU State courts such as Austria, Belgium, Germany and England, seems to reverse this trend and denies the arbitrability[53] of disputes regarding contracts of commercial agency.[54] As was seen above, EU agency law is deemed to be necessary for the achievement of the internal market. Hence, some courts have affirmed that disputes concerning commercial agency should be decided by courts of EU member States: choosing a court outside the EU, or choosing arbitration, may endanger the effective enforcement of EU law. This approach seems to go further than necessary or advisable.

There are parallels between these domestic courts' approach and the reasoning behind the already mentioned Advocate General Wathelet's opinion in *Genentech*. The same reasoning was at the basis of Advocate General Jääskinen's opinion in another case involving EU competition law, *CDC*.[55] However, as will be seen below, the mentioned domestic case law and AG Jääskinen in *CDC* go further than AG Wathelet, and reach results that the latter does not approve of in his opinion in *Achmea*.

---

51 Cordero-Moss (n 32) 246.

52 Radicati di Brozolo (n 19) 63f.

53 Or they deny the recognition of a contractual choice of forum in favour of a court not located within the EU. This responds to the same rationale, i.e. that matters relating to commercial agency shall be decided by courts located in the EU in order to ensure a uniform application of EU law. Therefore, it can be expected that the same courts would also deny arbitrability if the contract contained an arbitration clause.

54 In Austria: OGH 1.3.2017, 5ob 72/16y, Ecolex 520 (2017); in Belgium: Cour de Cassation, 16.11.2006, PAS. 2006, I, No. 11; Cour de Cassation, 14.1.2010, PAS. 2010, I, No. 12; Cour de Cassation, 3.11.2011 PAS. 2011, I, No. 1; in Germany: Bundesgerichtshof, 5.9.2012, *Neue juristische Wochenschrift* (2012); in England: *Accentuate Limited v. Asigra Inc.* [2009] EWHC (QB) 2655.

55 Case C-352/13 *CDC Hydrogen Peroxide v. Evonik Degussa and Others* [2015] ECR I-, Opinion of AG Jääskinen.

AG Wathelet argued in *Genentech* that restrictions upon the court's control are contrary to the principle of effectiveness of EU law[56] because they deprive the court of the possibility to ensure, by referring a question for preliminary ruling to the CJEU, compliance with EU law.[57]

In *CDC*, AG Jääskinen invoked the principle of effective enforcement of EU competition law. The AG recalled *Eco Swiss*, affirming that EU competition law may be regarded as a matter of *ordre public* and that questions about the compatibility of an arbitral award with EU competition law should be open to examination by national courts.[58] The *Eco Swiss* reasoning was made in the context of the court's review of an arbitral award. The AG in *CDC* extended this reasoning by analogy to the issue of arbitrability.[59] On one hand, the AG recognised that arbitration agreements do not necessarily deprive the victims of an alleged violation of EU competition law of the possibility of obtaining full compensation in arbitration. On the other hand, he described this as a theoretical possibility, and its implementation into practice as a 'matter of some delicacy.'[60] With respect to horizontal restriction of competition, as in the case at hand, the AG argued that an arbitration agreement would be compatible with the principle of effective enforcement only if the victims had expressly accepted arbitration and the arbitral tribunal was required to apply EU competition law as rules of public policy. As was mentioned above, the CJEU declined to answer on the issue of arbitrability, affirming that it did not have sufficient information.[61] The matter is therefore still open.

A clarification was expected in connection with the already mentioned *Achmea* case: the BGH requested confirmation that even though arbitration is not part of the mutual trust based on EU instruments, matters relating to EU law should be arbitrable – because the courts' second look ensures a uniform application of EU law. Embracing the maximalist view on court control was, in the eyes of the BGH, a sufficient counterweight to permit arbitrability of matters relating to competition law. This view was shared by the Advocate General Wathelet in the same case.[62] On this basis, AG Wathelet disapproved of AG Jääskinen's opinion in *CDC* on the non-arbitrability of disputes requiring interpretation of EU law.[63] The CJEU did not accept the AG's opinion and concluded that investment disputes are not arbitrable. However, according to the CJEU this conclusion did not apply to commercial disputes. The matter, therefore, is still open.

---

56 Case C-567/14 *Genentech v. Hoechst and Sanofi-Aventis* [2016] ECR I-, Opinion of AG Wathelet, para 58.

57 Ibid., para. 59.

58 Ibid., para. 123.

59 Ibid., paras 124–26.

60 Ibid., para. 126.

61 Case C-352/13 *Hydrogen Peroxide v. Evonik Degussa and Others* [2015] ECR I-, para. 58.

62 Case C-281/16 *Slovak Republic v. Achmea* [2016] ECR I-, Opinion of AG Wathelet, paras 251–60. The AG, however, considered this argument redundant, as in his opinion investment arbitral tribunals, as opposed to commercial arbitral tribunals, are to be considered permanent courts who may refer to the CJEU questions of EU law and are under a duty to apply EU law loyally. See n 29 above.

63 Ibid., para. 243.

The abovementioned case law, however, shows that domestic courts in a variety of EU member States are assuming a restrictive approach towards arbitrability. The BGH and AG Wathelet's understanding of the second look doctrine is more compatible with the arbitration-friendly regime based on the New York Convention than AG Jääskinen's approach in *CDC* and the mentioned domestic case law. Rather than excluding arbitration automatically and *a priori*, simply on the basis that the dispute regards an area regulated by laws that require accurate application,[64] it is better to permit arbitration and verify at the stage of challenge or enforcement whether the award is compatible with fundamental principles.[65]

Admittedly, the second look doctrine is not without flaws, as situations may still arise where the award is not brought to court and courts therefore do not get the possibility to give a second look.[66] AG Wathelet did not consider in *Achmea* that this is an obstacle to arbitrability.[67]

5. CONCLUSION

The foregoing shows that *Mitsubishi* opened a pro-arbitration era by expanding the scope of arbitrability. The court accepted to permit arbitration for disputes relating to regulatory matters such as competition law, because it knew it would be able to control the award after it was rendered. An award that infringes fundamental principles will be set aside or not enforced.

Insisting on arbitration's autonomy and restricting court control disturbs the balance foreseen in *Mitsubishi* between arbitrability and second look. As a consequence, courts may become more reluctant to permitting arbitration – and some domestic courts in EU States have recently rendered decisions that reduce the scope of arbitrability. Restricting courts' control thus leads to the result of restricting the scope of arbitrability. Accepting an independent court control, on the contrary, permits maintaining a broad scope of arbitrability. Court control does not create excessive interference with arbitration, if it is exercised in accordance with the principles laid down in the New York Convention and the Model Law. Courts are allowed to exercise control to ascertain serious violations of fundamental principles. This kind of court review is not equivalent to an appeal and does not restrict arbitration autonomy to an unacceptable extent. It seems to be a fair price to pay for being allowed to arbitrate a broader range of disputes, as the court has recognised in *Mitsubishi*.

---

64 Radicati di Brozolo (n 19) at 58 casts doubt on the assumption that arbitration is not capable of an accurate application of the law.

65 More extensively Cordero-Moss (n 32) 257f.

66 Massimo Benedettelli, '"Communitarization" of International Arbitration: A New Spectre Haunting Europe?' (2011) 73(4) *Arbitration International* 583, 597.

67 Case C-281/16 *Slovak Republic v. Achmea*, [2016] ECR I-, Opinion of AG Wathelet, paras 251–60.

5. By-passing sovereignty: *Trafigura lawsuits (re Ivory Coast)*

5.1 CASE BACKGROUND

The *Trafigura* case concerns corporate liability related to environmental damage in a transnational setting, which raises questions of ethical responsibility of multinationals. The main lawsuits took place in Ivory Coast, in the United Kingdom and in the Netherlands. In late 2005, a multinational trading company called Trafigura decided to buy large amounts of an unrefined gasoline in order to use it as a blendstock for fuels. The process of refining this product is known as caustic washing and it was carried out on a ship named Probo Koala. The company knew beforehand that the resulting chemical waste would be difficult to treat or dispose of. On 19 August 2006, Probo Koala unloaded the waste shipment at open-air sites at Abidjan, Ivory Coast. Soon afterwards, according to the allegations in this case, the people living near the discharge sites began to suffer from a range of illnesses. Subsequently, at least 100,000 sought medical attention for conditions which were attributed to the presence of toxic waste and a considerable number of people died.

In November 2006, the High Court of Justice in London agreed to hear an action by some 30,000 claimants from the Ivory Coast against Trafigura. Trafigura denied responsibility, claiming that the substances were standard waste from onboard operations of ships that were entrusted to an Ivorian disposal company. The English proceedings took an unexpected turn when Trafigura obtained, on the sidelines of the case, a super-injunction or 'gagging order' against the *Guardian*, and attempted to prevent the ensuing issue of the freedom of the press from being discussed in Parliament. However, on 23 March 2009, the High Court issued a temporary injunction barring Trafigura from contacting any of the claimants in the case, in view of evidence that the company had been asking individual claimants to change their sworn statements. In September 2009, the parties reached a settlement agreement. Meanwhile, on 22 January 2010, the Court of Appeals in Abidjan ruled in favour of the claimants against Trafigura. However, it seems that the victims never received the compensation thus ordered. In 2008, Dutch prosecutors filed criminal charges against Trafigura, based on the breach of Dutch environmental laws. In July 2010, the Dutch court ruled that the company had concealed the dangerous nature of the waste aboard the Probo Koala and fined the company €1 million. On appeal, however, in April 2011, it was ruled that the public prosecution department is not required to prosecute Trafigura for the waste dumping in Ivory Coast. Nevertheless, in a parallel lawsuit, in January 2012, the Court of Appeals of Amsterdam decided that Trafigura's co-founder and director could be personally prosecuted for the alleged illegal export of waste by Trafigura. In November 2012, the Dutch Public Prosecutor's Office and Trafigura reached an out-of-court settlement.

In February 2015, a lawsuit proposed by a foundation was presented before the Dutch courts. In view of the bodily, moral and economic injury that Trafigura caused, it requested 2,500-euro compensation for each victim and cleaning of the toxic waste. In November 2016, the court rejected the claim, finding that the foundation did not establish that the claim was in the best interests of the affected Ivorians.

Case: High Court of Justice. Queen's Bench Division. September 11, 2009

5.2 BUILDING AN ENVIRONMENTAL AND HUMAN DISASTER INTO A TRANSNATIONAL CASE: A SOCIO-POLITICAL PERSPECTIVE

Sara Dezalay

1. INTRODUCTION

In December 2005, large amounts of coker naphtha, an unrefined fuel, were bought by *Trafigura*, the world's third-biggest private oil and metals trader. Subjected to a process called caustic washing on board the *Probo Koala*, a ship registered in Panama, the refining of the fuel resulted in the creation of tonnes of hazardous waste. In July 2006, Trafigura attempted to deliver the waste in Amsterdam. When the price for treatment was increased upon finding that the waste was highly contaminated, Trafigura ordered it to be re-loaded on the *Probo Koala*. In August 2006, after a failed attempt to unload in Nigeria, Trafigura contracted a local company which dumped the waste in locations around the city of Abidjan in Ivory Coast, without receiving any treatment. A major medical emergency ensued, with tens of thousands of people reporting at local hospitals with headaches, vomiting, skin irritations and breathing problems, and at least 16 deaths.[1] Thus started the 'Trafigura saga': a media, political and environmental scandal with judicial ramifications across five jurisdictions – Abidjan, London, Amsterdam, Paris and Brussels. More than ten years after the *Probo Koala* disaster, over 100,000 victims have filed complaints against Trafigura. Yet, the company has never admitted any liability. Despite a sulphurous reputation,[2] Trafigura continues to thrive on the volatility of global markets for carbon commodities, advocating a public image neatly orchestrated by the PR firm Bell Pottinger as a 'decent global citizen' and agent of development in West Africa. Meanwhile, left largely untreated the waste continues its environmental and human damage. In Ivory Coast, which has since transitioned from a protracted civil war into one of Africa's booming economic hotspots, business with Trafigura, if it ever was interrupted, is thriving.

For the student interested in the complex articulation between law, multinational corporations and global value chains in late capitalism, the Trafigura saga seems to offer an exemplary case study. Firstly, the transnational dimension of the litigations around the Trafigura case underlines the multiple legal loopholes and the political resistance that are contriving to leave international law on hazardous waste and human rights, foremost the 1989 Basel Convention on the control of transboundary movements of hazardous wastes and their disposal, without much effect in the Global South. The case also underscores the difficulties to trace the chains of responsibilities within a multinational whose business spans the whole value chain involved in the sourcing and

---

1 Ivorian official records variously report 15–17 deaths, see Greenpeace and Amnesty International, *The Toxic Truth*, 2012: 58.

2 The company has been suspected of being involved in a number of legally suspect oil deals, including the smuggling of 500,000 barrels from Saddam Hussein's Iraq in 2001, and more recently the buying of oil said to have been 'looted' from South Sudan.

trading of carbon and mineral commodities across the globe: sourced in Mexico, the coker naphtha underwent a process of caustic washing both on land in various jurisdictions and at sea, along the long journey of the Probo Koala. Finally, the complex corporate structure of Trafigura seems specifically designed to disperse its chain of command across territorial boundaries, with Trafigura's head office, Trafigura Group Pte. Ltd, registered in Singapore, the group's holding company, Trafigura Beheer B.V., incorporated in Amsterdam, and Trafigura Ltd in London, acting as the coordinating entity for a substantial proportion of the group's oil operations including those related to the dumping of the waste in Abidjan, which, for its part, was managed by Puma Energy, Trafigura's wholly-owned subsidiary in Ivory Coast.

To overcome these difficulties, 'transnational litigation' seems a natural point of entry to study this case, that is: focusing on the strategic litigation opportunities (and barriers of entry) to bring claims against this multinational corporation domiciled and headquartered in one jurisdiction for its wrongful conduct in other jurisdictions, in Abidjan where the waste was dumped and along the journey of the Probo Koala. Yet: the complexity of the unravelling of the *Trafigura case* since 2006 seems to contradict a narrative that would see the fight for 'justice against corporate crimes' as a spontaneous uprising of civil society aided by 'cause lawyers' working around the strategic opportunities and barriers of access for transnational litigation. Emblematically, the *Trafigura case* grew into Britain's biggest ever group-action lawsuit, with staggering figures: representing 30,000 victims, the London-based firm Leigh Day & Co. negotiated an out-of-court settlement in 2009 which secured £30 million for the victims, £105 million in legal costs and a success fee of £40 million.[3] While the bulk of the settlement money was diverted by the self-claimed representative of the victims, the Trafigura saga imploded into several cases in Europe, with a jigsaw of actors … such that it now reads like a derailed Le Carré's *Mission Song*: elusive victims with a dozen associations claiming to represent them; another dozen European 'cause lawyers'; the media; NGOs; and a state in the background that is either apparently disempowered or complicit in the face of transnational corporate power in Ivory Coast, or benevolent towards group claims filed by foreign victims, though leaning to the considerable political clout of Trafigura in the United Kingdom.

A socio-political perspective would help illuminate these complex articulations. To be fully effective, such an approach would entail looking at the whole array of agents and national spaces that have contributed to the development of this scandal into a transnational litigation, to determine the combination of variables that shaped it: legal, but also social, economic and political. This necessarily includes looking at the legal entry-points and obstacles fostered by the interplay between (inter-)national legal frameworks, the corporate structure of Trafigura, and the specificities of the human and environmental damage in this case. It would also be necessary to trace carefully the constitutive roles played by the lawyers acting on behalf of each party, by being attentive not only to their technical interventions in the case, but also to their specific characteristics *qua* lawyers. A rich scholarship in political sociology has notably underscored how the strategies, trajectories and resources of lawyers could provide

[3] A. Hirsh and R. Evans, 'Lawyers for claimants in Trafigura case seek £105m in costs' *The Guardian*, 10 May 2010.

insights into globalisation patterns, across national scales and time.[4] As a social mobilisation, this case would further require tracing the roles of other actors – NGOs, the media, States and victims – their structural positions in relation to state and corporate power, as well as the cognitive alignments and dis-alignments that have contributed to build this case into a 'cause'.[5] In particular, this would imply reconstructing systematically the chains of intermediation between these different actors, notably the mobilisation and organisation of victims in Ivory Coast.

For reasons of space, but also of access to sources,[6] this chapter suggests some elements of answers by zooming in on specific aspects of this broad road-map. The first two sections follow a chronological sequencing to trace how the mobilisation of social, political and media resources contributed, along with legal opportunities, to the development of the scandal into a judicial battle, from Abidjan to London and other European jurisdictions. The third section focuses specifically on the London episode of the case, by looking at the resources mobilised by Leigh Day to build a civil claim against Trafigura. The third section opens up a wider interrogation on the contribution of this case to understandings of the transnational and transnational law, as it reflects broader articulations between law, politics and capitalism in the development of state power.

2. TURNING A HUMAN AND ENVIRONMENTAL SCANDAL INTO A JUDICIAL CASE

Sociological research on transnational litigation has emphasised the insights provided by a so-called pragmatic approach to law to trace the articulation between actors, discourses and substantive legal aspects in developing transnational claims.[7] Focusing on these connections helps understand how the case made its way from Abidjan to European jurisdictions. After the outbreak of the medical emergency in Abidjan in August 2006, several individuals across Trafigura's hierarchical structure were charged and imprisoned to face proceedings before Ivorian courts for offences relating to breaches of Ivorian public health and environmental laws, and breach of the Basel

---

[4] On the roles played by lawyers in state trajectories and globalization across Africa, see S. Dezalay, 'Lawyers in Africa: brokers of the state, intermediaries of globalization. A case-study of the "Africa" Bar in Paris' (2018) 25(2) *Indiana Journal of Global Legal Studies* 639–669.

[5] See D. Snow et al., 'Frame alignment processes, micro-mobilization and movement participation' (1986) 51 *American Sociological Review* 464–548.

[6] There is a specific problem with empirical sources in this case. In particular, beyond a limited legal scholarship, the plethora of sources (the media and advocacy organisations) reflect the positions of the actors who produced them. To gain a level of reflexivity, it would be necessary to interview agents involved in the case across the different sites partaking in its transnational landscape – Abidjan, London, Amsterdam, Paris, Brussels.

[7] E.g. focusing on the growth of universal jurisdiction in the 1990s, J. Seroussi, 'The cause of universal jurisdiction. The rise and fall of an international mobilisation' in Y. Dezalay and B. G. Garth (eds.), *Lawyers and the Construction of Transnational Justice* (Abingdon, Routledge 2011) 47–59.

Convention: two Trafigura executives who had travelled to Abidjan to negotiate with the Ivorian authorities, including its president Claude Dauphin, as well as the managing director of the Société Puma, the head of the Compagnie Tommy, the local company contracted to manage the waste, and other customs and ports officials. Ultimately, only these local companies' agents were convicted by the Tribunal de Première Instance d'Abidjan-Plateau.[8] At the time, Ivory Coast was still in the midst of a protracted civil war, which started in 2002 and had led to the *de facto* partition of the country between a North controlled by the so-called *Forces nouvelles*, and a South, including Abidjan, held by forces loyal to then President Laurent Ggagbo. While the imprisonment of Dauphin certainly gave Ggabgo and his negotiators the upper hand, the settlement he negotiated with Trafigura in February 2007 granted the multinational substantive and broad-sweeping[9] immunity from prosecution in Ivory Coast in return for a compensation of CFA 95 billion (€152 million) that, to date, has largely failed to deliver on its intended purpose to compensate the victims and clean up the contaminated zones.[10]

By then the Probo Koala disaster had already been built into a 'scandal' through the involvement of other actors: the media, the environmental NGO Greenpeace and a cluster of European lawyers specialised in transnational litigation.[11] The case was sparked first by the activism and media savvy of Greenpeace: in September 2006, Greenpeace activists blockaded the Probo Koala at the Estonian port of Paldiski, and the NGO filed a report with the Dutch Public Prosecutor requesting a criminal investigation into the dumping.[12] Involved early on, Leigh Day built on the London location of Trafigura Ltd and its direct role in the Probo Koala disaster to obtain a Group Litigation Order with the High Court of Justice in London in November 2006, to file a civil claim on behalf of thousands of Ivorian victims (ultimately 30,000) for damages for personal injury. To identify victims Leigh Day mobilised the firm's links with Greenpeace which launched a media campaign in Ivory Coast that same autumn.

Here, the position of Leigh Day in the legal field in the United Kingdom, and specifically the firm's senior partner Martyn Day, helps explain the opportunity for filing this claim in Britain, while also accounting for the unravelling of the case simultaneously on the terrain of the law and that of the media and politics in the United Kingdom, the Netherlands, Ivory Coast as well as in Norway, after the explosion of a Norwegian facility in May 2007 where Trafigura had continued caustic washing processes. Martyn Day, like other transnational litigation lawyers involved in the

---

[8] Salomon Ugborogbo, the head of Compagnie Tommy and Essoin Kouao, a shipping agent from West African International Business Services (WAIBS).

[9] With Trafigura identified under the broad sweeping terms of 'Trafigura Parties' to cover the whole corporate structure of the company.

[10] Including CFA73 billion to compensate for the harm caused to the State of Ivory Coast, and to the victims, and CFA 22 billion to treat the pollution caused by the waste See 'Protocole d'accord entre Trafigura et l'État de Côte d'Ivoire' 13 February 2007, www.probokoala.org (consulted 26 January 2018). Note that the victims are not identified in the agreement.

[11] Greenpeace has been at the forefront of claims filed in Amsterdam, and published a report in 2012, along with Amnesty International, to 'set out the case against Trafigura'. Greenpeace and Amnesty International (n 1).

[12] See Greenpeace and Amnesty International, ibid.

Trafigura saga,[13] combines a set of resources – legal, political and militant – that have contributed to the growth in Europe of strategic transnational litigation against corporate crimes from the end of the 1990s. These resources enabled Leigh Day to embed politics and media clout in the litigation of the Trafigura case in London.

Described in the press as 'the scourge of the corporations,'[14] Day was raised in Zimbabwe before returning to the UK as a young adult, where he obtained a law degree from Warwick University and qualified with Colombotti & Partners in 1981. A former Labour councillor, he helped draft *In Trust for Tomorrow*, the Labour Party's roadmap on the environment in 1994, whose key proposal was to encourage individuals to bring cases against polluting companies by scrapping the traditional 'loser pays' rules, under which a failed plaintiff must pay the winner's costs as well as his own.[15] Day has also had a long-standing involvement with Greenpeace, as member of the board of the NGO, Director of Greenpeace Environmental Trust, and chairman of Greenpeace UK until 2008. In 1981, Martyn Day first practised in the corporate firm Clifford & Co, before moving to Bindman & Partners, a firm set up in 1974 by a group of lawyers including Sarah Leigh,[16] that gained prominence as a defender of civil liberties and human rights. Leigh Day, co-founded with Sarah Leigh in 1987 to specialise in international, environmental and product liability claims, thus pioneered in transnational litigation.

3. FROM LONDON TO THE IMPLOSION OF THE *TRAFIGURA* LITIGATIONS

Particularly favourable opportunities within the British legal system – compared to other European jurisdictions – also help explain the development of a professional market for transnational litigation in the United Kingdom, notably the possibility to file group claims, and the opening up of this jurisdiction for claims made on behalf of foreign victims for wrongdoings in foreign jurisdictions. Leigh Day obtained a reversal of the *forum non conveniens* doctrine[17] in the *Cape Gencor lawsuits (re-South*

[13] E.g. William Bourdon, from the Paris Bar, who displays characteristics similar to that of Martyn Day – with a combination of resources across law, politics, economics and militancy. See his portrait in Dezalay (n 4).

[14] J. Vidal, 'Lawyers Leigh Day: troublemakers who are a thorn in the side of multinationals' *The Guardian*, 1 August 2015.

[15] Nick Gilbert, 'Profile: Martyn Day: Smoking out the tobacco giants' *The Independent*, 10 May 1997.

[16] All then solicitors at Lawfords, a trade union firm in Gray's Inn. Bindman & Partners whose original intent was to provide local residents eligible for legal aid, with legal services in family law, immigration, personal injuries, housing, social welfare and crime.

[17] The *forum non conveniens* doctrine enabled English courts to decline jurisdiction on the ground that there is a court in another jurisdiction which is clearly a more suitable forum for the trial of the action, in the interests of all the parties and justice of the case.

Africa).[18] The decision of the European Court of Justice in the case of *Owusu*[19] in 2005 further solved the question of jurisdiction. The British government's pro-active public legal aid policy until the early 2000s also played a key role: 'taxpayer cash has helped put (the) firm on the map.'[20] In 1997, the firm received £8.3 million from the Legal Aid Board. This contributed to position the firm as a key player in transnational litigation and establishing its strategy of promoting a low profile (defending 'the ordinary guy') in high profile cases from the end of the 1990s, ranging from the human and environmental wrongdoings of multinational corporations,[21] to political cases involving the British Department of Defence and British troops in wars of decolonisation[22] and Britain's involvement in Iraq from 2003.[23] The funding of such claims became an issue with the downsizing of legal aid from the turn of the 2000s. Leigh Day's last application for public funding for a group claim failed in 2005. The firm's strategy to counter this trend, such as in the *Trafigura case*, has been to bring these claims under a conditional fee basis. However, the amounts claimed by Leigh Day following the settlement of the case in 2009 have contributed to prompting governmental plans, still under review, to implement further cuts to legal aid and to restrict no win-no fee agreements[24] – thus potentially imperilling future possibilities to file group actions against transnational corporations in the United Kingdom.

The termination of the judicial proceedings in London with an out-of-court settlement in September 2009 emerged as one of the multiple political and media twists in the development of the case. The settlement agreed between Trafigura and Leigh Day stated that the waste had only caused 'flu-like symptoms' and did not admit any liability of the company. It also appeared as a last-minute deal, before the case was to be heard before the High Court in London, as parallel political, legal and media battles were unravelling. In May 2009 Trafigura sued (and won) a defamation case against the BBC. In autumn 2009, the Trafigura case also emerged as a test-case for the new 'super injunctions' which started being filed in Britain in the 2000s to allow companies and individuals to prevent the publication not just of the substance of allegations involving

---

18 UK House of Lords: *Judgments – Schalk Willem Burger Lubbe (Suing as Administrator of the Estate of Rachel Jacoba Lubbe) and 4 Others and Cape Plc. And Related Appeals*, 20 July 2000, [House of Lords decision].

19 Judgment of the Court (Grand Chamber) of 1 March 2005. *Andrew Owusu v N. B. Jackson, trading as 'Villa Holidays Bal-Inn Villas' and Others*. Case C-281/02.

20 Gilbert (n 15).

21 Starting with a first high-profile case against Gallaher & Imperial Tobacco on behalf of lung cancer victims in 1997; or, among other examples of group action claims against multinationals in the 2000s, the settlement secured in 2006 by Leigh Day on behalf of a group of Colombian farmers in a civil group action against BP.

22 E.g. the group action against the British government on behalf of 5228 former insurgents involved in the Mau Mau uprising in Kenya (the firm negotiated a settlement in 2010).

23 Day represented the family of Baha Mousa but faced (and succeeded in) a disciplinary prosecution before the Solicitors Disciplinary Tribunal launched by the Defence secretary in 2014, regarding the firm's conduct in the Al-Sweady inquiry. Phil Shiner, one of Day's main competitors in human rights litigation, faced similar charges and his Public Interest Lawyers firm was dismantled in 2016.

24 O. Bowcott, 'Impact of cuts to legal aid to come under review' *The Guardian*, 31 October 2017.

them, but even of the existence of such allegations. While the super-injunction granted to Trafigura spurred a public outcry as it was essentially preventing a parliamentary hearing over the case, the social media were leaking damning information demonstrating inside knowledge, within Trafigura, about the toxicity of the waste.[25]

Yet, Trafigura has consistently denied criminal liability for the damage created by the dumping of the waste in Abidjan. In 2010, a Dutch court did find the company guilty of illegally exporting waste from Europe, but it did not investigate events in Abidjan, the Public Prosecutor having decided that it would not be feasible to do so.[26] Attempts to date, in other European jurisdictions, to file criminal charges against Trafigura for the events in Ivory Coast have failed. These include a complaint brought in Amsterdam by Greenpeace in 2009 against the Public Prosecutor's decision not to prosecute Trafigura Beheer BV and Puma Energy, Trafigura Chairman, Claude Dauphin, and other employees of the Trafigura Group, for criminal offences related to the dumping in Ivory Coast; as well as, more recently, attempts made by Amnesty International in the United Kingdom to get the Crown Prosecution Services and the Environment Agency to open investigations for criminal conspiracy against the company.[27] In April 2010, two French NGOs, Robin des Bois and William Bourdon's Sherpa, filed complaints against Estonia and the Netherlands before the European Commission, so that the cases be referred to the European Court of Justice. Both complaints failed, the European Commission arguing in the first instance that Estonia did not have all the relevant information about the waste to take action, and in the second, that there were already criminal proceedings under way in Amsterdam.[28] An earlier complaint, filed in 2007 by French and Ivorian NGOs acting on behalf of Ivorian victims[29] against the two French Trafigura executives, Claude Dauphin and Jean-Pierre Valentini, before the Paris Prosecutor, was also dismissed in 2008, the Prosecutor arguing this time that there was not a sufficient link with France.

---

25 See D. Leigh, 'Revealed: Trafigura-commissioned report into dumped toxic waste' *The Guardian*, 17 October 2009.

26 In 2010, criminal charges were brought in Amsterdam against two relatively junior individuals, the tanker's captain, and a London-based Trafigura employee. Both were fined and convicted with suspended prison sentence, while the oil trader was fined £1m for concealing the dangerous nature of the waste when it was initially unloaded in Amsterdam. But the Court ruled that the company's chief executive, Claude Dauphin, would not face personal charges; and the prosecution did not cover the events after the tanker left Amsterdam.

27 Both public agencies have responded that they lacked the expertise and the resources to investigate the oil company for criminal prosecution: J. Ball and H. Davies, 'UK authorities "lack resources" to investigate Trafigura over toxic waste' *The Guardian*, 23 July 2015.

28 Greenpeace and Amnesty International (n 1) 168.

29 The Legal Action Group of the FIDH, the French League for Human Rights, the Ivorian League of Human Rights and the Ivorian Movement for Human Rights (MIDH).

4. CONCLUSION: THE ARTICULATION BETWEEN LAW, POLITICS AND ECONOMICS IN THE *TRANSNATIONAL LANDSCAPE* OF THE *TRAFIGURA* CASE

The various variables – political, social, economic – at play in the development of the *Trafigura case* have contributed to shape a legal trail – or *interlegality*[30] – across these national scales. Each nudge of the trail followed the structure of Trafigura as a multinational corporation, and opportunities in each jurisdiction to define legal entry-points for litigation. Meanwhile, this fostered the 'messiness of the landscape' of the case with competing norms and legal systems 'yielding their own characteristic excesses and omissions.'[31] Each nudge of the trail also reflected the specificities of the structure of the legal field and national field of state power in these diverse jurisdictions. These characteristics help account for the development of the case, notably the relative effectiveness of the strategies of the lawyers acting on behalf of each party. The failures of criminal claims, thus, can be explained in part by the legal specificities of each of these jurisdictions, as much as the apparent dis-alignment in the mobilisation of the cluster of actors involved in the development of the case – NGOs, lawyers and victims.

Emblematically, the controversies sparked by the embezzlement of the bulk of the settlement monies secured by Leigh Day in 2009[32] also contributed to the implosion of the *Trafigura* litigations in Amsterdam, with the emergence of a dozen competing organisations claiming to represent Ivorian victims set up with the help of Dutch lawyers from 2009, and a counter-claim in 2011 by yet another victims' organisation against Leigh Day in London to recover the disappeared funds. This elusiveness of victims, with accusations of theft identity or 'fake victims' a constant in Trafigura's defence, has also been one of the arguments to disqualify the Ivorian State – both for its role in the Probo Koala disaster, and as a valid forum to investigate the events. To be sure, 'the vulnerability of Ivory Coast officials to corruption formed part of the background to the original environmental disaster when the waste was dumped.'[33] With the country then at war, these propitious conditions certainly also contributed to

[30] B. de Sousa Santos, 'Law: A Map of Misreading – Toward a Postmodern Conception of Law' (1987) 14 *Journal of Law and Society* 279–302.

[31] C. Greenhouse and C. Davis (eds.), *Landscapes of Law: Practicing Sovereignty in Transnational Terrain*, manuscript under review.

[32] Leigh Day was to oversee the distribution of the settlement moneys to the 30,000 victims, but shortly after the settlement was agreed Martyn Day allegedly received a request to meet representatives of a senior Ivorian figure in Paris to agree to come to an 'arrangement'. This figure, claiming to be the president of the *National Coordination of Toxic Waste Victims of Côte d'Ivoire* (*Coordination nationale des victimes de déchets toxiques de Côte d'Ivoire*), managed to get the funds frozen in a move backed by the Abidjan State prosecutor. The compensation money was transferred a few days later, to the account of Claude Gohourou, 'one of the dozens of people representing the communities affected by the toxic waste' and henceforth partly disappeared, along with Gohourou. See X. Rice, 'Fears over £30m payment to toxic waste victims in Trafigura case' *The Guardian*, 22 January 2010.

[33] D. Leigh, 'Corruption fears over Ivory Coast toxic waste victims' £30m Trafigura payout' *The Guardian*, 4 November 2009.

positioning the country as one of the 'old margins' turned into 'new frontiers' described by the Comaroff, as 'places where mobile, globally competitive capital – much of it these days southern and eastern, finds minimally regulated zones in which to vest its operations.'[34]

Indeed, at a first glance, the *Trafigura case* reads like a by-passing of sovereignty, with the Ivorian State becoming seemingly a mere shadow in the background of the case, either disqualified due to the inefficiency of local jurisdictions and authorities, or their corruption. Yet this by-passing of sovereignty also applies to the other States involved in the landscape of the case, including the United Kingdom, with the super-injunctions granted to Trafigura in the London proceedings in 2009 demonstrating the political clout held by Trafigura in Britain. Thus, this apparent by-passing of sovereignty, importantly, also contributes to blurring the connections between Trafigura as a multinational corporation, the State – be it in Ivory Coast or the United Kingdom and other European jurisdictions – and the operations of transnational law, by drawing an image of transnationalism as primarily an expression of global capitalism *against* the State.

Yet, a recent body of scholarship[35] is endeavouring to locate, precisely, transnational law 'in the conceptual and practical spaces left open between borderless capitalism and bordered States.'[36] In this, focusing on the legal, but also social, political and economic landscape of the case across these different national forums could also help shed light on what remains largely a gap in the literature: the articulation between global value chains as a core feature of late capitalism, the State and transnational law.[37] Ongoing research on 'global wealth chains' is highlighting the 'constitutive significance of bifurcated sovereignty' for the development of capitalism, with law bifurcated to accommodate the mobility of capital and enabling the operations of multinationals across jurisdictions.[38] Though this can only be sketched here, this would imply a re-reading of the *Trafigura* case, not simply as a transnational litigation saga, but also as a reflection of the connections between a multinational corporation, London as a financial capital, and the 'flows and counter-flows'[39] between the national field of State power in Ivory Coast, and the European national fields of State power involved in this case. Drawing on long-standing scholarship in history and anthropology on the co-constitution of capitalism, imperialism and late colonialism could be adding a further layer to this insight, by tracing how this bifurcation of sovereignty is reverberated at the national level in differentiated political, economic and legal spheres.

---

34 J. Comaroff and J. L. Comaroff, *Theory from the South. Or, How Euro-America is evolving toward Africa* (Boulder, London, Paradigm Publishers 2012) 13.

35 C. Cutler and T. Dietz (eds.), *The Politics of Private Transnational Governance by Contract* (Abingdon, Routledge 2017).

36 Greenhouse and Davis (n 31).

37 With few exceptions, see The IGLP Law and Global Production Working Group (including: T. Ferrando), 'The role of law in global value chains: a research manifesto' (2016) *London Review of International Law* 1.

38 L. Seabrooke and D. Wigan, 'The governance of global wealth chains' (2017) 24(1) *Review of International Political Economy* 6.

39 B. Ibhawoh, *Imperial Justice. Africans in Empire's Court* (Oxford, Oxford University Press 2013).

Thus, though this is only one example, developments in the London side of the *Trafigura case* underscored that 'behind Trafigura is a little-known but wealthy group of London oil traders, who have high-level connections in the Conservative party.'[40] Conversely, in Ivory Coast, Trafigura is still conducting a thriving business, nimbly navigating the political transition, from war to peace in 2007, and from the regime of Laurent Gbagbo to that of his successor Alassane Ouattara in 2010. Thus, a nephew of Ouattara, Ahamadou Touré, is now heading the subsidiary of Trafigura in the country, Puma Energy: 'just like in Angola, where Trafigura holds the monopoly over the oil supply into the country based on close ties with the Presidency, Puma Energy relies in Ivory Coast on ties with the family in power.'[41] Both sets of examples illustrate the small world of oil trading in London and Abidjan, and its straddling across business and political interests. However, more than simply pockets of corruptive practices, these ties can also be seen as imperial legacies, specifically in the Ivorian case. Reflecting the co-constitution of global capitalism and late colonialism, these connections have contributed to shaping the very structure of the (post-)colonial State in Africa – what Cooper calls the 'gate-keeper State'[42] – by enabling a bifurcation of the State: with channels, built on inter-personal relations, enabling the flow of the capital generated by extractive boons to shape the unequal and uneven connection between Africa and global capitalism, and a domestic sphere left perfectly vulnerable to the violence of capitalist expansion. Thus, rather than weaving its way into, and despite, the loopholes of global capitalism, transnational law in this case as elsewhere could be constitutive of as much as it is constituted by bifurcated sovereignty.

5.3 THE *TRAFIGURA* ACTIONS AS PROBLEMS OF TRANSNATIONAL LAW

Simon Archer

1. INTRODUCTION

We are invited to comment on the *Trafigura* 'case' and its relationship to sovereignty. From the perspectives of both the development of transnational law discourse and a resurgence and reconsideration of forms of sovereignty, the task is timely. The Trafigura actions are, at one time, examples of the aspirations and pitfalls of transnational law, particularly vis-à-vis perceived challenges of domestic legal systems

[40] D. Leigh, 'Inside Trafigura: accusations, sour deals and friends in high places' *The Guardian*, 16 September 2009. In particular, Tory peer and former leader of the House of Lords Baron Strathclyde joined Trafigura as a non-executive director in 2013. He had previously stood down from the board of the group's hedge fund arm following the 2009 legal, media and political battles over the Probo Koala disaster in London.

[41] J. Tilouine, 'Probo Koala: drame écologique et bonnes affaires' *Le Monde*, 19 August 2016. My translation from French.

[42] F. Cooper, *Africa Since 1940: The Past of the Present* (Cambridge, Cambridge University Press 2002).

and States in the era of globalised production, communication and exchange.[43] Those aspirations, and the project of defining transnational law, has developed so as to reach something of a self-reflexive moment, in which it asks itself questions about initial assumptions, scope and method.[44]

Sovereignty was always part of the story of transnational law: often invoked for its diminishment under conditions of globalisation, upon closer reading we find its strong assertion, at least in some interests, and we see it continuing to shape the field of transnational law. Finally, transnational law itself has anxieties about its 'legitimacy' in both respects, that is, in positing the diminishment and the continuing presence and re-assertion of the importance of state forms.[45]

2. CASES AS METHOD IN TRANSNATIONAL LAW

Framing an inquiry into transnational private law through the examination of cases has made some decisions for us: cases are adversarial disputes over wrongful conduct, slow, expensive and uncertain in their outcomes both short- and long-term. They do not always or easily capture the ways in which law frames human interaction.[46] By focusing on transnational private law, we may be excluding from consideration other cooperative dimensions of transnational private law (patterns of contracting practices or corporate forms) and aspects of public international law, such as trade arrangements as

---

43 The scope and use of term 'globalisation' are not engaged for the purpose of this chapter. Among many sources problematising it see William Robinson, 'Theories of Globalization' in George Ritzer (ed.), *The Blackwell Companion to Globalization* (Oxford, Blackwell 2007), and for a discussion of the conceptual ambiguities in both 'globalisation' and 'transnational law' see Ralf Michaels, 'Globalization and Law: Law Beyond the State' in Reza Banakar and Max Travers (eds), *Law and Society Theory* (Oxford, Hart Publishing 2013).

44 Examples of these anxieties might include Martin Loughlin, 'Misconceived search for global law' (2017) 8(3) *Transnational Legal Theory* 353, responding to Neil Walker's proposals for how 'global law' obtains authority or legitimacy in *Intimations of Global Law* (Cambridge, Cambridge University Press 2014); Paul Berman offering three conceptions of global legal orders (sovereigntist, universalist or pluralist) in *Global Legal Pluralism: A Jurisprudence of Law Beyond Borders* (Cambridge, Cambridge University Press 2014); Nico Krisch's discussion of democratic reactions (containment, transfer or break) to the emergence of transnational law in *Beyond Constitutionalism: The Pluralist Structure of Post-national Law* (Oxford, Oxford University Press 2010), Peer Zumbansen, 'Defining the Space of Transnational Law: Legal Theory, Global Governance, and Legal Pluralism' (2012) 21(2) *Transnational Law and Contemporary Problems* 305, among others.

45 For example, the discussion by Claire Cutler of generating legitimacy through expertise in, 'The legitimacy of private transnational governance: experts and the transnational market for force' (2010) 8(1) *Socio-Economic Review* 157, or Andreas Maurer arguing legitimacy through participatory mechanisms in 'The Creation of Transnational Law – Participatory Legitimacy of Privately Created Norms' *Zentra Working Papers In Transnational Studies* No. 03/2012 <http://ssrn.com/abstract=2179584>. Finally, we find Ralf Michaels arguing that the state form *is* a transnational legal order: 'The State as Transnational Legal Order' (2016) 1 *UC Irvine Journal of International, Transnational, and Comparative Law* 141.

46 For a now-dated but useful summary of a modern legal realist approach in this vein, see Duncan Kennedy, 'The Stakes of Law: Hale and Foucault!' (1991) 15 *Legal Studies Forum* 327.

conditioning frameworks. From the perspective of transnational private litigation, we must examine the formation of cases, their actors, processes and outcomes, and build out an understanding of how they might be considered examples of transnational law, if not legal ordering more generally.[47]

In the study of law through the case method, it is common to start with 'the facts,' at least as they become stylised in a decision or summary. Eventually, we recognise that the framing of the factual basis of a case, or any series of events and people, has a powerful effect on the analysis that will follow. Similar observations apply and are amplified in transnational context, where problems of any proceeding are multiplied and magnified by two or more jurisdictions, institutional arrangements, systems of law, perhaps languages and other complicating factors.

The *Trafigura* facts are summarised elsewhere. It is easy to draw out several elements that suggest transnational legal dimensions: a ship registered in Panama and owned by a company headquartered in Greece is chartered by a corporation based in Singapore with head offices in Switzerland, and holding or operating subsidiaries in Amsterdam and London, which picks up raw fuels in Texas from a Mexican State-owned oil business, processes it on the open ocean, visits Amsterdam, then Abidjan, where it uses a recently-formed local company to distribute toxic waste (illegally) on 19 August 2006. According to the 'facts' before the courts, 17 people die and perhaps 30,000 are injured, although estimates run as high as 100,000.[48] The interim government under Prime Minister Banny (until presidential elections could be run) eventually agrees to a settlement for the dumping (US$195 million) and prosecution of the core Trafigura parties is ceased.[49] A clean-up is ordered, and eventually completed two years later. Some of the payment is used to compensate victims, although facts are unclear. The head of the local company that distributed the waste is sentenced to 20 years in prison. Claims are brought in the UK on behalf of victims, and a settlement agreed to after some back-and-forth.[50] Further prosecutions are brought in the Netherlands, which results in the issuing of fines for Trafigura companies, but a

---

47 For this reason, the rest of this comment uses 'transnational law' in relation to transnational private litigation, but recognises that this may only be one dimension or part of what could constitute transnational law.

48 Amnesty International/Greenpeace Netherlands, *The Toxic Truth About A Company Called Trafigura, A Ship Called Probo Koala And The Dumping Of Toxic Waste In Cote D'Ivoire* (Amnesty International Publications, 2012) ch 5.

49 State of Côte d'Ivoire and Trafigura Parties, *Protocol of agreement (Protocole d'accord) between the State of Côte d'Ivoire and the Trafigura Parties*, 13 February 2007. According to NGO reports, the settlement was paid in consideration of staying government prosecution against the Trafigura defendants. It is not clear from these reports whether the settlement precluded any third party claims (i.e., victims) in Ivorian courts, although this seems unlikely. Note that Prime Minister Banny was an appointed interim office; Laurent Gbagbo was then President, although his legitimacy in the position contested and a period of limited civil war ensued.

50 *Yao Esaie Motto & Ors v. Trafigura Ltd & Trafigura Beheer BV*, Case Nos HQ06XO3370, HQ06XO3342, UK High Court, (Macduff J), settlement approved 23 September 2009.

lawsuit on behalf of victims is dismissed.[51] Claims brought by Ivorian NGOs are attempted in France, but dismissed for lack of jurisdiction, and the European Commission also declined to bring a complaint.[52] How are these events a problem of 'transnational law'?

The Trafigura events could be viewed as an example of the failure of international arrangements respecting the movement and disposal of toxic waste to cope with the problem of transnational shipment of it, an example of a more general problem of transnational environmental regulation.[53] This approach could consider the actions and omissions of the exporting authority (Amsterdam Port Authority, Netherlands), the investigation and proceedings in the importing port (Abidjan, Ivory Coast), the broader problems of coordination of regulatory schemes across borders, the adequacy of the settlements and penalties eventually concluded and imposed. More broadly, there are two possible treaty regimes covering different forms of waste product that might have applied to the process by which the toxic slops were created, the MARPOL (normal ship waste) and Basel (toxic waste) regimes, but there may be gaps and ambiguities in and between them as well.[54] That was, in fact, the primary defence of Trafigura companies to the regulatory prosecution in the Netherlands. So, these events might be characterised as a failure of public international law, resulting from the lack of coordination between States in the manufacturing and transport of toxic waste. Through this lens, Trafigura is a 'public international law' problem.

A second, related approach views the Trafigura events as an example of the failure of domestic legal proceedings to provide a substantive justice outcome for the victims, either idiosyncratic to these particular circumstances (Abidjan in 2006), or, more frequently, as an example of the systemic failure of specifically those norms that are designed to come to the rescue of the most vulnerable and affected parties under the impact of transnational corporate conduct.[55] This view emphasises the possibilities of

---

51 *Stichting Union Des Victimes De Déchets Toxiques D'abidjan Et Banlieues v Trafigura Beheer BV*, C/13/581973 1 HA ZA 15-195 (Amsterdam) 30 November 2016.

52 *Toxic Truth* (n 48) 168.

53 For example, Gary Cox, 'The Trafigura Case and the System of Prior Informed Consent Under the Basel Convention – A Broken System?' (2010) 6(3) *Law, Environment and Development Journal* 263; Laura Pratt, 'Decreasing Dirty Dumping? A Re-evaluation of Toxic Waste Colonialism and the Global Management of Transboundary Hazardous Waste' (2011) 35 *Wm and Mary Envtl L & Pol'y Rev* 581; Rachel Anglin, 'International Environmental Law Gets Its Sea Legs: Hazardous Waste Dumping Claims Under the ATCA' (2007) 26(1) *Yale Law and Policy Review* 232; Robert Percival, 'Global Law and the Environment' (2011) 86 *Washington Law Review* 578.

54 These were discussed by the Netherlands court: *Trafigura Beheer BV, LJN* (National Case Law Number): BN2149, District Court of Amsterdam, 13/846003-06 (PROMIS); see also, *Toxic Truth* (n 48) 81.

55 For a volume applying a criminogenic lens to the Trafigura actions and defendants, but published too late for a fuller consideration in this chapter, see Thomas MacManus, *State-Corporate Crime and the Commodification of Victimhood* (Abingdon, Routledge 2018). Earlier work includes Lisbeth Enneking, 'Crossing The Atlantic? The Political And Legal Feasibility Of European Foreign Direct Liability Cases' (2009) 40 *Geo Wash Int'l L Rev* 903; Carmen Otero García-Castrillón, 'International Litigation Trends In Environmental Liability: A European Union–United States Comparative Perspective' (2011) 7(3) *Journal of Private International Law*

private transnational claims (in this case, toxic tort claims) brought in jurisdictions other than the Ivory Coast, the legal and administrative barriers to, and features of, such litigation. Transnational torts may be viable, or considered appropriate, on two related bases. First, there may be no viable claim possible in the jurisdiction of the harm due to the power of the defendant vis-à-vis the local courts or government, or merely ineffective local procedures (as was alleged by the plaintiffs in Trafigura). Second, a corporate actor may have no substantial assets in the jurisdiction where the harm occurs, and enforcing a judgment from that jurisdiction in the home jurisdiction of the corporate actor may be difficult (despite available principles of comity: this is, for example, the problem of enforcement in *Chevron*). Both are based on a particular understanding and, indeed, appreciation of the quality of domestic legal procedures in the jurisdiction of the harm. Cases such as *Trafigura*, however, prompt the question, in whose interest does the shift from domestic to transnational litigation occur?

Each of these approaches (failure of public international law, failure of private domestic remedies and need for trans-jurisdictional litigation) has something to say about the role of the State and sovereignty; in each case, we are inclined to point to a failure of some sort of a State role, either *narrowly* (as in government actors failing to prosecute) or more *widely* (referring to the dysfunctionalities of legal systems, perhaps aggravated by a recent civil war).

These views of the capacities of State and domestic legal systems fit within the view that those actors and processes are not appropriate or able to deliver desired justice outcomes and form, hence, a precondition for transnational claims, which justifies their potential characterisation as transnational law. Instead of basing transnational law's emergence on the fact alone that rising conflict phenomena have a border-crossing, spatialised character, the turn to 'transnational law' as an organising concept is, arguably, also a normative one.[56] The call for an adaptation of existing legal forms and instruments in order to more adequately respond to transnational ordering or governance challenges such as that informing the *Trafigura* case is a normative one in the sense that it forms a critique of 'State failure'. State failures, in other words, become, for some interests (the victims, the NGOs) a precondition for transnational law. This is the site of one of the anxieties of transnational legal theory: how have domestic legal proceedings been characterised as ineffective, unavailable or otherwise failed? In whose view, and interest? Are those views and interests just another form of 'environmental colonialism' or 'legal disaster capitalism', or more politely, a failure to fairly and properly evaluate the capacities of a State and its legal system in its own evolution?

As will be discussed below, the Ivorian government and court system's responses in the *Trafigura* actions are heavily criticised by the NGO actors, but we do not have available, absent close research, other perhaps more textured evaluations of the State's

---

551; Nicola Jägers and Marie-José van der Heijden, 'Corporate human rights violations: The feasibility of civil recourse in The Netherlands' (2008) 33(3) *Brooklyn Journal of International Law* 833, among others.

[56] Peer Zumbansen, 'Manifestations and Arguments: The Everyday Operation of Transnational Legal Pluralism' in Paul Berman (ed), *Oxford Handbook of Global Legal Pluralism* (Oxford, Oxford University Press 2019, forthcoming); TLI *Think!* Paper series 02/2018.

capacities at that time.[57] The second reason State failure is or should be a point of anxiety for transnational law is that, for some interests, State boundaries, especially as policed by legal systems, have a role in forming the boundaries and perhaps content of transnational law. In *Trafigura*, the NGO actors, Greenpeace Netherlands and Amnesty International, called for exclusively State-based actions to remedy the problems in the *Trafigura* case, in a traditional problem-policy response formulation. Another way that States define the boundaries of transnational law is in the ways transnational private tort litigation is formed and developed.[58] We turn next to this framework.

3. BUILDING A TORT CASE AS TRANSNATIONAL LAW

The issues that most of the (English language) legal literature on the *Trafigura* actions engaged with were those of corporate accountability, and more specifically, transnational tort claims as a framework to create such accountability. As just discussed, these accounts begin with 'the facts', or at least, the ones useful to framing a piece of transnational litigation – an intentional distribution of toxic waste in sites around Abidjan resulting in perhaps 100,000 victims of poisoning and further environmental harm, and there is assumed or express statement about the failings of the government and legal system in the Ivory Coast.

The next step is to discuss ways in which the primary defendants – a domestic corporation apparently created for the specific purpose of dumping the waste, but in reality, the Trafigura corporate entities based in the UK and Netherlands – can be held accountable within the bigger picture of the supply chain of which they are part.[59]

The next step is then to consider which defendants to bring a proceeding against, on behalf of whom, in which jurisdiction or jurisdictions, and under what procedures. This step brings up a series of questions that are in many ways the housekeeping of transnational tort, environmental and human rights litigation. These questions warrant deeper discussion on their own, because this moment is a key moment in the process of developing what we might call transnational private law.[60]

There are two claims in the *Trafigura* actions that are typically discussed as something we could consider transnational law: primarily the tort claim in the UK on behalf of victims, and secondarily the prosecutions in the Netherlands, one on behalf of victims (dismissed) and against the corporate defendants for breaches of environmental

57 But, see, for a parallel consideration, the critique of government failure in the context of the Haiti earthquake: Francois Pierre-Louis, 'Earthquakes, Nongovernmental Organizations, and Governance in Haiti' (2011) 42(2) *Journal of Black Studies* 186.

58 Richard Meeran, 'Tort Litigation against Multinational Corporations for Violations of Human Rights: An Overview of the Position Outside the United States' (2011) 3 *University of Hong Kong Law Review* 1.

59 Grietje Baars et al, 'The role of law in global value chains: a research manifesto' (2016) 4(1) *London Review of International Law* 57.

60 In this line of thinking see Peer Zumbansen, 'What Lies Before, Behind and Beneath a Case? Five Minutes on Transnational Lawyering and the Consequences for Legal Education' in Helge Dedek and Shauna Van Praagh (eds.), *Stateless Law: Evolving Boundaries of a Discipline* (Abingdon, Routledge 2015) 215.

laws. Generally speaking, there are both legal and administrative barriers to bringing these kinds of claims.

In the Anglo-American common law systems there are two significant legal barriers to transnational tort claims, one being the rules of private international law and in particular the *forum non conveniens* doctrine, and second, and perhaps more fundamentally, where there are related corporate entities, the doctrine of separate legal personality. Each has traditionally formed an effective defence to transnational claims in tort or some similar cause of action. The former requires[61] a proceeding in the jurisdiction the wrongful conduct took place, and the latter creates a legal separation of responsibility for actions that is difficult to overcome on the basis of common law theories.[62] These two defences to claims are typically argued in motions early on in litigation in common law countries (where corporate defendants are based or incorporated) in an attempt to deflect the claims to the jurisdiction of the harm (perhaps for the reasons that that jurisdiction was rejected in the first place), or to attempt to show no cause of action against the parent or lead corporate entity in its own jurisdiction. As many have wryly observed, globalised activity and porous borders are useful to conduct business, but a stiff assertion of sovereign barriers and rules remains important to corporate defendants; theorists call it bifurcated sovereignty or the bifurcated State.[63]

Different jurisdictions have addressed these legal barriers one way or another: in the EU, corporate actors may be sued in their jurisdiction of incorporation.[64] More creatively, Latin American jurisdictions have used 'blocking statutes' to manipulate the rules of private international law.[65] More generally, there was a period of optimism in the extraterritorial jurisdiction using the *Alien Tort Claims Act*,[66] which slowed down after the *Kiobel* case (also discussed in this volume), although key questions of whether corporate defendants are captured by that ordinance remain unresolved.[67] There were also proposals for similar assertions of global jurisdiction in other common law

---

61 Subject to exceptions one of which is discussed below.

62 The primary exceptions are statutory.

63 Among many examples: George Monbiot, 'Taming corporate power: the key political issue of our age' *The Guardian*, 8 December 2014, www.theguardian.com/commentisfree/2014/dec/08/taming-corporate-power-key-political-issue-alternative, accessed 28 February 2018; Dick Pountain, 'The battle between countries and companies' *Open Democracy* (10 July 2013) https://www.opendemocracy.net/ourkingdom/dick-pountain/battle-between-countries-and-companies, accessed 28 February 2018. The same observation applies to transnational treatment of taxation, the contours of which have been apparent through the Panama and Paradise Papers.

64 *Convention on Jurisdiction and the Enforcement of Judgments in Civil and Commercial Matters*, 27 September 1968, 1998 O.J. (C 27) 1 (consolidated version).

65 Henri Saint Dahl, 'Forum Non Conveniens, Latin America and Blocking Statutes' (2003–2004) 35 *U Miami Inter-Am L Rev* 21.

66 28 USC § 1350 ('ATCA') and much-discussed line of jurisprudence under it, including *Filártiga v. Peña-Irala* (1980) 630 F 2d 876 (2d Cir), *Sosa v. Alvarez-Machain*, (2004) 542 US 692.

67 *Kiobel v. Royal Dutch Petroleum Co*, (2013) 133 S Ct 1659. *Jesner v. Arab Bank*, PLC, 137 S Ct 1432 was granted leave by the US Supreme Court and may determine the question of corporate liability under this ordinance.

countries (but never adopted),[68] and expansion of universal jurisdiction to certain forms of claims.[69]

One line of these transnational cases – those dealing with the ATCA and those with universal jurisdiction – have entered periods of remission or retreat from initial expansion of jurisdiction, which some view as a form of defensive sovereignty re-asserting itself. US courts in particular have narrowed grounds on which transnational cases may be heard.[70] Finally, over the past 20 years, innovations in tort law have found ways around these traditional defences, although they are not yet widely established and fully tested. It is relevant to note that the firm that pioneered these developments in the UK – Leigh Day & Co. – was the firm that brought the action in the UK court against Trafigura. Most recently, the Leigh Day & Co. firm has engineered another interesting innovation, by conducting a part of a proceeding against a UK corporate defendant using UK courts, but sitting in the jurisdiction of the harm – Sierra Leone.[71]

The innovation in tort law just mentioned is worth a brief comment because it is perhaps stereotypically thought of as transnational private law. In order to 'work around' the two legal barriers just mentioned, a case is framed as one of wrongful conduct in the home jurisdiction of the defendant. In effect, it is the tort of negligent supervision of a subsidiary or related party.[72] That tort is alleged to have occurred in the boardroom of the parent or lead corporate actor; it is only the effect of that behaviour, somewhere down a longer chain of causation, that is the harm that occurs in another jurisdiction – whether it is asbestos poisoning for workers of a subsidiary, wrongful death caused by security guards hired by the subsidiary, or dumping of toxic substances. It is a clever theory and being tested in other common law jurisdictions,[73] at

---

68 For example, Private Member's Bill C-323 (2011) *An Act to amend the Federal Courts Act (international promotion and protection of human rights)*, October 16, 2013 <online: http://www.parl.ca/DocumentViewer/en/41-2/bill/C-323/first-reading?col=2>.

69 Craig Scott, *Torture as Tort: Comparative Perspectives on the Development of Transnational Human Rights Litigation* (Oxford, Hart 2001).

70 See *Kiobel* (n 67) and discussion of the case in this volume, but more generally, and not based on ATCA, *Morrison v. National Australia Bank*, (2010) 561 US 247. In that case, a securities fraud class proceeding that, despite sales taking place on a US exchange, did not have sufficient connection to the US to take jurisdiction. We might view these trends as a form of re-assertion of sovereignty, insofar as wider jurisdiction is denied and there is a stricter policing of legal borders.

71 See: AFP, 'Landmark case against British mining firm begins in Sierra Leone' *The Guardian*, 7 January 2018, <https://www.theguardian.com/global-development/2018/feb/07/landmark-case-against-british-mining-firm-sierra-leone-tonkolili-iron-ore-ltd-police-brutality>, accessed 28 February 2018.

72 *Lubbe v. Cape Plc* [1998] CLC 1559; [2000] 1 WLR 1545 and finally culminating in *Chandler v. Cape Plc* [2012] EWCA Civ 525.

73 Attempts elsewhere include *Das v. George Weston Limited*, [2017] ONSC 5583 (CanLII) (rejecting the applicability of the theory in *Chandler* on a supply chain); *Choc v. Hudbay Minerals Inc*, [2013] ONSC 1414 (CanLII) (dismissing preliminary motions to strike and permitting the theory in *Chandler* to be tried). In a case with comparable issues to the *Choc v. Hudbay* action, Leigh Day & Co is also prosecuting a case in Sierra Leone alleging corporate

least until corporate defendants find ways to organise to defeat it.[74] For the purposes of this discussion, it is relevant to note that this innovation might equally be viewed as entirely one of domestic law – the theory of the case rests on that fact.

The administrative barriers to these types of claims are both procedural (and hence, also legal) and economic, and these considerations raise several questions about who is involved in the case, and why. Again, each of these aspects is written on more thoroughly elsewhere, and so can be passed over more quickly here.[75] When considered as a commercial proposition, bringing a transnational claim only becomes viable when the expected fees from a case can sustain the costs and risks of it. Speaking very generally, to bring a transnational claim, a plaintiff law firm might budget €2–3 million in total costs, including disbursements and legal fees.[76] The categories of costs in a transnational litigation are similar to those in domestic mass tort litigation of the same type, but, unsurprisingly, considerably more. There may be significant fees associated with gathering and processing evidence, expert fees for both subject matter and procedural law, translation and travel costs, and not least, significant legal fees involved in dealing with standard legal tactics involving collateral motions and appeals designed to drive up costs of litigation, and fighting other related tactics like judgment-proofing.[77]

In order to achieve that as payment for the case, there must be an extraordinarily well resourced plaintiff or supporting group, or more likely, arrangement to be paid from the proceeds of an award or settlement of the claim – what are referred to as contingency fees in US and Canadian law, and as no-win no-fee in the UK. Contingency fees might reasonably range from 10% to 30% of total recovery, which implies at least €20 to 30 million in total damages to meet the proposed litigation budget.[78] Such damages are typically only available if a group proceeding is possible. And so procedural considerations – the type of fee arrangements permitted, and the availability of group proceedings – will be key determinants of viability of claims brought by private lawyers.

These law firms will then seek to diversify and mitigate their risks by developing a portfolio of cases across types, and seek outside financial assistance, by way of investors or insurance, in bringing them. As a result, we have a rapidly developing

control of local police force resulting in false imprisonment, assault and battery, trespass and theft of property. See n 71.

[74] It seems likely that this theory could be defeated by greater intermediation by formally independent actors (more subsidiaries or coordination along a supply chain) combined with careful due diligence steps at the lead or parent entity level.

[75] See, for example, Meeran (n 58) 29; for a standard textbook treatment, see John Haley, *Fundamentals of Transnational Litigation: The United States, Canada, Japan, and the European Union* (Durham, NC, Carolina Academic Press 2012).

[76] For a review of the costs issues in Trafigura UK action and settlement, see *Motto & Ors v. Trafigura Ltd & Anor* (Rev 3) [2011] EWCA Civ 1150. The costing was found disproportionate to the process and reduced to 58% of the original costs claimed.

[77] Meeran (n 58).

[78] In the Trafigura UK tort proceeding, the original claim was for about £100 million. The settlement amount of about £30 million was to be distributed to victims.

market in litigation insurance and third party financing.[79] These developments raise issues of possible conflicts of interest and the traditional common law rules against generating litigation ('champerty and maintenance').

There are other ways to finance and organise transnational litigation. Firms may partner with other firms in the jurisdiction of the harm, or more commonly, with non-governmental organisations who work with the communities and plaintiffs. Private firms may not be involved at all, and instead, cases may be brought by lawyers working with NGOs for purposes consistent with their mandates. The role of NGOs will be discussed more below.

These procedural and administrative considerations, which are primarily governed by the rules of domestic procedure, the impact of the domestic bar's regulation of its lawyers, and the economics of law firms, will cause some claims to be brought and others not; perhaps traditional issues of access to (transnational) justice, and likely to be highly idiosyncratic to events and actors. The fact that there are a small number of law firms and only some jurisdictions with the legal frameworks that permit the economics of a case to be viable means these factors will have considerable influence over the shape of transnational private law. The relatively small number of cases and actors will lead to closer consideration of them (as has been done with other transnational legal processes).[80] One such literature focuses on 'cause lawyering' as it is called in the US,[81] of which there are various typologies.[82] Their specificities have significant potential for research into what we think transnational law is or could be. The portfolio of cases of these firms could be a topography of these types of transnational legal cases; the backgrounds of the key lawyers and other actors in these firms a biography of the discipline.

The *Trafigura* case can fit into these analytic frameworks. A transnational toxic tort claim is brought in the UK by the Leigh Day & Co. firm, perhaps because domestic remedies were not preferred or available. The claim is eventually settled. The decision

---

79 Meeran (n 58) 24; Cassandra Robinson, 'The Impact of Third Party Financing on Transnational Litigation' (2011) 44 *Case Western Res J Int'L L* 159.

80 There are many variations. For activist networks and transnational environmental law, see Margaret Keck and Katherine Sikkink, *Activists Beyond Borders* (Ithaca, NY, Cornell University Press 1998); for transnational litigation and arbitration, see Walter Mattli, 'Private Justice in a Global Economy: From Litigation to Arbitration' (2001) 55(4) *International Organization* 919 and earlier seminal work by Yves Dezalay and Bryant Garth, *Dealing in Virtue* (Chicago, IL, University of Chicago Press 1996); for applications in West African legal contexts, see Sara Dezalay, 'African Extractive Economies and Connected Histories of Globalization – A Case Study of the Africa Bar in Paris' (18 July 2017) <https://ssrn.com/abstract=3004973>, accessed 18 February 2018 and 'Building a Political Sociology of Legal Professions in Africa: Stakes for an Open Research Agenda' (2 August 2017) <https://ssrn.com/abstract=3012719>, accessed 28 February 2018.

81 One well-known line in socio-legal literature is developed by Austin Sarat and Stuart Scheingold in several volumes beginning in the late 1990s. See for e.g., *Cause Lawyering and the State in a Global Era* (Oxford, Oxford University Press 2001) and *Cause Lawyers and Social Movements* (Palo Alto, CA, Stanford University Press 2006).

82 For example, Thomas Hilbink, 'You Know the Type: Categories of Cause Lawyering' (2004) 29 *Law & Soc Inquiry* 657; Anna-Maria Marshall, Daniel Crocker Hale, 'Cause Lawyering' (2014) 10 *Ann Rev L and Soc Sci* 301.

is a settlement, and not one we discuss for its doctrinal innovation – that had already been achieved by the Leigh Day & Co. firm as discussed above – but as an application of that innovation. The settlement we can place within the ranges of costs and risks mentioned above – a claim amount of initially about £100 million, a settlement for £30 million.[83] Distributions to the plaintiffs should have been in the range of €1,000 each. Those figures could be placed within the wider costs of the proceedings (apparently £14 million in defence costs in the UK action alone; see plaintiff cost claims of £100 million at footnote 76); compare to the NGO's estimates of the total economic cost of the dumping to the defendants (€254,000,000) and total revenues of the defendant of about US$122 billion. These figures represent a critique in themselves.

We might equally view the *Trafigura* claim (and if they are part of or become a pattern of claims, settlements and decisions, this form of transnational law) as the development and maturation of a business model: one of the portfolio of cases brought by the Leigh Day & Co. firm,[84] and a small number of firms like it, that developed a series of legal claims against corporate defendants operating transnationally out of the UK, and the realisation of the risks taken in that portfolio. Leigh Day & Co. now has a division of the firm named 'International Claims', and a portfolio of cases in over 14 jurisdictions. From this perspective, some of the initial preconditions to bringing a transnational claim, one being lack of viable domestic remedy for groups of victims in the Ivory Coast, might appear more as opportunities to diversify risk in a portfolio of claims and ultimate an opportunity for profit. The plaintiff law firms' economic incentives are, in a sense, based on there being a lack of domestic remedy, and the need to bring transnational claims. This raises several considerations which thicken the analysis: to what extent are the possibilities of domestic remedy really considered, exhausted or more to the point, inappropriate to the situation?[85] Furthermore, how are the relationships between the firms and plaintiffs created and mediated, how does the firm mitigate or syndicate its own risks?[86] From the 'business model' perspective, the *Trafigura* actions could be viewed, then, as twice an opportunity to profit, the first time in attempting to avoid expensive toxic waste processing in Amsterdam, and second, for

---

[83] Settlement amounts are often far less than claimed amounts for a variety of reasons. In the US, settlement amounts in (largely domestic) securities class proceedings are routinely less than 5% of the total claim, and declining for larger claims. For an example in a parallel field, see NERA Economic Consulting, Recent Trends in Securities Class Action Litigation: 2016 Full-Year Review, (NERA, 2017) <http://www.nera.com/content/dam/nera/publications/2017/PUB_2016_Securities_Year-End_Trends_Report_0117.pdf>, accessed 28 February 2018, 26. Settlement data is difficult to interpret, but the point for this discussion is a picture of the general economics of mass tort litigation.

[84] This portfolio is set out neatly (and not for the purpose discussed here) in Meeran (n 58) 24 and on the Leigh Day & Co. website.

[85] Chimène Keitner, 'The Three C's of Jurisdiction Over Human Rights Claims in U.S. Courts' (2015) 113 *Michigan Law Review First Impressions* 67.

[86] In this case we know that it was Greenpeace Netherlands that requested Leigh Day & Co. become involved in the case and presumably mediated the relationship with plaintiff groups, at least initially. Another French-based NGO, SHERPA, was also contacted by Leigh Day & Co.: see *Motto & Ors v. Trafigura Ltd & Anor* (Rev 3) [2011] EWCA Civ 1150 [11] et seq.

law firms from the global north to provide a form of justice outcome.[87] Is this, then, transnational law?

And, indeed, the role of Leigh Day & Co. in the *Trafigura* actions is not straightforward: while the claim was brought and settled, the distribution of the proceeds was not satisfactory; depending on the source of information, the funds were improperly appropriated by an Ivorian group with the aid of a domestic Ivorian proceeding, or were imprudently administered and lost by Leigh Day & Co. In the result, many victims did not receive compensation, and some resorted to claims against Leigh Day & Co. in the UK, which proceedings continued until 2016.

From this perspective the outcomes of the *Trafigura* actions are highly problematic. And that is certainly the view of the NGOs who have developed a lengthy report on the *Trafigura* actions,[88] and, in addition, their roles in these actions open another dimension of inquiry. Amnesty International and Greenpeace view the totality of the proceedings as effectively failing to properly sanction the key corporate defendants, a failure to properly compensate victims, a failure, even, for Trafigura to make a profit on the entire transaction.[89]

Interestingly, the NGO reports contain more detail about the domestic Ivorian legal procedures, settlement, clean-up and distribution of compensation to victims. These events are ultimately characterised as failing to make Trafigura accountable for the dumping, but consider the processes undertaken (at least formally) by the Ivorian government. Key local actors were immediately arrested, including Trafigura employees. Eventually an Ivorian court finds insufficient evidence for conviction in all but two cases, and those two are sentenced to 20 years in prison. The local environmental agency attempts to stop the ship leaving port. An emergency management team is appointed by the President a week later, and two commissions are established to investigate the dumping. A clean-up is undertaken by two different companies (French and Canadian). A settlement is eventually reached with Trafigura which releases their employees and pays nearly US$200 million for the clean-up. Some of this settlement fund is distributed to victims.

The NGO's report lists several failures of the Ivorian government to enforce existing laws that would have avoided the dumping, including licensing the domestic company and insufficient controls at the port of Abidjan. It also criticises the conditions of the settlements made by the Ivorian government and Leigh Day & Co., in particular for the Ivorian government's release from liability of the corporate defendants and Leigh Day & Co.'s agreement to keep terms of settlement confidential.[90] And the report is equally critical of state responses in the Netherlands and the UK. It even goes so far as to request Mexico commence an inquiry into why the raw, unprocessed fuel was sold in the first place.

---

[87] A third opportunity to profit lies, of course, with the eventual response of the corporate bar to the business model developed by the plaintiff firms.

[88] *Toxic Truth* (n 48).

[89] Ibid., 137.

[90] The report also notes the very limited number of actors willing to engage in these cases and criticised Leigh Day & Co. for agreeing not to pursue further litigation.

Although the conduct and effectiveness of these measures is criticised by the NGOs, even as purely formal exercises, the array of domestic responses do not fit easily within the typically brusque characterisation of the availability or quality of domestic justice often used as a practical precondition for a transnational claim.[91] We might expect a similar range of responses in any jurisdiction, and similar outcomes. There may have been serious problems in these processes, but it is too easy to gloss them as problems of developing countries' legal systems.

Although the report is lengthy, the thrust of it is that there should be a much more robust public enforcement of criminal or quasi-criminal sanctions against corporate actors in these circumstances by all States, and a more transparent process of remediation and compensation. It grounds its primary arguments on an international ordinance, the UN Convention on Economic, Social and Cultural Rights, and frames much of the report in terms of these rights.

Seen through the lens of transnational law, the NGOs frame it as a collective action problem of States and ground their analysis in 'rights talk' expressed in international agreements, in contrast to the innovation in private law of obligations used by the private law firms. It is one of the interesting features of the NGOs' perspective that in their description of the problem, we can simultaneously discern a wider legal lens – a socio-legal lens that renders a trenchant critique of all the actors involved in the problematic – while at the same time cleaving to State-based and rights-based solutions to the problem. We might call this solution the utopian formulation of transnational law; the properly coordinated State-State solution addressing pressing problems in the problem-and-policy-response mode. Put another way, these actors employ heterodox perspectives of socio-legal investigation combined with policy development, in which rights are conceived of as the justice outcome, and State instrumentality the mode of it. This approach may be quite consistent with the culture, modalities and objectives of the NGOs themselves; it is less clear whether this approach "fits" with the realities of a jurisdiction, politics and political economy. Further work into these NGOs, their cultures, economics and roles in the formation of transnational law is required.

4. SUBSTANCE OR APPROACH, DOCTRINE OR PROCESS

The *Trafigura* case is of course not a single case, but a series of them in several jurisdictions and with varying objectives. As an example of transnational private ordering it only has promise in the narrowest of senses, transnational tort law resulting in a settlement for victims where, for some reason, domestic remedies were not workable. This version of transnational law is still troubled in some ways: the innovation in tort law is one that is, essentially, not really transnational, but domestic, and in fact, relies on that to prove the theory of the case: the wrongful conduct was done in a boardroom in the UK; it is only the long chain of effects that causes injury in Abidjan. Doctrinally, the framing could be either domestic or international (the leading UK case is used as an example of how separate legal personality might be overcome in

[91] Recalling that a second reason for this 'precondition' may be difficulty enforcing a domestic claim in foreign jurisdictions.

UK corporate law textbooks),[92] but we can compare *Trafigura* to a number of other *cases*, like *Chevron*, or *Nike*, or *Kiobel*, and characterise them as a grouping of transnational legal cases in private law.

From another perspective, the Trafigura events are primarily about all States failing to act properly, to enact adequate controls, to co-ordinate properly over environmental problems and in each of these jurisdictions, about a failure to vindicate fundamental rights of the victims. This view of transnational law is closer to some form of public international law, using rights-talk to ground normative ordering. This perspective on transnational law is interesting when it is combined with socio-legal analysis of the actors in the NGO's perspective. This might be an example of a utopian transnational law, a call for better multi-State coordination vindicating rights articulated in UN conventions. This view of the *Trafigura* actions also includes a shift, namely one from adversarial litigation to ordering or governance outcomes: although the NGOs call for prosecution in support of corporate accountability, they ultimately propose solutions of better regulatory ordering and coordination.

Digging further into the different *cases* in the Trafigura events, legal proceedings, commissions of inquiry and other processes, it appears that they are riddled with problems of ultimate corporate accountability, enforcement and distribution. As the transnational litigation shows these problems are too complex to be addressed through the mode of adversarial litigation. They are problems of the interests, conflicts and power of actors and behavioural regulation.

If the objective is to consider prospects for transnational legal order, we must engage other perspectives and analytical tools, most notably from sociology of law and legal pluralism,[93] to begin to describe and understand these actors, particularly in relations to the State, and the processes they engage in and the norms they generate – if they generate them. Issues of enforcement of any order and legitimacy of any order – the latter always a difficult concept – arise immediately, in both the private transnational litigation driven by northern law firms' business models, as well as more traditional State roles. Using these methods and lenses leads the inquiry into transnational law away from the case method to those people and events that constitute what we later gloss as cases; the shift is toward some sort of Geertzian 'thicker' understanding. Here transnational law begins to conceive of itself as a process not a subject.

What is the *Trafigura* case about? Is it transnational law as a solution to a problem of sovereignty, or is it another example of the failures of it? Is it a story of failed domestic legal procedures during a period of domestic political instability? Or were domestic

---

92 See, for e.g., Paul Davies and Sarah Worthington (eds), *Gower: Principles of Modern Company Law* 10th edn (London, Sweet and Maxwell 2016) 201.

93 The literatures engaging in legal pluralism have become – plural – and the insights and methods of earlier work by Sally Moore, Sally Merry and John Griffiths and others have become correspondingly fragmented. For an enduring intervention not focused on transnational law, see Boa de Sousa Santos, *Toward a New Common Sense: Law, Science and Politics in the Paradigmatic Transition* (Cambridge, Cambridge University Press 1996, 2002); more recently Berman (n 44), Peer Zumbansen, 'Transnational Legal Pluralism' (2010) 1 *Transnational Legal Theory* 141 and in an application to private transnational law, Peer Zumbansen and Ralf-Peter Calliess, *Rough Consensus and Running Code: A Theory of Transnational Private Law* (Oxford, Hart Publishing 2010).

proceedings, which resulted in settlement of the claims in a standard way, and as such, perhaps an example of a functioning rule of law, despite the political context.

Is it a story of transnational corporate accountability for a toxic tort through the enterprising actions of a pioneering law firm from the UK, or another example of 'legal disaster capitalism' by law firms and their NGOs based in the global north? Are the strong domestic elements in transnational litigation – from defences asserted by corporate defendants which are systematically successful, to innovations by plaintiff law firms which rely almost entirely on framing the issues as purely matters of domestic law – part of transnational law? Is this not the opposite view to that of Jessup's famous definition of law that occurs across boundaries?

Are these small numbers of firms and lawyers engaged in transnational litigation forming the fabric of transnational law? Is it driven by their business models and those of their NGO partners? Is it a story of the possibilities of incremental improvements in coordination of transnational environmental regulation, or the impossibility of it through sovereign States in globalised networks of exchange?

Do we advance our understanding by conceiving of transnational law as a process of inquiry, not a substantive division in a typology of law?

PART II

THE RISE OF INFORMALITY: EMERGING NON-LEGAL NORMATIVITIES

6. Indigenous norms and judicial anthropology: *Song Mao*

6.1 CASE BACKGROUND

The Cambodian 'blood sugar' scandal was revealed to the general public in 2010 by the 'Cambodia Clean Sugar Campaign', which called for a boycott of sugar exported to Europe under the European Union's 'Everything But Arms' trade initiative. According to the campaigners, 'increasing production had resulted in human rights abuses' that required to be tackled at their origin, i.e. in the countries that were incentivising the exploitation and benefiting from ongoing land grabbing (http://www.cleansugarcampaign.net/). In this context, the *Song Mao* case illustrates several phenomena linked to global value chains: the generation and global circulation of value; multiple collateral damages (in terms of environmental harm, displacement of populations, forced labour, destruction of cultural forms of life and landgrabbing); and above all, the role of law, particularly in its private international avatar, in their construction and maintenance. Here, the claimants, some 200 villagers and former residents of the Koh Kong area in Cambodia, sued the multinational sugar giant Tate & Lyle in tort, alleging that they had been displaced from the land they inhabited; that the land and the sugar cane planted in that land was their property; that the raw sugar processed from the sugar cane was imported to England where it was converted by the defendants into refined sugar. Interestingly, they sought not the repossession of the land but a continued share in the profits generated by the refined sugar – targeting thereby the very core of the dynamic process of capital accumulation. As Tomaso Ferrando states, 'the "blood sugar chain" is deeply rooted in the soil, has geographical and financial structures that are dispersed in multiple jurisdictions, and is closely linked to Europe and the United States both as the final markets and crucial "chokepoints"'; mapping the chain, therefore, 'brings to light unexpected connections between productive and financial capital, domestic law and international human rights treaties, regional courts and the international criminal court, and private regulation and trade regimes'.[1] In this respect, the *Song Mao* case offers a prism through which to assess the place of private (international) law in the global political economy.

Case: *Song Mao & Others, and, Tate and Lyle Industry Ltd and T&L Sugars Ltd* (United Kingdom High Court of Justice, Queen's Bench Division, Commercial Court: Particulars of Claim, 28 March 2013; Defence and Counterclaim of the First and Second Defendants, 2 May 2013)

[1] T. Ferrando, *Land and Territory in Global Production: A Critical Legal Chain Analysis*, Doctoral dissertation, SciencesPo Paris, 2015 (dir. H. Muir Watt).

6.2 LITIGATING CAMBODIAN 'BLOOD SUGAR' IN THE ENGLISH COURTS

Alex Mills

1. INTRODUCTION

The *Song Mao* litigation[2] is, in many respects, an ordinary case. It involves a claim brought against English domiciled defendants, Tate & Lyle Industries Limited and T&L Sugars Limited,[3] in the English courts, for the tort of conversion. The fact that the claimants are foreign, in this case Cambodian, is not, in itself, a notable feature of the litigation. Cross-border disputes are an increasingly common feature of global economic and social relations, and indeed the significant majority of cases heard in the English commercial courts involve at least one foreign party. The fact that the dispute concerns questions and events which are very remote – geographically and culturally – from the practised formalities of the English bar is also not, in itself, remarkable. The disconnection of global dispute resolution from the location of the events giving rise to the claim is also a common feature of the legal dimension of global governance. With the growing influence of party autonomy in private international law,[4] multinational parties are themselves repeat consumers in a globalised law market, choosing for example between different systems of contract law, and between litigation in London, arbitration in Paris, or hybridised commercial courts in market disruptors such as Singapore.[5] The commencement of English proceedings against English domiciled defendants, even by foreign parties and relating to foreign acts, seems entirely unremarkable in the midst of such globalised legal activity.

There are, however, a number of reasons why this case is undoubtedly deserving of note, which are discussed in turn below. The first is that it raises some interesting questions of private international law, both in relation to choice of law, and as an illustration of certain peculiar features of the rules of jurisdiction applicable in the English courts pursuant to the EU Brussels I Regulation. These are points of technical debate among private international law scholars and in the courtrooms of the EU, but also raise important policy questions concerning the distribution of regulatory competence in cross-border disputes. The second is that the case is, at its heart, concerned with Cambodian land rights, and questions concerning title to immoveable property

---

2 *Song Mao v. Tate & Lyle Industries Limited*, EWHC (QB) Claim No 2013 Folio 451.

3 T & L Sugars purchased the sugar refining business of Tate & Lyle Industries in 2010, just after the shipment of sugar which formed the basis of the claim was delivered in London. The two defendants have since been involved in further litigation against each other over the terms of sale: see eg *T & L Sugars Ltd v. Tate & Lyle Industries Ltd* [2015] EWHC 2696 (Comm).

4 See generally e.g. Alex Mills, *Party Autonomy in Private International Law* (Cambridge, Cambridge University Press 2018); Horatia Muir Watt, '"Party Autonomy" in international contracts: from the makings of a myth to the requirements of global governance' (2010) 6 *European Review of Contract Law* 250.

5 Note e.g. the new Singapore International Commercial Court, <https://www.sicc.gov.sg/> accessed 23 April 2018.

have generally been exempted from the globalisation of dispute resolution, as they have been considered an aspect of the territorial sovereignty of the state. The third is the relationship between the case and the underlying supply chain which connects the Cambodian claimants with the English defendants. While supply chains exemplify the distance and the disconnections between the source and the ultimate consumer of goods, the case provides a striking illustration of the way in which supply chains also offer a relatively under-explored (but increasingly recognised) regulatory potential. The fourth is the curious lack of information surrounding the proceedings and their outcome – an element of mystery which suggests the potential of private litigation as a strategic regulatory technique, but also raises questions about its desirability.

2. QUESTIONS OF PRIVATE INTERNATIONAL LAW

Any cross-border dispute involving parties or events which occur in different jurisdictions raises issues of private international law. These include both questions of jurisdiction, regarding which court(s) or tribunal(s) may resolve the dispute, and questions of applicable law, determining which substantive law(s) will be applied.

The question of jurisdiction in this case depended on the Brussels I Regulation 2001,[6] as proceedings were commenced in 2013, prior to the 2015 commencement of the Recast Brussels I Regulation 2012.[7] The basic rule of jurisdiction in both versions of the Brussels I Regulation is that a defendant should be sued in the courts of their Member State of domicile, and there is no doubt that both defendants were English domiciled companies. The Tate & Lyle sugar refinery on the banks of the Thames, operational since 1878 and one of the largest in the world, is indeed a London landmark, particularly to frequenters of neighbouring London City Airport. A question might be raised, however, concerning whether the English courts were really the best forum in which to resolve this dispute. None of the facts or events in England appear to be contested in the case – it was accepted that the defendants took delivery of sugar in London, applying that sugar to their own use. It was contested, however, whether the sugar had derived from the land to which the claimants asserted title, or (even if it had) whether the claimants had any property interest in the sugar. Although (as discussed below) certain legal issues in the case were likely governed by English law, the factual questions which would require determination to resolve the claim were thus not English, but rather Cambodian.

Traditionally, the English courts would have dealt with this issue – whether the English courts were the appropriate forum to resolve the claim – through the exercise of their discretion to stay proceedings (or to refuse permission to commence them), under

[6] Council Regulation (EC) No 44/2001 of 22 December 2000 on jurisdiction and the recognition and enforcement of judgments in civil and commercial matters, OJ L 12, 16.1.2001.

[7] Regulation (EU) No 1215/2012 of the European Parliament and of the Council of 12 December 2012 on jurisdiction and the recognition and enforcement of judgments in civil and commercial matters, OJ L 351, 20.12.2012.

the doctrine of *forum non conveniens* (or *forum conveniens*).[8] The Court of Justice of the European Union has, however, held that this discretion is not available under the Brussels I Regulation.[9] Proceedings brought against English domiciled companies in the English courts must be heard by those courts, absent certain exceptions under the Regulation itself which are discussed in the next section. The Regulation, at least as interpreted by the CJEU, has prioritised the certainty and uniform application of its rules over the question of which forum is most appropriate to hear disputes. This creates a potential opportunity to commence proceedings in EU Member States against local companies in relation to their foreign activities, as explored further in other chapters of this book. The *Song Mao* litigation may thus in part be understood as an illustration of the potential of the Brussels I Regulation to open up avenues for holding EU corporate actors responsible for their worldwide activities – a perhaps unintended side-effect of the effort to create greater legal certainty in the functioning of the internal market. It should be noted, however, that this could also be read as having neo-colonialist undertones, as EU Member State courts assert regulatory competence over local companies regardless of where in the world their activities have taken place, and are unable to defer to a more closely connected foreign court which might resolve the dispute more efficiently and more closely to the affected community. On the other hand, a Cambodian NGO assisting some of the claimants has suggested that 'We are using international mechanism because the Cambodian judicial system is not independent'.[10] Even if the possibility of staying proceedings on *forum non conveniens* grounds were available, there is thus an argument that the English courts should nevertheless hear the case, on the well-recognised basis that the claimants would be denied justice if denied access to the English courts.[11]

The question of the applicable law in this case would, perhaps surprisingly, also raise some difficult questions. The first difficulty is that the common law tort of conversion is relatively unusual in that civil law systems generally deal with equivalent claims through the law of property.[12] This raises a potentially difficult problem in terms of characterising or classifying the cause of action for choice of law purposes. In EU Member States, the Rome II Regulation[13] deals with choice of law in non-contractual obligations, including torts, but it is unclear whether conversion would be classified as a 'tort' (or otherwise part of the law of obligations) for the purposes of the Regulation. If not, the choice of law question would fall back on national rules. One candidate would be the Private International Law (Miscellaneous Provisions) Act 1995, although

---

8 See eg Paul Torremans et al., *Cheshire, North & Fawcett: Private International Law* 15th edn (Oxford, Oxford University Press 2017) 351ff and 392ff.

9 Case C-281/02 *Owusu v. Jackson* EU:C:2005:120; see further e.g. Richard Fentiman, 'Civil Jurisdiction and Third States: Owusu and After' (2006) 43 *Common Market Law Review* 705.

10 See <https://www.foodnavigator-asia.com/Article/2014/06/24/Questions-to-answer-for-Tate-Lyle-in-Cambodian-land-grabbing-action> accessed 23 April 2018.

11 See generally eg *The Spiliada* [1987] AC 460; *The Vishva Ajay* [1989] 2 Lloyd's Rep 558; *Connelly v. RTZ* [1998] AC 854.

12 See Torremans et al. (n 8) 808ff; but see Lawrence Collins (ed.), *Dicey, Morris & Collins on the Conflict of Laws* 15th edn (London, Sweet and Maxwell 2012) para. 34-021.

13 Regulation (EC) No 864/2007 of the European Parliament and of the Council of 11 July 2007 on the law applicable to non-contractual obligations (Rome II), OJ L 199, 31.7.2007.

that would also require the classification of the action as a 'tort' for the purposes of that Act, which is again unclear.[14] Alternatively, the claim could be characterised as one in property, with the choice of law question governed by the common law. It is therefore possible that the choice of law question could be governed by the Rome II Regulation, the 1995 Act, or perhaps even by the common law choice of law rules in property.

Under each of these rules, it is likely that the applicable law would be English law, as it was by the Thames that the alleged interference with property rights and thus damage occurred. Under the Rome II Regulation or 1995 Act a flexible exception is available where the tort is considered to be more closely connected to another country, but would be unlikely to apply here because the events constituting the alleged tort occurred in England and both defendants are English. This still does not, however, quite resolve the complexity of the choice of law issues. For the tort of conversion to be established, the claimants would have to establish a property interest in the sugar. This arises as a subsidiary or incidental choice of law question, which would be governed by the law of the place of the property at the time the claimed acquisition of title arose.[15] This would undoubtedly be the law of Cambodia, as the claimants were claiming ownership in the sugar, derived from their asserted ownership of the land, from the time the sugar was harvested. Thus even if the claim were viewed as a tort governed by English law, the subsidiary question of ownership of the land would require application of Cambodian land law. The case thus provides an interesting illustration of both the complexity of questions of characterisation for choice of law purposes, as well as the potential application of multiple laws to a single claim through the incidental question doctrine.

3. FOREIGN LAND AND SOVEREIGNTY

A further feature of the *Song Mao* case which raises difficult legal issues is that it is at least partially concerned with foreign land title. Disputes concerning land have traditionally been considered matters which should be resolved solely by the territorial courts. This is because land title has been viewed as an aspect of state sovereignty, and also because – as Oona Le Meur demonstrates in her section – questions of land title may involve complex historical and cultural issues, which may best be decided by a local tribunal. If the English courts were to address these issues, they would need to engage with disputing claims of title to land – in this case, under different systems of land title which appear to co-exist in Cambodian law, which would present an undoubted forensic challenge. The proof of foreign law for the purposes of English proceedings is a complex enough task when the law is documented in formal sources, let alone when competing customary norms are relied on. The proof of customary law has long raised particularly difficult questions for the adaptation of the common law in India and in African commonwealth countries. The general approach has been that

---

[14] The 1995 Act offers, in Article 9(2), only the following somewhat delphic guidance: 'The characterisation for the purposes of private international law of issues arising in a claim as issues relating to tort or delict is a matter for the courts of the forum.'

[15] See e.g. Collins (n 12) para. 34-022.

customary law has to be ascertained as a matter of fact[16] – although this has been controversial in many instances (as prioritising English law over 'native' law),[17] this would not be the case where the ascertainment of customary law arises as part of foreign law, as all foreign law must be determined as a matter of fact under the common law.[18]

But should the English courts engage in such a task at all? The Brussels I Regulation includes, in Article 24, various grounds of exclusive subject matter jurisdiction – categories of claim considered to be so closely connected to a single legal order that only one court should be able to hear them. One such category, in Article 24(1), is disputes concerning title to immovable property located in a Member State. Infamously, however, the Brussels I Regulation does not include any rule dealing with cases which have equivalent connections to non-Member States, such as a dispute concerning title to Cambodian land. This is an aspect of the general problem that the Regulation, in its focus on improving the functioning of the internal market, does not deal adequately with 'external' effects, as it fails to take into consideration the connections which cases may have to non-Member States.[19] Many academics and national court decisions have supported the application of a doctrine of reflexive effect, under which Article 24 should have some (probably discretionary) effect in relation to equivalent non-Member State connections.[20] The difficulty with this argument is that it requires a strong purposive interpretation of the Brussels I Regulation, unsupported by the text. The argument has become more difficult under the Recast Brussels I Regulation 2012, because certain provisions of the Regulation (dealing with prior foreign proceedings)[21] have been given a reflexive effect directly in the Regulation.[22] Not only does this arguably imply that other similar effects should not arise implicitly, but the Regulation allows for exclusive jurisdictional connections to be taken into consideration in exercising the discretion to stay Member State proceedings where there are prior non-Member State proceedings.[23] This rule would appear to be redundant if indeed the rules on exclusive jurisdiction could be given reflexive effect. The consequence of all this is that, somewhat problematically, Member State courts may be *required* to hear claims against locally domiciled parties concerning title to non-Member State land, at least if they are first seised, regardless of the great difficulties which this presents.

---

[16] See e.g. *Angu v. Attah* [1916] Gold Coast PC 43; AN Allott, 'The Judicial Ascertainment of Customary Law in British Africa' (1957) 20 *Modern Law Review* 244.

[17] See e.g. Australian Law Reform Commission Report 31, *Recognition of Aboriginal Customary Laws* (1986).

[18] See generally e.g. Richard Fentiman, *Foreign Law in English Courts: Pleading, Proof and Choice of Law* (Oxford, Oxford University Press 1998).

[19] See generally e.g. Alex Mills, 'Private International Law and EU External Relations: Think Local Act Global, or Think Global Act Local?' (2016) 65 *International and Comparative Law Quarterly* 541.

[20] See generally e.g. Peter De Verneuil Smith, Ben Lasserson and Ross Rymkiewicz, 'Reflections on Owusu: The Radical Decision in Ferrexpo' (2012) 8 *Journal of Private International Law* 389; *Ferrexpo AG v. Gilson Investments Ltd* [2012] EWHC 721 (Comm).

[21] Articles 29 and 30.

[22] Under Articles 33 and 34.

[23] Recital 24.

Whether the *Song Mao* case should actually be considered to concern title to land is, however, a further difficult question. Clearly, a central issue in the case concerns the ownership of the Cambodian land from which the sugar was harvested. The form of the claim, however, was based on the tort of conversion, and the issue of land ownership arose only as an incidental question. Further, perhaps inadvisedly, the defendants disputed whether the sugar had actually come from the land in question.[24] This meant that there were other contentious central issues which did not concern land title, and the courts have shown a willingness to hear cases in which issues which would ordinarily be matters of foreign exclusive jurisdiction arise as subsidiary questions, to ensure that all issues are resolved efficiently in a single set of proceedings.[25]

Common law courts have traditionally applied a further doctrine under which disputes concerning title to foreign land are considered to be 'non-justiciable'.[26] The status of this doctrine is somewhat unclear – although expressed as a 'pre-jurisdictional' rule relating to the subject-matter authority of the court, it is perhaps best understood simply as a rule of 'preclusive jurisdiction', equivalent in effect to Article 24(1) of the Brussels I Regulation.[27] As such, in the English courts there should arguably be no place for non-justiciability in cases commenced pursuant to the Regulation, as it would (like *forum non conveniens*) affect the legal certainty and consistent application of the Regulation.[28] However, the defendants in the *Song Mao* case suggested in their defence an intention to rely on the doctrine.[29] The case thus raises a difficult question of the interaction between common law non-justiciability and European Union rules of jurisdiction, although in any case, once again, there would be an argument in this context that the issue of title to foreign land was only raised incidentally, and should not be covered by the common law doctrine.[30]

The *Song Mao* case thus illustrates some fractures which have emerged in the idea that disputes concerning title to land should be decided by the territorial court. First, the Brussels I Regulation may have inadvertently undermined the traditional deference to foreign sovereigns in respect of questions of title to their land, in respect of non-Member States. Second, courts have shown a willingness to examine such questions where they arise incidentally, prioritising efficient dispute resolution over sovereignty concerns. The fact that the English courts suggested a willingness to hear the *Song Mao* case exemplifies these trends, perhaps reflecting a tendency to emphasise the private dimension of property disputes, rather than their public territorial sovereignty dimension.

---

24 *Song Mao* (n 2) Defence and Counterclaim, [18.2].

25 See e.g. (by analogy) Case C-144/10 *BVG v. JPMorgan* EU:C:2011:300.

26 See e.g. *British South Africa Co v. Companhia de Mozambique* [1893] AC 602; *Belhaj v. Straw* [2017] UKSC 3; Torremans et al. (n 8) 484ff.

27 But see e.g. *Lucasfilm Ltd v. Ainsworth* [2009] EWCA Civ 1328 (overturned on other grounds at [2011] UKSC 39).

28 See e.g. Torremans et al. (n 8) 494.

29 *Song Mao* (n 2) Defence and Counterclaim, [8.5].

30 See e.g. *Hamed v. Stevens* [2013] EWCA Civ 911.

4. THE REGULATORY POTENTIAL OF THE SUPPLY CHAIN

A third aspect of the *Song Mao* case which is particularly notable is its reliance on the underlying supply chain which connects the Cambodian claimants with the English defendants. The supply chain is one of the defining architectural features of the modern global economy. It provides a powerful metaphorical image of the flow of material goods from origin to destination – from a mine or farm, via processors, manufacturers, assemblers, distributors, retailers and various other possible intermediary parties, through to the sale of goods to a consumer. The supply chain does not only show the links between these parties, however, but also their distance and separation. A consumer may purchase goods from a party who was not involved in any way in the initial stages of production, such as the extraction of raw materials or their processing and refinement. This distancing presents a regulatory challenge. Resource extraction in the developing world frequently raises concerns as to human rights compliance, environmental impact, and (as in the *Song Mao* case) questions as to the competing rights of local populations and foreign investors. Governance issues and economic pressures mean that these concerns are, however, often not met by local regulation. The final product of the supply chain frequently ends up purchased in the developed world, which may offer greater regulatory capacity, but is remote from these concerns. The remoteness is not merely geographical, although this remains undoubtedly relevant because of the territorial character of state regulatory power, but also cultural, as a polished retail experience may reveal little of the supply chain's story. The power differentials involved across the supply chain also raise distributive concerns, as little of the profit generated from sales of consumer goods may find its way back down the chain to developing world farmers, miners or factory workers.

It has been increasingly recognised, however, that the supply chain presents not only a regulatory challenge but also a regulatory opportunity. This is because pressure at the end of a supply chain may potentially be relied on to produce change along the line back to its origin. This prospect has arisen in a variety of forms, which need not be legal in character. If a publicity campaign or social media movement questions the ethics of the processes through which goods have been sourced and produced, consumers may simply boycott purchasing those goods, potentially leading to changes in production practices. To demonstrate compliance with ethical standards, companies may adopt private certification processes, such as the 'fair trade' movement, or the labelling of 'responsibly sourced' food or timber products. These market-driven processes are not themselves legal in character, although they may be supported by the law. For example, in the UK section 54 of the Modern Slavery Act 2015 requires certain commercial organisations carrying on business in the UK to prepare a 'slavery and human trafficking statement', providing information on the policies and procedures they have adopted to ensure that slavery and human trafficking have not been used in their supply chains anywhere in the world.[31] The statement must be published on an organisation's website, with a prominent link on its homepage. This provision of the Act thus does not directly seek to regulate the conduct of corporations extraterritorially,

---

31 See further <https://www.gov.uk/government/publications/transparency-in-supply-chains-a-practical-guide> accessed 23 April 2018.

but facilitates the possibility of market-based responses to organisations which fail to adopt sufficiently robust policies or procedures.

In other cases, the law may intervene more directly to affect the importation of raw materials sourced contrary to specified standards. The EU Conflict Minerals Regulation,[32] due to come into effect in 2021, requires EU importers of tin, tantalum, tungsten and gold to carry out due diligence on their supply chains to ensure that the resources they import have been mined and processed responsibly. The EU is thus relying on a form of territorial regulation to project its regulatory goals extraterritorially, to affect practices at the origin of these supply chains, although this is in the form of relatively weak due diligence and reporting obligations. Similarly but more generally, the EU has adopted non-financial disclosure requirements, under which:

> certain large undertakings should prepare a non-financial statement containing information relating to at least environmental matters, social and employee-related matters, respect for human rights, anti-corruption and bribery matters. … The non-financial statement should also include information on the due diligence processes implemented by the undertaking, also regarding, where relevant and proportionate, its supply and subcontracting chains, in order to identify, prevent and mitigate existing and potential adverse impacts.[33]

The *Song Mao* litigation represents a different regulatory approach, but with a similar objective. It seeks to leverage the power of private law and private international law to pressure Tate & Lyle, with the hope that in turn this will have an impact on the Cambodian sugar producers. Exactly what form this impact might take is somewhat unclear. The particulars of claim frame the action as a claim for damages, and if it were successful the litigation could lead to financial compensation for the lost productive value of the land. There is, however, evidently a bigger picture. The litigation might also seek to affect the viability of the Cambodian sugar production business based on the land whose ownership is contested by the claimants. The risk of litigation against prospective purchasers may affect the market value of the sugar produced on the disputed land, decreasing or even eliminating the profitability of the business. This could lead to the acceptance of a more general legally binding settlement agreement by the sugar producers who have control over the territory. The private law form of the cause of action in the English courts is thus mirrored in the potential for a contractual solution to the asserted dispossession of the claimants. However the desired outcome is framed, the mechanism is clear – the use of private litigation against third party recipients of produce from contested land, as a means of indirectly challenging the position of those who claim ownership of the land, reasserting the primacy of a frustrated customary title. As in other contexts, the possibility of disrupting a supply chain raises the potential for extraterritorial projection of regulation. In this case,

[32] Regulation (EU) 2017/821 of the European Parliament and of the Council of 17 May 2017 laying down supply chain due diligence obligations for Union importers of tin, tantalum and tungsten, their ores, and gold originating from conflict-affected and high-risk areas, OJ L 130, 19.5.2017.

[33] Directive 2014/95/EU of the European Parliament and of the Council of 22 October 2014 amending Directive 2013/34/EU as regards disclosure of non-financial and diversity information by certain large undertakings and groups, OJ L 330, 15.11.2014, Recital 6.

Cambodian villagers seek to invoke English tort law in the English courts as a mechanism for addressing their local concerns – they are themselves acting extra-territorially as claimants in seeking to invoke a projection of regulation back in their own territory, using what might perhaps be described as a 'regulatory boomerang' technique.

5. PROSPECTS AND LIMITATIONS OF 'PRIVATE' LITIGATION

A final aspect of the *Song Mao* litigation which is deserving of notice is the curious scarcity of information concerning the case, also noted by Oona Le Meur in her section. Proceedings were commenced in the High Court in London in 2013, and the Particulars of Claim filed by the claimants and the Defence and Counter-claim filed by the defendants are matters of public record and readily available online.[34] After initially receiving a mild flurry of academic note,[35] the case has since gone rather quiet. 'Did the Cambodian sugar case settle?', asked one human rights blog in 2015, reporting that inquiries to the Commercial Court revealed that the case had been removed from its listings.[36] Settlement negotiations have undoubtedly been at least attempted, including not only the parties to the English proceedings but also the Cambodian sugar producing company, but these have also proven highly controversial (as some parties have claimed that their acceptance of a settlement was under duress).[37] It is typical of settlement negotiations and settlement agreements that they impose confidentiality obligations on the parties, and this is the most likely reason for the relative lack of publicity of the action here.[38] This fact in itself raises a potential concern with the *Song Mao* regulatory technique – as a private law action, it is possible for the negotiations of a settlement of the proceedings to be carried out in secret and to remain secret. The characterisation of the action as 'private' thus carries a double-meaning. For the parties to the proceedings, this may be potentially beneficial. For the defendants, it may enable them to take the litigation off the public agenda, reducing the risk that they will be subject to

[34] See e.g. <https://business-humanrights.org/en/koh-kong-sugar-plantation-lawsuits-re-cambodia> accessed 23 April 2018.

[35] See e.g. Mahdev Mohan, 'The Road to *Songmao*: Transnational Litigation from Southeast Asia to the United Kingdom' (2014) 107 *AJIL Unbound* e-30.

[36] See <https://corporatewarcrimes.com/2015/05/01/did-the-cambodian-sugar-case-settle/> accessed 23 April 2018.

[37] See e.g. <http://www.phnompenhpost.com/national/sugar-companys-compensation-deals-leave-families-bitter-kampong-speu>; <https://www.cambodiadaily.com/archives/evictees-reject-latest-settlement-offer-from-uk-sugar-firm-60869/>; <https://business-humanrights.org/en/cambodia-evictees-in-land-dispute-claim-thai-company-made-them-sign-compensation-agreements-they-can%E2%80%99t-read-%E2%80%93-includes-company-comments>; <https://www.cambodiadaily.com/archives/evictees-sign-payout-deal-they-cant-read-without-lawyers-70997/> accessed 23 April 2018.

[38] See e.g. <https://business-humanrights.org/sites/default/files/documents/Tate-%26-Lyle-14-July-2014-response.pdf> ('Tate & Lyle Sugars responded with the following: "It has been agreed by all parties that these discussions should remain confidential, and it would therefore be inappropriate for us to say anything further at this time."') accessed 23 April 2018.

market-based activism. For the claimants, the possibility of entering into a confidentiality obligation provides them with leverage to increase the likelihood of a settlement of the dispute. The danger here is evidently that the broader public interest is left behind, in a way which would be less likely for other forms of legal or non-legal supply chain regulation. The wider issue may disappear – if the simile can be forgiven, dissolving from view like sugar in an English cup of tea.

As a counter-point, however, it must be noted that this litigation did have a short term impact on publicity surrounding the more general issue of Cambodian land rights, and as part of a broader campaigning strategy (centred around the concept of 'blood sugar')[39] it has potentially had a number of further indirect impacts. One such notable consequence is the 2013 suspension[40] of Tate & Lyle's membership of 'Bonsucro', a sugar industry organisation which seeks to advance and promote responsible production.[41] Tate & Lyle subsequently resigned its membership in 2014, citing the UK litigation as a reason why it was 'not able to play an active role in Bonsucro'.[42] On the one hand this may be cited as a failure of industry self-regulation procedures, which frequently prove to have no enforcement 'teeth' against breaches of the soft-law standards they promote. On the other hand, the wide reporting of this suspension and resignation is likely to have had at least some negative publicity impact for Tate & Lyle, and the threat of suspension alone may thus positively affect the practices of other members of Bonsucro.

A further counter-point to note is that private litigation need not suggest a broader confidentiality, because it can form a complementary part of the arsenal of legal and non-legal techniques which might be relied on to improve the human rights or environmental compliance of a supply chain. In the case of Cambodia's contested land issues and the sugar industry, this included, for example, complaints brought to the National Human Rights Commission of Thailand (based on the nationality of one of the parent companies of the Cambodian sugar production company). The Commission upheld the complaints in 2015, finding that human rights violations had indeed been committed.[43] A further avenue of legal complaint was the 2014 Communication to the International Criminal Court alleging that the land dealings in Cambodia constituted crimes against humanity.[44] This led to an announcement by the ICC in 2016 that it was broadening its scope of activity to include prioritisation of crimes based on, inter alia,

---

39 See e.g. <http://www.boycottbloodsugar.net/> accessed 23 April 2018.

40 See e.g. <https://www.cambodiadaily.com/archives/ethical-sugar-group-suspends-tate-lyle-over-plantations-35438/> accessed 23 April 2018.

41 See further <https://www.bonsucro.com> accessed 23 April 2018.

42 See e.g. <https://business-humanrights.org/en/cambodia-tate-lyle-resigns-from-bonsucro-company-claims-pending-uk-lawsuit-makes-them-unable-to-%E2%80%9Cplay-an-active-role%E2%80%9D-in-the-initiative> accessed 23 April 2018.

43 See e.g. <https://earthrights.org/media/human-rights-violations-in-koh-kong-sugar-plantation-confirmed-by-thai-human-rights-commission/> (with an unofficial English translation of the Report) accessed 23 April 2018.

44 <https://business-humanrights.org/en/cambodian-villagers%E2%80%99-intl-criminal-court-complaint-re-land-grabbing>; <https://www.reuters.com/article/us-icc-cambodia-landrights/landless-cambodian-farmers-look-to-international-criminal-court-for-justice-idUSKBN13H1J9> accessed 23 April 2018.

dispossession of land.[45] The possibility of a formal ICC investigation or even prosecution is likely to place further pressure on the sugar producers or government officials involved in their land grants to seek a fair settlement of the dispute. Finally, it may be noted that sugar imported from Cambodia to the European Union is given preferential treatment under the EU's 'Everything But Arms' initiative, which favours produce from 'Least Developed Countries'. However, this preferential status is subject to Cambodia demonstrating respect for human rights. In 2014 the EU launched an initiative jointly with the Cambodian government to investigate claims of forced displacement in the sugar industry, and to ensure redress for those affected.[46] Doubts have been expressed as to the progress which has been made on implementing this process,[47] although meetings continue.[48] The possibility for the EU to withdraw privileged trading status for Cambodian sugar remains a further potential (public law) mechanism by which the supply chain to the EU may be leveraged to address human rights concerns in Cambodia, and the issue remains on the agenda of the EU.[49]

6. CONCLUSIONS

The *Song Mao* litigation raises a range of complex legal questions. These include questions of private international law, including particularly the challenge the case presents to the traditional view that jurisdiction over disputes concerning title to land should be exercised exclusively by the territorial courts. An added difficulty in this case is that there is an underlying dispute between different systems of Cambodian land title, which multiplies the complexity of pleading and proving the content of foreign law. The potential for litigating these issues in the English courts arises in part because the case invokes a distinctive territorial regulatory claim – it seeks to regulate the source of the supply chain, but does so through regulating an English party further down the chain. The case therefore exemplifies the way that the supply chain presents a regulatory challenge, but also offers regulatory potential. The chain through which raw materials are assembled, generally from the developing to the developed world, may also be a device for the counter-flow of norms. This has been increasingly recognised in the context of non-legal and public law initiatives – the *Song Mao* case

45 See e.g. <https://www.theguardian.com/global/2016/sep/15/hague-court-widens-remit-to-include-environmental-destruction-cases>; <https://www.icc-cpi.int/itemsDocuments/20160915_OTP-Policy_Case-Selection_Eng.pdf> accessed 23 April 2018.

46 <https://www.theguardian.com/world/2014/dec/10/european-union-cambodia-sugar-industry-human-rights> accessed 23 April 2018.

47 <https://www.cambodiadaily.com/morenews/three-years-on-govt-eu-still-at-odds-over-sugar-evictions-124903/> accessed 23 April 2018.

48 <http://www.phnompenhpost.com/national/un-eu-reps-meet-officials-over-land-row> accessed 23 April 2018.

49 European Commission Report on the Generalised Scheme of Preferences covering the period 2016–17, Brussels, 19.1.2018, COM(2018) 36 final, p. 6 ('The EU is engaging with Cambodia to address human rights issues related to land disputes arising from sugarcane concessions and labour rights issues, in particular freedom of association. The EU needs to see real and sustained improvements, if further steps are to be avoided.').

adds to the potential range of techniques the possibility of pursuing private litigation as a further mechanism of projecting regulation back along the supply chain. This approach has significant potential, because the power to initiate the proceedings lies with private parties, although it also raises questions concerning the legitimacy of its distribution of regulatory authority and whether the public interest will be sufficiently accommodated. These concerns may also be reflected in the apparent disappearance of the *Song Mao* litigation from discussion in the public domain. Although in many respects the *Song Mao* litigation was (or is?) an ordinary case, it provides a striking and undoubtedly notable illustration of the complex interactions of public and private interests in the legal regulation of globalised commercial activity.

6.3 PROBLEMS OF DESIGNING A LEGAL INFRASTRUCTURE TO GLOBAL VALUE CHAINS IN GLOBALISED ECONOMIC SYSTEMS

Hisashi Harata

1. INTRODUCTION

Song Mao & Others v. Tate & Lyle and Tate & Lyle Sugars (referred to as the *Song Mao* case hereinafter)[50] has significant theoretical and practical implications in the context of Global Value Chains analysis. Various topical legal issues arise here in connection with the structuring of global production of sugar. Here, we focus on private law aspects, and particularly on often neglected choice-of-law problems that could play an important role in providing the legal infrastructure of value chains. Indeed, the globalised market economy depends upon private-law concepts such as contract, property, tort etc. Although the rules of municipal law can be and are different from each other, there is a common grammar of private law through which the globalised market economy operates. In this sense, the language of private-law is a constitutive part of our globalised society. The *Song Mao* case shows us emblematically how private-law is directly involved in structuring the global economy. Indeed, a conflict of laws perspective on this case shows up the limits and the problematic dimensions of such private-law tools for dealing with the darker side of global value chains, including issues of land grabbing. In this respect, such broadly acknowledged choice-of-law principles as *lex loci delicti* and *lex loci rei sitae* can be seen to provide multinational corporate groups with a large margin for manipulating the choice of applicable law.

[50] Particulars of Claim and Defence and Counterclaim of the First and Second defendants, Claim No 2013 Folio 451 in the High Court of Justice Queen's Bench Division Commercial Court between: Song Mao & others and Tate & Lyles Industries Limited and T & L Sugars Limited. An analysis of the Cambodian blood sugar campaign, the *Song Mao* case and more broadly, a critical legal theory of global value chains from which many elements in this note are borrowed, can be found in T. Ferrando, *Land and Territory in Global Production: A Critical Legal Chain Analysis*, Doctoral dissertation, SciencesPo Paris, 2015 (dir. H. Muir Watt).

This contribution analyses, first, certain contextual or background factors which, while invisible in the litigation, nevertheless weigh heavily on the legal structures involved in global sugar production. Secondly, it goes on to point out some of the legal characteristics of such production in terms of private law, particularly conflicts issues. It will be seen then that private law tools, at least in some respects, work to the advantage of global enterprise rather than to that of the local population. Furthermore, the reasons for these advantages will be discussed in the hope that this analysis will serve for further discussion on the governance of global value chains.

2. BACKGROUND AND CONTEXT

The case regards very specifically the civil dispute between local (Cambodian) people and the global sugar giant located (in England) far from the place where the raw-sugar is grown and processed. However, it is just a small particular part of the wider picture regarding the global structuring of food production. Here, first are some elements of context and background to consider, which are not necessarily apparent in the terms of dispute, but which are undoubtedly relevant to understanding the political economy of the relevant private law aspects involved in the value chain.

First, it is necessary to mention an EU trade policy called the 'Everything but Arms' initiative. This policy enabled EU Member States to import materials from 'least developed countries' with the privileges of duty-free and quota-free.[51] This policy also covered the sugar material import from Cambodia, as in this case. It is within this regulatory framework that one of the global sugar giants, T & L, proceeded to outsource significant parts of the process of sugar production to Cambodia, with a view to take advantage too, beyond these regulatory privileges, of lower market costs. A trade policy can have an impact for global value chain structuring.[52]

The second contextual element is provided by the Cambodian legal regime supporting private rights such as land ownership. In 2001, the Cambodian government enacted the Land Law for the purpose of re-stabilising title to land and wider societal relationships after the domestic conflicts. The domestic private law system is of course decisive as for whether and what kind of title the local people had over the disputed land; its applicability then depends on the operation of the choice-of-law rule pointing to the *lex loci rei sitae* for the recognition of title.

A third background factor is the Cambodian Government's call for foreign outsourcing and investment. In 2006, it enacted the Economic Land Concession Act and concluded a correlative Concession Agreement with the local companies that were engaged in the first stage of sugar production, viz. the sugar cane plantation and the processing of raw sugar. This granted them legal title for land usage and authorisation

---

[51] Council Regulation (EC) 980/2005 applying a scheme of generalised tariff preferences [2005] OJ L169, arts 12 and 13.

[52] For the EU's reaction after this 'Blood Sugar' issue, Council Regulation (EC) 732/2008 [2008] OJ L211/1. See, Maud Salber, '"Tout sauf les armes", une initiative européenne à double tranchant', *Grotius International*, 3 March 2014 <https://grotius.fr/tout-sauf-les-armes-une-initiative-europeenne-a-double-tranchant/#.WmfembkUk5s> accessed 28 April 2018.

of raw sugar production there.[53] This explains why it was alleged that the 'Land Clearance Agents', who (allegedly) expelled the local population from their land by force, acted on behalf not only of the local companies but also of the Cambodian Government. Indeed if it were the case that the acts of the agents involved several crimes (theft, destruction of homes etc.), and if they were also the agents of the government, the responsibility of the government under domestic law and international law could and should be addressed.

A. The Structure of the Chain

The first stage of global sugar production was carried out by local Cambodian companies, Koh Kong Plantation Co. Ltd. and Koh Kong Sugar Industry. Both companies were established under Cambodian law in 2006. The first local part of the global value chain was therefore outsourced to local companies in Cambodia. The production of raw sugar was then imported to England in the form of a sales contract with Tate & Lyle. Thus, the global value chain was divided into two parts, located in Cambodia and in the UK respectively, and combined by way of contracts between different legal entities. Two intriguing questions arise here. One regards the reason why local production was ensured not by one but by two companies. Another concerns the reason why the legal form of sales contract was adopted for connecting those two divided parts within the same global sugar production structure.

As for the first question, one fact worthy of note is that those two raw sugar production companies were incorporated at the same time (that is, in 2006) as the establishment of the sugar plantation. Yet the project was launched using distinct legal entities. Generally, in terms of structuring a global enterprise – typically, in respect of the choice between a local subsidiary rather than a foreign branch – various considerations may have weight, such as tax planning and competition-law in the host country. Similar considerations might have been taken into account in this case. But here there is also article 59 of the Cambodian Land Law, whose provision stipulates that 'land concessions areas shall not be more than 10,000 hectares'. The latter requirement explains why each of these two companies made a concession agreement with the government for less than 10,000 hectares. To all intents and purposes, there was no infringement of the law by either company individually. However, if we regard these two separate legal entities as one single unit of enterprise, the story would change. There would be a clear infringement of the local regulation. In this respect, it is possible to say that the domestic administrative law of a host country may influence the legal structure adopted by private enterprise. Furthermore, it may be that the host country actually welcomes such legal trickery to the extent that it encourages more investment.

---

[53] Regarding the Land Concession Agreement, Art. 58 of the 2001 Land Law stipulated that a land concession can only be granted on lands that are part of the 'private' [sic] property of the State. The disputed land is deemed to be private property of the Cambodian Government. And for the applicable law to Concession Agreement, the Art. 13 of the Land Concession Agreement stipulated that 'those agreements were to be governed by the laws of Cambodia.'

As for the second question regarding the role of the sales contract, we need to remember the aforementioned potential impact of foreign trade policy. If the tariff exemption is granted only for imports to the EU originating with a foreign local company, this would mean that the same advantage would not be extended if the same import concerned a simple foreign branch. When the import takes place as between distinct legal persons, it necessarily takes the legal form of sales contract, and an international one to boot. Therefore, once the contractual form is adopted, the relationship is governed by a substantive law chosen by the parties, in the name of the rapidly spreading principle of party autonomy. At this point, rules of property law also intervene, in the form of protection for the good faith purchaser, opening wider perspectives of legal title laundering.[54]

Additionally, we may wonder about the role of a consultancy agency in the structuring of the global sugar chain. PAPL is presented as a consultancy firm working for T & L, but it is not clear from the parties' files what kind of activities it was really engaged in.[55,56] Now if such a consultancy firm had actively been engaged in the construction of the part of raw-sugar processing to be outsourced from the UK, the UK side and the Cambodian side might start to look less separated. Rather, the first stage of raw-sugar processing outsourced in Cambodia could be regarded as part of T & L's well-planned structuring of global sugar production. Obviously, there is no direct capital relationship between both sides in the case, but a consultancy firm could work for a global major enterprise to plan a better structuring for covering the whole globe through local connecting actors.

B. The Identity of Investing Capital

While the raw sugar production was managed under the aforementioned legal form, the capital for this first stage of global production was expected to be raised through a multinational joint venture. At the beginning of the project, in 2006, this capital venture was composed of three investors, a Thai Company, a Taiwanese Company and a Cambodian individual. The first one, the KSL,[57] had half of the share of the local companies of raw-sugar processing. Remarkably, there is one individual person, Mr. Ly Yong Phat, engaged in this capital joint venture. He is not simply an individual investor but has been involved in the ruling party of the Senate since 2006 – again the same

[54] On this issue, Hisashi Harata, 'The Laundering of Legal Titles: The Antithesis of the Concept of a "secure and stable Transaction"' (2015) 12 *University of Tokyo Journal of Law and Politics* 75; on the laundering of legal title to cultural property in the context of the tort of conversion in private international law, see H. Muir Watt, 'La revendication internationale des biens culturels: à propos de la décision américaine Église autocéphale' [1992] *Rev. crit. DIP* 1.

[55] For PAPL, <http://www.paplconsultants.com/#> accessed 28 April 2018.

[56] An agent firm, often called 'consultancy firm', is easy to be established for foreign investment and also can be the place for bribes to a person on the side of host country. For instance, see *Konamaneni v. Rolls Royce Industrial Power (India) Ltd.* [2002] 1 WLR 1269.

[57] The KSL is the country's fourth-largest sugar miller, whose CEO, Mr. Chamroon Chinthammit, is also '2017 Thailand's 50 Richest Net Worth $615 Million', according to Forbes <https://www.forbes.com/profile/chamroon-chinthammit/> accessed 28 April 2018. So this case also shows up oligopolisation of sugar production in the region.

year of the launching of the project.[58] It might be that he had close connections with Cambodian government officials managing the granting of land concession, and also that he played a key role in the call for foreign investment from Thailand and Taiwan. If so, Mr. Ly should be deemed a 'connecting factor' for the first stage of global sugar production in Cambodia! Through his agency, the foreign capital, the local companies, and the concession granted by the Cambodian government all combined together.

Bonsucro is yet another element involved here in global sugar production. Bonsucro is the biggest Global Trade Association of Sugar Industry or the trade association of global sugar giants. It has its own private regulatory mechanisms for ruling the members' sugar business, such as Code of Conduct and the dispute-resolution mechanism.[59] One of the defendants, Tate & Lyle, was one of the founding members of Bonsucro. Perhaps surprisingly, Bonsucro showed independence in its review of the latter's production scheme. Indeed, in this case, Bonsucro's board urged Tate & Lyle to proceed with third party review of compensation and also to proceed with independent audit of compliance of T & L's Code of Conduct. But T & L refused to abide by this invitation, withdrawing instead from Bonsucro. So Bonsucro's self-private-regulation did not work as well in the case as expected!

3. PRIVATE-LAW ANALYSIS

The case makes it very apparent that the various actors (including the Cambodian Government, the local companies, the Joint Capital Venture, Mr. Ly, and PAPL), had a choice of possible legal and non-legal strategies. As for the parties themselves the choice of a particular type of claim has obvious strategic implications. These concern both the private law framework and the additional conflict of laws issues. Of course, at the very start, there is the choice of forum. The plaintiffs' civil and penal claim before a Cambodian court had already faced considerable obstacles.[60] Thereafter, their choice of an English forum and the determination of the defendants were strategically interrelated. The choice of English companies as defendants was designed to lead to the jurisdiction of the English court. This choice of forum may also have been led by the consideration of the foreseeable place of enforcement, or by non-legal considerations, such as the advocacy leading to the 'boycott campaign'.

But choice-of-law issues may also influence the plaintiffs' strategy in a case such as this. This requires looking a little more deeply into the private law categories at play here.

58 For his official profile, <http://lypgroup.com/president-profile.php> accessed 28 April 2018.

59 See <https://www.bonsucro.com/> accessed 28 April 2018.

60 Particulars of Claim [14.2].

A. 'Tort of Conversion'

The plaintiffs claimed 'damages for conversion'.[61] They alleged that 'Tate & Lyles wrongfully deprived the Villagers of the ownership, use and possession of the Sugar Cane processed into the Raw Sugar and converted into its own use' and that 'by reason of the conversion, the Villagers have suffered loss and damage'.[62] As the basis of this claim, they argued that 'in the premises it is averred that at all times the Villagers have been the owners of and are entitled to possession of the Sugar Cane' and that 'the Koh Kong Companies at all material times unlawfully held and dealt with both the Land and the Sugar Cane'.[63,64]

Under the tort of conversion, the fact of conversion as well as the question of ownership and its transfer are dealt with as 'preliminary questions', subject to the *lex rei sitae*. This detour via property might come as a surprise, since in English substantive law, 'conversion' is characterised as part of tort. In the present case, it means that Cambodian law will determine the original title. Moreover, characterisation in substantive law does not necessarily coincide with characterisation used for choice of law purposes. For instance, a claim based on the 'conversion' might be characterised as 'unjustified enrichment' and fall to be determined under EU Regulation Rome II[65] by the law of the place 'where the unjust enrichment took place' rather than, as in tort, that of the place of the damage.

In either case, a problematic point is how and where to identify the place of 'damage' and the place 'where the unjust enrichment took place'. The plaintiffs alleged that their land and sugar cane as fruit from the land were converted by the defendants into their own use. In the light of this argument, there might be two different possible places as the place of damage or unjustified enrichment: one is Cambodia where the title to land, the property of the sugar cane and their possession were directly interfered with; the other is England, where the sugar refinement from the disputed sugar cane and raw sugar was finally carried out. And of course, the two places are separated geographically as are the different moments in the 'conversion'. Whichever is chosen as the connecting factor for choice-of-law purposes, both possible points of reference, the place of raw-sugar processing or the place of final refinement, can to a large extent be freely located within the value chain, with the consequences explained above as to the choice of applicable law.

However, despite some unclear points regarding the choice of applicable law to the 'conversion', the plaintiffs themselves seem to have expected that the English court would apply English tort law. From the comparative-law perspective, conversion in English law is generally seen as instituting strict liability. In fact, the rules on tort and unjustified enrichment of many other countries institute an exemption from liability in

---

61 Particulars of Claim [33].

62 Ibid., [26], [27].

63 Ibid., [21].

64 Ibid., [29]. They argued similarly against Tate & Lyle Sugars Ltd., 'to the extent that Tate & Lyles Sugars has acquired Raw Sugar processed from the Sugar Cane'.

65 European Parliament and Council Regulation (EC) 864/2007 on the law applicable to non-contractual obligations (Rome II) [2008] OJ L117/6.

cases of no-fault. English law also acknowledges a similar exception in some cases, but it does not as a matter of principle require the plaintiff to prove negligence on the part of the defendant. This divergence between the substantive rules of English tort law and other municipal laws could lead the plaintiffs to choose an English court in the expectation that the stricter standard will be applied.

B. Property

As a prerequisite of the claim for damage of conversion, the plaintiffs alleged the breach of their property right and their possession of the disputed land and sugar cane. Within the whole structure of global sugar production, the issue of property and possession should be addressed at several different stages. It regards, first, title to the land in Cambodia; second, the status of the sugar cane as fruit of that land; third, the issue of property in respect of raw sugar; fourth, the transfer of property by the import sale to an English company, which might also involve the protection of the good faith purchaser from an untitled seller; and fifth, the ownership of the sugar refined in the United Kingdom.

According to English private international law as well as the choice of law rules generally adopted in many countries,[66] the acquisition and transfer of property rights, whether movable or immovable, are governed by the *lex loci rei sitae*, that is, the law of the place where the object is located. Under this principle, the issue of property regarding separation and specification occurring at different stages of production should be subject to the law of the place at each controversial moment. For the *Song Mao* case, the aforementioned first to third issues should be ruled by Cambodian law because of the location of the object at the moment when the relevant event happened. The last and fifth issue should be ruled by English law. (For the forth issue, see below.) In comparison with the choice-of-law issues regarding the tort of conversion, the choice-of-law issues regarding the property rights are relatively easier to deal with, due to the straightforward principle of *lex loci rei sitae*. Nevertheless, it is to be noted that the principle itself leaves room for the actors involved to change the applicable law by changing the physical location of the object from one place to another.

Due to this possibility of changing the applicable law by changing the location of the object, the divergence of property law in different territories may once again provide the global enterprise with room for manipulation. Obviously, the property law system of each country involves fundamental policy concerns, and a certain vision of economic development on the scale of national territory. In particular, regarding the rule on acquisition of title to fruits, their separation and specification, the substantive property laws of each country implement a certain system of allocation of cost and benefit for investment and production. In the context of global value chains, a global enterprise can take divergences between different systems into consideration when structuring such processes.

---

[66] Historically, until the first half of the 19th century, the criterion of the owner's (seller's) domicile was predominantly applied for ruling the transfer of movable property. In this regard, as historical critical analysis, see Harata (n 54).

Thus in the *Song Mao* case, Cambodian land law calls for careful scrutiny. As observed above, in the context of conversion, the first critical point to verify is the ownership of the land and the sugar cane grown there. In this regard, the applicable law will be Cambodian law as *lex loci rei sitae*. Article 30 of the 2001 Land Law of Cambodia states: 'Any person who, for no less than five years prior to the promulgation of this law, enjoyed peaceful, uncontested possession of immovable property that can lawfully be privately possessed, has the right to request a definitive title of ownership.'

This provision of the Land Law was enacted for stabilising land ownership after the long period of turmoil throughout the country. However, despite the invitation addressed to peaceful possessors to request a definitive title, the local villagers did not apply for registration of their land property. In fact, this newly established land law worked rather to deny any legal title over the disputed land to local inhabitants. Taking advantage of their ignorance, the Government had little difficulty in recognising the land as private property of the state, upon which it concluded the land concession agreement.

Moreover, in addition to this question of title to land, Article 94 of the 2001 Cambodian Land Law provides for the ownership of fruit of land in the following manner: 'The owner of immovable property is entitled to receive all types of fruits from such property.' Considered in isolation, if the land belonged to the local people, this provision would lead to the conclusion that the local people were also entitled to the sugar cane as the fruit of the land. However, another article (article 95) opposes this, insofar as 'the fruits resulting from cultivation of land belongs to the owner of such land provided he pays third parties for the cost of plowing and harrowing works, labor done by them and seeds.' The significance of the condition of payment by the land owner is very unclear in this text. Who does the fruit belong to, if the land owner has not made or completed the payment? Does it mean that the fruit belongs to third parties (if so, who among possibly different people)? Or that the property belongs to the land owner but that he/she has a monetary obligation to third parties?

In addition to the stage of sugar cane plantation observed above, there are other different stages in the global production structure at which value accumulates. Thus, sugar cane is transformed into raw sugar, and raw sugar into refined sugar. At each stage, we need to ask to whom the increased value shall be allocated and who shall assume the cost of the increase in value. This in turn requires addressing choice-of-law issues. The applicable law will govern the allocation of cost and benefit at each stage of the Global Value Chain. Therefore, taking account here of the room open to manipulation regarding the choice of the applicable law, we must conclude that the conventional principle of *lex loci rei sitae* facilitates arbitrage of cost-benefit allocation due to divergence of property laws. Capital, in structuring global production, can divide several stages of production and locate them one by one at the place where the local law is most favourable to accumulation at each stage of the production process.

There is also another kind of arbitrage open to global enterprises in terms of choice of law. It regards the protection of the good faith purchaser. Indeed, there are once again discrepancies between the legal regimes of different countries, as can be seen at the stage where raw sugar is imported. Under the *lex rei sitae* principle, the protection of the good faith purchaser should be ruled by the law of the place of the object at the time of the alleged transfer – that is, the sales contract. Whether the purchaser can protect his/her position as owner in relation to the previous true title-holder depends on the substantive rules of the *lex loci rei sitae* at that moment. For instance, in our case, it was open to Tate & Lyle (and T & L Sugars) to move the raw sugar from Cambodia to another country – wherever the law would protect them as good faith purchaser. Changing the physical location of the object of sale, the purchaser can make his or her ownership more stable. In the whole global production structure, if an enterprise uses different legal entities and the legal form of sales contracts between them, it can manipulate title in this respect, due to the broadly adopted principle of *lex loci rei sitae*. Thus there is ample margin for leverage of institutional divergence on the part of global capital.

4. CIVIL PROCEDURE

In private law in general, the position of the plaintiff and that of the defendant are not completely similar or symmetrical, even in an adversarial system of civil procedure. Usually the burden of proof will fall to the plaintiff. For instance, in the *Song Mao* case, the plaintiffs, having framed their claim as based on the tort of conversion, need to prove their ownership of land, and that of fruits, and the conversion of sugar cane by the defendants. However, it is sufficient for the defendants to disprove only one of these elements. This dissymmetry in the civil procedure is closely connected to the facts to be proved. In our case, the plaintiffs face several difficulties on this count. First of all, who can be identified as the local villagers deprived of their land? How can the plaintiffs prove this point? More than 200 families have filed the same claim and must prove that they were respectively using and possessing the land, living in the area at the moment of eviction. In addition, the plaintiffs also must show ownership of such land for justifying their title to the sugar cane as fruit of the land. As mentioned above, they did not go through with the registration as required by the 2001 Cambodian Land Law.[67] Therefore the proof of their legal title, at least at the level of customary law, is not an easy task at all. Even more difficult, the plaintiffs must prove that the raw sugar refined by the defendants in England is the same that was produced from sugar cane planted in the disputed land.[68]

[67] See Cambodian Land Law, art. 30, para. 1: 'Any person who, for no less than five years prior to the promulgation of this law, enjoyed peaceful, uncontested possession of immovable property that can lawfully be privately possessed, has the right to request a definitive title of ownership.'

[68] In this regard, it is critical for protection of local people's interests to stop the moving of the object toward abroad. The injunction for this stoppage might be potential. But it is still unclear for the author if and how the protection of possession works in Cambodia.

5. INVOLVEMENT OF A FOREIGN HOST COUNTRY: CROSSING THE PUBLIC/PRIVATE DIVIDE

There is an advantage for global enterprise to cross the public/private divide and involve a foreign host country (like Cambodia in this case). The involvement of a foreign country can have a significant impact for civil litigation before a domestic court. Acts of foreign state (such as the concession in this case) may be considered as non-justiciable, or (as claimed by the defendants here) protected by the 'Act of State' doctrine.[69] According to this doctrine the domestic court should treat the act of a foreign country as untouchable and thereby renounce any scrutiny of its validity. In this respect, the engagement of the Cambodian Government is likely to work as a powerful defensive tool for the global sugar giant. Whatever the legal defects of the land concession under Cambodian public law or public international law, no foreign court could question its validity.

All these points show that, at least according to conventional understandings of private law including private international law, a host country intervenes in the current global setting in ways that are highly advantageous for global capital. To the contrary, local populations face many obstacles in bringing their private-law claim.

6. CONCLUSION

The global production structure analysed in this note is just one aspect of contemporary economic globalisation as a whole. It indicates that the latter is by and large based on the market mechanisms grounded in private law. In this sense, the private law or the language of private law including some concepts such as contract, property, tort etc. are essential. However, even though the language of private law has been thus globalised, the substantive rules of municipal laws are different from each other. This is where conflicts issues appear and the risk of regulatory arbitrage by powerful private actors, in the form of forum shopping and the various strategies described above.[70] Needless to say, private law and private international law are just parts of the whole toolbox for legal regulation of the global economy. Civil litigation is indeed only one option for legal ruling. But, the focus of studies on global governance is usually on international trade law, international economic law and international human rights law, which are

---

69 See *A. M. Luther v. James Sagor & Co.*, [1921] 3 K.B. 532; *Anglo-Iranian Oil Company v. Idemitsu Kosan Kabushiki Kaisha*, Dist. Ct. of Tokyo (May 27, 1953) 4(5) Kakyu Saibansho Minji Saibanreishu 755, affirmed by High Ct. of Tokyo (September 11, 1953) 6 (11) Koto Saibansho Minji Hanreishu 702.

70 On the private law infrastructure of the global economy and the possibilities of regulatory arbitrage in value chains, see H. Muir Watt, 'Private International Law Beyond The Schism' [2011] 2(3) *Transnational Legal Theory* 347; H. Muir Watt, 'Empire Through Contract: A Private International Law Perspective' in A. Cutler and T. Dietz (eds), *The Politics of Private Transnational Governance by Contract* (Abingdon, Routledge 2016).

called upon to deal with land grabbing, environmental harm, displacement of populations and other damage linked to global value chains. Private international law is a missing piece of the puzzle …

6.4 INTEGRATING ORAL CUSTOMARY PRINCIPLES IN PRIVATE INTERNATIONAL LAW: FROM THE MOUTH TO THE PEN; AND FROM THE LAND TO THE COURT

Oona Le Meur

1. INTRODUCTION: SETTING THE SCALE(S)

The *Song Mao* case is one of the many attempts to stop the Blood Sugar phenomenon,[71] which denounces the correlation between international preferential trade schemes and an increased epidemic of land-grabbing,[72] frequently accompanied with a number of human rights violations.[73] The local land-grabbing phenomenon is indeed inserted in a global chain of production.[74] Although evictions and human rights violations were not prevented, the *Song Mao* case was an attempt by local communities and activists to strategically link the local wrongs and misconducts to a broader legal and economic frame. The increasing number of cross-border large-scale land deals can be referred to as a phenomenon of 'global land grab.'[75]

One major aspect of this case is the conflation of different scales. The *Song Mao* case as heard by the UK High Court of Justice comes once all domestic remedies before national courts and commissions have been exhausted. Despite courts' general reluctance towards extraterritoriality,[76] the villagers succeeded in persuading the UK High Court to hear their case, probably because of the location of both the defendant and the contested product (i.e. the sugar) in the UK. The *Song Mao* case thus 'lucidly

[71] See Clean Sugar Campaign [Online] available at: http://www.boycottbloodsugar.net/the-campaign/, accessed on 22 October 2017

[72] The *Everything but Arms* (EBA) European trade initiative which promised a preferential trade scheme, that provides a duty-free access to the European market and a guaranteed minimum price for sugar that is on average three times higher than the world market prices. While the initial aim intended to benefit the disfavoured fringes of the population, by creating jobs through the export-led growth, it was accompanied by an increased epidemic of land-grabbing in Cambodia.

[73] Cambodia Center for Human Rights, *Cambodia: Land in Conflict An Overview of the Land Situation* (Phnom Penh, Cambodian Center for Human Rights 2013).

[74] Tomaso Ferrando, 'Land Rights at the time of global production: leveraging multispatiality and 'legal chokeholds'' (2017) *Business and Human Rights Journal*, accessible at: http://wrap.warwick.ac.uk/89680, accessed on 23 September 2017.

[75] Saturnino M. Borras and Jennifer Franco, 'Political Dynamics of Land-grabbing in Southeast Asia: Understanding Europe's Role' *Transnational Institute in the context of the Just Trade project* (Amsterdam, January 2011) 14.

[76] See *Kiobel v. Royal Dutch Petroleum Co.*, 133 S.Ct. 1659 (2013); *Vava v. Anglo American South Africa Ltd.*, 2013, EWHC 2131 (QB).

exposes the links between the localism of violence and the globalism of capital accumulation.'[77]

The global dimension of this case should not make one lose sight of the particularisms of the local context. The transplant of this case to other scales and other legal systems is unlikely to go completely smoothly. There will be transplants – whether under the forms of appropriations or injunctions. The claims of the villagers have indeed to overcome several tensions. The first one is linked to a historical background of land regimes and modalities of ownership, where a customary principle of possession, or 'acquisition by the plough', confronts since the French Protectorate, the legal (and written) principles of property (2.A). This tension is enhanced by a cultural trait of Cambodian peasantry – that has taken an imposed and violent dimension in the second part of the 20th century, i.e. agricultural mobility (2.B). This tension between possession and property in the light of the various forms of agricultural mobility are reflected in the current domestic framework, and in particular in the 2001 Land Law that is mobilised in the Particulars of Claims (PoC) of the case[78] (2.C).

The historical contextualisation and consideration given to the *longue durée* allows to replace the tension between the historical principle of possession based on actual occupancy and the colonial-inherited property principle in the light of the tension provoked by the codification of certain customary principles, and more generally of the predominance of the writing form in the legal system (3.A), which leads to the translation, and adaptation of the claims of the villagers to the exigencies of a 'graphic reasoning.'[79] Submitting the *Song Mao* case to the British conversion law will bind the villagers to a certain type of procedure which will eventually standardise their demands (3.B).

2. HISTORICAL BACKGROUND

A. Possession: the Binder of the *Millefeuille* of Land Regimes

Pursuant to the Cambodian pre-colonial codes (*kram*), which bring together the legal texts concerning land tenure, the right to land was conditional on the fact of farming it. 'The King, theoretically at least, was the lord of all the land in the kingdom, which meant that it could reward people with the right to use it.'[80] It is important to note that 'collective property was unknown.'[81] Accordingly, the traditional ownership system of

---

[77] Ferrando (n 74) 1.

[78] See *Song Mao & Others, and, Tate and Lyle Industry Limited and T&L Sugars Limited* – before the English High Court of Justice, Queen's Bench Division, Commercial Court, Particulars of Claim, 28 March 2013, hereinafter PoC. See also *Song Mao & Others, and, Tate and Lyle Industry Limited and T&L Sugars Limited* – before the English High Court of Justice, Queen's Bench Division, Commercial Court, Defence and Counterclaim of the First and Second Defendants, 2 May 2013, hereinafter Defence.

[79] Jack Goody, *La raison graphique: La domestication de la pensée sauvage* (Paris, Les éditions de minuit 1979).

[80] David Chandler, *A History of Cambodia* (New York, Avalon Publishing 2009) 22.

[81] Jean Delvert, *Le paysan cambodgien* (Paris, L'Harmattan 1994) 489.

the Khmers before the French colonisation was similar to usufruct, the recognised right to use a piece of land and benefit from its outputs.[82] Ownership was hence acquired 'by the plough' by investing any form of labour in the land. Farmers who discontinued farming for more than three years lost any rights on the land. This system was enforced all over the country. The king probably aimed at encouraging farming through this system. Nevertheless, farmers enjoyed extended rights over the land, for example the right to inherit, donate, sell, mortgage, lend and rent it. Hence the traditional system of permanent usufruct allowed the farmers to hand over to their children the right to use the land.[83]

The French Protectorate (1863–1953) kept on with this orientation but started an official turn toward a cadastral policy of land ownership registration. The king's ownership was replaced by a dual, French and Cambodian (although practically French), authority on land, by a covenant signed in 1884.[84] A cadastral policy was gradually implemented from 1902, which really took off from 1930 to 1945. However, despite this shift in private ownership, the 1920 Civil Code by the Protectorate administration, recognised the right of possession, which was similar to the pre-colonial conception. In fact, the legal opposition between 'proprietor' and 'possessor' never really gained currency, as they had exactly the same rights and duties (i.e. transmission and alienation of land). Possession could be acquired through purchase, inheritance, or occupation and exploitation during five years of a land belonging to the state or local domain and for which the farmer was attributed a 'permit of cultivation.'[85] Incidentally, the colonial frame remained in force after independence in 1953 and until the Khmer Rouge victory in 1975.

Prior to the genocide operated by the Khmer Rouge regime – following which almost two million Cambodians died from overwork, starvation, disease and execution[86] – farmers would apply dye to the borders of their plots in waterlogged rice fields to mark out their property to other growers. Such traditional systems of land demarcation worked as everyone in the community understood which families controlled different plots based on historical claims and local knowledge, rather than title deeds.[87] These systems suffered severe alterations after the genocide with the important population displacement, especially the influx of urban residents, farmers.[88]

---

[82] Indira Simbolon, 'Access to land of highland indigenous minorities: the case of plural property rights in Cambodia' (2002) 42 Working Papers, *Max Planck Institute for Social Anthropology* 8.

[83] Anne Y. Guillou, 'The Question of Land in Cambodia: Perceptions, Access, and Use since De-collectivization' (2006) 9–10 *Moussons* 299–324, 302.

[84] Ibid., 304.

[85] Jan Ovesen, Ing Brigitte Trankell and Joakim Öjendal, *When every household is an island. Social organization and power structures in rural Cambodia* (Uppsala and Stockholm, Uppsala University and SIDA 1996) 47.

[86] Matthew S. Weltig, *Pol Pot's Cambodia* Revised Edn (Minneapolis, Twenty-First Century Books, 2012).

[87] Guillou (n 83).

[88] John Tully, *A Short History of Cambodia: From Empire to Survival* (Crows Nest, Allen & Unwin 2006).

The Khmer Rouge regime (1975–79) completely broke away from the dynamics described above. It implemented a Maoist communist system promoting ultra-collectivism where everything became common property of the state. Private property was totally abolished and the right to property – previously gained by working the land – became merely a right to work on it. All agricultural lands were collectivised. Market economy, as well as business activities, were abolished. All land records, including cadastral maps and titles were destroyed.

The following regime, the People's Republic of Kampuchea (PRK) (1979–89) put in place by the Vietnamese forces and the Soviet Union in 1979, did not have any register of legal titles to agricultural land, hence claims to ownership of residential land were mainly based on actual occupancy. Adding to the complexity, the PRK called for the internally displaced population to go back to their village of origin of the pre-Democratic Kampuchea period. Although a socialist economic model was implemented, and policies of solidarity and collectivism were adopted, the state reintroduced limited private ownership rights as they were defined by the French civil code, which has been abolished by the Khmer Rouge. The possession principle was nonetheless underlying, as these rights were only available to Cambodian citizens who had used and cultivated their land continuously for at least one year before the promulgation of these policies. The principle that land left vacant for more than three years reverted to state ownership, was readopted.

'[T]here are landowners only where cadaster has been achieved … and elsewhere possession was hegemonic.'[89] The importance of the principle of possession has been a central characteristic of land tenure dynamics from precolonial times, up until now, and even through colonisation. The idea of justifying possession by investment in labour has to be understood in light of a crucial characteristic of Cambodian peasantry, i.e. mobility.

B. Mobility as a Way of Life and Mobility for Survival

'Contrary to the representation of a peasantry deeply rooted in bounded localities and traditions, the history of Cambodian farmers bears the hallmark of mobility.'[90] These practices of 'fluid semi-nomadism'[91] are linked to the weak definition of the 'village' as a community or social entity. Villages – or *phum* – are administrative entities formalised under the colonial regime that never really acquired a strong social, political or administrative consistency. For Delvert and Ovesen, it is the house which is the essence of the rural Cambodian life.[92]

To this traditional agricultural mobility was added the displacements of populations following protracted situations of generating measures of village groupings, forced

89 Pel Sokha, Pierre-Yves Le Meur, Sam Vitou, Laing Lan, Pel Setha, Hay Leakhena and Im Sothy, *Land Transactions in Rural Cambodia A Synthesis of Findings from Research on Appropriation and Derived Rights to Land*, Gret online edition [www.gret.org] vol. 18, May 2008, p. 229.

90 Ibid.

91 Jacques Népoté, *Parenté et organisation sociale dans le Cambodge moderne et contemporain* (Geneva, Olizane 1992) 171.

92 Delvert (n 81) and Ovesen et al. (n 85).

displacements of population and escape strategies; especially the forced displacements during the Khmer Rouge regime and intense movement in the post-conflict 1980s. 'Almost at once, nearly everyone began moving. … [H]undreds of thousands of Cambodians crisscrossed the country looking for relatives, returning to their homes, trading, or seeking refuge overseas.'[93]

Today, new forms of mobility have emerged. They take roots on one hand in the development of land markets bought by external economic actors (entrepreneurs and officials). Farmers sell their land for various reasons (among them distress sale, increasing speculation, or even threat), and leave peri-urban areas to move to peripheral zones.[94] It would seem that a cycle of mobility is at play related to the development of peri-urban land markets pushing farmers to remote areas.[95]

C. The Domestic Legal Framework: the Ambiguities of the 2001 Land Law

In 1992 a Land Law was enacted, in order to rebuild a property registry to facilitate Cambodia's transition from a state-based to a market economy. The multiple conflicts over land were accentuated by the government's large-scale land titling programme which aims to have all of the country's land formally registered by 2023. Four million applications were submitted but in almost a decade, only 15 of them had been processed due to the limited capacity of the government.[96]

This land-titling programme shows how ownership and property are at the core of this Land Law. However other forms of property rights are also recognised, such as possession, concessions, leases, usufruct, easements, etc.[97] For example pursuant to article 30 of the 2001 Land Law:

> [A]ny person who, for no less than five years prior to the promulgation of this law, enjoyed peaceful, uncontested possession of immovable property that can lawfully be privately possessed, has the right to request a definitive title of ownership. In case the granting of a definitive title to ownership is subject to an opposition, the claimant has to prove that he himself fulfils the conditions of peaceful, uncontested possession for no less than five years over the contested immovable property or to prove that he purchased the immovable property from the original possessor or his legal beneficiary or from the person to whom the ownership was transferred, or from their successors.

The conditions to claim land ownership are detailed in article 38: '[I]n order to transform into ownership of immovable property, the possession shall be unambiguous, non-violent, notorious to the public, continuous and in good faith'.

---

[93] Chandler (n 80) 229.

[94] Sovannarit So, Sopheap Real, Uch Utey, Sy Rathmony, Brett Ballard and Sarthi Acharya, 'Social Assessment of Land in Cambodia. A Field Study' Working paper 20, Phnom Penh: Cambodia Development Resource Institute, 2001.

[95] Sokha et al. (n 89).

[96] Simbolon (n 82) 14.

[97] Sokha et al. (n 89) 222.

The lack of clarity led to a certain number of difficulties observed in practice[98] or recorded before tribunals.[99] The only exception to the generalisation of the private ownership category exists for the peoples considered as 'ethnic minorities'. These populations have been granted the possibility to apply for an 'Indigenous Community Property' title, which is a collective ownership title. 'This collective ownership includes all of the rights and protections of ownership as are enjoyed by private owners' (article 26), but it is inalienable. Although this policy was a concession made by the government for the respect of indigenous rights originally, it tends to rigidify the ethnic boundaries by defining them in the abstract and using these boundaries as an unambiguous basis for land-titling. Moreover, it relies on a common misconception of collective ownership whereas, these groups, as several others in the world, combine collective and individual forms of property rights.[100]

As previously discussed, the history of land regime as well as the current legal framework explain the grey area in which the villagers of the *Song Mao* case find themselves concerning their ownership rights. Looking carefully at the Particular of Claims, the villagers claim that they have been occupying the land 'since at least 1996' (§ 7).

Moorstein, the first lawyer that took the villagers' claim to the court, asserted that:

> [T]his case was a lot simpler than people really understood it to be because essentially what was happening was that if in fact this was an illegal taking, the crops still belonged to the villager – if we could establish that ownership really did reside in the hands of the villagers themselves. And wherever the crops went, so did title.[101]

Establishing that the villagers are the owners by virtue of the principle of possession, and not in terms of proprietory titles, is the real breakthrough of this case.

3. REVEALING LAW'S TEETH:[102] REPLACING THE 'ACQUISITION BY THE PLOUGH' WITH THE 'ACQUISITION BY THE PEN'

The heart of the problem lies in the coexistence of two types of ownership which are property and possession. Not only do these two notions carry a different conceptual and

---

98 Ibid.

99 Fabienne Luco, *Between a Tiger and a Crocodile: Management of Local Conflicts in Cambodia. An Anthropological Approach to Traditional and New Practices* (Phnom Penh, UNESCO 2002).

100 Jonathan Padwe, 'Highlands of history: Indigenous identity and its antecedents in Cambodia' (2013) 54(3) *Asia Pacific Viewpoint* 282–95.

101 Quoted by Joel Brinkley in 'Cambodia's government land grabs', *Politico*, 5 May 2013, available at: https://www.politico.com/story/2013/05/lawyer-works-to-put-end-to-cambodia-land-grabbing-090985?o=2, accessed on 23 October 2017.

102 Expression borrowed from Karl Llewellyn. See Karl N. Llewellyn and E. Adamson Hoebel, *The Cheyenne Way; Conflict and Case Law in Primitive Jurisprudence* (Norman, OK, University of Oklahoma Press 1941) 283.

theoretical weight, but they also differ in their modalities of recognition. Whereas property is usually recognised by a written land title; possession is based on oral customary notions of community consensus and existing occupation. According to Springer, 'the discrepancy between such orally recognized antecedents and the written word of law have been at the heart of the recent wave of dispossessions that have swept across the country.'[103] Springer goes as far as championing the idea that 'evictions in Cambodia are often literally underwritten by the articles of law'[104] and that the 'firm distinction between possessions and property, where the former is premised upon actual use and the latter is embedded in exploitation, [shows] how proprietorship is inextricably bound to the violence of law.'[105] Indeed between 1925 and 1975, 90% of private land in Cambodia was held in possession and 10% was held in formal ownership.[106] This leads to the paradox represented by the *Song Mao* case, where the villagers have been evicted 'illegally' through the written articles of the law. Besides, the legal framework is also unable to take into account the fact that agrarian contracts and the subsequent rights are much more diverse and context-specific than the broad categories of lease and loan recognised by (domestic) law.

The *Song Mao* case hence raises the issue of land rights' securing in the context of blurred frontiers and actors: the national and the international conflate in the global, as well as public and private categories overlap and combine, as in the case of a collusion between the state of Cambodia and private multinational actors.[107] The economic land concessions (ELC) that are at the heart of the dispute, have indeed been finger pointed by several NGOs as lacking a clear and transparent process of acquisition, which has allowed several arrangements with some state officials.[108]

If property is already a 'soft' category of law, that has evolved and extended over time,[109] possession is on the other hand a wide-open gap; a breach through which a different type of reasoning, other than the legal one, could infiltrate itself. In other words, possession is a logic that goes against legal categories. It is a possibility to think of normativity in a radically different way. Possession indeed stems from customs, usages and traditional practices. As shown in the extensive historical contextualisation, they have been prevalent until the French Protectorate, which imposed individual property without being able to completely erase the former practice of possession. What happens with the current land-grabbing phenomenon is that the 2001 Land Law,

---

[103] Simon Springer, 'Illegal Evictions? Overwriting Possession and Orality with Law's Violence in Cambodia', Conference Paper No. 14, Land grabbing, conflict and agrarian-environmental transformations: perspectives from East and Southeast Asia, Chiang Mai University, 5–6 June 2015, p. 2.

[104] Ibid.

[105] Ibid.

[106] Kheang Un and Sokbunthoeun So, 'Land Rights in Cambodia: How Neopatrimonial Politics Restricts Land Policy Reform' (2011) 84(2) *Pacific Affairs* 289–308, 305.

[107] There is for example a senator involved in the *Song Mao* case. See PoC paras. 4 and 6.3 and Defence para. 4.2.

[108] Un and So (n 106).

[109] Marie-Angèle Hermitte, 'Les concepts mous de la propriété industrielle: passage du modèle de la propriété foncière au modèle du marché' in Bernard Edelman and Marie-Angèle Hermitte, *L'homme, la nature et le droit* (Paris, Bourgeois 1988).

which promotes property through the promotion of land titles over possession, turns a blind eye on the violent appropriation of possessions based on actual use ('acquisition by the plough') and thereby legitimises the institution of property ('acquisition by the sword') – as shown by the numerous violations of human rights listed in the *Song Mao* case, which is far from being an isolated example) – hoping that it becomes an entrenched legal institution ('acquisition by the pen').[110] Hence the land-grabbing phenomenon is made possible by the legal structure and its operations,[111] such as transforming lands owned through possession into individual properties asserted by written titles of ownership. The violence of the institution of property is indeed erased through 'law's pen'.

A. Law's Pen and Custom's Mouth: listening for a Change?[112]

The written form, and especially the legal written documents, tend to decontextualise the objects from their history, traditions, cultural contexts. '*Le discours ne dépend plus d'une "circonstance": il devient intemporel. Il n'est plus solidaire d'une personne; mis sur papier, il devient plus abstrait, plus dépersonnalisé.*'[113] The written form, through the codification of some customs and usages, operates a selection among them. However, especially in terms of land registration, the legal reasoning can hardly be coupled to social practices.[114] Indeed, once the lands have been registered, its future does not reside in the customs practised by the people living on them, but by an administrative injunction. The land registration is not a means to secure rights anymore and to resolve conflicts, but an instrument of domination.[115]

There are several populations, especially those labelled as indigenous populations, that have been confronted by the de-legitimation of their oral traditions by the Western legal field, that only recognises and accepts written and cartographic documentations concerning territory and property. John Borrows for example shows how oral history was de-legitimised because it is multifaceted and spoken under the influence of present concern and values.[116]

In the *Song Mao* case, recognising that the villagers were the owners of the lands which they were farming, by virtue of the customary principle of possession, would be recognising that oral customary practices and written legal land titles are not mutually exclusive, but rather a continuum characterised by a plurality of situations of transition.[117] However, the quick diffusion of land titles is usually preferred to the recognition and valorisation of customary land occupation. The 2001 Land Law for

110 Springer (n 103) 9.

111 Yan Thomas, *Les opérations du droit* (Paris, EHESS Gallimard Seuil 2011).

112 Expression borrowed from John Borrows's article 'Listening for a Change: The Courts and Oral Tradition' (2001) 39(1) *Osgoode Hall Law Journal* 1–38.

113 Goody (n 79) 97.

114 Volker Stamm, 'Formaliser les pratiques coutumières. Europe médiévale, Afrique coloniale et contemporaine' (2013) 19(1) *Etudes rurales* 169–89, 172.

115 Martin Chanock, *Law, Custom and Social Order: the Colonial Experience in Malawi and Zambia* (Cambridge, Cambridge University Press 1985).

116 Borrows (n 112) 9.

117 Stamm (n 114) 170.

example was accompanied by a *Systematic Land Registration* (SLR) programme that encouraged the privatisation of land by integrating the titles distributed to a formalised cadastral registration system.[118] The primary minister Hun Sen pushed the country to open up to the global flows of capital, and the World Bank in particular, has been one of the primary drivers of a formal land registration process. Coupled with the SLR programme, a *Land Management and Administration Project* (LMAP) was launched in 2002, in order to improve land tenure security by establishing an institutional framework for land administration and especially encouraging the issuance and registration of titles.[119]

However, fieldwork has shown that the conversion of oral claims into written deeds did ultimately fail because those titles often sank into oblivion when land was bought or sold. The cadastral records hence quickly fell into disuse.[120] This shows that the significance of the Land Law and the Land Titles was not integrated yet and that the villagers' understanding of land holding continued to be rooted in the traditional principle of possession instead of property. Others have argued that titling conducted by LMAP was an exclusionary process in that it precisely avoided directing efforts toward those who were most vulnerable to eviction.[121]

Nevertheless, all these programmes launched by the Cambodian State under the impulsion of international donors have not mitigated land conflict but on the contrary increased the vulnerability of villagers especially to evictions by making the need for written titles to prove ownership unavoidable. Any possible recourse by the evictees is hence very limited as their claims on the land are based on the customary principle of possession and actual use, and not reflected in official documentation or legal titles. This is a stance that may contribute to the production of legitimacy for land-grabbing, even as it seeks to curb its excesses.

B. An Injunction of Analogy?

The choice to bring the *Song Mao* case to English Courts – even if few options were left – translating it into a case of conversion law necessarily submits the claims to an

---

[118] Marie Mellac and Christian Castellanet, *Histoires divergentes d'une convergence sous tension: les réformes foncières vers la propriété privée dans quatre pays du Mékong* (Birmanie, Cambodge, Laos et Viêt-Nam), Paris: Technical Committee on 'Land Tenure and Development', 2015.

[119] World Bank, *Land Management and Administration Project*, Cambodia, 2011, available at: http://web.worldbank.org/external/projects/main?pagePK=64283627&piPK=73230&theSitePK=40941&menuPK=228424&Projectid=P070875, accessed on 9 October 2017.

[120] See in particular Sokbunthoeun So, *Political Economy of Land Registration in Cambodia*, PhD Dissertation, Department of Political Science, Daniel Unger (director), Northern Illinois University, 2009.

[121] Mark Grimsditch and Nick Henderson, *Untitled Tenure Insecurity and Inequality in the Cambodian Land Sector*. Phnom Penh: Bridges Across Borders Southeast Asia, Centre on Housing Rights and Evictions, Jesuit Refugee Service, 2009.

'injunction of analogy.'[122] If a written title of property does already operate a process of abstraction, the translation of a claim into legal categories is a further step away from the social conceptions and relations that were at the origins of the claim.[123]

> When law comes to take on the form most familiar to us, that of authoritative rules and doctrines expressed in their own queer, technical language, gaining precision from the operations of technical specialists at work in their own peculiar context of technique, then Law becomes a world of its own. It is a world like *Alice's Looking-Glass* – both difficult to break into, and difficult, once one has become acclimated to it, to break out of.[124]

The claims, even if based on oral traditions and actual occupancy (as is the case for the notion of possession), necessarily will be submitted to the exigencies of conversion law procedures, such as in particular the evidence requirements. Conversion is often defined as an interference with a persons' right to property without the owner's consent and without lawful justification.[125] The burden is on the plaintiff to establish a conversion claim.[126] The villagers must establish at least the plaintiff's interest in the property, the identity of the property and of the defendant, the value of the property. They must also establish that the defendant exercised dominion over the property and that the exercise of dominion was intentionally committed. In other words, the plaintiff must prove that the defendant(s) intentionally interfered with the plaintiff's possession and that the defendant(s)'s acts are the legal cause of the plaintiff's loss of property. These are established through testimonies and documentary evidences. Looking at the Particulars of Claim, the villagers claim the land on the basis of the principle of possession but are not able to offer any written proof (§7), which the Defence does not fail to notice (§2.2 and 5).[127] Although the land-grabbing processes have been documented, notably because they have been the theatre of gross human rights violations,[128] it is not self-evident that English courts will be able to listen, let alone hear the Cambodian understanding of possession. Moreover, the Particulars of Claim is framed around a heavy insistence on the assumption that the Defendants knew or should have known about the land-grabbing and the human rights violations. However, in conversion law a defendant's intentions towards a plaintiff are not relevant.[129] Finally, for the courts to deliver a judgment over the land-grabbing in term of conversion would mean to take a stance on the legal validity of land titles issued by the Cambodian government in virtue

122 Expression borrowed from Louis Assier-Andrieu, 'Brève Théorie Culturelle du Droit', in Helge Dedek and Shauna Van Praagh, *Stateless Law, Evolving Boundaries of a Discipline* (Farnham, Juris Diversitas, Ashgate 2015) 88.

123 Marie Angèle-Hermitte, 'Le droit est un autre monde' (1998) *Enquête* 7–17.

124 Llewellyn and Hoebel (n 102) 41.

125 Andrew Burrows (ed), *English Private Law* 3rd edn (Oxford, Oxford University Press 2013), available at: Oxford Scholarship Online, 2013. doi: 10.1093/acprof:oso/9780199661770.001.0001, accessed on 23 September 2017.

126 Ibid.

127 See Defence (n 78).

128 PoC (n 78) paras 13–15.

129 Burrows (n 125).

of national laws, which would be an assertion of jurisdiction over the internal affairs of a foreign state. That is why the Defence relies on the 'Act of State' doctrine.[130]

4. CONCLUSION

Although the case was listed to start in the Commercial Court in London on 1 October 2014, it disappeared from the listings of the court.[131] A swap in the lawyers firm might have delayed the action at first,[132] but three years after it is impossible to obtain any information about the most recent developments of the case. We actively tried to contact the lawyers' firm that took on the case in 2014, Leigh Day, to learn more about the recent developments of the case. We were unable to obtain any answer. We will hence not be able to comment on the final decision in this case. This contribution nevertheless aimed to highlight crucial issues through the lens of legal anthropology by raising issues highlighting alternative understandings of ownership, different from property notions; emphasising the role of the writing in constituting a 'graphic reasoning'[133] which is overwhelmingly predominant in legal systems recognised by global law.

[130] Defence (n 78) para. 8.5.

[131] Russell Hopkins, 'Did the Cambodian sugar case settle?' *Corporate War Crimes. Issues around allegations of corporate complicity in human rights violations*, 1 May 2015, available at: https://corporatewarcrimes.com/2015/05/01/did-the-cambodian-sugar-case-settle/, accessed 24 October 2017.

[132] Peter Zsombor, 'Lawyer Swap Delays "Blood Sugar" Trial in UK' *Cambodian Daily*, 16 October 2014, available at: https://www.cambodiadaily.com/archives/lawyer-swap-delays-blood-sugar-trial-in-uk-69998/, accessed on 18 November 2017.

[133] Expression borrowed from the French Translation of Jack Goody's *Domestication of the Savage Mind* (n 79).

7. Non-state authority: *FIFA*

7.1 CASE BACKGROUND

The tragic deaths of hundreds of construction workers (allegedly) in the course of intensive building work of the stadiums for FIFA's 2022 Qatar World Cup are no doubt an inauspicious starting point for the analysis of the new spaces of normative interaction that are now generally considered to be a feature of the global legal order. The latter offers a complex body of different transnational rules that coexist and conflict, beyond the remit of nation-States – whose collective 'loss of control' is by no means accidental or inevitable.[1] The global labour market is perhaps the best example of a new paradigm of non-state (if not private) normativity. While domestic markets become increasingly flexible – take the new trend of zero-hour contracts practised by companies like Uber or Deliveroo – a new arena emerges in which multinational corporations control various industries all over the globe in accordance with their own corporate codes and soft law.

In 2010, the Gulf State of Qatar won the bid to host the 2022 World Cup. Following this, Qatar started carrying out multi-billion construction projects for numerous rail lines, roads, a new international airport, the world's largest green-field project and, of course, several stadiums that will host the World Cup matches. Qatar relies largely on migrant workers from South Asia (India, Sri Lanka, Nepal or Bangladesh) who according to some estimates comprise more than 90% of the country's workforce. They are employed under the controversial *kafala* system, that puts employees under near total control of their employers. Working in conditions that are close to a form of modern slavery, these workers are often subject to human rights abuses by their employers (i.e. confiscated passports and long work hours in extreme heat for very little or no pay). In 2013, the first report on the exploitation of migrant workers in Qatar was published in a report called 'The Case Against Qatar' by the International Trades Union Confederation. This has led to accusations that over 1,200 FIFA World Cup workers have died because of the harsh working conditions in Qatar, triggering a global wave of criticism against the Qatari Government and FIFA.

While nobody held FIFA directly accountable for the horrendous condition of the foreign workforce in Qatar, its failure to make pressure on the Qatari Government was stigmatised. Indeed, despite the fact that FIFA said it expected compliance with international standards from all host countries, it omitted to take any measures ensuring that Qatar was upholding its commitments in this respect. Arguably, FIFA wielded sufficient private power to impose minimum welfare standards upon non-compliant hosts. In other words, within a global network-like constellation made of public and private actors, FIFA constituted a 'pressure-point' through which international norms could be channelled. This seems to concord with a wider pattern in which private actors are entrusted with a duty of care that extends to places where more traditional modes of prescription and enforcement are impotent. Does this mean that a new form of transnational non-state authority is emerging?

---

1 Saskia Sassen, *Losing Control? Sovereignty in the Age of Globalization* (New York, Columbia University Press 1996).

7.2 FIFA AND HUMAN RIGHTS IN QATAR

Franck Latty

The question of FIFA's control on the working conditions of the people building the infrastructures for the 2022 World Cup in Qatar evidences some recent developments in international law. The weaknesses inherent in a global system based on the inter-state distribution of political power, coupled with low-level integration of international society, are offset by actions of global private actors. The deployment of transnational power, through a variety of legal processes, undermines traditional notions of public and private international law.

An overly formalist approach to the case *FIFA and the World Cup in Qatar* may obscure the underlying issues. Under such an approach, one might say that Qatar, a sovereign State, can freely regulate labour relations in its territory within the limits of its international obligations.[2] If it does not respect those obligations, it must assume the consequences imposed by the international legal order through existing procedures (albeit still limited) of control, sanction and responsibility.[3] By contrast, such responsibility does not apply to FIFA, a mere entity (incidentally far from exemplary)[4] incorporated under Swiss law that cannot interfere with the sovereignty of a State to decide its own laws and modes of implementation.

A more 'realist' approach would instead present FIFA for what it is: a leading political and financial power; the organisation responsible for the regulation of the world's most popular sport and unifying global event, the men's football World Cup. Qatar has done everything in its power to host the game on its territory in 2022[5] and will likely be willing to make more concessions to avoid losing this privilege. As a result, the balance of power works favourably for FIFA to impose obligations to

---

2 On 1 January 2018, Qatar is party to only six conventions of the International Labor Organization: Convention No. 29 on Forced Labor 1930; Convention No. 81 on the Labor Inspection 1947; Convention No. 105 on the Abolition of Forced Labor 1957; Convention No. 111 concerning Discrimination (Employment and Occupation) 1958; Convention No. 138 on the Minimum Age 1973; Convention No. 182 on the worst forms of child labor 1999. It is not a party to the two 1966 Covenants on civil and political rights and economic, social and cultural rights.

3 In 2014, the delegates to the 103rd Session of the International Labor Conference lodged a complaint against Qatar concerning the non-observance of Conventions 29 and 81 by that State as a result of the *kafala* system and conditions of work on the World Cup construction sites. In light of the legislative and other measures taken by Qatar and the initiation of the ILO technical cooperation program in Qatar, the ILO Governing Body closed the complaint process in November 2017 (ILO, Document GB.331/INS/13, § 5).

4 See Anne Brasseur's report on good football governance to the Committee on Culture, Science, Education and Media at the Parliamentary Assembly of the Council of Europe, Doc. 14452, 15 December 2017 (specifically §§ 1–13, recalling the latest scandals around FIFA).

5 The Swiss, French, American and Brazilian courts are investing the conditions of the FIFA award on the 2022 World Cup, due to serious suspicions of electoral fraud ('Mondial 2022: les charges s'accumulent contre le Qatar', *Le Monde* (1 December 2017)). The Parliamentary Assembly of the Council of Europe, in Resolution 2053 (2015) on the reform of football governance, considering that the decision to award the organisation of the 2022 World Cup in Qatar was 'radically flawed' (see Resolution 2053 (2015)).

improve the conditions of the workers who are building the infrastructures for the event and thereby to further advance human rights in Qatar.

As a compromise between the two approaches, FIFA, in its position as a global actor, should no longer be a passive player regarding the respect of human rights in the football industry. Clearly, as one observes the emerging role of non-State actors in global regulation, there is a need in order to attain such an end (1) for adequate legal means to do so (2).

1. THE END: FIFA'S OBLIGATION TO RESPECT AND ENSURE RESPECT FOR HUMAN RIGHTS

FIFA's status as an association under Swiss law does not prevent it from having an international dimension: FIFA is invested with power that is not confined within Swiss borders. FIFA unites national football associations from 211 'countries' (some of which do not correspond, for various historical or political reasons, to sovereign States). These national associations, subject to FIFA's *jurisdiction*, govern football on their respective territories. Footballers and their associated clubs constitute therefore the base of a global pyramid of which FIFA is the summit. As a result, a '*lex fifa*'[6] – which is the football version of the general *lex sportiva* – is produced, along the lines of the concept of *lex mercatoria* as a body of transnational norms created by private organisations. There is, however, much debate over *lex mercatoria*'s status as a legal system, particularly owing to the archipelagic nature of transnational commercial standards.[7] On the other hand, institutional rules created by international sports organisations, such as the Olympic Charter as the 'constitution' of the global sports events; the harmonisation of anti-doping laws through the World Anti-Doping Agency (WADA); and the establishment of an independent dispute resolution mechanism for sports, the Court of Arbitration for Sport (CAS), shape an authentic global legal order for sport.[8]

Notably, the *lex fifa* does not simply lay down the 'rules of the game,' or discipline, organisation of competitions, technical characteristics of the equipment, etc. It also is concerned with the status of its players (i.e. nationality of players as opposed to the nationality of the State[9]) and their activities in the field of sport. Thus, FIFA has adopted a Regulation on the Status and Transfer of Players, whose global reach is likely to supplant the application of domestic law. As an example, in the unilateral termination dispute between a Brazilian football player and the Qatari club Al Khor

---

6 Franck Latty, 'La *lex fifa*', in Mathieu Maisonneuve (ed.), *Droit et coupe du monde* (Paris, Economica 2011) 9s.

7 Cf. Paul Lagarde, 'Approche critique de la *lex mercatoria*', in *Le droit des relations économiques internationales. Etudes offertes à Berthold Goldman* (Paris, Litec 1982) 139. The author considers that due to the extremely diversified environment of international economic operators and its compartmentalisation, 'international trade looks like individual *islands* of organization, rather than a single organization.'

8 Franck Latty, *La* lex sportiva – *Recherche sur le droit transnational* (Leiden, Martinus Nijhoff Publishers 2007) 41s.

9 Johanna Guillaumé, 'L'autonomie de la nationalité sportive' (2011) *Journal du droit international (Clunet)* 313s.

SC, the CAS did not apply Qatari law, to which the employment contract referred. The CAS considered that

> the principle of universal application of FIFA rules … meets the requirements of rationality, security, and legal predictability. All members of the global football family are subject to the same rules … the resulting uniformity ensures equality of treatment for all recipients of these standards, irrespective of the country in which they are located.[10]

Quite evidently, the employment contracts of workers building the stadiums in Qatar are not regulated by FIFA regulations. The latter are thereby unable to challenge Qatari law. Moreover, neither Qatar nor the World Cup infrastructure construction companies, those outside of the 'global football family,'[11] come within the remit of FIFA's labour law. However, in accordance with its own statutes, FIFA aims to 'improve the game of football constantly and promote it globally in the light of its unifying educational, cultural *and humanitarian values*.'[12] As a member of the Olympic Movement, FIFA is obliged to respect the Olympic Charter, establishing as a 'Fundamental Principle' the goal of Olympism to 'place sport at the service of the harmonious development of humankind with a view to promoting a peaceful society concerned with the preservation of human dignity.'[13] These principles are integral to the transnational public sports policy, building on the fundamental values that animate the sports movement. Additionally, the CAS contributes to these goals by borrowing from both national and international law and applying the resulting principles to international sports organisations.[14]

In this regard, the *kafala* system and undignified conditions of Qatari construction workers undoubtedly conflict with the public policy of the *lex sportiva*. FIFA, therefore, has an obligation to ensure that preparations for its main competition (the men's World Cup) do not give rise to any serious breach of the principles relevant to the humanistic foundations supposedly at the core of the international sports movement.

The same obligation is likely to stem from international human rights law, which not only imposes obligations on States but also on private actors. Notwithstanding the question of direct horizontal effect of international conventions for the protection of human rights[15] (i.e. applicability to private interpersonal relations), various international instruments have been adopted to address corporations directly,[16] such as the

---

10 CAS 2014/A/3505, *Al Khor SC v. C.*, award of December 3 2014, § 85 (comm. Franck Latty in 'Chronique de jurisprudence arbitrale en matière sportive' (M. Maisonneuve ed.) (2005) 3 *Revue de l'arbitrage* 932s.

11 Ibid.

12 Art. 2, *litt. a*, FIFA Statutes, the FIFA Statutes and all documents from this organisation are available on <www.fifa.com>.

13 Fundamental Principle 2 of the Olympic Charter.

14 Latty (n 8) 341s.

15 With regard to the horizontal direct effect of certain conventions for the protection of human rights in French case law, see Y. Kerbrat, 'La responsabilité des entreprises peut-elle être engagée pour des violations du droit international ?', in H. Ghérari and Y. Kerbrat (eds.), *L'entreprise dans la société internationale* (Paris, Pedone 2010) 103, 104.

16 See Olivier De Schutter, 'The Challenge of Imposing Human Rights Norms on Corporate Actors' in O. De Schutter (ed.), *Transnational Corporations and Human Rights* (Oxford, Hart Publishing 2006) 1–22.

OECD Guidelines and those of the United Nations.[17] Though formally considered as soft law, these instruments contribute to the formation of customary corporate duties.[18] These principles are therefore equally applicable to FIFA, despite its status as an association, by reason of its transnational economic activities. The companies FIFA owns, their subsidiaries, and the profits it generates parallel those of a leading multinational firm.[19]

FIFA amended its statutes in 2016 to include Article 3, which stipulates 'FIFA is committed to respect all internationally recognised human rights and shall strive to promote the protection of these rights.' This clause does not seemingly codify a pre-existing obligation drawn from the sports legal order or from the international legal order. It is phrased as a voluntary commitment by FIFA ('FIFA is committed to …').

Nevertheless, the obligation exists regardless of its origins (i.e. from a statutory commitment, codification of a pre-existing obligation) and motives (i.e. sincere commitment to human rights, desire to improve its image or preserve the reputation and the future of the goose that lays the golden eggs: FIFA World Cup). In the 'specific instance' before the Swiss National Contact Point, FIFA has acknowledged that it

> follows guidance from the OECD Guidelines and the UN Guiding Principles on Business and Human Rights and accepts responsibility in terms of contributing to ensure, including through the use of its leverage, a due diligence process in the FIFA World Cup™-related construction sites and in collaboration with the relevant and competent actors …[20]

In doing so, FIFA contributes to reinforcing customary corporate guidelines.[21]

This raises the question of the extent to which FIFA can fulfil such obligations, given that FIFA's normative power is limited to the persons under its *jurisdiction*. FIFA can impose its human rights standards on football players, clubs, national or continental

---

17 OECD Guidelines for Multinational Enterprises, adopted in 1976 and several revisions; 'Ruggie Principles' adopted in 2011 by the United Nations Human Rights Council (Guiding Principles on Human Rights and Business, A/HRC/17/31).

18 *See Urbaser SA et al. v. Argentine* 2016 ICSID case No ARB/07/26, 1193s., where the tribunal considers that as a subject of international law an investor is likely obligated to respect human rights. From a doctrinal perspective, see Laurence Boisson de Chazournes, 'Conclusions', in SFDI, *L'entreprise multinationale et le droit international* (Paris, Pedone 2017) 514–15; Monique Chemiller-Gendreau, 'L'entreprise est-elle soumise aux règles du droit international?', in Alain Supiot (ed.), *L'entreprise dans un monde sans frontières. Perspectives économiques et juridiques* (Paris, Dalloz 2015) 100–01.

19 See the initial assessment by the Swiss National Contact Point (NCP) following referral by Building and Woodworkers' International (BWI) on violations of the *OECD Guidelines for Multinational Enterprises* related to the construction of the infrastructure for the 2022 World Cup in Qatar. The NCP noted that FIFA conducts international operations at a multinational level; and that FIFA's involvement in the organization of the 2022 World Cup could be considered a commercial activity, resulting in the applicability of FIFA to the OECD Guidelines (Initial assessment in the specific circumstance of FIFA submitted by BWI, 13 October 2015, 6). See also John Ruggie, *For the Game. For the World. FIFA and Human Rights* (Corporate Responsibility Initiative Report, No 68, Cambridge, MA, Harvard Kennedy School, 2016) 10.

20 Swiss National Contact Point Final Communiqué in the specific instance on FIFA submitted by BWI, 2 May 2017, § 6, 4.

21 See above.

football associations, all of which directly or indirectly operate under its umbrella of authority.[22] However, the *lex fifa* does not extend beyond those who are specifically affiliated. While FIFA cannot impose its transnational regulatory power on states or public works companies, FIFA can resort to original legal procedures to promote the respect for human rights obligations in international competitions.

2. THE MEANS: FIFA'S LEGAL SCHEMES TO ENSURE RESPECT FOR HUMAN RIGHTS

The construction site scandals in Qatar have led FIFA to present itself – ostentatiously – as an agent promoting respect for internationally recognised human rights. Following the introduction of Article 3 on the respect of human rights in its statutes, based on recommendations from John Ruggie,[23] FIFA created an Advisory Council on Human Rights that met for the first time in March 2017.[24] FIFA also adopted the 'FIFA's Human Rights Policy' in May 2017, which 'specifies FIFA's statutory human rights commitment and outlines FIFA's approach to its implementation in accordance with the UN Guiding Principles on Business and Human Rights.' Laying aside the 'advertising' dimension of such document, the policy includes a number of FIFA commitments that could be binding on it. These include, in tandem with its statutes, an obligation to make every effort in the promotion of human rights, notably that:

> FIFA will strive to go beyond its responsibility to respect human rights, as enshrined in the UNGPs, by taking measures to promote the protection of human rights and positively contribute to their enjoyment, especially where it is able to apply effective leverage to help increase said enjoyment or where this relates to strengthening human rights in or through football.[25]

What then are the legal means available for FIFA to fulfil its obligations to prevent or remedy situations such as those experienced by the Qatari construction workers?

First, FIFA can make sure that its affiliates handle the issue directly. The organisation of the World Cup is not directly managed by FIFA, but rather entrusted to a member association (namely the Russian Federation in 2018 and Qatari Federation for 2022) which has to create a local organising committee. As outlined in the FIFA Regulations for the 2018 World Cup in Russia, 'the Organising Association shall be subject to the supervision and control of FIFA, which has the last word on all matters relevant to

[22] See for example Article 3 of the FIFA Statutes, 'Non-discrimination and stance against racism.'

[23] Ruggie (n 19).

[24] See Human Rights Advisory Board Terms of Reference, November 2016. The Advisory Council issued its first report in September 2017 with a number of recommendations to FIFA. FIFA is also among the initiators of the establishment of the Centre for Sport and Human Rights (See the joint statement made by the committee director of the Mega-Sporting Events Platform for Human Rights, 'Diverse Coalition Commits to Establishing Centre for Sport and Human Rights in 2018', 30 November 2017).

[25] FIFA, FIFA's Human Rights Policy, May 2017, § 4.

the … World Cup …' (Article 1§4). Moreover, '[the] Organising Association undertakes to observe the FIFA Statutes, regulations, directives, decisions, guidelines, circulars as well as the HA [Hosting agreement, including the Biding Agreement]' (Article 1§5). The obligation to respect human rights, including the fundamental rights of workers, can be exercised in the name of FIFA's normative power through the national host association, particularly when it subcontracts infrastructure projects. The organising association should be obliged to use contractors who respect human rights standards (a clause to this effect should be included in the contracts). Thus, FIFA could indirectly impose obligations on companies outside of its direct control.[26]

However, not all responsibility falls under the World Cup organising association. Often, the host State of the competition pays questionable respect to human rights. With regards to the 2018 and 2022 World Cups, the limits of fundamental freedoms in Russia and Qatar are exemplary here. As one of several issues (freedom of expression, or freedom of press), associations promoting the defence of homosexual rights fear the penal sanctions that gays and lesbians participating or attending the 2018 or 2022 World Cups may face;[27] indeed, homosexuality remains a criminal offence under Qatari law while Russian law represses the 'promotion' of it to minors.

In this case, the legal mechanisms available to FIFA to impose upon on host states the respect of human rights obligations are at stake. While there is no contractual obligation between FIFA and the host state, FIFA has instead opted to integrate the human rights dimension within its application process. The alternative, which is to sanction countries with an unsatisfactory human rights situation, is politically complicated and likely to limit the organisation of the competition to democracies without furthering the cause of human rights. Thus, among the criteria for the bid, candidate associations are now assessed on this risk of adverse impact on human rights.[28] Additionally, the application of the football federations and the organisation contract concluded between FIFA and the selected national association must be supported with government guarantees so as to ensure that FIFA's various legal requirements are met.

These requirements typically concern a number of issues (i.e. access to the territory, security, currency exchange, FIFA commercial rights, use of national anthems and flags, telecommunications, import of necessary equipment for the organisation of the competition, broad tax exemptions). The State carries the responsibility to ensure that necessary legislative or regulatory changes are made. Recently, FIFA has decided that among the government guarantees, a declaration on the respect for human rights must

---

26 We can draw a comparison with the ban on *Third Party Ownership* (TPO) in the FIFA Regulations. Since FIFA is unable to directly regulate the activity of investment funds specialized in the purchase and resale of players, FIFA has prohibited clubs from using this type of financing to recruit players. See TAS, 2016/A/4490, *RFC Seraing v. FIFA*, arbitral award of 9 March 2017, § 117.

27 *Associated Press*, 14 December 2010; 'Gay fans warned holding hands at Russia World Cup will be dangerous', *The Guardian* (19 December 2017).

28 See Article 3.6 of the FIFA Regulations for the selection of the venue for the final competition of the 2026 FIFA World Cup™ that indicates the following selection criteria, 'The risk of adverse impacts on human rights, including workers' rights in the Host Country … , in connection with hosting and staging the Competition over the life cycle thereof, including the Member Association's … strategy and commitment to prevent or mitigate such risks.'

be included. The Guide to the Bidding Process for the 2026 FIFA World Cup includes a standard government declaration in which:

> (iii) The Government will fully support FIFA and the Hosting Association in their efforts to ensure that the hosting and staging of the Competition and any legacy and post-event related activities do not involve adverse impacts on internationally recognised human rights, including labour rights.
> (iv) The Government is committed to respecting, protecting and fulfilling human rights, including labour rights, in connection with the hosting and staging of the Competition and any legacy and post-event related activities, with particular attention to the provision of security, potential resettlement and eviction, labour rights (including those of migrant workers), rights of children, gender and other forms of discrimination and freedom of expression and peaceful assembly, and will ensure that access to effective remedies is available where such adverse impacts do occur, including judicial and non-judicial complaint mechanisms with the power to investigate, punish and redress human rights violations.

The legal value of such a declaration, even as a part of the organisation contract, may be questioned either under international law, under the domestic law of the host state, and/or under the governing law of the contract, Swiss law.[29] But in practice, governments observe the commitments made during the application process.[30] Examples include the amendment to Section 15A of the Merchandise Marks Act, No. 17 of 1941 by the South African government to ensure the 2010 FIFA World Cup is legally protected against ambush marketing.[31] In the 2014 World Cup, Brazil voted in Parliament a 'World Cup' exception to its law prohibiting the sale of alcohol in stadiums.[32]

Therefore, this type of instrument will hopefully be useful in making host states in future World Cups attentive to internationally recognised human rights. It remains, however, the responsibility of FIFA to verify that the respect for human rights is effectively part of the selection process and to evaluate the implementation of these commitments by governments, given that gaps (maybe too large even for football diplomacy) exist between texts and practice. Outside this legal framework, which is applicable only as from the 2026 World Cup, denunciation of the appalling work

---

[29] See Latty (n 8) 591s.

[30] Concerning the 2024 Olympic Games, the French parliament adopted in the beginning of 2018 an 'Olympic law' derogating from the common law, in accordance with the commitments in the French candidature file (as of 6 February 2018, the bill was expedited by two assemblies, due to the slight modifications made by the Senate, the text is submitted to a mixed joint commission).

[31] *General Notice* No.683 of 25 May 2006 adopted by the Minister of Industry and Commerce (see Annex 2 of the publication *FIFA Public Information Sheet (a guide to FIFA's Official Marks)*).

[32] 'La loi alcool adoptée' *L'Equipe* (29 March 2012). FIFA, having a partnership with Budweiser, has yet to obtain a similar waiver for the World Cup in Qatar. ('Mondial 2022: l'alcool aussi interdit dans les stades?' *L'Equipe* (9 November 2016)).

conditions in Qatar have already led to a significant improvement in that respect.[33] Various construction site inspection measures have been implemented on the initiative of FIFA.[34] It would even be possible, in efforts to substantiate the legal scope of the government's commitment, for FIFA and the host state to conclude an 'internationalised' contract (modelled after state contracts) setting out the rights and obligations of both parties in view of the World Cup, including respect for human rights.[35]

Another issue that arises is the long-term sustainability for human rights in host States. The preparation and hosting of the World Cup cannot be reduced to an exceptional circumstance with regard to human rights. Could FIFA use its political and legal power to maintain and uphold these standards, specifically implemented for the event? Non-governmental organisations and the Parliamentary Assembly of the Council of Europe advocate this.[36] FIFA's statutes allow it to suspend those national associations whose independence is interfered with by their government.[37] The implementation of these provisions is usually sufficient to encourage States to change their behaviour. The participation of the national team to international football competitions being a too big issue, FIFA can thus act indirectly on States.[38] Could FIFA suspend national associations whose government exhibit manifest violations of internationally recognised human rights, at least when such violations affect football?

Evidently, the global actor FIFA is not deprived of legal mechanisms to contribute to the improvement of human rights at a global level. The UEFA and the International

---

33 See Document GB.331/INS/13 in which the Governing Body of the International Labor Office records the measures taken by Qatar, particularly to put an end to the kafala system and improve working conditions immediately. See also the communiqué released by Amnesty International, 'FIFA under pressure over handling of World Cup construction abuse' (9 November 2017) <www.amnesty.org> accessed 23 April 2018.

34 Concerning the 2018 World Cup, see *Decent Work Monitoring System* launched by FIFA and the Russian organizing committee, outlining an inspection process executed by NGOs on infrastructure constitution sites. On these measures, see Thomas Grell, 'FIFA's Human Rights Agenda: Is the Game Beautiful Again?', 4 September 2017 <www.asser.nl/SportsLaw/blog> accessed 23 April 2018.

35 Since 2014, the Olympic Charter states that national authorities, 'at the discretion of the IOC', may be required to co-sign the host city contract. See Article 3.3 under the bye-law to Rule 33 of the Olympic Charter, amended in accordance with the Olympic Agenda 2020 recommendations, 'The IOC enters into a written agreement with the host city and the NOC of its country. At the discretion of the IOC, other local, regional or national authorities … may also be a party to such agreement. Such agreement, which is commonly referred to as the Host City Contract, is executed by all parties immediately upon the election of the host city.'

36 See Resolution 2200 (2018) adopted 24 January 2018 by the Parliamentary Assembly in the Council of Europe, § 11.2.2, where the Assembly recommends FIFA and the UEFA to 'insist with the governments of the host countries on the necessity of protecting the fundamental civil and political rights, and in particular the freedom of expression – including the freedom of the media – and freedom of peaceful assembly, and not only in connection with their competitions *but beyond*' (emphasis added).

37 See Articles 14, 16 and 19 of the Statutes.

38 See for example 'La FIFA lève la suspension du Koweït' *L'Equipe* (6 December 2017). The Kuwaiti federation was suspended in 2015 after adopting a law permitting government interference in sports institutions. The adoption of a new law by the Kuwaiti Parliament subsequently led to the lifting of the suspension.

Olympic Committee have taken a similar path,[39] which should soon be followed by other international sports organisations. While the profits gained in this sector often place considerations for human rights on a backseat, the core of the Olympic movement lies in humanist values that the aforementioned legal tools seek to address.

The activities of FIFA and other sports organisations are no longer limited to the regulation of their sports and to the organisation of competitions. The 'contractual' dimension of sports has been largely overtaken by practice. Through its (still simmering) action in favour of human rights, FIFA may play an important role in global regulation and may even be more efficient in this field than public international organisations.[40] The implementation by FIFA of these new functions through unorthodox legal means which may have effects on the behaviours of sovereign states blurs the classical boundaries of international law.

But taking into account the repeated scandals involving these organisations (and FIFA at first place), their legitimacy to address such issues may be challenged. Before wearing the gloves of virtue, should not one have clean hands?

[39] See the 2024 Olympic Games Host City Contract Principles (available on <www.olympic.org> accessed 23 April 2018), of which Article 13.2 obligates the host city, national Olympic Committee, and the organisation committee to 'protect and respect human rights and ensure any violation of human rights is remedied in a manner consistent with international agreements, laws and regulations applicable in the Host Country and in a manner consistent with all internationally-recognised human rights standards and principles, including the United Nations Guiding Principles on Business and Human Rights, applicable in the Host Country …'

[40] Cf. concerning the normative powers of companies, Hervé Ascensio, 'Les activités normatives des entreprises multinationales', in SFDI (n 18) 277.

8. Informal codes: *Nike v. Kasky*

8.1 CASE BACKGROUND

As non-State norms (codes, industry standards, various sources of transnational soft-law) multiply to fill the gaps left by the limited reach of national laws, the question arises as to how to give self-regulation 'teeth'. The answer may be easier in the context of arbitration. The courts, however, are usually constrained by the Westphalian paradigm which still governs private international law: they will only recognise as legal the laws of other nation-States. It is difficult to imagine a set of criteria with which to assess the legitimacy of normative claims by various groups or communities: Western legal systems adhere to political, not legal pluralism. Thus, a corporate code of conduct does not qualify formally as law-making under a State-centred methodology. However protective it is (or claims to be) of the rights of sub-contractors and stakeholders in far-away places, its 'private' origin has meant (at least until recently) that such a code does not provide grounds for contractual liability before the courts, nor does it serve as a legal foundation for tort liability. The lack of 'legal bite' of this code explains its very success among corporate manufacturers relocating industry to foreign environments. It is nevertheless possible to map various judicial attempts to 'harden' spontaneous promises made by private actors in code-like form.

In *Nike v. Kasky*, a private attorney general action was brought against Nike as employer and five of its corporate officers, alleging that, in the course of a public relations campaign, the employer made misrepresentations regarding its labour practices in its Asian factories, in violation of the Business and Professions Code. Nike attempted to shield itself from liability under consumer legislation by invoking the First Amendment and its right to free speech. Importantly, the Court decided that statements about labour policies, practices and conditions where athletic shoes and apparel were made consisted in 'commercial speech' for purposes of the First Amendment. This potentially opens the way to giving 'teeth' to self-regulation by harnessing it to formal sources of private law – that is, communal-garden private law tools.

For instance, reliance induced in its addressees may give rise to a right of redress. This can be seen in the case of Nike's spontaneous code of conduct for its own (or its 'sub-contractors') factories (or, similarly, Total's voluntary vetting process for its sea-bound oil-tankers). This *ex post* approach, balancing the equities, bypasses the legitimacy issue and looks straight at the effective impact of the code on those who are affected by it. Ultimately, however, the legal effect of that code derives from the (State) law governing the effects of the promise towards third parties. The advantage of this methodology is that the coordinating forum retains control over the applicability of the private norm, either making it enforceable or moderating its claim. Thus, for example, reliance on ISO 26000 could be used, despite its own self-denying claim not to provide the foundation of legal action. Properly employed, the methodology consisting in reinforcing the normativity of non-State sources through the tools of private law may even signal a move towards the 'constitutionalisation' of private codes.

Case: Supreme Court of California, *Mark Kasky v. Nike, Inc*, 27 Cal 4th 939, 45 P 3d 243, 119 Cal Rptr 2d 296 (2002)

8.2 THE DUAL PRIVATISATION OF LAW IN GLOBALISATION

Ralf Michaels

1. PRELIMINARIES: COURT CASES AS OBJECTS OF STUDY

In the 1990s, Nike, a leading seller of athletic footwear, was accused of selling shoes that had been produced in so-called 'sweatshops' in Asia under exploitative working conditions. The accusations were accompanied by a widespread boycott movement, which tried to hit Nike where it hurts most, in its profits. Nike responded with its own public relations campaign, claiming that working conditions in production sites were in compliance with applicable laws and norms. In response, it was sued for false advertising. The courts never reached the question whether Nike's statements were in fact true or not, because they had to deal with a prior legal question. Nike argued that such interference with its public relations campaign amounted to an infringement of its free speech rights. This argument was successful in the trial court and on appeal, but Nike lost before the California Supreme Court, the highest Californian state court.[1] Nike appealed to the US Supreme Court, but although the Court accepted the case and even held a hearing it subsequently dismissed it on the ground that *certiorari* had improvidently been granted[2] – though Justice Breyer wrote a long dissent in favour of Nike. The case was later settled for US$1.5 million.[3]

What then is this case ultimately about? The answer depends, dramatically, on one's perspective. From a social (or political) perspective, *Kasky* concerns core worries about globalisation. A myriad of issues are concerned: sweatshops, production chains, neocolonialism and exploitation, neoliberalism, globalisation and global justice, human rights, comparative advantage, the reclining of state regulation, corporate social responsibility, advertising. Not surprisingly, then, a number of rationalities interact: the economic rationality of profits and losses, the political rationality of power, the communicative reality of positive and negative images, the moral reality of right and wrong, and of course legal perspective. From the latter, i.e. the legal perspective, understood as a doctrinal perspective, on the other hand, *Kasky* concerns a narrow question. The sole issue at stake is whether a corporation can invoke protections of free speech for what it says about its own production conditions. Globalisation is absent from this perspective, and production conditions are mostly too: *Kasky* does not address whether Nike's claims are actually true or not.

What is an analyst of private international law to make of this discrepancy? The analyst can, as many legal analysts in the United States have done, confine herself to a doctrinal analysis. *Kasky* stands, then, for discussions about so-called 'commercial speech' and its protection under the First Amendment (the US constitutional provision on free speech). Such an analysis is not fully satisfactory, however: it is unable to

---

1 *Marc Kasky v. Nike, Inc.*, 27 Cal.4th 939 (Cal. Sup. Ct. 2002).

2 *Nike, Inc. v. Kasky*, 539 U.S. 654 (U.S. Sup. Ct. 2003).

3 Anitha Reddy, 'Nike Settles Case With an Activist For $1.5 Million' *Wall Street Journal* (13 Sep 2003).

unearth the political concerns that underlie the issue, and it ignores aspects of private international law altogether. And it feels disingenuous: commentators' views of the case are shaped by their political views of the underlying issues, but because those do not appear in the decision itself, they pretend that they are not relevant. All the criticism of the law's technical, formal character is relevant here.[4]

These insufficiencies appear to invite a different strategy for analysts: to use *Kasky* as little more than a starting point for general discussions of global conditions of production and consumption. From this perspective, *Kasky* is 'really' not about free speech, but about something else, and it is that something else that the analyst should focus on. At best, court decisions with their doctrinal debates are viewed as smoke-screens for the real underlying issues. Or, they are mere tools in a fight that is ultimately about politics: the law as a mere means to an end. As a consequence, the law itself, including its doctrinal arguments, is dismissed as irrelevant, at least in itself. This kind of analysis errs on the other side. It does not take the law seriously enough: the specific way in which the law negotiates, and often actually resolves, specific conflicts.

The proper analysis, it seems to me, must combine the doctrinal and the social/political analysis without prioritising one over the other. It must begin with a careful analysis of the court decision itself – an action called 'close reading' in literary analysis. A legal analysis that ignores court decisions would be like a literary analysis that ignores books. And a legal analysis that ignores the precise doctrinal argument would be like a literary analysis that ignores the book's language. Even those who think of legal language as a mere smokescreen that conceals real concerns and interest ought to acknowledge that the very form and nature of this smokescreen itself deserves attention.

Such an analysis must therefore focus on, and take seriously, the doctrinal arguments being made, but it need not and should not address these in isolation from the social and political situation that is being discussed. Technical, doctrinal legal language is never only that: the fact that politics is not openly discussed does not mean that it is absent. Rather, the technical language of doctrine serves as a way to make the political dispute resolvable. There are two ways to formulate this. The one is to say that legal doctrine operates in an 'as if' mode: it discusses legal concerns as if they could be separated from the underlying political concerns, even though it remains aware of these.[5] The other is to suggest that legal doctrine itself operates as a language in which the political conflicts themselves are expressed.[6] In order to make this implicit political element, the analyst must demonstrate (one could say: 'reverse engineer') the way in which social and political concerns are translated into, or expressed in, the language of

---

4 Horatia Muir Watt, 'Theorizing Private International Law' in Anne Orford and Florian Hoffmann (eds), *The Oxford Handbook of the Theory of International Law* (Oxford, Oxford University Press 2015).

5 Annelise Riles, 'Is the Law Hopeful?' in Hirokazu Miyazaki (ed.), *The Economy of Hope* (Philadelphia PA, University of Pennsylvania Press 2016) 126, 129ff.; Karen Knop, Ralf Michaels and Annelise Riles, 'From Multiculturalism to Technique: Feminism, Culture and the Conflict of Laws Style' (2012) 64 *Stan. L. Rev.* 589–656, 647–48.

6 Ralf Michaels, 'Post-Critical Private International Law: From Politics to Technique—A Sketch' in Horatia Muir Watt and Diego P Fernández Arroyo (eds), *Private International Law as Global Governance* (Oxford, Oxford University Press 2014).

the law. She must resist the temptation to view the formal language of the law as less real than that of other disciplines focusing on the same issue: international relations, political theory, etc.

And, unlike the purely legal analysis, which starts and ends with doctrine, the proper interdisciplinary study will branch out from the doctrinal discussion. It will identify the points of friction within that discussion and instead of resolving them (as the law ultimately must) instead use them as indicators of frictions in the world that are reflected. Moreover it will identify the gaps in the decision, the issues that are not addressed at all, and thematise both why they are not addressed in doctrine and how their absence in the law relates to their existence in the world.

What follows has therefore two functions. It is a discussion of *Kasky v. Nike* and the issues it raises, both within and without the court decision. And it is, at the same time, a practical example of the method of analysis proposed above.[7]

2. COMMERCIAL SPEECH AS ENTRY

Starting with the doctrinal perspective, *Kasky v. Nike* is a free speech case. The question is as follows: Was Nike protected to provide information about its production conditions that were wrong, or at least misleading? This is not an absurd question. Although US law does not protect a freedom to lie, it does protect speech from the need to justify itself. Free speech is, in US constitutional law, a kind of super-right: its protection in the First Amendment is broader than in other constitutions, because it allows, in principle, not for any limitations. And its scope is broader, too, because speech is defined so as to encompass, for example, donations to political parties and other kinds of conduct that is only very indirectly expressive.

However, the protection is not unlimited. In particular, the US Supreme Court has distinguished, since 1942,[8] political speech, which benefits from broad protection, and commercial speech, which is far less protected. Where to draw the border has long been problematic. The Supreme Court, in its *Bolger* decision of 1983,[9] named three criteria to identify speech that is commercial and therefore deserves less protection: its form as an advertisement, its character as the reference to a product, and its motivation as that of creating or maintaining commercial relationships. That case concerned advertising for contraceptives (which was then illegal), facts very different from those in *Kasky.*[10] Indeed Nike's conduct in *Kasky* did not fit these criteria very well: it consisted of public statements not advertisements, it referenced production conditions not a product,

---

7 An earlier attempt of a combination of close reading and critique in this spirit is Ralf Michaels, 'Empagran's Empire: International Law and Statutory Interpretation in the U.S. Supreme Court of the Twenty-First Century' in David L. Sloss, Michael D. Ramsey and William S. Dodge (eds), *The U.S. Supreme Court and International Law: Continuity or Change?* (Cambridge, Cambridge University Press 2011).

8 *Valentine v. Chrestensen*, 316 U.S. 52 (U.S. Sup. Ct. 1942).

9 *Bolger v. Youngs Drug Products Corp.*, 463 U.S. 60 (US Sup. Ct. 1983).

10 The *Bolger* criteria had been applied before to cases more similar to *Kasky*. For example, in *Association of Nat. Advertisers, Inc. v. Lungren*, 44 F.3d 726 (9th Cir. 1994), the defendant had claimed its products to be biodegradable.

and the economic motivation concerned goodwill at large, not the sale of specific products. The California Supreme Court in *Kasky* therefore established a slightly different triad of criteria in order to define commercial speech: a speaker engaged in commerce, an intended audience of consumers, and commercial content of the message defined as 'representations of fact about the business operations, products, or services of the speaker (or the individual or company that the speaker represents), made for the purpose of promoting sales of, or other commercial transactions in, the speaker's products or services.' Whether the speech came in the form of an advertisement, as in *Bolger*, or in a public relations campaign, like in *Kasky*, was not relevant.

This list of criteria is problematic, and the two dissenters on the Court, in particular Judge Brown (who was later to become America's most libertarian federal judge) mercilessly point out the flaws in the argument. The first such problem concerns the last factor, the commercial content of the speech. The speech at issue here mixed political and commercial issue: it concerned matters of public interest, namely the working conditions in Asian countries, and it concerned commercial matters, in particular Nike's good will. Indeed, it is hard to imagine *any* corporate speech that does not at least also concern commercial matters, as Judge Brown in dissent points out: 'Because all corporate speech about a public issue reflects on the corporate image and therefore affects the corporation's business goodwill and sale value, the majority's test makes all such speech commercial notwithstanding the majority's assertions to the contrary.'

This leads to the second problem in the majority's argument: to use the speaker's identity as a factor in assessing whether speech is commercial or not. This runs against the idea of free speech as speaker-independent, and also against Supreme Court jurisprudence. It also creates problems for a level playing field of debate over employment conditions, if critics of a corporation are protected by the First Amendment, but the corporation is not. The majority tries to defend the differentiation with two arguments: the corporation has better access to the truth, and false statements deserve no protection. But the first point is not always true, and the second is not useful towards the characterisation of speech as commercial or not.

There may have been a time when an economic sphere could be separated from a political sphere. This is the world that the Supreme Court's free speech doctrine, with its separation of political speech, has in mind. But that world is not our world. Corporations have long been political actors as well – as have boycott movements. The court recognises this when it downplays the question whether the corporate speech comes in the form of an advertisement or not. This seems appropriate: in our world advertising comes in many forms. But the Court is unable to develop a doctrine that appropriately grasps these issues – even though Judge Brown's dissent proposes various such doctrines. And the US Supreme Court has so far been unwilling to help.

3. THE PUBLIC REGULATORY GAP

One notable point about this case is what it is not about. Nike is sued for lying about its compliance with applicable employment laws; it is not being sued for actually breaking them. The reason is that such a claim would have been hard to bring, on either the law of the developing countries of production, or the developed countries of sale.

Why not? This ultimately links to a well-known regulatory gap which exists between the developing countries of production and the developed countries of sale. The developing countries in which production took place often have no laws protecting workers. When they have such laws, they lack the institutions to enforce them. And even when such institutions exist, they lack incentive to actually enforce them. Giant world producers like Nike bring in valuable investment. Exploited workers, by contrast, often have fairly little political clout. Moreover, complicating the analysis, many of these workers are actually not interested in workers' protection, because they rely so much on the jobs that the investor brings in. For the developing countries, lax employment standards often translate into a comparative advantage because they lower production costs and thereby attract investors.

The developed countries, on the other hand, are constrained in different ways. One constraint is legal: the general restrictions in international law on extraterritorial regulation mean that regulating working conditions in developing countries was not unproblematic. The United States has international law jurisdiction over Nike, which is a US company. But it has no clear jurisdiction over Nike's independent subcontractors in Vietnam. Relatedly, developed countries have mixed incentives as to the regulation of workers' conditions elsewhere, beyond the general incentive to do good (and to implement international law). On the one hand, states want to protect their own workers from competition at places with lower production costs, On the other hand, they want to enable their consumers to benefit from the lower prices for products that emerge, and they want to support their own corporations, like Nike.

We face, then, a public regulatory gap with regard to workers' conditions. That gap is characteristic of globalisation: the fact that production and sale happen in different countries with different regulations and different economic conditions, and they happen via different actors, between Nike as the multinational corporation on the one hand, and local contractors and subcontractors on the other. How should this gap be filled? Traditional responses concern state law: either international law, or more expansive application of existing state laws. Those solutions are addressed in other chapters. Here, the focus lies on privatised law (or soft law).

4. THE DUAL PRIVATISATION OF ENFORCEMENT

We have previously discussed that Nike was not sued for breaking public laws. Nike was however sued for false advertising. But the false advertising itself contains a claim that is, in itself, quasi-legal in nature. Nike's claim had been that they and their subcontractors complied with applicable laws, and also with Nike's own, stricter, Code of Conduct. They claimed, in other words, that they complied with the law. The plaintiff, in calling this false advertising, implicitly claimed that Nike failed to comply with the law. Accordingly the free speech conflict in reality hides a conflict about actual compliance. This suggests that the consequence of this gap of public regulation has not been a complete vacuum of regulation. The public law conflict is translated as a conflict about private speech. What we see is privatisation of law.

This privatisation happens, interestingly, in a multiple sense. A first sense concerns lawmaking. Nike, aware of both the complaints and the lax enforcement of local laws abroad, had established a Code of Conduct in 1992 and changed it repeatedly. According to this Code, Nike's contractors were banned from use of forced labour and child labour, required to pay local minimum wages and provide legally mandatory benefits, and forced to comply not only with local work time and environmental regulations, but also Nike's own factory/vendor health and safety standards. The Code, thus, is a mix of privately made law and of a reference to existing state law. It is not law in a formal sense, but performs many of the same functions. It is generally referred to as soft law: texts that have the appearance of formal law but are not formally binding.[11] Codes of Conduct are different from traditional forms of self-regulation in several ways.[12] Their goal is not to smooth market conditions and lower transaction costs but instead to ensure compliance with non-economic values. Their nature lies somewhere between economy and politics (reflecting, here, the law's distinction between commercial and political speech). And their governance invites contestation, thereby making them more similar to law in a traditional sense.

Such codes can emerge from individual companies, but this is not always the case. Some of these codes are established by whole industries, which eliminates the problem of companies which follow such a code potentially being at a competitive disadvantage with regard to production costs of those companies which do not follow such a code. And some of these codes are of public origin. For example, ISO 26000 (Social Responsibility) was established by the International Organization for Standardization. The OECD Guidelines for Multinational Enterprises (2003) also contain standards, as do the so-called 'Ruggie Principles', the 'Guiding Principles on Business and Human Rights: Implementing the United Nations 'Protect, Respect and Remedy' Framework'. The UN Global Compact, an attempt to ensure sustainable development, is a further example.

It is worth realising how much Nike's Code of Conduct resembles existing legislation. The code in this case binds not only Nike itself and its employees, but also its contractors. Where a formal legislator is able to bind individuals through its sovereign power, Nike can do the same through its bargaining power: it can, and does, make acceptance of its Code of Conduct a prerequisite for contracting with Nike. What is at play here is a frequent feature of neoliberal globalisation. Not only is state law replaced with privately made codes; in addition, legislation is replaced with contractual agreements.

Legislation alone, private or not, does not resolve issues on its own. In addition, enforcement is needed. Enforcement too is privatised here, in even two ways. The first concerns Nike's own enforcement. In 1996, Nike established an internal compliance

---

11 See, e.g., Harry Arthurs, 'Private Ordering and Workers Rights in the Global Economy: Corporate Codes of Conduct as a Regime of Labour Market Regulation' in Conaghan Joanne, Richard Michael Fischl, and Karl Klare (eds), *Labour Law in the Era of Globalization: Transformative Practices & Possibilities* (Oxford, Oxford University Press 2002); André Sobczak, 'Are Codes of Conduct in Global Supply Chains Really Voluntary? From Soft Law Regulation of Labour Relations to Consumer Law' (2006) 16 *Business Ethics Quarterly* 167–84.

12 David Vogel, 'The Private Regulation of Global Corporate Conduct; Achievements and Limitations' (2010) 49 *Business and Society* 68–87, 70.

department. In addition, Nike engaged in announced audits of its contractors. All of these mechanisms served a dual purpose: to make sure that the Code of Conduct was actually followed, but also to make sure that Nike is immune from criticism. The problem of such self-enforcement is evident. Nike, unlike an ordinary legislator, has no real interest in finding violations of its Code of Conduct: it has an incentive for the public to trust that such violations do not occur, regardless of whether they actually do. It was, in fact, the leaking of results of such an internal audit that spurred some of the strongest criticism against Nike.

In this situation of insufficient internal enforcement, it is not surprising, therefore, that we also find external enforcement: enforcement by others. Boycott movements provide, in this sense, one way of external private enforcers: they evaluate whether a corporation complies with certain norms, and punish the corporation for violations. Of course, the norms that are enforced need not necessarily be those of a Code of Conduct: they can be any norms, from formal laws to perceived moral norms.

Another way of external private enforcement is the bringing of a legal claim, as in *Kasky v. Nike*. Nike cannot be compelled directly to comply with its own Code of Conduct, which is only soft law. It can, however, be compelled indirectly, as in a false advertisement claim. In this sense, we can speak of a re-entry of non-state law (soft law) into the procedures of state law. This remains private enforcement as long as private individuals are entitled to bring such claims in the general interest, as is the case here. Kasky brought his suit, explicitly, in the public interest as a so-called private attorney. US competition law provides for such a rule, which means that a plaintiff, in order to have standing, need not prove that he is personally affected.

This leads to the question of adjudication. Public adjudication is only incompletely capable of enforcing soft law, for the reasons given above, but it is not toothless, as the *Kasky* case demonstrates. In addition, adjudication can be private. Companies eager to gain trust in the eyes of activists can voluntarily subject themselves to the verdict of an ombudsman, of an auditor, or of a private tribunal, which may or may not find them compliant with their own rules. ISO 26000 comes with a certification procedure; although certification is not an adjudication process, it does lead to a certain control of compliance.

5. BETWEEN PUBLIC AND PRIVATE

This privatisation of lawmaking, enforcing and adjudication, is sometimes presented as a new development of globalisation, i.e. of a law that exists ‘without’ or ‘beyond’ the state. This is partially true. Current privatisations happen after a long history of a mutual back and forth between state and industry. During the first globalisation, in the 19th century, very little protective legislation existed, and very little production was therefore delocalised outside industrialised countries like the UK. When conditions in factories were shown to be unacceptable, the state stepped in with protective legislation. Companies responded by moving production abroad, to low level production countries. In turn lobby groups lobbied for enhanced protection – through state laws, but also through international law, hard and soft.[13] It is in part against this development that corporations responded by establishing codes of conduct and monitoring mechanisms, in an attempt to fend off public enforcement. This is unlikely to be the last stage.

There are reasons to celebrate the privatisation of law as a response to the problems of under-regulation, arising from globalisation and the limits of nation state laws. These limits are sometimes exaggerated, as students of private international law especially know. Public law is not as strictly confined within national borders as it is sometimes made to be. Law can apply extraterritorially, and doctrines exist, between private international law and public international law, to determine when and how. Still, state law has lags, and international law cannot fill these completely. Privatised law can cross borders in ways in which public law, as long as it remains tied to the territorialised state, cannot.

In addition, privatised enforcement can go a long way towards remedying shortcomings of public enforcement. Developing countries often lack functioning court systems; courts in developed countries sometimes show insufficient sensitivity for foreign interests. Private interest groups are not confined by such limitations. This is a reason why the private attorney general, introduced in US law, plays an especially important role on an international scale.[14]

Nonetheless, the hope often placed in privatised law seems misplaced. Soft law codes can contain attractive rules, but the lack of hard enforcement power behind them severely weakens their appeal. Compliance is still uneven. *Kasky* describes a case in which, arguably, a code of conduct had been mere window-dressing: Nike had set it up but did not actually mean for it to be binding. Still today, many codes of conduct are not strictly enforced: corporations use them to improve their brands, not to actually improve conditions. This is not surprising: industries writing such codes are influenced by competing incentives; only one of them is to provide actual protection even where that hurts their economic interests. Shareholder interests as the main incentives for corporations are focused on profit, not human rights. Relatedly, codes of conduct lack the democratic legitimacy that state law, at least in democracies, enjoys. This is so especially for corporation-specific or industry-wide codes (depending on the lack of stakeholders participation). Quasi-public codes like the ISO 26000 may fare a little better.[15]

Privatised enforcement is also problematic. Boycott movements, celebrated when they came up in the 1990s, have shown to be problematic for a number of reasons: they tend to pick corporations on the basis of visibility; they are run by organisations that lack formal democratic legitimacy; their information is not always correct, and they tend to be very imprecise in their regulation. Nike's story is a good example: Nike's own response to the boycott movement is taught in business schools around the world

13 The International Law Organization, or ILO, is an example of a global enforcer.

14 Hannah L. Buxbaum, 'The Private Attorney General in Global Age: Public Interests in Private International Antitrust Litigation' (2001) 26 *Yale J Int'l L* 219–63.

15 Rüdiger Hahn and Christian Weidtmann, 'Transnational Governance, Deliberative Democracy, and the Legitimacy of ISO 26000: Analyzing the Case of a Global Multistakeholder Process' (2016) 55 *Business and Society* 90–129.

as a success story for the company and for workers' rights alike, but at the same time protesters still criticise working conditions and boycotts still exist. Which side is right? And should we really trust the marketplace to decide this question? Internal enforcement is marred by structural problems: control of compliance stands in the way of building structures of cooperation and trust.[16] Boycott movements tend to have their own special interests, and those are not always benevolent; we have seen 'astroturf' movements that allegedly call out certain behaviour in the interest of consumers but are in reality financed by corporate competitors of the companies whose conduct is called out. External audits might be superior.[17]

The core problem can be identified in terms of legal theory: privatised law, frequently, performs the functions of law but is not really law itself. Both privatised lawmaking as codes of conduct and privatised enforcement through contract and through the power of the purpose replace the logic of law and justice with the logic of economics and rational self-interest. This has problematic consequences. First, privatised law is deficient where justice and self-interest diverge. Second, perhaps, the hope to control markets and abuse of market powers with more markets and different market powers is, ultimately, self-defeating as it is the endorsement of capitalism in order to keep capitalism in check. Human rights are being commoditised. Consumers' 'power of the purse' becomes a substitute for democratic votes, with many unattractive implications (among them the fact that rich consumers have more influence than poor consumers).

In view of this, the law remains relevant, at least in connection with privatised law. At least as long as meaningful legal institutions outside the state are still nascent, that law and its institutions must remain those of states.[18] *Kasky v. Nike* demonstrates the need to rely on the courts, though it also demonstrates the insufficiencies of an approach that translates hard social and political concerns into the language of free speech. What it regulates, directly, is not compliance with norms, but only how to speak about such compliance. This cannot fully get at the core concerns.

There are, in fact, promises of a more direct legal response to the underlying problems. Some such solutions are legislative. In 2017, France adopted a new Social Responsibility Code, which requires multinational firms that carry out all or part of their activity on French territory to adopt mechanisms to prevent human rights violations and environmental damages throughout their supply chain.[19] The law is not

---

[16] See Richard Locke, Thomas Kochan, Monica Romis and Fei Qin, 'Beyond corporate codes of conduct: Work organization and labour standards at Nike's suppliers' (2007) 146 *International Labour Review* 21–40.

[17] See Kristen Bell DeTienne and Lee W. Lewis, 'The Pragmatic and Ethical Barriers to Corporate Social Responsibility Disclosure: The Nike Case' (2005) 60(4) *Journal of Business Ethics* 359–76, 370ff.

[18] Vogel (n 12) 81ff.

[19] LOI n° 2017-399 du 27 mars 2017 relative au devoir de vigilance des sociétés mères et des entreprises donneuses d'ordre, https://www.legifrance.gouv.fr/eli/loi/2017/3/27/2017-399/jo/texte.

perfect[20] – it requires due diligence in supervision only and does not hold corporations liable for the conduct itself – but it goes a long way. Another example is the Modern Slavery Act that the UK passed.[21] EU legislation has been proposed.[22]

Other solutions are adjudicatory, though they often tackle the issues directly not indirectly.[23] In Germany, a case is pending against a chain store company which the plaintiffs want to hold responsible for the rights violations of their suppliers in Bangladesh.[24]

None of this is to say that state law should play the exclusive role in the regulation of global production chains, or that an indirect regulation through the regulation of speech, as in *Kasky v. Nike*, is irrelevant. Both hard and soft law, direct and indirect regulation, will retain their roles in the new global legal pluralism, sometimes as supplements, sometimes as substitutes for each other.[25] What we can see, however, is that pure economic responses that leave the law outside are insufficient, and that indirect attempts as in *Kasky v. Nike* fail to grasp, fully, the relevant issues. This area, like many in transnational law, remains in flux.

---

20 See Pierre Lequet, 'Loi "devoir de vigilance": de l'intérêt des normes de management des risques' (2017) 42 *Revue juridique de l'environnement* 705–25; Sandra Cossart, Jérôme Chaplier and Tiphaine Beau de Lomenie, 'The French Law on Duty of Care: A Historic Step Towards Making Globalization Work for All' (2017) 2 *Business and Human Rights Journal* 317–23.

21 UK Modern Slavery Act 2015, s 54 on Transparency in Supply Chains. See Shuangge Wen, 'The Cogs and Wheels of Reflexive Law—Business Disclosure under the Modern Slavery Act' (2016) 43 *Journal of Law and Society* 327–59.

22 Angelica Dziedzic, Celine Lelievre, Jonathan Povilonis, *Towards EU legislation on human rights due diligence: Case study of the garment and textile sector* (2017) <https://ssrn.com/abstract=2976330>.

23 See, generally, Juan José Àlvarez Rubio and Katerina Yiannibas (eds), *Human Rights in Business: Removal of barriers to access to justice in the European Union* (Abingdon, Routledge 2017).

24 LG Dortmund, 7 O 95/15 ('Kik'). See Marc-Philippe Weller and Chris Thomale, 'Menschenrechtsklagen gegen deutsche Unternehmen' 46 *Zeitschrift für Unternehmens- und Gesellschaftsrecht* 509–26; Chris Thomale and Leonhard Hübner, 'Zivilgerichtliche Durchsetzung völkerrechtlicher Unternehmensverantwortung' (2017) 72 *Juristenzeitung* 385–97; Ingrid Heinlein, 'Zivilrechtliche Verantwortung transnationaler Unternehmen für sichere und gesunde Arbeitsbedingungen in den Betrieben ihrer Lieferanten' (2018) 35 *Neue Zeitschrift für Arbeitsrecht* 276–82; Matthias Weller and Alexia Pato, 'Local Parents as "Anchor Defendants" in European Courts for Claims against Their Foreign Subsidiaries in Human Rights and Environmental Damages Litigation: Recent Case Law and Legislative Trends' (2018) 23/2 *Unif LR*.

25 Davi M Trubek and Louise G Trubek, 'New governance and legal regulation: complementarity, rivalry, and transformation' (2007) 13 *Columbia Journal of European Law* 539–64.

8.3 PRIVATE CODES OF CONDUCT AS AN INSTRUMENT OF GLOBAL LAW

Ludovic Hennebel[*]

The *Kasky v. Nike* case showcases the transformations of contemporary law from several angles.[26] From a technical point of view, it is above all a landmark case on the definition of commercial speech,[27] which also deals with the extent of protection afforded to the freedom of expression as applied to commercial discourse. However, a constitutional approach shows up as a creative legal practice[28] the fact of invoking misleading advertising practices in order to compel multinational companies to change their behaviour in the field of human rights and social responsibility.[29] Above all, however, *Kasky* illustrates the regulatory effect of norms contained in private codes of conduct, or even in voluntary commitments and commercial speech of private actors. It is therefore a testimony to the strategic use of non-legal tools in order to regulate the behaviour of such actors who seem to escape any regulatory control in our global world.

The purpose of this note is to show the normative dynamic that characterises this case. At the outset, there was a wave of indignation against violent injustice that offended a certain 'universal conscienceness'; it gave voice to a sufficiently influential public opinion (1). However, positive legal engineering does not necessarily afford adequate leverage in response. Positive law – both national and international – lacks the strength to lead the fight against such injustice in a global world. Other modes of regulation emerge, such as the voluntary commitments of multinational companies, which, prima facie, are not binding and usually arise out of communication and marketing sectors (2). Standards of conduct then compete with one another, in response to economic considerations (3). *Kasky* illustrates the unusual encounter between the code of conduct of a private company and national law, through litigation. This encounter enabled the former to produce legal effects in a (state's) legal order (4),

---

* Contribution originally written in French, translated to English by Chloe Njamfa.

26 John Gerard Ruggie, 'Business and Human Rights: The Evolving International Agenda' (2007) 101(4) *The American Journal of International Law* 819–40.

27 William Warner Eldridge IV, 'Just Do It: Kasky v. Nike, Inc. Illustrates That It Is Time to Abandon the Commercial Speech Doctrine' (2003) 12(1) *George Mason Law Review* 179–210; Victoria Dizik Teremenko, 'Corporate Speech under Fire: Has Nike Finally Done It' (2003) 2(1) *DePaul Business & Commercial Law Journal* 207–50. See also: Jennifer L. Close Pomeranz, 'Are We Ready for the Next Nike v. Kasky' (2014) 83(1) *University of Cincinnati Law Review* 203–28.

28 Julia Fisher, 'Free Speech to Have Sweatshops – How Kasky v. Nike Might Provide a Useful Tool to Improve Sweatshop Conditions' (2006) 26(2) *Boston College Third World Law Journal* 267–310.

29 Lena Ayoub, 'Nike Just Does It–And Why the United States Shouldn't: The United States' International Obligation to Hold MNCs Accountable for Their Labor Rights Violations Abroad' (1999) 11(2) *DePaul Business Law Journal* 395–442; Ryan P. Toftoy, 'Now Playing: Corporate Codes of Conduct in the Global Theater, Is Nike Just Doing It' (1998) 15(3) *Arizona Journal of International and Comparative Law* 905–30.

while at the same time reinforcing certain hypotheses that help us to conceptualise and define the emergence of a global law (5).

1. CONSTRUCTIVE INDIGNATION

Indignation provides the anchor for the emergence of these new attempts towards global regulation. It echoes a deontological moral philosophy that places human dignity at the forefront of supreme and universal values. At times, the protection afforded to this universal value runs counter to the economic and financial interests that benefit from worldwide deregulation and a utilitarian market rationale (albeit disguised as morally tinged ethics). This market rationale boosted the offshoring of American production in the clothing sector, which began to take place in the 1970s. The low costs of both the local workforce in developing countries and import taxes, as well as the benefits of global trade deregulation, all favoured massive offshoring.[30]

But such profits were – and are – accrued to the detriment of the protection of the social and human rights of workers, exploited in 'sweatshops' both in developing countries and in the United States. A group of civil society actors composed of students, activists from non-governmental organisations, and trade unions launched a strong militant movement against these 'sweatshops' in the United States during the 1990s, denouncing the deplorable working conditions in these factories and foreign workshops in which American companies made their products, which were then resold on the American market.[31]

The *Kasky v. Nike* case fits within this context of indignation. Marc Kasky is none other than an outraged American consumer who decided to use the tools available to him to bring the controversy against the American company before an American judge. He is not a direct victim of the sweatshops, but a citizen of the world who feels deceived by Nike's discourse that asserts irreproachable ethics, while all the while conducting abusive practices abroad as denounced by the media.

2. THE STRUGGLE BETWEEN MODES OF REGULATION

The global fight against 'sweatshops', which is still relevant today, was long and difficult due to insufficient legal engineering and the unreliable effects of the commercial boycott tactics.[32] In the absence of legislative reform, the short-lived media interest could not ensure that the embers of indignation disturb well-established commercial practices, nor indeed weigh upon the conduct of private actors harnessing their deregulated environment.

---

30 See in particular the analysis of Fisher (n 28) 267–310.

31 See A. Ross (dir.), *No Sweat: Fashion, Free Trade and the Rights of Garment Workers* (London and New York, Verso 1997).

32 Tim Bartley and Curtis Child, 'Movements, Markets and Fields: The Effects of Anti-Sweatshop Campaigns on U.S. Firms, 1993-2000' (2011) 90(2) *Social Forces* 425–51.

What the fight against sweatshops illustrates is, above all, the inadequacy of our pre-global methods of regulating conduct. Governing global actors, such as multinational companies operating in a transnational environment, through regulation that corresponds to the classical model of 'command and control' is both unsuitable and impracticable.[33] Under this traditional paradigm of regulation, global actors are legally untouchable when they operate in weak or authoritarian countries. They do so within the jurisdiction of states that either lack the legal instruments to protect workers' rights and human rights, or do not have the technical, economic, legal or financial means to implement these laws, at the risk of driving foreign investments away.[34] International law, including the standards of the International Labour Organization, is still insufficient in this respect, and no American extraterritorial legal instrument was applicable to regulate the behaviour of American companies abroad in the area of social rights and labour law. Behind the scenes, there is a regulatory struggle, in itself indicative of the confrontation between models of legal thought, and a cold war of normative instruments. Should we regulate, co-regulate or self-regulate?[35] Is conventional law – in its 'command and control' form – adapted to or overtaken by global affairs, the permeability of borders and the rise of private actors? More than that, how should we think about codes of conduct? Are these instruments normative? Are they legal? Or do they produce at the very least some regulatory effects?

While positive law does not offer regulatory or judicial solutions to the problem of sweatshops located in weak or authoritarian states, and is ill-equipped to regulate global problems, it may be that awareness campaigns and public outcry will lead multinational companies to voluntarily committing themselves to certain minimum standards. Indeed, initiatives to create binding norms aimed at regulating the behaviour of companies have not succeeded or have been insufficient, leaving room for companies to self-regulate.[36] This is the project of corporate social responsibility, seen as an alternative to binding regulation. Corporate social responsibility convinced capital that it was an opportunity to develop a communication strategy adapted to the evolution of global public opinion, while escaping coercive norms.[37] But it also convinced non-governmental organisations that perceived in self-regulation as an effective mode of governance, as well as States that saw it as a way to preserve an acceptable form of

---

[33] On the regulatory dilemma of capital-importing countries and its consequences on the design of conduct regulation in the transnational sphere, see H. Muir Watt, 'Aspects économiques du droit international privé (Réflexions sur l'impact de la globalisation économique sur les fondements des conflits de lois et de juridictions)' (2004) 307 *Recueil des cours*; Robert Baldwin and Martin Cave, *Understanding Regulation: Theory, Strategy, and Practice* (Oxford, Oxford University Press 2013) 568 p.

[34] Ayoub (n 29) 422.

[35] Darren Sinclair, 'Self-Regulation Versus Command and Control? Beyond False Dichotomies' (1997) 19(4) *Law & Policy* 529–59.

[36] D. Collins, 'The Quest to Improve the Human Condition: The First 1500 Articles Published in Journal of Business Ethics' (2000) 26 *Journal of Business Ethics* 1–73.

[37] T. Bartley, 'Corporate Accountability and the Privatization of Labor Standards: Struggles over Codes of Conduct in the Apparel Industry' (2005) 14 *Research in Political Sociology* 1–52.

political balance, thanks to a mode of regulation that did not block the neo-liberal project for the world economy.[38]

The underlying idea of corporate social responsibility is to bring a certain moral and ethical tinge to the neoliberal paradigm of global commerce, which is devoid of such values. It seeks to determine the moral philosophy[39] that governs companies, in the form of a minimal ethic. Corporate social responsibility is the response of the economic world to the emergence of a moral conscience of consumers and to the concomitant globalisation of business and indignation. But of course, corporate social responsibility is not disinterested. It is fundamentally political because it allows multinational companies to join the starting line of key players within the emerging field of global governance. Its ethical appearance is the concession that gives purchase to a form of democratic legitimacy on a global scale. But of course, it is also economic: it serves the interests of the market because it attracts consumers and investors while avoiding more restrictive state regulation.

The *Kasky* case highlights the inherent tensions between two opposing trends: that of a global deregulated market and that of a minimal moral ethic.[40] Nike perfectly controls the rules of the game of a deregulated market and the relocation of its production, in order to maximise its profits by reducing its production costs. However, producing is not enough! Nike must sell its production and cannot neglect that its market is composed of American and European consumers potentially endowed with a moral conscience. It is this other face of globalisation – that of moral values – that the corporate giant has a harder time mastering; it has to bear the costs of a battle that plays out in the courts.

3. THE MARKET OF STANDARDS

Multinational corporations act as standard entrepreneurs by adopting various codes of conduct with diverse content,[41] dealing with human rights, the environment, corruption, consumer rights, labour law or other themes. They define the social and environmental standards to which they voluntarily submit themselves, as they please.[42] In order to

---

38 Willem van Genugten and Sophie van Bijsterveld, 'Codes of Conduct for Multinational Enterprises: Useful Instruments or a Shield against Binding Responsibility' (1998–99) 7(2) *Tilburg Foreign Law Review* 161–78.

39 J. Dienhart, 'Rationality, Ethical Codes, and an Egalitarian Justification of Ethical Expertise: Implications for Professions and Organizations' (1995) 5(3) *Business Ethics Quarterly* 419–50. *Contra:* M. S. Schwartz, 'Why Ethical Codes Constitute an Unconscionable Regression' (2000) 23 *Journal of Business Ethics* 173–84.

40 M. S. Schwartz, 'Universal Moral Values for Corporate Codes of Ethics' (2005) 59 *Journal of Business Ethics* 27–44.

41 Emily Carasco and Jang Singh, 'The Content and Focus of the Codes of Ethics of the World's Largest Transnational Corporations' (2003) 108(1) *Business and Society Review* 71–94.

42 The role of codes of conduct as regulatory instruments is not new, see: Joel Davidow and Lisa Chiles, 'The United States and the Issue of the Binding or Voluntary Nature of International Codes of Conduct Regarding Restrictive Business Practices' (1978) 72(2) *American Journal of International Law* 247–71.

standardise the content of these voluntary commitments, various public, private or hybrid initiatives have sought to propose universal codes. This was the purpose of the OECD Guidelines for Multinational Enterprises revised in 2000; the Tripartite Declaration of the International Labour Organization; the United Nations Global Compact; or private initiatives such as Amnesty International's Human Rights Principles for Companies, the *Ethical Trading Initiative Code* or the *Global Sullivan Principles*, to name but a few.[43] These codes have not necessarily imposed themselves as exclusive norms, but rather as references that have structured the private response to a normative gap. Thus, they have found their place in an anarchic set of voluntary, public, private or hybrid norms. Most of these instruments will refer to other standards, such as the 1948 Universal Declaration of Human Rights, a tool of reference of quasi-constitutional value. In reality, these references have little legal or technical interest. They are mainly used to determine a framework of values embodied in relatively indeterminate standards that the company asserts it wishes to respect in the context of its commercial or financial activities.

The adoption by a corporation of a code of conduct does not mean that that corporation will be invested with an ethical and virtuous mission. The incentive for adopting codes of conduct must be found elsewhere, and particularly in the agent's rational interest. There are several reasons[44] that can drive a business to adopt a code of conduct, the primary one being the competitive advantage and the economic and financial benefits that it provides.

The adoption of a code allows for the anticipation of how standards will be applied. For instance, a corporate code adopted by a market leader is likely to become a reference standard very quickly. This is also true of multi-company or sectorial codes of conduct that provide a normative structure for an entire industry. Thus, when a company adopts a code of conduct, it can anticipate the emergence of these wider standards and thereby engineer them according to its own economic interests. Other companies in the same industry will have to comply sooner or later, but will have fallen behind the leading company, that will benefit from a competitive advantage. This explains the emergence of a competitive market for standards. In the textile sector, for instance, China has promoted a social responsibility standard CSC9000T offering less protection for human rights than SA8000, a reference standard in Europe and the United States, with which the Chinese norm was directly seeking to compete.[45]

Additionally, there is a series of incentives that is likely to convince companies to adopt codes of conduct for commercial and financial reasons. Several examples can be mentioned. Some companies may be required by co-contractors either to comply with certain codes of conduct or even to adopt such a code. The leading companies of certain industries can thus contractually impose standards on all the actors in the chain

[43] For an analysis of the emergence of these codes of conduct, see: Robert Grosse, 'Codes of Conduct for Multinational Enterprises' (1982) 16(5) *Journal of World Trade Law* 414–33.

[44] L. J. Brooks, 'Corporate Codes of Ethics' (1989) 8(2–3) *Journal of Business Ethics* 117–29.

[45] Qingxiu Bu, 'Migrant Labour Standards and Human Rights Or Multinational Companies' Supply Chains: Reshaping a Playing Field in China: Part I' (2016) 37(4) *Business Law Review* 129–33.

of production.[46] As a rational agent that seeks to invest in a sector of activity in which one or more codes of conduct are imposed by contract, the adoption of such a code is an economic necessity for a company. This also applies to companies wishing to compete in public tenders or obtain public aid. Governments are now increasingly requiring these private companies to respect social and environmental standards and are inviting them to adopt codes of conduct that reflect these commitments.

These few examples demonstrate that, while the adoption of a code of conduct by a company was originally conceived as purely commercial discourse, resulting from the free choice of each company and responding to a purely voluntary philosophy, the examination of practices and incentives makes it clear that this voluntarism is constrained or at least strongly incentivised. The code of conduct becomes an indispensable tool to operate and participate in the global economy. However, the critical question concerning the emergence of these codes and escalating communication remains that of their real or supposed impact on behavioural change.[47] Since we now understand that companies adopt codes of conduct, voluntarily from a legal point of view but constrained to do so from an economic standpoint, what is the fate of these instruments? How can they be used to amend behaviour and respond, if necessary, to the constructive indignation that was our starting point?

4. BEHAVIOURAL ANALYSIS

The adoption of a code of conduct in response to general outrage seems like a very slight move in light of the numerous and serious human rights violations that are being perpetrated daily and which go hand in hand with a deregulated and amoral liberal economy. One wonders if these codes of conduct play any part in changing the culture, softening the violations, or at the very least controlling the violence that attaches to this economy. If they do not offer a structural solution, codes of conduct can nevertheless play a reforming role through appropriate sanctions. Indeed, these codes of conduct, as voluntary and non-binding instruments that are conceived to be outside the legal prism, are nevertheless likely to produce legal effects. In some cases, failure to comply with the codes results in penalties – legal, economic or reputational – that are costly for the company. Following some calculations and analyses, a company may choose to comply with the social and environmental standards of the code of conduct. For instance, this applies to codes of conduct that are incorporated into contracts.[48] They can be legally

---

[46] A. Sobczak, 'Codes of Conduct in Subcontracting Networks: A Labour Law Perspective' (2003) 44 *Journal of Business Ethics* 225–34.

[47] R. C. Warren, 'Codes of Ethics: Bricks without Straw' (1993) 2(4) *A European Review* 185–91.

[48] Haley Revak, 'Corporate Codes of Conduct: Binding Contract or Ideal Publicity' (2011–12) 63(6) *Hastings Law Journal* 1645–70; J. Klabbers and T. Piiparinen (dir.), *Normative Pluralism and International Law: Exploring Global Governance* (Cambridge, Cambridge University Press 2013) 193 et seq.

sanctioned as contractual terms enforceable against subcontractors,[49] or may be invoked by employees.[50] This is also illustrated in the misleading advertising allegation invoked by Mr. Kasky. The Nike code of conduct is a communication tool conveying information about the products or services of a company. It is part of a set of communication tools used by companies to assert their image. The media denouncing Nike's sweatshops abroad in 1996 led to an escalation of public communication, with the corporate giant refuting these allegations, releasing multiple statements and brandishing its code of conduct which forbade this type of practice. According to Mr. Kasky, these elements of communication were misleading; indeed, they provided the grounds on which, as a consumer, he would file a lawsuit, using California legislation on commercial practices. The legal battle mostly focused on whether the code of conduct was protected by freedom of expression or whether it should be equated with a form of commercial speech that does not enjoy the same constitutional protection. Understandably, the decision of the Californian Supreme Court, which opted for the latter option, will have significant effects for businesses. Companies' communication policies, which emanate from marketing departments, suddenly produce legal effects: companies can now be held liable for misleading statements in their communication, regardless of the medium, including statements contained in their code of conduct.

The subtlety of these lawsuits is that, rather than focusing on the violations of fundamental rights committed abroad – which usually escape the jurisdiction of the home courts of the multinational enterprise – they focus on its misleading statements, which violate local law. Commercial normative tools – in this case, the standards of unfair practices and misleading advertising – are used to compel private actors to modify their extraterritorial behaviour. The company is not likely to comply with the standard per se, but is directly incentivised by a cost-benefit analysis. Indeed, deregulated commercial practices violating social and environmental standards do not generate sufficient benefits to neglect the reputational, financial and commercial costs of breaching the standards of these codes – depending of course on the profile of the company, the level of activity and the particular industry concerned.

The same dynamics are replicated elsewhere,[51] especially in Europe, since advertising refers to 'the making of a representation in any form in connection with a trade, business, craft or profession in order to promote the supply of goods or services, including immovable property, rights and obligations.'[52] This potentially includes corporate codes of conduct, given that is deemed misleading

[49] Sobczak (n 46) 225–34; A. Sobczak, 'Are Codes of Conduct in Global Supply Chains Really Voluntary? From Soft Law Regulation of Labour Relations to Consumer Law' (2006) 16 *Business Ethics Quarterly* 167–84.

[50] Lance Compa and Tashia Hinchliffe-Darricarrere, 'Enforcing International Labor Rights through Corporate Codes of Conduct' (1995) 33(3) *Columbia Journal of Transnational Law* 663–90.

[51] Tamieka Spencer, 'Talking about Social Responsibility: Liability for Misleading & Deceptive Statements in Corporate Codes of Conduct' (2003) 29(2) *Monash University Law Review* 297–315.

[52] Directive 84/450/EEC on misleading advertisement (OJ 1984, L.250/17), amended and codified: Directive 2006/114/EC of 12 December 2006 concerning misleading and comparative advertisement (OJ 2006, L.376/21).

> any advertising which in any way, including its presentation, deceives or is likely to deceive the persons to whom it is addressed or whom it reaches and which, by reason of its deceptive nature, is likely to affect their economic behaviour or which, for those reasons, injures or is likely to injure a competitor.

Moreover, in accordance with the Unfair Commercial Practices Directive,[53]

> a commercial practice shall also be regarded as misleading if, in its factual context, taking account of all its features and circumstances, it causes or is likely to cause the average consumer to take a transactional decision that he would not have taken otherwise, and it involves [inter alia] non-compliance by the trader with commitments contained in codes of conduct by which the trader has undertaken to be bound where i) the commitment is not aspirational but is firm and is capable of being verified and, ii) the trader indicates in a commercial practice that he is bound by the code.[54]

5. THE REGULATION OF THE GLOBAL WORLD

Although it is already over ten years old, one can draw useful lessons from the *Kasky* case. This case showcases, from a certain angle, the emergence of global law and emphasises the importance of its conceptualisation. The starting point of this case is what we can call a global problem, a situation that escapes the influence of state-centric law. The State is no longer an adequate regulator when it comes to countering human rights violations by companies acting on a global scale. These violations can no longer be controlled by a sovereign State in accordance with a standard 'command and control' type regulation, whether it is the State of the company's headquarters or the host State. State-centric normative tools are unable to effectively regulate private behaviours due to the extraterritorial character of activities, the fluidity of capital and investment, and the overwhelming economic and financial power of multinational companies.

The impact of globalisation on the law requires revisiting the premises and paradigms on which the state-centric conception of law is usually based.[55] Borders disappear in favour of a global space in which private actors act as producers of standards. Private codes of conduct emerge, in a disorderly manner, as responses to an outraged public and consumer opinion, on a global scale. They are then structured, institutionalised and integrated into contracts, markets and legislation, and become indispensable instruments on both a commercial and economic level. However, these codes of conduct are far from being a satisfactory response to the outrage over a violent deregulated liberal economy. At most, they act as instruments of socialisation for the economic actors in a global space that resembles the state of nature. This return to the state of nature, and this failure of international law and the sovereign state, is a unique

53 C. M. D. S. Pavillon, 'The Interplay between the Unfair Commercial Practices Directive and Codes of Conduct' (2012) 5(4) *Erasmus Law Review* 267–88.

54 Directive 2005/29/EC on Unfair Commercial Practices (OJ 2005, L.149/22).

55 B. Frydman, *Petit manuel pratique de droit global* (Bruxelles, Collection L'Académie en poche 2014).

opportunity to revisit the foundations of law, in order to conceive a neo-naturalist law[56] that puts humankind at the heart of its reasoning and purpose. The global space should thus be based on humanist values. These values would be conveyed by social and environmental standards that codes of conduct would help promote, at least from a formal point of view. Codes of conduct also respond, as pointed out by some theorists, to the de-statisation that characterises globalisation, which is accompanied by the rise of global operators seeking legitimacy and accountability.[57] As regulatory instruments, corporate codes are likely to meet these expectations at least partially, as long as their content and control mechanisms are adequate. Some authors see in corporate codes of conduct the expression of a societal constitutionalism,[58] which echoes the normative project of the theories of global constitutionalism. In this perspective, *Kasky* reveals the 'constitutional' emergence of codes of conduct, which seek to respond to the pressure caused by public outrage over the human rights abuses in which multinational corporations are complicit. Of course, one cannot analyse these codes in isolation and consider them to be a foolproof solution to the abuses of a deregulated liberal market in anarchic globalisation. However, the constitutional metaphor points to the potential role of these codes of conduct with their varied content, forms and authors, as part of a complex and subtle piece of global engineering that can contribute to changing conduct. This is the main lesson of the *Kasky* affair; it highlights the point of contact between private normative production (the Nike code of conduct) and the consumer protection law. This transnational litigation[59] emphasises the creativity and strategy of the actors – a consumer playing the role of 'private prosecutor' against a company that acts as a 'producer of standards' and a judge – strengthening the normative basis of private codes of conduct and their legal potential.

---

[56] On global law as part of this general perspective, see R. Domingo, *The New Global Law* (Cambridge, Cambridge University Press 2010); A. Cançado Trindade, *International Law for Humankind: Towards a New Jus Gentium*, General Course on Public International Law (La Haye, Leiden/Boston, Martinus Nijhoff 2006); H. Berman, 'World Law' (1995) 18 *Fordham Int'l L.J.* 1617; N. Feldman, 'Cosmopolitan Law?' (2007) 116 *Yale L.J.* 1022.

[57] See B. Kingsbury, N. Krisch and R. Stewart, 'The Emergence of Global Administrative Law' (2005) 68 *Law & Contemporary Problems* 15; S. Cassese, *Au-delà de l'Etat* (Bruxelles, Bruylant 2011) (this book contains eight texts written by Cassese translated into French. This is undoubtedly the most complete and useful bibliographic reference in French to get acquainted with GAL).

[58] Gunther Teubner and Anna Beckers, 'Expanding Constitutionalism' (2013) 20(2) *Indiana Journal of Global Legal Studies* 523–50.

[59] B. Frydman and L. Hennebel, 'Le contentieux transnational des droits de l'Homme: une analyse stratégique' (2009) *R.T.D.H.* 73; H. H. Koh, *Transnational Litigation in United States Courts* (New York, Foundation Press 2008).

9. Arbitration and religion: *Jivraj v. Hashwani*

9.1 CASE BACKGROUND

Are arbitrators employees for the purpose of the Employment Equality (Religion or Belief) Regulations, 2003? This is an unlikely question to open a debate about the role of religious norms in the global sphere! Yet it arose in the context of an international commercial contract with a religious arbitration clause, triggering controversy not only within the arbitration community (which feared the potential fiscal and other consequences of a legal characterisation of arbitration as employment) but also far beyond. In a world where religious norms are gaining (or regaining) increasing prominence, how exactly do our multiple belief systems fit with global economic governance by contract?

The case arises from a joint venture agreement between Mr. Jivraj and Mr. Hashwani, that contained the controversial arbitration clause. It provided that any dispute between the parties should be resolved by arbitration before three arbitrators, all of whom should be 'respected members of the Ismaili community' (a religious community comprised of Shia Ismaili Muslims). The parties terminated their joint venture agreement in 1988 (seven years after its inception) and appointed three Ismaili arbitrators to assist them in dividing the joint venture assets. However, as the panel was unable to resolve all the issues between the parties, they remained in dispute for some years. In 2008, Mr. Hashwani initiated another arbitration and appointed Sir Anthony Colman as an arbitrator, despite the fact that he was not a member of the Ismaili community. Mr. Jivraj started proceedings in England in the Commercial Court, seeking a declaration that the appointment of Sir Anthony Colman as an arbitrator was invalid. Upon which, in turn, Mr. Hashwami sought a judgment validating the appointment on the basis that the agreement violated the Employment Equality (Religion and Belief) Regulations 2003, which protects employees from being discriminated against on grounds of religion or belief in relation to their employment.

The Court of Appeal held that arbitrators were employees for the purpose of the Regulations and that the requirement that arbitrators be members of the Ismaili community contravened the prohibition of discrimination in those Regulations. The provision was therefore void and, being inseparable from the arbitration clause, rendered that clause void in its entirety. The holding sent shockwaves through the arbitration industry, since the procedural rules of many arbitral institutions (such as the International Chamber of Commerce) accept restrictions on arbitrators' nationality. Hundreds of arbitration clauses became potentially unenforceable overnight. Very rapidly, a unanimous decision by the Supreme Court overturned the decision of the Court of Appeal on that point. However, beyond the issue of the legal status of arbitrators as employees or service providers, the place of religion in global economic governance remains moot, as does the assumed neutrality in this respect of non-religious legal norms and the principles that govern choice in private international law.

Case: *Jivraj v. Hashwani* [2010] EWCA Civ 712

9.2 BEYOND LEGAL PLURALISM: SOME THOUGHTS ON PAIDEIC ARBITRATION

*François-Xavier Licari**

1. INTRODUCTION

> In spite of what so many Enlightenment thinkers would have predicted, religious identities are still central to ethical identity.[1]

The *Jivraj v. Hashwani* case was essentially apprehended for the momentary disturbance it caused to the 'arbitration community'. The judgment of the Court of Appeal for England and Wales was castigated because it had intolerably damaged the image of arbitration: the arbitrator would be an employee and a clause requiring him to be Ismaili would constitute a discrimination prohibited under English law.[2] In contrast, the judgment of the United Kingdom Supreme Court was praised for the reassurance it provided to the various actors of the London arbitration market;[3] everything went back to normal: the arbitrator is an independent service provider,[4] the parties are free to choose him according to whatever criteria they deem appropriate, including ethnic and religious ones.[5] *Much ado about nothing?* asked an author.[6] One is tempted to say yes. However, the case is of particular interest if addressed for what it brings to the understanding of the diaspora, its institutions, transnational legal systems, legal pluralism and *paideic arbitration* (2). From a more technical point of view, the case is also interesting for the questions it has not answered, but that are often raised by such an arbitration, such as the question of the validity of the religious arbitration clauses included in a contract of adhesion, the impartiality of the arbitrator or the relationship

---

* Contribution originally written in French, translated to English by Nedra Ben Miled.

[1] Kwame Anthony Appiah, 'Causes of Quarrel: What's Special about Religious Disputes?', in Thomas Banchoff (ed.), *Religious Pluralism, Globalization, and World Politics* (Oxford, Oxford University Press 2008) 41, 57.

[2] *Jivraj v. Hashwani* [2010] EWCA Civ 712.

[3] On this topic: Audley Sheppard and Marie Berard, '*Jivraj v. Hashwani* – Faith in English Arbitration Is Restored' (2011) *Cahiers de l'arbitrage* 1079.

[4] On this specific issue, see: Christopher McCrudden, 'Two Views of Subordination: The Personal Scope of Employment Discrimination Law in *Jivraj v Hashwani*' (2012) 41 *Industrial L. J.* 30.

[5] *Jivraj v. Hashwani* [2011] UKSC 40, *Rev. arb.* 2011, 1007, comment J.-B. Racine; Christopher Style and Philomena Cleobury, '*Jivraj v Hashwani*: "Public Interest and Party Autonomy"' (2011) 27 *Arbitration International* 563; C. Mark Baker and Lucy Greenwood, 'The Regionalisation of International Arbitration: Maintaining International Standards in Appointing Arbitrators – A Comment on *Jivraj v Hashwani*' in P. Wautelet, T. Kruger and G. Koppens (eds), *The Practice of Arbitration – Essays in Honour of Hans van Houtte* (Oxford, Hart Publishing 2012) 15; Umar A. Oseni and Hunud Abia Kadouf, 'The Discrimination Conundrum in the Appointment of Arbitrators in International Arbitration' (2012) 29 *Journal of Int'l Arbitration* 519; Jeff Dasteel, 'Arbitration Agreements That Discriminate in the Appointment and Selection of Arbitrators' (2012) 11 *Rich. J. Global L. and Bus.* 383.

[6] Racine (n 5).

between religious arbitration and the main constitutional principles such as the religious neutrality of the State (3).

2. ARBITRATION AS A PAIDEIC INSTITUTION

It is tempting to put the case of *Jivraj v. Hashwani* under the banner of religious arbitration.[7] Yet, the facts show a singularity that has been neglected by commentators: the clause did not designate the *Sharia* in general, nor the Ismaili law in particular,[8] but *English law* as applicable to the merits of the case. What mattered was only the arbitrators' religious belonging to a transnational Shia Muslim community, the Nizarite Ismailis, whose spiritual and temporal leader is the Agha Khan. It says that beside the religious arbitration *sensu stricto*, there is a kind of arbitration which we will call *diasporic* or *paideic*.

To fully appreciate the richness of the *Jivraj v. Hashwani* case, it is first necessary to introduce the notion of *diaspora*. The term was originally used to refer almost exclusively to the condition of the Jewish people. The word *diaspora*, of Greek origin, designates, since the beginning of modern times, the state of a people dispersed geographically, therefore installed in different political organisations, but which, despite this dispersion, maintains a form of unity and solidarity.[9] The term refers to a certain number of more or less connoted elements; a people or an ethnic group, a real historical or an imaginary collectivity, and constantly reinvented, a religious affiliation.

---

[7] We have defined 'religious' or 'denominational' arbitration as being directed 'to adherents of a particular faith wishing to have their dispute settled by judges adhering to the same faith and according to the norms and principles of that faith. The adjective "religious" thus designates both the substantive law and the procedural law that the arbitral tribunal must apply as a result of a choice of law clause': François-Xavier Licari, 'L'arbitrage rabbinique, entre droit talmudique et droit des nations' (2013) *Revue de l'arbitrage* 57, 59. On the religiously binding nature of arbitration for Jews and Muslims: François-Xavier Licari, '*Dieu est mon droit*: la place des modes alternatifs de règlement des litiges dans les trois religions du Livre' (2018) *Annuaire Droit et Religion* 392. On religious arbitration, *inter alia*: Mark Hill, 'Resolution of Disputes within Religious Communities', in Richard Potz and Wolfgand Wieshaider (eds), *Religious Adjudication and the State* (Granada, Editorial Comares 2015) 5; Michael J. Broyde, *Sharia Tribunals, Rabbinical Courts, and Christian Panels – Religious Arbitration in America and the West* (Oxford, Oxford University Press 2017).

[8] On which, Arif A. Jamal, 'Principles in the Development of Ismaili Law' in Eugene Cotran (ed.), *Yearbook of Islamic and Middle Eastern Law*, Volume 7 (Leiden, Brill 2000) 115.

[9] Dominique Schnapper, 'De l'Etat-nation au monde transnational. Du sens et de l'utilité du concept de diaspora' (2001) 17 *Revue européenne des migrations internationales* 9; Michel Bruneau, *Diasporas et espaces transnationaux* (Paris, Anthropos 2004); Chantal Bordes-Benayoun and Dominique Schnapper, *Diasporas et nations* (Paris, Odile Jabob 2006); Prakash Shah and Werner F. Mensky, 'Introduction : Migration, Diasporas and Legal Systems in Europe', in Prakash Shah and Werner F. Mensky, *Migration, Diasporas and Legal Systems in Europe* (Abingdon, Routledge 2006) 1; Daniel Boyarin, *A Traveling Homeland. The Babylonian Talmud as Diaspora* (Philadelphia PA, University of Pennsylvania Press 2015) 1–32.

Essentially used in humanities and social sciences, the notion of diaspora experienced a success and an inflation that made its promoters fear the erasure of any heuristic value. To avoid this pitfall, we will adopt the definition proposed by Daniel Boyarin: the word diaspora designates a

> synchronic cultural situation applicable to people who participate in a doubled cultural (and frequently linguistic) location, in which they share a culture in the place in which they dwell but also with another group of people who live elsewhere, in which they have a local and a trans-local cultural identity and expression at the same time.[10]

The author, breaking with the common opinion, adds: 'None of this needs imply trauma, an original scene of forced dispersion, a longing for a homeland or even the existence of a myth of one homeland'.[11] The Nizari Ismailism certainly corresponds to this ideal type: a minority within a minority who enjoyed political autonomy for a short time belonging to a distant past, scattered to the four corners of the planet, sharing a Shiite religious culture, modernist, whose cement is the Agha Khan's Imamate.[12] The Ismailis (*Shia Imami Ismaili*) belong to the Shia branch of Islam. The foundations of Shiite Islam do not differ from Sunni Islam: strict monotheism and recognition of Muhammad as the messenger of God and ultimate prophet. The fundamental difference is rather of a dynastic nature. Like the other Shiites, the Ismailis consider that at the death of Muhammad, Ali b. Abi Talib, Muhammad's son-in-law and cousin, became the first Imam, that is, the spiritual leader of the Muslim community. They also consider that this spiritual directorate, the imamate, is hereditary, transmitted by Ali and his wife Fatima, the daughter of Muhammad. Prince Karim Aga Khan IV is considered by the Nizarite Ismailis to be the 49th Imam. Born in Switzerland in 1936, he succeeded his grandfather, Sir Sultan Mohamed Shah Aga Khan III (1877–1957) in 1957, at the age of 20 years. This diaspora presents the unique case, it seems to us, of obeying a political regime that could be described as an *enlightened theocracy. Theocracy*, because the authority of the Aga Khan rests on his quality of hereditary Imam;[13] *enlightened* because the Aga Khan IV endowed his nation with a transnational

---

[10] Boyarin (n 9) 19.

[11] Ibid.

[12] Farhad Daftary, *The Isma'ilis – Their History and Doctrines* 2nd edn (Cambridge, Cambridge University Press 2007); Karen Leonard, 'Transnational and Cosmopolitan Forms of Islam in the West' (2009) 8 *Harvard Middle Eastern and Islamic Review* 177, 181 seq.; Jonah Steinberg, *Isma'ili Modern: Globalization and Identity in a Muslim Community* (Durham NC, The University of North Carolina Press 2011); Teena Purohit, *The Aga Khan Case: Religion and Identity in Colonial India* (Cambridge MA, Harvard University Press 2012); M. Boivin, *L'âghâ khân et les khojah.- Islam chiite et dynamiques sociales dans le sous-continent indien* (Paris, Karthala 2013).

[13] Harold Stephen Morris, 'The divine kingship of the Aga Khan: A study of theocracy in East Africa' (1958) 14 *Southwestern Journal of Anthropology* 454; Soumen Mukherjee, 'Being "Ismaili" and "Muslim": Some observations on the politico-religious career of Aga Khan III' (2011) 34 *South Asia: Journal of South Asian Studies* 188.

constitution[14] in 1986[15] and a whole network of institutions (*The Aga Khan Development Network*) that allow Ismailis to take an active part in political, social and economic affairs of the diaspora[16]; *enlightened* because the Agha Khan tirelessly promotes education and integration, shaping his community in his cosmopolitan[17] and pluralistic[18] image. Also under his authority, this diaspora has an official language, English.[19]

The Ismailis constitute not only a diaspora, but also a *paideic community* in the sense that Robert Cover gives to this expression.[20] In ancient Greek, the word *paideia* means 'education,' 'culture,' or 'civilization.'

> Whether it is the *paideia* described by Homer, Cicero's *humanitas* or the *adab* in Arab-Islamic culture, what is meant by the word 'culture' is somewhat universal in the sense that, far from being a professional training, it is a body of knowledge whose acquisition aims at the harmonious development of the body and mind and at the self-fulfillment from a theoretical as well as from an ethical point of view.[21]

---

14 The official text of this Constitution is available at the following address: http://www.ismaili.net/Source/extra1.html.

15 The official title of this constitution is 'The Constitution of the Shia Imami Ismaili Muslims' (art. 2.1.). At first, it was the Aga Khan III who endowed his East African community with a constitution in 1905. Then similar constitutions were gradually promulgated for various communities in the Indian subcontinent. From the 1970s, the current Aga Khan continued this practice to take into account the development of Ismaili communities in the United States of America, Canada, Europe, South and East Asia, some Gulf States, Syria, Iran and Afghanistan. In 1986, a panismaili constitution was promulgated: see Arif A. Jamal, 'Religious Authority and Constitutional Order: A Case Study of The Conciliation and Arbitration Boards (CABs) of the Shia Imami Ismaili Community' (2013) 2 *Journal of Law, Religion and State* 235; Mohamed Jindani, 'Dispute Resolution in the Shai'a Isma'ili School in Islamic Law: A Case for Legal Pluralism in the United Kingdom' (2005) 12 *YB Islamic and Middle EL* 141, 145 seq.

16 Paul J. Kaiser, *Culture, Transnationalism, and Civil Society – Aga Khan Social Service Initiatives in Tanzania* (Westport CT, Praeger 1996); Daryoush Mohammad Poor, *Authority without Territory: The Aga Khan Development Network and The Ismaili Imamate* (Basingstoke, Palgrave 2014); Karim H. Karim, 'Aga Khan Development Network: Shia Ismaili Islam', in Stephen M. Cherry and Helen Rose Ebaugh (eds), *Global Religious Movements across Borders: Sacred service* (Abingdon, Routledge 2014) 143; Karim H. Karim, 'Shia Ismaili Leadership: Past and Present' (2016) 33 *The American Journal of Islamic Social Sciences* 102.

17 Aga Khan, *The Memoirs of Aga Khan* (New York, Simon and Schuster 1954); M. Roch, *L'Aga Khan: une identité transversale*, Institut Universitaire des Hautes Etudes Internationales, Mémoire, January 2005, http://www.ismaili.net/Source/martinroch.pdf.

18 Sahir Dewji, 'The Aga Khan's Discourse of Applied Pluralism: Converging the "Religious" and the "Secular"' (2017) *Studies in Religion/Sciences Religieuses* 1.

19 Brook Bolander, 'English and the transnational Ismaili Muslim community: Identity, the Aga Khan, and infrastructure' (2016) 45 *Language in Society* 583.

20 Robert M. Cover, 'The Supreme Court, 1982 Term – Foreword: Nomos and Narrative' (1983) 97 *Harv. L. Rev* 4.

21 Laetitia Monteils-Laeng, 'Paideia : éducation et accomplissement humain dans la Grèce antique', in Houari Touati (ed.), *Encyclopédie de l'humanisme méditerranéen*, Printemps 2014, http://encyclopedie-humanisme.com/?Paideia-216.

Cover endorses the thesis that a human being does not fit into a physical world or *cosmos*, but also into a normative universe, or *nomos*. According to this author, any legal system (state or non-state, as is the case of the Ismailis) mixes two elements, present in varying degrees: a 'paideic' component and an 'imperial' component. The first component corresponds to the 'construction of a world.' It is formed by the adherence to ideals, to a religion, or an *ethos* that federate the human group, constituting a society and generating a right (*jurisgenerative*). The Ismaili society is a very united and relatively homogeneous society that shares the same *Weltanschauung* – largely shaped by the past and by its constant reinterpretation by the various Aga Khans – and living according to a common nomos. The modern liberal societies in which most Ismailis live have a weak paideic link and a multiplicity of narrations, which constitutes a danger for a society with a strong paideic bond, like the Ismailis. In more or less a short time, this situation can lead to a dissolution of the nomos, an evil that threatens any diaspora.[22] To avoid such an outcome, it is necessary to ensure a narrative and nomic unity. This harmony is ensured by the various educational institutions of Ismaili society in the forefront of which is the Institute of Ismaili Studies.[23] It is mainly ensured by the Aga Khan who sees his quality of hermeneute and supreme narrator enshrined in Article 1 of the Ismaili Constitution. This narrative and hermeneutic activity takes the form of *farmans* (or *firmans*). The Constitution defines the *farman* as: 'Any pronouncement, direction, order or ruling made by Mawlana Hazar Imam'.[24]

The unity of the nomos is ensured by Articles 12 and 13 of the Ismaili Constitution, establishing a true transnational private justice system, *the Conciliation and Arbitration Boards* (*CABs*). The importance of *CABs* for the sustainability of the Ismaili diaspora as a paideic community is evident in the words of Mr. Nanji, heard as a witness in the *Jivraj* case: 'The primary objective of the CAB system is to assist Ismailis to resolve disputes in an equitable, speedy, confidential, cost effective, amicable and constructive manner and in *an environment, that is culturally sensitive …*'.[25] In other words, it is not only a question of resolving a conflict but of restoring peace in the respect of the community ethos, of ensuring that the conciliator or arbitrator respects and protects the values of the litigants in a liberal society where traditional values have taken a back seat.[26] It is a question of adapting the right to the aspirations of the parties and not to

---

22 The dissolution of the nomos is part of the more general and fundamentally ambivalent phenomenon of assimilation: David N. Myers, '"The Blessing of Assimilation" Reconsidered: An Inquiry into Jewish Cultural Studies' in David N. Myers and William Rowe (eds), *From Ghetto to Emancipation: Historical and Contemporary Reconsiderations* (Chicago IL, University of Chicago Press 1997) 17.

23 http://iis.ac.uk/home.

24 See e.g.: A. K. Adatia and N. Q. King, 'Some East African Firmans of H. H. Aga Khan III' (1969) 2 *Journal of Religion of Africa* 179.

25 Quoted by Jamal (n 15) 242.

26 E. Gary Spitko, 'Judge Not: In Defense of Minority-culture Arbitration' (2000) 77 *Wash. U.L.Q.* 1065; Michael J. Broyde, 'Faith-Based Private Arbitration as a Model for Preserving Rights and Values in a Pluralistic Society' (2015) 90 *Chi.-Kent L.R.* 111.

reconstitute a personal status[27] or to create a religious right detached from any state control, an undertaking anyway utopian in Western democracies.[28] Paideic arbitration promotes personal autonomy.[29] It promotes recognition of the cultural specificity of communities that coexist within a state community.[30]

3. MISCELLANEA

Paideic arbitration raises many other interesting questions that were not asked by *Jivraj*. Some of them will be briefly introduced in the following lines.

A. The Jewish Arbitrator and the Descendant of Nazis

Is an arbitrator required to disclose his Jewishness? This is the question to which the California Court of Appeal answered negatively in the case of *Rebmann v. Rohde* on 28 June 2011.[31] Arbitration proceedings were initiated in California between a Californian company and Mr. Rohde, its majority shareholder, on the one hand and a German company and Mr. Rebmann, its German majority shareholder, on the other hand in a dispute over a joint venture created between these parties in California. The arbitrator appointed by the arbitration centre designated in the arbitration clause rendered in California an award in favour of the German parties. Californian parties brought a legal action before Californian courts to overturn the award. They criticised the arbitrator for failing to reveal that he was Jewish, born in the United States of German Jewish parents who emigrated to the United States before the Second World War and that he was a member of an organisation, the '1939 Club', intended to prevent the occurrence of a new Holocaust. In support of this surprising reproach is a family history: the father of the California majority shareholder had been a soldier in the *Wehrmacht* during the Second World War and his father-in-law, a member of the *SS*. Mr. Rohde did not hesitate to maintain that if he had known the Jewishness of the arbitrator, he would have never accepted his appointment. The question asked to the Californian judge was therefore whether the genealogy of the arbitrator constituted a fact capable of creating in the mind of a reasonable person a doubt as to his impartiality. Based on a precedent of the California Supreme Court, the Court of Appeal held that impartiality must be objectively assessed from the perspective of a well-informed and thoughtful observer. Firstly, the Court of Appeal noted that Mr. Rohde's family situation could not have had

---

27 H. Patrick Glenn, 'L'arbitrage religieux au Canada: un statut personnel qui n'ose pas dire son nom?' in Michel Aoun (ed.), *Les statuts personnels en droit comparé. Evolutions récentes et implications pratiques* (Leuven, Peeters 2009) 265.

28 Nomi M. Stoltzenberg, 'Is There Such a Thing as Non-State Law? Lesson from Kiryas Joel', in Michael Helfand (ed.), *Negotiating State and Non-State Law: The Challenge of Global and Local Legal Pluralism* (Cambridge, Cambridge University Press 2015) 261.

29 Farrah Ahmed and Senwung Luk, 'How Religious Arbitration Could Enhance Personal Autonomy' (2012) *Oxford J. of Law and Religion* 1.

30 On the topic of 'recognition', see Charles Taylor, *Multiculturalism: Examining the Politics of Recognition* (Princeton NJ, Princeton University Press 1994) 25–75.

31 196 Cal.Ap.4th 1283 (Cal.Ct.App. 2011).

any role in the arbitrator's decision, since it was unknown to him. The Court of Appeal also noted that the case of the arbitrator concerned neither the Second World War nor the Holocaust. The Court of Appeal then goes on to say, and above all, that an arbitrator's impartiality should never be questioned simply *because of who he is*. The fact that an arbitrator belongs to a minority does not render the arbitrator biased, even if the matter before the arbitrator has any connection whatsoever with his affiliation to a minority. As the court put it: 'That one is black does not mean, ipso facto, that he is anti-white; no more than being Jewish implies being anti-Catholic, or being Catholic implies being anti-Protestant'.

B. Scientological Arbitration and Contract of Adhesion

A recent case concerning the Church of Scientology hit the headlines.[32] To the members of the Scientology, the legal system of their church supersedes and fully displaces the mainstream legal system.[33] This case deals, inter alia, with the decried practice of inserting a religious arbitration clause in a contract of adhesion.[34] Mr. and Mrs. Garcia are former members of the Church of Scientology. They complained that they had been fraudulently led to contribute financially to a construction project and various humanitarian actions related to the Florida Church of Scientology. They also complained that they had paid for services that had never been provided to them and that they had never been reimbursed. They then assigned two Scientology organisations before a district judge. The defendants argued that the contracts signed with the plaintiffs included an arbitration clause and that, therefore, the judge seized must refer the plaintiffs to arbitration. The existence of such a clause was not disputed. In essence, it required parties involved in any dispute with the Church of Scientology to submit it to the arbitration of an internal ecclesiastical commission to the Church of Scientology that would decide according to a body of rules entitled 'Internal Ethics' of the Scientology. The plaintiffs invoked the *unconscionability* of the arbitration clause to impede its enforceability. This basis is particularly interesting because the concept of *unconscionability* is not only present in American law and in English law, but also in the various European statutes which sanction 'leonine' or 'lesionary' contracts (*contrats léonins ou lésionnaires*) under various names: 'unfair' or 'unreasonable' clauses, 'significant imbalance', etc. The judge began by recalling that American law is fundamentally in favour of arbitration; it is only in exceptional circumstances that a judge will not sanction the parties' willingness to avoid state justice. However, the validity of arbitration clauses is not limitless: under Section 2 of the FAA it can be overturned on various grounds such as *fraud*, *duress* or *unconscionability*. Under

---

[32] U. S. District Court, *Maria del Rocio Burgos Garcia, and Luis A. Garcia Saz v. Church of Scientology Flag Service Organization Inc., Church of Scientology Flag Ship Service Organization, Inc.*, 2015 WL 10844160.

[33] Phil Lord, Scientology's Legal System, https://ssrn.com/abstract=3232113

[34] Michael Corkery and Jessica Silver-Greenberg, 'In Religious Arbitration, Scripture Is the Rule of Law' *New York Times* (2 November 2015), https://www.nytimes.com/2015/11/03/business/dealbook/in-religious-arbitration-scripture-is-the-rule-of-law.html; Jeff Dasteel, 'Religious Arbitration Agreements in Contracts Of Adhesion' (2016) 8 *Yearbook on Arbitration and Mediation* 45.

Florida law, a contractor invoking the unconscionability of the contract must prove both *procedural unconscionability* and *substantive unconscionability*. Procedural unconscionability relates to the circumstances surrounding the conclusion of the contract, including the unequal bargaining power of the parties and a person's ability to understand the contract to which she or he has been subject to. Substantive unconscionability requires the judge to determine whether the terms of the contract are so 'outrageously unfair' as to 'shock the judicial conscience' or 'unreasonably favorable' to the more powerful party. The judge carefully examined whether these two standards were met. First of all, the judge recalled that one of the tests that make it possible to know whether there is procedural unconscionability is to verify whether the plaintiff was deprived of a meaningful choice when the contract was concluded. In this case, the contract is a contract of adhesion (*contrat d'adhésion*) and, in particular, the arbitration clause was not negotiable. However, the judge reminded that even though the fact that the contract of adhesion is a strong evidence of procedural unconscionability, it is not enough to characterise it. What is crucial is the lack of meaningful choice. In this case, the judge considered that the Garcias cannot invoke the lack of choice or even surprise.[35] The judge noted that the plaintiffs stated during the hearings that they had read and generally understood the contracts they signed on many occasions. The judge pointed out that at least one of the plaintiffs was aware of the existence of the 'Committee on Evidence' and its operation. The judge further noted that Luis Garcia had attended a training entitled 'Ethics Specialist Course' during which he had studied the procedures of the 'Committee on Evidence' and the rules of ethics and law internal to Scientology. Another interesting argument raised by the plaintiffs was that the procedural unconscionability would come from the fact that there are no substantive rules or procedures governing Scientology arbitration. The judge noted that, as a matter of facts, there is no document from the Church of Scientology organising the arbitration procedure and that the person who acts as supreme judge within this Church himself recognises that the few rules that exist are contradictory. According to the judge, this was yet not enough to invalidate the clause. Indeed, Florida law is liberal in this regard. It is sufficient that the clauses allow the parties to have at least some ideas of the issues to be submitted to arbitration and establish some procedural elements by which the dispute will be settled. More specifically, the clause must contain the following essential elements: the mode of appointment of the arbitrators, the number of arbitrators, the questions submitted to arbitration, the mandatory nature – or not – of the arbitrator's decision. Examining the clauses, the judge considered that they met the requirements of Florida law and that the absence of detailed rules was not problematic. The judge then responded to the parties' arguments on substantive unconscionability. The question is particularly interesting because it emphasises some of the issues related to religious arbitration. According to the plaintiffs, the substantive unconscionability would result from the fact that the planned arbitration could not be fair and neutral. The

---

[35] Comp. U.S. District Court, *Maynard v. Valley Christian Academy, Inc.*, 2017 WL 3594670 (Westlaw) where the judge rejects the complaint of procedural unfairness given the applicant's high level of education (Christian arbitration clause in a contract of employment between a Christian private school and one of its executives); comp. U. S. District Court, *Easterly v. Heritage Christian Schools, Inc.*, 2009 WL 2750099 (Westlaw).

partiality of the arbitrators would come from the fact that Mr. and Mrs. Garcia were declared by the Church of Scientology 'suppressive persons'. According to the Church of Scientology such persons are anti-social and therefore excluded from the Church of Scientology and stripped of their rights and benefits.[36] They are, in the terminology of this Church, 'disconnected' from the other members of this Church, which forbids them to communicate with them. Mr. and Mrs. Garcia drew the consequence that 'reputable Scientologists', among whom the arbitrators must necessarily be chosen, would necessarily be hostile to suppressive persons. The 'supreme judge' of the Scientology stated during the trial that this would not be the case, as the arbitrators would be ordered to be fair. The judge did not take a side regarding the question of the objectivity of the arbitrators because he considered that the first amendment to the American Constitution ('Non-Establishment Clause') prohibited him from doing so. This is an exaggeratedly broad conception of the 'hands-off doctrine' with a rather serious consequence here, since this conception led to not answering the important question of the neutrality of the arbitrators.

9.3 INTERMINGLED RATIONALITIES: USING PRIVATE INTERNATIONAL LAW TO DEAL WITH 'UNSOLVABLE' CASES?

*Sandrine Brachotte**

In this comment, I suggest that *Jivraj* is an 'unsolvable' case. By this, I mean that the legal reasoning employed at various levels of the courts up to the Supreme Court seems disconnected from the true issue at hand. Even if, arguably, the practical consequences of the decision appear fair and reasonable (although of course, there is controversy on this point), the underlying process 'does not feel right.'

I further argue that the reason for this is the involvement in *Jivraj* of a complex intermingling of rationalities.[37] In that perspective, this contribution examines whether private international law (or conflict of laws) techniques might enable us to see the situation in a better light.

1. INTERMINGLED RATIONALITIES: MAPPING THE WORLD WITH HYBRID, INTERTWINED, NORMATIVE SYSTEMS

What are rationalities? For the purpose of this contribution, rationalities should be understood as 'worlds of meaning', which reflect distinct ways of seeing the world.

---

[36] http://www.scientologie.fr/faq/scientology-attitudes-and-practices/what-is-a-suppressive-person.html.

* Many thanks to Patrik Garon-Sayegh, Rory Gillis, Nadia Lambek, and Sarah Mason-Case for their decisive comments on earlier drafts.

[37] Andreas Fisher-Lescano and Gunther Teubner, 'Regime-Collisions: The Vain Search for Legal Unity in the Fragmentation of Global Law' (2004) 25 *Mich J Intl L* 999.

They can be divided into sub-rationalities. For instance, in *Jivraj*, there are three rationalities and sub-rationalities involved: state law[38] (rationality) and UK law[39] (sub-rationality); religion (rationality) and Ismailism (sub-rationality); and the economic market (rationality) and investment (sub-rationality).

Many scholars accept that our 21st century world is a global network of overlapping (sub-)normative systems, which materialise (sub-)rationalities.[40] In *Jivraj*, three normative systems are concerned: the UK, the Ismaili community, and the investment market. Yet, the lines between these systems are blurred. I identify two main reasons why.

First, normative systems are not the only representatives of rationalities: individuals are, too.[41] In fact, people may identify and/or claim to identify with one or several rationality(-ies) in a given instance. Such identification depends on many factors – e.g. ethical, economic, cognitive. Individuals may also vary in their definition and interpretation of the same rationality. In *Jivraj*, Mr. Hashwani signed a joint venture agreement with Mr. Jivraj, for the purpose of multinational investments. This agreement is subject to English law, pursuant to Article 9 of the contract. Moreover, the contract includes an arbitration clause (Article 8) that provides for the appointment of Ismaili arbitrators. Hence, at the time of the conclusion of the contract, Mr. Hashwani was claiming two identities: his identity as a UK citizen, on the one hand, and his identity as member of the Ismaili community, on the other hand. When, several years later, Mr. Hashwani appointed Sir Anthony Colman, who is not a member of the Ismaili community, as an arbitrator, he detached himself from his Ismaili ethos, or at least changed his narrative of it.

Second, normative systems are not isolated from each other. They constantly influence one another, including via the transposition of norms belonging to one given system into another system. For instance, the UK recognises the normative power of arbitration, which is an institution that represents, notably, two normative systems, i.e. the Ismaili community and the economic market. Conditions therefore are laid down in the Arbitration Act 1996.

Not only are the limits between normative systems unclear, but also do normative systems' institutions hold unequal power. These institutions speak for one normative system in an authoritative way. In particular, dispute resolution bodies play a crucial role in the maintenance and development of normative systems. Hence, regarding

---

38 Here, I call 'state law', 'law' in the Modern sense of the term, i.e. norms produced by states or by the community of states.

39 For the purpose of this contribution, it is referred alike to both UK law and English law, i.e. the part of UK law that is applicable in England and Wales.

40 Gunther Teubner, *Constitutional Fragments: Societal Constitutionalism in Globalization* (Oxford, Oxford University Press 2012). See also, among others, Paul Schiff Berman, *Global Legal Pluralism: A Jurisprudence of Law Beyond Borders* (Cambridge, Cambridge University Press 2012); Christopher Thornhill, *A Sociology of Transnational Constitutions: The Social Foundations of the Post-National Legal Structure* (Cambridge, Cambridge University Press 2016); William Twinning, *Understanding Law from a Global Perspective* (Cambridge, Cambridge University Press 2009); Neil Walker, *Intimations of Global Law* (Cambridge, Cambridge University Press 2015).

41 This point was inspired by Annelise Riles, 'Cultural Conflicts' (2008) 72 *Law Contemp Probl* 273. See for the idea more generally, Gunther Teubner, 'La Matrice anonyme: de la violation des droits de l'homme par des acteurs "privés" transnationaux' (2016) 4 *Rev crit DIP* 591.

Jivraj, state courts are crucial to the UK system; the Conciliation and Arbitration Boards (CABs) system is vital to the Ismaili community; and commercial arbitration institutions such as the International Chamber of Commerce (ICC) and the London Court of International Arbitration (LCIA) are critical to the investment market and to the economic market in general. Nonetheless, dispute resolution bodies representing normative systems other than states need judicial sanction for their decisions to become legally binding. Thus, neither the CABs system nor institutions of commercial arbitration can work as a full alternative to the courts system. Among other issues, one party may refuse to commence arbitration proceedings or to enforce an arbitral award. The other party has then no choice but to request the assistance of state courts. As a result, compared to dispute resolution bodies representing rationalities other than state law, state courts hold a special position. They must decide on cases that affect other rationalities than state law, while being the warrant of state law.

As a result of the above, the world to which law should fit is imagined as presenting the following features: (i) states are normative systems among others, including religious and economic communities. However, state courts are the only dispute resolution body that can make the decisions of other normative systems' dispute resolution institutions legally binding; (ii) the lines between normative systems are blurred, so that their norms happen to reflect more than one rationality, which generates hybridity; (iii) aside from normative systems, individuals also drive rationalities in various ways, which adds complexity to the interaction of different rationalities. In the following sections, I examine whether one recent theory of private international law techniques could enable law to adapt to the above features: Karen Knop, Ralf Michaels and Annelise Riles' 'theory through technique', as described in their article 'From Multiculturalism to Technique: Feminism, Culture and the Conflict of Law Style.'[42]

In order to do so, this contribution tests Knop et al.'s account, by applying it to *Jivraj* and suggesting alternative ways in which the courts could have reasoned. After surveying the context of the case (2), Knop et al.'s 'theory through technique' will be outlined (3) and then applied to *Jivraj* (4). The comment ends with several reflections (5).

2. CONTEXT: THE ISMAILIS, THEIR ARBITRATION SYSTEM AND THEIR LAWS

The Shia Imami Ismail community (the Ismailis), or the Nizari Ismailis, are a transnational, Muslim, community, belonging to various ethno-geographic and linguistic traditions, including those of Arabia, India, Central Asia, Western China and South

---

[42] Karen Knop, Ralf Michaels and Annelise Riles, 'From Multiculturalism to Technique: Feminism, Culture and the Conflict of Law Style' (2012) 64(3) *Stan L Rev* 589.

Asia.[43] In more recent decades, they have established significant communities in Europe and North America.[44]

The Ismailis have counted remarkable individual business successes among their members, due to strong efforts of both integration within the economic market and increase of wealth.[45] Since the 15th century, they also have engaged in a very efficient communitarian society, under the guidance of the living Imam, the Aga Khan.[46] The current Aga Khan is promoting a cosmopolitan and pluralistic Islam, which moves with the times and promotes integration into Western society.[47] He has further gotten involved in common projects with states such as Canada and several non-religious NGOs, for the benefit of the society as a whole.[48]

In line with these undertakings, the dispute resolution institution of the Ismaili community, the CABs system appears, not as a religious arbitration body, but as a hybrid structure. The CABs system operates all over the world, under the supervision of both the International CAB (ICAB) and the Aga Khan. According to the general spirit of the 1986 Ismaili Constitution,[49] when the dispute involves commercial matters (including investment contracts), the CABs apply the state law of the seat of arbitration.[50] Distinct from state court, however, the CABs system further aims at complying with the broader ethics of the Ismaili faith. The reason therefore is, in Islam, law, ethics and faith are inseparable from each other.[51] Pursuant to the Ismaili ethics, Ismailis are encouraged to use that internal institution to solve their dispute. They are also strongly recommended to make their best efforts to settle the case before opting for arbitration.[52]

---

43 Arif A Jamal, 'Religious Authority and Constitutional Order: A Case Study of the Conciliation and Arbitration Boards (CABs) of the Shia Imami Ismaili Community' (2013) 2 *J L Religion and St* 235, 236.

44 Ibid.

45 Jean-Claude Penrad, 'Identités Disséminées. Musulmans d'origines indopakistanaises en Afrique orientale' (2008) 15(1) *Lusotopie* 125, 126–33.

46 See Jamal (n 43) 236–37; see also the official website of the Ismaili community (<https://the.ismaili/community> accessed 25 January 2018).

47 See Karim H. Karim, 'Speaking to Post-Secular Society: The Aga Khan's Public Discourse' in Aziz Nurjehan, *The Relevance of Islamic Identity in Canada* (Toronto, Mawenzi House 2015) 97.

48 *Jivraj v. Hashwani* [2011] UKSC 40, [2011] 1 WLR 1872, Witness Statement of Noordin Nanji [2.5].

49 The English text is available on the website of The Heritage Society, the Ismaili electronic database and library: <http://ismaili.net/Source/extra1.html> accessed 26 January 2018. According to Arif Jamal, the Ismaili Constitution, enacted by the Aga Khan, may be the preeminent legal source of Ismaili law today, aside from Qur'an and the traditions of the Prophet that are foundational for Ismaili law (Arif Jamal, 'Authority and Plurality in Muslim Legal Traditions: The Case of Ismaili Law' *American Journal of Comparative Law* (2018) NUS Working Paper 2018/008, 12 <https://papers.ssrn.com/sol3/papers.cfm?abstract_id=3141048> accessed 20 November 2018).

50 Witness Statement of Noordin Nanji (n 48) [3.7].

51 See Ismail K. H. Poonawala, *The Pillars of Islam. Volume II. Laws Pertaining to Human Intercourse* (Asaf Fyzee tr, Oxford, Oxford University Press 2002) editor's introduction. Sharia contains five legal qualifications of every human action, which all bear an ethical quality: obligatory duties; recommended duties; indifferent actions; reprehensible actions; and forbidden actions. Only the first and the last categories fit to the definition of state law.

52 Witness Statement of Noordin Nanji (n 48) [5.5].

3. PRIVATE INTERNATIONAL LAW TECHNIQUES FOR A RE-MASTERED LEGAL REASONING: 'THEORY THROUGH TECHNIQUE'

Karen Knop, Ralf Michaels and Annelise Riles' 'Multiculturalism Through Technique' focuses on the virtues of private international law in managing multicultural societies. Their theory is particularly addressed to traditional Western feminist views. It highlights the value of conflict as an intellectual style, which can, its authors say, be applied to any question of overlap among normative communities.[53] The implementation of this intellectual style consists of applying the steps of a private-international-law analysis to solve a case, according to the bilateralist method,[54] even if the dispute is not otherwise subject to private international law.[55]

The first step in the conflict of laws approach is to recognise the existence of a *foreign element* before beginning any legal reasoning. This serves as a constant reminder to the judge that there are many frameworks of understanding relevant to any particular, normative, question, of which state law is only one. In that regard, the common law approach to proof of foreign law is valuable. That approach allows parties to defeat proper outcomes by choosing not to plead the foreign law. This, Knop et al. argue, gives agency to the parties to decide whether to situate themselves within one culture or another on a particular issue.[56]

The second step is the *characterisation* of the issue, which includes the application of the 'as-if' technique.[57] The 'as-if' technique requires characterising the issue in full appreciation of the fact that, indeed, the very question of how one characterises the issue is highly malleable.[58] Conflict of laws, by definition, involve two or more legal systems imagined as laterally rather than hierarchically related to one another. As a result, the very structure of a conflicts problem recognises that even the initial characterisation of the issue must take place from the situated viewpoint of one system or another. So there is no right answer.[59]

---

53 Knop, Michaels and Riles (n 42) 627–28.

54 The bilateralist approach, applied in Europe and in Canada, as opposed to the US unilateralist method, considers two sets of national laws (from State A and from State B) that could equally apply to the case. To choose between these two laws, e.g. the lex fori and a foreign law, the judge applies an external, neutral, criterion (i.e. a connecting factor, e.g. in civil contracts, the place of contract performance) (Dominique Bureau and Horatia Muir Watt, *Droit International Privé. Tome I. Partie Générale* (3rd edn, Paris, PUF 2014 (3rd. ed.) paras 330–331).

55 The full reasoning includes six steps (Knop, Michaels and Riles (n 42) 627). Only fourth of these steps are relevant to this comment, which are summarized here, and adapted to the description of the world suggested under section 1.

56 Knop, Michaels and Riles (n 42) 629.

57 Ibid., 634.

58 Ibid., 645.

59 Ibid., 636.

Third, the *applicable law* is identified according to the particular choice of law methodology in use in that jurisdiction. Jurisdictional and choice of law questions are split.[60] It is acknowledged that just because an authority has the power to impose its value system on all the parties does not necessarily mean that it must or should do so. It can exercise jurisdiction and still remain open to the possibility that it might defer to another body of law – another normative system. This process of 'dépeçage' (i.e. slicing issue by issue)[61] that qualifies the two last steps, opens the door to a case-by-case contextual analysis. The benefit of such analysis is that it can mediate conflicts in the particular case at hand.[62]

Fourth, if foreign law – i.e. another normative system – is applicable, the judge verifies whether the *international public policy exception* bars the application of such law. Judges can approach the potential conflict with public policy in the concrete rather than in the abstract.[63] They may hence conclude that what appeared to be a fundamental difference is, when more deeply understood in each culture, a superficial one.[64] If the conflict is fundamental, however, the judges' only choice is not to apply foreign law to the issue at hand. Conflicts ultimately do not make room for policy compromise.[65]

4. FROM THEORY TO CASE: ALTERNATIVE REASONING IN *JIVRAJ*

Pursuant to Knop et al.'s 'theory through technique', I suggest to re-frame the legal reasoning in *Jivraj* following a conflict of laws analysis. This section considers how UK courts would judge the dispute, if they could do so another time, by applying private international law techniques. Before getting there, however, I should cover some of the findings in the dispute.

A. The Courts' Decisions

In First Instance[66]

The Commercial Court – i.e. the sole judge David Steel – answered, among others, the following questions: (i) do the Employment Equality Religion or Belief Regulations 2003 (the Regulations 2003)[67] apply to the arbitration clause provided under Article 8

60 Ibid., 632.
61 Ibid., 636.
62 Ibid., 637.
63 Ibid., 641.
64 Ibid., 642.
65 Ibid., 641.
66 *Jivraj v. Hashwani* [2009] 2 All ER (Comm) 778.
67 This statutory instrument has been replaced by the Equality Act 2010 c. 3, which reinforces the uniformity of the law relating to all areas where discrimination is forbidden.

of the joint venture agreement?;[68] (ii) if so, is the latter discriminatory on the grounds of religion or belief?;[69] (iii) if so, is that discrimination justified?; (iv) if the Regulations 2003 do not apply, is Article 8 invalid under the Human Rights Act 1998, or otherwise at common law as contrary to public policy?

The Commercial Court denied that Article 8 was discriminatory on the grounds of religion or belief, be it with regard to the Regulations 2003, the Human Rights Act 1998, or UK public policy. Judge Steel found that neither of these laws was applicable to the case. He found on each of those grounds, respectively, that an arbitrator was not an employee, and therefore, the Regulations 2003 were not applicable;[70] Mr. Hashwani was not the direct victim of the claimed discrimination;[71] and public policy was no 'holdall' notion.[72] The court further stressed that, as 'not surprisingly' argued by Mr. Jivraj, the claim did not make much sense. Under English law, it was 'clearly time barred' so any arbitrator that would decide on the case would deny his claim.[73]

Alternatively, the judge ruled that, if the Regulations 2003 were applicable, the discrimination based on religion would be justified. It would indeed fall under the exception provided in Article 7(3) of the Regulations 2003. This Article, read together with Article 6.1(c), provides that it is lawful to refuse to offer employment to someone for a religious reason, if: (i) the employer has an ethos based on religion or belief; (ii) being of a particular religion or belief is a genuine occupational requirement for the job; (iii) it is proportionate to apply that requirement in the particular case. In that respect, Judge Steel held that containing dispute resolution within the Ismaili community corresponded to 'one of the more significant and characteristic spirits of the Ismaili sect.'[74] It thus constitutes an 'ethos based on religion.'

In Appeal[75]

Mr. Hashwani appealed the decision, which was authorised on the violation of the Regulations 2003 only.[76] The Court of Appeal reversed the first judgment. It determined that the arbitration clause was invalid regarding the Regulations 2003. It ruled that an arbitrator was an employee.[77] It further held that the case did not fall under Article 7(3) of the Regulations 2003. The Court of Appeal did not see the requirement

68 Pursuant to Article 2(3), the Regulations 2003 apply to a contract of service or of apprenticeship or a contract personally to do any work.

69 Article 6.1(c) of the Regulations 2003 forbids the refusal to offer employment to someone on the ground of religion.

70 See *Jivraj v. Hashwani* [2009] 2 All ER (Comm) 778 [27].

71 Ibid., [62].

72 Ibid., [71]: 'Even allowing for the need to move with the times, it is inappropriate for the courts to trespass further than parliamentary intention by way of filling what is suggested as a "lacuna" under the guise of public policy.'

73 Ibid., [10].

74 Ibid., [45].

75 *Jivraj v. Hashwani* [2010] EWCA Civ 712, [2010] All ER 302.

76 Ibid., [11].

77 Ibid., [16].

of being Ismaili as a qualification because English law was the governing law, which did 'not call for any particular ethos'.[78] The Court hence applied a necessity test.

At the Supreme Court Level[79]

Mr. Jivraj's counsel brought the case before the Supreme Court. The ICC, the LCIA, the ICAB and the Aga Khan intervened in the proceedings.

The Supreme Court reversed the appeal judgment and aligned its position to that of the Commercial Court. Notably, alternatively, the Court confirmed the assessment of the Commercial Court that the arbitration clause fell under Article 7(3) of the Regulations 2003. According to the Supreme Court, the Court of Appeal's reasoning that an arbitration dispute governed by English law did not require an Ismaili arbitrator, took a very narrow view of the function of arbitration proceedings. This characterisation reduced arbitration to no more than the application of a given national law to a dispute.[80] Instead, the Court of Appeal should have considered the *raison d'être* of arbitration, that is, to provide for final and binding dispute resolution 'by a tribunal with a procedure that is acceptable to all parties, in circumstances where other fora (in particular national courts) are deemed inappropriate.'[81] The Court of Appeal, as the Supreme Court ruled, also failed to consider the Ismaili ethos, as described by the Commercial Court.

B. Alternative Reasoning

This section suggests an alternative reasoning based on the intellectual style of private international law described above (section 3), taking the position of any UK court dealing with the *Jivraj* case. This reasoning is proposed in an analytical perspective (not in a prescriptive view).

Foreign elements

First, the court would acknowledge that there is a *foreign element* involved, that is Ismaili arbitration. This probably means to acknowledge that, in the case, arbitration is foreign to the UK, in spite of the Arbitration Act 1996. In fact, this act integrates, in a certain way and only to a certain extent, arbitration proceedings into UK law. Consequently, the court can note that the CABs system holds for the Ismaili community the status of primary, internal, dispute resolution body, just as courts do for states. It is thus not an alternative dispute resolution, contrary to what conciliation and arbitration proceedings represent under state law. Both the Commercial Court and the Supreme Court have actually reasoned that way. However, one could contend that Knop et al.'s theory includes the parties' freedom not to regard foreign elements (section 3). It should therefore be verified whether, in *Jivraj*, giving legal meaning to the

78 Ibid., [29].

79 *Jivraj v. Hashwani* [2011] UKSC 40, [2011] 1 WLR 1872.

80 Ibid., [60].

81 ICC's written argument as quoted by the Supreme Court (ibid., [61]).

circumstance of Ismaili arbitration would meet Mrs. Hashwani and Jivraj's will. I believe that this would be so, indeed: the Commercial Court noted that its description of Ismaili arbitration, which grounded its decision, was based on the documents brought by the parties.[82]

Characterisation

Second, the court would *characterise* the issues. There are, I suggest, three possible characterisations. *Jivraj* can be examined regarding: (i) the principle of non-discrimination on the ground of religion; (ii) arbitration law, especially the principle of party autonomy; or (iii) the Ismaili ethos.

Applicable norms

Third, the court would determine the *norms applicable to the case.* Depending on the characterisation (previous section), the court would ground its decision on three distinct legal bases: (i) the Regulations 2003, or alternatively, the Human Rights Act 1998, or UK public policy; (ii) Article 1(b) of the Arbitration Act 1996; (iii) the relevant rules that relate to the Ismaili ethos, i.e. the need to resolve disputes within the Ismaili community.

Of course, these legal grounds are only available if the choice-of-law rules of the normative system to which they belong provide so. In that respect, as stated above (section 1), one should remember that *Jivraj* involves three normative systems: the UK, the Ismaili community, and the investment market. The question is then to which of these systems the legal bases belong. Clearly, the Regulations 2003 belong to the UK, and the Ismaili ethos belongs to the Ismaili community. As for party autonomy, it also reflects a legal provision produced by the UK, i.e. Article 1(b) of the Arbitration Act 1996.[83] Hence, none of the legal bases refer to the investment market *per se*. Consequently, only the Ismaili ethos appears as a foreign norm that could be applied instead of the law of the forum, i.e. UK law. In order to verify the applicability of that norm, the court should examine whether this is required under the choice-of-law rules of the Ismaili community. Hence, the court must put itself in the Ismaili dispute resolution bodies' shoes, that is, CABs. As explained above (section 2), CABs give priority to UK law. The Ismaili ethos comes in as a second, complementary, source of law. Therefore, CABs would not rely on the Ismaili ethos as a legal basis. Instead, they would regard such ethos in addition to state law, to the extent that it would not lead to a decision that is contrary to state law. As a result, the court would be left with two, domestic, possible legal grounds: the Regulations 2003, and the Arbitration Act 1996.

Application of state law: the internal conflict

The choice between the Regulations 2003 and the Arbitration Act 1996 does not involve any conflict between normative systems concerned by the case. Instead, it shows a conflict that is internal to state law, i.e. to domestic law. Which of these legal

---

82 *Jivraj v. Hashwani* [2009] 2 All ER (Comm) 778 [41].

83 Ibid., [46].

sources is the most pertinent to ground the court's decision? Taking the Ismaili ethos into account would, it seems, enable the court to select the arbitration principle of party autonomy as legal ground. In fact, characterising the facts in terms of arbitration appears more respectful of the Ismaili community's view that arbitration is a main dispute resolution body – not an alternative one. The Ismaili principle that requires the internal resolution of dispute further supports the binding force of the arbitration clause.

Yet, the question remains as to whether the Ismaili ethos must be regarded or ignored instead. In order to answer to that question, the fourth step of Knop et al.'s reasoning on the public policy exception (section 3) is not helpful, because the conflict is internal to state law. Instead, the court should find out whether the doctrine of conflict of laws requires the court to consider foreign norms when interpreting domestic norms, even where it has already been determined that domestic and not foreign law applies. There is no direct, certain and unvarying answer to such question.[84] In any event, one could argue that the Ismaili ethos belongs to the critical facts of the case.

As a result, the court would rule the case based on the arbitration principle of party autonomy. This does not automatically mean, however, that the parties should indeed put their dispute in the hands of Ismaili arbitrators. In fact, Article 1(b) of the Arbitration Act 1996 limits party autonomy to the safeguards that are 'necessary in the public interest.' Public interest covers, on the one hand, mandatory, arbitration, rules that aim at: (i) guaranteeing natural justice; (ii) protecting the weaker party; (iii) and protecting the public good.[85] Nevertheless, the 1996 Arbitration Rules do not include any provision that forbids, directly, or indirectly, the appointment of religious arbitrators as such. On the other hand, public interest includes public policy. But, as pointed out by the Commercial Court, UK public policy does not prohibit parties from stipulating that arbitrators be of a religious character (section 'In First Instance' above). Consequently, pursuant to Article 1(b) of the 1996 Act, Article 8 of the joint venture agreement demanding the appointment of Ismaili arbitrators is valid.

5. CONCLUSION: FROM CASE TO THEORY

The analysis of *Jivraj* proposed above was based on the application of Knop et al.'s account of the intellectual style of private international law to state courts' legal reasoning. I wish to end this contribution by pointing out three important questions that I think it raises.

First, the conflict of laws reasoning would have required that, in *Jivraj*, the courts consider the existence of a conflict within UK law, between two norms: (i) the Regulations 2003 against religious discrimination of employees; and (ii) Article 1(b)

[84] There is no space to discuss that question here.

[85] Mia Louise Livingstone, 'Party Autonomy in International Commercial Arbitration: Popular Fallacy or Proven Fact?' (2008) 25(5) *J Intl Arb* 529, 531–32.

of the Arbitration Act 1996 protecting party autonomy. Nevertheless, it is doubtful whether this would have been possible under UK procedural law. In fact, the 1998 Civil Procedure Rules[86] do not allow courts to fix a legal basis for the decision different from the one(s) invoked by the parties.[87] The current feasibility of the conflict of laws reasoning therefore appears limited. In addition, Knop et al.'s 'theory through technique' itself praises the common law approach to proof of foreign law, which allows parties not to plead the foreign law even when this defeats proper outcomes (section 3).

Second, because of such a procedural limitation, the most crucial question becomes, intriguingly, the one that should have probably been answered, would the Ismaili ethos have been the relevant legal basis to rely on. Why did Mr. Hashwani not want Ismaili arbitration? The joint venture agreement that he signed requires Ismaili arbitrators. Why did he stop wanting that, and appoint a non-religious arbitrator instead? And why did he commence arbitration proceedings so long after that the dispute occurred? It is hardly convincing that he wanted to protect non-Ismaili arbitrators from discrimination. There are valid reasons that could have explained his choice, at least partially, such as the perception that Ismaili arbitrators lack neutrality and expertise in business law. These are actually the types of arguments that should have been pushed to the fore to allow the courts to connect judgments to reality.

This generates a third and broader reflection. In fact, a great part of the reason why Mr. Hashwani started court proceedings lies in his identification with one of the three normative systems involved in *Jivraj*: the investment market. This belonging is, nonetheless, not unveiled by the conflict of laws analysis, in spite of Knop et al.'s comment that a dispute can be 'further complicated by the opportunities but also the demands of a global economy'.[88] One could wonder, then, whether there exists another legal technique that would uncover the role played by neoliberalism in cases like *Jivraj*. Or whether this is just where law proves its limits.

[86] No. 3132 (L.17).

[87] Neil Andrews, *English Civil Procedure. Fundamentals of the New Civil Justice System* (Oxford, Oxford University Press 2003) 90.

[88] Knop, Michaels and Riles (n 42) 621.

9.4 RELIGIOUS IDENTITY: BETWEEN NON-DISCRIMINATION AND PARTY AUTONOMY

*Nathalie Najjar**

Much has been written about the *Jivraj* case.[89] Although it was resolved several years ago already, a convincing view has not yet been reached. It raises different issues, relating to sensitive matters in international trade, freedom of contract and its limits, the role of religion, and, more generally, whether religious factors should be involved in arbitration-related contractual choices in international commercial cases, in view of the worldwide scene of conflicts. While policies on these points are usually implicit, it should be asked whether they should eventually be established as clear and generally accepted principles.

The facts have already been summarised, yet it will be importantly recalled that, in this case, two Pakistani parties, Messrs. Jivraj and Hashwani, created a joint-venture agreement including an arbitration clause providing that in case of a dispute, it shall be submitted to one or more arbitrators who are from the Ismaili community, in these terms 'All arbitrators shall be respected members of the Ismaili community and holders of high office within the community.' This community is a branch of Shia, which in short considers the Aga Khan as its spiritual leader; it operates according to the same modalities as those of Shia, that is, by having a very deep faith in its spiritual leader.[90] The nature of this community and its influence on the matters in dispute did not however raise any particular issue in that case.

Parallel to the constitution of an arbitral tribunal composed of three Ismaili arbitrators whose mission was not yet complete, one of the parties, Mr. Jivraj, initiates parallel proceedings and appoints Sir Anthony Colman. Dissatisfied with this appointment, Mr. Hashwani, also a Pakistani national, refers the matter to the High Court of Justice Queen's Bench division (Commercial Court), in order to annul this appointment which conflicts with the agreed criteria. The 'Court of Appeal' (Civil division) overrules the decision and, on the grounds of the 'Employment Equality Regulation of

---

* Contribution originally written in French, translated to English by Marion Creach.

89 Short bibliography: Inae Yang, 'Nurdin Jivraj v. Sadruddin Hashwani: The English Court of Appeal Erects a Regulatory Barrier to Appointment of Arbitrators in the Name of Anti-Discrimination' (2011) 28(3) *JIA* 243–54; Latham & Watkins, 'Jivraj v. Hashwani: arbitrator nationality and the law of unintended consequences', http://www.executiveinsights.law.com/abstract/jivraj-hashwani-arbitrator-nationality-law-unintended-consequences-6536 (last accessed 30 April 2018); *Jivraj v. Hashwani* [2011] UKSC 40, *Rev. arb.* 2011, p. 1007, comment by J.-B. Racine; C. Style and P. Cleobury, '*Jivraj v. Hashwani*: Public Interest and Party Autonomy' (2011) 27(4) *Arb. Int'l* 563; C. M. Baker and L. Greenwood, 'The Regionalisation of International Arbitration: Maintaining International Standards in Appointing Arbitrators – A Comment on *Jivraj v Hashwani*' *in* P. Wautelet, T. Kruger and G. Koppens, *The Practice of Arbitration – Essays in Honour of Hans van Houtte* (Oxford, Hart Publishing 2012) 15; U. A. Oseni and H. A. Kadouf, 'The Discrimination Conundrum in the Appointment of Arbitrators in International Arbitration' (2012) 29 *JIA* 519; J. Dasteel, 'Arbitration Agreements That Discriminate in the Appointment and Selection of Arbitrators' (2012) 11 *Rich. J. Global L. & Bus.* 383.

90 On the Ismaili community: F. Daftary, *Les Ismaéliens, histoire et traditions d'une communauté musulmane* (Paris, Fayard 2003).

2003', in which is enshrined non-discrimination and freedom of belief and religion for employees, considers the arbitrator as an employee, and subjects him to relevant rights and obligations. The Court of Appeal therefore considers that the agreed arbitration clause must be annulled and rejects the arguments of the respondent.

Much has been written on the decision of the Court of Appeal, which made quite some noise among the arbitration community in general and in institutional spheres in particular. It has been seen as undermining the neutrality of the arbitrator and especially the nationality clauses provided for in institutional arbitration rules, but also as introducing imponderable factors in the resolution of international commercial disputes, and probably moreover as putting an end to party autonomy. Jivraj brings the case before the British Supreme Court, which overturns the appellate ruling and thereby confirms the decision of the High Court and validates the agreed clause. The ICC and LCIA had also requested to join in the appeal as *amici curiae* to provide their insights on the case, which was granted.

Through examining the comments on the *Jivraj* case, it can be noted that most of the time they have been written to highlight particular aspects of the case, that is to say, the characterisation of the arbitrator's mission, discrimination, the status of the arbitrator, etc. These comments are undoubtedly relevant. The insight here is, however, slightly different. Our main focus will be the role that religion should play in the resolution of international commercial disputes, and more generally as to the scope of freedom of contract and its limits with regard to truly international concerns outside domestic frameworks. There is no doubt that freedom of transactions, whether or not the transnational public policy is recognised as a fundamental principle, is a founding element of international commercial relationships, grounded in the freedoms provided for in international conventions such as the Universal Declaration of Human Rights, or the Declaration of the Rights of Man and of the Citizen. The question being asked is thus whether limits should be imposed on it and, if limits should be drawn, which they might be, and by what method should they be defined?

This contribution is subdivided into two parts. On the one hand, it aims at assessing the various consequences of including religious factors in the resolution of international commercial disputes (1). On the other hand, it intends to show that, even though there is no particular sanction or specific authoritative text – at least yet – that could limit the risk of discrimination resulting from introducing religious factors into contractual choices, perhaps efforts should be directed towards refining the limits that must be imposed on freedom of contracts in international commercial relationships (2).

1. THE VARIOUS CONSEQUENCES OF INCLUDING RELIGIOUS FACTORS IN THE RESOLUTION OF DISPUTES THROUGH INTERNATIONAL COMMERCIAL ARBITRATION

The practice consisting of including religious factors in the resolution of disputes through international commercial arbitration has not been identical in all parts of the world. In this regard, Arab countries and Western countries must be distinguished.

Although in Western countries generally speaking the appointment of arbitrators based on religious considerations is not a common practice, as shown by the *Jivraj* case

(B), in Arab countries, however, and in Islamic countries in particular, this assertion must be reassessed (A). The subsequent consequences are not the same.

A. In Arab-Islamic Countries

The role of religion in appointing the arbitrator in Islamic Sharia

Sharia law is not unfamiliar with the practice of appointing arbitrators based on religious considerations.[91] Arbitration in Islamic law is in general considered as a spontaneous, if not improvised, mechanism through which two or more parties agree to entrust a third party, named *hakam* or *mouhakkam* (arbitrator) who has the characteristics of an Islamic judge, to settle a dispute that has arisen, in accordance with sharia. The *tahkim* (arbitration) in sharia cannot be equated with Western-type arbitration, as the arbitrator settles the dispute in a way to bring the parties together, based on their common interest. It is a religious mechanism.[92] Sharia arbitration, therefore, although quite similar to Western-type conciliation or mediation, remains distinct.[93] Therefore, the arbitrator, in Islamic law, like the Islamic *qadi*, promotes justice as the Prophet, supreme judge among believers, does. Consequently, the arbitrator must, like the *qadi*, conduct the arbitral proceedings and rule on the merits of the dispute in accordance with sharia and must above all meet the requirements applicable to a *qadi sharhi*, and, especially, be a Muslim, since, in strict Islam, he is the only person who has the authority to rule on Islamic law, after the *ulema*, the imam or the caliph.

This conception of arbitration is the one that prevails in all of the Fiqh Schools, whether Shia or Sunni. This stems from the verses of Quran in which arbitration is a mission undertaken like that of the Prophet:

> and if you render your judgment, pronounce it fairly, even if a near relative is involved and so comply with God's mission. But if they come to you, be judge and settle among them, or decline. And if you decline, they will not harm you. But if you judge, judge between them by being fair, because Allah loves those who judge in equity …[94]
>
> we sent you the Book (the Quran) as the truth for you to judge among men guided by God …[95]
>
> Judge therefore among them according to what Allah has revealed and do not submit to their vain desires …[96]

---

91 See Nathalie Najjar, *Arbitrage dans les pays arabes et commerce international* (Paris, LGDJ 2016) 35 n° 62 et seq.; *Arbitration and International trade in the Arab Countries* (Leiden, Brill-Nijhoff 2018), 45 n° 62 et seq.

92 Verse 65 Surah of the Women.

93 See Nathalie Najjar, 'The Arab World', in *ADR in business* 2nd edn (Alphen aan den Rijn, Kluwer Law International 2011) 559; *Arbitrage dans les pays arabes et commerce international* (n 91) 35; *Arbitration and International Trade in the Arab Countries* (n 91) 45.

94 Verse 152 Surah of the Women.

95 Verse 105 Surah of the Women.

96 Verse 49 Surah of the Cow.

> Oh believers, obey Allah and the Prophet and those among you who are vested with authority. And if you violate, refer to Allah and his Prophet. And if you believe in Allah and the last judgment, this will be the strongest and most equitable resolution.[97]

The case of Saudi Arabia

In Arab-Islamic countries, the arbitration laws in force have changed a lot. Currently, only the regulations of Saudi Arabia impose, as before the arbitration regulation of 2012, an indirect requirement to appoint the arbitrators based on their religion.

In fact, in Saudi Arabia, before the 2012 arbitration regulation, the regulation of 1983–1985[98] required that the arbitrator be a 'national or a *foreign Muslim*.'[99] Saudi regulation was therefore different from other Islamic systems, especially the Omani and Qatari systems which also derived from the Majallat, and required that the arbitrator be, like the judge, 'of male gender, of sound mind, free, Muslim and fair'. This requirement was even considered in Saudi Arabia as 'a fundamental principle of Saudi law imposed upon all the faithful.'[100] The requirement of religion did not reflect a sense of 'religious fanaticism' of the Saudi legislator; it was related to the function and role of the arbitrator in Islam. Nevertheless, requiring the arbitrator to belong to the Islamic community was unsuitable for domestic arbitration and, all the more so, for international arbitration. Contrary to the judge who strictly applies sharia and who scrupulously follows its prescriptions, the arbitrator may settle the dispute as an *amiable compositeur*, depart from legal rules or comply only with fundamental principles of sharia without following doctrinal teachings of the Fiqh. The modern attitude toward the function of an international arbitrator, which features prominently in the Saudi arbitration regulation of 2012, thus requires that the arbitrator be not enshrined within a particular legal or judicial domestic order; his mission has a conventional basis. This is why the new arbitration regulation has not kept the requirement of an Islamic arbitrator.

It is also in practical terms that the requirement of an arbitrator that belongs to the Islamic community has been criticised and thus officially rejected: on the one hand, there are technical disputes which do not require any thorough or particular knowledge of Islamic law; the religion-related requirement obstructs the appointment of any non-Islamic arbitrator as long as the case relates in some way to the Saudi kingdom. Non-Muslims could, besides, have perfect knowledge of Islamic law; why reject them all? Finally, what if the dispute relates to several countries, including Saudi Arabia? Could the arbitrator, in this case, decide in accordance with a non-Islamic foreign law? Even though the ties with the Kingdom of Saudi Arabia are weak, aren't the parties required, for purposes of efficiency, to comply with the religious community condition provided for in the Saudi regulation? As many factors that explain the official abandon of the requirement of Islamic community in respect of the arbitrator, which had been

---

[97] Verse 59 Surah of the Women.

[98] See Nathalie Najjar, *L'arbitrage dans les pays arabes face aux exigences du commerce international* (Paris, LGDJ 2004) 225.

[99] Article 3 of the 1985 Saudi implementing decree.

[100] B. Bin Sultan Al-Saoud, 'The Centre and the International Arbitration Commission request the appointment of sharhi arbitrators' *El-Mouslimoun* (Saudi Arabia), n° 693, of 16 May 1998 (in Arabic).

responsible for the isolation of the Saudi system; this restriction dissuaded international investors and harmed the best Saudi interests.

However, if the requirement of religion was abandoned, it was substituted by other conditions, no less restrictive, especially that of obtaining a university degree in *sharhi* and legal sciences. If the arbitral tribunal is composed of more than one arbitrator, these conditions are required only from the president of the arbitral tribunal (article 14 of the Saudi arbitration regulation of 2012). It should be recalled that in fact, Saudi arbitration regulation, which officially results from the UNCITRAL Model Law, introduces significant modifications to the latter by giving sharia a prominent place in the system: any arbitral proceedings and any choice cannot be carried out unless they comply with divine law; this is all the more the case when freedom of contract is at stake.

Yet, the condition thus laid down is not uncontroversial and raises various questions. It is known that the new Saudi regulation does apply subject to conformity with the provision of Islamic sharia. Additionally, both the arbitration agreement and the arbitral award cannot be executed in the kingdom if they do not comply with divine law. Knowledge of the latter thus seems essential. Furthermore, this condition of obtaining a particular degree is required only for the president of the arbitral tribunal; this makes its scope more flexible and allows the appointment of co-arbitrators who do not hold a degree in Islamic legal sciences, or even non-Muslims.

Nonetheless, the requirement of a degree in *sharhi* sciences remains of limited relevance to the needs of trade and leads to complications. On the one hand, this condition depends upon the award of a degree in *shareh*: are universities that are approved and authorised by Saudi authorities the only ones empowered to award them? What about jurists who are not Islamic? Are they eligible for obtaining these degrees? This requirement amounts to requiring, by indirect means, the Islamic religion of the president of the arbitral tribunal, although it was officially abandoned by the new arbitration regulation. Why not accept that jurists may have knowledge of sharia without being awarded a particular degree in that respect? Additionally, arbitral proceedings taking place in Saudi Arabia may not be enshrined within the Saudi legal order. Why extend the condition to all arbitral proceedings taking place locally, even to those that produce effects abroad, all the more so that the reform of 2012 at least in theory allows for the application of foreign laws? The new condition seems even more restrictive than the one previously required in the arbitration regulation of 1983–1985, which required a mere 'knowledge of sharia.'

Moreover, should this requirement be imposed on an arbitral tribunal composed of a single arbitrator such as required under the previous regulation? As many factors support the idea of continuation of the practice of appointment of Islamic arbitrators even though it was officially abandoned, and such practice remains, indirectly, in prominent place both in fact and law.

B. The Case of Confessional Systems: the Lebanese Example

The selection of an individual based upon the criteria of religious community is not totally alien to the functioning of the Lebanese system. The latter is a consensual democracy based upon political confessionalism as enshrined in the Constitution, which underpins the distribution of the powers in the State.

The Lebanese Criminal Code enshrines nevertheless, thereby differentiating itself from other Arab criminal codes, a provision (article 317) according to which 'any individual who, by act, written or verbal statement whose object or effect is an incitement to conflicts between communities, discrimination, or conflicts between communities and the rest of the population' is subject to criminal sanctions. In other words, in the Lebanon, even though the community factor is integrated within the conduct of public affairs, confessionalism finds a limit when it triggers discrimination. The nature of this discrimination is not specified in the texts. It is not clear whether it is an inclusive discrimination on religious grounds or whether it is exclusive altogether. There are however strong reasons to believe that any selection of an individual based upon his or her religious affiliation may be considered as a form of discrimination that leads to the exclusion of other individuals who could have been considered for appointment. In any event, since the legality of this clause is not based on any text or custom, it raises certain legal concerns.

C. Informal Practices

It may be common to select an arbitrator, because he is Muslim, or at least to preclude the choice of a non-Muslim arbitrator, in order to prefer the appointment of an arbitrator from the Islamic community. Admittedly, these practices are informal to the extent that they reflect only an intention, or custom, that are not institutionalised practices; it is also important, however, to say that in view of the significance of religious factors, not only in sharia but also in some Arab-Islamic systems, these practices are fairly common although not talked about.

In Arab-Islamic countries, there is arguably a genuine common practice that sees religion as a key factor in the selection of an individual for functions in both the public and private spheres. This approach should not be considered as being detrimental to freedoms and intrinsic values of individuals but rather as a factor in easing religious tensions in order to prevent them from resurging once the arbitrator is appointed and subsequently taken on too prominent a role.

In other words, it should perhaps be acknowledged that, in Arab-Islamic countries, there is a general understanding of the significance of the religion-related community of arbitrators, although the texts have officially moved away from these requirements and do not provide for sanctions for their infringement, at least in arbitration law.

D. In Western Countries: the Example of the *Jivraj* Case

The *Jivraj* case shows that religious factors may raise quite a few interrogations in the context of the business world.

The English Court of Appeal considered, on what was later held to be an erroneous ground, that the arbitrator should be treated as an employee, and thereafter that it is discrimination to enforce an agreement that appoints an arbitrator on the basis of his religious community. This reasoning resulted in an exacerbated sense of outrage towards the selection of an arbitrator based upon a criteria that is not 'objective': in this case, since the arbitration was commercial, it was therefore unrelated to the Ismaili community, so that the religious community of the parties was not a justifiable criterion for the selection of the arbitrator.

However, it is also important to note that in the *Jivraj* case, sharia was not involved; it was a commercial international dispute. It is uncommon that arbitrators be selected based upon their religious community, at least in a non-religious dispute without any religious overtone. In this regard, the decision of the Court of Appeal is understandable, even though its grounds are questionable.

In any case, the discrepancies between the decision of the UK Supreme Court and that of the Court of Appeal show that the question is far from being addressed through a single solution, at least when the community and religious element of the case are not clearly characterised, as in this particular case.

2. ABSENCE OF SPECIFIC SANCTION FOR CONSIDERING RELIGIOUS FACTORS IN THE PROCESS OF SELECTING THE ARBITRATOR AND NECESSITY TO REFINE THE LIMITS TO FREEDOM OF CONTRACTS IN INTERNATIONAL COMMERCIAL RELATIONSHIPS

In view of the increasingly frequent inroads of religious factors in daily life, especially with regard to the political tensions and religious wars arising here and there, should the religious approach to the process of selecting the arbitrator be acknowledged, become common practice, and be accepted as a given fact? Should the parties be allowed to waive by their agreement the obligation of non-discrimination in the process of selecting the arbitrator?

The answer to those questions must be balanced: as further discussed, although it is currently possible that the practice become common, due to the absence of any sanction or legal characterisation of discrimination by an agreement that includes religious factors in the process of selecting the arbitrator (A), it should nevertheless be restricted to the principles that govern the discipline (B).

A. Absence of Specific Sanction and of Characterisation in the Instruments of International Trade

The arguments endorsed by the English Court of Appeal did not convince the Supreme Court and showed only that currently there is no textual basis or clear legal characterisation of discrimination that would allow a judge, or even an arbitrator, to put an end to party autonomy with discriminatory intent. This could be detrimental to the stability and safety of international trade.

This absence of legal characterisation results, on the one hand, from the fact that the choice by the two parties of an individual based upon his or her nationality, gender or religious community is most of the time implicit; it represents a real practice of international trade, even though it is not talked about; on the other hand, and most importantly, contrary to the nationality issue (regarding which, for example, the principle that 'no person shall be precluded by reason of his nationality from acting as an arbitrator, unless otherwise agreed by the parties' is clearly stated in the UNCITRAL Model Law, article 11.1), no text among the international trade instruments applicable to arbitration governs the religious issue.

The international instruments which could have been targeted would have been, for example, the European Convention of Human Rights in which the principle of non-discrimination based on religious community is enshrined (article 21) or some domestic texts, such as Article 225-4 of the French Criminal Code (or its equivalent in the Lebanese Criminal Code).[101] These texts remain nevertheless of general application and not specific to arbitration; it could not be said whether, for example, an agreement could stipulate otherwise when both parties agree that the religious affiliation of the arbitrator is a criterion for selection. By analogy, Article 11.1 of the UNCITRAL Model Law allows, in terms of nationality, parties to agree otherwise.

In other words, in view of the current provisions of international trade instruments, the requirement of non-discrimination between individuals based upon their nationality or religious community are not a sufficient basis to sanction freedom of contract. Hence the necessity to rely on another mechanism, which would be a truly international public policy rule, that is balanced and specific to international commercial arbitration, based upon the provisions expressed in the above-mentioned instruments.

B. Necessity to Refine the Truly International Public Policy in View of the Issues that Undermine Safety of International Commercial Transactions

When all the parties agree to select an arbitrator based on religious community, this is not a form of discrimination that is 'exclusive,' but rather 'inclusive.' This means that discrimination does not occur to the detriment of the rights of the other party but in accordance with the latter. Even though the element of discrimination is not substantial here, it is however necessary to stick to the principles governing the discipline.

As a general rule, it is an illusion to believe that regarding a dispute or a claim for which religious issues are inherently at stake, religious affiliation is not a criterion that must be taken into account in selecting the arbitrator. This is the case in particular when a dispute has a community element and when sharia law – or religious law – is applied to the merits of the dispute. We must agree with an author who does not hesitate to assess that

> arbitration is not monolithic. Based on party autonomy, it may also be used as community justice. It is even a dispute resolution mechanism well suited for disputes between members of a same religious community or not. Therefore, it is conspicuous that arbitration may be both a justice relying on ideas of cosmopolitanism, as it is a system of world justice, and justice relying on the premises of multiculturalism, as it allows to each community to build a dispute resolution system that suits its needs, customs, and community spirit (with obviously, when appropriate, an post arbitral review of the award that must comply with public policy.) It is the wealth of arbitration that reflects legal pluralism.[102]

---

[101] See above.

[102] J. B. Racine, comments under UK Supreme Court, 27 July 2011, (2011) *Rev. arb.*, 4, 1026–41 and in particular 1040.

However, as far as international commercial arbitration is concerned, it must be dissociated from religious or domestic frameworks. It is essential to preserve its disconnection and autonomy from these frameworks even when the parties themselves want to depart from it. It is not reasonable that freedom of contract be limitless. The consideration of religion in non-religious arbitration is a form of discrimination which undermines the neutrality essential to the peaceful and serene resolution of international commercial disputes. The claims of religious criteria here do not rest on any strong basis. It is not because an arbitrator is affiliated to Ismailism that he is necessarily and exclusively able to apply the Ismaili *shareh*. There are arbitrators who can very skilfully apply the rules of Islamic *shareh* although not Muslims. In other words, religion is not a sufficient and exclusive indication of a proper knowledge of religious law. This element is discriminatory, even though discrimination occurs only through a refinement of the required qualifications of the arbitrator. If the parties want to designate an arbitrator who has knowledge of a particular law, they should maybe start from there, that is, by stating it in those terms, and not by inducing it from his affiliation to a particular religious community.

The risks of colouring arbitration with religious factors are substantial. It is to be feared that discrimination finally becomes common and trivialised and that neutrality of arbitration be undermined. These factors disrupt not only the elements upon which the principle of party autonomy relies but also, and more importantly, safety of international transactions.

Admittedly, terminating an agreement on the ground of international or truly international public policy may disturb the 'sacrosanct' principle of freedom of contract in international trade. But it is also in order to preserve this freedom from its own risks that limits must be imposed on it, and which could exceed the mere issues of the process of designating the arbitrator.

It has been shown that in similar proceedings, it is accepted that one may limit contractual freedom, when the international public order is at stake; this is in particular the case in the process of selecting the law applicable to the merits of the dispute. In the *Dutco* case,[103] the French *Cour de cassation* did not hesitate to reject the agreed appointment mechanism, and even to sanction it, on the ground that it affects a fundamental principle of arbitration, that is, equality of the parties.

Freedom of contract should not therefore be enshrined without limits. These limits must currently also be applied to the mechanism of selecting the arbitrator. The latter must not, at least in arbitration proceedings that have no religious or community nature, be designated on a confessional basis. The freedom of the parties should find its proper limits in the imperative of safety of international commercial transactions.[104] The truly international public policy includes non-discrimination and must also operate within the arbitral process in international commercial disputes, at least when the public policy of a particular State is not at stake and when the arbitral proceedings do not have a religious nature. The future of arbitration requires this.

---

[103] Cour de cassation, First Civil Chamber, 7 January 1992, *Rev. arb.* 1992.470, comments by P. Bellet; (1992) *JDI*, 707 comments by Ch. Jarrosson.

[104] See Najjar, *Arbitrage dans les pays arabes et commerce international* (n 91) 8, n° 17; *Arbitration and International trade in the Arab Countries* (n 91) 10, n° 17.

In short, one should advocate a limitation, not only of the scope of party autonomy, but also to the sanction imposed when it appears overly broad. Perhaps, for this matter in particular, a limitation should be recommended not only regarding the mere soundness of contractual choices, but also regarding the sanction of the latter when discrimination is not justified by the nature of the dispute. This limitation would result in an appropriate sanction: the sole discriminatory stipulation should be considered as unwritten; the annulment should not reach the whole arbitration clause, unless the agreed qualifications are considered decisive. In sum, reliance should be placed on the judiciousness in this respect not only of the contracting parties but also of the institutional bodies called upon to assess the arbitration clause and resulting award.

PART III

CHANGING STRUCTURES: NEW FOUNDATIONS OF THE PRIVATE GLOBAL ECONOMY

10. Emerging global giants: the legal infrastructure and structural causes of economic monopoly: *Samsung*

10.1 CASE BACKGROUND

Samsung controls a large part of the world market in electronics and related goods. In this respect, it provides a fascinating example of economy-wide specialisation in global value chains. The comments below look at the legal and institutional infrastructure that supports this situation of economic quasi-monopoly. One focuses on the power derived from intellectual property and looks at the anatomy of the recent high-profile smart phone dispute in the US Supreme Court. The other explores the makings of the corruption, bribery and political scandal that has dogged the footsteps of the chaebol electronics conglomerate as it takes off as a world player. It provides a perfect opportunity to compare the structural, political and cultural conditions in which similar phenomena affect emerging varieties and forms of monopolistic capitalism across the globe. In a high-profile patents case in US federal court, a jury found that various smartphones manufactured by Samsung infringed design patents owned by Apple Inc. These covered a 'rectangular front face with rounded edges and a grid of colorful icons on a black screen'. Apple was awarded $399 million in damages – Samsung's entire profit from the sale of its infringing smartphones. Under Section 289 of the Patent Act, a person who manufactures or sells 'any article of manufacture to which [a patented] design or colorable imitation has been applied shall be liable to the owner to the extent of his total profit' (35 U.S.C. §289). The Federal Circuit affirmed the damages award, reasoning that the entire smartphone was the only permissible 'article of manufacture' for the purpose of calculating damages under §289, because consumers could not separately purchase components of the smartphones. The question was whether that reading was consistent with §289. The Supreme Court judged that it was not, holding that in the case of a multicomponent product, the relevant 'article of manufacture' need not be the end product sold to the consumer but may be only a component of that product (Compare too in Europe, CJUE, 3e ch., 21 déc. 2016, aff. C-618/15, "Compétence juridictionnelle en matière de cyber-délits: le cas des pratiques restrictives de concurrence" *Revue critique de droit international privé*, 2018, p. 105, note Tristan Azzi). However, beyond the literal reading of *Samsung v. Apple*, the case illustrates the ways in which the relationship between firms and States is changing dramatically, heralding in a new global business paradigm in which nations and firms compete with one another through intellectual property law and the private international rules that allow for private 'State shopping' by highly mobile capital or ubiquitous firms. This perspective is to be related to the wider context in which highly concentrated market power is exercised, as an explanation for the recurring bribery and corruption scandals that have affected Samsung but also other global giants such as Petrobras (encountered infra chapter 18) or Siemens according to very similar schemes. In the case of Samsung, for example, the interpersonal practices highlighted in South Korea, or its embedded market-society State relationship through *chaebol* conglomerates, do not suffice to explain the events that ultimately led to impeachment or arrest of key governmental and corporate players. The source of these reiterative corruption scandals is certainly structural and lies in the capacity to capture government officials.

Case: *USSC Samsung Electronics Co., Ltd., Et Al. V. Apple Inc.* No. 15–777. Argued October 11, 2016—Decided December 6, 2016

10.2 HOW FIRMS AND NATIONS COMPETE THROUGH INTELLECTUAL PROPERTY LAW

Darren Rosenblum

1. INTRODUCTION

Samsung allegedly stole designs of key features of iPhones to compete with Apple for smartphone market share, an infringement that gave rise to a case that went to the US Supreme Court and has drawn notice from around the world.[1] Intellectual property ('IP') debates concern who owns the ideas that people use, and to what extent inventors can exercise dominion over that property. But that debate sidesteps another, perhaps central element – the radical shift in the relationship between firms and states in the wake of globalisation. Within international business law, a perennial debate around intellectual property focuses on the need for more effective international protections. However, this is not the issue here – because of cross-border recognition of intellectual property rights, firms no longer depend entirely on a single state to determine and protect their rights and responsibilities; they've begun state shopping to achieve the most favorable interpretation of their rights and responsibilities.

It is for that reason that a literal reading of *Samsung v. Apple* falls short. It overlooks how the relationship between firms and states has begun to change dramatically, as reflected by the phenomenon of traveling corporations. This critical reading of the case will first articulate the traditional narrative around this case – one of coherent state law with clear property rules contested by firms competing for market share. Second, it will explain how that traditional narrative overlooks the reality that some firms, 'travelling corporations,' alter their structures to cherry-pick the laws that will apply to them. Third, this commentary will explore how this state-firm battle functions in a cat/mouse evolutionary dynamic, as firms compete not only against each other but also against states themselves. While IP may fortify a state in its defence against 'travelling corporations,' it is simply more palatable for states to pretend that corporate persons function in a realm of *state* law that governs their actions, rather than a realm in which firms themselves choose, define, or even dictate the legal terms that govern their market activity.

---

[1] Within intellectual property debates, questions arise about the nature of creation and the rights of inventors over their designs; opinions range along a spectrum from rigid adherence to inventors' rights toward unencumbered use of inventors' designs.

2. THE TRADITIONAL STORY – FIRM COMPETITION ALONGSIDE STATE COMPETITION

Apple and Samsung are the two largest manufacturers of mobile phones.[2] Beyond phones, the firms have divergent market shares in distinct product lines. The overlap is undeniable, and their market shares in key countries rival each other. The common way to view their relationship is that of a typical clash of the titans. Consumers, media commentators and scholarly observers largely adhere to this perspective.

However, the firms operate with highly distinct relationships toward their respective states. Apple has often had an adversarial relationship with the US government. At a 2012 dinner, President Obama met with Apple CEO Tim Cook to encourage greater US domestic production of Apple products.[3] Unrepentant, Cook asserted that the US simply did not have the labour force or regulatory flexibility to increase its US-based production. Apple products would remain 'designed in California,' but produced elsewhere, largely in China.[4] Security has been another source of tension: in 2016 Apple fought a federal court order requiring them to write a code to allow the FBI to bypass the security features on the iPhone of one of the San Bernardino shooters.[5] A recent law review article explained that the front-end encryption on certain messaging apps causes further friction between tech companies and the government, increasing their competition with each other.[6] Finally, several US political and business leaders have derided firms, like Apple, that bank hundreds of billions of dollars in profits outside the US to avoid tax liability.[7]

---

[2] Don Reisinger, 'Samsung is Back atop the Smartphone Market' *Fortune* (11 April 2017) <http://fortune.com/2017/04/11/samsung-apple-market-share/> accessed 16 April 2018.

[3] At a Presidential dinner with several of Silicon Valley's leaders, Obama asked Steve Jobs about bringing jobs back to America and Jobs said 'Those jobs aren't coming back.' Keith Bradsher and Charles Duhigg, 'How the U.S. Lost Out on iPhone Work' *NY Times* (21 January 2012) <http://www.nytimes.com/2012/01/22/business/apple-america-and-a-squeezed-middle-class.html> accessed 16 April 2018; Jobs's successor, Tim Cook, promised to bring some jobs back. Jay Yarow, 'Here's How Many Jobs Apple Will Bring to the US to Make Macs' *Business Insider* (13 February 2013) <http://www.businessinsider.com/heres-how-many-jobs-apple-will-bring-to-the-us-to-make-macs-2013-2> accessed 16 April 2018.

[4] Yoni Heisler, 'Barack Obama References Apple During State of the Union Speech' *Network World* (13 February 2013) <https://www.networkworld.com/article/2224030/data-center/barack-obama-references-apple-during-state-of-the-union-speech.html> accessed 16 April 18.

[5] James Estrin, 'Samsung and the South Korean Success Story' *NY Times: Lens* (13 November 2015) <https://lens.blogs.nytimes.com/2015/11/13/samsung-and-the-south-korean-success-story/> accessed 16 April 2018.

[6] Matthew Weber, 'Warning—Weak Password: The Courts' Indecipherable Approach to Encryption and the Fifth Amendment' (2016) 2016 *U Ill JL Tech and Pol'y* 455, 459–60; Mr. Weber explains that when tech companies are served with a warrant they typically provide the requested information 'if they have access to it, and have no reason to object to [the warrant].' Ibid.; This is still likely the case, but with the prevalence of encrypted messaging (like iMessage or WhatsApp) the companies 'often do not have access to the unencrypted data.'

[7] 'Media Deride Tax Haven "Cheats" and "Loopholes;" Ignore Benefits' *Meida Research Center* <https://www.mrc.org/articles/media-deride-tax-haven-cheats-and-loopholes-ignore-benefits> accessed 16 April 2018.

In marked contrast to this story, Samsung's relationship with the state of South Korea is successfully interwoven. As with many corporatist firms, the state plays a central role, and in turn, Samsung's success is critical to South Korea's economic prowess. It accounts for a fifth of South Korean exports, and nearly a fifth of its GDP.[8] South Korea's chaebols (family-controlled conglomerates) rose in power thanks to state benefits such as reduced taxes, special loans, anti-labour policies and government subsidies.[9] Recently, Lee Jae-yong, the former leader of Samsung, was convicted on charges of corruption for bribery intended to acquire government approval for a controversial merger and to cement family control of the company (Lee Jae-yong is the grandson of Samsung's founder, Lee Byung-chul).[10] These tightly intertwined relations between South Korea and Samsung have led some in the press to call the country the 'Republic of Samsung.'[11] Such domination by one firm used to exist in the US – where it was said that 'as General Motors goes, so goes the nation.'[12] No longer – the US economy has diversified and many of its firms have gone on to become traveling corporations.

Legal scholarship on this particular issue has stayed within a traditional IP framework rather than grappling with the political economy surrounding it.[13] The debate rests on how broadly to understand the article of manufacture. Since Apple alleges that Samsung focused its illicit copying on certain design elements within a complex product, the US Supreme Court suggested that the standard of whether there is a violation should focus on the scope of the design claimed in the patent and its prominence within the design.[14] Legal scholars have explored the legitimacy of this test and challenged it from various perspectives. Given the discord among large technological firms, it is no surprise that legal scholars dispute what test might be appropriate. Some focus on the relationship between design elements and profitability,[15] while others note the intensely competitive relationship between Apple and

---

8 Estrin (n 5).

9 Ibid.

10 Elise Hu, 'Will Samsung Case Mark a Turning Point for South Korean Business Ties to Government?' *NPR* (25 August 2017) <https://www.npr.org/sections/parallels/2017/08/25/546041137/will-samsung-case-mark-a-turning-point-for-south-korean-business-ties-to-govern> accessed 16 April 2018; See also, Choe Sang-Hun, 'Samsung's Leader is Indicted on Bribery Charges' *NY Times* (28 February 2017) <https://www.nytimes.com/2017/02/28/world/asia/lee-jae-yong-samsung.html?_r=0> accessed 16 April 2018.

11 Ibid.

12 As Charles Wilson, former President of General Motors, said in a confirmation hearing for his nomination to serve as Secretary of Defense, 'I cannot conceive of one because for years I thought what was good for our country was good for General Motors, and vice versa. The difference did not exist. Our company is too big.'

13 For a discussion of political economy of intellectual property, see Christopher May, *A Global Political Economy of Intellectual Property Rights: The New Enclosures?* (Abingdon, Routledge 2000).

14 Thomas DaMario, 'Samsung Electronics Co. v. Apple Inc., 137 S. Ct. 429 (2016)' (2017) 27 *DePaul J Art, Tech and Intell Prop L* 285.

15 Perry Saidman, Elizabeth Ferrill, Damon Neagle and Tracy Durkin, 'Determining the "Article of Manufacture" Under 35 U.S.C. § 289' (2017) 99 *J Pat and Trademark Off Soc'y* 349; the authors argue that the default article of manufacture should be the end product, but that the

Samsung.[16] As with much IP scholarship, some argue in favour of a strong vision of the rights of the inventor, since they fear that undermining creators' rights might serve as a disincentive to creation.[17]

To conclude, the typical narrative about the Apple-Samsung dispute is about the existence of two companies competing for global market share, one of them maintaining close links to its host state. At the national level, the US and South Korea present distinct state contexts in which firms operate; these nations compete for investment and trade, even as they cooperate through a contested but successfully negotiated bilateral trade agreement.[18] This narrative presumes above all that the US and South Korea have dominion over Apple and Samsung, respectively. However, as the rest of this commentary argues, in many cases, firms such as Apple have exceeded the framework of the Westphalian nation state.

3. COMPETITION IN THE WORLD OF TRAVELLING CORPORATIONS

The traditional narrative falls short when we consider how firms have begun to flip sovereignty with states. Until the turn of this century, states presumed their dominion

---

infringing party could offer evidence that the relevant article of manufacture is only a component of that end product. The authors leave the ultimate determination of what the relevant article of manufacture is to the finder of fact based on four factors: (1) visual contribution to the appearance of the end product in the eye of an ordinary observer; (2) whether the article(s) of manufacture were sold separately from the end product at the time of the infringement; (3) the intent of the infringer; and (4) the degree of difficulty in calculating the profit attributable to the article(s). The authors also suggest that, if only a component of the end product is the relevant article, calculation of the profit should include the identification of: (1) total profit associated with the end product; (2) relative revenue and costs associated with the article of manufacture compared to the end product; and (3) other evidence showing the profit attributable to the relevant article.

[16] Elizabeth M. Gil, 'Samsung v. Apple: Taking a Bite Out of the Design Patent "Article of Manufacture" Controversy' (2017) 25 *U Miami Bus L Rev* 67; after a history and analysis of the design patent law in the U.S., this article presents the United States' proposed test and assesses advantages of that test. It then situates the dispute within the broader corporate competition between Samsung and Apple, in which 'each company is determined to take down the other.'

[17] Sarah Burnick, 'The Importance of the Design Patent to Modern Day Technology: The Supreme Court's Decision to Narrow the Damages Clause in Samsung v. Apple' (2017) 18 *NC JL and Tech On* 283; the author fears the Supreme Court decision will weaken design patents, and draws on the support of other major technology firms such as Google, Facebook, and eBay for a looser standard, even as some designers supported Apple, such as the fashion designer Calvin Klein and the architect Norman Foster. The latter would favour obligating the infringer to forfeit all profits from the product infringing the copyright. Conversely, the article notes that several major tech companies signed on to an opposing brief claiming that it would be absurd to require a forfeit of all profits for infringement of a design patent for one component.

[18] See Free Trade Agreement Between the United States of America and the Republic of Korea (2007) <https://ustr.gov/trade-agreements/free-trade-agreements/korus-fta/final-text> accessed 16 April 2018.

over the world. Firms went along with that political economy narrative, but after the 2008 financial crisis, firms started undermining that Westphalian reality. States generally organised their polity according to the two principles of the Westphalian model of sovereignty: territoriality and state's autonomy.[19] States chose and enacted intellectual property protections based on national priorities, a reflection of the fact that protections for intangible property depended principally on the state.[20]

Sovereignty means far less in our globalised and largely privatised world; firms have more information and often command more resources than the state. Despite the highly contested nature of sovereignty, states and civil society leaders continue to take at face value the false pretence of Westphalian sovereignty: that states control what occurs within their borders and what passes across their borders. While globalisation does not completely obviate the state, it has sharply reduced national sovereignty as firms increasingly assume the ability to establish global norms for trade, production and consumption.

Globalisation's expansion, however, saw firms assemble global empires, some of which competed with or even surpassed nation states. As free trade expanded and tariffs came down, many firms began to manufacture abroad. Then came the wave of outsourcing – first products, then services – to the developing world. Cross-border M&A expanded, always driven by synergies and other efficiencies. Globalisation has also led firms to establish subsidiaries abroad or buy foreign firms. The result was a set of truly multinational corporations, with distinct workforces in many countries that maximise efficiencies of labour, capital and natural resource markets. Before the turn of the 21st century, multinationals had already begun this process of creating global supply chains to produce the most profitable combination of workers, products, and consumers. Toward the end of the first decade, it became clear that law, as well, was just another efficiency to maximise. Corporations have become increasingly mobile, essentially allowing firms to relocate to a preferred jurisdiction with relative ease.[21] This corporate mobility marks a radical decline in the Westphalian notion of state sovereignty, as firms grab the power to decide which laws will govern them. In this extreme form of regulatory arbitrage, global firms locate subsidiaries and intellectual property in jurisdictions that provide them with the most favorable business environment. As we see within the United States and within the European Union, jurisdictions compete openly with advantageous tax rules and other regulatory benefits.[22] While this game is not new – firms have managed their earnings to minimize tax exposure at least since the early 20th century – it has reached a new level with the recent wave of inversion mergers that have been specifically designed to avoid tax liability.[23]

---

[19] Stephen Krasner, 'Pervasive not Perverse: Semi-Sovereigns as the Global Norm' (1997) 30 *Cornell Int'l L.J.* 651, 656; "States exist in specific territories. Within these territories, domestic political authorities are the only arbiters of legitimate behavior. The basic rule of Westphalian sovereignty is non-intervention in the internal affairs of other states."

[20] Ibid.

[21] Tsilly Dagan, 'Pay as You Wish: Globalization, Forum Shopping, and Distributive Justice' (manuscript at 3) (20 June 2014), <https://ssrn.com/abstract=2457212> accessed 16 April 2018.

[22] See Joseph McWeeney, 'Cat and Mouse—How Can the U.S. Government Keep American Companies in America' (2016) 14 *De Paul Bus and Com LJ* 357, 383–84.

[23] Some argue that Henry Ford's reticence to issue dividends was a response to the high tax rate. More recently, tax credits motivated the merger involved in the *Smith v. Van Gorkom* case.

For firms like Apple, engineering profitability moves beyond the mere question of assembling hyper-efficient supply chains. It requires a mastery of regulatory arbitrage. Firms not only game which state's rules govern which contracts, but they also manage which laws govern them when. As Tsilly Dagan eloquently writes with regard to tax laws, firms can 'pay what they choose,' accepting taxation rules in jurisdictions with light tax burdens and avoiding states with heavier responsibilities.[24] Thanks to their capacity to relocate based on legal frameworks, such firms may be called 'travelling corporations.'

Intellectual property plays a central role in the life of a travelling corporation, which depends on certain property regimes to amass and maintain capital.[25] Firms like Apple, as well as other leading technology companies, have to secure their intellectual property rights by locating them in jurisdictions where they are most secure. In this way, firms cherry-pick nations based on their IP, tax and other regulatory structures, and they subdivide to maximise profit. Thus, the ruling by the US Supreme Court in the *Samsung v. Apple* case, to the extent that it takes a position protecting intellectual property, invites larger firms to house their intellectual property, if not production, in the United States. Were the US to adopt a looser set of protections, it would risk losing this intellectual property to other states. International norms may create IP rights that are 'more than optimal,'[26] – meaning they restrict innovation – but they still remain an ideal for many large firms who would benefit most, although such enforcement would likely exacerbate existing global North-South inequalities.[27] Without those norms, firms constantly engage in forum shopping.[28]

Firms like Starbucks and Apple credit protected IP as the source of substantial revenues. Some states require taxation on that revenue, but other states allow firms to house their intellectual property in their jurisdiction, then allow that subsidiary to pay out the earnings to a different jurisdiction with a lower tax rate: the famous 'Double Irish with a Dutch Sandwich,' by which Google protected its property and avoided tax on its earnings.[29] Such travelling corporations, with their armies of expert accountants

---

Early in the 2010s firms began to see law – in particular tax law – as a cost to engineer across national lines. The advent of inversion mergers brought this technique to a new level as firms began to use their domicile as a fungible element subject to advantageous tax regimes.

[24] Dagan (n 21).

[25] May (n 13) 17–18 ('There is the process of the development of property as an institution which protects certain interests in society in a specified manner.').

[26] Scotchmer argues that IP harmonisation on minimum protections may produce asymmetric protections which may be more efficient than universal protections. It may also create IP rights that are more than optimal. Suzanne Scotchmer, 'The Political Economy of Intellectual Property Treaties' (2002 Working Paper) NBER. See Frederick Abbott, Carlos Correa and Peter Drahos, *Emerging Markets and the Patent Order* (Cheltenham, Edward Elgar 2015); Matthias Lamping et al., 'Declaration on Patent Protection Regulatory Sovereignty Under TRIPS' (2014) Max Planck Institute for Innovation and Competition Research Paper No. 14-19. See also, May (n 13) 12, 14.

[27] Scotchmer (n 26). See Abbott, Correa and Drahos (n 26); Lamping et al. (n 26).

[28] Laurence Helfer, 'Regime Shifting: The TRIPs Agreement and the New Dynamics of Intellectual Property Making' (2004) 29 *Yale J Int'l L* 1; Laurence Helfer, 'Regime Shifting in the International Intellectual Property System' (2009) 7 *Perspectives on Pols* 39.

[29] Dagan (n 21).

and lawyers, easily outpace even the most effectively governed states. The firms learn what legal rules govern where, and how to skirt those rules, whether with mere paperwork compliance, or with more complex endeavours such as setting up subsidiaries or inversion mergers.

For travelling corporations in the technology sector, such as Apple, even more pronounced competition sits with firms that constitute 'regulatory entrepreneurs.' For such firms, the line of business itself requires changing the law. This category of company has jumped to the forefront of the corporate sector as Uber and Airbnb now provide more taxi rides and evening stays than traditional companies. These companies succeed by targeting local contexts to raise their business model as a political issue, in which they motivate those involved with the firm to advocate on their behalf.[30] Apple's dispute with the US over relinquishing codes to the FBI involved a similar use of customers to fight back against a political threat to their commercial venture.[31] Apple views its competition not only as other firms but as the state itself, and may move further in that direction. With regulatory entrepreneurship, firms may view rules enacted by the state as inefficient systems that should be undermined for efficiency and profit.

Not all multinationals challenge state sovereignty, however. Indeed, Samsung plays by rules set in the 20th century, in which large firms functioned in tandem with the states in which they resided. Samsung's close links with the South Korean government provide it with regulatory benefits, tax benefits, and access to capital it might not receive if it were any other company. One cannot underestimate the value of the link between a large firm and the state, as Calixto Salomão Filho notes in his commentary in this volume on the same case. Much of this connection may veer toward corruption, and indeed that word has described some of Samsung's relationship to the South Korean state. At the same time, Samsung's link with South Korea frames its competition with Apple not only as a competition between a South Korean firm and a US firm, but perhaps more importantly as one between a traditional multinational and a travelling corporation.

The link to the state could not be more divergent – for Apple, the United States is a competitor, each ranking their need for profits (or tax revenue) as paramount. Samsung may achieve similar ends from South Korea – avoiding tax liability for instance, but it does so in concert with the state. Evolutionary dynamic theory involves understanding how beings evolve in relation to each other. In this model, Apple and the US evolve against each other, while Samsung and South Korea evolve together, as a co-dependent species, in a symbiotic relationship, against other predators and prey – the US and Apple, for instance.

A counterargument is that industrialised-country firms and their home states pressure emerging market states to conform to their standards.[32] Dominant states such as the US and the EU use the carrot of granting access to their intellectual property markets (and

---

30 Jordan Barry and Elizabeth Pollman, 'Regulatory Entrepreneurship' (2017) 90 *S Cal Rev* 383.

31 Hal Hodson, 'Apple vs FBI: First Salvo in the Information War' (2016) 229 *New Scientist* 24 <http://www.sciencedirect.com/science/article/pii/S0262407916600283> accessed 16 April 2018.

32 Ibid. at 27–28.

the stick of refusing such access) to pressure other countries to raise their IP standards.[33] IP disputes then become battlegrounds for competition among nations. Arguments between international companies (such as Apple and Samsung) over their intellectual property may be framed as a microcosm or even a sideshow of the overarching competition between the nations that provide those protections.[34]

I attempt to account for these perspectives in Figure 10.1, to account for the state-centered framework, the travelling corporation framework, and how they interact within the Apple-Samsung dispute.

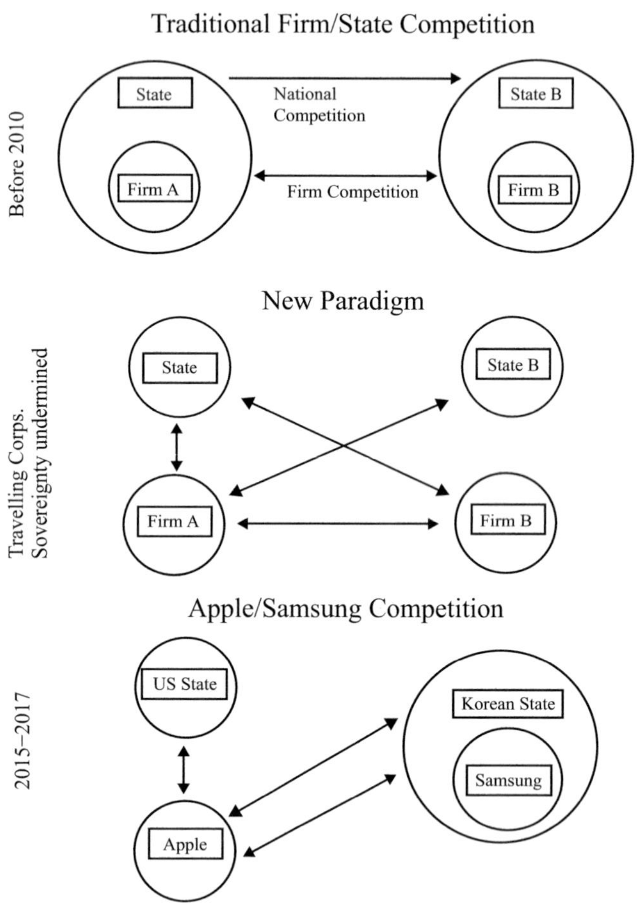

Source: Author's own source.

Figure 10.1 The contrast between the evolving paradigm of relationships among firms and states

---

[33] Ibid. at 103.

[34] Abbott, Correa and Drahos (n 26) 27–29.

Figure 10.1 depicts the contrast between the evolving paradigm of relationships among firms and states. The figure makes it clear that with travelling corporations, firms sit outside the state in which they came into being. This is not entirely accurate because of course firms, such as Apple, do have deep links to their home states, but those links are far fewer than was traditionally the case. Many such firms draw greater revenue from abroad than from their home state, and some even have more employees abroad. However, as depicted in the third time frame, travelling corporations relate differently both to their home state but also to other firms and other states.

4. TRAVELLING CORPORATIONS, IP AND THE STATE

As Figure 10.1 shows, states no longer compete only with each other but also with firms themselves. Gary Shteyngart's dystopic novel *Super Sad True Love Story* envisions this world.[35] In it, the area of the United States is divided up into territories in which foreign states and multinational firms hold power. Given the radical increase in power by travelling corporations, it may be a future, akin to a 'new feudalism' that is not so distant. The internet fosters this radical increase of firm power, as cybertrade enables individuals to provide or receive services worldwide without leaving home. Anupam Chander, for one, worries that the internet's end run around local law might imperil domestic laws. Firms may replace local laws with those of the provider's home state, or avoid many laws altogether.[36] In the same way that travelling corporations avoid tax liability through their clever manoeuvering, firms can, through the internet, shift jurisdictional hold on their transactions away from states that impose other liabilities. It may be that, as Chander says, 'law itself [is] at risk, now avoidable by a mere single click.'[37]

A traditional understanding of the relationship between states and patent-impinging firms frames the dispute as between states as cats and patent-impinging firms as mice.[38] But the evolutionary dynamic theory that describes the games of cat and mouse may prove more fruitful than that. As evolutionary dynamic theory argues, predator and prey constantly mutate to better catch or avoid capture. Likewise, it's not only that the state seeks to 'capture' the IP violators, but the firms transform themselves to avoid capture. Thus, firms establish and move subsidiaries around the globe to protect their IP and to avoid paying taxes on their revenue.

---

35 Gary Shteyngart, *Super Sad True Love Story* (New York, New York 2010) 256–57.

36 Ibid. at 6.

37 Ibid.

38 Daria Roithmayr et al., 'Cat and Mouse: The Evolutionary Dynamics of Getting Around the Law' (last revised 7 March 2017) <http://papers.ssrn.com/sol3/papers.cfm?abstract_id=2808718> accessed 16 April 2018; See also, Susan K. Sell, 'Cat and Mouse: Forum-Shifting in the Battle Over Intellectual Property Enforcement' (Draft/Presentation paper 6 September 2009) <http://papers.ssrn.com/sol3/papers.cfm?abstract_id=1466156>; Sell frames her argument as a game of cat and mouse between those who seek to ration access to IP and those who seek to expand access where forum-shifting is used by strong states to optimise advantages and minimised opposition, and by 'weaker' parties in efforts to reshape the rules. Ibid.

In order to better capture revenue, states adapt as well, albeit to a lesser extent; because states depend on tax revenue to operate, their incentive could not be greater. With the extensive support of global accounting and law firms, travelling corporations display far greater efficacy in mutating to avoid capture of their resources, allowing many prey actors to grow far larger than some of their predators. Firms become travelling corporations, beyond their birth state's dominion.

Not only do states hold less and less power as the world globalises and interconnects through trade and the internet, but both states and citizens seem willing to avoid a frank assessment of this topic as it confirms their collective powerlessness and impotence with regard to mass capital. In this sense, the competition between Apple and Samsung over mobile phone technology is not a battle of titans but almost a sideshow over the true competition, between the firms and their home states. Focusing on the titanic sideshow within the juridical boxing ring of the legal sphere provides insecure states, leaders and citizens with a balm assuring the continued relevance of the state in decision-making; in fact, however, firms actually constantly compete with and undermine the states in which they operate. IP law provides this boxing ring – it serves as a front for the legitimacy of law in a world where far weaker tax laws allow firms like Apple to amass an unprecedented fortune beyond any state's dominion.

Such firms also depend on states to enforce their IP rights, without which they would cease being profitable. IP law buttresses corporate power, but some of those same firms avoid state commitments such as taxes. An honest assessment of this corporate power is essential to states' maintaining some sway over the lives of their individual and corporate citizens.

Even as firms depend on state IP enforcement, they attempt to avoid state claims on their profits through taxes. States should consider enforcing IP rights in response to firms' broader regard for the law. In that sense, states can use IP as a tool not only against competing states but also against travelling corporations. They can mould their IP systems to suit their public social, cultural, and economic needs and priorities, and not just those of firms.[39] The fact is, stronger states such as the US actually fund a lion's share of technological research and development, and that share approaches 80% when one considers funding by nonprofits.[40] Taking into account the role the state plays in the development of IP, even in liberal democracies such as the US, justifies greater state action with regard to travelling corporations. As we examine transnational IP disputes, we should view the state's relationship with the firm through a holistic lens, one that allows us to recognise other ways in which firms not only submit to the state's will but compete with and even undermine the state.

---

[39] Lamping et al. (n 26) 1.

[40] Amy Kapczynski, 'The Cost of Price: Why and How to Get Beyond Intellectual Property Internalism' (2012) 59 *UCLA L Rev* 970, 972. Given the public origins of so much IP, it may make sense for the state to enforce IP more loosely and incentivize innovation instead, as Amy Kapczynski suggests. Ibid. at 973.

5. CONCLUSION

This commentary has tried to assess the *Samsung v. Apple* case by questioning the traditional narrative of how IP law works. The question is not simply how states recognise IP rights but rather how the recognition of IP rights relates to the changing nature of the relationship between the firm and the state. The IP dispute between Apple and Samsung reflects how IP law insufficiently describes the battle not only between these two firms, but that between two models of firms: the travelling corporation and the traditional corporatist firm. Whether corporatist firms will continue to thrive in a world dominated by travelling corporations remains to be seen. It may be that states with strong links to specific firms continue to develop their power, while others wither as travelling corporations avoid liability for public goods in their home states. For all these firms, intellectual property figures prominently in firm development, success, and ultimately in the allocation of resources among states and firms.

10.3 GLOBAL CORRUPTION AND ECONOMIC POWER

Calixto Salomão Filho and Vitor Henrique Pinto Ido

1. INTRODUCTION

As a global phenomenon, corruption is neither isolated nor exclusive to certain countries and/or cultures. For some, corruption is an unavoidable burden most commonly seen in the 'Global South', a feature of extractivist and patrimonialist elites who harm the quality of national institutions and the path of development.[41] For others, corruption is a natural part of human relations as a whole and a consequence of never-ending individual's utilitarian aspirations, somehow regardless of geography and history. Be it one or the other, law struggles to properly address corruption.

This is due to its multiple forms, leading to a seemingly 'impossible' regulation, in a way every legal effort sounds irrelevant. On one hand, corruption is attached to local and personal private interests, making it hardly controllable by conventional public policies and institutions. On the other hand, economic power has an intrinsic transnational dimension, which only turns such debate into a much more complex legal issue, as national states, per se, cannot control corruption. All in all, as definitions, regulatory dilemmas, and cost-benefit analyses are all unclear, corruption seems a problem not solvable by law at all.

Taking a step back, a critical reflection on corruption requires a discussion on what is and should be the role of law in its regulation, especially in (re)designing structures and avoiding the consequences of the concentration of both political and economic power.[42]

---

[41] Susan Rose-Ackerman and Bonnie J. Palifka, *Corruption and Government: Causes, Consequences, and Reform* 2nd edn (Cambridge, Cambridge University Press 2016).

[42] Calixto Salomão Filho, *A Legal Theory of Economic Power – Implications for Social and Economic Development* (Cheltenham, Edward Elgar 2011).

This implies more than the creation of incentives and compensation mechanisms, but the development of truly structural measures against corruption. It also makes critical empirical descriptions important to materialise the conditions under which corruption ultimately happens. More than that. Through this lens, it is possible to see the shortcoming of the aforementioned institutional approach to corruption. Much more than a product of institutional underdevelopment, corruption should be seen as a consequence of global economic structures and its variations across different regions (Global South, Global North) – which are themselves a consequence of the particular ways these structures have been established and nowadays operate in each of these regions.[43]

Bearing this in mind, this article compares three landmark cases: i) the Petrobras oil scandal in Brazil, ii) The Siemens bribery system, and iii) Samsung's influence in South Korea's political arena. These major cases highlight some of the main elements of how corruption tends to take place, and allow further considerations on the possible role of legal strategies to address it. The selection of examples coming from different parts of the world has the ultimate purpose of analysing differences and similarities of a phenomenon happening everywhere. However, as we seek to argue, corruption practices are intertwined with the degree of economic power's concentration, and a (global) law approach aiming to establish an adequate regulatory framework needs to take this structural element into account.

2. PETROBRAS OIL SCANDAL

Petrobras is Brazil's biggest company and was founded in 1953 as part of a strong developmentalist policy. It is one of the world's largest oil companies, working on several parts of oil's supply chain and a leading player in deep water oil extraction.[44] From a corporate law point of view, Petrobras is currently a public-private corporation ('*sociedade de economia mista*'), being the Union of Brazil its controller shareholder, but having its remaining shares in the hands of private individuals/companies. It has also several subsidiaries and international branches, being listed at New York Stock Exchange, as well as Brazil's B3. It had legal monopoly in Brazil on all oil industries until 1997, when a constitutional amendment allowed for its flexibilisation and the entrance of new economic players.[45]

On 17 March 2014, 17 people, including then directors of Petrobras, were arrested for corruption charges involving the company. The Brazilian Federal Police investigation was named 'Lava Jato' (Operation Car Wash). Throughout 2015 and 2016, various other politicians and businessmen were also arrested, many of whom eventually

[43] Deepak Nayyar, *Catch-Up – Developing Countries in the Global Economy* (Oxford, Oxford University Press 2013).

[44] Petrobras, 'Our History – Travel time in 50 years and know Petrobras' (2017) <http://www.petrobras.com/en/about-us/our-history/our-history.htm> accessed 20 October 2017.

[45] Ibid.

negotiated plea bargain.[46] Petrobras' board members and directors, as well as many prominent political characters, have been formally accused. Some were deemed guilty for corruption-related crimes. Critics argued the plea bargaining system, inspired by common law systems, actually created incentives for corruption, as several plaintiffs simply found a way out of punishment. Critics also pointed out the politically oriented focus of the operation, with a bias against left-wing parties, which was actually made clear by some judges' statements. Those in favour of Car Wash highlighted how much elites (including some relevant businessmen) were 'for the first time ever' being sent to trials in Brazil. Regardless of the point of view, Operation Car Wash led to unprecedented years of still on-going investigations and trials in the country. It is Brazilian Federal Police' largest investigation in its history.[47]

As a whole, the corruption involved, among others, bribery of politicians and company employees in order to benefit private companies in large contract bids and to the appointment of certain directors inside Petrobras. Several private actors, especially those related to civil construction, have directly participated in the scheme, in some cases their controlling shareholders and some of their directors have also been charged with corruption.

Politically, despite the media's focus on the then ruling party Partido dos Trabalhadores (PT – Workers Party), the Petrobras scandal actually dealt with most of the existing political parties with representation in Brazilian Congress, including Mr. Aecio Neves, an opposition member from the Partido da Social Democracia Brasileira (PSDB – Party of Brazilian Social Democracy).

Operation Car Wash has been also consistently remembered for its similarities to 1990s Italy's Mani Pulite operation – including its arguably questionable aftermath: the political rise of Berlusconi to power.[48] Through media coverage, Operation Car Wash took central attention of Brazil's public sphere and somehow created its very own central characters. The first is a federal judge, Mr. Sergio Moro, criticised by many as be overly political, and praised by others for the same reasons. The other side of the investigation is focused on Mr. Luiz Inácio Lula da Silva, Brazil's former president and the first worker to run the country in its history, now accused of corruption charges involving political choices to Petrobras' board and personal benefits, such as a beach apartment and a pedal boat (although until now no charges have been demonstrated).[49]

As the 'commodity boom' of the late 2000s vanquished, Brazil's economy, once praised as one of the most stable and promising emerging markets in the 21st century, eventually ended up being caught in a huge economic and political turmoil. In this context, Operation Car Wash and corruption were ubiquitous in all political discussions,

---

46 'Cronologia da Operação Lava-Jato' (*El País*, 18 April 2017). <https://brasil.elpais.com/brasil/2017/04/12/politica/1492018492_100094.html> accessed 20 October 2017.

47 Ministério Público Federal, Caso Lava-Jato (2017). <http://www.mpf.mp.br/para-o-cidadao/caso-lava-jato/entenda-o-caso> accessed 20 October 2017.

48 Luiza Bandeira, 'Operação que inspirou Lava-Jato foi fracasso e criou corruptos mais sofisticados, diz pesquisador' *BBC Brasil* (17 March 2016) <http://www.bbc.com/portuguese/noticias/2016/03/160316_lavajato_dois_anos_entrevista_lab> accessed 19 October 2017.

49 Jonathan Watts, 'Operation Car Wash: Is this the biggest corruption scandal in history?' *The Guardian* (1 June 2017) <https://www.theguardian.com/world/2017/jun/01/brazil-operation-car-wash-is-this-the-biggest-corruption-scandal-in-history> accessed 19 October 2017.

a main theme for the big manifestations occurred during that year.[50] Amid tensions, President Mrs. Dilma Roussef, the first and only female ruler of the Federal Republic of Brazil, was ultimately impeached in 2015 under accusations of 'fiscal pedaling' (*pedaladas fiscais*), i.e., artificially making up national accounting results. Its critics argue with good reason that Mrs. Roussef's impeachment was actually a coup d'état, and that her accusations were only the excuse found to undemocratically take her out of power. Since then, her Vice President, Mr. Michel Temer, became the president of Brazil to unprecedented popularity rates as low as 3 per cent. Despite his own (and more serious) accusations of corruption, Mr. Temer has not been impeached – he has in fact been judged by Brazilian Congress, composed in its majority by his allies.

The legal and economic consequences are particularly relevant as Petrobras is not only the country's biggest company, but also part of a strategic sector for the Brazilian economy, being one of the few sectors not fully privatised during the 1990s and 2000s. Operation Car Wash may still lead to several changes in corporate structure. Apart from new corporate governance mechanisms and a renewed attempt to recreate its corporate image,[51] arguments for the privatisation of Petrobras reappeared. One must take into account how those against turning it into a privately-owned firm controlled by international shareholders (as the authors of this essay) refer not only to Brazil's own corporate history of strong state participation, but do have in mind real and in fact justified concerns about national economy and foreign 'dependency' (a long and ongoing debate[52]).

Moreover, the losses in investment ratings and market value were enormous, and had an impact on not only Petrobras' brand and reputation, but for its various stakeholders – not only minority shareholders. This all led to various shareholder legal claims and arbitration procedures in Brazil and abroad, such as New York, with still unfinished results. The impacts of outsourced litigation and shareholder primacy interpretations in corporate law[53] are still unclear, but might be detrimental to Petrobras' finances. As an important argument for these claims, corruption has been argued as a breach of fiduciary duties by the company itself and by the State of Brazil (its controlling shareholder) towards its shareholders.

In Peru, former president Alejandro Toledo was arrested in February 2017 due to Petrobras' corruption-related practices.[54] For similar reasons, two Mossack Fonseca

---

50 'Brazil's Fall' *The Economist* (2 Jan 2016) <https://www.economist.com/news/leaders/21684779-disaster-looms-latin-americas-biggest-economy-brazils-fall> accessed 19 October 2017.

51 Daniel Silveira, 'Petrobrás aposta em nova campanha para "resgatar reputação" após Lava Jato' *G1* (8 November 2017) <https://g1.globo.com/economia/midia-e-marketing/noticia/petrobras-aposta-em-nova-campanha-publicitaria-para-melhorar-reputacao-de-sua-marca.ghtml> accessed 8 November 2017.

52 Celso Furtado, *Desenvolvimento e Subdesenvolvimento* (Fundo de Cultura, 1961).

53 Peer Zumbansen and Cynthia A. Williams, *The Embedded Firm – Corporate Governance, Labor and Finance Capitalism* (Cambridge, Cambridge University Press 2011); Lynn Stout, *The Shareholder Value Myth* [2011] Paper 771.

54 'Ex-presidente do Peru tem prisão decretada: Lava-Jato avança no exterior e põe governos da América Latina sob suspeita' *BBC Brasil* (10 Feb 2017) <http://www.bbc.com/portuguese/brasil-38907251> accessed 8 November 2017.

lawyers, a law firm in Panama, have also been sent to jail.[55] These examples highlight some of the consequences that go far beyond Brazilian legal system and society. In another dimension, the federal antitrust agency Cade (Conselho Administrativo de Defesa Econômica), which had in its history vetoed corporate mergers only on very few cases, started to change its policy to impede in some cases the concentration of economic power. Many have understood this as a sign of response to the events in Petrobras.[56] It is unclear by now if it is a durable change or just a transitory political response.

Generally speaking, this case makes explicit the ties between political and economic power and its various consequences. Despite the fact most of media attention in Brazil has exclusively focused on the individual morality of the politicians involved, it is actually deeply intertwined with the power of major companies contracting with Petrobras (an oligopoly of constructing companies) and Petrobras itself. The case could hardly be explained and legally debated in purely political science, corporate law or criminal law terms. Its roots are structural: they are also profoundly linked to the way monopolistic and oligopolistic structures developed in Brazil. Furthermore, it is linked to how the use or abuse of economic or market power is embedded in their rationale.[57] Under these lenses, the corruption scandal was another instance in both the abuse of economic power (the private constructing companies oligopoly – the corruptors) and the capture of an also monopolised entrepreneurial state (represented by Petrobras – the corrupted). In this sense, it seems absolutely in line with the structures that have been established during and survived the colonial monopolistic system of exploitation established for centuries in those regions.[58]

3. SIEMENS BRIBERY SYSTEM

In 2005, Siemens AG, one of Germany's biggest and most well-known corporate groups, was accused of bribery activities in several parts of the world over the course of decades. They included, among others, officials for the Athens Olympic Games in 2004, Israeli officials for the construction of a power plant, and some others to win a bid in Argentina for the making of national identity cards.[59] Names as diverse as

---

55 'Sócios da Mossack Fonseca são detidos no Panamá por investigações relacionadas com a Lava Jato' *G1* (10 Feb 2017) <https://g1.globo.com/mundo/noticia/socios-da-mossack-fonseca-detidos-no-panama-por-investigacoes-relacionadas-com-a-lava-jato.ghtml> accessed 8 November 2017.

56 Leticia Toledo, 'Veto à fusão entre Kroton e Estácio revela transformação no Cade' *Exame* (13 Jul 2017) <https://exame.abril.com.br/revista-exame/o-tribunal-diz-nao/> accessed 8 November 2017.

57 Calixto Salomão Filho, *Teoria Crítico-Estruturalista do Direito Comercial* (Madrid, Marcial Pons 2015).

58 Calixto Salomão Filho, *Monopolies and Underdevelopment – From Colonial Past to Global Reality* (Cheltenham, Edward Elgar 2015).

59 Siri Schubert and T. Christian Miller, 'At Siemens, bribery was just a line item' *New York Times* (20 Dec 2008) <http://www.nytimes.com/2008/12/21/business/worldbusiness/21siemens.html> accessed 8 November 2017.

Saddam Hussein were pointed out, and there was an annual budget specific to bribery of (also) corrupt foreign governments. Up until then, this was considered the biggest private corruption scandal in the world's history.

Its corruption practices are better described as a whole corruption system, as it was actually fully institutionalised. As most of the practices themselves occurred out of German territory – yet from decisions taken and approved in Germany – this transnational scheme would even get deductions under German tax law, as bribes were registered as 'business expenses.'[60] Despite the fact German State was not directly involved in the facts, it has been criticised for the excessive openness and lack of accountability regarding foreign activities of German companies, despite important changes in 1999, when foreign corruption was finally criminalised in the country.

Even though this scandal was by no means the first in the Global North's contemporary history, the degree and extent of the briberies undertaken by Siemens AG were remarkable. They had become a fully corporate policy to expand markets and either sustain or gain its presence and power abroad. The government officials involved were both democratic and autocratic, left-wing and right-wing, aligned or not to Germany, large and small, and with quite different living standards. It seems the distance between the ones taking corporate decisions in German offices and the countries affected were partly responsible for such detachment, similar to how moral values tend to erode when market relations become denser and larger.[61] Many of the employees felt they were simply following orders or securing local jobs of a company that, undoubtedly, hires thousands of people with major economic benefits. However, taking such events as purely individual decisions would be completely inaccurate, as there were clear economic benefits (in violation of competition standards) rising out of corruption. This was thus a whole structural scheme promoted, and authorised, in its turn, by corporate structure.

Siemens AG has actually had a much longer history of bribery, tracing back to at least January 1914 in Japan, in a scandal involving naval contracts.[62] Siemens was obviously not a bad apple among pristine and fair companies, but effectively took such practices to a whole new level. The extension of the scandal is also in part responsible for its widespread reaction, as it managed to harm virtually every side of the narrative, be it European or not, lower or high-ranking, liberal or conservative.

In 2008, Siemens had been fined US$1.6 billion for bribery, the largest in modern corporate history. It was charged under the USA's Foreign Corrupt Practices Act, as the company also traded its shares on the New York Stock Exchange, but also in several different jurisdictions through different claims. The biggest legal suit was the one in Greece, related to the 2004 Olympics. Following the scandal, German law and institutions have been further amended to create better control of transnational practices of corruption, and to avoid new cases, since they had consequences far beyond the corporate brand itself.[63]

---

[60] Ibid.

[61] Armin Falk and Nora Szech, 'Morals and Markets' *Science* (10 May 2013) 340 707, 711.

[62] Richard Sims, *Japanese Political History Since the Meiji Restoration 1868-2000* (Basingstoke, Palgrave Macmillan 2001).

[63] Schubert and Miller (n 60).

However, the more serious consequences were in corporate governance and structure. Internationally, more than 80% of the top level, 70% of middle, and 40% of lower executives of Siemens were replaced,[64] and a rather robust full-time compliance team has been created. The creation and almost complete change in internal practices were brought about by a highly specialised international team.[65] Peter Löscher, then Merck CEO, was hired to lead the structural reforms, and, according to his own view, this was a unique opportunity to promote such drastic changes.

The company redesign was actually much needed after the huge negative impact on the brand and the company, rather than a moral decision. Investors were unpleased as much as shareholders, but also the German government, the OCDE and the European Commission. Similar and somehow equivalent changes have been since then undertaken, for instance, by Royal Dutch Shell after the Kiobel scandal in Nigeria, one of the most prominent cases in business and human rights.[66] In fact, it would be no exaggeration to try to hold Siemens AG accountable for indirect human rights violations under the current international framework.

This case highlights the opportunity to promote structural changes in times of major crises, even though results are always unclear and context-dependent. It is always easier, and less bureaucratic, to perform reforms in companies than in public institutions, as much as it's more efficient to create changes in corporate structure than to pretend general international norms will work by themselves. However, Siemens AG has never been in an empty void, and its case should not be taken as an exclusively private matter. Again here the structural explanations seem relevant. The existence of a huge multinational willing to expand its market power internationally and willing to abuse its economic power through bribes specially in the Global South is consistent with a view of a continuous metropolitan monopolistic enterprise. The help provided by the state includes the – to say the least – curious legal authorisation until 1999 to deduce bribes paid in foreign countries as expenses. The 'state-business colonial monopolistic structures'[67] seems also here to survive in a transformed way. The fact that Germany is not perceived as a corrupt country but that it allowed such a widespread system of corruption abroad is a relevant counterfactual to institutional explanations of this case. It seems to strengthen the case for structural explanations of corruption.

---

64 Peter Löscher, 'The CEO of Siemens on Using a Scandal to Drive Change' *Harvard Business Review* (Nov 2012) <https://hbr.org/2012/11/the-ceo-of-siemens-on-using-a-scandal-to-drive-change> accessed 8 November 2017.

65 Siemens AG, 'Responsible Behavior – Compliance at Siemens' (2017) <https://www.siemens.com/content/dam/internet/siemens-com/global/company/sustainability/downloads/responsible-business-behavior-compliance-at-siemens.pdf> accessed 11 November 2017.

66 John Ruggie, *Just Business – Multinational Corporations and Human Rights* (London, W. W. Norton & Company, 2013).

67 Salomão Filho (n 58).

4. SAMSUNG AND GOVERNMENT RELATIONS

Samsung Group is South Korea's largest and most powerful business group. Founded in 1938 by Lee Byung-chul, it eventually emerged to become one of the world's leading firms in electronics and also other industries. It accounts for around 15% of the country's GDP, and, as a joke puts it, one can be born in a Samsung hospital, go to a Samsung school, use Samsung house-ware, have a Samsung phone, until you die in another Samsung hospital.[68]

In 2016, then President Mrs. Park Geun-Hye, the first female president in East Asia, was impeached following a controversy over its ties to Mrs. Choi Soon-Sil, her personal advisor and, to some, her spiritual leader.[69] Mrs. Park is the daughter of former dictator Mr. Park Chung-Hee, who is deemed responsible for South Korea's very 'economic miracle'. A self-proclaimed conservative candidate, Mrs. Park's had as one of the campaign's strongest mottos her alleged distance from patrimonialistic relations as she is a single independent woman, who had thus 'no one' to benefit. Albeit gender inequality issues obviously arise from this narrative, it served as a way to place her as a possible exception to the already long list of investigated and sanctioned South Korean presidents since the 1980s. The 18 charges against her, which included taking or soliciting bribes worth 59.2 billion won (US$52 million), would prove this thesis wrong.

During the development of the case, the strong relation between Mrs. Park and Mrs. Choi was expanded to include other important links, specially the one of Mr. Lee Jae-Yong, Samsung's heir and de facto CEO. In the most controversial allegation, Mr. Lee would have given or promised to Mrs. Park, in the benefit of Mrs. Choi, the amount of 43.3 billion won (US$38.3 million) to guarantee a corporate merger in 2015.[70] The money was ultimately destined to two private non-profit associations led by Mrs. Choi, then resident of Germany, but for unclear purposes.

On 31 March 2017, Mrs. Park was arrested, being later convicted for corruption-related practices that included bribery, abuse of power, traffic of influence, and leaking of government secrets. Dozens of other politicians and businessmen from South Korea's biggest groups (chaebols), such as Lotte, SK, Hanwha and Hanjin, have been also investigated and/or convicted. Mrs. Park later publicly apologised for the incidents and was said to deeply regret her own conduct. Mrs. Choi denied the accusations, and was later sentenced to three years of imprisonment. Mr. Lee was arrested and convicted to five years in prison for corruption charges.

Most of the media follow-up focused on either the personal ties between the two women or the 'uniqueness' of the case, as Mrs. Choi has been depicted as a 'religious

---

68 Zahra Ullah, 'How Samsung dominates South Korea's economy' *CNN* (17 Feb 2017) <http://money.cnn.com/2017/02/17/technology/samsung-south-korea-daily-life/index.html> accessed 11 November 2017.

69 'South Korea's Presidential Scandal' *BBC* (25 Aug 2017) <http://www.bbc.com/news/world-asia-37971085> accessed 11 November 2017.

70 Justin McCurry, 'Former South Korean president Park Geun-hye on trial for corruption' *The Guardian* (23 May 2017) <https://www.theguardian.com/world/2017/may/23/former-south-korean-president-park-geun-hye-on-trial-for-corruption> accessed 11 November 2017.

cult leader'. She is herself the daughter of Mr. Choi Tae-Min, the founder of a religious group, and who was also personal advisor to Mrs. Park's father. These aspects of the case were an entry point to analyses based on South Korea's specific social relations, including the role of Christianity, Confucianism and Buddhism, as well as intense group and social pressure towards individuals. In other words, individual morals or culture as main explanations for the scandal.

Some have also consistently argued for such proximity between market and State as a trait of South Korea's society, in the sense that competition has actually never been the paradigm that oriented its own variety of capitalism,[71] similar to post-War developmentalist Japan[72] and China, among others. This argument is important. If understood as a specific set of socio-economic, as well as historical and political structures, and not as a peculiar situation of an Asian country or culture, this case allows for serious considerations about the entanglement between law, corruption and economic power.[73]

As to the consequences of the case, South Korea's economy was not directly hit by the scandal, nor were the profits of Samsung, which remained largely intact. Many have criticised the relatively short punishments of both Mrs. Park, Mrs. Choi and Mr. Lee, as some had even expected life in prison sentences.[74] No corporate restructuring processes happened so far, apart from the temporary dismissal of Mr. Lee from Samsung Group's positions. Samsung has in fact experienced a hard crisis following its Galaxy Note 7 recall, which both damaged the company's confidence and its financial turnover for a few years, but few remembered the corruption scandal. Even still, it experienced its biggest operating profit ever in 2017's third quarter. Corruption seems to have affected Samsung's brand to a much lesser degree than it has Petrobras' or Siemens', an aspect yet to be comprehended. Either way, in its big corporate reorganisation, Samsung will for the first time have separate chairman and CEO positions, a typical – and praised – corporate governance move.[75]

In the political arena, centre-left and former human rights lawyer Mr. Moon Jae-in was elected on 9 May 2017. This scenario was completely unexpected until the scandal.[76] In June, Mr. Moon appointed Mr. Kim Sang-Jo as chief of South Korea's

---

71 Kaoru Sugihara, 'The East Asian path of economic development. A long-term perspective' in Giovanni Arrighi, Takeshi Hamashita and Mark Selden (eds) *The Resurgence of East Asia. 500, 150 and 50 year perspectives* (Abingdon, Routledge 2003).

72 Chalmers Johnson, 'The Developmental State: Odyssey of a Concept' in Meredith Woo-Cumings (ed.) *The Developmental State* (Ithaca NY, Cornell University Press 1999).

73 In fact, it is also relevant to understand the liberalization process that South Korea's economy went through in the 1990s, which has changed the transnational dynamics of capital flows in the country. See Jong-Il You, 'The Long and Winding Road to Liberalization: The South Korean Experience' in Lance Taylor (ed.) *External Liberalization in Asia, Post-Socialist Europe, and Brazil* (Oxford, Oxford University Press 2006).

74 Hansoo Choi, 'Samsung, Lee Jae-yong's Conviction, and How Business in South Korea Is Changing' *Harvard Business Review* (29 Sep 2017) <https://hbr.org/2017/09/samsung-lee-jae-yongs-conviction-and-how-business-in-south-korea-is-changing> accessed 11 November 2017.

75 Saheli Roy Choudhury, 'Samsung just completely shook up its leadership' *CNBC* (31 Oct 2017) <https://www.cnbc.com/2017/10/30/samsung-electronics-search-for-new-ceo.html> accessed 11 November 2017.

76 McCurry (n 70).

Fair Trade Commission, the antitrust organ. Mr. Kim is a well-known scholar who has long fought against chaebol's economic and political power, nicknamed 'chaebol sniper' by some. The move has been seen as a clear statement by South Korea's new government concerning the ties between market and State. However, as of now, the effective impacts of such change in the 'fight against chaebol dominance and monopoly' are still quite unclear at best.[77]

Again here the scandal and its real life consequence seem in line with the structural explanation. As in the case of Brazil the close relationship of State–private monopolies reveals itself in the bribery system established. However, differently from Brazil, the fact that the company involved is all private is also in line with the general Asiatic colonial tradition of monopolistic structures, basically private with State support since colonial times,[78] but also with South Korea's more recent tradition of oligopolistic structures based on private chaebols.[79]

5. CONCENTRATION OF ECONOMIC POWER AND GLOBAL CORRUPTION: A LEGAL FRAMEWORK

Among different historical and sociological explanations of capitalism and market societies, Germany, South Korea and Brazil are placed in quite different theoretical schemes.[80] Germany has been analysed as a specific capitalist model based on its co-management system, conceived after the direct participation of employees in the conduction of corporate activities.[81] The harmonious ties between labour and capital would be specific to a German variety, and a big reason for its social and economic success. Siemens would be a fruit of this process.

South Korea, in its turn, modelled after the Japanese developmentalist experience, was based on a strong state control, major educational and Research & Development (R&D) investments, and the development of huge chaebols such as Samsung. The Korean variety of capitalism, based on a great articulation between market and state, would explain the huge economic success of post-war South Korea's economic miracle.[82] This and the former cases, of course, largely benefited from (highly politically biased) American financial aid as well.[83]

---

77 Hyo-sik Lee, 'FTC chief urges chaebol to institute "self-reform"' *Korea Times* (1 Sep 2017) <http://www.koreatimes.co.kr/www/biz/2017/09/367_235731.html> accessed 11 November 2017.

78 For the structural pattern set by the 'East Indian Company' type of colonisation in South East Asia see Salomão Filho (n 58).

79 Alice Amsden, *The rise of the rest – Challenges to the West from late-industrializing economies* (Oxford, Oxford University Press 2001).

80 Peter A. Hall and David Soskice, *Varieties of Capitalism. The Institutional Foundations of Comparative Advantage* (Oxford, Oxford University Press 2001).

81 Michel Albert, *Capitalisme contre Capitalisme* (Paris, Seuil 2001).

82 Sugihara (n 71).

83 Giovanni Arrighi, *The Long Twentieth Century: Money, Power and the Origins of our Times* (New York, Verso 2010).

Finally, Brazil, after the creation of Petrobras, would become part of 'the Rest' that eventually rose in the 1960s through developmentalist policies and heavy industrialisation.[84] It became one of the biggest economies in the world and has been considered a main new global player, despite its levels of inequality. How could it be possible, for such different countries, to give rise to such grand corruption scandals, similar at least in terms of scale?

The comparison of what happened in Siemens, Petrobras and Samsung cannot be oversimplified. Would it be an (exclusive) matter of culture or variety of capitalism (VoC), ascetic German ethos or institutions would not have allowed such a broad bribery system to be created in the first place, even or especially under private realm. It clearly did, though. The somewhat 'odd Asian' interpersonal practices highlighted in South Korea, or its embedded market-society-state relationship through chaebol conglomerates, would suffice to explain the events that ultimately led to Park's impeachment and Lee's arrest, but they don't. After all, this was neither the only nor the first case. Brazilian cultural informality and alleged lack of separation between public and private (sometimes summarised as '*jeitinho*', or 'little way out') could serve as a shortcut explanation to Petrobras' corruption scheme, but is opposed by empirical analyses of how effectively corrupt the country really is,[85] and takes the highly concentrated political and economic structures for granted, as if they were natural and immutable.

Actually, as discussed in the previous paragraphs, the best explanation for all cases seems to be structural – and not institutional or cultural, and even less individual. The source of corruption scandals is in the economic market power of its respective actor and to the degree of capture of government officials they are capable of. Its different manifestations also vary according to the historical environment of each region since colonial times. This is not all. Also the respective responses to the scandal can be seen under structural lenses.

The fact that Brazil seems more willing through its judiciary to put in check a big part of its political elite, shows the bigger involvement between State officials and abuse of monopolistic position, but highlights at the same time its urgent need to do away with these practices. Additionally, the fact that no relevant regulatory or corporate law interventions have been made in the companies involved demonstrates the continuing power of such economic structures. The same can be said about South Korea. The difference here seems to lie again in the fact that the corporate structure involved is private and therefore the involvement of the political arena is reduced to certain (albeit very relevant) individuals.

Finally, in the case of Germany, the measures taken, of corporate nature, have to do with the private character of the structure involved (Siemens) and the small relevance to the State involved (Germany) of the acts practised, all in foreign countries. Again here,

---

84 Amsden (n 79).

85 As Transparency International has recently reported, Brazil is not among the most corrupt countries in the world, and it is the country with the highest percentage of persons who feel 'ordinary people could make a difference [in corruption]' (83%). See Transparency International, *Global Corruption Barometer: Citizens' Voices from Around the World* (14 Nov 2017) <https://www.transparency.org/_view/publication/8064> accessed 15 Nov 2017.

as previously noted, this seems completely in line with the economic structures involved and their historical path dependencies that can be traced back to the behaviour of metropoles in colonial and postcolonial times.

6. CONCLUSION

Samsung Group controls around 15% of South Korea's GDP; Siemens is one of the leading conglomerates and brands in Germany; Petrobras is Brazil's biggest company. Their degree of internationalisation, technical expertise and R&D in their own fields place them among the most important multinational companies in the world. Reducing their own financial success to corruption practices would be demeaning. Nonetheless, ignoring their role in the global economy dynamic, especially in order to stabilise and guarantee profits to the benefit of private interests, would be equally wrong.

As we have shown, the relation between corruption and power (both political and economic) is strong: sometimes, power leads to corruption – either for direct private interests, either to avoid others from having power, and sometimes, corruption fosters power. In different ways, this was at stake in all three cases, thus the need to address power in order to fight corruption.

Addressing corruption in a global perspective urges jurists to treat it as a phenomenon magnified by the structural concentration of economic and political power in a world-system context. Therefore, it should not be conceived as a 'cultural' or '(i)mmoral' set of practices, allegedly typical only to non-developed nations. This is even more relevant to the extent which the whole world is inheriting characteristics of the Global South: inequality, poverty, violence and oppression are definitely not exclusive traits of certain countries, but rather global issues. The experienced life of a South Chicagoan may not be that much different, in broader terms, to that of a person living in Kibera, Rocinha or Dharavi.[86] In fact, inequality has been consistently rising on a global scale,[87] and the world's most unequal place is actually, by a huge margin, the world itself, and not one single country.[88] Under global capitalism, thus, corruption becomes a consequence and reproduction of old concentrating economic and political structures.

Transnational transparency practices, new corporate liability for extraterritorial activities and compliance programmes are different attempts to investigate and sanction corruption practices around the world. The evidence from the Petrobras, Siemens and Samsung cases highlight to what extent, and how, corruption may take place at the very 'core' of different economic activities, and generate a discussion on who should be held accountable. Despite its different characteristics, more or less transnationalised and more or less related to private and/or public agents, they all benefit from the lack of accountability rendered possible by their monopoly or quasi-monopoly status. Either a

---

[86] Mike Davis, *Planet of Slums* (New York, Verso 2006); Salomão Filho (n 58).

[87] Thomas Piketty, *Capital au XXe siècle* (Paris, Seuil 2013).

[88] Branko Milanovic, *Global Inequality – A New Approach for the Age of Globalization* (Cambridge MA, Harvard University Press 2017).

trait of current global capitalism or a never-ending characteristic of economic operations, corruption drains both knowledge and material resources that could be used elsewhere for better social and economic results.

Accordingly, 'fighting corruption' requires jurists to unpack the broader contexts of how, where and when corruption actually occurs. In this case, the 'why' question is actually less relevant, and tends to lead regulators, politicians and general public to an inefficient and moralist 'naming and shaming' policy. If contextualisation does not take place, 'compliance' measures will be ineffective at best, and cynical at worst. Therefore, in order to address corruption, the need for real structural legal measures against political and economic power is clear.

It all shows that 'compliance', just as corporate governance, cannot be reduced to a formal legal commitment to norms of transparency and adjustment of conduct. The shareholder primacy epitomised by most of current corporate law makes corruption seem a deviation from the norm, but when economic activity is reduced to become an entirely abstract entity working for the profit of a few shareholders, corruption may actually be the norm. In this case, transfer of corporate control of companies involved in corruption, new or reregulation of sectors involved in corruption scandals and new transnational liability regimes may be better-suited answers.

Finally, the construction of a global corruption framework is not an exclusive task of international institutions, either of national governments or private actions. It is rather a complex interaction, to be put forward by mutual development between several different actors, public and private, large and small, jurists and non-jurists. The recurrent danger, whatever the measures taken, is to simply reproduce the old structures of political and economic power on softer terms, allowing for new forms of legal transplants and 'magical solutions' to be implemented without prior notice or consent of those involved and directly affected by the drains of resources – not surprisingly, workers, peasants, indigenous peoples always at the forefront. This would be simply a continuation of how law has mistakenly understood the role of economic structures for a long time. The risk is clear: allowing equal or more corruption practices, despite the increase of formal accountability. Law has not yet internalised structural issues and concerns, but urgently needs to do so.

11. Global supply chains: *Doe v. Nestle*

11.1 CASE BACKGROUND

This is a (purported) child slavery case involving cocoa farms in the Ivory Coast. Such farms supply the cocoa which is transformed and ultimately marketed worldwide by the defendant(s) (Nestle USA, Archer Daniels Midland and Cargill), powerful multinational actors in the agro-food industry. It was alleged that the defendant corporations aided and abetted child slavery by providing assistance to Ivorian farmers. First filed in 2005 as a class action in federal court, in the name of the (purported) child slaves, the case raised two sets of jurisdictional issues under the Alien Tort Statute. One was the geographical scope of that statute. On this point the question, shrouded in controversy since the Kiobel case, is whether the situation in dispute 'touches and concerns' the territory of the United States. But for the purposes of this chapter, it is the second issue concerning the *material* scope of the statute which elicited from the Ninth Circuit the most remarkable response. According to the Alien Tort Statute, federal courts have jurisdiction over torts committed by aliens in violation of the law of nations. Jurisdiction depended therefore on whether or not there had been a violation of the law of nations on the part of the defendants. While the law of nations forbids aiding and abetting a crime (that is, providing assistance or other forms of support towards its commission), the question arose as to whether the defendants had acted, as required by the rule of international law, with 'knowledge' or (more stringently) 'purpose' of facilitating the criminal act. The Ninth Circuit answers that a myopic focus on profit over human welfare drove the defendants to act with the purpose of obtaining the cheapest cocoa possible, even if it meant facilitating child slavery. They might have used their economic leverage in the cocoa market either to ensure that the farms did not have recourse to such methods, or that farms using slavery were excluded from the supply chain.

This case draws attention to the ways in which the structure and operation of global value chains are largely dependent upon the often invisible work done by private international law rules. The way in which the jurisdictional requirements play out here can impact upon the whole political economy of such arrangements. Moreover, it illustrates the conflicting claims, values, interests, ideals, and norms which appear beyond the remit of state law, in varied spheres and with diverse stakes, and which require new modes of legal expression. Remarkably, neither territory, nor sovereignty, nor the requirements of foreign policy are part of the legal reasoning used by the Ninth Circuit, although they have been the focus of (private international) law's more familiar approach to the governance of corporate conduct abroad. On the other hand, what the Court is clearly attempting to do, within the formal confines of a determination of jurisdiction, is to bring the pressure of the legal system on a point (in various vocabularies, a 'hub', weakest link or 'pressure point', or a point of 'jurisdictional touchdown') in a global value chain.

Cases: Court of Appeals for the Ninth Circuit: Case No. 10-56739 (9 April 2014; 4 September 2015); Central District of California, Judge Wilson, 2 March 2017

11.2 ABOUT CAPITALISM AND PRIVATE INTERNATIONAL LAW

Tomaso Ferrando

1. PRIVATE INTERNATIONAL LAW AND THE PRODUCTION OF 'DARK VALUE'

The internationalisation of production and the shift from vertical integration to contractual links are presenting courts with new challenges when judges are asked to redress violations that occur at different points of the supply chain. In the struggle for global governance and corporate accountability, the fact that slavery, forced labour, violations of *jus cogens* and environmental disasters take place beyond borders already poses legal concerns and raises significant obstacles. When the same events are realised by third party contractors that only have a contractual obligation and that may operate several tiers away from the lead firm, the possibility that victims obtain some form of satisfaction appears even more unlikely.[1]

This is recognised by Susan Marks when she states that

> [n]ational governments, even the most powerful among them, face growing difficulty in controlling the activities of business, and especially finance, is today very widely acknowledged. The question of the significance of this development for nation-state-based systems of power is considered by many to be one of the most important political questions of our age.[2]

The case under analysis, along with others that were brought in the past and others that will follow, reflects the evolving interactions between law, territory and corporate accountability. In particular, it is characterised by the Ninth Circuit Court's attempt to elaborate a legal framework that can cope with the dual nature of supply chain capitalism as contemporary constructed around the ideas of order and coherence, on the one hand, and of chaos and fragmentation, on the other hand. As discussed below, firms that occupy a leading position in transnational supply capitalism are increasingly paying attention to the transparency, traceability and standardisation of their supply chains: control, organisation, efficiency and public concern require it. On the other

---

1 See, e.g. Mark Anner, Jennifer Bair and Jeremy Blasi, 'Towards Joint Liability in Global Supply Chains: Addressing the Root Causes of Labor Violations in International Subcontracting Networks' (2013) 35(1) *Comparative Labor Law and Policy Journal* 1–43; Kevin B. Sobel-Read, 'Global Value Chains: A Framework for Analysis' (2014) 5 *Transnational Legal Theory* 364–407; Naomi Jiyoung Bang, 'Unmasking the Charade of the Global Supply Contract: A Novel Theory of Corporate Liability in Human Trafficking and Forced Labor Cases' (2013) 35 *Houston Journal of International Law*; Galit A. Sarfaty, *Shining Light on Global Supply Chains* (2014), available from http://papers.ssrn.com/abstract=2512417 (last visited 29 Dec 2014); Stephanie Barrientos, '"Labor Chains": analysing the role of labour contractors in global production networks' (2011), https://ideas.repec.org/p/bwp/bwppap/15311.html (last visited 29 Dec 2014).

2 Susan Marks, 'Empire's Law (The Earl A. Snyder Lecture in International Law)' (2003) 10 *Indiana Journal of Global Legal Studies* 1. See also Michael Hardt and Antonio Negri, EMPIRE (Cambridge MA, Harvard University Press 2001).

hand, it can be claimed that the goal of profit maximisation is best achieved by deciding not to control some areas and some aspects, i.e. by refraining from assessing the dark spots of production, favouring their preservation, and profiting from the cheapness of labour, nature, food and resources.[3] It is the engagement with the boundary between chaos and order that makes *Doe v. Nestle et al.* important and that would require to be addressed further.

2. TAKING CONTRACTS-BASED CAPITALISM SERIOUSLY

It may seem anachronistic to discuss an Alien Tort Statute case after the *Kiobel* judgment. It is known, in fact, that most of the decisions that were issued in the aftermath of that milestone decision had to bow to the stringent concept of 'touch and concern' formulated by Justices Scalia and Alito. Almost all the cases were thus dismissed at the jurisdictional stage, without even the possibility of questioning the matter of convenience of the forum – let alone the substance of the claim. As a consequence, the non-jurisdictional points that are raised in these cases – both by parties and judges – often end up forgotten. This may be the future of the case under scrutiny, which would be a shame given the Court of Appeal's innovative proposal to move beyond the idea of legal and territorial chaos and to identify ways to make the productive and economic coherence of supply chains legally relevant.

In fact, the *Nestle* case offered the plaintiffs and the court a unique opportunity to deal with an issue that several authors consider among the most problematic aspects of supply chain capitalism, i.e. subcontracting and the allocation of liability that it generates among its actors. For example, Stephanie Barrientos stated that '[t]hird party labour contractors are increasingly prevalent in Global Production Networks, and are a potential channel for 'new forms of slavery.'[4] Similarly, Anner, Bair and Blasi conclude that '[t]here is widespread consensus that twenty years of efforts to address poor working conditions and violations of workers' rights in global supply chains for apparel products have been mostly unsuccessful.'[5]

More recently, Naomi Jiyoung Bang intervened in the debate defining supply chain contracts as a charade that covers the fact that '[c]orporations using global production chains, containing multiple levels of subcontracting and outsourcing, breed human trafficking and forced labor' and allow them to 'easily avoid accountability given the extraterritorial location of the suppliers, and the appearance of 'arm's length' contracts with their suppliers.'[6] For Hayashi 'Contracting out the production part of their

---

[3] Anna L. Tsing, *The Mushroom at the End of the World: on the Possibility of Life in Capitalist Ruins* 1st edn (Princeton NJ, Princeton University Press 2015); Jason W. Moore, *Capitalism in the Web of Life* 1st edn (London and New York, Verso Books 2015).

[4] Barrientos (n 1).

[5] Mark Anner, Jennifer Bair and Jeremy Blas, 'Buyer Power, Pricing Practices, and Labor Outcomes in Global Supply Chains', IBS working paper (2012) available from http://www.colorado.edu/ibs/pubs/pec/inst2012-0011.pdf (last accessed 29 January 2015).

[6] Bang (n 1) (footnotes omitted). See also Special Rapporteur on the Human Rights of Migrants, Specific Groups and Individuals Migrant Workers, Comm'n on Human Rights, U.N. Doc. E/CN.4/2006/73 (2005), at 2; ESCOR, 62d Sess. (Dec. 30, 2005).

business has enabled manufacturers to minimize their investment and insulate themselves from instability and risk. By characterizing their relationship with contractors as independent, they have avoided legal responsibility for workers' compensation, unemployment insurance and fringe benefits.'[7]

Facing a system of production that is increasingly global and shifting from property (direct control through foreign direct investments and shareholding) to contract (purchase agreements and mediated connections), the Circuit Court tried to develop a legal reconstruction of the supply chain that may be capable of addressing this double transition and providing responses to violations and forms of exploitation that may take place behind the contract veil. Although temporarily frustrated by the trump card of jurisdiction, *Nestle* represents an attempt to engage with the complexity of production and to move beyond the double use of contractual agreements both as sources of unity for the chain and as tools to create legal distance, fragmentation and impunity.

As discussed below, the Ninth Circuit's opinion in *Nestle* offers a combination between territory, contracts and lead firms' actions to overcome the geographical and legal fragmentation that are crucial to the economic success of transnational chains. The claim highlights the extent to which contemporary legal understanding of transnationality are lagging behind the reality on the ground. It brings to light the need to combine the economic and legal elements of the cocoa supply chain to define a distribution of legal responsibilities that is ultimately more reflective of the value distribution and economic power of that specific chain. Whether this position will be successful in the future also depends on the possibility for its elements to be known and discussed.

3. REDEFINING 'AIDING AND ABETTING' AT THE TIME OF SUPPLY CHAIN CAPITALISM

When it comes to providing solutions to the fact that contracts normally shield lead companies (in the Global North) from accountability, different approaches have been suggested. For example, Anner et al. propose a proactive intervention and to extend the idea of the 'jobbers agreements' at the transnational level, i.e. to expand the use of the trilateral contracts concluded between contractors, intermediaries (jobbers) and workers' unions that were useful to improve the labour conditions in sweatshops in the 20th century in the USA.[8] Another possibility would be to transnationalise the doctrine of

---

[7] Dennis Hayashi, 'Preventing Human Rights Abuses in the U.S. Garment Industry: A Proposed Amendment to the Fair Labor Standards Act' (1992) 17 *Yale J. Intl'l L.* 195, 199.

[8] See Anner, Bair and Blasi (n 1) p 13 ('The jobbers agreement served as the lynchpin of a system that was sometimes called triangular collective bargaining – so named because the goal was to regulate, via a set of paired contactors and jobbers agreements, relations between the three 'sides' of the production triangle: the workers as represented by the union, and the jobbers and contactors, each represented by their own employers association. Yet among these three parties to the agreement, the jobber was clearly recognized to be the most powerful industry actor and the only one capable of safeguarding the wages and working conditions of garment workers in contracting shops'). Such contracts would deprive corporations of the possibility to deflect responsibilities by the interposition of intermediaries and would multiply standing and

the 'joint-employer doctrine', i.e. the recognition that independent contractors often are simply interposed between workers and final beneficiaries and the identification of common responsibilities towards workers.[9] This was, for example, the attempt advanced in *Doe v. Wal-Mart Inc*, a case that was brought – and dismissed – against the US parent and several subsidiaries to recognise the former's liability for misconducts of the latter.[10]

Recently, Bang proposed to extend the economic reality test from the national to the transnational level, an operation to be realised by adopting an elaborated *ex post* jurisdictional strategy that consists of two prongs: first, the courts of the corporations' home state should apply the 'economic realities test as a vehicle to determine the existence of joint employment between a corporation and their contractor.'[11] Secondly, courts should extend the scope of domestic legislation to cover extraterritorial conduct, if it can be indirectly attributed to national corporations.[12]

Another pattern followed by plaintiffs and courts in the USA is represented by the notion of 'aiding and abetting', i.e. the possibility to recognise secondary liability to a violation of law without direct participation. In the US national context, the parameter is generally satisfied when

> (1) the party whom the defendant aids must perform a wrongful act that causes an injury; (2) the defendant must be generally aware of his role as part of an overall illegal or tortious

---

the venues to obtain their enforcement. However, they would require an active involvement of all the parties – unlikely to happen without sufficient pressure both on buyer corporations and subcontractors – and attention in the definition of the governing rules and adjudicatory venues.

[9] *Castillo v. Case Farms of Ohio* [1999] W.D. Tex 96 F. Supp. 2d 578, 596.

[10] *Doe v. Wal-Mart Inc* [2009] 9th Cir. 572 F.3d 677. In that case, the court affirmed that the common law test for joint-employment required 'the right to control and direct the activities of the person rendering service, or the manner and method in which the work is performed.' The court equated the concept of 'control' to physical proximity as well as frequency of contact, holding that '[a] finding of the right to control employment requires … a comprehensive and immediate level of "day-to-day" authority over employment decisions.' The content of the supply-contract and the allocations of rights and obligations that it produced were thus considered irrelevant.

[11] Bang (n 1) at 258.

[12] Bang's application of the economic reality test to the global system of production would thus require courts to take patterns of capital seriously. Judges should move beyond the territorial fragmentation of multiple jurisdictions and at the same time recognise the role of law (in this case of contracts) in distancing the observer from the underlying distribution of power and control. Courts would recognise that global value chains represent the new transnational space of jurisdictional operation and that legal formalism is inconsistent with the way in which capital operates. Foreign subcontractors would thus be 're-territorialised' and considered operating under the control of the domestic corporation, so that buyer and subcontractor would be both equally liable for injuries suffered by overseas factory workers. Borders and contractual formalism would be replaced by transnationality and economic reality, and judges would be the craftsmen. 'Essentially', Bang concludes, 'the logic is that if the contractor is found to be an employee of a corporation, then its workers are also the corporation's employees' and therefore they could be considered a unity when responsibilities have to be allocated. See Bang (n 1) at 279.

activity at the time that he provides the assistance; (3) the defendant must knowingly and substantially assist the principal violation.[13]

However, its standards have been at the centre of jurisdictional challenges in the context of the ATS and of transnational litigation, in particular because of the transplantation of the notion of 'purpose' from international criminal law (Rome Statute) to private international law and corporate accountability cases.[14]

Nestle operates within this framework. However, its innovation is represented by the Court's attempt to fulfil the requirements of 'aiding and abetting' by embedding the violations in their economic and legal context, i.e. the cocoa supply chain controlled by the plaintiffs and based on the extraction of value from slave labour. What the Court tried to do, was to give relevance to the plaintiffs' active involvement in enforcing coherence and control along the chain (by enforcing standards, checking production, having access to the land where the cocoa was produced, etc.) and, at the same time, to the actions or omission aimed at maintaining a space of darkness, chaos and lack of accountability.

> In the court's interpretation of the link between supply chains and law, the contractual construction of supply chains as a commercially reliable space and the existence of dark spots of unaccountability represent the two sides of the same coin which cannot be read separately. Therefore, the exclusivity of the contractual relationship, the quality control exercised by the defendants in order to satisfy their own self-regulation and the interests of the consumers, and the transfer of technology and resources to guarantee the needed supply (all expressions of order and coherence), must be read together with the omitted use of the economic leverage deriving from the exclusive buyer/seller contractual agreements, the cost-cutting delocalisation which is proper of supply chain capitalism, and the exercise of political lobby in the United States to avoid the introduction of mandatory labelling and reduce the level of transparency.

4. CHEAPNESS AT THE BEGINNING AND END OF SUPPLY CHAIN CAPITALISM

Another element that deserves attention is the Ninth Circuit's attempt to prove the existence of *mens rea* by the identification of the profit motive as an indication of purpose. In the Court's reconstruction, child slaves represented a central element in the establishment and maintenance of the cocoa chain because of the cost-cutting benefits that they represent. Although the defendants were not directly interested in harming children, they were interested in lowering their cost of production – whatever it takes.

According to the Court:

---

[13] *Doe*, 654 F.3d at 34 (citing *Halberstam v. Welch* [1983] D.C. Cir. 705 F.2d 472, 477). *Hauser v. Farrell* [1994] 9th Cir. 14 F.3d 1338, 1343, rev'd on other grounds, *Central Bank of Denver, N.A., v. First Interstate Bank of Denver, N.A.* [1994] 511 U.S. 164; accord *Halberstam v. Welch* [1983] D.C. Cir. 705 F.2d 472, 477.

[14] *Aziz v. Alcolac, Inc.* [2011] 4th Cir. 658 F.3d 388, 399–400; *Presbyterian Church of Sudan v. Talisman Energy* [2009] 2nd Cir., Inc., 582 F.3d 244, 259.

> [T]he defendants placed increased revenues before basic human welfare, and intended to pursue all options available to reduce their cost for purchasing cocoa. Driven by the goal to reduce costs in any way possible, the defendants allegedly supported the use of child slavery, the cheapest form of labor available. These allegations explain how the use of child slavery benefitted the defendants and furthered their operational goals in the Ivory Coast, and therefore, the allegations support the inference that defendants acted with the purpose to facilitate child slavery.[15]

In the reasoning of the Court, profit, exploitation and responsibility are circularly constructed. The use of cheap labour is seen as a prerequisite to the increase in return and the obtainment by the defendants of a dominant position in the supply chain (at least in Ivory Coast). It is through the exploitation of slave labour and children, the Court concludes, that foreign corporations can produce 'dark value' (generate non-internalised externalities) in the Ivory Coast and appropriate a higher rent.[16] However, the same market power achieved through exploitation would have required the defendants to intervene and act against their own economic interest. For the Court it is not important how the leading position in a supply chain is obtained: what matters is that this implies obligations and lowers the standard for accountability.

On the contrary, the defendants decided to use their resources and their political power to allegedly lobby against a 2001 United States Congressional proposal to require chocolate manufacturers and importers to certify and label their products as 'slave free.' As a result, the mandatory law was replaced by a 'voluntary arrangement known as the Harkin-Engel protocol, in which the chocolate industry agreed upon certain standards by which it would self-regulate its labor practices.'[17] In a circular way, if slavery and cheap labour lie behind profit and revenues, they also provide the resources that are needed to avoid political and legal interventions that may impact the way in which value is produced and accumulated.[18]

5. LAW AND TRANSNATIONAL GLOBAL PRODUCTION

To conclude this short note, I would like to stress the importance of the Ninth Court's focus on the just mentioned lobbying operations realised by the defendants in a jurisdiction that is not the same where the violations occurred. Implicitly, the judges recognise that legal interventions at the domestic level can introduce disturbances in the

---

15 *Doe*, 654 F.3d, at 22.

16 It is my opinion that the massive violations of human rights committed by the government in Sudan should not be kept separated from the case of child labour in Ivory Coast. If the threshold to determine that the defendant purposefully aided and abetted a violation of international law is represented by the economic benefit that it obtains, it could be claimed that Talisman Energy obtain an economic benefit because of the reduced social opposition, the lower costs of labour and the cheaper access to resources.

17 *Doe*, 654 F.3d, at 1066.

18 Raj Patel and Jason W. Moore, *A History of the World in Seven Cheap Things: a Guide to Capitalism, Nature and the Future of the Planet* 1st edn (Oakland CA, University of California Press 2017).

supply chain and impact the way in which value and power are allocated throughout all actors and nodes.[19]

Although lobbying is not considered a violation per se, the position of the Court reveals two aspects of the complex interaction between value chains and legal structures: a) that corporations are aware that the mechanism of extraction and appropriation of capital throughout the chain could be modified by legal interventions that do not take place there were exploitative conducts take place – for example by reforming the legal framework in the country where the final products are sold rather than where natural resources are extracted; b) that the current system of law is, in most cases, incapable of coping with transnational forms of production and that the status quo is reproductive of inequalities and legalised violence.

From the perspective of law in Global Production, courts' lax attitude toward misconducts realised beyond national boundaries produces a judicially-created incentive for incorporating, offshoring and outsourcing. The geography and forms of production are, therefore, deeply intertwined with the spatial extension of jurisdiction and the identification of the content and applicability of a set of legal tools, in particular those of private international law and tort law. More than one decade ago, Saskia Sassen noted that the relation between the global capital economy and national states is not adequately or usefully captured by the use of a clear-cutting distinction between global and national. According to Sassen,

> [t]his duality is conceived of as a mutually exclusive set of terrains where what the global economy gains the national economy or the national state loses. It is this type of dualism that has fed the proposition of declining significance of the national state in a globalized economy. Such a dualist perspective also resists the recognition that we may be dealing with a new bundle of practices that are stabilizing new meanings of sovereign power and constituting new institutional locations for components of this power.[20]

Instead of passively suffering for the globalisation processes that operate beyond the scope of government, courts all over the world have been increasingly required to interrogate this duality. To paraphrase Anna Tsing, these interventions may create spaces of transformative encounters along the supply chains, making new legal assemblages and new distribution of power possible.[21] Where they take, it is often hard to foresee. In this context, some courts – including the Supreme Court in *Kiobel* – have adopted territorial reconstructions of their jurisdictions that 'do not fit globalization and

---

[19] Tsing (n 3) 160; Tomaso Ferrando, 'Land Rights in Global Production: Leveraging Multi-Spatiality and "Legal Chokeholds"' (2017) 2 *Business and Human Rights Journal* 2.

[20] Saskia Sassen, 'Territory and Territoriality in Global Economy' (2000) 15 *International Sociology* 2, at 376.

[21] I do not share the plaintiffs' position that the introduction of a certification scheme would have been such that 'Defendants' cocoa plantations would not have been able to use child labor.' A critical approach to law requires considering the indeterminacy of regulation, the multiplicity of its interpretation, and the role that context, power and asymmetries play in determining its consequences. However, the existence of a mandatory system of labelling and certification, supported by an appropriate mechanism of control and complaints, may have improved the conditions of cocoa workers throughout the chain (and not only in Ivory Coast).

the transcendence of territorial border'[22] or dismissed the role of control and chaos as two complementary elements of supply chains. Thus, they take legal decisions that create spaces of legal impunity that contribute to the consolidation of an exploitative form of supply chain capitalism based on the combination between 'dark and bright value'.[23] Others have tried to think differently.

Among these, the Ninth Circuit in *Doe v. Nestle et al.* teaches us that the 'allegedly "external" processes of globalization should be seen as distinctly co-evolving with and as being produced, constructed and conceived *within* the nation state.'[24] It also proves that Moore and Princen may be right when they affirm that contemporary transnational capitalism is constructed on the extraction of dark value via the production and accumulation of cheap labour, cheap nature, cheap food and cheap natural resources.[25] At the same time, it highlights the potential implications of higher levels of control that are imposed in the name of sustainability of their supplies and safety of the consumers. In this tension between order and chaos, *Nestle* suggests to engage with the role of law in the production and extraction of value along the supply chains (both through control and darkness) and sounds like a clear invitation to private international lawyers to be at the forefront of this new intellectual and practical endeavour.

11.3 GRAPPLING WITH (GLOBAL SUPPLY) CHAINS: TRANSNATIONAL HUMAN RIGHTS LITIGATION IN THE AGRIBUSINESS SECTOR

Samuel Fulli-Lemaire

For the most part, human rights litigation against transnational corporations (hereafter TNCs) belies the well-known saying that a chain is no stronger than its weakest link. The conundrum which lies at the heart of these cases is easily expressed: while meaningful reparation can only be obtained if the ultimate parent is held liable,

---

22 Ralf Michaels, 'Empagran's Empire: International Law and Statutory Interpretation in the US Supreme Court of the Twenty-First Century', in David L. Sloss, Michael D. Ramsey and William S. Dodge (eds.), *International Law in the US Supreme Court* 1st edn (Cambridge, Cambridge University Press 2009) at 539.

23 See Donald A. Clelland, 'The Core of the Apple: Dark Value and Degrees of Monopoly in Global Commodity Chains' (2014) 20 *Journal of World-Systems Research* 1.

24 Peer Zumbansen, 'Defining the Space of Transnational Law', in Günther Handl, Joachim Zekoll and Peer Zumbansen (eds), *Beyond Territoriality: Transnational Legal Authority in an Age of Globalization* (Queen Mary Studies in International Law, Leiden, Brill 2012). See also some of the seminal works by Saskia Sassen, e.g. Saskia Sassen, 'Globalization or denationalization?' (2003) 10 *Review of International Political Economy*; Saskia Sassen, *The Global City: New York, London, Tokyo* (Princeton, Princeton University Press 2001); Saskia Sassen, *The Mobility of Labor and Capital: A Study in International Investment and Labor Flow* (Cambridge, Cambridge University Press 1988).

25 Thomas Princen, 'The Shading and Distancing of Commerce: When Internalization Is Not Enough' (1997) 20 *Ecological Economics* 3; Moore (n 3); Patel and Moore (n 18).

proceedings can often be brought successfully only against the direct perpetrators.[26] The relative impunity thus enjoyed by TNCs from the Global North[27] when they have profited from human rights violations in the Global South, and the correlative difficulty in coming up with remedies within the traditional frameworks of both public and private international law, are thrown into sharp relief by *Doe v. Nestlé*. This case also offers the much-needed reminder that, even though the manufacturing and extractive industries provide perhaps the most famous or striking cases at the intersection of the transnational human rights violations and global supply chain issues, the agribusiness sector cannot be ignored.[28]

The three plaintiffs in *Doe v. Nestlé* claim to be former child slaves who were forced to work on Ivorian cocoa plantations and subjected to other abuse. They allege that the defendants – Nestlé USA Inc., Archer Daniels Midland Company and Cargill Inc. Company – are liable under the Alien Tort Statute (hereafter ATS) for aiding and abetting child slavery. Since the plaintiffs filed in 2005 a proposed federal class action, several orders have been rendered by both the District Court of the Central District of California and the Court of Appeals for the Ninth Circuit,[29] the latter turning out to be

---

26 Naturally, cases where the abuse can be attributed *directly* to the TNCs themselves also raise fascinating issues and obtaining compensation for the victims is a taxing endeavour in this context as well. Nonetheless, the challenges posed by human rights violations committed by actors of a supply chain which are not the ultimate parent are turning out to be particularly vexing, for reasons that will be made clear over the course of this paper.

27 On the notion of regulatory gaps, see Robert Wai, 'Transnational Liftoff and Juridical Touchdown: The Regulatory Function of Private International Law in an Era of Globalization' (2002) 40 *Colum. J. Transnat'l L.* 209, 251–54, and the references cited.

28 For an overview of the pivotal role played by TNCs in the agribusiness sector and the complex interplay with their suppliers, see Kaitlin Y. Cordes, 'The Impact of Agribusiness Transnational Corporations on the Right to Food', in Olivier De Schutter, Kaitlin Y. Cordes (eds), *Accounting for Hunger – The Right to Food in the Era of Globalization* (Oxford, Hart 2011). The part of the article devoted to the cocoa industry (37–44) makes for very sobering reading and contains an indictment of the manufacturers' (economic) responsibility in the persistence of child and forced labour every bit as damning as the Ninth Circuit's: 'The Ivorian cocoa industry's dependence on child labour or forced labour demonstrates the desperation of cocoa farmers that arises from the low prices they are paid. This subsequently implicates the right to food: because cocoa farmers in the Côte d'Ivoire receive insufficient income from their cocoa products, they are unable to purchase sufficient food without resorting to illegal labour and human rights abuses' (38–39). Nestlé's role in relation to the murders of ten Colombian union members by presumed paramilitaries between 1986 and 2005 has also been questioned. Again, the firm's refusal to increase the price it paid for milk deliveries was singled out as a decisive reason why conflicts between milk producers and union members escalated during that period, see Éric David, Gabrielle Lefèvre, *Juger les multinationales – Droits humains bafoués, ressources naturelles pillées, impunité organisée* (Brussels, Mardaga/Grip 2015), esp. 45–48. Kraft has also been accused by Oxfam of buying cocoa harvested by enslaved children, see Fabrizio Marrella, 'Protection internationale des droits de l'homme et activités des sociétés transnationales' (2017) 385(33) *RCADI* 199.

29 At the time of writing, the case in a broader sense is made up of four judgments, the two most recent of which will be discussed here: *Doe I v. Nestlé USA Inc* 766 F 3r 1013 (9th Cir 2014) which was rendered in September 2015; *Doe I v. Nestlé USA Inc.* 05-cv-05133 US District Court, Central District of California (Los Angeles) 2 March 2017.

markedly more sympathetic to the purported victims' case than the former, or the Supreme Court for that matter.

Doe v. Nestlé, which is again pending in the Ninth Circuit,[30] exemplifies the considerable uncertainty which surrounds the scope and thus the potential of ATS litigation before US federal courts (1). That is not to say, unfortunately, that other approaches would necessarily fare better if they were applied in similar circumstances; in that sense *Doe v. Nestlé* can be used as a test case and a basis for comparison (2).

1. THE UNCERTAINTIES SURROUNDING ATS LITIGATION IN THE UNITED STATES AFTER *KIOBEL*

Doe v. Nestlé perfectly illustrates both the considerable uncertainty that still surrounds ATS litigation before US federal courts and the reasons why this uncertainty now appears unlikely to be resolved in a way that would benefit victims of human rights abuses. The ATS is a 1789 law which reads, in full: 'The district courts shall have original jurisdiction of any civil action by an alien for a tort only, committed in violation of the law of nations or a treaty of the United States'.[31] As recounted in the Ninth Circuit judgment of 2015,[32] this law was 'almost never invoked' for the first 200 years of its existence. This changed dramatically during the 1980s however,[33] and since then the ATS has been a focus of litigation on the initiative of foreign victims of violations of international law, and consequently of academic study. A number of difficulties remain, three of which can be usefully discussed using the Ninth Circuit judgment:[34] the delineation of corporate liability for aiding and abetting under the ATS (A), the role of international law in the context of ATS litigation (B), and how the presumption against the extraterritorial application of the ATS can be overcome (C).

A. The Delineation of Corporate Liability for Aiding and Abetting Under the ATS

For the sake of clarity, this first question must actually be broken down into two sub-questions, which are both discussed comprehensively in the Ninth Circuit judgment.

---

[30] John Bellinger, Andy Wang, '*Jesner v. Arab Bank*: The Supreme Court Should Not Miss the Opportunity to Clarify the "Touch and Concern" Test' (Lawfare Blog, 10 October 2017) <https://www.lawfareblog.com/jesner-v-arab-bank-supreme-court-should-not-miss-opportunity-clarify-touch-and-concern-test> accessed 15 February 2018.

[31] USC § 1350.

[32] 766 F 3r 1013 (9th Cir 2014) 10ff.

[33] See *Filártiga v. Peña-Irala* 630 F 2d 876 (2nd Cir 1980) and *Sosa v. Alvarez-Machain* 542 US 692 (2004).

[34] The District Court's 2017 ruling, by contrast, only deals with the third issue, that is to say the possibility of overcoming, in the circumstances of the case, the presumption that the ATS should not apply extraterritorially. Because the Court 'finds that the complaint seeks an impermissible extraterritorial application of the ATS, [it] does not reach the merits of Defendants' remaining arguments' (2).

The first is the possibility of corporate liability under the ATS, that is to say 'whether and under what circumstances corporations can face liability for ATS claims'.[35] This issue was initially at the heart of the *Kiobel* case, but the Supreme Court did not settle it because it redirected the discussions towards the determination of the extraterritorial scope of the ATS.[36] Deciding that corporations can indeed be held liable for violations 'of the law of nations' implies accepting, first, that the law of nations applies to private actors, and second that it can apply to legal persons as well as to natural persons. The latter contention is addressed at length by the Ninth Circuit, which finally concludes that 'the prohibition against slavery is universal and may be asserted against the corporate defendants in this case'.[37]

The second sub-question is specific to aiding and abetting ATS claims, and regards the two constitutive elements of the crime.[38] As far as the objective element is concerned, the Court merely observes that 'the *actus reus* of aiding and abetting is providing assistance or other forms of support to the commission of a crime', an assistance which furthermore must be 'substantial', but the Court declines to go beyond and does not address the point of 'whether international law imposes the additional requirement that the assistance must be specifically directed towards the commission of the crime'.[39]

Regarding the subjective element, the tone is decidedly sharper.[40] The Ninth District alludes to the controversy surrounding the *mens rea* standard for aiding and abetting liability: is it enough to prove that the defendants knew that their acts would facilitate the commission of the underlying offence, or should the claimant show that they had acted with the purpose of facilitating the criminal act? The Court deems it unnecessary to choose between the competing *knowledge* and *purpose* standards, because it declares itself satisfied that the allegations satisfy the latter, more stringent standard: 'the allegations suggest that a myopic focus on profit over human welfare drove the defendants to act with the purpose of obtaining the cheapest cocoa possible, even if it meant facilitating child slavery'. To reach this inference of purpose, the Court emphasises that the defendants are alleged to have directly benefitted 'from the use of child labour', to have refrained from using their 'control over the Ivory Coast cocoa market … to stop the use of child slavery', and to have 'participated in lobbying efforts designed to defeat federal legislation that would have required chocolate importers and manufacturers to certify and label their chocolate as "slave free"'. It should be kept in mind that deciding on a motion to dismiss requires the Court to '[read] the allegations

---

35 766 F 3r 1013 (9th Cir 2014) 15.

36 On this point, see Dominique Bureau and Horatia Muir Watt, *Droit international privé* vol 2, 4th edn (Paris, PUF 2017) para. 1024-2; Philip Liste, 'Transnational Human Rights Litigation and Territorialised Knowledge' (2014) 5(1) *TLT* 1, 14–18, who analyses the switch as 'spatial politics of the law at work'.

37 766 F 3r 1013 (9th Cir 2014) 18.

38 On this point, see Inés Tófalo, 'Overt and Hidden Accomplices: Transnational Corporations' Range of Complicity for Human Rights Violations' in Olivier De Schutter (ed), *Transnational Corporations and Human Rights* (Oxford, Hart 2006).

39 766 F 3r 1013 (9th Cir 2014) 26–27.

40 Ibid., 20–26.

in the light most favourable to the plaintiffs'; nonetheless, the Court's language is extremely striking and reveals a determination to make the defendants accountable.

B. The Role of International Law in the Context of ATS Litigation

The reasoning developed regarding both these points underlines the pivotal role that (public) international law plays in defining the contours of liability under the ATS. That role, however, is not entirely unproblematic. US federal courts have to engage with the complex array of sources that make up international law[41] and, ultimately, decide which norm should prevail in case of conflict. This seemingly technical exercise naturally provides ample scope for policy considerations to interfere, as Scheffer points out:

> this paradox, of American courts fully embracing tribunal jurisprudence to determine the fate of claims under federal law while some political, academic, and judicial dialogue paints foreign and international rulings as somehow poisonous to the American system, becomes particularly stark when some senior conservative judges on the federal bench warmly invoke the Rome Statute of the International Criminal Court and then misinterpret it to establish both a narrow purpose standard for aiding and abetting and the denial of corporate liability under the Alien Tort Statute altogether.[42]

C. Overcoming the Presumption Against the Extraterritorial Application of the ATS

Whether or not claims based on an extraterritorial application of the ATS can succeed is, of course, arguably the most decisive and critical issue raised by ATS litigation in its current state. It should then come as no surprise to find it at the heart of the *Doe v. Nestlé* case. Because the two key Supreme Court cases of this discussion, however, are covered by other entries in this case-book,[43] this dimension of *Doe v. Nestlé* will only be touched upon here.

It is by now well-known that, in its eagerly awaited *Kiobel* ruling of 2013,[44] the Supreme Court 'severely diminished'[45] the scope for ATS litigation by holding that the statute did not rebut the general 'presumption against extraterritoriality'. As a result, ATS suits could only be filed if they 'touch[ed] and concern[ed] the territory of the United States … with sufficient force to displace the presumption'.[46] Beyond making

[41] The statutes and case-law of international and hybrid war tribunals assume particular relevance, notably the Rome Statute of the International Criminal Court, see the Ninth Circuit's judgment at 13–27. On this point, see David Scheffer, 'The Impact of the War Crimes Tribunals on Corporate Liability for Atrocity Crimes under US Law' in Charlotte Walker-Said, John D. Kelly (eds), *Corporate Social Responsibility? Human Rights in the New Global Economy* (Chicago IL, The University of Chicago Press 2015).

[42] Scheffer (n 41) 156.

[43] See below the '*RJR Nabisco Inc v. European Community*' and '*Kiobel v. Royal Dutch Petroleum Co*' entries.

[44] 133 US 1659 (2013).

[45] Geert van Calster, *European Private International Law* 2nd edn (Oxford, Hart 2016) 366. See also the various articles in 'Agora: Reflections on *Kiobel*' (2013) 107(4) *AJIL* 829, 829–63.

[46] 133 US 1659 (2013), 1669.

clear that 'the ATS did not give US courts jurisdiction over so-called foreign-cubed cases, that is, cases brought by foreign victims, against foreign defendants, for violations occurring in countries other than the United States',[47] *Kiobel* was characterised as raising more questions than it answered.[48] Two points stood out as particularly vexing.

The first, which is tackled by both the Ninth Circuit in its 2015 judgment and the District Court in its 2017 judgment, relates to the content of the 'touch and concern' test put forward in *Kiobel*. To summarise briefly, proponents of the restrictive view – including the defendants, unsurprisingly – argued that this test was equivalent to the focus test set out in the earlier *Morrison* case of 2010,[49] according to which 'courts first determine the "focus of congressional concern" for a statute, and allow the statute to be applied to a course of conduct if the events coming within the statute's focus occurred domestically'.[50] Following another, more expansive interpretation however, which seems to have satisfied the Ninth Circuit in 2015, *Kiobel* 'did not incorporate *Morrison*'s focus test', which leaves open the possibility that the 'touch and concern' test might be less stringent. In 2016, the Supreme Court in *RJR Nabisco* explicitly brought together *Morrison* and *Kiobel* as reflecting a unitary 'two-step framework for analyzing extraterritoriality issues',[51] with the focus test at its heart. On this base, the District Court in 2017 ruled – convincingly, it must be said – that the view had prevailed and that the focus test should be applied to ATS claims.[52]

But even on the assumption that the first, methodological issue, has now been so resolved, the second, more concrete issue, remains: which contracts with the United States will be sufficient to overcome a presumption against extraterritoriality?[53] The District Court, in its 2017 ruling, disqualifies all the factors put forward by the plaintiffs: US-based decision-making, the provision of funds originating in the US, the provision of supplies and training, public statements against child slavery, and

---

47 Nadia Bernaz, *Business and Human Rights – History, Law and Policy – Bridging the Accountability Gap* (Abingdon, Routledge 2017) 269.

48 Ralph G. Steinhardt, 'Kiobel and the Multiple Fractures of Corporate Liability for Human Rights Violations' (2013) 28 *Md. J. Int'l L.* 1, 10.

49 *Morrison v. National Australia Bank* 561 US 247, 130 US 2869 (2010).

50 Ninth Circuit's ruling, 30.

51 *RJR Nabisco Inc v. European Community* 136 US 2090 (2016), 2101: 'At the first step, we ask whether the presumption against extraterritoriality has been rebutted – that is, whether the statute gives a clear, affirmative indication that it applies extraterritorially. … If the statute is not extraterritorial, then at the second step we determine whether the case involves a domestic application of the statute, and we do this by looking to the statute's "focus." If the conduct relevant to the statute's focus occurred in the United States, then the case involves a permissible domestic application even if other conduct occurred abroad; but if the conduct relevant to the focus occurred in a foreign country, then the case involves an impermissible extraterritorial application regardless of any other conduct that occurred in U.S. territory'.

52 At 2–3.

53 On this point, see also Bellinger and Wang (n 30). The dissenting opinion in *Adhikari v. Kellogg Brown & Root Inc* 845 F 3d 184 (5th Cir 2017), which accepts that it follows from *RJR Nabisco* that a two-step framework must be applied in ATS cases, and that a 'focus' reasoning is relevant, but disagrees with the majority as to the implementation of the test, shows that some room for manoeuvre remains even after *RJR Nabisco*.

lobbying against (timid) federal legislation aimed at combating child slavery – for the Court, the first three are 'ordinary business operations'.[54]

Despite the uncertainty which led to a split in the federal courts of appeals and the resultant doctrinal criticism, the Supreme Court has proved unwilling to revisit the topic of ATS litigation in the years that followed *Kiobel*, denying at least six petitions for writs of certiorari.[55] However, it has recently granted one in the *Jesner et al v. Arab Bank PLC* case,[56] which could then provide an opportunity for much-needed clarification.

Moving a little away from the specifics of ATS litigation, it is apparent that the mechanical application of rules which were not designed specifically for the purpose of addressing human rights violations in global supply chains – here, the ATS statute –, as evidenced by the formalistic reasoning of the District Court and the restrictive interpretations of the Supreme Court, cannot be expected to lead to accountability in a reliable manner. Conversely, the more flexible arguments relayed by the Ninth Circuit hint at what a holistic approach could achieve if it were allowed to thrive. This insight can now be studied in other contexts.

2. *DOE V. NESTLÉ* AS A TEST CASE FOR OTHER APPROACHES TO CORPORATE LIABILITY FOR HUMAN RIGHTS VIOLATIONS

Two very different directions can be explored. The first involves turning to the other side of the Atlantic and switching from a public to a private international law-grounded reasoning. In other words, it amounts to testing the existing, traditional, European private international rules, by applying them to a *Doe v. Nestlé*-type situation (A).[57] The shortcomings that will thus be revealed encourage the investigation of other, decidedly more prospective avenues, which appear particularly suited to global supply chain scenarios (B).

A. The Application of European Private International Law Rules

From a European perspective, *Doe v. Nestlé*-type cases appear quite different, mainly because this time the crux of the matter does not reside in jurisdiction. This, in turn, comes about as a result of the general ground for jurisdiction of article 4 of Brussels I

---

[54] For the record, the Supreme Court in *Kiobel* had specified that 'mere corporate presence' would be insufficient to disprove the presumption, see 133 US 1659 (2013), 1669.

[55] Note 'Clarifying *Kiobel*'s "Touch and Concern" test' (2017) 130 *Harv. L. Rev.* 1902, 1923.

[56] <http://www.scotusblog.com/case-files/cases/jesner-v-arab-bank-plc/> accessed on 15 February 2018.

[57] Despite what is sometimes described as a European preference for redressing human rights violations through criminal law rather than civil law (see e.g. Caroline Kaeb and David Scheffer, 'The Paradox of Kiobel in Europe' (2013) 107 *AJIL* 852, 855; George P. Fletcher, *Tort Liability for Human Rights Abuse* (Oxford, Hart 2008) 9–10), 'prosecutions of business and human rights violations have been rare', see Bernaz (n 47) 285, who does refer to a single French case.

Recast Regulation: if victims of a human rights violation bring proceedings, the court of the defendant's domicile will be able to assert jurisdiction regardless of the type of claim.[58] 'Consequently truly multinational corporations may in theory at least be quite easily pursued in the courts of an EU Member State, even for actions committed outside the EU'.[59]

The difficulty, however, is merely postponed; more specifically it resurfaces at the stage of the determination of the applicable law. Because the Rome II Regulation on the law applicable to non-contractual obligations does not contain a specific rule for human rights violations, the applicable law is, under the general rule of article 4 (1), 'the law of the country in which the damage occurs irrespective of the country in which the event giving rise to the damage occurred'. As van Calster puts it, 'given that plaintiffs generally do not pursue the case with a view to having the law of a non-EU Member State apply … , this general rule of the Rome II Regulation in all likelihood is not the goal of the plaintiffs',[60] in whose interest it is to aim for the (presumably) greater compensation that could be awarded under the law of a Member State. Moreover, it appears unlikely that this outcome can be avoided in a *Doe v. Nestlé* scenario through the use of the Regulation's exceptions, in particular the exception clause of article 4 (3).[61] Ultimately, the only way to avoid the application of the *lex loci damni* could be the public policy exception,[62] which furthermore provides a classic channel for human rights to intervene within private international law reasoning. Even then, however, a requirement that the dispute be sufficiently connected to the forum might in some cases thwart the whole strategy.[63]

Once again, some of the shortcomings of the European approach can be traced back to the absence of a rule specifically designed to bring accountability to TNCs implicated in human rights violations in the Global South.[64] With this in mind, the notion of global supply chain can perhaps be put to good use.

---

58 According to article 4 (1) of Regulation (EU) No 1215/2012 on jurisdiction and the recognition and enforcement of judgments in civil and commercial matters (recast), 'Subject to this Regulation, persons domiciled in a Member State shall, whatever their nationality, be sued in the courts of that Member State'. Regarding the determination of the domicile of a corporate defendant, see art. 63 (1) of the Regulation.

59 van Calster (n 45) 367. Interestingly, the European Commission submitted to the US Supreme Court an *amicus curiae* brief in the *Kiobel* case 'arguing in favour of universal civil jurisdiction for victims of violations of human rights, which would also attract universal criminal jurisdiction', see Bernaz (n 47) 276.

60 van Calster (n 45) 369.

61 Ibid.

62 See article 26 of the Rome II Regulation.

63 Horatia Muir Watt, 'Les enjeux de l'affaire Kiobel: le chaînon manquant dans la mise en œuvre de la responsabilité des entreprises multinationales en droit international public et privé' [2010–2012] *Travaux du comité français de droit international privé* 233, 241. It should be pointed out that, during the debates which followed Muir Watt's presentation, a *Cour de cassation* judge weighed in favour of triggering the public policy exception (247).

64 Other factors are naturally at play, for instance 'the absence of collective redress mechanisms' in most European countries, see Bernaz (n 47) 275.

B. Global Supply Chains as Catalysts of New Adjudication Strategies

In what is far from its least important merit, *Doe v. Nestlé* draws attention to those cases where the idea of parent company liability is virtually useless because the conduct giving rise to liability cannot be traced back to a subsidiary of the TNC. This is significant, because the interest generated by this thriving approach, as well as the advances it has brought about,[65] is such that it could overshadow other, equally valuable, developments. *Doe v. Nestlé* thus demonstrates that a strategy aiming at imposing accountability on multinational firms for their activities outside their home country must go beyond the issue of lifting the corporate veil. One such avenue, which relies on the concept of global supply chains, will be briefly described.

The basic idea is to involve the TNCs themselves more closely in policing the behaviour of their sub-suppliers established abroad, in a way that goes beyond trusting blindly in their ability and willingness to self-regulate. This implies, first, that TNCs adopt meaningful corporate social responsibility (hereafter CRS) codes and, second, that they manage to enforce them down their respective supply chains. The main obstacle, naturally, comes from privity of contract: while the buyer's CSR policy can become part of a contract with a first-tier supplier by incorporation through the buyer's general terms and conditions, through an expressly negotiated contract or through an invitation to tender,[66] the sub-suppliers will not directly be bound because they are not party to the first contract. This obstacle, at least in theory, is not entirely insuperable: 'if the buyer's general terms and conditions impose a duty on the first-tier supplier to implement the buyer's CSR policy further down its own supply chain (perpetual clause) then this term constitutes a contractual duty on the supplier to do so'.[67] By iteration then – and, again, in theory – the CSR duties could be passed down the chain and enforced.

The TNCs' ability to police the behaviour of their sub-suppliers nonetheless remains limited at best, especially if the difficulty of becoming aware of breaches is factored

---

65 For the possibility that, under English law, a parent company may owe a duty of care to employees of its subsidiary (in a domestic case), see *Chandler v. Cape Plc* [2012] EWCA Civ 525. For a tentative step towards an extension of that duty of care to other third parties beyond employees (in a cross-border case), see *Lungowe v. Vedanta and Konkola* [2017] EWCA Civ 1528. On the *Shell* case in the Netherlands, see Bernaz, above n 47, 279–80; Claire Bright, 'Affaire *Shell* aux Pays-Bas (Tribunal de district de La Haye): Quelques réflexions' in Laurence Dubin and others (eds), *L'entreprise multinationale et le droit international* (Paris, Pedone 2017). For a critique of the distinction between supply chains structured through contracts and supply chains structured through equity ownership from the point of view of liability of TNCs, see Peter Rott and Vibe Ulfbeck, 'Supply Chain Liability of Multinational Corporations?' (2015) 23(2) *ERPL* 415, who argue that supply chain liability could be based on control in both contexts. For an in-depth look at various innovative approaches to production liability, see Jaakko Salminen, 'From National Product Liability to Transnational Production Liability: Conceptualizing the Relationship of Law and Global Supply Chains' (Doctoral Dissertation, University of Turku 2017), available from the author upon request.

66 On these three techniques, see Andreas Rümkorf, *Corporate Social Responsibility, Private Law and Global Supply Chains* (Cheltenham, Edward Elgar 2015) esp. 85–95.

67 Ibid., 99.

in.[68] In all likelihood, this makes Western TNCs unlikely to invest the significant resources that would be necessary to contractually enforce CSR.[69] Moreover, as shown by *Doe v. Nestlé*, the TNCs can actually *profit* from violations of their own CSR codes, in this instance by reaping the benefits of the low prices for raw materials which suppliers can only accept by resorting to forced or child labour. How, then, to remove the incentive to turn a blind eye to transgressions down a supply chain? This objective should be pursued, because the various ways to fight human rights abuses are not mutually exclusive but, on the contrary, can be mutually reinforcing. A multipronged approach, which includes consumer activism and more effective sanctions, should then be favoured.

From the latter point of view, initiatives like the French legislator's recent corporate duty of vigilance Act, which imposes a nucleus of legal responsibility on parent companies and commissioning companies for the acts of their subsidiaries, suppliers and sub-contractors, appear extremely significant.[70] All in all, the notion that duties should be imposed on actors in relation to acts that unfold within their 'spheres of influence'[71] seems to be gaining ground – this notion, incidentally, could in the future find application in public as well as in private international law. This could for instance, perhaps through the conclusion of an international treaty,[72] lead to a duty being

---

68 Ibid., 102–22.

69 Ibid., 123. Rümkorf concludes: 'It is [the decision of Western buyers] how they include, monitor and enforce CSR in their supply chain. The fact that the research for this chapter has not shown a single decided case about the breach of CSR terms reveals the economic reality of CSR'. For an exploration of other techniques, see Jaakko Salminen, 'Contract-Boundary-Spanning Governance Mechanisms: Conceptualizing Fragmented and Globalized Production as Collectively Governed Entities' (2016) 23(2) *Indiana Journal of Global Legal Studies* 709.

70 On the 2017-399 Law of 23 March 2017 on the duty of oversight of parent companies and commissioning companies, see Béatrice Parance and Élise Groulx, 'Regards croisés sur le devoir de vigilance et le *duty of care*' [2018] *Journal du droit international (Clunet)* doctr 2; Horatia Muir Watt, 'Devoir de vigilance et droit international privé. Le symbole et le procédé de la loi du 27 mars 2017' (2017) 50 *Revue internationale de la compliance et de l'éthique des affaires* 48–53.

71 Alain Supiot reasons in terms of 'allegiance networks', see 'Introduction' in Alain Supiot (ed.), *Face à l'irresponsabilité: la dynamique de la solidarité* (Paris, Collège de France 2018) 7–11, and the references cited.

72 See Olivier De Schutter, 'Towards a New Treaty on Business and Human Rights' (2015) 1 *Business and Human Rights Journal* 41. See also point (I-A-2) of the non-binding 'Guiding Principles on Business and Human Rights: Implementing the United Nations "Protect, Respect and Remedy" Framework (A/HRC/17/31)', the so-called 'Ruggie principles', according to which 'States should set out clearly the expectation that all business enterprises domiciled in their territory and/or jurisdiction respect human rights throughout their operations'. For an overview of the discussions to which the Ruggie principles have given rise, see Francisco Javier Camora Cabot, Lukas Heckendorn Urscheler and Stéphanie De Drycker (eds), *Implementing the U.N. Guiding Principles on Business and Human Rights – Private International Law Perspectives* (Zurich, Schulthess 2017). On the role played by the notion of a TNC's 'sphere of influence' in the earlier 'Global Compact' proposed at the 1999 Davos summit by the then-UN Secretary General Kofi Annan and the 'Norms on the Responsibilities of Transnational Corporations and Other Business Enterprises with regard to Human Rights' approved by the UN Sub-Commission for the Promotion and Protection of Human Rights in Resolution 2003/16 of 14 August 2003

imposed on home states to ensure that their (corporate) citizens respect fundamental rights 'when exercising an economic activity' abroad.[73]

Postscript: after this chapter was delivered to the editors, the US Supreme Court handed down its eagerly-awaited decision in the *Jesner v. Arab Bank* case,[74] which delivers a near-fatal blow to ATS litigation before US federal courts. In an opinion authored by Justice Kennedy, the Court ruled by a 5-4 majority that, absent congressional instructions, foreign corporations may not be defendants in suits brought under the ATS.[75] Naturally, this controversial ruling dramatically alters the discussion described in the first part of the chapter. This makes the alternatives discussed in the second part all the more relevant.

(UN doc E / CN.4 / Sub.2 / 2003 / 12 / Rev.2 (2003)), see Olivier De Schutter, 'The Challenge of Imposing Human Rights Norms on Corporate Actors' in Olivier De Schutter (ed.), *Transnational Corporations and Human Rights* (Oxford, Hart 2006) esp. 9–17.

[73] Horatia Muir Watt, 'Future directions?' in Horatia Muir Watt and Diego P. Fernández Arroyo (eds), *Private International Law and Global Governance* (Oxford, Oxford University Press 2014) 353. See also, by the same author (n 63) 242; 'Private International Law Beyond the Schism' (2011) 2(3) *TLT* 347, passim.

[74] See above n 56.

[75] *Jesner et al v. Arab Bank PLC* 584 US ___ (2018).

12. Global market for sovereign debt: *Argentina v. NML Capital, Ltd.*

12.1 CASE BACKGROUND

The *NML* case points to an inversion of sovereignty, when debt makes purportedly sovereign actors dependent upon their access to global capital markets. NML Capital, Ltd. (NML), a vulture fund specialised in distressed sovereign debt, purchased at extreme discounts Argentine public bonds off a panicking market. In 2001, the Republic of Argentina defaulted on $103 billion of debt due to a severe economic crisis. The government announced that it would not pay its debts, but gave the investors a choice of accepting new bonds worth 70 per cent less. NML Capital did not accept and commenced a collective action against Argentina in Manhattan Federal District Court. The District Court decided in favour of NML, ordering Argentina to pay over US$2 billion to the vulture fund and to prioritise NML Capital's position over other creditors.

In order to execute the judgment against Argentina, NML served subpoenas on Bank of America and Banco de la Nación Argentina, requesting information about Argentina's assets held worldwide. Argentina moved to quash the subpoenas and argued, under the Foreign Sovereign Immunities Act (FSIA), that the locations of its assets were immune from discovery. Nevertheless, the District Court ordered the banks to comply with the subpoena requests. Argentina appealed and the Second Circuit affirmed the discovery order, since it was directed at commercial entities that did not have a claim to sovereign immunity.

Argentina then petitioned for a writ of certiorari from the Supreme Court of the United States, and the petition was granted. The question was whether a subpoena that requires a bank to disclose information about all assets of a foreign State without respect to their location or use violates the Foreign Sovereign Immunities Act.

The Court, in a majority opinion delivered by Justice Scalia on 21 April 2014, held that a foreign-sovereign judgment debtor is not immune from post-judgment discovery of information concerning its extraterritorial assets. Based on an originalist interpretation, tracing the history of foreign sovereign immunity in the United States, Justice Scalia reasoned that any claimed immunity must stand or fall on the FSIA's text alone. Since Congress did not mention foreign sovereign immunity from post judgment discovery in the FSIA, there can be no such immunity.

The Court also noted that the fact that some property may be immune from attachment under the FSIA does not mean that it is immune from discovery. Besides, the FSIA only grants immunity to property held within the United States; hence, NML could find foreign property held outside the United States that is attachable under the law of the foreign jurisdiction.

Justice Ginsburg dissented, writing that the discovery request under the FSIA should have been limited to property used in connection with commercial activity, which is a necessary requirement under U.S. law for attachment.

Case: *Republic of Argentina v. NML Capital, Ltd.*, 573 US ___ (2014)

12.2 MEASURING THE STRENGTH OF CONTRACT AGAINST SOVEREIGN IMMUNITY

*Jérôme Sgard**

The judgment rendered in 2014 by the New York Court of Appeals in the *NML v. Argentina* case will remain in the annals of sovereign debt. First, this decision paved the way for the resolution in March 2016 of Argentina's payment default – one of the longest (2001–16), largest ($93 billion) and most complex defaults in history. Further, this decision confirms the critical role henceforth granted to national courts in the resolution of sovereign defaults, and therefore in the interpretation of the underlying contracts. Finally, the New York court has considerably strengthened the position of minority investors who refused a collective restructuration agreement, by confirming a controversial interpretation of the *pari passu* clause, and by giving them new powerful means to pressure the sovereign issuer.

This chapter reviews the principal stages of the resolution of Argentina's default, as well as the immediate conclusions one may draw from this episode. It then compares the rules for debt restructuring that found their full expression on that occasion to the core principles that back up two somewhat similar experiences: one is the generic bankruptcy rule as developed historically at the national level, the other is the practice adopted by the IMF during the debt crisis of the 1980s. These two comparisons highlight the scope of the evolutions observed in this field since 1990, but also the unbalanced (and thus unstable) nature of the current non-regime.

1. THE RESOLUTION OF ARGENTINA'S DEFAULT

The main stages of the long Argentine saga are well known. Following the December 2001 default, the local authorities proposed an exchange of bonds in 2005 and again in 2010: investors who accepted a 70% write-off on the face value of their debt contracts would benefit from an immediate resumption of debt service. This would have set the stage for Argentina's return to international capital markets. The fact that 93% of the total bondholders accepted the bond exchange should have reinforced the expectation of such a normalization. However, in 2009, vulture funds that held 7% of the bonds and had refused to participate in the first exchange took the whole case to American courts in order to obtain a complete service (at par) on their non-restructured bonds.

As a first step, they obtained in December 2011 the confirmation by the US District Court for the Southern District of New York of a radical and controversial reinterpretation of the *pari passu* clause that had been written into the new 'exchange-bonds'. This latter clause is actually quite venerable, establishing a vague principle of equality or non-discrimination between two or more issuances of bonds, but whose practical implications have long remained limited.[1] An isolated decision rendered by the

* Contribution originally written in French, translated to English by Yanis Rahim.

[1] Mitu Gulati and Robert E. Scott. *The 3½ minute transaction, Boilerplate and the Limits of Contract Design* (Chicago IL, University of Chicago Press 2013).

Brussels Court of Appeal in 2000 had however paved the way for a much more restrictive reading of this clause: each party was entitled to the same payment terms, whether it held old or new bonds. Hence if new bonds received full interest payments, older ones should as well, though under their own terms. This decision was rendered in the context of a similar case to that of Argentina, though smaller in size, opposing the Republic of Peru to the Elliott Associates group, of which NML is a subsidiary. In 2011, the District Court for the Southern District of New York, that has jurisdiction over Wall Street, confirmed the principle: if Argentina was to serve, entirely, its new exchange bonds, then it must also serve, entirely, the residual, 7% of non-restructured bonds.

Then came the issue of enforcement. At first, minority investors had tried to seize assets owned by Argentina in third countries, but the rules of sovereign immunity proved too powerful and prevented such seizures. This is where the second dimension of the December 2011 decision came into play: the court injunction that prohibited the Argentine Government from servicing the restructured bonds only, also bound any financial intermediaries that purported to act as 'agents' of Argentina ('in active concert or participation'). If one of them were to execute Argentina's payment orders, it could be sued directly for 'contempt of court.' This provision was then further strengthened and clarified (District Court, decision as of 21 November 2012)[2] upon express request of the Court of Appeals (decision as of 26 October 2012).

The District Court's decision thus opened an entirely new avenue to back up the *pari passu* clause as it shifted the remedial action from stocks of assets to flows of money, relying at this point on the American payment system. Because the Argentine debt was denominated in US dollars and had been issued in New York, payments had to be processed, logically, through an American bank and American clearing houses. This strategy – which leverages the payment system infrastructure – is both new and highly powerful, in that it builds on the dollar's dominant position at the international level in order to achieve the extraterritorial reach of the decision of the US court. Other things being equal, this strategy could probably not be implemented as effectively from London, for example.

After a series of interim decisions, the District Court judgment was upheld by the US Court of Appeals for the Second Circuit in New York, so that once the US Supreme Court had declined to grant certiorari in 2014, the injunction became effective. In July 2014, Argentina decided to test its real efficacy and transferred $539 million to the Bank of New York for interest payments owed to holders of its 2005 and 2010 bonds. The District Court judge immediately ordered this transfer to be frozen and in one month later Argentina was duly declared in 'selective default' by Standard & Poor's and Fitch. Holders of restructured bonds were no longer paid, and the Argentine public and private borrowers' access to international markets was closed.

The last episode of this saga followed the victory of center-right candidate Mauricio Macri in Argentina's presidential election of October 2015. His programme provided for a quick resolution of the debt problem, which had put a heavy strain on the economy since 2001. Discreet negotiations rapidly began and were supported by the New York District Court, who announced that it would lift the injunction on 30 April

---

2 Mark C. Weidemaier, 'Sovereign debt after *NML v Argentina*' (2013) (8)2 *CMLJ*. 123.

2016[3] as a consequence of Argentina's new, more conciliatory position. This was rightly expected to support a rapid settlement with minority bondholders and to open the door to a large bond issue in New York. The Argentine federal government soon issued $19.5 billion and brought at last to an end the 2001 default.

While the creditors who had accepted the 2005 and 2001 bond exchange had received approximately 30% of the bonds' initial face value, minority investors eventually obtained 75% thereof. NML in particular achieved a total capital gain of 392% on its initial investment. A series of separate agreements were later concluded with small groups of creditors in the months that followed, including by way of arbitration.

2. INTERMEDIARY CONCLUSIONS

The immediate lessons of this long case are relatively easy to draw. First, minority creditors, in particular vulture funds, achieved their goal. Moreover, a number of guidelines have now been put in place, notably in US law, which strengthen the ability of minority investors to resist a debt restructuring agreement, even when an overwhelming majority of creditors support it (93% in the present case). Other things being equal, this development should make it more difficult in the future to agree on such an operation, especially where the number of bond issues and categories of holders is high.

For sure, a lot may depend upon the future interpretation of the 2014 decision by the New York Court of Appeals as to the exact wording of the debt contracts and the pari passu clause, which may evolve in response to the NML case. Still, we are in no way in a stable, consolidated regime of sovereign debt restructuring which would guarantee predictable effects, broadly oriented towards an orderly resolution of payment defaults. On the contrary, the risk in the future is that restructurings will be long, costly, unpredictable and subject to dilatory tactics. Moreover, minority creditors would also be in a position to exercise considerable, potentially damaging pressures on the economy of the debtor State, hence too on local society as a whole. The decision declaring Argentina in 'selective default' in July 2014 is exemplary in that regard, since it immediately entailed major difficulties in financing all foreign trade operations. The risk moreover is that these rules, or close variants of them, may also prove dangerous for the capital markets as whole. The classic example at this point is the series of sovereign defaults of 1931–33 which were resolved only twenty years later, because of the absence of a structured framework for restructuring.

---

[3] See Tomas M. Araya, 'A Decade of Sovereign Debt Litigation: Lessons from the NML v Argentina Case and the Road Ahead' (2016) 17(2) *Business Law International* 83; Lee C. Buccheit and Mitu Gulati, 'Restructuring Sovereign Debt after *NML v Argentina*' (2017) 12(2) *CMLJ* 224.

3. THE BANKRUPTCY RULE

Furthermore, it is striking how far the present 'non-system' is from the basic rules of a generic bankruptcy procedure, envisaged as a collective action by creditors acting under the protection of courts, along with guarantees of execution. Of course, everyone knows that there is no supranational authority similar to that of a public judge who is able to suspend the performance of private contracts, to coordinate creditors and to confirm decisions taken on a qualified majority basis. Such top-down authority is in fact intrinsic to the classical, liberal constitutional framework and to the way it structures the core interaction between public and private spaces, or rights. However, in sound legal doctrine, the creditors' vote in a bankruptcy procedure only indicates or reveals to the judge what is probably the 'least bad' outcome after the common debtor's default. But he is the only one who can make this decision legally binding in order that, in particular, the minority's contractual rights will be neutralized.

From this vantage point, the New York Court of Appeals' decision does more than remind us that there is no such thing as a supranational court for sovereign debtors. By defending the rights of minority bondholders at all costs against the "least worst" preference of the majority, the New York judge refused to consider the collective of creditors as a single body with a recognised capacity to make up its opinion and have it defended. This may lead to outcomes that would be both neither economically effective nor socially fair.

Remember here that in a market economy, bankruptcy is also the final stop at which the effects of distressed debt contracts are suspended. The legislator, probably informed by historical experience, knows that debt contracts left on their own can lead to oppressive results – debt bondage, indentured servitude, coolie labour, loan sharks … All things being equal (and admittedly, these things are numerous), the current non-regime on sovereign debt may raise similar problems. Deliberately causing obvious harm to the debtor State's economy to satisfy the rights of a tiny minority of creditors raises serious problems of efficiency and fairness. Note that this is not a problem of the 'odious debt' type, a line of argument that questions the conditions under which the contracts were initially negotiated and entered into. The argument here is about how strong the hand of creditors should be, and how far it should be allowed to extend – in particular the hand of minority creditors.

4. THE COUNTER-EXAMPLE OF THE 1980s

A second entry into the discussion over sovereign debt contracts and their restructuring is offered by the experience of the International Monetary Fund (IMF) during the 1980s debt crisis. After the near-default of Mexico in 1982, dozens of developing countries soon followed suit, so that a total of 109 restructurings were agreed upon up until 1989, following very similar, stable, though non-formalized rules of negotiation and decision-making. That year, the Brady Plan opened the door to debt write-offs of 30–40% that were associated with a massive loan-for-bond exchange. Intermediated finance was replaced by bond finance.

The main actor in the 1980s restructurings was the IMF, which stood as a third party interposed in the debt dispute, displaying a presumption – or a claim – of neutrality.[4] However, the Fund was less 'above' the parties than 'between': it acted simultaneously as a strong broker between debtor States and creditor banks, as an expert in economic policy, as the financier of crisis countries, and finally as the medium-term guarantor of the agreements concluded by the parties (through the monitoring of conditionality). In the end, however, the justification for this complex model of intervention rested on a notion of common good: 'burden sharing' among the parties to a given agreement and 'comparability of treatment' across cases referred ultimately to the multilateral nature of the IMF's action – a dimension that is entirely absent from the current 'non-regime.'

Remarkably, during all these years, the final decision on each restructuring depended neither upon a judgment by a national or an international judge, nor upon an arbitration, nor upon a more or less friendly mediator. Rather, it resulted from a very original, three-way decision rule based on a right of veto given successively to each party in the final outcome. The IMF could thus refuse the debt financing agreement if it considered for instance that the banks had not made enough concessions, thereby jeopardising the success of the overall plan. But the banks in turn could reject an agreement on economic policy that they considered too soft, perhaps because the country in question was protected by one of the IMF's major shareholders. And of course the country also had to formally accept these two agreements, which altogether formed a whole in which everyone had to contribute. Lastly, the execution of this three-way settlement over time was guaranteed by the IMF's usual ways of monitoring and enforcing conditionality.

Thus, let us underline this point: this stable, predictable procedure did not have any jurisdictional dimension. Furthermore, its practice typically implied a fair amount of power relationship and arm-twisting between the IMF and public authorities in the creditor countries on the one hand, and debtor countries *and* commercial banks on the other. A judge or a trustee would not have been in a position do enter that terrain, for fear of undermining their legitimacy.

But the very specific legal character of this regime was also underlined by the fact that all *ad hoc* clauses inserted in the initial debt contracts, all norms of private international law, all national laws or statutes applicable to the debt contracts were systematically suspended or circumvented. Even the Articles of Agreement of the IMF resulting from the Bretton Woods Conference had been ignored when it was assumed (albeit in a non-written way) that the decision to lend to a Member State could be *de facto* vetoed by a group of commercial banks. Not least, this group of banks itself had no legal existence. Hence the rule-based, predictable dimension of decision making came with a largely informal character: no treaty, no official decision, no discrete announcement ever made clear how exactly the Fund was dealing with debt restructurings.

---

[4] Jerome Sgard, 'How the IMF Did It? Sovereign Debt Restructurings during the 1980s' (2016) 11(1) *CMLJ* 103.

5. HOW DID THE IMF NEGOTIATE WITH SOVEREIGNS?

Let us try however to better characterise this unique, extraterritorial procedural space. In fact, the forum was neither the IMF as such, nor an *ad hoc* instance created in the IMF's shadow, nor the proxy of an international court. In fact, the rules of the game were written in the Stand-By Agreement *as such*, i.e. an original model of transaction, invented and developed by the IMF from 1953 onwards, that has allowed it to conjoin lending and conditionality. The key point however is that contrary to what the usual vocabulary suggests, the *Stand-By Agreement is not a contractual arrangement.* Joseph Gold, the founding father of the IMF's legal doctrine and main architect of the Stand-By, often underlined the point: the two parties in a Stand-By commit themselves separately and successively on the terms of their transaction.[5] A country in crisis thus sends to the Fund a *Letter of Intent* (which formalises its policy commitments), and the IMF then announces that a Stand-By Agreement had been decided and makes the money available to the country. Critically, no text is ever signed jointly by both parties.

Gold justified this principle by the fact that the conduct of the economic and financial policy of a sovereign borrower is far too complex, and exposed to too many influences and external shocks, for the notion of a contractual commitment to apply in its hard, legal sense. If a contractual reading of conditionality were to be adopted, any deviation from the terms of the initial agreement, voluntary or not, would have entailed legal consequences, and possibly sanctions. In turn, this might well have generated excessive – if not dangerous – rigidity in the interaction between the parties, before and during the life-cycle of the Stand-By.[6] In particular, a break-up between the parties, possibly followed by sanctions, had to be avoided at all costs: the return to the negotiation table and to the bilateral transaction had to remain the normal option. This is why for instance the IMF has always ruled out any recourse to arbitration proceedings for resolving disputes with Member-States, just as it never asks for the confirmation of Stand-By agreements by national parliaments or supreme courts. In short, one had to take into account the economic context in which the sovereign operates, but also the inevitably open, renegotiable and therefore flexible nature that a transaction with a sovereign always presents.

Put another way, the Stand-By is a transaction whose rules respond to the classic forms of action of the sovereign State on the international scene: an actor that is altogether realistic, rational, hard-headed, calculating and independent from any superior authority. Significantly, the Fund interacts exclusively with executive powers (and with central banks). The rules of the Stand-By aim, in essence, at placing the borrowing sovereign within a cooperative framework of interaction from which it may not easily exit and which should lead hopefully to economic stabilisation and a return to international market. The realist character of the Stand-By should thus be assessed by looking at the eventual results of the economic program, not at the process, or the path that led to that result. This is why the very idea of the country 'complying' with each clause of the *Letter of Intent* makes no sense at all.

---

[5] Joseph Gold, 'The Law and Practice of the International Monetary Fund with Respect to "Stand-By Arrangements"' (1963) 12(1) *ICLQ* 1.

[6] Joseph Gold, 'The "Sanctions" of the International Monetary Fund' (1972) 66(5) *AJIL* 737.

The debt restructurings of the 1980s were thus negotiated and sealed within this very curious, yet familiar setting. The Stand-By was in fact the jurisdictional space within which these contracts were renegotiated. Commercial banks (with all their credits in quasi-default) were thus literally co-opted into this very particular arena which the IMF had built and developed, by way of trial and error, since the early 1950s. The 'three-ways veto rule' that was adopted in 1982 just signalled the usual two-way exchange of unilateral commitments had been extended to a triangular transaction. Significantly, the debt financing agreement between the debtor country and the Steering Committee of banks had no legal value in itself: its scope was limited to the triangular relationship with the IMF and to the practice of the triple veto. Each single creditor bank would later have to confirm the terms of this agreement in the language and forms of the respectively applicable contract law. The concessions granted to the indebted country then became legally binding: they would impact overall the bank's balance sheet and its fiscal or regulatory obligations.

6. *ARGENTINA V. NML*, RETROSPECTIVELY

Here are therefore the two main elements that become apparent when comparing the experience of the 1980s with that of Argentina after 2001: the first is the absence today of any binding multilateral rule, as a corollary of the emergence of the national courts of justice as the jurisdiction of reference; and the second is the emergence of a set of hard legal norms, in particular contractual norms, whose language now structures the entire discussion on sovereign debts. The regulating principle of these negotiations has thus shifted from a weak standard of justice (resting on the idea of a transaction subject to mutual veto) to a standard of very high substantive and procedural formalisation.

Between these two poles – Mexico in 1982 and *NML* in 2014 – one finds however in 2001 the attempt to create an intermediary or mixed regime: the proposal by the IMF to establish a "Sovereign Debt Restructuring Mechanism" (SDRM) would have given jurisdiction over sovereign debt contracts to a new, *de facto* supranational entity, closely linked to the IMF, though with some guarantees of procedural independence.[7] One could interpret this as an attempt to set up an *ad hoc* jurisdiction, probably of a rather loose arbitral character, where substantive legal constraints would not have weighed too heavily on the capacity to deal and bargain – just as in the 1980s, though in a more settled forum. This feature was illustrated particularly by the clause advocated by the IMF at that time that it would be itself part of the deliberation, to which it would bring its expertise and economic assessment. The overall assumption, therefore, seems to have been that the sustainability and success of the new regime would have hinged upon the balance it reached between two demands: the pressure by private investors for strong procedural guarantees and an a priori judgment that sovereign debt restructurings should not be constrained by too strict substantive and procedural legal rules.

---

[7] IMF, *The Design of the Sovereign Debt Restructuring Mechanism – Further Considerations*. Prepared by the Legal and Policy Development Reviews Departments. 27 November 2002, 76 pages.

The SDRM proposal was however rapidly rejected by private financial actors, who clearly did not want to put their assets in the hands of a supranational adjudicator. At that time, in the early 2000s, the influence of contractual norms and language was already too powerful to allow for the adoption of such a forum. The transfer of jurisdiction over sovereign defaults to the national courts was already a *fait accompli*, a feature that was indeed fully reflected in the way the Argentine debt was dealt with. In other words, the new regime rests on the assumption that sovereign debt contracts can be read and broadly interpreted like private contracts, while their specific, international and sovereign dimensions only emerges when questions of enforcement and remedies have to be addressed.

Here is ultimately the paradox of the current non-regime of sovereign debt restructuring. On the one hand, a strict contractual reading has been instrumental in the destruction of all formal multilateral dimensions in these operations: multilateralism is rightly perceived as implying a substantial degree of de-formalisation and relative autonomisation that de facto leaves room for transactions, power relationships and settlements. By the same token, many features that are specific to sovereign borrowers have also been largely whittled away. Macroeconomic uncertainty, the domestic political economy, and sovereign realism on the international scene are not expected to shape the behaviour of a sovereign debtors' court.

On the other hand, the current rules of the game, as illustrated by the *NML v. Argentina* case, reflect the rejection of any binding limit to the practical reach of contractual rights: in the matter of sovereign debts, they are now conceived as thoroughly and exclusively individual, so that the collective and social dimension that is a full part of the generic bankruptcy rule at the domestic level just has no equivalent here. This was illustrated both by the unconditional defence of the rights of a tiny minority of Argentine bondholders, and by the remedies they obtained from the New York court. The disproportion between the value of those claims and the costs induced by the forced default of July 2014 will remain for this reason a striking illustration of a highly dangerous rule.

12.3 THE NEW GUANO: LEGAL ENFORCEMENT IN MODERN SOVEREIGN DEBT MARKETS

Mark Weidemaier

1. INTRODUCTION

For most of the two-century history of sovereign bond markets, a borrower government could pledge little more than its reputation to lend credibility to its promise to repay. When a private borrower defaults, its assets can be seized and liquidated to satisfy creditor claims, but the doctrine of sovereign immunity often denies creditors a remedy against government borrowers. In consequence, the general view is that legal actors, such as courts, and legal tools, such as contracts, play little role in sovereign debt markets.[8] In a world without legal enforcement, even a pledge of customs or export revenue might mean little to investors. Absent some non-legal enforcement mechanism, investors would have no reason to trust such a pledge.[9] To take a prominent historical example, Peru borrowed abroad extensively in the 19th century while pledging guano export revenues as security. What made the pledge credible, according to Vizcarra,[10] was that Peru contracted with a British merchant house to collect export revenues abroad and to retain a share of the proceeds to cover loan payments. These contracts provided some assurance of repayment, at least while Peru remained dependent on guano export revenues, as the merchant house had its own reputation to protect and was itself subject to the coercive power of English courts. This example comes from the era of absolute sovereign immunity, when national courts had no power to enforce creditors' claims against foreign governments.

By the 1970s, the law had changed, permitting creditors to sue foreign governments in national courts and to enforce money judgments through attachment and liquidation of some government assets.[11] A creditor owed a great deal of money will probably not find enough assets to satisfy its claim in full. But in theory, this is unproblematic, for the creditor's primary goal is to use the threat of asset seizure to disrupt the sovereign's foreign commercial and financial transactions. If costly enough, this disruption may induce the sovereign to settle on favorable terms.[12] Indeed, the evidence suggests that creditors increasingly turn to the courts after a sovereign's debt default.[13]

2. THE NML LITIGATION

Despite the shift away from absolute immunity, and the increasing frequency of litigation, the perception remains that courts can do little to enforce sovereign debt obligations.[14] The persistence of this view may explain the intense interest in the litigation between the Republic of Argentina and NML Capital (an affiliate of the Elliott Management hedge fund). Put simply, in the two-century history of the sovereign bond

---

[8] Mark Weidemaier and Mitu Gulati, 'Market Practice and the Evolution of Foreign Sovereign Immunity' (forthcoming) *Law and Soc. Inq.*

[9] Chabot and Santarosa, for example, describe how London Stock Exchange rules denying listing privileges to foreign governments that had defaulted on such pledges operated as an enforcement mechanism. Benjamin Chabot and Veronica Santarosa, 'Don't Cry for Argentina (or Other Sovereign Borrowers): Lessons from a Previous Era of Sovereign Debt Contract Enforcement' (2017) 12 *Cap. Mkts. L. J.* 9.

[10] Catalina Vizcarra, 'Guano, Credible Commitments and Sovereign Debt Repayment in Nineteenth-Century Peru' (2009) 69 *J. Econ. Hist.* 358.

[11] Weidemaier and Gulati (n 8); Mark Weidemaier, 'Sovereign Immunity and Sovereign Debt' [2014] *Univ. of Ill. L. Rev.* 67.

[12] Mark Weidemaier and Anna Gelpern, 'Injunctions in Sovereign Debt Litigation' (2010) 31 *Yale J. Reg.* 189.

[13] Julian Schumacher, Christoph Trebesch and Henrik Enderlein, 'What Explains Sovereign Debt Litigation?' [2015] CESifo Working Paper No. 5319.

[14] Ugo Panizza, Federico Sturzenegger and Jeromin Zettelmeyer, 'The Economics and Law of Sovereign Debt and Default' (2009) 47 *J. Econ. Lit.* 651.

markets, the *NML* litigation is one of only a handful of cases where courts have clearly *mattered*.

In assessing the significance of the litigation, it is tempting to emphasise the extraordinary remedy that finally brought closure. Yet the litigation is more important for what it reveals about the evolving structure of sovereign debt markets. Effective legal enforcement does not require new law – or, anyway, not much new law. It requires specialised litigants, ready access to capital, and the ability to further mitigate the risk of investing in litigation through portfolio diversification. Such actors and mechanisms are routinely present in other forms of civil litigation.[15] The lasting significance of the NML litigation is that it marks their arrival in force in sovereign debt markets.

A. Does Legal Enforcement Require Extraordinary Remedies?

Although the dispute spanned nearly two decades, most accounts focus on the so-called *pari passu* injunction: the extraordinary remedy that ultimately induced Argentina to pay.[16] Frustrated by Argentina's steadfast refusal to pay the money judgments won by holdouts like NML, US federal courts fashioned a different remedy. This was an injunction designed to enforce a covenant in Argentina's bond contracts, the *pari passu* clause,[17] which the courts interpreted as a commitment to treat all bondholders equally. To give effect to this covenant, the courts forbade Argentina to pay bondholders who had participated in its prior debt restructurings without also paying all outstanding principal and interest owed to non-participants.[18] To prevent Argentina from defying the injunction – for example, by making payments on its restructured debt abroad – the courts threatened financial and other intermediaries with contempt sanctions, and they reached extraterritorially to target intermediaries with limited US contracts.[19] The remedy ultimately brought the government to heel; in 2016, Argentina settled with NML and other holdouts.

Legal actors feature prominently in this story, but the emphasis on the *pari passu* injunction arguably reinforces the view that the law usually plays little role in sovereign debt markets. After all, for more than a decade, the usual legal remedies – a money judgment, followed by efforts to execute that judgment against sovereign assets – put little money in NML's pocket. To make a difference, US courts had to fashion an atypical remedy and go to extraordinary lengths to enforce it. The fact that the very judge who created this remedy subsequently limited its reach – explaining that the injunction resulted from 'extraordinary circumstances' not present in typical cases of

[15] Herbert Kritzer, *Risks, Reputations, and Rewards: Contingency Fee Legal Practice in the United States* (Stanford CA, Stanford Univ. Press 2004).

[16] Laura Alfaro, 'Sovereign Debt Restructuring: Evaluating the Impact of the Argentina Ruling' (2015) 5 *Harv. Bus. Law Rev.* 47.

[17] Tim Samples, 'Rogue Trends in Sovereign Debt: Argentina, Vulture Funds, and *Pari Passu* Under New York Law' (2014) 35 *Northwestern J. Int'l. L. and Bus.* 49.

[18] *NML Capital v. Republic of Argentina* 727 F.3d 230 (2d Cir. 2013).

[19] Weidemaier and Gelpern (n 12); Karen Halverson Cross, 'The Extraterritorial Reach of Sovereign Debt Enforcement' (2015) 12 *Berkeley Bus. L. J.* 111.

sovereign default[20] – arguably drove home the point: just as Peru's pledge of guano revenue meant little absent a mechanism for enforcing it, the covenants in Argentina's bond contracts meant little absent herculean judicial intervention.

B. A Counter-Narrative: the Changing Landscape of Legal Enforcement

With this background, it may initially seem surprising that the introduction to this chapter describes, not the extraordinary *pari passu* injunction, but a relatively quotidian aspect of the *NML* litigation. In its quest for payment, NML tried multiple strategies, including the usual creditor's route of obtaining a money judgment and looking for assets to seize. As in every case involving a foreign sovereign, the primary difficulty was that Argentina kept few assets in the United States, and most of what it did keep in the country was protected by sovereign immunity. Argentina also took pains to obscure the presence of assets in other jurisdictions where creditors might reach them. To solve this problem, NML asked US courts to order financial institutions with extensive dealings with Argentina to provide information about the government's financial assets worldwide. In a 2014 decision, the United States Supreme Court approved such discovery, ruling that the Foreign Sovereign Immunities Act (FSIA) does not limit the right of a judgment creditor to demand information about the whereabouts of a foreign government's assets.[21] For convenience, I will refer to this as the 'Discovery Ruling.' The ruling established the United States as a global 'discovery clearinghouse' – i.e., a one-stop forum for creditors to uncover information about a foreign government's assets.

If the Discovery Ruling is important, it is not for doctrinal reasons. At least under US law, the discovery requested by NML was not very noteworthy, and nothing in the text of the Foreign Sovereign Immunities Act suggests that foreign governments are subject to different discovery rules.[22] Perhaps the most noteworthy aspect of the Discovery Ruling is that it exists at all. If courts do not matter unless they fashion extraordinary remedies, why would a creditor bother litigating such a quotidian matter all the way to the US Supreme Court? Indeed, one might ask this question about nearly all of NML's litigation tactics, which reportedly cost tens of millions of dollars and included filing dozens of independent lawsuits and initiating nearly 1000 separate proceedings to seize Argentine assets.[23] The story of the *NML* litigation is not about any single lawsuit or judicial decision. In many respects, it is not even about courts. It is, instead, a story about litigating creditors and their financiers.

---

[20] *White Hawthorne LLC v. Republic of Argentina* No. 16-cv-1042 (TPG) (S.D.N.Y. Dec. 22 2016).

[21] *NML Capital Ltd. v. Republic of Argentina* No. CV 14-02262 SVW (C.D. Cal. Mar. 6 2015); *Republic of Argentina v. NML Capital* 134 S. Ct. 2250 (2014).

[22] However, courts have less power to enforce discovery-related orders against foreign sovereigns. A court can penalise a foreign sovereign's discovery misconduct by imposing litigation-related sanctions, such as adverse evidentiary inferences, and perhaps through contempt. But aside from imposing monetary fines – which may prove uncollectible – the court has little power to compel compliance.

[23] Schumacher, Trebesch and Enderlein (n 13).

C. Managing Litigation Risk in Sovereign Debt Markets

From a creditor's perspective, sovereign debt litigation is an acute exercise in risk management. A single lawsuit will be expensive and time-consuming. To be sure, it is often simple to get a money judgment; after all, the sovereign has borrowed money and not repaid. But the prospects of enforcing that judgment are highly uncertain. At minimum, the creditor will have to retain expensive lawyers with expertise in litigating cases against foreign governments and in the difficult and specialised process of enforcing judgments across national boundaries. In the modern era, creditors often recover something for their efforts – whether measured by the ultimate satisfaction of a judgment in the creditor's favour or by an out-of-court settlement – but the process can last a decade or more and cost tens of millions of dollars.[24]

It is obvious that, to make such a proposition worthwhile, the creditor's claim must be large enough, after discounting for litigation risk, to justify the expense. But even then, risk averse creditors will think twice before initiating suit. As with any investment, diversification can reduce this risk.[25] For example, an investor who assembles a portfolio of claims against multiple debtors reduces the variance associated with litigation outcomes and spreads litigation costs across multiple investments.[26] Of course, all of this follows straightforwardly from portfolio theory. The important point is that, until recently, the actors capable of efficiently managing litigation risk played little role in sovereign debt markets.

During the 1970s and 1980s, when the bulk of private lending to sovereigns consisted of syndicated bank loans, the commercial banks involved in sovereign lending did not relish this role, and indeed there were relatively few lawsuits against sovereign borrowers during this era.[27] To be sure, distressed debt investors have long been part of sovereign debt markets, but investment funds intent on assembling portfolios of claims for litigation appeared on scene in the 1990s.[28] More recently still, entities specialising in litigation finance have arrived,[29] enabling litigation by entities that would not otherwise relish the prospect of a decade-long litigation against a foreign government. For example, bankrupt mining company Crystallex, whose only significant asset is a claim based on Venezuela's expropriation of mining rights, obtained debtor-in-possession financing from a litigation finance entity associated with hedge fund Tenor Capital Management. These funds allowed it to vigorously pursue

---

24 Julian Schumacher, Christoph Trebesch and Hendrik Enderlein, 'Sovereign Defaults in Court' (7 March 2018) <http://papers.ssrn.com/sol3/papers.cfm?abstract_id=2189997> accessed 14 April 2018.

25 Harry Markowitz, 'Foundations of Portfolio Theory' (1991) 46 *The Journal of Finance* 469.

26 Jessica Erickson, 'The Market for Leadership in Corporate Litigation' [2015] *Univ. Ill. L. Rev*. 1480.

27 Schumacher, Trebesch and Enderlein (n 13).

28 Ibid.

29 Maya Steinitz, 'The Litigation Finance Contract' (2012) 54 *Wm. and Mary L. Rev*. 459; Catherine Rogers, *Ethics in International Arbitration* (Oxford, Oxford University Press 2014).

claims against Venezuela on multiple fronts and ultimately to extract a favourable settlement (though it remains unclear how much of the settlement will actually be paid).[30]

D. A Broader View of *NML*'s Significance

The *NML* litigation is important not because it produced changes to legal doctrine, but because it reveals the depth of these changes in the structure of sovereign debt markets. As noted, a creditor need not seize assets whose value exceeds its claim against a foreign government. Instead, its goal is to cause enough disruption to induce a settlement. Ex ante, however, the creditor cannot easily identify the right strategy to produce this outcome. The difficulty is magnified by the fact that only so many strategies can be deployed in each lawsuit. At the outset of the NML litigation, for instance, it was not clear whether a creditor could pursue both a money judgment and a *pari passu* injunction in the same lawsuit.

NML initially diversified its investment in Argentine debt by filing at least nine separate lawsuits seeking money damages.[31] It held additional bonds in reserve, which it later used as the basis for a lawsuit seeking injunctive relief based on the *pari passu* clause.[32] Between 2006 and 2009, these lawsuits yielded money judgments totalling well over $1 billion. Both before and after these judgments, it launched efforts to seize or freeze Argentine assets. At times, it swung for the fences – i.e., made low-probability attempts to seize assets of enormous value. As examples, consider attempts to seize central bank funds on deposit at the Federal Reserve Bank of New York and the Bank for International Settlements.[33]

On other occasions, NML tried to exploit unique moments of leverage, when seizing an asset would impose costs on Argentina far beyond the asset's value. For example, along with other creditors it tried to seize defaulted bonds tendered by bondholders who had agreed to participate in Argentina's 2005 debt exchange.[34] When government bonds include so-called collective action clauses (CACs), they can be restructured with a vote of a majority or super-majority of creditors. But Argentina's debt lacked CACs; no bond could be restructured without the assent of the affected bondholder. Thus, Argentina attempted an exchange offer, in which bondholders willing to give debt relief tendered their old, defaulted bonds for new ones the government intended to pay. Argentina intended to cancel the tendered bonds after the exchange was consummated, thereby negating the debt they represented. NML's strategy was to seize the tendered bonds at the point of exchange. Although the law supported its position, US courts

[30] Katia Dmitrieva, Katia Porzecanski and Bob Van Voris, 'Crystallex, Venezuela Agree to Settle $1.2 Billion Mine Dispute' *Bloomberg* (24 Nov. 2017) <http://www.bloombergquint.com/business/2017/11/24/crystallex-venezuela-agree-to-settle-1-2-billion-mine-dispute>.

[31] NML was just one of many such litigants, some of whom received judgments earlier.

[32] Weidemaier and Gelpern (n 12).

[33] Ibid.

[34] *EM Ltd. v. Republic of Argentina*, Nos. 05–1525–CV(L), 05–1642–CV ETC., 05–1543–CV(L), 05–1544–CV(CON) (2d Cir. May 13 2005).

rejected NML's request on equitable grounds, deeming the restructuring 'of critical importance to the economic health of the nation.'[35]

On other occasions, NML pursued assets of low economic value but high political salience. These searches were seemingly motivated by the potential to embarrass government officials or to disrupt the government's relations with other countries. Examples include the attempted seizure of a training vessel used by the Argentine navy[36] and an attempt to levy on rights held by a government agency in a contract to launch observational satellites, which were intended to contribute to an international mission to study the global environment.[37] NML also capitalised on the fortuitous revelations of the Panama Papers, a leaked trove of documents revealing the role of Panamanian law firm Mossack Fonseca in helping wealthy clients exploit tax loopholes. NML demanded information from a Mossack Fonseca affiliate in Nevada, alleging that the firm had helped launder state assets appropriated by associates of President Cristina Fernández de Kirchner and her family.[38] The apparent goal, once again, was to embarrass Argentine officials and possibly even to threaten personal assets held by ruling elites.[39]

3. CONCLUSION

The *pari passu* injunction remains the proximate cause of Argentina's decision to settle with NML. Nevertheless, NML's aggressive pursuit of assets shut the country out of foreign capital markets, disrupted its attempts to participate in global commerce, and routinely complicated the professional and personal affairs of government actors. It is worth remembering that, compared to many governments, Argentina was substantially insulated from the effects of creditor enforcement. For example, although shut out of foreign capital markets, it was able to borrow substantial sums in foreign currency in domestic capital markets. Even for Argentina, however, the functional embargo imposed by NML's collection efforts imposed substantial costs. It remains to be seen whether other governments, more dependent on foreign capital markets and export revenues, will prove as resilient. Venezuela is the latest test case. Mired in economic crisis, the country has already been sued aggressively by creditors backed by firms specialising in litigation finance. As the country nears default, other creditors wait in

---

35 Ibid.

36 Camila Russo, 'Evading Singer's Dragnet Means $800,000 Flight' *Bloomberg* (10 Jan. 2013) <http://www.bloomberg.com/news/2013-01-10/evading-singer-s-dragnet-means-880-000-flight-argentina-credit.html>.

37 *NML Capital v. Space Expl. Tech. Corp.*, No. CV 14-02262 SVW (C.D. Cal. Mar. 6 2015).

38 Simon Bouvier, 'American Billionaire's Hedge Fund Sues Mossack Fonseca' *International Consortium of Investigative Journalists* (1 Sept. 2016) <http://www.icij.org/blog/2016/09/american-billionaires-hedge-fund-sues-mossack-fonseca/>.

39 Michael Goldhaber, 'Argentine Bond Litigation Wins Global Legal Award for Disputes' *The American Lawyer* (26 Sept. 2016).

the wings to pursue claims against it and state-owned oil company Petróleos de Venezuela.[40]

Two decades ago, it would have been rather remarkable to have creditors queuing up to sue a sovereign borrower on the verge of default. Now, aggressive legal enforcement is taken for granted. The *NML* litigation did not cause this development; creditors are not lining up to seek injunctive relief equivalent to that awarded against Argentina. Rather, *NML* is a symptom of underlying changes in the sovereign debt markets, which have ushered in new investors and financiers capable of making the substantial investments necessary to successfully litigate against foreign governments. This, more than anything else, is the lasting legacy of the *NML* litigation.

40 Katia Porzecanski, 'Why Venezuela Doesn't Get it Over With and Default' *Bloomberg* (9 Aug. 2017) <https://www.bloomberg.com/news/articles/2017-08-09/why-venezuela-struggles-so-hard-to-avoid-default-quicktake-q-a>.

13. Autonomising financial markets: *Lehman Brothers v. BNY Corporate Trustee*

13.1 CASE BACKGROUND

When the bankruptcy of Lehman Brothers Holdings, Inc. (LBHI) produced shockwaves throughout the global financial market and calls for regulation of systemic risk, the role of private international law was hardly a central preoccupation with either financial institutions or the general public. It is well known that Lehman's over-the-counter (OTC) derivatives portfolio (containing over 900,000 OTC derivatives transactions) was governed by the default provisions of the ISDA Master Agreement. On the terrain of private law, the question arose in the aftermath of the crisis as to whether the Master Agreement played any meaningful role in Lehman Brothers' bankruptcy and its catastrophic outcome and more generally whether a modification of its terms could reduce the systemic risk associated with derivatives transactions. In respect of the transnational dimension of the Agreement, a more theoretical debate concerned the extent to which attempts to create global certainty by the financial industry through the use of standardised agreements could be seen as a present-day renewal of the *lex mercatoria*. Might privately created norms provide an alternative frame of reference for the governance of contracts concluded in global financial markets? In such a perspective, the interference of divergent local laws was seen to thwart the operation of uniform contractual terms. However, the presence of a conflict of laws in relation to the interpretation of the ISDA Master Agreement also suggests that private international law plays an essential role in constituting the rules of the game against the backdrop of which the Master Agreement is given legal effect. Such issues surfaced when the courts of New York and London, under their respectively applicable laws, reached opposite conclusions on the enforceability of a term in the Agreement that conferred a charge over property by way of security for a loan. While the courts of New York held the term to be invalid, their London counterparts ordered that charge to be enforced...

Case: *Lehman Brothers Special Financing Inc v. BNY Corporate Trustee Services Ltd* Case no. 09-01242 (Bankr. SDNY) January 25 2010;

Similar case: in the UK, *Perpetual Trustee Co Ltd, Belmont Park Investments PTY Ltd v. BNY Corporate Trustee Services Ltd, Lehman Brothers Special Financing Inc* [2009] EWCA Civ 1160

13.2 FINANCIAL GOVERNANCE THROUGH PRIVATE INTERNATIONAL LAW AND THE GLOBAL POLITICAL ECONOMY

Horatia Muir Watt

1. INTRODUCTION

In the wake of the 2008 financial crisis, the black hole left by the collapse of Lehman Brothers revealed a juridico-financial construction of unprecedented complexity. The ensuing transatlantic judicial struggle that gave rise to the conflicting judgments discussed here, draws attention to the ways in which the technologies of private international law – often abstruse or undecipherable, when indeed they are not more generally invisible in such a context – have provided the ultimate but crucial nail in the edifice which constitutes the global political economy. Here, in the shadow[1] of conflicting and parallel procedures,[2] a private settlement emerged in May 2011 between the failed Lehman galaxy and its creditors. From a global governance perspective, this outcome is important because it reminds us that although this particular financial crisis triggered, progressively, a variety of public regulatory responses on both sides of the pond, markets are still made of contracts while global markets continue to function under the banner of party autonomy: they are still the stuff of judicial determination in private international law. It also draws attention to the ensuing calls for a transnational set of norms, based on practice within the financial industry and particularly the virtues of the ISDA (International Swaps and Derivatives Association) Master agreement as a self-sufficient regime. Our analysis below will start by looking at the background framework in which the private settlement took place in this case, constituted by conflicting legal regimes and the divergent responses of the courts (2). It will then enlarge on a political economy perspective, which questions the lure of contract as a self-constituting regime beyond the state (3).

2. THE SHADOW OF PRIVATE INTERNATIONAL LAW

Contrary to much conventional wisdom about the causes of the sub-prime disaster, there is nothing inevitable about the much-deplored legal 'gap' or 'lag' that represents law as in some way powerless to keep up with the lightening development of finance,

[1] The reference is to the shadow of the law, as in Robert H. Mnookin and Lewis Kornhauser, 'Bargaining in the Shadow of the Law: The Case of Divorce' (1979) 88 *The Yale Law Journal* 950.

[2] UK Court of Appeal [2009] EWCA Civ 1160, *Perpetual Trustee Co. Ltd. c. Corporate Trustee Services Ltd & Lehman Brothers Special Financing Inc*; US Bankruptcy Court (SDNY 2010, 422 B.R. 407.) *Lehman Bros. Special Fin. Inc. v. BNY Corp. Trustee Servs. Ltd. (In re Lehman Bros. Holdings Inc.).*

technology or science.[3] Beyond the evident inadequacy of public regulation of financial and property markets, private law played an essential, distinctive role *ex ante* in laying out the invisible background rules governing both title to property and contract. Both mortgage-backed securities (MBS) and collateralised debt obligations (CDO) are quite obviously creations of private legal technique. Private international law also contributed here by bolstering such constructs in the transnational sphere, when foreign investors were led to entrust their savings to the Lehman galaxy. In this respect, the ISDA (International Swaps and Derivatives Association) Master Agreement governing the swap agreements (to which we shall revert) provides for the application of English law under the jurisdiction of the English courts (A). However, the global extent of the catastrophe meant that multiple fora had cause to intervene *ex post*, with a high risk of collision with other legal regimes. Such a clash materialised in 2010 in the context of the ensuing bankruptcy (Chapter 11) proceedings initiated by Lehman Brothers Holdings in New York (B).

A. Swapping and Flipping: the Exigencies of Contract Law

The players were Saphir, a predatory 'special purpose vehicle' to which Lehman Bros Special Financing Inc. (LBSF) was a swap counterparty, and its creditors hailing from as far as Papua New Guinea,[4] whose investments Saphir had engulfed to a tune of many billions of dollars. The core operation bore the deceptively romantic name of 'Dante' … but turned out to be, in the words of Hugh Collins, a 'flipping wreck'.[5] Indeed, the first transatlantic private international legal issue which arose in this context concerned the validity of a particular clause in the swap agreements known as a 'flip clause'. According to this contractual 'flipping' device, any priority of payment stipulated in favour of Lehman Bros (here in the guise of LBSF) would shift automatically to its creditors in case of default. As we know, default took place when the Federal Reserve decided to refrain from bailing out the failed bank, leading Lehman Bros. Holdings, followed on its heels by LBSF, to file for bankruptcy in the Southern District of New York. This event prompted the Dante creditors' trustee to obtain a declaratory judgment from the High Court in London, confirming the binding effect of the flip clause and the shift of the priority of payment to the creditors. Such a declaration could then be invoked as res judicata in the New York insolvency.

The High Court and the Court of Appeal approved this line of reasoning and determined that the clause was valid. Arguably, however, such a conclusion was not easily reached, despite the nesting of the ISDA Master Agreement under English law and the presumably attentive verifications to which its drafters must have proceeded. Indeed, LBSF, the swap counterparty, had raised some powerful objections, which

---

3 Sheila Jasanoff, 'Making Order: Law and Science in Action' in Edward J. Hackett (ed.), *The Handbook of Science and Technology Studies* 3rd edn (Cambridge MA, MIT Press 2007) 761–86.

4 https://www.ft.com/content/b1a0de4c-811c-11de-92e7-00144feabdc0, *Financial Times* report by Anousha Sakoui, 4 August 2009.

5 Hugh Collins, 'Flipping Wreck: Lex Mercatoria on the Shoals of Ius Cogens' in Stefan Grundmann, Florian Möslein and Karl Riesenhube, *Contract Governance: Dimensions in Law and Interdisciplinary Research* (Oxford, Oxford University Press 2015) 383.

could be disregarded only by isolating the legal issue of the validity of the flip clause from the specific context of the bankruptcy proceedings that constituted the default. The English Insolvency Act 1986 contains 'anti-deprivation' provisions, while the common law disqualifies any attempt to transfer title by contract to a third party in the event of insolvency.[6] A similar prohibition can be found elsewhere.[7] It is true however, that practice pulls in a different direction in the case of arrangements involving 'flawed assets', which would appear to have carved out a derogation from the general rule and shrouded the latter in uncertainty as to its actual purport. In this case, the judges seemed sensitive to the simple economy of the financial arrangement under which those who provided the capital for the operation to continue should be allowed to recover their outlay.

But another more legalistic and somewhat contorted argument seems to have been decisive here. The default event that triggered the flip clause was necessarily the failure of the parent company, which dragged its subsidiary down the road to bankruptcy in its fall. Therefore, by the time the swap counterparty filed for bankruptcy, two weeks after the parent, the flip clause had already operated in favour of its creditors. This meant that its own bankruptcy was irrelevant and the anti-deprivation provisions equally so. These did not affect the validity of the clause under English law. Given the existence of Chapter 11 proceedings in New York, it was surmised that the American bankruptcy court might see the clause in a different light. However, this could have no impact on the assessment of its validity under the applicable (English) law. The sole concession to the existence of parallel and possibility conflicting proceedings in the United States was the declaratory nature of the English judgment, which stopped short of ordering that the priority be shifted to the creditors. The rest was up to the res judicata effect of the English judgement before the New York bankruptcy court.

B. Bankruptcy Backfires: the Interference of Comity

However, the creditors were less successful across the Atlantic. Despite the English ruling, the flip was paralysed and the interests of Lehman's bank prevailed. Such an outcome is hardly surprising, at least at first glance. Under paragraph 365 (e) (1) of Chapter 11 USC, the effect of the bankruptcy proceedings was to deactivate the flip clause, and the latter provision was indisputably applicable to bankruptcy proceedings opened in the United States. However, the determination of the respective scope of the laws governing the contract, on the one hand, and the insolvency, on the other, is notoriously difficult. For instance, article 9 of the EU Insolvency Regulation provides that the effects of insolvency on the rights and obligations of parties to a payment or settlement system or financial market are to be defined by the law applicable to that system.[8] The existence of a conflict of substantive outcomes is doubled over therefore

[6] *British Eagle International Airlines v. Compagnie Internationale Air France* (1975) 1 WLR 758, HL.

[7] In France, for instance, to similar effect, art. L.621-28, Law of 26 juillet 2005.

[8] Under article 12 of Regulation (Eu) 2015/848 of 20 May 2015 on insolvency proceedings (recast), 'the effects of insolvency proceedings on the rights and obligations of the parties to a payment or settlement system or to a financial market shall be governed solely by the law of the

with a divergence, or at least uncertainty, as to the characterisation of the legal issue: is it for the law of the contract to decide on the effects of bankruptcy on the contract, or for the law of bankruptcy to determine how contract survives in bankruptcy?

This explains no doubt why the disregard for the authority of the English judgment was clothed here, once again, in a highly sophisticated argument, under which one senses that the Dante creditors' trustee (or perhaps the English court that found in favour of the latter's interests) was hoisted as it were with his own petard. Thus (so the reasoning goes), the English judgment is indisputably part of English law, and English law is applicable to the contract. Now, that judgment ruled that the swap counterparty had lost the benefit of the flip clause due to the prior failure of its parent company, before its own collapse. That legal effect is incorporated into the governing law and deprives the swap counterparty of any priority in the context of the bankruptcy proceedings in federal court.

Furthermore, the bankruptcy court saw fit to add an argument based on the principle of Comity, which also seemed to contain more moral statement than legal content. Comity (says the American court), should have led its English counterpart to take account of the bankruptcy proceedings which had commenced across the Atlantic and of which it had been made fully aware. A form of inverted Comity required therefore that the American court impose its own conception of the impact of the bankruptcy on the contract, despite the contract being governed by English law, with its radically contrary outcome.

Such transatlantic conflicts are not without precedent. A spectacular example is the Laker airways litigation in the 1980s, in which anti-suit (and anti-anti-suit) injunctions were launched from both sides of the pond in a high-stakes antitrust case.[9] Colluding banks and established airlines attempted (ultimately successfully) to thwart Freddie Laker's daring low-cost commercial venture and then to stop his claim for treble damages in US federal court. The judicial conflict ended only after diplomatic intervention and the case became emblematic of the blurring of traditional divides between the public and the private, the geopolitical and the judicial, the legal and the political. However, in the present case, the judicial struggle was more demure. It nevertheless suggested very clearly that while the 'background rules' for the functioning of markets are (more or less) identifiable in a domestic context, they become entirely foggy beyond the State.

Member State applicable to that system or market'. The Regulation rests on the idea that there is 'a need for special protection in the case of payment systems and financial markets, for example in relation to the position-closing agreements and netting agreements to be found in such … For such transactions, the only law which is relevant should be that applicable to the system or market concerned. That law is intended to prevent the possibility of mechanisms for the payment and settlement of transactions, and provided for in payment and set-off systems or on the regulated financial markets of the Member States, being altered in the case of insolvency of a business partner …' (recital 21).

[9] On which see Daryl A. Libow, 'Laker Antitrust Litigation: The Jurisdictional Rule of Reason Applied to Transnational Injunctive Relief' (1986) 71 *Cornell L. Rev.* 645 and https://www.washingtonpost.com/archive/business/1985/07/13/laker-airways-antitrust-suit-is-settled/33c63e60-96d7-41cc-aaf3-c24445d73a5b/?utm_term=.59cc0be724c7.

Bargaining in the shadow of shifting laws is an art that requires a considerable degree of strategic anticipation of the potentially diverse positioning of different fora. It leads to forum shopping in various forms (reverse or otherwise) but also to the creation by private actors of autonomous contractual space dis-embedded as it were from any local context or pressure. In the present case, the parties reached a settlement on 25 May 2011, the existence of which was revealed to the public only after a further battle over banking secrecy. This means that the destiny of the enterprise that shook the world banking system was left to out-of-court bargaining: the bang ended in a whimper. It also explains the lure of the *lex mercatoria* and its promise of a transcendent form of uniform rules,[10] far from the madding muddle of national laws. Why not acknowledge the *de facto* prevalence of the ISDA Master Agreement as governing the global market for derivatives? The global financial industry – so the argument goes – provides ample opportunity for competition between private contractual norms[11] and 'public' (state-made, or state-approved) laws – of which the performance in this particular case was admittedly extremely poor ...

3. THE LURE OF GLOBAL GOVERNANCE BY CONTRACT

It is easy to see that contract emerges as the core organisational scheme under which the contemporary forms of global capitalism have put down their roots – within the law and through the law.[12] In our 'world of struggle',[13] contract has facilitated the creation of private, autonomous systems (from the global financial markets at stake here, to delocalised industries or global value chains) in which informal power flourishes untrammelled, protected from external constraints or social pressures. Contemporary critical theory in international law has traced this largely invisible role of private law in the constitution of informal empire back to the work of the Spanish scholastics.[14] A similar analysis is relevant to contemporary forms of power in the global political economy today, where – dwarfed by public (international) law and its institutions, associated in turn with the formal governance of political authority – creatures of private law provide the legal infrastructure for the concentration and growth of private

---

[10] On which see Collins (n 5).

[11] On the issue of normativity beyond the State, see Part II of this book and the developments in the Introduction.

[12] See A. Claire Cutler and Thomas Dietz, *The Politics of Private Transnational Governance by Contract* (Abingdon, Routledge 2017).

[13] See David Kennedy, *A World of Struggle. How Power, Law, and Expertise Shape Global Political Economy* (Princeton NJ, Princeton University Press 2016).

[14] Marty Koskenniemi ('Empire and International Law: The Real Spanish Contribution' (2011) 61 *University of Toronto Law Journal* 1) shows that the Spanish scholastics provided the institutions of private law needed here; notably credit. As will be seen below, contract and property have worked hand in hand to create markets and ensure credit and insurance since the very beginnings of Western capitalist expansion in the direction of the New World. Similarly, corporations as 'bundle of contracts' emerged as forces to be reckoned with in a domestic setting, before driving the global economy in largely unregulated 'multinational' form.

economic power beyond, and above, the state (A).[15] The key resides in the migration from the domestic to the international context at the turn of the 20th century, of the libertarian idea of contract as untrammelled 'party autonomy' (B).[16]

A. The Invisibility of Private Power

Indeed, one of the most significant effects of the public/private divide in classical liberal thought has been to divert attention away from the ways in which private law structures and justifies power. It does so to a large extent invisibly, as if its institutions were perfectly natural. Even within the field of public (international) law, as David Kennedy forcefully points out, it is usual to think of law as *regulating* the basic elements of global political and economic life, in providing 'the sinews of a constituted order' but not as involved in the very *creation* of markets, or money, or debt.[17] Similarly, in his discussion of the 'constitution of private law', Harm Schepel observes that

> as the current financial crisis shows only too well, blaming the markets for the inadequacies of public—domestic and international—policies, as if the markets were 'out there', skittish, autonomous, unshaped by law and policy, and subject to whims of their own invention—is more than suspect. As emphasised so forcefully in the domestic sphere by American legal realism, markets are social—and therefore, legal constructs, so that not plying discipline is, of course, in itself a form of regulation.

There is no such thing, then, as an 'unregulated market'. 'Markets are always already regulated, insofar as political intervention into markets is not a question of regulating a void, but of how to interact with the wider normative universe that constitutes markets'.[18] Moreover, as L. Pauly writes, 'markets have always obscured distributive issues and helped diffuse blame for negative economic consequences'.[19] That markets themselves are creatures of the law is 'what private lawyers know'[20] about economic governance – although such knowledge may be unconscious or deliberately repressed. Furthermore, the split within the law between its public and private spheres means that

---

15 This in no way implies that public law has not used contract. In its public dimension, international law has always sovereign states – the legal creatures of Westphalia – have always depended upon the recourse to contract in the form of fictional or implied consent, which serves as a device both in liberal political theory (the social contract) and in conciliating state sovereignty with subordination to higher principles. Moreover, the heart of modern public international law remains the treaty.

16 As seen below, the principle of party autonomy in private international law is so unquestioned as to have attained mythical status.

17 *Op cit*, p. 11: depicting the 'world of struggle' over law and expert knowledge which shapes the global political economy, 'the basic elements of global economic and political life – capital, labour, money and liquidity, as well as ower and right – are creatures of law'.

18 Harm Schepel, *The Constitution of Private Governance* (Oxford, Hart Publishing 2005) 406.

19 L. Pauly, 'Global Finance, Political Authority, and the Problem of Legitimation' in Rodney B. Hall and Thomas J. Biersteker (eds), *The Emergence of Private Authority in Global Governance* (Cambridge, Cambridge University Press 2002) 76, 77.

20 Henry James, *What Maisie Knew* (London, Penguin Classics 1896).

private law's relationship to markets is rarely expressed in terms of power or framed as affecting the global political economy. Indeed, the classical theorisation of private law as a-political or 'merely technical'[21] has lent credence to the idea that issues of power are beyond its remit, and this idea dies hard even after the emergence of more 'social' or regulatory models.

However, within the sphere of private law, the specific contribution of private *international* law theory and institutions to the workings of power within the global economy have remained less obvious still. This invisibility is paradoxical. Arguably, *private* international law is the closest the law gets at present, to understanding, framing and governing the 'global' dimension of social and economic interaction in any systematic way. We know that its traditional scope has been the activities of private actors that straddle the boundaries of sovereign States. Now the 'private', in this conception, is taken as a clear indicator of the absence, beyond interaction between States, of any issue involving transnational political power.[22] It expresses the confluence between a field of law (private law) and a category of interests (issues not involving the public order). It is clear however that the private and the non-State can be the loci of highly political conflicts.[23] In this respect, the discipline has played a crucial role in extending the private law infrastructure of power beyond the domestic setting; indeed, it has worked to ex-filtrate from transnational governance the more regulatory dimensions of contemporary private law, particularly insofar as it subordinates individual interests to wider considerations of solidarity or proportionality. How else indeed did multinationals straddle State boundaries, how did cross-border markets extend to judicial services, how did foreign investment gain protection round the world, how did value chains globalise … despite conflicting policies on a local level? Why do various shared, countervailing, tendencies within domestic jurisdictions, which seek to curb the excesses of individual interests – concern for weaker parties, protection of non-contracting stakeholders, intervention of human rights – lose their relevance whenever economic flows take place beyond State boundaries?

B. The Centrality of Party Autonomy

This is all the work of the complex technologies specific to the discipline of the conflict of laws. The latter has, arguably, been the single most significant enabling factor in the transition from liberalism to neo-liberalism,[24] which has seen sovereign states relinquish political control,[25] individually and collectively, over the global economy. Its specific understandings of contract have undoubtedly played an essential

---

21 Duncan Kennedy, 'The Political Stakes in "Merely Technical" Issues of Contract Law' (2001) 19 *European Review of Private Law* 7.

22 Conversely, classical public international law takes the view that all political interaction outside the domestic sphere occurs through the medium of nation-States.

23 Just as sovereignty understood as supremacy or autonomy may vest in powerful private actors.

24 For the difference between classical and neo-liberalism, see M. Foucault, *La Naissance de la biopolitique. Cours au Collège de France, 1978–1979* (Paris, ed. Seuil 2004).

25 S. Sassen, *Losing Control? Sovereignty in an Age of Globalization* (New York, Columbia University Press 1996).

role in facilitating the global turn within the political economy. Under the umbrella of the 'principle of party autonomy', contract is apprehended as the unrestricted power of private actors to soar above domestic regulations and circumvent local court systems. First used at the beginning of the 20th century to justify a derogatory regime for international transactions,[26] it has had profound implications in terms of global governance, which could not possibly have been foreseen at the time. Unquestioning acceptance of the principle of party freedom points to its status as a foundational myth of private international economic law. Indeed, its success has been unimpeded by the fact that significant issues as to its real ambit remain unsettled, as will be shown below. Nor does it seem to matter that despite its Kantian pedigree, its dominant justification is essentially utilitarian, linked to the needs of international trade. Although methodological, political and economic objections do appear from time to time, albeit outside mainstream doctrine, they remain largely unheeded; thus, neither the functionalist arguments drawn from governmental interests analysis, nor the potential democratic deficit resulting from the permission to contract out of local rules, nor indeed the uncertain economic rationality underlying the apparent indifference of states to free-riding by foreign parties on proven or novel regulatory models, detract from its remarkable success. The latter is, most recently, illustrated by the Hague Principles Principles on Choice of Law in International Commercial Contracts (2015), which 'sets forth general principles concerning choice of law in international commercial contracts. They affirm the principle of party autonomy with limited exceptions'.

The centrality of private choice of law in the European tradition is so taken for granted, or at least, appears to be so solidly rooted in the history of Western private international law, that astonishingly little attention has been paid to the function it fulfils within the changing economic and political environment induced by globalisation. The cloak of tradition is reinforced by more recent law and economics doctrines, which tend to promote party autonomy as efficiency, in the form of predictability, reduced transaction costs or facilitated risk-management. No doubt these virtues exist, at least for the party whose skills in contract negotiation and drafting are strongest. It is highly probable however that the interests purportedly served by unbridled freedom of choice, whether cast as those of the market or of a purported community of merchants, do not allow for adequate governance of the cross-border activities of private actors. In this respect, the (in)famous Lloyd's litigation serves as a cautionary illustration of the cumulative effect of contract doctrine and private international law theory.[27] Thus, under a wider perspective than that offered by various

---

26 V. Cass com, 5 décembre 1910 (*Rev. Dr. Int.*, 1911. 395, *Clunet,* 1912. 1156, S. 1911. 1. 129). This decision goes further than contemporary understandings of party autonomy as freedom to choose any state law. Here, it allows parties to derogate from the chosen state law by agreement (on the issue of a clause of non-liability) so that, ultimately, the contractual regime was not provided by any identifiable existing positive law. Such a choice is now widely possible in international arbitration, but rarely before state courts.

27 *Roby v. Corporation of Lloyd's*, 996 F.2d 1353 (2d Cir 1993); *Bonny v Society of Lloyd's*, 3 F.3d 156 (7th Cir 1993); comp. in France, the '*Monster Cable*' case: Cass civ 1re, 22 octobre 2008, JCP (G) 2008, II, 10187, note L. d'Avout; JCP (E) 2008, 2535, note N. Mathey; *Contrats, conc consom* 2008, comm 270, note M. Malurie-Vignal; D 2009, 200, note F. Jault-Seseke,

dimensions of private law doctrine, it becomes clear that party autonomy no longer serves to free private enterprise from entrenched parochial constraints under the benign supervision of a community of liberal states, but works to transform national public regulation into a disposable private good in a deregulated economy. As shown by the Lehman case under discussion, this holds true even after the various recent financial crises and the disastrous role played by self-regulation in subordinating wider public concerns to speculative interests. In this respect, the implications of party autonomy for what has been aptly described as 'regulatory liftoff'[28] must be seen in the context of the various legal tools[29] that provide the private legal infrastructure of global markets and foreign investment.

The question is, of course, where we go from here. Re-embedding financial markets through more vigilant and coordinated public regulation is of course a significant step. It is also important, as we have attempted to do here, to deconstruct the legal 'plug-in' device underlying such markets and acknowledge the constitutive role of private (international) law. There is a clear need in this context for new intellectual schemes adapted to the complex interaction of market actors. Networks, here, are a promising candidate.[30] But whatever the legal technology involved, the lesson of the *Lehman* case presented here is that it is essential today to move beyond governance by contract, so as to introduce novel modes of collective responsibility. This is both an ethical and political project, as much as it creates a challenge in terms of the existing technologies of private international law.

D. Bureau and H. Muir Watt, 'L'impérativité désactivée? (à propos de Cass civ 1re, 22 octobre 2008)' *Rev crit DIP* 2009, 1.

[28] See Robert Wai, 'Transnational *Liftoff* and Juridical Touchdown: The Regulatory Function of Private International Law in an Era of Globalization' (2002) 40 *Columbia Journal of Transnational Law* 209.

[29] Among these, within the European context, free movement of goods and services entertains a symbiotic relationship with party choice, the latter being the metaphorical expression of cross-border mobility and regulatory arbitrage. More globally, party autonomy also structures transnational production and supply chains (generating what can been described as a 'plug-in effect' in respect of sub-contractors and suppliers), and can moreover be linked in this context to direct investment, of which it supports the international (contractual) regime. The private legal regime thus created is reinforced, on the one hand, by private international law rules in tort, when they work to keep any obligation to pay attention to third party interests under the sway of local law, itself often constrained to lower the level of reparation by reason of competition to attract foreign investment. On the other hand and furthermore, the private international law regime governing the structure of multinational enterprise reinforces the autonomy of corporate entities when it comes to the duty to care or repair in respect of industrial accidents, environmental damage, or human rights abuse.

[30] Testing out this idea, see Horatia Muir Watt, 'Party Autonomy in Global Context: The Political Economy of a Self-Constituting Regime' (2015) 58 *Japanese Yearbook of International Law* 175.

PART IV

MODES OF REASONING: DOING LAW BEYOND THE STATE

14. Mysteries of extraterritoriality: *RJR Nabisco, Inc. v. European Community*

14.1 CASE BACKGROUND

This is yet another case where the US Supreme Court was called upon to determine the reach of a federal statute. It held, on the one hand, that 'the Racketeer Influenced and Corrupt Organizations Act' (RICO) could be applied to conduct that occurs outside the United States. According to the Court, Congress intended certain provisions of RICO, such as §§1962 (b) and (c), to apply extraterritorially. This was significant, as it involved the rebuttal of the presumption against extraterritoriality in respect of those provisions. On the other hand, it also ruled that §1964(c), which provides for a private action, must prove an injury within the United States. It was, therefore, a bitter-sweet victory for the claimant, the European Community, who had brought a claim under §1964(c). As it alleged only foreign injuries, it failed to meet the test under this provision.

The European Community and 26 of its Member States brought an action against RJR Nabisco and its related entities ('Nabisco'), alleging that Nabisco participated in a global money laundering scheme in association with various organised crime groups, which violated RICO. This Act prohibits certain activities of organised crime groups, including the investing income derived from racketeering activities in an enterprise involved in interstate and foreign commerce; acquiring or maintaining an interest in an enterprise, and conducting affairs through a pattern of racketeering activity; and conspiring to violate any of these prohibitions. The European Community claimed that drug traffickers smuggled narcotics into Europe and sold them for sums which, through transactions involving black market money brokers, cigarette importers, and wholesalers, were then used to pay for large shipments of Nabisco cigarettes into Europe. It also alleged that Nabisco engaged in a pattern of racketeering activity, including money laundering, material support to foreign terrorist organisations, mail fraud, and violations of the Travel Act.

The District Court granted Nabisco's motion to dismiss on the ground that RICO did not apply to racketeering activity occurring outside the U.S. territory or to foreign enterprises. The Second Circuit reinstated the claims and held that RICO applied extraterritorially and that it could permit recovery of a foreign injury. The Supreme Court, once again, reversed this decision and held that while §§1962 did not involve an impermissibly extraterritorial application of RICO, the right of private action under §1964(c) did not overcome the presumption against extraterritoriality. Justice Ruth Bader Ginsburg delivered a dissenting opinion, joined by Justices Stephen Breyer and Elena Sagan. She argued that a domestic-injury requirement is not supported by the text of the statute, is inconsistent with its purpose and unnecessary to protect the interests of international comity. Moreover, in her own words, 'this case has the United States written all over it'.

Case: *RJR Nabisco, Inc. v. European Community* 579 US ___ (2016)

14.2 RICO'S EXTRATERRITORIAL APPLICATION: REBUTTING THE PRESUMPTION?

*Hannah Buxbaum**

1. INTRODUCTION

In 2000, the European Community filed a lawsuit against RJR Nabisco (RJR) in US federal court, alleging violations of the Racketeer Influenced and Corrupt Organizations Act (RICO).[1] After more than 15 years and a number of intermediate judicial decisions, the litigation came to its likely close in 2016 with the US Supreme Court's ruling in *RJR Nabisco, Inc. v. European Community*.[2] The Court held that RICO's private cause of action does not extend to claims based on injuries suffered outside the United States, denying the European Community any recovery.

The case was the third in recent years in which the Supreme Court applied the 'presumption against extraterritoriality,' a tool of statutory interpretation, to determine the geographic reach of a US federal law. In *Morrison v. National Australia Bank*[3] and *Kiobel v. Royal Dutch Petroleum*,[4] it had applied the presumption to the general anti-fraud provision of US securities law and to the Alien Tort Statute, respectively. Those opinions effected a shift in the Court's jurisprudence toward more expansive application of the presumption – a shift whose effect is to constrain quite significantly the application of US regulatory law in cross-border cases.

The Supreme Court's opinion in *RJR* proceeds in two parts. The first addresses the geographic scope of RICO's substantive provisions, analysing whether the statute's prohibition of certain forms of conduct applies to acts occurring outside the United States. The second addresses the private cause of action created by the statute, asking whether it permits a plaintiff to recover compensation for injury suffered outside the United States. After beginning with a brief overview of the lawsuit, this contribution discusses each of these parts in turn.

2. BACKGROUND

RICO, enacted in 1970, created four criminal offences prohibiting certain forms of organised crime: investing income derived from a pattern of racketeering activity, acquiring or maintaining an interest in an enterprise through a pattern of racketeering

---

* This contribution was initially published in 37 Praxis des Internationalen Privat- und Verfahrensrechts (IPRax) 106 (2017) as 'RICO's Extraterritorial Application: RJR Nabisco, Inc. v. European Community,' and is reprinted here with the permission of the publishers.

1 18 U.S.C. Chapter 96.

2 136 S.Ct. 2090 (2016). The Court remanded the case to the Second Circuit Court of Appeals; however, as discussed herein, its ruling forecloses recovery by the European Community for the injuries alleged.

3 *Morrison v. Nat'l Australia Bank Ltd.*, 561 U.S. 247 (2010).

4 *Kiobel v. Royal Dutch Petroleum Co.*, 569 U.S. __, 133 S. Ct. 1659 (2013).

activity, conducting an enterprise's affairs through a pattern of racketeering activity, and conspiring to violate any of these three prohibitions.[5] The statute defines 'racketeering activity' to include a wide range of both state and federal offences, which are referred to as the 'predicates' to liability.[6] The existence of multiple related predicates – together suggesting a pattern of criminal activity – is required to establish a violation of RICO.[7] In addition to creating criminal penalties for these offences, the statute also created a private cause of action allowing '[a]ny person injured in his business or property' by a RICO violation to sue in US federal district court for treble damages.[8] This cause of action became a popular tool for private plaintiffs seeking damages in a broad range of cases, often involving fraud in business transactions rather than the sort of activity typically associated with organised crime.[9]

The European Community sued RJR and a number of related entities on behalf of itself and 26 member states. It alleged that RJR, acting in concert with other participants including Colombian and Russian drug traffickers, participated in a scheme to smuggle narcotics into Europe and use the proceeds of their sale to pay for shipments of RJR cigarettes.[10] It identified a number of predicate offences, including 'acts of money laundering, material support to foreign terrorist organizations, mail fraud, [and] wire fraud.'[11] The European Community stated that the harms it had suffered as a result of these violations included 'competitive harm to their state-owned cigarette businesses, lost tax revenue from black-market cigarette sales, harm to European financial institutions, currency instability, and increased law enforcement costs.'[12]

At an earlier stage of the litigation, RJR had moved to dismiss certain portions of the claim on the basis of the so-called 'revenue rule.' This rule, rooted in traditional principles of territorial sovereignty, provides that the courts of one country need not assist other countries in recovering unpaid taxes.[13] Its primary justification is the concern that the enforcement of a foreign sovereign's tax laws (particularly in the form of enforcing a foreign judgment for the payment of taxes) would require inquiry into the purposes behind those laws, and would therefore involve policy decisions that

---

5 18 U.S.C. s 1962.

6 18 U.S.C. s 1961(1).

7 18 U.S.C. s 1961(5) (defining 'pattern of racketeering activity' to require at least two acts of racketeering activity within a ten-year time period).

8 18 U.S.C. s 1964(c).

9 See *Sedima, S.P.R.L. v. Imrex Co., Inc.*, 473 U.S. 479 (1985) [499]-[500] (recognising that '[i]nstead of being used against mobsters and organized criminals, [civil RICO] has become a tool for everyday fraud cases brought against "respected and legitimate enterprises." … [I]n its private civil version, RICO is evolving into something quite different from the original conception of its enactors' (quoting *Sedima, S.P.R.L. v. Imrex Co., Inc.*, 741 F.2d 482 (2d Cir. 1984) [487]).

10 136 S.Ct. [2098].

11 Ibid.

12 Ibid.

13 See Restatement (Third) of the Foreign Relations Law of the United States s 483 (1987) ('Courts in the United States are not required to recognize or to enforce judgments for the collection of taxes, fines, or penalties rendered by the courts of other states.').

might embarrass foreign governments.[14] In the United States, the doctrine also protects against judicial interference in matters of foreign relations that lie within the sphere of the political branches of government.[15] Concluding that the substance of the European Community's claims implicated the 'sovereignty and separation of powers concerns' underlying the rule, the Second Circuit Court of Appeals held that it barred the portion of the European Community's claims based on lost tax revenue.[16] The Court permitted the remainder of the claims to proceed.

RJR subsequently moved to dismiss the complaint on a different basis: that RICO has no extraterritorial effect. It argued that the statute applies neither to racketeering activity occurring outside the borders of the United States nor to the activity (wherever located) of foreign enterprises. The District Court for the Eastern District of New York dismissed the claim on this basis;[17] however, the Second Circuit Court of Appeals reversed the judgment and reinstated the claims.[18] The Supreme Court granted certiorari in 2015.

3. APPLYING THE PRESUMPTION AGAINST EXTRATERRITORIALITY

A. To RICO's Substantive Provisions

The first part of the Supreme Court's opinion was unanimous. It addressed the question whether RICO's substantive provisions apply to conduct occurring in foreign countries. The Court begins by noting the 'basic premise of our legal system that, in general, "United States law governs domestically but does not rule the world."'[19] Stating that this principle 'finds expression' in the presumption against extraterritoriality,[20] it then analysed whether Section 1962 had overcome the presumption.

The presumption against extraterritoriality is a judicially created doctrine of statutory interpretation. In one leading case, the Supreme Court summarised it as follows: 'legislation of Congress, unless a contrary intent appears, is meant to apply only within the territorial jurisdiction of the United States.'[21] Like the revenue rule, it is rooted in traditional principles of territorial sovereignty. And as with the revenue rule, courts offer a number of other justifications for its application, including the desire to 'avoid the international discord that can result when US law is applied to conduct in foreign

---

14 See Hannah Buxbaum, 'Transnational Regulatory Litigation' (2006) 46 *Va. J. Int'l L.* 251, 284–87 (describing and critiquing this justification).

15 Ibid. at 283.

16 *European Community v. RJR Nabisco, Inc.*, 355 F.3d 123 (2d Cir. 2004), aff'd, *European Community v. RJR Nabisco, Inc.*, 424 F.3d 175 (2d Cir. 2005).

17 *European Community v. RJR Nabisco, Inc.*, 2011 WL 843957 (E.D.N.Y. 2011).

18 *European Community v. RJR Nabisco, Inc.*, 764 F.3d 129 (2d Cir. 2014).

19 136 S.Ct. [2100] (quoting *Microsoft Corp. v. AT&T Corp.*, 550 U.S. 437 (2007) [454]).

20 Ibid.

21 *EEOC v. Arabian American Oil Co.*, 499 U.S. 244 (1991) [248] (quoting *Foley Bros. v. Filardo*, 336 U.S. 281 (1949) [285]).

countries.'[22] The Supreme Court's application of the presumption has been somewhat inconsistent over time. Although many of the Court's decisions in the area of legislative jurisdiction refer to it, some do not;[23] moreover, the formulation of the test for determining when the presumption has been overcome has varied from case to case.[24] In 2010, however, the Supreme Court issued its decision in *Morrison*, which in two respects marked a turning point in the Court's extraterritoriality jurisprudence. Because *RJR* relies heavily on that case – adopting, and in some respects expanding, its approach – it is worth outlining those aspects of the *Morrison* decision.

First, *Morrison* articulated a particularly stringent version of the presumption. The Court stated that the relevant question is not to '"discern" whether Congress would have wanted the statute to apply' in a certain situation, but simply to ascertain whether the statute clearly indicates that it has extraterritorial reach.[25] The Court emphasised that the presumption in this form was *not* intended to operate as a 'clear statement rule,' if by that is meant a requirement that a statute say 'this law applies abroad,' and stated that '[a]ssuredly context can be consulted as well.'[26] Nevertheless, the opinion was widely read as requiring a more explicit indication of Congressional intent to overcome the presumption than previous cases had required.[27]

Second, *Morrison* introduced a further analytical step to determine when a 'non-extraterritorial' statute (that is, a statute lacking clear indication of extraterritorial reach) could permissibly be applied to cases involving both foreign and domestic conduct. The plaintiff's securities fraud claim in that case arose from a foreign investment transaction, but alleged that the defendant had engaged in some fraudulent conduct in the United States.[28] The Court had concluded that the Securities Exchange Act lacks an affirmative indication that its anti-fraud provision was intended to apply extraterritorially.[29] On the basis of the US-based conduct, however, the plaintiff argued that it sought merely 'domestic application' of the statute.[30] The Court stated that the presumption against extraterritoriality was relevant in this context as well.[31] It held that

---

22 136 S.Ct. [2100]. See also William Dodge, 'Understanding the Presumption Against Extraterritoriality' (1998) 16 *Berkeley J. Int'l L.* 85 (outlining the application and purpose of the presumption).

23 See, e.g., *F. Hoffmann-La Roche Ltd. v. Empagran S.A.*, 542 U.S. 155 (2004); *Steele v. Bulova Watch Co.*, 344 U.S. 280 (1952); see also Dodge (n 22) at 85–86.

24 The *Aramco* case, for instance, suggested that a statute must contain a clear statement regarding extraterritorial reach in order to overcome the presumption. *EEOC v. Arabian American Oil Co.*, 499 U.S. [248].

25 561 U.S. [255].

26 Ibid. at 265.

27 See Lea Brilmayer, 'The New Extraterritoriality: Morrison v. National Australia Bank, Legislative Supremacy, and the Presumption Against Extraterritorial Application of American Law' (2011) 40 *SW L. Rev.* 655, 656 (describing the opinion as 'raising the evidentiary standard for rebutting the presumption').

28 561 U.S. [251]–[253].

29 Ibid. at 265.

30 Ibid. at 266.

31 Ibid. ('[I]t is a rare case of prohibited extraterritorial application that lacks *all* contact with the territory of the United States. But the presumption against extraterritorial application would

in such cases, the court must identify the 'focus of congressional concern' in enacting the statute in question.[32] If the conduct relevant to that focus occurred outside the United States, then the statute's application would be impermissibly extraterritorial despite the presence of other US-based conduct.[33]

In *RJR*, the Supreme Court summarises and adopts the *Morrison* approach. Its analysis begins with a concise and admirably clear description of *Morrison*'s 'two-step framework for analyzing extraterritoriality issues.'[34] In the future, lower courts are likely to rely on this test for applying the presumption against extraterritoriality:

> At the first step, we ask whether the presumption against extraterritoriality has been rebutted—that is, whether the statute gives a clear, affirmative indication that it applies extraterritorially. ... If the statute is not extraterritorial, then at the second step we determine whether the case involves a domestic application of the statute, and we do this by looking to the statute's 'focus.' If the conduct relevant to the statute's focus occurred in the United States, then the case involves a permissible domestic application even if other conduct occurred abroad; but if the conduct relevant to the focus occurred in a foreign country, then the case involves an impermissible extraterritorial application regardless of any other conduct that occurred in US territory.[35]

In accordance with this framework, the Court in *RJR* began by considering whether RICO gives a clear and affirmative indication that it applies to foreign conduct. Section 1962 itself does not contain a statement regarding its geographic scope.[36] However, as noted above, the statute defines 'racketeering activity' by reference to a range of predicate offences included in other state and federal laws.[37] Many of those offences *do* apply explicitly to foreign conduct.[38] The Court correctly recognised this as an 'obvious textual clue' that Congress did intend RICO to apply extraterritorially – at least in cases involving those forms of activity.[39] It therefore held that the presumption against extraterritoriality had been overcome with respect to claims based on predicate

---

be a craven watchdog indeed if it retreated to its kennel whenever *some* domestic activity is involved in the case.')

[32] Ibid.

[33] Interpreting Section 10(b) of the Securities Exchange Act, the Court held that the statute's focus was not on regulating domestic fraud, but rather on regulating domestic securities transactions. Thus, regardless of where the fraudulent conduct in question occurred, an application of that provision to claims arising from foreign securities transactions was impermissibly extraterritorial. 561 U.S. [266]–[267].

[34] 136 S.Ct. [2101].

[35] Ibid.

[36] Interpreting *Morrison* as imposing a 'clear statement' rule, the district court had concluded that RICO's silence on this point 'prohibits any extraterritorial application of RICO.' *European Community v. RJR Nabisco, Inc.*, 2011 WL 843957 (E.D.N.Y. 2011) [*4].

[37] See supra at n 6.

[38] The Court provides as examples the prohibitions against 'engaging in monetary transactions in criminally derived property, ... assassination of Government officials, ... [and] hostage taking,' each of which expressly applies to conduct outside the United States. 136 S.Ct. [2101].

[39] Ibid.

offences that themselves have extraterritorial effect.[40] In other words, it held that RICO's geographic scope tracks the geographic scope of the predicate offences involved in a particular case.[41]

In this passage of its analysis, the Court reaffirmed its observation in *Morrison* that the presumption is not intended to operate as a 'clear statement rule.' It stated that '[w]hile the presumption can be overcome only by a clear indication of extraterritorial effect, an express statement of extraterritoriality is not essential.'[42] It would be reading too much into this, however, to conclude that the Court intended to relax the standard for overcoming the presumption. First, the Court elsewhere signaled its commitment to a rigorous evidentiary standard – for instance, stating that the question is whether Congress has 'affirmatively and unmistakably instructed' the statute in question to apply to foreign conduct.[43] Second, each of the particular predicate offences the Court used as examples does contain an express statement as to its application to foreign conduct. Third, in concluding this part of its decision, the Court went out of its way to describe RICO's 'unique' structure, characterising it as 'the *rare* statute that clearly evidences extraterritorial effect despite lacking an express statement of extraterritoriality.'[44] Overall, the decision supports the Court's recent move toward a robust and restrictive interpretation of the presumption against extraterritoriality.

B. To RICO's Private Cause of Action

In the second part of its decision, the Supreme Court turned to what it characterised as a separate question: whether the portion of RICO creating a private cause of action had extraterritorial effect – that is, whether it permitted a private plaintiff to recover for injuries suffered outside the United States. On this question, the Court divided 4-3.

The civil remedies section of RICO creates a private right of action allowing '[a]ny person injured in his business or property by reason of a violation of section 1962' to recover treble damages for the resulting harm.[45] In addressing this provision, the Court expressed its concern that 'providing a private civil remedy for foreign conduct creates a potential for international friction beyond that presented by merely applying US

---

40 'We therefore conclude that RICO applies to *some* foreign racketeering activity. A violation of § 1962 may be based on a pattern of racketeering that includes predicate offenses committed abroad, provided that each of those offenses violates a predicate statute that is itself extraterritorial.' 136 S.Ct. [2103] (emphasis added).

41 'RICO's extraterritorial effect is pegged to the extraterritorial judgments Congress has made in the predicate statutes …' 136 S.Ct. [2105]. The Court went on to state that in claims based on predicates with extraterritorial reach, RICO applies to *all* partly or wholly foreign patterns of racketeering. Ibid. at 2104. It therefore rejected RJR's argument that, even if it applies to extraterritorial conduct, RICO does not reach the activities of foreign rather than domestic enterprises. Ibid. at 2103–05.

42 136 S.Ct. [2102].

43 Ibid. at 2100.

44 Ibid. at 2103 (emphasis added).

45 18 U.S.C. s 1964(c). The section also permits the successful plaintiff to recover costs, including attorneys' fees.

substantive law to that foreign conduct.'[46] In describing the extent of this potential friction, the Court hoisted the European states with their own petard. In previous lawsuits, many European states had filed amicus briefs highlighting various differences between the US system of private enforcement and their own justice systems.[47] They argued that the application of US law to foreign conduct would generate significant conflict and undermine their sovereignty. In *RJR*, the Court quoted from several of these opinions, reading back to the European states the objections they had previously raised.[48]

It is critical to note that the Court ignored two important differences between the cases in which those arguments had been made and *RJR*. First, as the European Community pointed out, those concerns had been raised in the context of litigation initiated by private plaintiffs – who would be unlikely to 'exercise the type of self-restraint or demonstrate the requisite sensitivity to the concerns of foreign governments' expected in actions initiated by public regulators.[49] Indeed, many of those cases involved efforts by a state's own citizens (as investors in a securities case, for instance, or as purchasers in an antitrust case) to 'bypass' the remedial scheme of their home jurisdiction in favour of a more attractive US forum. In this case, the European Community argued, there was no such risk, since the plaintiffs were the foreign countries themselves. The Court rejected this argument as an invitation to create a 'double standard.'[50] Because the rule it adopted would henceforth govern suits by private as well as governmental plaintiffs, the Court concluded, it could not overlook the potential for friction created by private actions under RICO.

Second, the focus of the European states' previous objections was the application of US law to conduct occurring either entirely or primarily in a foreign jurisdiction – and, frequently, involving a foreign defendant. As Justice Ginsburg points out in her dissent, *RJR* looks entirely different: '[a]ll defendants are US corporations, headquartered in the United States, charged with a pattern of racketeering activity directed and managed from the United States, involving conduct occurring in the United States. ... In short, this case has the United States written all over it.'[51] Given the location of the conduct and the nationality of the defendants, applying US law in this case would have been well within the limits of customary international law on jurisdiction and therefore

---

46 136 S.Ct. [2106].

47 For instance, the preference for public rather than private enforcement of economic laws, or the general policy against treble damages. See 136 S.Ct. [2107] (summarising the arguments made in these briefs).

48 Ibid. at 2106–08.

49 Ibid. at 2117, n. 9 (quoting one of the amicus briefs).

50 Ibid. at 2108.

51 Ibid. at 2114–15 (Ginsburg, J., dissenting). In this passage, Justice Ginsburg echoes a statement she made during oral argument in the *Morrison* case: 'I mean, this case is Australian plaintiff, Australian defendant, shares purchased in Australia. It has "Australia" written all over it.' Oral Argument at 7:21–23, *Morrison v. Nat'l Australia Bank*, 561 U.S. 247 (2010), No. 08-1191.

unlikely to cause international friction. The majority opinion makes one oblique reference to this distinction,[52] but otherwise ignores it.

Having identified the particular form of international discord that private enforcement may create, the Court turned once again to the presumption against extraterritoriality, stating that where the risk of friction is evident, the need to 'enforce' the presumption is particularly strong.[53] It concluded that although the presumption had been overcome with respect to RICO's substantive provisions, it must nevertheless be applied *separately* to the provision creating a private cause of action. In justifying this conclusion, the Court said something quite surprising about the presumption against extraterritoriality: it stated that the presumption must be applied to any statute 'regardless of whether [it] regulates conduct, affords relief, or merely confers jurisdiction.'[54]

This is a dubious proposition. First, it represents a startling expansion of the presumption's scope. That doctrine has traditionally been understood to concern the conduct to which federal statutes apply; its own sphere of application, accordingly, was limited to conduct-regulating rules. *Kiobel* already represented a significant departure from this approach in that it applied the presumption to claims brought under a jurisdictional statute, the Alien Tort Statute (ATS).[55] In that case, however, the Court offered a justification for applying the presumption to that particular statute: applying the ATS requires courts to recognise substantive causes of action based on international-law norms, and thus creates the same danger of 'unwarranted judicial interference in the conduct of foreign policy' that conduct-regulating statutes do.[56] *RJR* goes much further. Second, it sweeps far too broadly. To apply the presumption against extraterritoriality to general jurisdictional statutes, for instance, would deprive federal courts of subject-matter jurisdiction Congress clearly intends them to enjoy.[57] Third, as *RJR* itself demonstrates, the Court seems to envision that the presumption can be applied piecemeal to separate sections of federal statutes.

To apply the presumption separately to sub-provisions of substantive statutes with extraterritorial effect – as in *RJR* itself – is likely to frustrate congressional intent. Many statutes contain sections creating private rights of action. Consider, for example, the laws on employment discrimination. Following the Supreme Court's holding in *EEOC v. Arabian American Oil Co.*[58] that Title VII lacked extraterritorial effect, Congress amended that law to include the 'clear statement' the Court sought: in the

---

[52] 'This is not to say that friction would necessarily result in every case, or that Congress would violate international law by permitting such suits.' 136 S.Ct. [2107].

[53] Ibid. at 2107.

[54] Ibid. at 2101.

[55] *Kiobel*, 133 S.Ct. [1664].

[56] Ibid. Even so, as commentators at the time pointed out, the Court's rationale in this regard was incompatible with its own distinction in *Morrison* between subject-matter jurisdiction and legislative jurisdiction under the securities laws. See, e.g., Anthony Colangelo, '*Kiobel*: Muddling the Distinction Between Prescriptive and Adjudicative Jurisdiction' (2013) 28 *Md. J. Int'l L.* 65.

[57] William Dodge, 'The Presumption Against Extraterritoriality Still Does Not Apply to Jurisdictional Statutes' *Opinio Juris* (1 July 2016) <opiniojuris.org/2016/07/01/32658/> accessed 14 April 2018.

[58] *EEOC v. Arabian American Oil Co.*, 499 U.S. 244 (1991).

portion of the law defining covered employment relationships, Congress clarified that the law protects US citizens employed abroad.[59] Yet, the provisions that allow the victims of intentional employment discrimination to sue for compensatory and punitive damages (contained in other sections of Title VII as well as in the Civil Rights Act of 1991) do not contain a separate statement that they apply extraterritorially. Surely, though, Congress intended that remedy to be available to any covered employee harmed by intentional discrimination, not just those whose injury is suffered within the United States.

Nevertheless, having concluded that the presumption must be applied separately to the section of RICO creating a private cause of action, the Court turned to Section 1964(c). This section provides simply that 'any person injured in his business or property' by a violation of the substantive provisions of RICO may assert a cause of action. Although it recognized 'any' as a term that 'ordinarily connotes breadth,' the Court held that use of that term failed to rebut the presumption against extraterritoriality.[60] Similarly, it concluded, the unqualified reference to 'business or property' failed to communicate Congressional intent that business or property interests located outside the United States would be protected by the private cause of action. Stating that '[n]othing in § 1964(c) provides a clear indication that Congress intended to create a private right of action for injuries suffered outside of the United States,' it held that RICO creates a cause of action only for *domestic* injury to business or property.[61] Because the European Community's injuries were suffered overseas,[62] it was barred from recovering for those injuries.

4. JURISDICTIONAL CONFLICT AND THE PRESUMPTION AGAINST EXTRATERRITORIALITY

As Justice *Ginsburg* noted in her dissent, the majority could have used other means to address the threat of international discord that private enforcement of RICO creates. The presumption against extraterritoriality is just one of many tools traditionally used to deal with jurisdictional conflict in cross-border disputes – others being, for example, the *Charming Betsy* presumption that ambiguous statutes should be interpreted in accordance with international law,[63] the doctrine of *forum non conveniens*, and comity. Standing alone, the presumption is not well suited to deal with all instances of conflict. Indeed, in both *Kiobel* and *RJR*, some of the Justices sketched out an alternative path. In his concurring opinion in *Kiobel*, Justice Breyer pointed out that the ATS 'was

---

59 42 U.S.C. s 2000e(f).

60 136 S.Ct. [2108].

61 Ibid. at 2111.

62 As the Court notes, the European Community had waived any claims based on domestic injuries. Ibid.

63 See *Murray v. Schooner Charming Betsy*, 6 U.S. (2 Cranch) 64 (1804) [118] (establishing a presumption that 'an act of congress ought never to be construed to violate the law of nations if any other possible construction remains.')

enacted with "foreign matters" in mind.'[64] As a result, in his view, the presumption – which reflects the understanding that Congress ordinarily legislates with domestic matters in mind – 'does not work well' in that context.[65] He set out an alternative approach under which the geographic scope of the ATS would be determined by international jurisdictional norms (citing Sections 402–404 of the Restatement (Third) of Foreign Relations Law), and any international friction resulting from its application would be minimised by recourse to 'limiting principles such as exhaustion, *forum non conveniens*, and comity,' as well as judicial deference to the views of the executive.[66] Justice Ginsburg's dissent in *RJR* takes a similar approach. She notes that '[t]o the extent extraterritorial application of RICO [in private litigation] could give rise to comity concerns not present in this case, those concerns can be met through doctrines that serve to block litigation in US courts of cases more appropriately brought elsewhere.'[67]

RJR was a 4-3 decision, as Justice Sotomayor had recused herself.[68] She (along with Justices Ginsburg and Kagan) joined Justice Breyer's concurring opinion in *Kiobel.* Had she participated in *RJR*, she would presumably have joined Justice Ginsburg's dissent, which rests on similar arguments. At the moment, then, it appears that the eight current Justices[69] are divided, with four supporting a broader analysis that views the presumption as one mechanism – but not the only mechanism – for managing jurisdictional conflict in cross-border cases. Thus, *RJR* may not be the Court's last word on the scope and application of the presumption against extraterritoriality.

14.3 THE IMPLAUSIBILITY OF COORDINATING TRANSBORDER LEGAL EFFECTS OF DOMESTIC STATUTES AND COURTS' DECISIONS BY INTERNATIONAL LAW

Jean d'Aspremont

1. INTRODUCTION

International lawyers like to think of the world as constitutionally organised in spheres of domestic jurisdictions where cross-border legal effects of domestic statutes and courts' decisions are carefully and smoothly coordinated by international law. It is to satisfy this organisational craving that international lawyers have designed a grand and sophisticated doctrine of attribution of prescriptive and adjudicative jurisdiction among

64 *Kiobel*, 133 S.Ct. 1659 (2013) [1672] (Breyer, J., concurring).

65 Ibid.

66 Ibid. at 1673–74.

67 *RJR*, 136 S.Ct. [2115] (Ginsburg, J., dissenting).

68 As a judge on the Second Circuit Court of Appeals, Justice Sotomayor had participated in earlier stages of the lawsuit that did not address RICO's extraterritorial application.

69 At the time of writing, Justice Scalia's successor (Justice Gorsuch) had not yet been appointed.

states. Yet, the debate swirling around the judgment of the United States (hereafter US) Supreme Court in the *Nabisco* case[70] and the controversy about the scope of the traditional presumption against extraterritorial effects of US legislation – which are discussed in this chapter – sheds new light on the very (un)plausibility of a coordination of the cross-border legal effects of domestic statutes and courts' decisions by international law. In fact, as it is shown here, the *Nabisco* case not only shows that international legal considerations have been absent from that debate, but also – and more fundamentally – that extraterritoriality is primarily calibrated along the lines of how successfully the most central constitutional actors of the State(s) concerned vindicate their own views as to the ambit of domestic legislation as well as the role of courts with respect to claims with cross-border elements. In discussing the implications of the *Nabisco* judgment from the perspective of a possible international coordination of cross-border legal effects of domestic statutes and judicial decisions, this chapter simultaneously argues that it is unavailing to approach questions of cross-border effects of domestic statutes and judgments from the perspective of international law and that these questions should be reduced to matters of domestic constitutional law and foreign relations law.

The discussion is structured as follows. After recalling the main features of international lawyers' dream about a constitution-like coordination of cross-border effects of statutes and judicial decisions across spheres of jurisdictions by international law and sketching out some of the central paradigmatic premises of the argument made here (2), this chapter provides a short overview of the *Nabisco* case and the scholarly debate that followed (3). It continues with a few evaluative remarks on the consequences of the recalibration of the presumption against extraterritoriality operated by the Court on this occasion and argues that international law offers no useful vocabulary for the battle between domestic actors as to how debates on cross-border legal effects of domestic statutes and courts' decisions ought to be arbitrated and settled (4).

2. INTERNATIONAL LAWYERS' CONSTITUTIONAL DREAM OF A WORLD ORGANISED IN SPHERES OF DOMESTIC JURISDICTION

It is a commonplace to assert that international law provides for grounds of prescriptive and adjudicative jurisdiction. According to that view, States are prohibited to exercise jurisdiction either through legislative or adjudicative channels unless there is a permissive rule to the contrary, that is a ground of jurisdiction found under international law. Such an international coordination of jurisdiction at the international level is said to reflect customary international law[71] and constitute what is called an 'international

70 *RJR Nabisco, Inc. v. European Community* [2016] 136 S Ct 2090, 195 L Ed 2d 476.

71 Cedric Ryngaert, *Jurisdiction in International Law* (Oxford, Oxford University Press 2008) 21.

law of jurisdiction'.[72] This idea is dominant in international legal scholarship.[73] It also finds some support in the Restatement of the Law (Third) of US Foreign Relations,[74] the case law of the European Court of Justice,[75] or that of the United Kingdom House of Lords.[76] Such a construction has strong constitutionalist overtones, for it conveys the impression that international law operates like a constitutional instrument that defines the competence of all public actors.[77]

It is not the place to revisit the idea of such a coordination of prescriptive and adjudicative jurisdictions by international law and the possibility of positive rules on this matter. This has already been done critically elsewhere.[78] For the sake of this short chapter, it suffices to recall that the doctrine of the grounds of jurisdiction originated in a scholarly systematisation of the main constitutional traditions of States. In fact, it is the 1935 Harvard Research on International Law – which built on US law and case law[79] – that proved most instrumental in the emergence of such a construction.[80] The 1935 Harvard Research built on domestic practice as domestic judges that had been confronted with cases that reach out of a purely domestic context in cases and who had been trying to justify their exercise of jurisdiction. It is these grounds 'invoked' by domestic judges and reported in the work of the 1935 Harvard Research that were subsequently turned into international rules about jurisdiction by international lawyers in order to build an international law framework on jurisdiction.[81]

It is contended here that translating convergences of domestic practices into rules about the distribution and coordination of sphere of jurisdictions and cross-border legal effects by the 1935 Harvard Research constituted an argumentative shortcut that is far from being self-evident. It is true that international law can possibly limit some exercises of public authority by States with a cross-border ambit. In this respect, mention is

---

72 The expression has been used by Ryngaert, see ibid., 1.

73 For a few examples, see John E. Ferry, 'Towards Completing the Charm: The Woodpulp Judgement' (1989) 19 *EIPR* 21; J.-M. Bischoff and R. Kovar, 'L'application du droit communautaire de la concurrence aux entreprises établies à l'extérieur de la communauté' (1975) 102 *JDI* 675; Hannah L. Buxbaum, 'Transnational Regulatory Litigation' (2006) 46 *Va J Int'l L* 251, 304; see Ryngaert (n 71) 21.

74 1 Restatement of the Law (Third) of U.S. Foreign Relations 235-319, paras. 402–23 (1987).

75 *Wood Pulp*, Joined Cases C-89, 104, 114, 116, 117 and 125 to 129/85 [1993] ECRI-1307.

76 See, e.g., *Jones v. Saudi Arabia* [2006] UKHL 26 [34], [2007] 1 AC 270.

77 For instance, Christian Tomuschat claimed in his provisional report to the *Institut de Droit international* that 'International law has one of its primary functions to delimit the areas of competence (or jurisdiction) of all the States in order to ensure peaceful coexistence side by side under the rule of law'. See Christian Tomuschat, 'Provisional Report on Universal Criminal Jurisdiction with Regards to the Crime of Genocide, Crimes Against Humanity and war Crimes' (2005) 71 *Ann Inst Droit Int'l* 128.

78 I have myself ventured in such criticism. See Jean d'Aspremont, 'Multilateral Versus Unilateral Exercises of Universal Criminal Jurisdiction' (2011) 43 *Israel L Rev* 301–29.

79 Ryngaert (n 71) 153.

80 Ibid., 28.

81 Ibid., 25.

sometimes made – albeit unconvincingly – of the 'principle of reasonableness'[82] or the 'abuse of rights' doctrine.[83] It is similarly argued that the principle of non-intervention in internal affairs also provides for some limits to the exercise of jurisdiction – although it is difficult to construe any exercise of prescriptive or adjudicative jurisdiction as a coercive action that would fall within the ambit of the principle of non-intervention.[84] Yet, even if international law were to contain rules that actually limit certain cross-border exercises of public authority, it remains that it would still fall short of a grand constitutional scheme coordinating grounds of jurisdiction and cross-border effects of domestic statutes and judicial decision as the one vindicated by international lawyers. It is argued in the next sections that the *Nabisco* judgment of the US Supreme Court provides a useful heuristic perspective to revisit debates on cross-border effects of statutes and judicial decisions and further challenge international lawyers' constitutional ambitions.

[82] Judge Fitzmaurice in his separate opinion in the *Barcelona Traction* case lent his support to the idea that reasonableness constrains the exercise of jurisdiction. See *Belgium v. Spain* [1970] ICJ 3, 105. The Restatement of the Law elevates it to a principle of public international law ([402]–[403]). Some elements of reasonableness are also enshrined in the abovementioned 2005 Resolution of the Institut de Droit international (n 8 [3d]): 'Any State having custody over an alleged offender, to the extent that it relies solely on universal jurisdiction, should carefully consider and, as appropriate, grant any extradition request addressed to it by a State having a significant link, such as primarily territoriality or nationality, with the crime, the offender, or the victim, provided such State is clearly able and willing to prosecute the alleged offender.'

See also Rosalyn Higgins, 'The Legal Bases of Jurisdiction', in Cecil J. Olmstead (ed.), *Extra-Territorial Application of Laws and Responses Thereto* (Oxford, ESC Publishing 1984) 12; Andreas F. Lowenfeld, *International Litigation and the Quest for Reasonableness: Essays in Private International Law* (Oxford, Oxford University Press 1996) 77.

[83] In his preliminary report to the Institut de Droit international, Tomuschat alluded to the possibility of abuse (n 77). See also Michael Akehurst, 'Jurisdiction in International Law' (1972–73) 46 *Brit Y B Int'l L* 145, 189. It must be acknowledged that the theory of abuse of rights is not totally unprecedented in international law. It usually is applied in the context of international judicial proceedings. See Case Concerning the *Gabcikovo Nagymaros Project (Hungary v. Slovakia)* [1997] ICJ 95, sep op Judge Weeramantry; WTO Appelate Body, 'United States-Import Prohibition of Certain Shrimp and Shrimp Products' (1998) WTO Doc, WT/DS58/AB/R. In the context of substantive rights, see Nicolas Politis, 'Le Problème des limitations de la souveraineté et la théorie de l'abus de droit dans les rapports internationaux' (1925-I) *RCADI* 6; A. C. Kiss, *L'abus de droit en droit international* (Paris, LGDJ 1952); P. J. Kuyper, 'European Community Law and Extraterritoriality: Some Trends and New Developments' (1984) 33 *Int'l Comp L Q* 1012, see especially 1015.

[84] Ryngaert is of the same opinion, see n 71, at 145. See generally Michael Wood and Maziar Jamnejad, 'The Principle of Non-Intervention' (2009) 22 *Leiden J. Int'l L.* 345–81 or Joe Verhoeven, 'Non-intervention: "affaires intérieures" ou "vie privée?' in Michel Virally, *Le droit international au service de la paix et du développement* (Paris, Pedone 1991) 493–500.

3. THE *NABISCO* CASE AND ENSUING SCHOLARLY DEBATES

The substance of the judgment in the *Nabisco* case[85] is summarised above and it is therefore not necessary to provide another snapshot thereof. It suffices to recall that the judgment pertains to the scope of application of the Racketeer Influenced and Corrupt Organizations Act (hereafter RICO), a statute enacted by the US Congress to fight organised crime.[86] Indeed, RICO imposes enhanced criminal penalties and civil liability for offences created by other bodies of law in a context that the statute defines as racketeering.[87] It is on the basis of RICO that the European Union took action against the company RJR for its role in an international money-laundering scheme in Europe with a view to holding it liable under RICO. For its part, RJR sought to dismiss the complaint by claiming that RICO bears no extra-territorial effect and does not apply to racketeering activity occurring beyond the borders of the United States. As summarised above, the US Supreme Court, drawing on the presumption against extraterritoriality of US statutes that had been regularly affirmed in its case law since the 1990s, came to deny any private right of action to the European Union. More precisely, the Court found that the presumption against extraterritoriality has been overcome regarding RICO's substantive provision, but not as far as the provision creating a private cause of action are concerned. It thus came to limit RICO's private right of action provided in Section 1964(c) of RICO to injuries suffered in US territory. In practical terms, the specific spin given to the presumption against extraterritoriality by the Court in this case – and which is meant to be applied by lower courts – curbs the ability of plaintiffs to litigate foreign claims against foreign defendants in US Courts and to deprive foreign plaintiffs of the right to sue in US Courts for harms suffered abroad. As a result, the ability of any private litigants – like the European Union – is limited to injuries suffered in the US territory, unless otherwise explicitly provided by Congress.

At first glance, it can be said that correcting the scope of a statute like RICO by the Supreme Court is, as such, very banal for a high judicial authority. Indeed, adjusting and calibrating the scope of a statute is part of the normal business of high courts. Yet, it is the way in which the Court built its argument in favour of a curbing of the ability of plaintiffs to litigate foreign claims against foreign defendants in US courts, and more specifically, its interpretation of the presumption against extraterritoriality of US Statute, that has drawn the attention of commentators and fuelled controversy; most commentators agreeing that the resort to the presumption against territoriality bears consequences far beyond the restriction of the scope of RICO at stake in *Nabisco*.[88] In this respect, it was found that the specific use of the presumption by the Court goes far beyond the requirements previously set in *Morrison v. National Australia Bank* where the Court satisfied itself with a 'clear indication' of Congress's intent to allow

[85] *RJR Nabisco, Inc v. European Community* [2016] 136 S Ct 2090.

[86] See Racketeer Influenced and Corrupt Organizations Act (RICO) 1970, 18 US Code, c 96.

[87] See the overview of Paul B Stephan, 'Private Litigation as a Foreign Relations Problems' (2016) 110 *ASL* 40, 42.

[88] In the same sense, see Maggie Gardner, 'RJR Nabisco and the Runaway Canon' (2016) 102 *Virginia Law Review* 134, 150.

extraterritoriality.[89] In fact, in *Nabisco*, the Court required an explicit consent to extraterritoriality from Congress. As a result of the judgment in *Nabisco*, a statute must now affirmatively and unmistakably indicate that it applies extraterritorially. What is more, such congressional consent ought not to be general, but specifically ascertained for each provision. Last but not least, the judgment generalises the presumption to all US federal statutes as the presumption is meant to apply 'whether the statute in question regulates conduct, affords relief, or merely confers jurisdiction',[90] which is another significant departure from its earlier case law.[91]

Criticisms of the expansion of the presumption against extraterritoriality vindicated in *Nabisco* abound. For instance, some severe objections have been raised from the perspective of the US Constitution and the separation of powers that has allegedly been jeopardised by the *Nabisco* decision.[92] In this regard, mention has been made of the empowerment of courts as to the definition of the proper scope of litigation in US Courts[93] or the use of the presumption against extraterritoriality to keep an upper hand on Congress.[94] By the same token, it has been said that the limitation to private actions in *Nabisco* will prove very disruptive for jurisdictional provisions.[95] Others have contended that the use of the presumption in *Nabisco* no longer corresponds to a search for Congressional intent, but simply boils down to judges' intervention to bar to extraterritorial effect when they deem it appropriate[96] and 'myopic quest to quash the private right of action in transnational cases'.[97] As far as the search for intent from a constitutional perspective is concerned, it has also been found that it is unrealistic to expect Congress to express its extraterritorial intent for each provision[98] and that extraterritorial intent may be expressed by reference to other statutes having such a scope.[99] It has also been argued that the specific use of the presumption in *Nabisco* is at odds with the rationale behind the construction of the presumption of the 19th

89 *Morrison v. National Australia Bank Ltd* [2010] 561 US 247, 255. See also *Kiobel v. Royal Dutch Petroleum Co.* [2013] 133 S Ct 1659.

90 See (n 70) 1201. See the remarks of Pamela K. Bookman, 'Doubling Down on Litigation Isolationism' (2016) 110 *ASIL* 57, 58.

91 See *Kiobel v. Royal Dutch Petroleum Co.* [2013] 133 S. Ct. 1659. In *Kiobel* the Court reversed several decades of expansive use of Alien Tort Statute litigation that followed *Filartiga v. Pena-Irala* (630 F. 2d 876 (2d Cir. 1980) by applying the presumption against extraterritoriality and finding that the ATS fails to rebut the presumption. *Kiobel* innovated in applying the presumption to the cause of action authorised by a jurisdictional statute. See Ingrid Wuerth, 'Kiobel v. Royal Dutch Petroleum Co.: The Supreme Court and the Alien Tort Statute' (2013) 107 *AJIL* 601; Gardner (n 88) 136–37. See also Pamela K. Bookman, 'Litigation Isolationism' (2015) 67 *Stanford Law Review* 1081.

92 Gardner (n 88) 134.

93 Ibid.

94 Anthony J. Colangelo, 'The Frankenstein's Monster of Extraterritoriality Law' 110 *AJIL Unbound* 51; Gardner (n 88) 134.

95 William S. Dodge, 'The Presumption Against Extraterritoriality Still Does not Apply to Jurisdictional Statutes' *Opinio Juris* (1 July 2016).

96 Gardner (n 88) 142.

97 Colangelo (n 94) 51.

98 Gardner (n 88) 139.

99 Ibid., 140.

century. Indeed, the presumption is said to have been invented by the Supreme Court in *United States v. Palmer* in 1818,[100] by virtue of the Court's assumption that Congress legislates with only domestic concerns in mind and that this construction helps avoiding international friction provoked by US jurisdictional overreach.[101] In this respect, it has been contended that, if the intention of the Supreme Court is to limit the risk of international friction and conflict with foreign law as the Court indicates,[102] resort to other tools may have been more appropriate.

Criticisms have not been limited to the perspective of the US Constitution and the previous case law of the Court. From the vantage point of legal argumentation, it has been stressed that the use of the presumption to deny a right of private action to foreign litigants when the injury occurred abroad did not constitute the only argumentative construction available to the Court. In that sense, calibrating the legal effects of statutes and curbing the possibility of litigation of a 'transnational'[103] character, and especially their extraterritorial effect, could have been carried out through many constructions. The presumption against extraterritoriality is only one of them.[104] Resort could have been equally made to the famous *Charming Betsy* interpretation principle according to which statutes should be interpreted in a way that reconciles them with the international legal obligations of the United States, the doctrine of *forum non conveniens*, or comity, in order to adjust the legal effects of statutes. It is in this context that it has been found that the use of the presumption against extraterritoriality performs the very role of comity and *forum non conveniens*.[105]

The calibration of the presumption against extraterritoriality put forward in *Nabisco* has similarly been deemed harmful for US business operating abroad[106] because such a limitation to private action ignores that commodity markets are now international.[107] In the same vein, it has been contented that denying foreign plaintiffs access to US Courts for the wrongdoing of US nationals fuels foreign resentment and damages the image of the US.[108]

Last but not least, *Nabisco* has been criticised for its 'anti-internationalism' and its alleged 'disengagement with international law'.[109] According to this type of criticism, the Court is said to have ignored that 'we live in a post-national word'[110] and is found

---

100 *US v. Palmer* [1818] 16 US (3 Wheat.) 610 (1818). Colangelo (n 94) 53.

101 For a discussion of the rationale of the presumption, see also the remarks of Carlos M. Vazquez, 'Out-Beale-Ing Beale' (2016) 110 *AJIL Unbound* 68, 69.

102 *RJR Nabisco, Inc.* v *European Community* [2016] 136 S Ct 2090, 2107.

103 The expression is from Bookman (n 90) 57.

104 Hannah L. Buxbaum, 'The Scope and Limitations of the Presumption Against Extraterritoriality' 110 *AJIL Unbound* 64, 65; of Bookman (n 90) 57.

105 This is an argument made by Judge Ginsburg in her dissent. Gardner (n 88) 144.

106 Bookman (n 90) 61.

107 On this point, see the remarks of Stephan (n 87) 40, 41.

108 Colangelo (n 94) 51; Gardner (n 88) 144.

109 Stephen B. Burbank, 'International Civil Litigation in US Courts: Becoming a Paper Tiger?' (2012) 33 *University of Pennsylvania Journal of International Law* 663.

110 Austen L. Parrish, 'Fading Extraterritoriality and Isolationism? Developments in the United States' (2017) 24 *Indiana Journal of Global Legal Studies* 207, 208.

to have disengaged from the broader world.[111] As a result of what is accordingly seen as 'litigation isolationism',[112] the decision in *Nabisco* has been bemoaned for allowing foreign countries to be 'calling the shots',[113] for US and foreign plaintiffs can now be expected to increasingly resort to foreign law and foreign courts to pursue similar cases.

Some of these objections have been extensively debated and met by some counter-arguments. For instance, it has been argued that the Court is not necessarily anti-international or isolationist[114] and denotes no anti-international animus and no anti-internationalist effect.[115] For these scholars, *Nabisco* is simply a decision about the separation of power and federalism.[116] In the same vein, it has been said that the *Nabisco* use of the presumption does not prohibit extraterritorial regulation[117] nor does it bring about a more limited role for national courts.[118] Likewise, it has been said that such interpretation neither prevents incorporation of international norms[119] nor prevents judges from engaging with international law.[120] According to this line of argument, *Nabisco* could even be seen as an 'invitation' to reinvigorate multinational negotiation as extraterritorial statutes have taken the pressure off the US to engage with international lawmaking.[121] For those authors, the decision may actually be read as being more consistent with international law principles' like non-intervention as well as international jurisdictional principles that allegedly prevent adjudication in the absence of a close factual nexus between the dispute and the State seeking to adjudicate it.[122] Similarly, the abovementioned functionalist charge against the *Nabisco* decision as denying the original rationale of the presumption against extraterritoriality has been questioned, for such a criticism is not congruent with the recent use of the presumption in the case law of the US Supreme Court. Indeed, it is counter-argued, after the presumption fell into oblivion in the 20th century – it was not even mentioned in the 1987 Restatement (Third) of Foreign Relations law[123] – it is for the very purpose of curbing litigation with a transnational dimension in US courts that the Supreme Court resuscitated the presumption in the last two decades.

This short section is not the place to evaluate the merits of this great variety of arguments and counter-arguments. Observers can bicker indefinitely – and probably inconclusively – on the question of the most appropriate scope of the presumption against extraterritoriality and the consequences of the interpretation of the Court. It

---

111 Ibid., 209.
112 Bookman (n 91) 1081; Bookman (n 90) 57.
113 Bookman (n 90) 61.
114 Parrish (n 111) 209.
115 Ibid., 224.
116 Ibid., 215.
117 Ibid., 222.
118 Ibid., 220.
119 Ibid., 221.
120 Ibid.
121 Ibid., 222.
122 Ibid., 217.
123 American Law Institute, Restatement (Third) of Foreign Relations Law of the United States, 1987.

would be of no avail to perpetuate such debates here. Instead, the following section focuses on one specific aspect of the decision, namely its alleged *disengagement* with international law and especially with the so-called international law of jurisdiction.

4. THE POLITICS OF ENGAGEMENT WITH THE 'INTERNATIONAL' LAW

It is noteworthy that, whether one approves or disapproves the Supreme Court's take on extraterritoriality in *Nabisco* as it has been sketched out in section 3, very few commentators justified their claim by reference to international lawyers' doctrine of grounds of jurisdiction as was described in section 2. It is submitted in this section that such indifference to international law is not surprising, let alone idiosyncratic. Indeed, according the paradigmatic view developed in section 2, international law does not coordinate the spheres of domestic jurisdiction and the cross-border effects of domestic statutes and judicial decisions. There is accordingly very little that both actors and commentators engaged in the *Nabisco* controversy could extract or gather from international law. Put differently, that Congress could possibly want that its legislation applies to behaviour with foreign elements – whether it is consequential or causal – whilst the Supreme Court wants to discharge US courts of cases with a cross-border dimension is not a debate that international law can resolve or arbitrate. As a result, it can be argued that the *Nabisco* controversy can be seen as boiling down to a mere battle between domestic actors vindicating their own views as to the scope of domestic legislation as well as the role of courts, including whether courtrooms ought to be loaded with claims with cross-border elements. In other words, the contention at the heart of *Nabisco* can be crudely construed as pitting two actors, namely those purporting to give US statutes a cross-border outreach as well as a right of action for foreign claimants and those seeking to keep transnational claims outside US courtrooms, international law therefore providing no useful vocabulary for the articulation of any of such claims. It follows that, in the battle of the outreach of statutes grappling with a transnational phenomena and the content of the docket of courts, international law is simply not the platform on which the domestic actors concerned can fight against one another.

This argument can even be pushed further. It is not only that the debate triggered by the Supreme Court's decision in *Nabisco* cannot be a matter for international law. It is also that the positions that any of these actors take in the debate – like the position of the Supreme Court in the *Nabisco* case – reveal nothing about how the actors concerned situate themselves *vis-à-vis* international law. In this sense, the position of the Supreme Court in the *Nabisco* case cannot plausibly be construed as manifesting any kind of 'disengagement with international law',[124] for international law was not engaged in the first place. Any argument pertaining to some international legal isolationism of sorts or to disrespect for international law is unwarranted.

[124] Burbank (n 109) 663.

That being said, even if the merits of the Supreme Court's position cannot be evaluated from the perspective of international law according to the argument made herein, the *Nabisco* controversy discussed in this chapter continues to raise questions as to the weight with which domestic actors provide themselves in global legal debates. In this respect, it is submitted here that the Supreme Court's decision in *Nabisco* can be seen as potentially debilitating the say of US judges in global legal battles, whether of a criminal, commercial or civil nature. For this reason, the author of these lines is sympathetic to the argument that the *Nabisco* decision can possibly end up obliterating the voices of US judges in global debates while correlatively bolstering the say of foreign judges.[125]

In sum, *Nabisco* cannot be reduced to a disengagement from international law, but simply as a – conscious or unconscious – move by a specific actor in the US constitutional structure that bears the effect of scaling down the weight of US judges in global legal debates. Whether such a stifling of the possible say of US courts in global legal debates is a good or bad thing is not a question that ought to be examined here.

In light of the foregoing, it can be concluded that the judgment of the US Supreme Court in the *Nabisco* case usefully illustrates how domestic actors battle with one another about the outreach of legislation and the content of the docket of courts. More fundamentally, and irrespective of the societal functions of dreams and myths like the constitutional organisation of the world by international law in spheres of jurisdiction, the *Nabisco* controversy is yet another reminder that international law not only falls short of coordinating domestic spheres of jurisdiction among states, but provides no useful vocabulary to understand – let alone fight – the battles about the cross-border outreach of statutes and judicial decisions at the domestic level.

---

125 Bookman (n 90) 61.

15. Beyond the State: how far can rights reach? *Kiobel v. Royal Dutch Petroleum Co.*

15.1 CASE BACKGROUND

Kiobel is a landmark decision, handed down by the United States Supreme Court in 2013, in the field of jurisdiction for corporate human rights violations. The claims here were brought under the Alien Tort Statute, by Esther Kiobel and other Nigerian nationals, in a putative class action against The Shell Petroleum Development Company of Nigeria and other related entities before the United States District Court for the Southern District of New York. It was alleged that the respondents, while operating oil production facilities in the Ogoniland region of the Niger Delta between 1992, were complicit with the Nigerian government's human rights abuses. The crimes consisted of murder, torture, unlawful detention, expropriation and exile of the group of petitioners and their relatives. The District Court dismissed the claims.

Both parties cross-appealed to the US Court of Appeals for the Second Circuit. The question was whether civil liability could be attached to corporations under the law of nations for the purposes of the Alien Tort Statute, which provides that 'the district courts shall have original jurisdiction of any civil action by an alien for a tort only, committed in violation of the law of nations or a treaty of the United States.' On 17 September 2010, the Second Circuit found that claims could not be brought against corporations under the Alien Tort Statute. The petitioners asked the Supreme Court to grant a review of the Second Circuit's decision.

Oral arguments were held on 28 February 2012. However, the case took an unexpected turn when on 5 March 2012, the Supreme Court announced that it would hold an additional hearing on the question 'Whether and under what circumstances the Alien Tort Statute, 28 USC § 1350, allows courts to recognize a cause of action for violations of the law of nations occurring within the territory of a sovereign other than the United States.'

On 17 April 2013, the Supreme Court, in an opinion delivered by Chief Justice John G. Roberts Jr., held that according to a traditional canon of statutory interpretation, there is a presumption against the extraterritorial application of US law. This presumption serves to prevent unintended clashes between US law and the law of other nations. The Court reasoned that nothing within the text, history or purpose of the Alien Tort Statute is of a nature to rebut that presumption. Furthermore, the latter could only be displaced, according to the Court, when claims 'touch and concern the territory of the United States… with sufficient force.' Since the statute did not apply, the Court did not address the question of whether corporations are immune from tort liability for violations of the law of nations.

Case: *Kiobel v. Royal Dutch Petroleum Co.*, 133 S.Ct. 1659 (2013)

15.2 THE DEMISE OF INTERNATIONAL HUMAN RIGHTS LITIGATION IN THE US COURTS?

Patrick Kinsch

1. INTRODUCTION

This note addresses the issues arising under US law in the *Kiobel* case and in the cases having preceded and succeeded it, leaving to the companion note by Professor Marchadier the task of generalising (and, to a certain extent, Europeanising) these issues.[1] It will be seen that the issues that confronted the US courts in dealing with the tersely worded Alien Tort Statute (ATS[2]) were numerous, and that the answers given have always been surprising and at the same time important for the pursuit of remedies for human rights violations. Pursuing theses remedies under universal international law norms in a national forum – the US federal courts – has been proven, by the US Supreme Court's holding in *Kiobel*, as being largely a noble and utopian dream. This does not prevent the case from being a highly instructive case on the importance of private international law for human rights litigation.[3]

2. THE ATS: EUROPEAN SIMPLIFICATIONS AND THE COMPLEXITIES OF US LAW

The ATS has in the past frequently been (mis-)understood, in Europe, as providing for a type of universal civil jurisdiction of the US courts over human rights violations occurred abroad and harmed foreign nationals. In fact, the ATS is not about having 'international jurisdiction' (in the European sense) or about personal jurisdiction (its equivalent in US law in international cases) at all. It is not a statute providing for 'universal civil jurisdiction.'[4] Under US law, personal jurisdiction depends, in ATS proceedings as in other civil proceedings, on compliance with the ordinary rules of civil jurisdiction as laid down by state statute. These may be based on the defendant's residence within the territorial jurisdiction of the court,[5] or (in the case of physical persons) on actual service of process within the jurisdiction on a defendant habitually

---

1 See Marchadier note *infra* at p. 319. The other companion note, by Chris Thomale (*infra* at p. 310) essentially deals with aspects of American law, in a different perspective from that of the present author.

2 For its wording, see the introduction to *Kiobel, supra* at p. 302.

3 On international human rights litigation in national courts, see generally F. Marrella, 'Protection internationale des droits de l'homme et activités des sociétés transnationales' (2016) 385 *Rec. des Cours* 33.

4 On universal civil jurisdiction, see Andreas Bucher, 'La compétence universelle internationale' (2014) 372 *Rec. des Cours* 9.

5 As in the first modern ATS case: *Filartiga v. Pena-Irala*, 630 F.2d 876 (2d Cir. 1980), where the defendant was illegally residing in Brooklyn, New York.

resident abroad but temporarily present in the jurisdiction.[6] As for corporations, and contrary to the halcyon days of the so-called 'doing business' jurisdiction, it is not easy to obtain general jurisdiction of a US court over a foreign corporation in an ATS case.[7] Alternatively, rules of 'specific jurisdiction' may be applicable. These refer to liability-creating behaviour taking place, or producing effects, in the forum and are generally not appropriate for 'foreign cubed' cases, where a foreign plaintiff (an 'alien' within the sense of the ATS) brings proceedings for injuries suffered abroad against a foreign defendant, especially a corporate defendant.

The ATS is jurisdictional in a very different sense: it creates subject matter jurisdiction for the US federal courts, as opposed to the courts of the different States. But it does have another aspect of 'universality' – that of the legal norms which are enforced through ATS lawsuits. As noted in the *Kiobel* opinion, the ATS does not directly regulate conduct or afford relief; it instead allows federal courts to recognise certain causes of action based on sufficiently definite norms of international law.[8] The US Supreme Court cases have started from the assumption that in substance, the *lex fori* applies to ATS proceedings: federal common law applies to enforce international legal norms.[9]

3. THE ATS SAGA: THE RISE OF HUMAN RIGHTS LITIGATION IN US COURTS

The last mentioned aspect explains the fascination that ATS proceedings have always held for human rights lawyers, in particular for international law academics. These proceedings showed that international law truly mattered in practice.[10] But it also explains conservative opposition to the ATS thus construed, which was seen by legal conservatives as a tool for '*unelected federal judges* [to] apply customary [international] law made by *the world community* at the expense of state prerogatives.'[11]

---

[6] *Kadic v. Karadzic*, 70 F.3d 232 (2d Cir. 1995), where Radovan Karadžić had been physically served with process while in Manhattan as an invitee of the United Nations.

[7] *Daimler A.G. v. Bauman*, 134 S. Ct. 746 (2014): see below, section 4.

[8] *Kiobel v. Royal Dutch Petroleum Co.*, 569 U.S. 108, 115 (2013).

[9] *Sosa v. Alvarez-Machain*, 542 U.S. 692 (2004). In contrast, *Filartiga v. Pena-Irala* had tried to distinguish the international law aspect which only arises at level of federal jurisdiction, and the choice of the applicable law, which might be the law of the foreign country where the conduct took place: 630 F.2d 876, 889 (2d Cir. 1980). For criticism of the 'calamitous substantive law approach' by a European PIL legal scholar, see Chris Thomale, 'The Forgotten Discipline of Private International Law: Lessons from *Kiobel v Royal Dutch Petroleum*' (2016) 7 *Transnational Legal Theory* 155 (Part I) and 287 (Part II), 303.

[10] Early enthusiastic articles include Anne-Marie Burley, 'The Alien Tort Statute and the Judiciary Act of 1789: A Badge of Honor' (1989) 83 *AJIL* 461 and Harold Hongju Koh, 'Transnational Public Law Litigation' (1991) 100 *Yale Law Journal* 2347.

[11] Curtis Bradley and Jack Goldsmith, 'Customary International Law as Federal Common Law: A Critique of the Modern Position' (1997) 110 *Harvard Law Review* 815, 868 (emphasis in original). See also Judge Bork's concurrence in *Tel-Oren v. Libyan Arab Republic*, 726 F.2d 774, 808-820 (D.C. Cir. 1984) and Justice Scalia's concurrence in *Sosa v. Alvarez-Machain*, 542 U.S. 692, 750 (2004).

In the courts, the modern history of the ATS started with the 1980 case of *Filartiga v. Pena-Irala*, involving claims for torture and murder against a former Inspector General of Police in Paraguay.[12] While a possible extension of the class of defendants to foreign sovereign States failed before the Supreme Court on grounds of foreign sovereign immunity,[13] the idea of suing (United States or foreign) corporate defendants for complicity in human rights violations committed by foreign governments[14] proved an attractive option, including 'for plaintiff attorneys seeking deep pockets, but it backfired, not least since corporate defendants could – and did – hire the best lawyers money could buy to defend themselves.'[15]

4. THE MORAL (BUT ALSO THE HEGEMONIC) DIMENSION OF ATS LITIGATION

ATS litigation for violation of human rights outside the United States has thus always attracted a coalition: the victims' attorneys (without whom these cases could not be brought in practice), international law specialists in the United States and, increasingly, abroad. Apart from those cases that ended in settlement – the Holocaust cases are perhaps the most prominent of these[16] – relatively few cases have ended in money judgments, and few of them have been enforced.[17] Yet, these cases have had the effect of 'formally holding accountable those responsible and making clear that future perpetrators might face consequences'.[18] They have also served the cause of international law at least superficially, by making it appear relevant before the courts of the foremost power of the Western world.

At the same time, when looked at objectively, the ATS litigation saga was an instance of US hegemony (benevolent hegemony in this case) making claims of universalism.[19] It is quite clear that no one would have thought of bringing a foreign-cubed case for the

---

12 *Filartiga v. Pena-Irala*, 630 F.2d 876 (2d Cir. 1980). See the important *amicus curiae* brief in those proceedings for the United States (at that time, the Carter Administration), 19 ILM 585 (1980).

13 *Argentine Republic v. Amerada Hess Shipping Corp.*, 488 U.S. 428 (1989).

14 The first such case was *John Doe I v Unocal Corp.*, 395 F.3d 932 (9th Cir. 2002).

15 Samuel Moyne, 'Why the Court Was Right About the Alien Tort Statute' *Foreign Affairs* (May 2013).

16 Leora Bilsky, 'Transnational Holocaust Litigation' (2012) 23 *European Journal of International Law* 349.

17 Beth Stephens, 'The Curious History of the Alien Tort Statute' (2014) 89 *Notre Dame Law Review* 1467, 1487–90.

18 Ibid., 1490.

19 See Ugo Mattei and Jeffrey Lena (applying, in their own words, a Gramscian analysis), 'U.S. Jurisdiction Over Conflicts Arising Outside of the United States: Some Hegemonic Implications' (2001) 24 *Hastings International and Comparative Law Review* 381; Ugo Mattei, A Theory of Imperial Law: A Study on U.S. Hegemony and the Latin Resistance' (2003) 10 *Indiana Jounal of Global Legal Studies* 383; see also Horatia Muir Watt, 'Privatisation du contentieux des droits de l'homme et vocation universelle du juge américain: réflexions à partir des actions en justice des victimes de l'holocauste devant les tribunaux des Etats-Unis' 2003 *Revue internationale de droit comparé* 883.

violation of human rights in the courts of countries like, say, Senegal or Venezuela. Such power as the ATS may have had has never been the power of international law as such. It has been the power of that part of the US Government that is embodied in the US court system. The popularity of the ATS in the worldwide community of international human rights activists and international lawyers has always been deeply ambiguous.

5. THE PROBABLE END: *KIOBEL* AND THE PRESUMPTION AGAINST EXTRATERRITORIALITY OF FEDERAL STATUTES

The decision of the Second Circuit Court of Appeals that had adjudicated the *Kiobel* case against the plaintiffs had held that corporate liability is not a norm of customary international law and that, as a consequence, the subject matter jurisdiction of the federal courts over Royal Dutch did not exist.[20] The plaintiffs appealed the dismissal of their suit to the Supreme Court, which agreed to hear the case – presumably because the contrary had been held by other Courts of Appeals on the issue of the applicability of the ATS to corporate liability under international law. The Supreme Court, after having heard initial arguments of the case, ordered the case to be reargued on an additional, and quite different, question: '[w]hether and under what circumstances the [ATS] allows courts to recognize a cause of action for violations of the law of nations occurring within the territory of a sovereign other than the United States.' It then went on to apply that particular presumption used for the purposes of US federal statutory law, the presumption against extraterritoriality. Under that doctrine – which is a canon of statutory construction, not a rule of constitutional law – there is nothing preventing Congress from expressly making a law with extraterritorial applicability. But extraterritoriality cannot be a matter of implication by the courts. It is the political branches of government that are responsible for international relations. The presumption 'serves to protect against unintended clashes between our laws and those of other nations which could result in international discord.'[21]

That is the political function of the presumption against extraterritoriality, which is grounded in separation of powers concerns. The application of the presumption, which normally is applied to statutes regulating conduct abroad, to the ATS, a merely jurisdictional statute, is explained in the opinion of Chief Justice Roberts as follows. There is an implied link, made in earlier case law of the Supreme Court, between the jurisdiction of the federal courts and the applicability of federal common law under the ATS: the ATS may not be a statute regulating conduct, but by providing a cause of action under federal common law to enforce a norm of international law, it has the potential to cause the courts to interfere with the managing of foreign affairs.

The opinion of the Chief Justice does not apply the presumption radically to decree the unavailability of federal subject matter jurisdiction in all cases involving extraterritorial conduct. The formula chosen is that when ATS claims 'touch and concern the

---

20 *Kiobel v. Royal Dutch Petroleum Co.*, 621 F.3d 111 (2d Cir. 2010).

21 *EEOC v. Arabian American Oil Co.*, 499 U.S. 244, 248 (1991). See also *Morrison v. National Australia Bank Ltd.*, 561 U.S. 247 (2010), and other cases.

territory of the United States, they must do so with sufficient force to displace the presumption against extraterritorial application'. At any rate, 'mere corporate presence' in the United States is insufficient.[22] The Kiobel plaintiffs' case fell under the presumption against extraterritoriality of the ATS because it involved a wholly foreign conduct (no part of it having taken place in the United States) and a Dutch company. While the true 'foreign cubed' cases – those that had been thought to justify the ATS's reputation as an instrument of 'universalism' – therefore generally fall outside of the federal courts' jurisdiction, it is far from certain whether the same holds true for "foreign squared" cases: where the defendants are US corporations held accountable for their conduct abroad, it might be said that the 'touch and concern' standard of *Kiobel* is met, although that has been questioned in the post-*Kiobel* case law of the Courts of Appeals.[23] That question is of obvious importance and may be the object of a future decision of the Supreme Court.

Before that, however, the Supreme Court agreed to take on another case on the issue that it had originally planned to review in *Kiobel* before deciding that case on the presumption against extraterritoriality: in the recent case of *Jesner v. Arab Bank, PLC*, it decided that corporate liability (of foreign corporations – the case does not concern the liability of US corporations) is not a norm of customary international law for ATS purposes, or at least that the courts lack the power to declare it to be so in the absence of a clear statement to that effect by the political branches of the United States government: Congress and the President. It was held therefore that foreign corporations can never be defendants in suits brought under the ATS.[24]

A further case, decided by the Supreme Court in 2014, that is highly relevant to such future as international human rights litigation in American courts still may have is the personal jurisdiction case of *Daimler A.G.* v. *Bauman*, decided the year after *Kiobel*.[25] In that case, an ATS claim against a German automobile manufacturer based, *inter alia*, on the conduct of its subsidiary in Argentina during the years of the 'Dirty War' waged by the Argentinian military government was dismissed, this time on grounds of lack of personal jurisdiction of the US court seized. It was held that personal jurisdiction could

22 *Kiobel v. Royal Dutch Petroleum Co.*, 569 U.S. 108, 125 (2013). The opinion ends by saying: '[i]f Congress were to determine otherwise, a statute more specific than the ATS would be required.'

23 In particular the Court of Appeals for the Second Circuit has held that a defendant's citizenship was irrelevant to the presumption against extraterritoriality and that only the place of the conduct was of relevance: *Balintulo v. Daimler AG*, 727 F.3d 174, 190 (2d Cir. 2013).

24 *Jesner v. Arab Bank, PLC*, __ U.S. __ (No. 16-499, 24 April 2018). This was a case against a foreign corporation (a bank incorporated in Jordan) accused of complicity in armed attacks in Israel, the West Bank and the Gaza Strip. The conduct in United States territory that was alleged by the plaintiffs to be relevant was the mere clearing of dollar-denominated transactions through New York. The (radical) disposition given to the case by the Supreme Court rendered unnecessary a decision on the sufficiency of that conduct for the purposes of the 'touch and concern' standard of *Kiobel*.

25 *Daimler A.G. v. Bauman*, 134 S.Ct. 746 (2014).

not be founded simply on the presence in the United States of another US subsidiary.[26] With the end of general jurisdiction based on 'doing business' in the United States, bringing a 'foreign cubed' law suit in a federal court against a foreign corporation became almost impossible (even before it was finally precluded by *Jesner v. Arab Bank, PLC*), except in those rare cases where the relevant conduct on US territory was not only sufficient to meet the 'touch and concern' standard of *Kiobel* for purposes of subject matter jurisdiction, but also sufficient under the (constitutional) due process standard for purposes of personal jurisdiction.

6. NEW BEGINNINGS (I): LITIGATION IN STATE COURTS

The holding of the US Supreme Court in *Kiobel* only applies to the subject matter jurisdiction of the US federal courts. It has no incidence, as we have seen, on the personal jurisdiction of the US courts generally. Therefore litigation in US State courts – the courts of California, of Texas or of New York – is not impacted at all by that ruling. Since neither *Kiobel* nor any other specific aspect of ATS litigation ever touches on issues of personal jurisdiction, the personal jurisdiction rules of the several states will apply, subject however to the federal Constitution's due process restrictions. This is where the impact of *Daimler A.G. v. Bauman* is likely to be felt, for the same restrictions on general jurisdiction that result from that case will apply to the (personal, or 'international') jurisdiction of the State courts.

Assuming that the *Daimler* obstacle can be overcome in some exceptional cases, what will the bringing of proceedings in state courts, not based on the ATS, mean in terms of applicable law? The litigation would be much less prominently about customary international law norms – torture will appear as a tort,[27] subject not to US federal law nor even necessarily to the common law of the forum. Depending on the (State) choice of law rules, the issues that would arise might be subject to the law of the forum, but might also be subject to the foreign law of the place of the human rights violations alleged in the proceedings.[28] The extent to which international law norms are relevant to State court proceedings – as part of the substantive law of the forum, or of its public policy – is likely to become an issue of the same degree of intellectual interest, and at present of greater practical relevance, than the ATS-related discussions of similar issues. A potential defence however, as a State law case in the Court of Appeals for the Ninth Circuit has shown, is the highly politicised defence of 'adjudicatory comity,' under which the courts can be expected to defer to the judgment

[26] The case repeats the holding of *Goodyear Dunlop Tires Operations, S.A. v. Brown*, 564 U.S. 915 (2011) that for purposes of the due process clause of the federal Constitution the corporate defendant against whom general jurisdiction is invoked must be 'essentially at home' in the forum State. Mere 'doing business,' as that concept used to be understood, is insufficient.

[27] Craig Scott (ed.), *Torture as Tort: Comparative Perspectives on the Development of Transnational Human Rights Litigation* (Oxford, Hart Publishing 2001).

[28] See Donald J. Childress, 'The Alien Tort Statute, Federalism, and the Next Wave of International Law Litigation' (2012) 100 *Georgetown Law Journal* 709, 744–45.

of the political branches of government, and in particular the State Department, on the desirability of human rights cases based on conduct abroad going forward.[29]

7. NEW BEGINNINGS (II): HUMAN RIGHTS LITIGATION IN A EUROPEAN FORUM

The other possibility that remains open to victims of corporate involvement in human rights violations is to bring the proceedings outside the United States. If, as is usually the case, suing in the country where the violations were committed is not an option, a lawsuit for the tort of violating human rights can be brought in the country of the headquarters of the corporation involved. That will transform what would appear a 'foreign cubed' case, if brought in a US forum, into a mere 'foreign squared' one, which can then be handled by the traditional instruments of private international law.

Many of the corporations sued in the US courts have been European. A European approach to jurisdiction would be based on the Brussels I Regulation (recast), which provides for jurisdiction of the courts of the domicile of the corporate defendant, without the complications arising from a *forum non conveniens* analysis.[30] Once the 'anchor' defendant is domiciled within the jurisdiction of a European court, other defendants can be joined in the proceedings, and jurisdiction over all the defendants will exist by virtue of the *litisconsortium* among them (article 8(1) of the Regulation, or similar provisions of national law if the joined defendants are not domiciled in the EU). The applicable law would be determined pursuant to the Rome II Regulation on the law applicable to non-contractual obligations. Determining the applicable law would be unspectacular; the Regulation would point, *prima facie*, towards the application of the law of the place where the harm occurred; however, the fundamental conceptions of the law of the forum (including such international law norms as are incorporated into them) would exercise a corrective function through the public policy exception. The case would be handled, in other words, like an ordinary case, which may be preferable to the US way of handling these cases, with direct applicability of international law on the one hand and the ever-present prudential concerns of 'foreign acts of state,' 'political questions' and 'comity,' on the other.[31]

The case of *Kiobel v. Royal Dutch* ultimately failed on jurisdictional grounds because it was brought in the United States; had it been brought in the Netherlands, the Dutch courts might have treated it as they treated the real-world case against Royal Dutch and its Nigerian subsidiary for oil spills brought by Nigerian farmers and fishermen supported by the Dutch branch of Friends of the Earth. The case proceeded to the merits and damages were awarded to the plaintiffs against the Nigerian subsidiary of Royal Dutch.[32]

---

[29] *Mujica v. Airscan, Inc.*, 771 F.3d 580 (9th Cir. 2014).

[30] Case C-281/02, *Owusu*, ECLI:EU:C:2005:120 (ECJ, 1 March 2005).

[31] Some of the latter are the, perhaps regrettable, common heritage of the law of England and of the United States, and may play a role in proceedings in English courts.

[32] See Nicola Jägers, Kantinka Jesse and Jonathan Verschuuren, 'The Future of Corporate Liability for Extraterritorial Human Rights Abuses: The Dutch Case Against Shell' 2014 *AJIL*

Other opinions, it is true, are more skeptical. In Germany in particular – another country whose corporations were not infrequently sued in the US federal courts – the effects of *Kiobel* on human rights tort litigation have already been the object of careful study; it is said in one thoughtful piece that the Rome II Regulation mandates application of the law of the place where this particular tort has been committed; but that if that law provides for unsatisfactory remedies, German law cannot be applied in its stead (public policy, in particular, is said to be unavailable on account of a lack of *Inlandsbeziehung*, the necessary proximity of the facts to the German forum, in cases involving the conduct of German companies in Third World countries).[33] That opinion turns law into a dismal science. It remains to be hoped that it will not be followed by the German courts.

8. CONCLUSION

In the conclusion of her post-*Kiobel* article, 'The Curious History of the Alien Tort Statute,' Beth Stephens writes: 'ATS litigation was never as powerful as its supporters hoped or its opponents feared. But it has been successful as a modest effort to impose some accountability for a small number of human rights violations.'[34] The 30-odd years of transnational ATS litigation from *Filartiga* to *Kiobel* have had an impact on thinking about remedies for violations of human rights. Whether or not this thinking can, in turn, have a lasting effect on practice, remains to be seen.

15.3 THE *KIOBEL* TRAGEDY: MISSED CHANCES FOR CORPORATE SOCIAL RESPONSIBILITY

Chris Thomale

1. INTRODUCTION

Taking stock of the *Kiobel* case before US federal courts, one should remind oneself exactly why it has triggered such close attention and comment worldwide. To be sure, there may be sheer empathy and resentment involved: empathy towards the Nigerian Ogoni tribe having to suffer atrocities, which beyond rape and manslaughter may have amounted to genocide; resentment towards the corporate sector ('Big Capital' and other protagonists), which has been growing since the Global Financial Crisis. However,

Unbound e-36. The case (*Akpan v. Royal Dutch Shell*) is apparently still on appeal. In a partial judgment on appeal, the Gerechtshof Den Haag confirmed jurisdiction against the Nigerian subsidiary on 18 December 2015, ECLI:NL:GHDHA:2015:3586.

33 Gerhard Wagner, 'Haftung für Menschenrechtsverletzungen' (2016) *RabelsZ* 717 (see especially at 744–49). A more optimistic view is that of Marc-Philippe Weller, Luca Kaller and Alix Schulz, 'Haftung deutscher Unternehmen für Menschenrechtsverletzungen im Ausland' (2016) *AcP* 387.

34 Stephens (n 17) 1543.

there is something more substantial behind this attention, namely, a growing awareness and dissatisfaction with the poor status of global corporate social responsibility, multinational corporations seemingly being able to outplay both national and international regulation. From this point of view, the *Kiobel* decisions fly in the face of many hopes and expectations on two grounds.

First, after the Second Circuit Court had decided that the Alien Torts Statute does not extend, *ratione personae*, to corporate legal persons, the US Supreme Court after its second hearing dropped the issue,[35] thereby avoiding an affirmation or refutation of this controversial claim. The gravity of this omission can only be appreciated fully by looking at the Second Circuit Court's reasoning. According to Judge Cabranes, speaking for the majority, it was left for international law to determine, whether it 'extends the scope of liability for a violation of a given norm to the perpetrator being sued, if the defendant is a private actor such as a corporation or an individual.'[36] This goes to show that while on the face of it, the Second Circuit Court was interpreting a federal statute only, in substance, the personal ambit of internal law in and of itself was discussed. In other words: the *Kiobel* case concerned the very existence of corporate social responsibility in international law.

The second criticism goes to the heart of the US Supreme Court's decision. Extending a doctrine first coined with regard to the extra-territorial reach of the Securities Exchange Act of 1934,[37] the Court on the foreign-cubed[38] facts declined jurisdiction. This decision is questionable on ever so many grounds. From a global corporate social responsibility perspective, the main concern is that it represents a huge set-back to unilateral efforts to provide relief for the unavailability of effective *fora* where to challenge corporate actors.

In the note to follow, we will deal with both points, personal ambit and extra-territorial reach.

2. THE CORPORATION AS A SUBJECT OF INTERNATIONAL LAW

It is questionable whether the personal ambit of the Alien Tort Statute raises questions of international law at all. An alternative theory would be that the Statute's reference to 'a tort only, committed in violation of the law of nations or a treaty of the United States'[39] refers to international law only with respect to the rule of conduct, leaving it to US national law to determine whether torts can be attributed to corporations or not.

---

35 See the Transcript of Oral Argument at 23–35 <https://www.supremecourt.gov/oral_arguments/argument_transcripts/2017/16-499_n24m.pdf> accessed 17 April 2018.

36 *Kiobel v. Royal Dutch Petroleum Co* 621 F 3d 111, 126 (2d Cir 2010), affirmed 133 S Ct 1659, 185 L Ed 2d 671 (US 2013), relying on *Sosa v. Alvarez-Machain* 542 US 692, 732 n 20, 124 S Ct 2739, 2761–62, 159 L Ed 2d 718 (2004).

37 *Morrison v. National Australia Bank Ltd* 561 US 247, 130 S Ct 2869, 2878, 177 L Ed 2d 535 (2010).

38 This means: first, foreign plaintiffs, second, foreign defendants and, third, foreign subject matter.

39 28 U S C § 1350.

After all, this wording does 'not distinguish among classes of defendants'[40] just as US common law in general recognises corporate entities as fully-fledged persons, i.e. as legal subjects, being able to hold rights as well as duties.[41] This issue of statutory construction set aside,[42] the claim of the Second Circuit Court's majority that corporations by virtue of their corporate personality as such fall outside the personal scope of public international law, seems far from convincing, as will be shown.

Let us start by appreciating that States themselves are legal persons, meaning that although they are no human beings, they can undoubtedly enjoy rights and duties under public international law. Thus, it can hardly be corporate personality in and of itself, on a theoretical or morphological level, exempting business corporations from international law. Rather, this exemption has to flow from the specific private nature of business corporations. It is precisely within the realm of business law, however, where corporate personality is an optional matter of purposive calculation. This opportunistic nature starts with incorporation as such, but also comprises conglomeration, i.e. building a network of corporate persons forming groups and conglomerates, and choice of law, i.e. the selection of specific places of incorporation in order to profit from regulatory advantages. Hence, in international business more than anywhere else, it seems odd that it should be possible to set aside public international law through mere incorporation. Similar observations have been made before, even in the very context of Alien Tort Statute liability.[43] What is more, significant express authority treating business corporations as subjects, i.e. obligation-bearers, of international law, can be found in the Universal Declaration of Human Rights 1948[44] as well as in certain

---

40 *Argentine Republic v. Amerada Hess Shipping Corp* 488 US 428, 438, 109 S Ct 683, 690, 102 L Ed 2d 818 (1989) (giving the Foreign Sovereign Immunities Act priority with regard to immunity issues despite the absence of an amendment pro tanto to the Alien Tort Statute).

41 See *New York Cent & HRR Co v. US* 212 US 481, 495–96, 29 S Ct 304 US 1909 (holding corporations responsible for criminal conduct); see also *Citizens United v. Federal Election Commission* 558 US 310, 342, 130 S Ct 876, 899, 175 L Ed 2d 753 (2010) (holding that corporations enjoy First Amendment protection); *Burwell v. Hobby Lobby Stores Inc* 134 S Ct 2751 (2014) (considering for-profit corporations entitled under the 1993 Religious Freedom Restoration Act).

42 For further details see Chris Thomale, 'The forgotten discipline of private international law: lessons from Kiobel v Royal Dutch Petroleum – Part 1' (2016) 7 *Transnational Legal Theory* 155, 160 seqq.

43 See *In re Agent Orange Prod Liability Litigation* 373 F Supp 2d 7, 58–59 (EDNY 2005), affirmed sub nomen *Vietnam Assn for Victims of Agent Orange v. Dow Chem Co* 517 F 3d 104 (2d Cir 2008); see also the sarcastic comment by Judge Posner in *Flomo v. Firestone National Rubber Co LLC* 643 F 3d 1013, 1017 (7th Cir 2011): 'So, according to [the defendant], a pirate can be sued under the Alien Tort Statute but not a pirate corporation (Pirates of the Indian Ocean, Inc, with its headquarters and principal place of business in Somalia); … .'

44 'The General Assembly proclaims this Universal Declaration of Human Rights as a common standard of achievement for all peoples and all nations, to the end that every individual and every organ of society, keeping this Declaration constantly in mind, shall strive by teaching and education to promote respect for these rights and freedoms and by progressive measures, national and international, to secure their universal and effective recognition and observance.' (GA res 217A (III), UN Doc A/810 at 71 (1948)).

treaties.[45] Special attention should also be drawn to the fact that the virtual absence of corporate criminal liability at the international level, upon which the Second Circuit Court's majority heavily relied,[46] does not speak to the question of corporate civil liability. This is because constructive hurdles like corporate *mens rea*, corporate guilt and the enforcement stage, where sanctions like incarceration need to be adjusted to the fictitious nature of corporate personality, do not affect corporate civil liability. This civil liability, however, is being 'enforced throughout the world'[47] and at the same time is the only way to avoid a clearly unsustainable result: that for violations of non-derogable international law, corporate 'immunity' exceeds state immunity.[48]

3. EXTRATERRITORIAL JURISDICTION

As mentioned before, the US Supreme Court did not decide *Kiobel* based on the question of corporate civil liability in international law. Rather, the court took a different angle, focusing on the extra-territorial nature of the case. The intellectual approach of the majority, however, was strictly national, one might even say: parochial, simplifying an African-European-American case to a mechanical exercise of statutory construction. Admittedly, the more profound question of international jurisdiction was

---

45 For example: Convention on Civil Liability for Oil Pollution Damage 1969, UNTS 3, Art III; UN Convention on the Law of the Sea 1833, UNTS 3, Art 1371; See also *Presbyterian Church of Sudan v. Talisman Energy Inc* 244 F Supp 2d 289, 316–17 (SDNY 2003); For a more sceptical view see Carlos Manuel Vázquez, 'Direct vs Indirect Obligations of Corporations Under International Law' (2005) 43 *Colum J Transnational L* 927–59 and Markos Karavias, *Corporate Obligations Under International Law* (Oxford, Oxford University Press 2013) 12 seqq.

46 *Kiobel v. Royal Dutch Petroleum Co* 621 F 3d 111, 132 (2d Cir 2010), affirmed 133 S Ct 1659, 185 L Ed 2d 671 (US 2013). See also *Jesner v. Arab Bank, PLC*, 138 S.Ct. 1386, 1400 (U.S., 2018): 'It does not follow, however, that current principles of international law extend liability—civil or criminal—for human-rights violations to corporations or other artificial entities. This is confirmed by the fact that the charters of respective international criminal tribunals often exclude corporations from their jurisdictional reach.'

47 *Kiobel v. Royal Dutch Petroleum Co* 621 F 3d 111, 170 (Leval, J, concurring) (2d Cir 2010), affirmed 133 S Ct 1659, 185 L Ed 2d 671 (US 2013); Similarly: *Flomo v. Firestone Nat Rubber Co LLC* 643 F 3d 1013, 1019 (7th Cir 2011); it should be made clear, however, that there has to be a norm of conduct, which according to its own personal scope extends to civil actors such as corporations at all. Corporations cannot e.g. generally be held accountable for complying with treaty obligations incumbent upon states only; See the recent French case *AFPS and OLP v. Alstom and Veolia*, 22 March 2013, Cour d'appel de Versailles (on charges against the defendant corporations abetting the alleged Israeli occupation of Palestine, holding 'Les sociétés morales de droit privé qui ne sont pas signataires des conventions invoquée, ni destinataires des obligations qui les contiennent, ne sont pas, en conséquence, des sujets de droit international. Dépourvues de la personnalité internationale, elles ne peuvent se voir opposer les différentes normes dont se prévaut l'appelante.'); see for a comparative analysis: M. D. Goldhaber, 'Corporate Human Rights Litigation in Non-US Courts: A Comparative Scorecard' (2013) 3 *UC Irvine Law Review* 127.

48 E. Engle, 'Kiobel v Royal Dutch Petroleum Co: Corporate Liability Under the Alien Torts Statute' (2012) 34 *Hous J Intl L* 499, 512.

briefly alluded to by Justice Breyer, who wanted to seek guidance 'in part by principles and practices of foreign relations law.'[49] Even Justice Breyer, however, despite listing a few exceptions to assuming jurisdiction – namely: exhaustion of local remedies, comity, *forum non conveniens* and the duty not to provide a safe harbor for pirates and other enemies of all mankind – did not take a position as to whether these notions should be regarded as domestic self-restraint driven by political prudence or as binding public international law. This is regrettable, as international jurisdiction, meaning the power of the United States to adjudicate upon a foreign-cubed liability case, seems highly unclear.[50] In fact, the former US state practice under the Alien Torts Statute by its 'unilateral exercise of the function of guardian of international values … has not attracted the approbation of States generally.'[51] Therefore, the US Supreme Court, theoretically, could have based its abstention on the recognition of public international limits of universal civil jurisdiction combined with a presumption of compliance,[52] i.e. construing the Alien Tort Statute such as to yield no title of jurisdiction, whose exercise would be in breach of international law. In *Kiobel*, however, we find little evidence for the Supreme Court's restrictive construction of the Alien Tort Statute being based on considerations of public international law. While the majority entirely avoids it, admittedly, the dissenting opinion of Justice Breyer at least declares to be 'guided in

---

49 *Kiobel v. Royal Dutch Petroleum Co* 133 S Ct 1659, 1671, 185 L Ed 2d 671 (2013).

50 The leading authority is PCIJ, *SS Lotus (France v. Turkey)* [1927] PCIJ Ser A, No 10; Although the PCIJ held therein, considering jurisdiction in general, that every State enjoys 'a wide measure of discretion which is only limited in certain cases by prohibitive rules', this referred to the *kind* of principles of jurisdiction adopted domestically, not to their boundaries at public international law: While a State in its municipal law can avail itself of a 'great variety of rules' not prescribed by International Law, it may still not 'overstep the limits which international law places upon its jurisdiction.' (ibid. at 19); with regard to universal jurisdiction, according to the foregoing reasons a transgression has to be rebuttably presumed. Such public international jurisdiction cannot be taken for granted but has to be shown in state practice amounting to an exceptional permissive rule of customary international law. See D. Donovan and A. Roberts, 'Emerging Recognition of Universal Civil Jurisdiction' (2006) 100 *AJIL* 142, 142–43; Thomale (n 42) 166 seqq.

51 Arrest Warrant of 11 April 2000 (*Democratic Republic of the Congo v. Belgium*), Joint Separate Opinion of Judges Higgins, Kooijmans and Buergenthal, 2002 ICJ Rep 3, 63 (Feb 14), para. 48; Amicus curiae brief by Australia, Switzerland and the United Kingdom in *Sosa* at 6: 'International law does not … recognize universal civil jurisdiction for any category of cases at all …'. This is additionally evidenced in the amicus briefs of Germany, the United Kingdom, the Netherlands and the European Commission in *Kiobel*, arguing for a limitation of the Alien Tort Statute; See also *Tel-Oren v. Libyan Arab Republic* 726 F 2d 774, 781 n 7, 788 (DC Cir 1984) (recognising public international law limits to the exercise of universal jurisdiction).

52 See the long-standing principle, by which 'an act of Congress ought never to be construed to violate the law of nations if any other possible construction remains.'; *Murray v. Schooner Charming Betsy* 6 US (2 Cranch) 64, 118 (1804) (Marshall, CJ); *McCulloch v. Sociedad Nacional de Marineros de Honduras* 372 US 10, 21, 83 S Ct 671, 678, 9 L Ed 2d 547 (1963); See also Restatement (Third) of Foreign Relations Law §114 (1987): 'Where fairly possible, a United States statute is to be construed so as not to conflict with international law or with an international agreement of the United States.'

part by principles and practices of foreign relations law'[53] and urges that 'we should look to international jurisdictional norms to help determine the statute's jurisdictional scope.'[54] Having said that, Justice Breyer relies on §§ 402–404 of the Restatement (Third) of Foreign Relations Law (1987),[55] which concern prescriptive jurisdiction, i.e. essentially the power to legislate – not to adjudicate.[56] The Alien Tort Statute, however, does not legislate on foreign conduct as it in fact presupposes existing norms of conduct at public international law.[57] Rather, it provides a forum to try alleged violations of those preexisting norms of conduct, rendering it a piece of legislation, which – from a public international outside perspective – assumes *adjudicative* jurisdiction. The Alien Tort Statute is 'strictly jurisdictional' in the sense of 'addressing the power of the *courts* to entertain cases concerned with a certain subject.'[58]

So the US Supreme Court in *Kiobel* chose to solve an international case without international law. But the troubles do not stop there, for the so-called presumption against extra-territoriality allows for at least two readings. First, the doctrine may be presuming the sheer empirical fact that Congress usually does not contemplate foreign application of its legislation,[59] which would mean that the presumption equally applies in the absence of international legal conflicts. This was the original meaning coined in the *Morrison* case.[60] The majority in *Kiobel*, however, seems to lean towards a different meaning. According to them, the presumption 'serves to protect against unintended clashes between our laws and those of other nations which could result in international discord.'[61] This purposive account of the presumption led the majority to conclude that piracy, despite taking place abroad and still being contemplated as a historical

[53] *Kiobel v. Royal Dutch Petroleum Co* 133 S Ct 1659, 1671, 185 L Ed 2d 671 (2013) (Breyer, J concurring).

[54] Ibid.

[55] Ibid.

[56] See Restatement (Third) of Foreign Relations Law IV Intro Note (1987).

[57] See text around n 48 above.

[58] *Sosa v. Alvarez-Machain* 542 US 692, 713–14, 124 S Ct 2739, 2755, 159 L Ed 2d 718 (2004), cited by the majority in *Kiobel v. Royal Dutch Petroleum Co* 133 S Ct 1659, 1664, 185 L Ed 2d 671 (2013), emphasis added.

[59] *Smith v. United States* 507 US 197, 204 in n 5, 113 S Ct 1178, 1190, 122 L Ed 2d 548 (1993): 'But the presumption is rooted in a number of considerations, not the least of which is the commonsense notion that Congress generally legislates with domestic concerns in mind.'; *Foley Bros v. Filardo* 336 US 281, 285, 69 S Ct 575, 577, 93 L Ed 680 (1949): 'Congress is primarily concerned with domestic conditions.'

[60] *Morrison v. National Australia Bank Ltd* 561 US 247, 130 S Ct 2869, 2877–78, 177 L Ed 2d 535 (2010): 'The canon or presumption applies regardless of whether there is a risk of conflict between the American statute and a foreign law.'

[61] *Kiobel v. Royal Dutch Petroleum Co* 133 S Ct 1659, 1664, 185 L Ed 2d 671 (2013) citing *EEOC v. Arabian Am Oil Co* 499 US 244, 248, 111 S Ct 1227, 1230, 113 L Ed 2d 274 (1991); See also *Weinberger v. Rossi* 456 US 25, 32, 102 S Ct 1510, 1516, 71 L Ed 2d 715 (1982), linking a presumption against extraterritorial reach directly with weak monism and *Kiobel v. Royal Dutch Petroleum Co* 133 S Ct 1659, 1669, 185 L Ed 2d 671 (2013): 'Moreover, [assuming adjudicative jurisdiction], also applying the law of nations, could hale our citizens into their courts for alleged violations of the law of nations occurring in the United States, or anywhere else in the world. The presumption against extraterritoriality guards against our courts triggering such serious foreign policy consequences, and instead defers such decisions, quite appropriately,

paradigm example of the Alien Tort Statute's substantive scope, does not turn the Alien Tort Statute into an extra-territorial statute:

> piracy typically occurs on the high seas, beyond the territorial jurisdiction of the United States or any other country. … Applying U.S. law to pirates, however, does not typically impose the sovereign will of the United States onto conduct occurring within the territorial jurisdiction of another sovereign, and therefore carries less direct foreign policy consequences.[62]

The cited reasoning fails to recognise basic principles of public international law.[63] In the words of the Court's own minority:

> the majority cannot wish this piracy example away by emphasizing that piracy takes place on the high seas. … That is because the robbery and murder that make up piracy do not normally take place in the water; they take place on a ship. And a ship is like land, in that it falls within the jurisdiction of the nation whose flag it flies.[64]

As a result, the very claim in itself that the Alien Tort Statute should be presumed not cover foreign cases does not find convincing support in the reasoning of the Court. It is hard to avoid the irony: of all statutes, the *Alien* Tort Statute, speaking in the broadest language of any 'violation of the law of nations,' is construed to be limited to US internal affairs. But there is method to the madness: it is the absence of any consideration of public international law leading the majority to a blatant misrepresentation of the international status of ships on the high seas.[65]

It seems understandable why the reasoning of the US Supreme Court's majority was criticised so heavily by commentators. But these formal insufficiencies set aside, can we subscribe to the upshot of all these deliberations, i.e. was the court right to decline jurisdiction in *Kiobel*? This may well be so. In Alien Tort Statute litigation as much as in any transnational litigation, US courts are officially anxious not to interfere with foreign policy by creating international discord.[66] As the Court had observed in an

---

to the political branches.' This line is picked up by recent case law, see notably *Al Shimari v CACI Premier Tech Inc* 758 F 3d 516, 529–30 (4th Cir 2014).

62 *Kiobel v. Royal Dutch Petroleum Co* 133 S Ct 1659, 1667, 185 L Ed 2d 671 (2013).

63 Art 91, 92 United Nations Convention on the Law of the Sea (UNCLOS); See also H. Muir Watt, 'L'Alien Tort Statute devant la Cour Suprême des Etats-Unis' (2013) *Rev crit DIP* 595, 597.

64 *Kiobel v. Royal Dutch Petroleum Co* 133 S Ct 1659, 1672, 185 L Ed 2d 671 (2013) (Breyer, J dissenting).

65 On further misconceptions such as the so-called transitory torts doctrine, see Chris Thomale, 'The forgotten discipline of private international law: lessons from Kiobel v Royal Dutch Petroleum – Part 2' (2016) 7 *Transnational Legal Theory* 287, 302 seqq.

66 See e.g. *Benz v. Compania Naviera Hidalgo SA* 353 US 138, 147, 77 S Ct 699, 704, 1 L Ed 2d 709 (1957); *Sosa v. Alvarez-Machain* 542 US 692, 727, 733 n 21, 124 S Ct 2739, 2763, 159 L Ed 2d 718 (2004); *Kiobel v. Royal Dutch Petroleum Co* 133 S Ct 1659, 1664, 185 L Ed 2d 671 (2013); On the act of state doctrine and its limits see *WS Kirkpatrick & Co Inc v. Envtl Tectonics Corp Intl* 493 US 400, 405, 110 S Ct 701, 704, 107 L Ed 2d 816 (1990); On the related political question doctrine see *Hwang Geum Joo v. Japan* 413 F 3d 45, 48 (DC Cir 2005) and *Al Shimari v. CACI Premier Tech Inc* 758 F 3d 516, 531 (4th Cir 2014), both referring to *Baker v. Carr* 369 US 186, 82 S Ct 691, 7 L Ed 2d 663 (1962).

earlier decision: 'the creation of a private right of action raises issues beyond the mere consideration whether underlying primary conduct should be allowed or not, entailing, for example, a decision to permit enforcement without the check imposed by prosecutorial discretion.'[67] In foreign-cubed cases, the application of the Alien Torts Statute thus seems to encroach upon policy decisions made by foreign countries to either provide or not provide private law enforcement for international crimes committed in their territory, let alone less drastic policy decisions on limitation periods and measure of damages. But is there no legal solution to coordinate such decisions in the sense that if, e.g. Nigeria does provide private law enforcement under certain constraints, such relief can also be given before US federal courts? In fact, there is, but it is yet another aspect completely overlooked in the *Kiobel* case: private international law and choice of law analysis. We can observe an emerging 'universal customary law'[68] of certain choice of law rules. Such consensus is especially noticeable at choice of torts law as pertinent to Alien Tort Statute cases. In Europe and in the United States, personal injury cases are generally governed by the tort law of the legal order of the country in which the harm was suffered, the *locus damni*.[69] Admittedly, US law is less clear insofar as the place where the conduct causing the injury occurred, the *locus delicti commissi*, maintains some importance.[70] The same is true for China, where 'tortious liability is governed by the law of the place of [the] tortious act.'[71] However, this dispute is immaterial for *Kiobel*-like cases, in which *locus damni* and *locus delicti commissi* coincide. As explained in the Commentary to the Restatement (Second) of Conflict of Laws, 'when the injury occurred in a single, clearly ascertainable state and when the conduct which caused the injury also occurred there, that state will usually be

---

67 *Sosa v. Alvarez-Machain* 542 US 692, 727, 124 S Ct 2739, 2763, 159 L Ed 2d 718 (2004).

68 So predicted by Friedrich Carl von Savigny, the founding father of modern European continental choice of law, in 1849: 'A treatise on the conflict of laws, and the limits of their operation in respect of place and time.' (William Guthrie transl, Edinburgh 1869) §360, 92.

69 Europe: Rome II Regulation 2010, Art. 4(1): 'the law applicable to a non-contractual obligation arising out of a tort/delict shall be the law of the country in which the damage occurs …'; United States: Restatement (Second) of Conflict of Laws 1971, §146: 'In an action for a personal injury, the local law of the state where the injury occurred determines the rights and liabilities of the parties' where 'state' denotes any 'territorial unit with a distinct general body of law' (§3).

70 Restatement (Second) of Conflict of Laws 1971, §145(2)(b); A similar intermediate position is taken by Japan: Japanese General Rules of Application of Laws 2006, Art 17; Russia: Russian Civil Code 2003, Art 1219(1) and Switzerland: Swiss Choice of Law Code 2014, Art 133(2).

71 Law of the People's Republic of China on the laws applicable to foreign-related civil relations 2010, Art 44 (translation by Professor LU Song <http://conflictoflaws.net/News/2011/01/PIL-China.pdf>); while Indian law of torts is still rather underdeveloped, K. B. Agrawal and Vandana Singh, *Private International Law in India* (Alphen aan den Rijn, Kluwer Law International 2010) 135 seqq. observe a certain adherence to the old English rule of a combined *lex fori* and *lex loci delicti commissi* approach, according to which a tort is actionable in England only, if it is considered wrongful in both England and the place where it was committed, cf Dicey, *A Digest of the Law of England with Reference to the Conflict of Laws* (2nd edn 1908) 38, 645–54 with further references.

the state of the applicable law with respect to most issues involving the tort.'[72] This rule coincides with the one chosen in the 1948 Federal Tort Claims Act, according to which in tort litigation against the United States, the 'law of the place where the act or omission occurred' applies.[73] The application of the law of the place where the act occurred and the harm was suffered has a compelling rationale as all interests involved point towards the same substantive law: the plaintiff-creditor is protected by the law applicable at 'her' place of harm, which incidentally, in the case of Mrs. Kiobel, also coincides with her nationality, domicile and habitual residence at the time. Likewise, the defendant-debtor is held accountable to tort rules which are in effect where he deliberately conducted his business as much as his alleged wrongful acts. Finally, the local state's interest in controlling behaviour in its sovereign territory is unreservedly respected, as a competing interest of the forum state is not evident.[74] Such interest and margin of discretion of the local state is recognised even in the face of international norms of conduct: 'international law imposes substantive obligations and the individual nations decide how to enforce them.'[75] Given this broad consensus, a better way to reconcile both the plaintiffs' interest to be given a forum and the court's interest not to interfere with foreign policy could have been to hear the case, while at the same time applying Nigerian substantive law on torts.

4. CORPORATE SOCIAL RESPONSIBILITY AFTER *KIOBEL*

When the US Supreme Court rendered its *Kiobel* decision in 2013, the Alien Torts Statute was deemed moribund and so were the prospects of corporate social responsibility. Recent history, however, has shown a growing international consensus, fueled by the UN Guiding Principles on Business and Human Rights of 2011, to strengthen the liability of notably multinational corporations. All we see is a shift of efforts from adjudicative to prescriptive jurisdiction, i.e. while being content to sue corporations at their seat, regulators concentrate on tightening the screws of substantive corporate and

---

72 Restatement (Second) of Conflict of Laws 1971, §145 comm e; See also §146 comm c.

73 28 USCA §1346 (West); See J. Shapiro, 'Choice of Law Under the Federal Tort Claims Act: Richards and Renvio Revisited' (1991–92) 70 *N C L Rev* 641 (arguing that this reference to local law does not include local choice of law); See also *Am Banana Co v. United Fruit Co* 213 US 347, 356, 29 S Ct 511, 512, 53 L Ed 826 (1909) (J Holmes): 'The general and almost universal rule is that the character of an act as lawful or unlawful must be determined wholly by the law of the country where the act is done. ... For another jurisdiction, if it should happen to lay hold of the actor, to treat him according to its own notions rather than those of the place where he did the acts, not only would be unjust, but would be an interference with the authority of another sovereign, contrary to the comity of nations, which the other state concerned justly might resent.'

74 Cf Restatement (Third) of Foreign Relations Law 1987, §403(3).

75 *Flomo v. Firestone Nat Rubber Co LLC* 643 F 3d 1013, 1020 (7th Cir 2011); See also *Sosa v. Alvarez-Machain* 542 US 692, 727, 124 S Ct 2739, 2763, 159 L Ed 2d 718 (2004): 'The creation of a private right of action raises issues beyond the mere consideration whether underlying primary conduct should be allowed or not, entailing, for example, a decision to permit enforcement without the check imposed by prosecutorial discretion.'; *Kiobel v. Royal Dutch Petroleum Co* 621 F 3d 111, 172 (2d Cir 2010) (J Leval, concurring).

torts law in order to hold mother corporations responsible for violations committed by their foreign subsidiaries. This seems convincing, especially in light of the *Kiobel* case. It is difficult to imagine that suing Shell and Royal Dutch Petroleum at their place of incorporation in the UK or the Netherlands should have been any less accessible to the plaintiffs than the New York District Court. Providing a convenient forum does not exert the permission of forum shopping. Conversely, what really troubled US courts has not been the question of jurisdiction in and of itself, but which substantive rules to apply if and once jurisdiction were to be affirmed. In the meantime, a chance for the US Supreme Court to reconsider its *Kiobel* decision has been wasted: In *Jesner v. Arab Bank, PLC*, argued before the Court on 11 October 2017, both issues mentioned above, personal ambit and extra-territorial reach, have been combined. The majority opinion decisively held that 'absent further action from Congress it would be inappropriate for courts to extend ATS liability to foreign corporations.'[76] In effect, we find the understandable hesitance against regulating extra-territorial behaviour and the appropriate judicial deference that follows from that somewhat misdirected towards an immunity privilege for corporate actors. This is to show that *Kiobel* is but an Act in a larger tragedy of US courts declining to use the ATS in order to strengthen international corporate social responsibility.

15.4 EXTRATERRITORIAL APPLICATION OF DOMESTIC STATUTES: TIP-TOEING AROUND THE ISSUE OF INTERNATIONAL COMPETENCE

Fabien Marchadier[77]

The reach of rights is not determined *a priori*. It moves between the different scales of strict territoriality and universality. From an international law perspective, a State is free to adopt or apply within its territory a norm with an extraterritorial dimension,[78] or in a broader sense, a norm which 'is applied outside its territory, from its enacted scope to its concrete enforcement'.[79] More specifically, this relates to the judicial authority of the forum's application of a foreign (general or specific) standard, rule or decision, to a person, act, or object situated abroad. However, does the freedom of States to extend the reach of their own law to situations beyond its territory (that is, to persons, objects, acts or facts) through means provided by its own judicial order, go so far as to imply that no real connection with that State is necessary?

---

[76] *Jesner v. Arab Bank, PLC*, 138 S.Ct. 1386, 1403 (U.S., 2018).

[77] Contribution originally written in French, translated to English by Megan Ma and Leia Shin.

[78] An absolute freedom according to P. Mayer ('Droit international privé et droit international public sous l'angle de la notion de compétence' (1979) *RCDIP* 345 et and 537), the only limit is defined by default and one that contains the exercise of constraint; in comparison to B. Stern ('Quelques observations sur les règles internationales relatives à l'application extraterritoriale du droit' (1986) 32 *AFDI* 7, 20) who, on the contrary, considers that the *Lotus* case subjects States to the reasonableness test in exercising its jurisdiction.

[79] Stern, ibid., 9.

The Supreme Court of the United States in the *Kiobel* decision has answered negatively. It maintained and confirmed its earlier case-law which confines the reach of US laws, regardless of whether they are substantive (such as the federal securities legislation[80]) or procedural (such as the Alien Tort Claims Act;[81] 'ATCA').[82] Cautious to preserve US diplomatic relations and not to hinder the executive and legislative branches in matters of foreign policy,[83] the Court ruled that, absent a clear indication of the contrary, there exists a presumption against extraterritoriality in respect of the laws passed by Congress. According to the majority opinion of the Supreme Court, this presumption was applicable to the claims based on ATCA, meaning that this law does not aim to regulate acts which occur in the territory of other States. Neither the black letter of the ATCA nor its history or purpose were of a nature to reverse this presumption. However, arguably, the arguments presented by the Court in support of this reasoning were neither decisive nor in line with the relevant legal issue (1). Furthermore, on a different register, one may ask why extraterritoriality should be questioned when allowing such extraterritorial application of local standards provides the only solution that can ensure a comprehensive protection of the most fundamental human rights (2)?

1. DISCUSSION OF THE ARGUMENTS IN FAVOUR OF THE PRESUMPTION AGAINST EXTRATERRITORIALITY

The presumption against extraterritoriality is based on grounds such as (A) the weakened interests of the state to rule on situations that are too remote; (B) the principle of international comity; and (C) a reluctance to intervene on diplomatic relations.

A. The Weakened Interests of the State

At first glance, the *Kiobel* judgment appears to belong to a broader group of cases which purport to limit the exercise of a State's normative jurisdiction within the boundary of reasonableness.[84] The situation presented before the Court concerned an individual who claimed enforcement of the rights recognised and protected by that State (although these rights arose out of specific international norms with universal

---

80 *Morrison v. National Australia Bank*, 561 U.S. 247 (2010).

81 *Kiobel v. Royal Dutch Petroleum Co.*, 133 U.S. 1659 (2013).

82 On this movement, see for example, V. Grosswald Curran, 'La jurisprudence récente de la Cour suprême des États-Unis sur l'extraterritorialité et d'autres questions d'importance internationale' (2014) *Dalloz* 2473.

83 This issue was already a central matter in *Sosa* (*Sosa v. Alvarez-Machain*, 542 U.S 692 [2004]). On this argument and its relevance, see C. D. Fabre, 'Réflexions sur l'Alien Tort Statute' (2016) *RSC* 505, §§ 10–11.

84 Approach in which doctrine of *forum non conveniens* is also applied to *personal jurisdiction* (*general or specific*).

application and public policy)[85] through an award of damages for tort, despite the fact that the situation was not of a domestic nature. As a matter of fact, the case had a triple layer of extraneity (foreign-cubed action), given that both the plaintiffs and the defendants were nationals of foreign states and that the wrongful acts were committed abroad (and, moreover, were alleged to violate not domestic or local law but the Law of Nations). The plaintiffs in *Kiobel* were Nigerian nationals, the defendants were two companies respectively incorporated in the Netherlands and England, and the acts took place in Nigeria where the plaintiffs had their residence at the time. From a European perspective, the remoteness of the situation in relation to the court would have justified the same outcome, even when the claim concerned harm suffered from acts of torture committed in foreign territories. In such circumstances, the Court's denial of jurisdiction would probably not result constitute a violation of the individual's right of access to justice.[86]

The majority opinion of the Court further suggests that the United States was not the only eligible forum. Other States may have had a more direct link with the dispute: for instance, the State in which the wrongful acts were committed. Additionally, the Torture Victim Protection Act ('TVPA'),[87] which directly refers to and complements the provisions of ATCA,[88] provides that any review of claims brought before the US court must be subject to the exhaustion of all available and adequate remedies provided by the State of the place of the tort (i.e., torture, extrajudicial killings).

It goes without saying that there must be a sufficient link between the forum and the cause of action. The stronger the link, the less likely it becomes for a State to deny access to its courts. States should always be able to examine whether the quasi-domestic claims brought to its courts are well founded.[89] The requirement is transformed into a simple possibility when that link is weakened. The individual right of access to justice, including and perhaps most importantly in an international context, does not imply an unlimited right to choose a competent court.[90] Meanwhile, it must be noted that foreignness is first and foremost a construct. While the mere presence of a subsidiary in the US may not have been sufficiently significant given that the parent company was established abroad (either in terms of place of business or of place of incorporation),[91] additional factors were present to reduce the distance between the United States and the violence denounced by Esther Kiobel. Perhaps the foreignness of

85 *Sosa v. Alvarez-Machain*, 542 U.S. 692 (2004), that specifies more precisely the norms 'specific, universal and obligatory.'

86 *Naït-Liman v. Switzerland* App n° 51357/07 (ECHR, 15 mars 2018). See F. Marchadier (2018) *RCDIP* 658.

87 See, for example, J. Correale, 'The torture victim protection act: a vital contribution to international Human Rights enforcement or just a nice Gesture?' (1994) 6 *Pace Int'l L. Rev.* 197.

88 See, I. Moulier, 'Observations sur l'Alien Tort Claims Act et ses implications internationales' (2003) 49 *AFDI* 129, 140.

89 *Arlewin v. Sweden* App n° 22302/10 (ECHR, 1 March 2016). See F. Marchadier (2016) *RCDIP* 560.

90 *Bayrak v. Germany* App n° 27935/95 (ECHR, 6 July 2000).

91 Similar to the mere presence of the parent company when the action arises out of the actions of one of its subsidiaries or subcontractors (*Comilog v. Fidèle X* (2017) C. cass. Soc. n°s 15-26737 et 15-26738. See É. Pataut (2018) *RCDIP*).

the matter would have been less debatable if emphasis had been put on the plaintiffs' US residency at the time the US courts were seized with the claims, or their refugee status granted by none other than the United States. Interestingly, the facts in *Kiobel* are analogous to those of the *Naït-Liman* case,[92] whereby the European Court of Human Rights (ECtHR) did not consider it unreasonable that the Swiss courts chose to emphasise the foreignness of the situation (Tunisian nationality of the victim, domiciled in Italy, and tortured by Tunisian government agents in Tunisia), without considering the factors contemporaneous to their claims (plaintiff's residency in Switzerland and his status as a refugee).[93] This type of reasoning, adopted by the US Supreme Court and loosely supported by the ECtHR in Strasbourg,[94] is regrettable considering that the purpose of the claim cannot be reduced to mere monetary compensation for damages. In *Kiobel*, the underlying context is that of corporate torts committed by multinationals who engaged in, or encouraged, significant violations of human rights. ATCA allows a foreign national to bring an action in tort before the US federal courts against perpetrators of violations of customary international law or international treaties signed by the United States. The actions sanctioned under this Act are those that are universally condemned. The decision in *Kiobel* confirmed that acts of torture, genocide, crimes against humanity and other war crimes fall within its scope. The prohibition for such crimes is enshrined as a mandatory international norm, the compliance with which is imposed upon all states.[95] This is the reason why ATCA is frequently associated with the most egregious violations of human rights and is often interpreted as a domestic response to such violations, particularly since *Filartiga*.[96]

On this note, the decision in *Kiobel* provides us with a single answer to the question of the reach of rights – the most restrictive imaginable. If recourse to obtain a domestic sanction against a conduct expressly prohibited by international norms is open to a plaintiff with foreign nationality against a defendant, either a national of the forum or that of another foreign state, it is only to the extent that the conduct in whole or in part occurred in US territory. Therefore, one might say that the Court's answer is marked by a 'strong imprint' of territoriality. Other factors linking the situation to the United States were deemed unimportant. And yet, the domicile of the defendant or the minimum contact (however limited) that the defendant had with the United States might normally have sufficed to justify the exercise of jurisdiction by the US courts, subject to *forum non conveniens*. Nevertheless, these factors will not meet the requirements of the Alien Tort Statute, which determines subject-matter jurisdiction as opposed to the extent of the court's jurisdiction in international context.[97] Victims

---

92 Ibid.

93 Moreover, shortly after the final decision, he acquired Swiss citizenship.

94 In the *Naït-Liman* case, a relatively high threshold was set for determining arbitrariness and unreasonableness.

95 *Belgium v. Spain* (case of Barcelona Traction and Power Company Limited) (1970) ICJ, §§ 33–34.

96 *Filartiga v. Pena-Irala*, 630 F 2nd 876, 880 2nd Circuit 1980.

97 C. Kessedjian, 'Les actions civiles pour violation des droits de l'homme – aspects de droit international privé' (2005) *TCFDIP 2002–2004* 151, 152.

would, therefore, be unable to get compensation for any damage, unless the wrongful act is deemed to have happened on US soil.[98]

B. The Principle of International Comity

The principle of international comity requires that a State does not exceed its jurisdictional purview by imposing its own rules on other States extraterritorially. This principle is clearly present in *Kiobel*, whereby the Supreme Court, by reiterating its decision in *EEOC*,[99] justified the presumption against extraterritoriality based on its role to 'protect against unintended clashes between our laws and those of other nations which could result in international discord'. A broad interpretation of the scope of the Alien Tort Statute would lead to a diminished capacity of the 'judicial authority of the sovereign state, on the territory of which the violations of international law have been committed'.[100] The decision to assume such consequences should be left to the Congress alone: such was the conclusion of the Supreme Court in *Kiobel*. It would have been excessive to apply US law to a corporation based solely on its presence in the United States. The Court even specifies that if Congress wished to extend the applicability of the act to such situations, it should adopt a more specifically tailored legislation than the current Alien Tort Statute, the same way it has dissipated the doubts hovering over the legal regime of acts of torture committed on foreign soil by enactment of the TVPA in 1991.

The Supreme Court has again confirmed the importance of international comity in defining general personal jurisdiction in the case of *Daimler AG v. Bauman*.[101] The case called into question the reasoning of the Ninth Circuit Court of Appeals, which had heavily relied on the circumstances surrounding the case (serious human rights violations committed in Argentina in the 1970s under the military regime) and on the necessity to avoid a denial of justice detrimental to the victims. The Supreme Court pointed to the weak link between the defendant and the State of California. The US courts will not exercise jurisdiction over a German company relying solely on the fact that its subsidiary has made sales in the State of California, especially given that none of the corporate bodies were registered in that state. Any decision to the contrary would have been seen as a disregard of the 'fair play and substantial justice' requirement deriving from the Due Process clause set out in the XIVth Amendment as well as its interpretation in *International Shoe v. Washington*.[102]

The same argument can equally be observed in litigation before the ECtHR. The European Court has ruled on the respect for the jurisdictional immunity of States and the inherent limitation it may impose on the right of access to justice.[103] Similar to the

98 See specifically, U.S. District Court of Massachusetts June 5, 2017 *Sexual Minorities Uganda v. Scott Lively*, which viewed that the presumption against extraterritoriality was not rebutted by defendant's domicile and nationality, since his role was limited to providing rhetoric inciting violence against the LGBT population, without necessarily engaging in direct provocations, financing of such actions or personally taking part.

99 *EEOC v. Arabian American Oil co.*, 499 U.S 244, 248 1991.

100 C. D. Fabre, 'Réflexions sur l'Alien Tort Statute' (2016) *RSC* 505, § 35.

101 *Daimler AG v. Bauman*, 571 U.S. (2014).

102 *International Shoe v. State of Washington*, 326 U.S. 310 (1945).

103 See *Al-Adsani v. United Kingdom*; ibid.

reasoning of the US Supreme Court, the ECtHR sets out a solution neutralising the proportionality test. However, the European Court has not always taken this avenue. In the case of *Naït-Liman*,[104] having considered the remoteness of the situation vis-à-vis the forum, and having regard to Article 6 of the European Convention on Human Rights ('ECHR') on the right to access of justice, the European Court ruled that those courts can indeed decline to exercise their jurisdiction. The underlying rationale was that, in those circumstances, such exercise of jurisdiction would have bordered on excess and unreasonableness, even balanced by the parties' right to a fair trial (the extent of which remains largely uncertain in relation to international jurisdiction).[105] On this note, the European Court stresses that accepting the notion of universal jurisdiction may lead one country to cause undesirable interference in the internal affairs of another (paragraph 127). International comity tolerates a violation of the right of access to justice. Proportionality depends on other factors.

Nonetheless, these numerous rulings are not demonstrative of a set principle. International comity is a vague and imprecise notion without a precise content. In which circumstances would the strict application of territoriality by the forum supersede the requirements of international Comity? How exactly would the extraterritorial reach of laws impact and diminish the authority of another sovereign State, either the one of which the defendant is a national and/or in the territories where the wrongful acts amounting to serious violations of human rights were committed? Theoretically, the latter has no obligation to recognise (and has even less reason to enforce) the decision to be rendered by foreign courts condemning the acts. The enforcing State may simply argue that the foreign judge lacked jurisdiction or that it was contrary to its international public policy, for instance by neglecting the particular circumstances of the local society and the operation of transitional justice which brought peace to society and reconciled its people. Although international comity requires that States shall not be completely oblivious to the judicial activity of its peers, it does not suggest that foreign judgments take effect independently without any kind of control nor does it identify any particular methodologies thereof.

Moreover, foreign sovereign interests could sufficiently be preserved by requiring the victims to first seek recourse in the foreign forum, particularly in that of the state where the wrongful acts were committed. Just as in the case of jurisdiction grounded on the risk of denial of justice (forum of necessity), an action based on TVPA is grounded on the principle of subsidiarity. Even if such principle is not expressed in black letters in the Alien Tort Statute, it can be introduced through the doctrine of *forum non conveniens*.[106] Raising an action abroad could be much more feasible than waiting for a significant change in the political context, either by popular vote or by more or less

---

104 Ibid.

105 See on this topic, L. Sinopoli, *Le droit au procès équitable dans les rapports privés internationaux (recherches sur le champs d'application de l'article 6, § 1 de la CEDH en droit international privé)*, thèse Paris 1, 2000; P. Kinsch, 'Droits de l'homme, droits fondamentaux et droit international privé' (2005) 318 *CCHAIL*; F. Marchadier, *Les objectifs généraux du droit international privé à l'épreuve de la CEDH* (Brussels, Bruylant 2007) 37.

106 Although its application in the context of the ATCA raises serious objections (on this debate, see D. Bureau and H. Muir Watt, *Droit international privé. Tome 1* 4th edn (Paris, PUF 2017) 68).

soft types of revolutions – the collapse of the Soviet Union, or the Arab Spring are the standing proof. Perhaps it may be preferable for a State to put in place other types of reparation or procedures designed to restore the national unity, promote reconciliation and peace, especially in the aftermath of a period of devastation (as in the case of Rwanda, South Africa, South America or Cambodia). Nevertheless, such solutions are not always put in place. In other instances, they may not be conceivable, due to the risk of causing additional human rights violations. The TVPA, like the principle of *forum non conveniens*, therefore sets out the exercise of only the available and adequate recourses. The conditions for invoking a forum of necessity are stricter, in the sense that they require the plaintiff to demonstrate a 'general and persistent'[107] impossibility to take legal action in the foreign state. However, arguably a state of impossibility should be acknowledged when foreign justice is failing, either due to inefficiency of the judicial system[108] or corruption. Is not such impossibility salient when the perpetrators of tort remain in political power or have benefited from an amnesty law which was put in place solely for the purpose of evading prosecution and has never evolved into a reconciliation scheme for society?

C. Reluctance to Intervene on Diplomatic Relations

Amnesty law creates diplomatic tensions. Allowing a legal action without any consideration for foreign law on amnesty will always be met with strong resistance,[109] even when particular types of crime, namely such as torture, are in question and there exists a doubt on the compatibility of such amnesty law with the norms of international and European law.[110] An extraterritorial application of ATCA could give way to one State's claim over adjudicating the events and situations localised in another State, but such a claim is 'riddled with strong foreign policy implications'.[111] The simple act of bringing an action can therefore affect the diplomatic relations between States and can seriously impede the works of the administration to different degrees. Such a hindering effect is also intensified by the fact that the claims lie in the hands of the victims.[112] The privatisation of claims is apparent in civil matters as much as in criminal matters

---

[107] *Israel v. Société NIOC* (2005) C. cass. Civ. 1ère nos 01-13.742 et 02-15.237 Bull. I n° 53 p. 45. See G. Kessler (2005) *JCP G* II-10101; S. Hotte (2005) *Dalloz* 2727; H. Muir Watt (2005) *Rev. arb.* 693; T. Clay (2005) *RCDIP* 140; F. Marchadier (2005) *Ann. dr. eur.* 781.

[108] In comparison to the surprisingly restrictive and formalistic approach of the Cour de Cassation in *Comilog* (préc.) where it refused to equate inefficiency with the denial of justice (comp. L. Favoreu, *Du déni de justice en droit public interne* (Paris, L.G.D.J. 1964)).

[109] On the difficulties created by Amnesty laws in cases of serious violations of human rights, see R. Koering-Joulin, 'De quelques difficultés posées en droit français par la mise en œuvre de la compétence répressive universelle' (2009) *TCFDIP 2006-2008* 49.

[110] *Le Procureur c. Anto Furundzija* (1998) TPIY aff. n° IT-95-17/1-T, §§ 153 et s.

[111] C. D. Fabre, 'Réflexions sur l'Alien Tort Statute' (2016) *RSC* 505, n° 33; *Ould Dah c/ France* App n° 13113/03 (ECHR, 17 March 2009).

[112] The exception of terrorism from jurisdictional immunity has led to a similar phenomenon and has triggered, for this precise reason, a very strong opposition (see for example, D. Gartenstein-Ross, 'A critique of the terrorism exception to the Foreign Sovereign Immunities Act' (2002) 34 *Journal of International Law and Politics* 887).

(a civil action brought within criminal proceedings known as '*constitution de partie civile*'), and opens doors to legal actions by associations.

The harmfulness of such actions and their related impact on diplomatic relations are perhaps not so significant. The privatisation of public claims is an undisputable trend, but it is only partial.[113] Under the French system, the public prosecutor has the exclusive right to bring public actions and to assess the value of bringing an action. A lack of responsiveness on the part of the prosecution would provide an opportunity for the suspect to escape, which would result in a failure of criminal justice.[114] A civil action brought within criminal proceedings ('*constitution de partie civile*') could help overcome the inertia of the prosecution, but will nonetheless be unable to stop the judge in charge from issuing an order of refusal to investigate, or from rendering a decision to dismiss. In any case, an argument derived from the logic of institutional equilibrium leads to a serious confusion of issues. At what point must a court inquire into the impact of its decision on diplomatic relations? In the French perspective, the essence of a judicial decision is that it be rendered in complete independence, free from all influence of the executive power. Therefore the concern over preserving diplomatic relations could never be a justification for trampling the guarantee to a fair trial.[115] Meanwhile, however, it is clear that law and politics are closely interlinked and it would therefore be an illusion to pretend that a clear border demarcates the two: that a court rules on legal grounds and that the law is a notion completely free of all political influence.

On a separate note, there were criticisms of imperialism on the part of the United States and those States which took upon themselves to exercise jurisdiction over acts committed on foreign soil by acknowledging the competence of its courts to hear the claims and by applying its own set of laws. However, given the seriousness of the issues involved – i.e., claims for damages for the most serious violations of fundamental human rights – these accusations seem exaggerated and rather dubious. The criticism could have been relevant, had the standards of protection for the affected rights been those defined by the forum state. Yet, this is not the case in these matters. Application of the Alien Tort Statute opens the possibility to claim damages for violations of only a handful of universal international norms. Most or all of these rights are recognised as *jus cogens*. Also, under any assumption, application of domestic standards would not come as a shock if it concerned the assessment of an act in foreign territories by parties having their centre of interest in the forum.

---

[113] With regard to civil matters, there were instances where diplomatic constraints have heavily influenced the issues before the court, to the detriment of the private parties. (see H. Muir Watt, 'Privatisation du contentieux des droits de l'homme et vocation universelle du juge américain: Réflexions à partir des actions en justice des victimes de l'Holocauste devant les tribunaux des Etats-Unis' (2003) 55 *RIDC* 883).

[114] See the progress of the *Naït-Liman* case recounted in the fact part of the decision by the Court of Strasbourg (Ibid.).

[115] Regarding the interpretation of international treaties that France is a party to, see *Beaumartin c/ France* App n° 15287/89 (ECHR, 24 nov. 1994) and on the assessment of the reciprocity requirement which is decisive in determining their applicability *Chevrol c/France* App. n° 49436/99 (ECHR, 13 Feb. 2003).

In turn, those seeking retribution for humanity are faced with two risks. On one hand, they are not sufficiently involved themselves with the foreign courts, more or less directly. In the history of any and all States exist dark moments and turmoil (slavery, war crimes, torture committed at the occasion of certain historic events – according to the modest and inappropriate expression often used as a synonym for civil war). On the other hand, if the court's jurisdiction is defined too broadly, it would attract victims from the entire world and would then result in a blockage of judicial process, with cases bearing little or no relevance to domestic interests. Considering the interests of the residents of the forum who contribute through tax to the proper functioning of the courts of public service, this signifies an important diversion of public, human and financial resources, not to mention a loss of precious time. Such an issue is not completely inevitable however, and the criticism comes along with solutions. The interests at play in these matters are not strictly foreign. All societies are or should be concerned by a massive violation of human rights. The jurisdiction of courts will never be universal, but subordinate to the existence of a link with the forum. Such a link remains a constant factor in principles dedicated to forum of necessity.[116] Even when the link is weak, there are always mechanisms to check that bringing an action before a particular forum was not coincidental nor a part of a procedural strategy to harass the defendant by dragging the latter to multiple proceedings and/or before an onerous and inconvenient jurisdiction.

2. EXTRATERRITORIALITY IN THE SERVICE OF THE GLOBAL PROTECTION OF THE FUNDAMENTAL HUMAN RIGHTS

As in the case of TVPA, the Alien Tort Statute contributes to ensuring the effectiveness of the most fundamental human rights – the right to life, the right to physical integrity, the right to non-discrimination. Is it acceptable to reduce the reach of a legislation resting on universal rights, when these rights are attributed to mankind by virtue of the status of human being without regard for concepts of nationality, residence and conditions of life – be it men, women or children? It must be noted that the US Supreme Court has defended its disregard of the universality of rights, reasoning that these rights do not impose upon the courts in the US to act. Put differently, according to this line of argument, the reach of rights does not depend solely on the nature of the rights or on the way they have been prescribed. Rights endowed with universal scope would never oblige States, correlatively, to provide courts with universal jurisdiction for the purpose of understanding what constitutes a violation of such rights, and would certainly not demand that States prescribe their universal application without consideration of the existence of a link between the situation and their territory.

This view does not clash with international law, whether in relation to civil remedies or criminal sanctions of international crimes. Setting aside the question of jurisdictional immunity, this view encourages States to define their jurisdictional reach in the widest

[116] V. Rétornaz and B. Volders, 'Le for de nécessité: tableau comparatif et évolutif' (2008) *RCDIP* 225.

manner possible, without ever having to impose a truly universal jurisdiction. Therefore, in France, in all cases where the French court finds itself competent to exercise criminal jurisdiction on the basis of an international convention, the requirement of a minimum link with France comes into play.[117] The presence of the prosecuted individual is obligatory in all cases.[118] Also, quite curiously, it can be observed that the requirement of link intensifies rather than loosens, when facing punishment of crimes as serious as genocide.[119]

Is the approach of the European Court of Human Rights so different from that of the US Supreme Court? When States ratified the ECHR, they did not undertake to respect the rights and liberty proclaimed therein under all circumstances and in all places. They undertook to recognise these rights only in respect of the persons within their respective jurisdiction. While the European Court's approach is essentially territorial, it also holds the potential to extend its reach over the territories of another State.[120] On this particular note, the rights protected by the ECHR appear to possess a high degree of extraterritoriality, supported by public coercion. Wherever the State establishes its authority, it also has an obligation to respect the rights enshrined in the Convention. In contrast, wherever the State's authority weakens, its obligation to respect the ECHR does so too. The Court of Strasbourg does not have the authority to compel third party states nor to impose upon them responsibilities for which they have never signed up. In this respect, they are on an equal footing as the State parties. The Court has said that the ECHR 'does not govern the acts of the third-party states, and does not purport to impose on State parties to impose these norms on third States'.[121] In other words, the ECHR does not govern the entire array of activities of the authorities of the State parties. The fact that the courts of State parties have been seized to deal with a particular claim, even when they are competent to hear such claim, is not sufficient to establish that they are expected to behave in a certain way or to render a decision which is compatible in context with the ECHR. This is the reasoning by which the Court of Strasbourg relieved Great Britain of its obligations in the case of *Al-Adsani*.[122] The case revolved around the allegations of torture in foreign territories (Kuwait) inflicted on a British national (more specifically, the applicant had dual nationalities of Britain and Kuwait) by foreign government agents. The applicant claimed before the Court of Strasbourg that the English court's refusal to examine the merits of his claim was a violation of article 3 (protection against torture) of the Convention. Independently of its

[117] Articles 689-1 and s. of the Code on Criminal Procedure (*Code de procédure pénale*).

[118] On the french situation, see Koering-Joulin (n 109) 49.

[119] The Constitutional Council (Le Conseil Constitutionnel) has not questioned this approach (Déc. n° 2010-612 DC du 5 Août 2010 Loi portant adaptation du droit pénal à l'institution de la Cour pénale internationale). It stipulated that no principle of constitutional value would impose more strongly the pursuit of an individual situated in France than the principle of human dignity. It also acknowledged the principle of equality in context with the specific situations at hand and the degree of discretion that the legislator holds in this regard (pt. 11–16).

[120] On all relevant questions, see F. Sudre et al., *Les grands arrêts de la Cour européenne des droits de l'homme* 8th edn (Paris, PUF 2017) 70.

[121] *Soering c/ Royaume-Uni* App n° 14038/88 (ECHR, 7 July 1989), § 86.

[122] *Al Adsani c/ Royaume-Uni* App n° 35763/97 (ECHR, 21 Nov. 2001). See J.-F. Flauss (2003) *Dalloz* 1246; F. Massias (2002) *RSC* 149.

determination of the issues related to jurisdictional immunity of which Kuwait had conveniently opted out (discussed in more depth with regard to article 6 of the ECHR and the right to access of justice), the Court rejected the claims on the grounds that the prohibition of torture does not have any extraterritorial reach whatsoever. The English courts had not failed in any of their obligations, once the acts were found to have been committed outside of their jurisdiction. The question of who bears the obligation to lead an official investigation into allegations of torture committed by agents of a State then comes with an obvious answer. Investigating the agents of another State would be excluded, since it might be read as a duty to adopt preventive measures that prohibit individuals from engaging in acts of torture. However, in concrete terms, what other measures could a foreign State be expected to take in this regard, besides warning its own nationals of the risks that exist in those States associated with allegations of torture? Therefore, the duty of a State under the Convention to lead a thorough and effective investigation fails in its practical implementation. All of the correlative rights are subject to the strict territoriality of any preventive measures. As a consequence, they require the cooperation of the foreign State where the acts of violation were committed.

This of course is a different issue from that of the provision of damages, or more specifically the obligation to offer recourse through civil action for compensation of damages resulting from acts of torture. Yet, in its decision in *Al-Adsani*, the Court of Strasbourg reached a curious conclusion. The Court begins its analysis with the obligations to investigate and to prevent, which are heavily marked by territoriality, to deduce there onwards the scope of application of an obligation to provide civil damages. In the respect of the latter, extraterritoriality (the fact that the tortious acts took place in foreign territories) disappears through the fact that the proceedings in the forum will lead to a decision in the forum. The question before the court was simply that of the jurisdiction of the British courts to examine a civil action claiming compensation for injuries suffered abroad.

The similitude between *Al-Adsani* and *Kiobel*, and between article 3 of the ECHR and the scope of applicability of the Alien Tort Statute, is actually a misconception. The situation described in *Al-Adsani* was not within its scope, since the acts were exclusively committed by foreigners (a quality that could have been disputed in the case of the applicant, who had dual nationality) and, more importantly, torture cases are governed by a separate text. Recognising the jurisdiction of the US courts would have been much more favourable under TVPA. The act provides recourse to all victims of torture, national or foreigner, and unlike in the case of Alien Tort Statute, there is no doubt over its extraterritorial application. The requirement upon the victim to exhaust all available and adequate remedies within the state of the place of wrongful acts is necessarily present.

One cannot always remain insensible to the context and the nature of the litigation. Clearly, in France, these factors prompted the Cour de Cassation to neutralise the rules of international jurisdiction and the conflict of laws rules in a case known as

Moukarim.[123] Barely one year after the decision in *Siliadin*,[124] by which the European Court of Human Rights found France to be in violation of the Convention, it was indeed unimaginable that the Cour de Cassation would leave a gaping hole in the sanction of domestic slavery situations. In *Moukarim*, the Cour de Cassation adopts a line of reasoning that is as daring as it is unique, to deprive the French rules on private international law of any effect by invoking, not article 4 of the ECHR which prohibits slavery, servitude and forced labour, but the concept of international public policy! The typical role of the public policy exception in private international law is that of preventing the application of foreign norms, general or individual, which are incompatible with the basic principles of French law. However, public policy had the mandate here to exclude the application of French rules on conflict of laws or international jurisdiction when these principles would apply to the detriment of the victims of serious violations of human rights, depriving them of the possibility to seek compensation before French courts under French law. This issue was at the core of the decision. It is unimportant that the centre of gravity of the case was situated in Nigeria (the case involved a British employer with a residence in Nigeria, a Nigerian victim, the employment and the habitual place of work of the employee took place both in Nigeria), once the case was found to have a link (even tenuous) with France (ownership of a residence in France and the victim's presence in France). In this case, international public policy was reduced to a simple and technical cover for a fair solution. Instead, public policy could have been introduced by application of the forum of necessity principle (as grounds for establishing the jurisdiction of a French court), and/or failing such, as an exception justifying the exclusion of Nigerian law, or even through an interpretation of article 4 of the ECHR.[125]

What are the elements that lead to prioritising one right over another? From the perspective of the global protection of fundamental rights, the ECHR aligns the reach of rights along that of the obligations of States, which do not necessarily stop at the borders of the European legal community. The various duties prescribed therein – the duty to ensure that decisions dismissing an individual from the forum do not expose the latter to a serious risk of being treated in a manner contrary to the ECHR in a foreign forum,[126] the duty to assess that a foreign judgment was obtained through fair trial prior to granting exequatur,[127] as well as the duty to recognise the status of an individual

---

[123] *Époux Moukarim c/ Mademoiselle Isopehi* (2006) C. cass. Soc. n° 03-46593. See E. Pataut and P. Hammje (2006) *RCDIP* 856; S. Bollée (2006) *JCP G* II-10121; P. Guiomard (2006) *Dalloz* 1400.

[124] *Siliadin c/ France* App n° 73316/01 (ECHR, 26 July 2005). See D. Roets (2006) *Dalloz* 346; J.-P. Marguénaud (2005) *RTD. civ.* 740.

[125] On this topic, *see* H. Muir Watt, 'Les enjeux de l'affaire Kiobel : le chaînon manquant dans la mise en œuvre de la responsabilité des entreprises multinationales en droit international public et privé' (2013) *TCFDIP 2010-2012* 233, 241.

[126] *Soering c/ Royaume-Uni* App n° 14038/88 (ECHR, 7 July 1989).

[127] *Pellegrini c/ Italie* App n° 30882/96 (ECHR, 20 July 2001). See J.-P. Costa (2002) *RTDH* 263; L. Sinopoli (2002) *Gaz. Pal.* 2002-2-Doctr 1157; L. Christians (2004) *RCDIP* 106; F. Sudre (2002) *JCP G* I-105-7; J.-P. Marguénaud (2001) *RTD civ.* 986; Marchal (2004) *RIDC* 231. – *Avotins c/ Lettonie* App n° 17502/07 (ECHR, gde ch., 20 May 2016). See Burgorgue-Larsen

acquired on foreign soil[128] – all point, albeit to different degrees, to the extraterritoriality of fundamental rights and their potential to address situations occurring in foreign territories.[129]

(2016) *AJDA* 1743 (decision of the chamber of 25 February 2014, s. F. Marchadier (2014) *RCDIP* 679; J.-S. Bergé (2014) *RTDE* 361; C. Picheral (2016) *Rev. UE* 426.

128 *Wagner c/ Luxembourg* App n° 76240/01 (ECHR, 28 June 2007). See J.-F. Flauss (2007) *AJDA* 1918; F. Marchadier (2007) *Dalloz* 2700; P. Courbe et F. Jault-Seseke (2008) *Dalloz* 2008 1507; P. Kinsch (2007) *RCDIP* 807; J.-P. Marguénaud (2007) *RTD civ.* 738; L. D'Avout (2008) *JDI* 5. Comp. European Court of Human Rights, déc., 6 July 2010, *Green et Farhat c/ Malte* App n° 38797/07 (ECHR, dec., 6 July 2010), see L. D'Avout (2011) *RCDIP* 665.

129 Bearing in mind that a situation (reasonably) perceived as very remote from the forum does not require the state to hear it in its courts (such was the judgment of the chamber in the case of *Naït-Liman*, ibid.).

16. Interpretation at cross-purposes: *Dallah v. Pakistan*

16.1 CASE BACKGROUND

This case arises out of a controversy between Dallah Real Estate & Tourism Holding Co ('Dallah') and the Government of Pakistan regarding the validity of an ICC arbitration commenced by Dallah in 1998. Dallah was a Saudi Arabian company that provided services to pilgrims travelling to Saudi Arabia. In 1995, Dallah signed a Memorandum of Understanding with the President of the Islamic Republic of Pakistan, whereby Dallah agreed to build housing for Pakistani pilgrims. In January 1996, the President of Pakistan then established an Awami Hajj Trust ('Trust'), whose principal objective was to facilitate activities related to the pilgrimage. In the same year, the Trust and Dallah concluded a contract for the construction of housing for 45,000 Pakistani pilgrims. The contract referred to the terms that had been previously negotiated with the Government and also contained an arbitration clause, under which the parties agreed to refer all disputes to ICC arbitration in Paris. However, the Government of Pakistan was not a party to this contract. In November 1996, the Trust ceased to exist and the contract was never really executed. As a result, in 1998 Dallah initiated an arbitral proceeding against the Government of Pakistan before the ICC. The tribunal sided with Dallah awarding approximately US$20 million in damages and legal costs. Sitting in Paris, the tribunal composed of distinguished arbitrators (Lord Michael Mustill, Nassim Hasan Shah and Ghaleb Mahmassani) delivered three awards – on jurisdiction, applicable law and on the merits. For the purpose of the present analysis, its first decision on jurisdiction is the most significant, because the tribunal held that it had jurisdiction over the Government of Pakistan, despite the fact that it had not signed the arbitration agreement. The tribunal applied French law and held that the Government of Pakistan was the *alter ego* of the Trust. This meant that the Government was the successor to the Trust in regards to all its rights and obligations under its contract with Dallah, including its consent to an arbitration clause. Dallah then sought the enforcement of the award in England. The Government of Pakistan opposed enforcement by the English courts and simultaneously asked the Paris Court of Appeal to annul the award. In November 2010, the UK Supreme Court, applying French law, refused to enforce the award on the grounds that the arbitral tribunal had incorrectly decided on its jurisdiction over Pakistan. Only a few months later, in February 2011, the Paris Court of Appeal, while also applying French law to the same facts, came to the opposite conclusion and rejected Pakistan's application for setting aside of the ICC award. The (in)famous legacy of this case lies in the conflicting decisions by the English Supreme Court and the Paris Court of Appeals, only four months apart from each other and applying the same law. The decision of the UK Supreme Court was widely criticised for its refusal to stay the enforcement proceedings pending the French court's decision on the annulment of the award.

Case: *Dallah Real Estate & Tourism Holding Co v. Ministry of Religious Affairs, Government of Pakistan* [2010] UKSC 46, 3 November 2010;

Cour d'appel de Paris, 17 February 2011, *Gouvernement du Pakistan – Ministère des Affaires religieuses c. Société Dallah Real Estate and Tourism Holding Company*, n° R/G 09/28533

16.2 JUST PICK ONE? THE REASONS FOR A LAMENTABLE DIVERGENCE

Hayk Kupelyants

1. INTRODUCTION

The saga of *Dallah v. The Government of Pakistan* revolves around a well-trodden problem of contract and third parties. However, it raises more than textbook issues of contractual formation: it raises concerns about the design of the international commercial arbitration framework.

The conflicting decisions in *Dallah* provide a fertile ground for debate on the fragmentation in international commercial arbitration and the decisional harmony across jurisdictions. While at first blush the inconsistency of decisions rendered by the courts of two leading arbitration jurisdictions is disconcerting, a more subtle analysis is required. Two main questions arise: 1) is there anything lamentable in the fact that the English and French courts reached diametrically opposite conclusions? 2) Assuming there is, how do we achieve consistency of decisions in the recognition and enforcement of arbitral awards?

2. OPPOSITE CONCLUSIONS IN THE *DALLAH* SAGA

Turning to the first issue, the starting point is that the task of a court is to apply a correct legal test to the facts of the case. The English courts first found that under section 103(2)(b) of the English Arbitration Act 1996 (reflecting Article V(1)(a) of the New York Convention on the Recognition and Enforcement of Foreign Arbitral Awards of 1958 ('New York Convention')), French law was applicable to assess the Ministry's consent to arbitration and that the French law test required a common intention to be bound by the arbitration agreement. This was indeed common ground between the experts of French law.

Applying this test to the facts of the case, the Supreme Court concluded that no common intention to subject the Government of Pakistan to the arbitration agreement was discernible. Dallah signed the contract with the trust and there was no evidence establishing a common intention necessary to bind the Ministry to the contract and, therefore, the arbitration agreement. Lord Mance further considered that the test applied by the arbitral tribunal was not really consistent with French law: the tribunal applied the test of direct involvement, whereas the correct test under French law was that of common intention. In fact, the test of common intention was more demanding than the test applied by the arbitral tribunal.[1]

It has been argued that the correct legal test under French law is not that of common intention but instead that of 'implication' of a person in the performance of the

---

[1] *Dallah Real Estate and Tourism Holding Company v. The Ministry of Religious Affairs, Government of Pakistan* [2010] UKSC 46, [39]–[40].

contract.[2] This denotes an even lower threshold for identifying consent to arbitration than the 'common intention'. The first point to mention is that, even if the test is different under French law, no blame attaches to the Supreme Court (or indeed lower instances) for applying the test of common intention. English judges were exposed to detailed evidence on the state of affairs in French law and they carefully analysed the relevant French authorities. The (distinguished) experts on French law were cross-examined before Aikens J in the first instance[3] and they agreed that the test under French law is that of the common intention of parties.[4] While, under the English law, the courts may diverge from the common agreement of the parties' experts regarding the content of foreign law,[5] they may only do so based on the evidence produced by the parties: a court cannot conduct its own research into the content of foreign law.

The second point arises from the statement of Lord Mance who, having clarified the test of common intention, noted that: 'It is difficult to conceive that any more relaxed test would be consistent with justice and reasonable commercial expectations, however international the arbitration or transnational the principles applied.'[6] Can this statement of Lord Mance be a reference to English public policy or overriding mandatory norms of English law? The statement refers to the consistency with 'justice', irrespective of how 'international the arbitration or transnational the principles applied' are. Of course, the New York Convention does not contain a reference to the doctrine of public policy in Article V(1)(a) (validity of an international arbitration), but nothing stands in the way of implying a public policy defence into an international convention.[7] If the position in French law is that in the absence of consent, whether express or implicit, a party may be considered bound by an arbitration agreement on the ground of being 'involved' in the negotiations, Lord Mance's statement may be taken to indicate that such position may infringe a principle of English law that a person is only bound by an agreement if he consented to such agreement in one way or another.

Apart from the legal test applicable to the issues of consent, the English and French courts assessed differently the factual matrix of the case, as well.[8] In identifying the consent to the arbitration agreement, the Paris Cour d'appel relied on various indications suggesting that Pakistan was bound by the arbitration clause. First, the Paris Cour d'appel referred to the pre-contractual negotiations and correspondence where the Government of Pakistan acted as the contracting party. It was also indicative for the Court that after the contract was executed, two officials from the Government, with no

---

2 Isabelle Michou, 'Note to Dallah' 2011(2) *JDI* 395, 411.

3 *Dallah Real Estate and Tourism Holding Company v. The Ministry of Religious Affairs, Government of Pakistan* [2008] EWHC 1901 (Comm), [73], [89].

4 Ibid., [85].

5 *Bumper Development Corporation v. Commissioner of Police of the Metropolis* [1991] 1WLR 1362 (CA).

6 *Dallah Real Estate and Tourism Holding Company v. The Ministry of Religious Affairs, Government of Pakistan* [2010] UKSC 46, [18].

7 *Application of the Convention of 1902 Governing the Guardianship of Infants (Netherlands v Sweden)* [1958] ICJ Reports 55.

8 For an English translation, see *Gouvernement de Pakistan, Ministere des Affaires Religieuses v. Société Dallah Real Estate and Tourismes Holding Co.*, Cour d'appel de Paris, 17 Feb. 2011, (2011) XXXVI Yb Comm Arb 590.

liaison to the trust, wrote to Dallah in respect of the pilgrimage services. The Court held that '[n]o reason can justify the intervention of these two state functionaries'. All of this, in the eyes of the Paris Cour d'appel, indicated that the Ministry behaved as the true Pakistani party to the 'economic operation'.

By contrast, Lord Mance found that the Government's involvement in these two respects was 'clear but understandable', and added 'little if any support to the case for saying that, despite the obvious inference to the contrary deriving from the Agreement itself, any party intended or believed that the Government should be or was party to the Agreement'.[9]

It seems that at the heart of the outcomes in both jurisdictions lies the letter from Mr. Lutfullah Mufti, who was the Secretary of the Ministry and *ex officio*, the secretary to the trust. After the trust ceased to exist, he sent a letter to Dallah on the letter-paper of the Ministry to inform Dallah that its conduct had the effect of repudiating the contract and the Ministry accepted such repudiation. The Paris Cour d'Appel considered that the letter showed 'the quality of the Ministry'. The Court then decided to ignore the fact that in 1997, after the letter had been sent, Mr Mufti initiated proceedings against Dallah in the courts of Islamabad but this time in the name of the trust.

Conversely, Lord Collins considered that the use of letterhead was irrelevant since

> the Trust had no separate letterhead and it is plain from the surrounding circumstances, and particularly the way in which the 1997 Pakistan proceedings were commenced on behalf of the Trust, and verified by Mr Mufti, that the letter was written on behalf of the Trust and in ignorance of its dissolution.[10]

For Lord Collins, the initiation of proceedings in Islamabad in the name of the trust was good evidence that the letter was not sent on behalf of the Ministry.

Much criticism has been levelled against the conflicting decisions in *Dallah*. It was often said that the UK Supreme Court did not apply the French law as a French court would have done: it did not look at the case through the prism of French law.[11] While it is true that issues of consent are fact-related, the facts are to be construed according to legal rules. What level of factual consent has to be reached for an arbitration agreement to exist is a mixed issue of law and fact, which requires a legal characterisation of the facts. Further, it is arguable that the law should be understood in a wide manner so as to include any guidance or inclinations of judges.[12] Given how interwoven the legal and factual aspects of the question were, the disparity in the conclusions reached by each court may be a matter for concern.

However, again, no blame should be attached to the English judges. Both Aikens J at first instance and the Supreme Court analysed the facts of the case and applied the legal test, which the French law experts have agreed upon. Lord Collins in particular referred

---

9 *Dallah Real Estate and Tourism Holding Company v. The Ministry of Religious Affairs, Government of Pakistan* [2010] UKSC 46, [44].

10 Ibid., [143].

11 See, e.g., Pierre Mayer, 'Conflicting Decisions in International Commercial Arbitration' (2013) 4(2) *JIDS* 407, 412.

12 *Wall v. Mutuelle de Poitiers Assurances* [2014] EWCA Civ 138 (where French soft law (practices, guidelines and conventions) was treated as part of French positive law).

to the *affaire Pyramids* where a private company signed a contract with an Egyptian state-owned entity to construct a tourist centre near the pyramids. The Egyptian Minister for Tourism endorsed the contract with the phrase 'approved, agreed and ratified' on the last page of the agreement. The Paris Cour d'appel held that the Egyptian Government was not a party to the contract and the arbitration agreement therein, since the words under the Minister's signature were to be read as an indication of the approval by the Minister in his capacity as a supervising authority of the Egyptian tourist sites.[13] The outcome in the *affaire Pyramids* was a good indication that the French courts will not be quick to identify a third party's intention to be bound by a contract.

The complex and ambivalent nature of the facts of the case perhaps explains the divergence in the conclusions of the two courts. The characterisation of the letter from Mr. Mufti is a perfect example of such ambivalence. An official wearing two hats sent a letter to Dallah on the letterhead of the Ministry. However, he then initiated proceedings under the name of an already defunct trust. Reasonable people may disagree on the proper characterisation of this factual pattern. National courts, and arbitral tribunals alike, in the exercise of their procedural discretion, may reach different conclusions on the assessment of facts, even when applying the same legal test.

The fact that French and English courts decided differently is thus perhaps part of the legal process and the application of widely drafted legal provisions or existing legal principles. However, it seems that the problem is more systemic. The jurisdictional disparity, perhaps inevitably, arises from the fragmented design of international arbitration. *Dallah* is merely an infamous and (publicised) example of a situation where the system of international arbitration has manifested its flaws.

3. DECISIONAL HARMONY IN INTERNATIONAL ARBITRATION

In light of the *Dallah* case, one is left perplexed as to how to ensure international harmony of decisions in international arbitration. It may simply be that the decisional harmony is impossible to achieve since every state has exclusive jurisdiction over the enforcement of judgments/awards in its own territory. This is reflected in the New York Convention which recognises the jurisdictional mosaic at the level of recognition and enforcement of awards (with the only (quasi-)exception of arbitral awards set aside at the seat (Article V(1)(e))).

The correction of the system of international arbitration clearly falls beyond the scope of this case comment. However, some tentative suggestions will be made, organised below under four sub-headings.

---

[13] *République Arabe d'Egypte v. Southern Pacific Properties Ltd*, Paris Cour d'appel, 12 July 1984, (1985) 10 Yb Comm Arb 113, 117–18.

A. The Compétence-Compétence Principle

One suggestion could be to vest arbitral tribunals with *compétence-compétence* to decide matters of jurisdiction. Counsel for Dallah proffered a very nuanced position before the UK Supreme Court whereby the courts of the seat may undertake a *de novo* and in-depth review of the findings of the arbitral tribunal, whereas the review of the enforcing courts in other jurisdictions should be limited due to the principle of *compétence-compétence*.[14] Lord Mance was sceptical of this view and cited from *Fouchard, Gaillard and Goldman on International Commercial Arbitration* to the effect that *compétence-compétence* does not result in leaving the question of the arbitrators' jurisdiction in their own hands alone.

Lord Mance also considered that Articles V(1)(e) and VI of the New York Convention did not have the effect of vesting *compétence-compétence* in the arbitral tribunal or the courts of the seat:

> It is true that Article V(1)(e) of the Convention and s.103(2)(f) of the 1996 Act recognise 'the courts of the country in which, or under the law of which' an award was made as the court where an application to set aside or suspend an award may appropriately be made; and also that Article VI and s.103(5) permit a court in any other country where recognition or enforcement of the award is sought to adjourn, if it considers it proper, pending resolution of any such application. But Article V(1)(a) and s.103(2)(b) are framed as free-standing and categoric alternative grounds to Article V(1)(e) of the Convention and s.103(2)(f) for resisting recognition or enforcement. Neither Article V(1)(a) nor s.103(2)(b) hints at any restriction on the nature of the exercise open, either to the person resisting enforcement or to the court asked to enforce an award, when the validity (sc. existence) of the supposed arbitration agreement is in issue. The onus may be on the person resisting recognition or enforcement, but the language enables such person to do so by proving (or furnishing proof) of the non-existence of any arbitration agreement. This language points strongly to ordinary judicial determination of that issue. Nor do Article VI and s.103(5) contain any suggestion that a person resisting recognition or enforcement in one country has any obligation to seek to set aside the award in the other country where it was made.[15]

Lord Mance was also doubtful of the theoretical confusion which arose from this proposition:

> Yet Miss Heilbron's submissions invoke in one and the same breath a transnational view and a view attaching a special and dominant significance to the law of the seat. They also invite the spectre of dual sets of proceedings, conducted in two different countries (that of the seat and that of enforcement) involving different levels of review in relation to essentially the same issue – whether the award should be enforced in the latter country.[16]

The proposition advanced by Dallah's counsel was perhaps forced by the Supreme Court's earlier refusal to stay the proceedings in favour of the French courts. Once the

---

14 *Dallah Real Estate and Tourism Holding Company v. The Ministry of Religious Affairs, Government of Pakistan* [2010] UKSC 46, [20]–[21].

15 Ibid., [28].

16 Ibid., [27].

prospects of the stay in favour of French courts were eliminated, counsel sought to argue deference for the arbitral tribunals.

Following Lord Mance's pronouncement in Dallah, the extent of deference to the arbitral tribunals or the courts of the seat is limited. It seems that the only avenue for ensuring decisional harmony is at an earlier stage of proceedings – by requesting a stay. English courts (or for that matter any other enforcing court) may consider the possibility of staying their proceedings in favour of the courts of the seat. On 25 January 2010, the UK Supreme Court refused an application to stay its proceedings pending the set aside proceedings in France. The Ministry brought set aside proceedings on 21 December 2009, and on 17 February 2011, the Paris Cour d'appel rendered its decision. A stay of English proceedings could have acted to prevent the decisional inconsistency between the judgments. The reasons for refusing the stay of proceedings are unclear but this case comment will address some of the salient questions.

B. Exclusive Jurisdiction

Before addressing the possibility of staying the proceedings, one needs to decide a preliminary question – whether the enforcing court has exclusive jurisdiction. A stay of proceedings in favour of the courts of the seat seems only possible if the enforcing court does not possess exclusive jurisdiction over the enforcement of arbitral awards in its own territory. If, by contrast, a court enjoys exclusive jurisdiction, a stay of proceedings is not apposite.

This is what Lord Mance seems to have hinted in the following passage:

> Further, what matters, self-evidently, to both parties is the enforceability of the award in the country where enforcement is sought. Since Dallah has chosen to seek to enforce in England, it does not lie well in its mouth to complain that the Government ought to have taken steps in France.[17]

The exclusive jurisdiction of the enforcing court is echoed in the Brussels I Regulation recast on jurisdiction and the recognition and enforcement of judgments in civil and commercial matters ('Brussels Regulation'), which is not applicable to arbitration. Article 24(5) of the Brussels Regulation stipulates that the court of the EU Member State in which the judgment has been or is to be enforced shall have exclusive jurisdiction in proceedings concerned such enforcement.

However, such jurisdiction can be circumscribed by international conventions: Article VI of the New York Convention permits the stay of proceedings if an application for the setting aside or suspension of the award has been made before the courts of the seat. Further, while the English courts may have a special interest in deciding on the enforcement of a foreign arbitral award, the special nature of the relationship between the seat and the arbitration may justify a stay of proceedings in favour of the courts of the seat.

It thus stands to reason that the stay of proceedings in favour of the courts of the seat is clearly conceivable. The issue of the binding effect of the decision of the courts of

---

17 Ibid., [29].

the seat, and the decision to stay proceedings in the anticipation of such decision, may be analysed on two levels: the effect of the set aside decision under the New York Convention and its effect under the national law of the enforcing court.

C. Article VI of the New York Convention

The position under the New York Convention is subject to great debates well known to the reader. Article V(1)(e) (mirrored in section 103(5) of the English Arbitration Act 1996) provides that the enforcing court *may* refuse recognition and enforcement if the award has been set aside by the courts of the seat. The enforcing courts enjoy discretion, evidenced by the use of 'may', to give effect to the set aside by the courts of the seat. Based on this provision some jurisdictions have decided that even if the arbitral award has been set aside, the arbitral award may still be enforced under certain circumstances.[18]

To ensure that effect is given to the decision of the courts of the seat to set aside the arbitral award, Article VI of the New York Convention provides a mechanism for staying the proceedings when there is an application before the courts of the seat. Again, Article VI is not couched in mandatory terms – it merely provides a power to stay the proceedings. Quite how this power is to be exercised is unclear.

While there is no doubt that there is no obligation to seek the setting aside of the award at the seat of the arbitration, once proceedings have been initiated at the place of the seat, Article VI imposes an obligation at the very least to consider the stay of proceedings in favour of the courts of the stay. Albert Jan van den Berg in his classical treatise reasons that

> '[i]n conformity with the division made between the second part of Article V(l)(e) and Article VI, it is likely that the court before which the enforcement is sought will adjourn its decision on enforcement if it is *prima facie* convinced that the request for the setting aside or suspension of the award in the country of origin is not made on account of dilatory tactics, but is based on rather reasonable grounds.[19]

The exercise of discretion is multifactorial. Factors relevant in the exercise of discretion may include the following:

1. Are the proceedings pending before the courts of the seat or some other enforcing court?
2. How well advanced are the proceedings in the court of the seat?
3. When are the proceedings likely to conclude?
4. To what extent is the decision of the court of the seat binding?
5. Will proceeding in the courts of the seat give rise to the breach of natural justice?
6. Other factors relevant to the stay of proceedings in favour of the courts of the seat.

---

[18] For a discussion, see Gary Born, *International Commercial Arbitration* Vol III, 2nd edn (Alphen aan den Rijn, Wolters Kluwer 2014) 3624–34.

[19] Albert Jan van den Berg, *The New York Arbitration Convention of 1958* (Alphen aan den Rijn, Wolters Kluwer 1981) 353.

D. Case Management Stay

In addition to Article VI of the New York Convention, the English courts may stay their proceedings under national law. English courts retain broad case management powers permitting a court to regulate the content and progress of civil litigation so as to achieve the overriding objective of dealing with the case justly (CPR 1.1). To achieve this aim, the court holds a general case management power to stay proceedings (CPR 3.1(2)(f)), which it may exercise when either the parties agree, or the court, of its own initiative, considers that a stay would be appropriate.

In deciding to stay its proceedings, the court will be guided by the imperative of whether 'the outcome of one set of proceedings may have an important effect on the conduct of the other.'[20] It bears emphasis that in English law the court may stay its proceedings to see whether a foreign judgment will be set aside in the courts of the jurisdiction which had issued the judgment.[21]

The proceedings at the seat may reach two outcomes: to set aside the arbitral award or to refuse the application to set aside. Only if both outcomes have 'an important effect' on English proceedings, then one can be reassured that the case may be stayed on case management grounds.

For the first eventuality, Article V(1)(e) allows the enforcing court to resist the enforcement of the arbitral award on the ground that the award was set aside at the seat. It is accepted that the setting aside of the arbitral award at the seat may bind, subject to a residual level of discretion, the courts of the place of enforcement. Much has been written on the subject and this case comment will not expand on the topic.[22]

The difficulty is the haze that overlies the effect of the decision to recognise/enforce or confirm an arbitral award at the seat. Does it have any binding effect on the courts where enforcement proceedings are initiated? Some academic commentary responds in the negative.[23] The old adage *titre exécutoire sur titre exécutoire ne vaut* suggests an answer in the negative: a decision to recognise/enforce or confirm an arbitral award at the place of the seat should bear no consequence for an enforcing court.

This case comment suggests that much can be said in favour of giving effect to the decision at the seat to confirm an arbitral award. While the New York Convention does not mention the possibility of giving effect to judgments at the seat that recognise/enforce or confirm arbitral awards, nothing prevents conferring such effect under

---

20 *Reichhold Norway ASA v. Goldman Sachs International* [2000] C.L.C. 11, 15.

21 *Colt Industries Inc v. Sarlie (No 2)* [1966] 3 All ER 85.

22 For a recent writing on the subject, see Linda Silberman and Nathan Yaffe, 'The US Approach to Recognition And Enforcement of Awards after Set-Asides: The Impact of the Pemex Decision' (2017) 40 *Fordham Int'l L.J.* 799.

23 Lord Collins et al. (eds.), *Dicey, Morris, Collins on the Conflict of Laws* 15th edn (London, Sweet & Maxwell 2012) [16-165] (countenancing the possibility that the English courts may enforce, even under the New York Convention, a judgment of the courts of the seat that recognised/enforced an arbitral award but only in exceptional cases); Linda Silberman and Maxi Scherer, 'Forum Shopping and Post-Award Judgments' in Franco Ferrari (ed.), *Forum Shopping in the International Commercial Arbitration Context* (Berlin, De Gruyter 2013) 313, 329; Maxi Scherer, 'Effects of Foreign Judgments Relating to International Arbitral Awards: Is the "Judgment Route" the Wrong Road?' (2013) 4(3) *JDIS* 587.

national law. Under the English doctrine of issue estoppel, a foreign judgment issued by a competent court and which resolves factual or legal issues in the course of foreign proceedings may bind subsequent English proceedings.[24] Denying issue estoppel effect to the judgments of the seat which confirm or recognise/enforce awards may undermine the case management stay of English proceedings: why wait for the courts of the seat, if their positive action is without effect? Having said that, this case comment does not consider that on balance, such effect is to be conferred to arbitration awards themselves or the judgments of the courts other than at the seat.

The pronouncements of English courts do largely support the possibility of according issue estoppel effect to the decisions at the seat. The Court of Appeal in *Yukos Capital S.A.R.L v. OJSC Rosneft Oil Company* proceeded on the assumption that the decision of the Dutch courts to reject may in principle produce issue estoppel effect before the English courts.[25] Lord Collins in *Dallah* considered that 'in some cases a determination by the court of the seat may give rise to an issue estoppel or other preclusive effect in the court in which enforcement is sought.'[26]

Lord Mance's rejection of the compétence-compétence of the arbitral tribunals or the courts of the seat has the overtones of limiting the application of the issue estoppel effect of the judgments from the court of the seat. He considered that: 'The very issue is whether the person resisting enforcement had agreed to submit to arbitration in that country. Such a person has, as I have indicated, no obligation to recognise the tribunal's activity or the country where the tribunal conceives itself to be entitled to carry on its activity.'[27]

However, Lord Mance then goes on to countenance the possibility that the courts of the seat may accord issue estoppel to the findings of the English court:

> I note, however, that an English judgment holding that the award is not valid could prove significant in relation to such proceedings, if French courts recognise any principle similar to the English principle of issue estoppel (as to which see The Sennar (No. 2) [1985] 1 WLR 490). But that is a matter for the French courts to decide.[28]

4. CONCLUSION

The divergence of outcomes in the *Dallah* saga is lamentable but is perhaps explainable by the uncertainty of the legal process and widely drafted legal tests. After all, legal training and legal culture are embedded at an almost subconscious level. Examples abound of lawyers trained in the same legal system arriving at diametrically opposite conclusions in hard cases. Instead, the way forward for international decisional harmony may lie in preventing the concurrent proceedings arising in the first place. This may be achieved through according preference to the courts of the seat. This will

---

[24] See, for instance, *Good Challenger Navegante SA v. Metalexportimport SA* [2003] EWCA Civ 1668, [50].

[25] *Yukos Capital S.A.R.L v. OJSC Rosneft Oil Company* [2012] EWCA Civ 855, [138] et seq.

[26] *Dallah Real Estate and Tourism Holding Company v. The Ministry of Religious Affairs, Government of Pakistan* [2010] UKSC 46, [98].

[27] Ibid., [29]. See also ibid., [23].

[28] Ibid., [29].

of course have the effect of reducing the say of enforcing courts. But it could be the price to pay for those willing to attain a higher international judicial harmony.

16.3 THOUGHTS ON THE *DALLAH* CASE: THE HYPOTHESIS OF THE INDETERMINACY OF THE LEGAL SYSTEM

*Sylvain Bollée**

On the surface, the *Dallah* case primarily seems interesting in that it illustrates a remarkable legal glitch, exposing the curative limitations of conflict of laws: two courts, although agreeing on the applicability of the same rules to the same legal question, issue decisions that are diametrically opposed.[29] Whereas the English courts, in applying French law, held that the Republic of Pakistan was not bound by the arbitration clause signed by the Trust that it had established, the Paris Court of Appeal, also applying French law, reached the precisely opposite conclusion.

At first glance, such a result appears to constitute an aberration and even – to be frank – the result of a *mistake* made by one of the courts. It would be quite natural to cast a sideways glance at the English court: after all, is it not the French court that presumably wields and expresses the truth in regards to its own legal system? It is even more tempting to consider, as several commentators have suggested, that the English court's analysis essentially reflects a particular legal-cultural orientation. In short, the English court could not have escaped the notions that permeate its own law, particularly with regard to contractual interpretation (more objective) and consent to arbitration (stricter); the court thus ended up misapplying French law.[30]

The suggestion that the English court remained subject to the influence of its own legal culture likely does provide part of the explanation. One should, however, add a substantial degree of nuance to this hypothesis and, in particular, question its premise: that the divergent interpretations of the law provided on either side of the Channel should be considered a pure anomaly and as a reflection of a mistake committed by one of the courts. If the international context (1) does not provide a complete explanation, the potential role of legal culture (2) should not overshadow the part of explanation attributable to what shall be referred to as legal indeterminacy (3).

---

* Contribution originally written in French, translated to English by Sean Croft.

29 The singularity of this outcome did not escape the notice of commentators in France on the Paris Court of Appeal's decision (see Isabelle Michou (2011) 2 *JDI* 395 (note); Gilles Cuniberti (2011) 2 *Cah Arb* 433 (note); Christophe Seraglini (2011) 51 *JCP* 1432 (note); François-Xavier Train (2012) 2 *Rev Arb* 374 (note)).

30 See Gary Born, 'Dallah and the New York Convention' (2011) *Kluwer Arbitration Blog* <http://arbitrationblog.kluwerarbitration.com/2011/04/07/dallah-and-the-new-york-convention/> accessed 22 December 2017: 'It is difficult to avoid the conclusion that the UK Supreme Court is not able to understand the substance of the law'. See also Jacob Grierson and Mireille Taok, 'Dallah: Conflicting Judgments from the U.K. Supreme Court and the Paris Cour d'Appel' (2011) 4 *JIntlArb* 407; Pierre Mayer, 'The Extension of the Arbitration Clause to Non-Signatories – The Irreconcilable Positions of French and English Court' (2012) 4 *AmUIntlLRev* 831.

1. INTERNATIONALITY

To put the apparent disorder into perspective, one should first consider the consequences of the litigation's international character. Admittedly, the fact that the same question of law may be answered in two contradictory ways is clearly not compatible with the kind of legal thinking that a jurist habitually applies in the domestic context. For each question, the law is supposed to provide a single answer: like an on or off switch, behaviour is either lawful or unlawful, a contract is either formed or it is not, a party is either bound by an arbitration clause or it is not, etc. How can the legal system properly fulfil its function if it does not, as a fundamental prerequisite, obviate the possibility of contradictory conclusions?

But this reassuring framework, assuming that it corresponds to reality (see *infra*, p. 343), falls apart as soon as we adopt an international perspective. From this vantage point emerges the fundamental issue of a plurality of legal systems that may independently entertain competing and divergent perspectives in regards to particular legal situations. According to F. Rigaux's superb characterisation, legal systems are situated in a 'system of general relativity'.[31] Law is no longer interchangeable with truth given that, from one legal order to another, the same situation can be addressed in a variety of logically incompatible ways. This is the history of 'limping situations' (*situations boiteuses*), the appearance of which private international law generally endeavours to avoid insofar as possible.

The outcome of the *Dallah* case can be reduced to this unfortunate, although hardly uncommon situation, that international arbitration law seeks however to resist with all its strength. While contemporary private international law appears generally open – at least in Europe – to the recognition of judgments, this favourable attitude toward legal continuity is only occasionally applied in international arbitration: according to the dominant approach in comparative law,[32] only certain judicial decisions reviewing arbitral awards are recognised as internationally binding (those rendered in the country of the seat annulling an award), and French law is distinct in going so far as even to refuse to recognise any foreign judicial ruling as to the validity of an award whatsoever.[33] The discrepancy between the rulings in the *Dallah* case can therefore hardly be regarded as a complete aberrance, given that it was understood that the French court would be required to deliver its own assessment as to arbitral jurisdiction,

---

[31] 'Les situations juridiques individuelles dans un système de relativité générale' (1989) 213 *RCADI* 9.

[32] An approach reflected by the 1958 New York Convention, and in particular Article V § 1(e).

[33] See, in particular, the emblematic decisions rendered in Cass civ (1) 23 March 1994 *Société Hilmarton v. Société OTV* (1994) 2 *Rev Arb* 327 (See Charles Jarrosson (1994) 2 *Rev Arb* 329 (note); Bruno Oppetit (1995) 2 *Rev Crit DIP* 356 (note); Emmanuel Gaillard (1994) *JDI* 701 (note); Jean-Claude Dubarry and Eric Loquin (1994) *RTDC* 702 (note)) and in Cass civ (1) 29 June 2007 *Société PT Putrabali Adyamulia v. Société Rena Holding et Société Mnogutia Est Epices* (2007) 3 *Rev Arb* 507 (Emmanuel Gaillard (2007) 3 *Rev Arb* 517 (note); Matthieu de Boisséson (2007) *LPA* 20 n 192 (note); Thomas Clay (2007) 4 *JDI* 1236 (note); Philippe Pinsolle (2007) 326 *GazPal* 14 (note); Christophe Seraglini (2007) 51–52 *JCP* 216 n 1 (note); Sylvain Bollée (2008) 1 *Rev Crit* DIP 109 (note).

irrespective of the English court's conclusion. At most, it could be said that English law, which unlike many other legal systems is open to recognising decisions that have *validated* an award,[34] was clearly in a position to avoid the juridical contradiction; the United Kingdom Supreme Court could have stayed its ruling until the Paris Court of Appeals had ruled on the action for annulment.

2. LEGAL CULTURE

Such an analysis could, of course, be faulted as incomplete if it were to ignore the most deeply disturbing point: it was in applying the same rules – those found in French law – that the English and French courts arrived at contradictory conclusions. In some sense, both courts claimed to adopt the point of view of the same legal order, which, as previously mentioned, is presumably meant to be uniform. The rules of French law were intended to provide a definite answer; is not the fact that two separate decisions were reached *necessarily* indicative that these rules were incorrectly applied by one of the courts?

Clearly the supposition that the English court misapplied French law appears to enjoy a degree of merit in theory, as this explanation corresponds to a more general divergence that must not be ignored: the difference between French and English legal cultures in regard to the interpretation of contractual intent. This yardstick is relevant because, in determining whether an arbitration clause should be extended to a non-signatory, French law can be said to examine whether there was tacit consent – consent that the third party's involvement in the conclusion and execution of the contract is likely to evidence (*see infra*, p. 347). The United Kingdom Supreme Court, in fact, focused on an assessment of the parties' intent in the *Dallah* case.

French law traditionally addresses the issue of contractual interpretation beginning with the presumption that the parties essentially shared a common intent; the whole question is then to determine what that intent was. There is a long history of objective interpretative guidelines. But these are secondary and only serve precisely as guideposts – from which a court can deviate – in applying the primary interpretive requirement to seek the common intention of the parties.[35] This order of operation was admittedly undermined by the introduction of article 1188 paragraph 2 of the Civil Code during the 2016 contract law reform: 'When this intention cannot be ascertained, the contract shall be interpreted in the sense to be given to it by a reasonable person in the same situation.' That said, it is reasonable to think that it will take time for this provision (which did not exist when the *Dallah* case was decided) to potentially influence the courts' interpretative practices. Not only is the classic approach to

---

[34] See Maxi Scherer, 'L'autorité de chose jugée des décisions relatives au contrôle des sentences: l'approche anglaise' (2016) 1 *Rev Arb* 187.

[35] This state of affairs does not seem to have been called into question by the contract law reforms carried out in 2016, even though the texts are not explicit in this respect (see Olivier Deshayes, Thomas Genicon and Yves-Marie Laithier, *Réforme du droit des contrats, du régime général et de la preuve des obligations* (New York, LexisNexis 2016) 369, 374, 390 concerning Article 1190 of the Civil Code).

contractual interpretation deeply rooted in tradition, it also accords with a logic more broadly pervading French contract law. The existence of a contract stems from the fact that the parties *jointly wanted something*, and it would seem paradoxical to unearth the contract's meaning in any other fashion than by seeking the contours of this common intent.

English law adopts a profoundly different interpretive approach. It is far less concerned with a subjective search for the intention of the parties than it is with an analysis of its objective manifestation, which results above all from the contract's text and the manner in which it could be understood by a reasonable person.[36] According to one jurisprudential formulation, 'interpretation is the ascertainment of the meaning which the document would convey to a reasonable person having all the background knowledge which would reasonably have been available to the parties in the situation in which they were at the time of the contract.'[37] This far more objective approach has significant repercussions in terms of which elements are relevant to interpretation. It is reflected in the '*Parol Evidence Rule*', which in principle prohibits the production of evidence outside the text of the contract, particularly those relating to pre-contractual negotiations.[38] This description of course is only general and does not do justice to the many nuances of English law,[39] but the fact remains that, in comparison with French law, the English approach provides courts with less room to seek an outward manifestation of the parties' common consent beyond the contractual documents themselves.

It would be quite unfair to reduce the English court's approach in the *Dallah* case to a disguised application of the principles of English contractual interpretation. A reading of the decision undeniably reveals that the court examined the parties' common intention. But the question remains whether, from the point of view of French law, it did so *poorly* or not. In this sense, it is obviously tempting to explain the Paris Court of Appeals and the United Kingdom Supreme Court's divergent decisions by presuming that the latter could not have escaped the undue influence of its own legal culture, characterised by a stronger focus on the contractual document itself than that prescribed by French law.[40] The fact is that the decision adopted by the English court corresponds to the contract's terms (according to which the Trust, and not the Republic of Pakistan, was a party), whereas the French court considered that it was appropriate to look beyond the contractual terms themselves.

---

[36] See in this regard, an analysis of recent case law in the superb article by David McLaughlan, 'A Better Way of Making Sense of Contracts?' (2016) 132 *LQR* 577.

[37] *Investors Compensation Scheme v. West Bromwich Building Society* [1997] UKHL 28; [1998] 1 All ER 98; [1998] 1 WLR 896.

[38] See Joseph Chitty and Hugh G Beale, *Chitty on Contracts*: *General Principles* vol 1 (London, Sweet & Maxwell 2015) 13-99.

[39] In fact, the Parol Evidence Rule has significant exceptions. See Chitty and Beale, ibid., 13-100 et seq.

[40] See e.g., François-Xavier Train (2012) 2 *Rev Arb* 374 (note) n 16.

3. LEGAL INDETERMINACY

The proposition that the English court erred in applying French law by tainting it with its own legal and cultural heritage, nevertheless, seems to require significant qualifications.

Above all, one should emphatically reject the idea that the divergence of the French and English decisions necessarily reveals in and of itself a failure to correctly apply French law – that one court was necessarily right and the other court was necessarily wrong. The simplistic proposition that a legal system provides, on every question of law, one unique answer should be held in check.[41] This view is plainly contradicted by everyday experiences of contemporary legal systems. Often, legal rules, like facts themselves, open themselves up to several possible interpretations, one interpretation enjoying no greater objective validity than the other. To this extent, contemporary legal systems fail to live up to their ambitions of ensuring uniform substantive content. Of course, one of these interpretations will ultimately be imposed through a judicial decision, which we desire to embody the expression of a pre-existing truth: in retrospect, the rule of law has always been deemed to function accordingly, in general and in this particular case. But this understanding is a fiction, its only merit being to conceal an unthinkable reality that is difficult to reconcile with the legal system's professed objective (legal certainty, the precedence of the rule of law over personal judgments, equality before the law …). A more lucid understanding of law – which is also more disturbing – is to recognise its partial indeterminacy, maintaining in regards to each legal question, not necessarily a single point of view, but sometimes, or even often, a *diversity of potential viewpoints* corresponding to the various possible outcomes resulting from the application of laws and coexisting as long as a judicial decision has not adopted one point of view to the detriment of the others. This plurality of potential legal points of view, a phenomenon that is both banal and yet constantly repressed, is only rarely manifested as a result of the mechanisms designed to prevent contradictory judgments, beginning with the authority of res judicata. It is possible, however, to perceive fleeting apparitions,[42] and it is perhaps in these terms that the issue in the *Dallah* case should be considered: by relinquishing the view that two contradictory decisions were the result of one correct and one incorrect application of French law, in order to discern instead the adoption of two potential points of view under French law, equally valid in theory, on the question of arbitral jurisdiction.

To substantiate what is at this stage only a theory, it is necessary to focus on one crucial point: the degree to which legal rules and situations are open to a plethora of potential points of view. Rules differ in the degree to which they are subject to a variety

[41] The ideas that follow owe much to the reflections provoked by the work of Pierre Bayard (e.g., Pierre Bayard, *Il existe d'autres mondes* (Paris, ed. Minuit 2014)).

[42] The discussion surrounding the reversal of French jurisprudence regarding the issue of the retroactivity is symptomatic in this respect (for a summary, see Pascal Deumier, V 'Jurisprudence' *Rep Dalloz Dr Civ* (2017) Ch 2 n 119 et seq.). Moreover, as has already been explained elsewhere, the concept of indeterminacy is particularly pronounced in international arbitration given the absence of rules that are *a priori* binding on the arbitrator (Sylvain Bollée, 'L'impérativité du droit choisi par les parties devant l'arbitre international' (2016) 3 *Rev Arb* 675).

of interpretations, courts are afforded more or less discretion, and the facts themselves are more or less susceptible to various understandings. In regards to the *Dallah* case, all the variables seemed to combine to favour the emergence of potentially conflicting points of view.

First, the rules of French law bearing on the potential extension of the arbitration clause to a non-signatory hardly lend themselves to a definite and mechanical application. A review of jurisprudence does not necessarily provide an overall sense of consistency; an extension of the clause to a non-signatory State has previously been rejected in circumstances that might seem at least as favourable as those present in the *Dallah* case.[43] What renders French law somewhat elusive in regards to this issue, moreover, does not only lie in the casuistry involved in assessing the non-signatory's involvement in the course of the contractual relationship and the inevitable weighing of initial motivating factors, in this respect, in order to admit or reject the extension.[44] It is a much more fundamental problem, which is that French law lacks precision and clarity as to the respective weight to be given to subjective factors – reflecting the will of the parties – and objective factors – reflecting the third party's involvement in the contract's conclusion or execution phase. Accordingly, one can furnish two readings as to jurisprudential theory pertaining to the extension of arbitration clauses to third parties.[45]

According to the first reading, objective criteria are considered only in so far as they support the presumption of tacit consent to arbitration.[46] It is clearly possible to reach very far in seeking this consent, but to quote one author, 'the need for consent to the arbitration agreement is greatly watered down, but it is not completely thrown out.'[47] An argument along these lines is that it is difficult to see how, from a principled point of view, there could be any different approach, as this would amount to imposing forced submission to arbitral jurisdiction upon a third party, which would offend the fundamental principles of arbitration law – including under French arbitration law.[48] There is nevertheless a second reading possible, one, moreover, adopted by excellent

---

[43] See, e.g., CA Paris 26 March 2009 *Société Papillon Group Corporation v. République Arabe de Syrie et autres* (2010) 3 *Rev Arb* 525; Vincent Chantebout (2010) 3 *Rev Arb* 533 (note); Cass civ (1) 29 June 2011, 3 *Rev Arb* 959; Vincent Chantebout (2011) 3 *Rev Arb* 962 (note).

[44] See François-Xavier Train, 'L'extension de la clause compromissoire – Chronique des années 2012-2017' (2017) 2 *Rev Arb* 389 n 68.

[45] Regarding this ambiguity, see e.g., Mathias Audit, Sylvain Bollée and Pierre Callé, *Droit du commerce international et des investissements étrangers* (Paris, LGDJ 2016) n 887.

[46] See accordingly, in the *Dallah* case, François-Xavier Train (2012) 2 *Rev Arb* 374 n 9 (note).

[47] Jean-Baptiste Racine, *Droit de l'arbitrage* (Paris, PUF 2016) n 325.

[48] See in particular Cass Civ (1) 20 December 1993 *Comité populaire de la municipalité de Khoms v. Société Dalico Contractors* (1994) 4 *Rev Crit DIP* 663, note Pierre Mayer; Emmanuel Gaillard (1994) *JDI* 432 (note); Eric Loquin (1994) *JDI* 690 (note); Hélène Gaudemet-Tallon (1994) 1 *Rev Arb* 118; Jean-Claude Dubarry and Eric Loquin (1994) *RTDC* 254 (note): 'according to a substantive principle of international arbitration law, the arbitration clause is legally independent from the main contract that incorporates it directly or by reference and its … existence and effectiveness are assessed, subject to the mandatory rules of French law and international public policy, *according to the common intention of the parties*, without the need to refer to domestic law.' (emphasis added)

commentators. It provides a purely objective foundation to the extension: 'The binding effect does not rest on tacit consent; it rests on an objective situation: the fact of having been involved.'[49] Analysed in these terms, the French theory of extension is tricky to justify and no less than iconoclastic.[50] But in regards to the situation at issue, these aspects are secondary. What matters is the existence of a fundamental ambiguity that creates difficulties as soon as one has to answer this sensitive question: to what extent can the objective criterion of involvement be tempered by adducing evidence that, on another level, attests to a lack of common intent to extend the clause?

This question is far from having been clearly resolved under French law, and it is certainly key to explaining the divergent decisions of the French and English courts in the *Dallah* case. If one detects in the English decision a particular emphasis on the contract's stated intention, a comparative reading of both decisions demonstrates that the fault line is, in fact, situated elsewhere: strikingly, it was the English court alone that made an explicit effort to elicit the protagonists' common intention. In comparison, it is the approach of the French court that somewhat paradoxically exudes a more objective character: in justifying the extension, the Paris Court of Appeals' emphasis only considers the attitude of the Pakistani government, which 'behaved as if the Agreement was its own' – its involvement 'confirm[ing] that the establishment of the Trust was purely a formality' and that it had 'behaved like the real Pakistani party during the economic transaction.' Behind both decisions, there were obviously two possible manners of proceeding, given the government's involvement, in addition to the potentially contradictory factors applicable to examining the existence of a common intention. The French court was much more sensitive to the first aspect, to the point of appearing to neglect anything that might support the existence of a common intention to exclude the State as a party to the contract. The English court, on the other hand, adopted a possible reading of French law that incorporates what is at least supposedly fundamental to the theory of extension, namely consent to arbitration. This led the court to attach greater importance to elements that appeared more persuasive than objective considerations as to the parties' common intention, focusing on the State's role in the formation and life of the contract. It could be debated at length which of these two approaches best corresponded to the 'correct' application of French law. But the relativity of either conclusion, given *the ambivalence* of French law, should itself be underscored. This ambivalence also emerges from French case-law which, at times, like the English judge in the *Dallah* case, seems to treat the issue of extension far more in terms of an overall assessment of the parties' common intention, without appearing to attach overwhelming importance – as the Paris Court

---

49 Pierre Mayer, 'Extension of the Arbitration Clause to Non-Signatories under French Law' in *Multiple Party Actions in International Arbitration* (Oxford, Oxford University Press 2009) 189 n 5.11; See also Christophe Seraglini (2011) 51 *JCP* 1432 n 3.

50 Compare the recent work of Gilles Cuniberti, arguing for a renewed approach that tempers the importance of consent to arbitration: Gilles Cuniberti, *Rethinking International Commercial Arbitration – Towards Default Arbitration* (Cheltenham, Edward Elgar 2017). See also, in the *Dallah* case, the pragmatic observations made by Pierre Mayer noting that a refusal to recognise the award made against the Republic of Pakistan would have amounted to a denial of justice (Pierre Mayer, 'The Extension of the Arbitration Clause to Non-Signatories – The Irreconcilable Positions of French and English Court' (2012) 27(4) *Am U Intl L Rev* 836 et seq.).

of Appeals does here – to the State's objective involvement in the contractual circumstances.[51]

The facts in the *Dallah* case reinforce the proposition that two divergent, yet equally legitimate points of view on French law are possible. The facts could give rise to substantial uncertainty because they intermingle contradictory elements: the terms of the contract, the circumstances of its negotiation and execution, as well as the sudden demise of the Trust as a legal entity. In light of this complex information, two of the three arbitrators, while considering the extension of the clause as justified, frankly stated that they were deciding 'with some hesitation, considering that the case lies very close to the line.' Such a confession is remarkable, especially if considered that by itself, the 'line' designated by French law is far from thin, but rather, in its thickness, presents a broad range of possible legal interpretations.

Instead of standing for a conceptually unjustifiable anomaly, the *Dallah* case's dual outcomes appear to echo a recurrent situation – although generally concealed from view – illustrating legal systems' fundamental indeterminacy given the existence and persistence of contradictory and yet equally tenable views. Acknowledging the presence of indeterminacy in legal systems (and, correspondingly, in particular legal situations) does not necessitate neglecting this cause of dissatisfaction any more than it means seeking out decisional conflicts; but it does permit a more accurate and nuanced understanding of the legal reality in abandoning the illusion of a normative order that speaks with only one voice and that forever contains, deep down, a single truth. The *Dallah* case represents, in this respect, a salutary opportunity.

[51] See in this respect, the decisions rendered in CA Paris 26 March 2009 *Société Papillon Group Corporation v. République Arabe de Syrie et autres* (2010) 3 *Rev Arb* 525. See also CA Paris 12 July 1984 *République arabe d'Egypte v. Southern Pacific Properties Ltd, Southern Pacific Properties (Middle East)* (1986) 1 *Rev Arb* 75 note Philippe Leboulanger; Berthold Goldman (1985) *JDI* 129 (note) (affirmed by Cass civ (1) 6 January 1987 (1987) 4 *Rev Arb* 469, note Philippe Leboulanger; Berthold Goldman (1987) *JDI* 638 (note)).

17. Economic transplants: *Lafonta v. Autorité des marchés financiers*

17.1 CASE BACKGROUND

European financial markets operate as a highly integrated regime that promotes transparency and tackles systemic financial risk. It is no surprise that insider trading and market manipulation are heavily regulated. And one of the key instruments that have been used to combat market abuse – the Market Abuse Directive 2003/124 – was the focus of this 2015 Court of Justice of the European Union (CJEU) case.

In *Lafonta v. Autorité des marchés financiers*, the CJEU interpreted the meaning of 'precise information' in the context of inside information under the 2003 Directive, which was applicable at that time. Inside information referred to any undisclosed information relating to financial instruments, which could have a significant effect on the prices of those instruments if it were made public. The Implementing Directive further specified that information was to be considered precise if it allowed an investor to draw conclusions on the price movement of an investment. It was, however, unclear whether one was also required to predict a particular direction of the price movement – up or down – to meet this part of the test.

Mr. Lafonta was a chairman in a company called Wendel that concluded a swap agreement with a number of credit institutions in September 2007. The underlying assets of the swaps were shares in Saint-Gobain. Wendel acquired more than 66 million shares in Saint-Gobain, which represented 17.6% of its share capital. Wendel informed the AMF, the French market regulator, that it exceeded the thresholds of 5%, 10%, 15% and 20% of the company's share capital. However, in its inquiry AMF found that Wendel had intended to acquire a significant shareholding in Saint-Gobain's capital from the very beginning. AMF went on to accuse Wendel of failing to disclose the inside information concerning the financial operation that led to acquiring a substantial shareholding in Saint-Gobain's capital. This led to AMF imposing a financial penalty on Wendel and Mr. Lafonta amounting to 1.5 million euro. After the Paris Court of Appeal dismissed Mr. Lafonta's action for the annulment of that decision, he appealed before the French Cour de Cassation. Mr. Lafonta argued that as it was impossible to predict whether the disclosure of the information concerning Wendel's acquisition of a shareholding in Saint-Gobain would result in an increase or decrease of the share price – he, in fact, did not possess an inside information. The Cour de Cassation then decided to stay proceedings and refer this point to the CJEU.

The CJEU held that in order for information to be regarded as being of a precise nature, it need not be possible to infer from that information, with a sufficient degree of probability, that once it is made public, its potential effect on the prices of the financial instruments concerned will be in a particular direction. In other words, being able to determine the possible direction of the price movement is not necessary. This decision has important practical implications, particularly for investors, as it lowers the threshold for what is considered as inside information by financial markets.

The 2003 Market Abuse Directive was repealed in 2016, when it was replaced by the Regulation No. 596/2014 on Market Abuse. It extended the scope to new markets and trading strategies and strengthened the existing framework. Nonetheless, the provisions on inside information and precise information remained largely unchanged, which means that the Lafonta case still constitutes a 'good law'.

Case: *Jean-Bernard Lafonta v. Autorité des marchés financiers* (Case C-628/13)

17.2 A COMMON LANGUAGE OF LAW AND ECONOMICS? INTEGRATING ECONOMIC TRANSPLANTS INTO THE LEGAL WEB

*Katja Langenbucher**

1. A BRIEF INTRODUCTION INTO 'ECONOMIC TRANSPLANTS'[1]

The question how law and legal scholarship interact with other disciplines has been an evergreen of global legal theory. Inward-glancing strands of thought have stressed the specifics of legal methods and techniques and drawn a clear dividing line not only between law and other disciplines, but also between different national jurisdictions. 'Legal transplants' were ogled suspiciously by those who understand the law as a distinctly local matter, tied to a specific historical, linguistic, sociological and cultural background. More external-looking legal theories often display a more consequentialist, pragmatic approach to the law. Legal rules, principles and institutions are conceived of as tools to advance a certain goal such as economic efficiency. If input from another legal order or a different discipline could help establish such goals or make the legal tools work better, there would be no reason to object to that.

The law dealing with listed stock corporations and with financial markets has a tradition of being rather open to input of both, different legal orders and different disciplines, especially if it came from economics. The often global nature of stock corporations and capital markets accounts for some of that, with economic thinking offering something like a common language to converse across borders. The seemingly natural proximity of the topics discussed in this area of law to economics faculties and to business schools explains low thresholds for communication across disciplines. The

---

* I am most grateful to Pauline Bruant for very helpful assistance on French law.

[1] See the title of Katja Langenbucher, *Economic transplants, on lawmaking for corporations and capital markets* (Cambridge, Cambridge University Press 2017). The term has, to my knowledge, only been used by Ioannis Lianos in 'Lost in Translation? Towards a Theory of Economic Transplants' (2009) 1 *Current Legal Problems* 346; and '"Judging" Economists. Economic Expertise in Competition Law Litigation. A European View' (2009) 1 CLES Working Paper Series. He describes 'analytical concepts, such as market power, barriers to entry, consumer welfare, efficiency gains' in a competition law context, ibid., 56. He distinguishes this use from 'economic authority', ibid., 61. The term in the way it is used here encompasses both.

fact that this dialogue largely concerns legal, not natural persons muted many critics of earlier 'law and economics' movements.[2] Today, we not only see lawyers tackling research questions with methods borrowed from empirical disciplines. We also witness the introduction of economic premises and concepts into legal contexts.

A. The Internalist and the Externalist

Such 'economic transplants' raise a number of problems. Lawyers working from what H.L.A. Hart called the 'internal point of view'[3] will be doubtful as to the employability of economic thinking and techniques in the law. They will understand themselves as *participants* in one legal community and say things like: 'this may be efficient from the economic point of view, but this is not what the law prescribes'. Economic parlance may facilitate global policy and scholarly dialogue, but, for them, will clash with established national legal cultures. Their techniques are typically hermeneutic ones, focusing on the text of a rule or a statutory code and suggesting how to interpret it in light of the code's history, inner coherence and judicial precedents. They will try to distinguish good arguments from unconvincing ones or flag out points of view which are in line with one jurisdiction's spirit and those which are not. They will usually place a premium on inner coherence, legal security and, often, display a conservative bias. French and German jurisprudence, along with most of continental Europe, largely follows this pattern.

What happens if such a traditionally internalist way of understanding, teaching and practising the law, due to the nature of the cases it deals with, is exposed to what we may call 'externalist', *observing* accounts of the law, still loosely borrowing from H.L.A. Hart? The externalist does not follow any hermeneutic, interpretative methodology. Instead, we may compare him to an anthropologist or ethnographer. He observes a legal system 'from the outside', noting how a certain legal rule (or a class of legal rules) affects human behaviour. Where the internalist's main tools are words, arguments and discourse rules, the externalist will tend to work with numbers, formal models, data or regression analyses. Let us picture him doing research on judicial verdicts in private law cases. While the internalist will understand a judicial verdict as exposing the law, may concur or criticise their reasoning, the externalist will have a very different research interest in mind. He could, for instance, try to show how a certain class, gender, race or political party affiliation will determine the outcome of the judicial decision. Such research 'from the outside' will often overlap with other social sciences, perhaps psychology, sociology or the political sciences.[4] Unsurprisingly, the law on financial markets offers a prime example for an overlap between externalist legal research and economics.

Usually, an externalist will be occupied with things such as building theoretical models or sampling data, and establishing correlations. Traditionalists will understand

---

[2] See pars pro toto Ronald Dworkin, 'Why Efficiency? – A Response to Prof. Calabresi and Posner' (1980) 8 *Hofstra L Rev* 563; Roberto Mangabeira Unger, *The Critical Legal Studies Movement* (first published 1983, New York, Verso Books 2015).

[3] H.L.A. Hart, *The Concept of Law* 1st edn (Oxford, Clarendon Press 1961).

[4] More on this example at Langenbucher (n 1) 49.

their job as describing the world as it inductively emerges from such work. Others may do it the other way round and, instead of *inferring* a correlation, start with a prediction of what they think is most likely to happen. They will then test their hypothesis with data they collected or models they built. Philosophers of science speak of 'the problem of underdetermination' when they discuss ensuing methodological and epistemic problems.[5]

Both economists, traditional or not, may sometimes do 'policy work'. They will suggest to change legal rules or to interpret them in a different way. This is where the externalist meets the internalist, suggesting what I would like to call an 'economic transplant'. We shall see in the following section that, again, financial markets law is illustrative of such an encounter.

B. Financial Markets Law as a Paradigm Example of Economic Transplants

Continental European securities and capital markets law's tradition is short, if compared to the United Kingdom and to the United States. Many countries formerly belonging to the Soviet Union had traditionally focused on different forms of ownership and financing for corporations. Many western countries, notably Germany and France, share a culture of credit financing and bank lending, rendering equity financing via capital markets less important, hence not developing a strong legal tradition in that area. This changed when the European Union focused on establishing liquid and efficient capital markets, lowering thresholds to cross-border investment and creating a 'level playing field' as to investing and financing via capital markets. The Segré Report of 1966 was a first step, stressing the importance of a union-wide law on capital markets. Further milestones were the 1999 Financial Services Action Plan, triggering an impressive amount of lawmaking at the level of the European Union, and the de Larosière report, meant to help prevent financial crises in the future.

The lack of a distinguished body of continental European capital markets law suggested a look abroad, most notably to the US and, to a somewhat lesser extent, to the UK. Both legal orders have hosted large financial centers, have a tradition of reliance on equity finance and, consequently, a well-developed body of law and legal practice. With the look abroad came not only an increase in legal transplants from jurisdictions where 'reasonable investors', 'material impact on stock prices' or 'inside information' were long established concepts. The prevalence of scholarship from an 'external point of view' in the US also accounts for a surge of 'economic transplants'.[6]

C. Legal Transplants and Economic Transplants

Legal transplants are known to imply 'displacement. For the lawyer's purposes, the transfer is one that occurs across jurisdictions: there is something in a given jurisdiction that is not native to it and that has been brought there from another.'[7]

[5] More at ibid., 109 et seq.

[6] What follows is a quote from ibid., 1–2.

[7] Pierre Legrand, 'The Impossibility of Legal Transplants' (1997) 4 *Masst J Eur & Comp L* 111.

The concept of 'economic transplants' addresses a similar form of displacement. However, while legal transplants are transferred 'across jurisdictions',[8] economic transplants are relocated across disciplines. Naturally, they are 'not native'[9] to the law because they origin in a different discipline. But what is being transferred? It cannot be 'the moving of a [legal] rule … from one country to another, or from one people to another'.[10]

Instead, 'economic transplants' encompass any concept, research finding or policy conclusion being transplanted from the economist's to the legal world. Think about a court relying on a prediction how capital markets will react to disclosure of inside information, based on input from the world of theoretical modelling of market processes. Imagine an empirical study presented to the legislator, benchmarking the strength of a country's shareholder rights against numerous other countries. Consider a neo-institutionalist scholar contributing an article to a law review where he describes the incentives determining the conduct of a CEO when going about his daily work. Imagine this work is later referred to in recitals of a European Directive or in a judicial opinion.

We have seen above[11] that taking an externalist perspective sometimes involves suggesting to change the law. Hence, transplanting insights from economics into a legal context will usually be a matter for the legislator. He may hear experts during legislative proceedings, define goals and, while doing so, will rely on descriptions of the world or predictions made, based on the methodology of economics. An instrumentalist concept of the law, characteristic for the external point of view, fits in with this. Let us caricature: economic research frames a goal to be achieved – for example efficient capital markets, delivering prices which closely reflect the fundamental value of the corporations traded on those markets. Legal rules are technical instruments, employed to serve that goal. Success in doing so may be measured, again using economic techniques. A 'non-performing rule', unable to measurably contribute to better working capital markets, will be abolished and replaced by a new one.

Against this background, economic transplants will, in many respects, raise similar problems to those discussed in research on legal transplants. Economic transplants, just like legal ones, are 'not native'[12] to the law. Consider Legrand's claim that 'rules cannot travel' and the conclusion that 'legal transplants are impossible'.[13] For economic concepts, engendered according to economics' specific methodology, to travel from there to an 'external perspective' on the law, to then be translated and transformed into a legal rule, fitting in with the internal perspective's point of view seems a frightening task. Even more frightening seems the chore to seamlessly integrate a rule born in this way into an existing legal order and to expect a judge to apply the economic reasoning behind it.

---

8 Ibid.

9 Ibid.

10 Alan Watson, *Legal Transplants: An Approach to Comparative Law* 2nd edn (Athens GA, University of Georgia Press 1993) 21; Legrand (n 7) 112 more finely elaborates on this quote.

11 Above at s 1.A.

12 Legrand (n 7) 111.

13 Ibid., 114.

D. The Plan of this Section

In what follows, we will elaborate on the *Lafonta* case as an example of a legal rule which one may trace back to an economic concept. We shall, *first*, briefly explain how an economic transplant was introduced into the European market abuse law and, *second*, try to understand the complexities this transplant has caused in judicial practice.

2. THE MARKET ABUSE REGULATION AND THE EFFICIENT CAPITAL MARKETS HYPOTHESIS

A. The Economic Theory

The 'efficient capital markets hypothesis' is a paradigm example of an economic theory having had tremendous traction in both legal scholarship and legislative discourse. It suggests that financial instruments which are being traded on capital markets have a clearly identifiable 'fundamental value' based on their expected return and on the risk inherent in the investment. Because capital markets 'price securities with payoffs extending out in time',[14] they involve a certain 'hope that they can be used to forecast the future [which] has long fascinated both scholars and practitioners'.[15]

How could trading on a financial market help to predict future developments? This depends on the information to be had on what is being traded. If any conceivable information of relevance to risk or return of a financial instrument was publicly available without transaction costs, so the hypothesis assumes, investors would look out for and then trade on the basis of such information. Most models, in order to achieve manageable results, assume that investors act rationally. Good news will then be reflected in rising prices, bad news will account for prices going down. Many models claim that even if not every investor takes each piece of available information into account, aggregating all investors allows to assume that prices will be moved to 'where they belong'. Keeping this enormously simplified version of the efficient capital markets hypothesis in mind,[16] let us take a look at the Market Abuse Regulation's recitals.[17]

B. Transplanting into the Market Abuse Regulation

We learn that

> reasonable investors base their investment decisions on information already available to them, that is to say, on *ex ante* available information. Therefore, the question whether, in making an

[14] Steve Ross, 'The Recovery Theorem' (2015) 70 *J Finance* 615.

[15] Ibid.; quoted in Langenbucher (n 1) 26.

[16] For some more detail see Langenbucher (n 1) 95 et seq.

[17] Regulation (EU) 596/2014 on market abuse (EU market abuse regulation) [2014] OJ L173/1.

> investment decision, a reasonable investor would be likely to take into account a particular piece of information should be appraised on the basis of the *ex ante* available information. Such an assessment has to take into consideration the anticipated impact of the information in light of the totality of the related issuer's activity, the reliability of the source of information and any other market variables likely to affect the financial instruments.[18]

Note how the recital accepts as a given that investors base their investment decisions on information.[19] The assessment the legislator has in mind concerns all available information on the issuer's activity, market variables and the reliability of the source of information. On that basis, we find 'reasonable' investors making their investment decision, closely reminding us of the premise of 'rational' investors the efficient capital markets hypothesis uses.

Understood in that way, the term 'reasonable investor' provides us with a good example of an economic transplant. An economic theory, namely on the workings of capital markets, suggests to help with both, the legislator's task of bringing about a good regulatory regime, and with judicial work when interpreting the rules of the Market Abuse Regulation.

i. Disclosure of inside information to the market, article 17 MAR

Article 17 paragraph 1 MAR[20] requires the issuer of certain financial instruments to 'inform the public as soon as possible of inside information which directly concerns that issuer'. Inside information, under Article 7 paragraph 1 (a) MAR,[21] is non-public information of a precise nature, relating to an issuer or a financial instrument which, if it were made public, would be likely to significantly impact prices. Compare this to the efficient capital markets hypothesis, assuming that all relevant information is available to investors: if we can arrange for the law to make sure that relevant information will be published by all issuers, we are moving the 'real world' one step closer to the economic model. By requiring issuers to disclose information, we are relying on the model's prediction: more information in the market will lead to better informed investment decisions. These, in turn, will lead to better pricing and to the value of all shares aggregated being the equivalent of the fundamental value of the corporation.

ii. Significant price impact, article 7 MAR

It follows from there that the decision on which information has to be disclosed under this rule has to do with the potential of this information to move prices. Therefore, a

---

[18] Regulation (EU) 596/2014 on market abuse (EU market abuse regulation) [2014] OJ L 173/1, recital 14.

[19] After the financial crisis, that same legislator mused that investment firms and clients are not capable of a good 'understanding of the risk involved' (Directive (EU) 2014/65 on markets in financial instruments (MiFID II) [2014] OJ L173/349, recital 80); quoted in Langenbucher (n 1) 28.

[20] The case was decided under the identical wording of Art. 6 of the Directive (EU) 2003/6 on insider dealing and market manipulation (market abuse) [2003] OJ L96/16.

[21] Directive (EU) 2003/6 on insider dealing and market manipulation (market abuse) [2003] OJ L96/16, art. 1 para 1.

significant price impact, under Article 7 paragraph 4 MAR,[22] refers to information '*a reasonable investor* would be likely to use as part of the basis of his investment decisions'. Again, we see an economic transplant creeping in. The model 'reasonable investor' will help us to define which information to disclose to the market. Whatever an investor of this genre would consider relevant for his decision to buy or to sell falls under Articles 7, 17 MAR.

iii. Expected return and a change in stock prices

Some more economic theory enters into the picture here. Our model rational investor will calculate his potential risk and his potential return before making a decision. For each potential investment, he will try to define how high his return could be (say, 30%), how high his loss may be (say, 20%) and what the odds are for either option (say, 50:50). By multiplying the odds with the potential profit/loss and adding up the chances, he arrives at the expected return (in our example: 5%). Inside information will often influence the odds. Good news about an issuer may move the chance of a profit from 50:50 to 60:40. Bad news will lower the probability of making a profit. Under the MAR regime, issuers will have to ask themselves if their piece of good (or bad) news is likely to have investors re-think investment decisions they made. If this is the case, release of this information is likely to change the price of that issuer's stock and, consequently, is price-significant.

iv. Economic transplants as a common European language?

Note how 'the clarity and precision that math brings to our shared vocabulary'[23] has entered legislation. An insider trading and disclosure case requires us to calculate the expected return of an investment decision and infer from there if stock prices are going to budge. The burdensome work of case-by-case reasoning, which the internalist lawyer is used to undertaking, has partly been replaced by an exercise in financial mathematics.

This is not the place to discuss the extent to which it is indeed 'clarity and precision' what we have transplanted into legislation.[24] Finance, obviously, follows its own methodology with its own methodological debates, struggles and fights between 'schools' such as neo-classical and behavioural. Understanding the extent of a causal relationship between disclosure to the market and efficient price-building as such is as hotly debated an issue as the conclusions we may draw on the basis of the stylised assumptions that a theoretical model relies on or that the selective data empirical work uses. This is even more so when individual cases have to be assessed. We would usually need an 'event study' showing that the information in question led to a rise or fall in prices. This would require for data to be collected on the corporation in question, for such data to be compared with more general market developments and for running a regression to understand if we are not comparing apples with pears. The confidence

---

[22] Council Regulation (EC) 2003/124 [2003] OJ L339/70, art. 1 para 2.

[23] Paul M. Romer, 'Mathiness in the Theory of Economic Growth' (2015) 105.5 *AER: Papers&Proceedings* 89, 90, talking, however, about the relationship between maths and economics; discussion of this at Langenbucher (n 1) 84.

[24] For more detail see Langenbucher (n 1) 85.

this exercise will give us will depend on whether we are happy to rely on standard normal distribution. Unfortunately, in cases involving sudden disclosure of new information to the market it is difficult to find a large number of events in relevant markets to compare the case in question to. This will lead us to different methodological tools, for example to conducting a large number of single-event studies. But, there again, we find economists arguing that such methodology will lead to 'substantial inferential errors'.[25]

Unimpressed by methodological considerations like these, we find scholars suggesting to view the MAR's 'reasonable investor' as 'the *alter ego* of the efficient capital markets hypothesis'.[26] They propose for a judge sitting on an insider case to defer to finance experts when having to rule on what a 'reasonable investor' would have done. In this way, an economic transplant from the externalist's world would, through the 'gateway' of this term, enter the internalist's world.

An economic transplant of this type seems not only intriguing due to its potential for bringing 'clarity and precision'. Seen from the point of view of European law (and its judges) economic transplants could be viewed as offering a common language, spanning national borders and jurisdictions.[27] European secondary law, instead of requiring complicated comparative studies and lengthy debates on common principles, would refer to economic concepts. Because these depend much less on language and national legal systems, they could recommend themselves as a lowest common denominator for both, legislators and judges. Interestingly, this is not at all what the ECJ did in *Lafonta*.

3. *LAFONTA* AND ECONOMIC TRANSPLANTS IN ACTION

Why had Wendel been confronted with failure to properly disclose his transactions regarding the shares of St Gobain in June? Had it not reported crossing the thresholds of 5%, 10%, 15% and 20% to the AMF between September and November of 2007?

The *Lafonta* case concerns what is often called a 'creeping-in' situation. A corporation that is interested in acquiring a significant number of shares of another corporation faces a problem. As soon as the market realises its plan, the price of the target company's shares is very likely to rise. As this makes the acquisition more expensive, the buying company has a natural interest in keeping its transactions secret. However, as we have seen above, European market abuse laws require to disclose transactions of this kind as soon as they become price significant. In *Lafonta*, the transactions in question were the total return swaps Wendel had concluded with several banks between June and July 2007, regarding St Gobain shares.

25 Jonah B. Gelbach, Eric Helland and Jonathan Kick, 'Valid Inference in Single Firm, Single-Event Studies' (2013) *American Law and Economics Review* 495, 496.

26 Lars Klöhn, 'Wertpapierhandelsrecht diesseits und jenseits des Informationsparadigmas – Am Beispiel des "verständigen Anlegers" im Sinne des deutschen und des europäischen Insiderrechts' (2013) 177 *ZHR* 349, 364, 377.

27 In more detail: Langenbucher (n 1) 68, 162 et seq., 199 et seq.

A total return swap is a derivative financial instrument to hedge risk exposure. Imagine you would like to count on the stock price of a certain type of share to remain stable during a certain period of time. With markets being by their very nature volatile, you can never be sure. If you enter into a total return swap, your counter-party promises to pay you the difference between the stock price on a specific date (e.g.: today) and a future date (e.g.: the end of the period you are interested in). Its business logic is an insurance against price volatility. However, total return swaps have also surfaced in a context where the reason for entering into them was not to be insured against a rise in prices. Instead, the buyer of the swap (in our case: Wendel) knew that the seller of the swap (in our case: several banks) would buy the underlying shares (in our case: of St Gobain) to minimise its own risk exposure. The buyer (Wendel) also knew that when phasing out the swap the banks would be selling those shares again. This allowed him to arrange the timing to a moment when the market seemed favourable to his own plans – namely to buy these shares (in our case: 66 million shares of St Gobain) from his counter-parties (in our case: the banks, having bought 85 million shares of St Gobain). *Lafonta* illustrates this strategy: Wendel had not only entered into the swaps but *at the same time* arranged funding agreements to be able to buy these shares once the banks were going to sell them. It is with this business logic in mind that the AMF claimed Wendel should have reported these transactions in June, rather than only in September and November.

Under French law, two different rules were violated. Article 223-6 of the Règlement Générale de l'AMF (RGAMF) relates to financial transactions which are likely to have a significant price impact on that instrument or on its holder(s). The AMF claimed that the combination of the swaps and the funding agreements were proof of Wendel's intent not only to minimise its risk exposure regarding St Gobain shares during the duration of the swap, but to acquire those shares altogether, hence had a price effect on St Gobain's shares. While the EU market abuse regime only requires the issuer of the share in question to disclose any information relating to his own shares,[28] this French rule requires *anyone* who enters into a relevant financial transaction to disclose. Under Article 223-6, the AMF held, the market should have been informed by the end of June, when the last swap and the last funding agreement had been entered into. This ruling under article 223-6 was not brought before the ECJ.

What was referred to the ECJ was the alleged violation of articles 223-2 and 621-1 RGAMF. These rules transpose EU market abuse rules into French law. Under this regime, it was assumed that we would have seen a significant price impact on Wendel shares, had the markets realised that their 'hidden' plan was to buy a significant amount of St Gobain shares. The AMF argued that the relevant date for this was early July, when Wendel had not only concluded the swaps and the funding agreements, but also started buying St Gobain shares. Disclosing not before September was considered too late.

What was Mr. Lafonta's argument for not having disclosed? He claimed that at that time, it was not clear whether the market would approve or disapprove of Wendel's plans to buy a stake in St Gobain. Consequently, it was not clear whether Wendel's share prices were to go up or down.

---

[28] See above 2.B.i.

What would a model rational investor do in this case? Of course, he would calculate expected return! Along those lines, we find scholars arguing that, clearly, the model investor would not have had an incentive to trade, because he cannot be sure whether prices will go up or down.[29] Not much legal reasoning seems to be necessary to arrive at that conclusion.

The ECJ, by contrast, took a very different route. We find no sign of deference to economic input.[30] The Court stressed what it understood as the goals of the market abuse regime, namely to provide integrity, investor confidence and placing investors on an equal footing.[31] All of those goals, to the court, pointed towards a broad reading of the rule, encompassing everything which might grant the one 'in the know' an advantage over those who are unaware of the information held back, acting 'to the detriment of the other actors on the market'.[32]

In very traditional 'internalist' fashion, the judges point to the plain and ordinary meaning of the rule and cite the *travaux préparatoires*,[33] none of which suggest to them that the potential direction of a price movement has to be discernible. Interestingly, they place the case in the broader context of criminal law, reminding us of deterrence and wary of opening up 'a pretext'[34] for insiders who claim that they did not know whether prices would go up or down.

4. WHAT WE CAN LEARN

What can we learn about economic transplants as a 'common language' of global law, bringing insight gained from an observing, externalist viewpoint to the judiciary? *Lafonta* seems to mainly teach us caution:[35] economic transplants do certainly display attractive features such as a good grasp of a relevant financial context, 'clarity and precision' and the possibility to communicate across the borders of languages and jurisdictions. However, they stem from a very different methodological background than the law. At times, this will impair their usefulness for the decision of an individual case. At other times, we will find that integrating them in a judicial context, shaped by

---

29 Lars Klöhn, 'Inside information without an incentive to trade? What's at stake in Lafonta v AMF' (2015) 10 *CMLJ* 162, 166, 174. In passing, let us note that there are of course derivatives the prices of which vary with the volatility of the underlying shares, irrespective of their direction. Hedge funds are paradigm users of such options. Without delving into details, this provides us with a warning against too readily ascribing 'clarity and precision' to what seems to be a clear-cut economic transplant.

30 See Langenbucher (n 1) 178 quoting Scott Brewer, 'Scientific Expert Testimony and Intellectual Due Process' (1998) 107 *Yale Law Journal* 1586 et seq. on 'epistemic deference'.

31 Case C-628/13 *Lafonta v. AMF* [2015] ZIP 2015 627, para 21.

32 Ibid., para 36.

33 Ibid., para 37.

34 Ibid., paras 36–37.

35 For a different example of using economic transplants, namely to hide decision taken on the basis of a certain interpretation of freedom of movement, see Toni Marzal, 'From Hercules to Pareto: Of bathos, proportionality, and EU law' (2017) 15 *I.Con* 621.

participatory, internalist paradigms and a closely knitted 'legal web',[36] proves enormously difficult. The best we can do in the face of this predicament is probably transparency: bringing the differences in methodology to the fore and using economic transplants to critically challenge legal answers, without hoping to replace them.

17.3 ON ECONOMIC TRANSPLANTS IN JUDICIAL PRACTICE AND THE DYNAMICS OF LEGAL ACCULTURATION

Toni Marzal

1. FROM LEGAL TO ECONOMIC TRANSPLANTS

One of the most well-known theories in comparative law is that of the 'legal transplant'. It can be said to be a theory in that it proposes an abstract account of the dynamics of legal development. A considerable portion of this development, so goes the argument, can be attributed to the reception and importation of legal ideas and norms from foreign jurisdictions. Legal ideas can of course travel by force (e.g. colonisation), but the legal transplant theory focuses mainly on the diffusion of law through voluntary borrowings (e.g. the reception of Roman law in Medieval Western Europe).

The legal transplant theory is as much an account of legal development as of the relations between legal systems[37] (hence its appeal to private international lawyers). The choice of the metaphor of a 'transplant' to refer to one of the possible forms that these relationships might take is far from indifferent. The comparison of legal development to a surgical procedure projects a certain representation of the law. This representation involves three main propositions. First, that there is a certain need that requires addressing in the receiving legal system (like the patient who is desperate for a new kidney). Second, that the transferring legal system has what is necessary (the spare kidney here being a well-functioning set of regulations). Third, that it is at least possible to remove that legal material from the transferring system (like the body that can function on a single kidney) and implant it in the receiving legal system. Conversely, the metaphor also opens up the possibility that the operation might not work: perhaps the receiving law will reject the transplant, as its legal antibodies perceive it as a foreign body and attack it.

There are certain underlying ideas that support this representation. We leave aside here the fact that a transplant involves not only an act of reception and displacement but also of removal from the original source, which is of course entirely absent here. More importantly, it should first be underlined that law is viewed in functional terms, as a tool that fulfils certain needs. As the kidney allows the body to survive by processing blood, contract law might be said to allow for the economy to function and

[36] Langenbucher (n 1) 150 et seq.

[37] Alan Watson, *Legal Transplants. An Approach to Comparative Law* 2nd edn (Athens GA, University of Georgia Press 1993).

for people to peacefully coexist. Second, the legal transplant theory assumes that some form of deliberate intervention is responsible for the reception of the legal material, which, absent such agency, would not leave its domestic setting. Third, the theory also assumes that legal systems can be said to be more or less enlightened on the way they approach various social issues, and that they can be said to be equipped with better or worse tools to deal with them. It follows that, to less advanced jurisdictions, legal transplantation offers the possibility to rapidly catch up with the more developed ones, simply by borrowing suitable rules rather than coming up with such rules by themselves through experience or experimentation.

These ideas can of course be shown to be, at the very least, contestable. We will limit ourselves to the most obvious and well-known. Law is not only a set of copy-pastable rules, nor can it be reduced to a mere social tool. It is also the expression of a certain worldview and values, a set of coherent principles, the affirmation of a sovereign will, the product of destructive contestation, etc. (none of which alternative conceptions can be said to sit well with the pragmatically-oriented theory of legal transplants). Moreover, legal development does not seem in many instances to follow a path of progress or ascendancy, but rather moves through oscillations, back and forth between opposite visions (as conflict of laws specialists know well, given the history of shifts in their field between private law and public law conceptions, and between domestic and international ones).[38] Finally, transplants do not only fail because they might be perceived to be excessively foreign or structurally unsuited for implantation in the receiving legal system. More frequently, transplantation is only a surface phenomenon. Some argue that transplants inevitably fail, since transplanted rules immediately acquire a new meaning in their new, local environment.[39] We may refer to this critique as the 'acculturation thesis'. The circulation of legal ideas across jurisdictions might be said to resemble more the translation of a text from one language to the other:[40] no matter how skilled the translator, the English version of Don Quixote will never fully capture the full meaning of the original Spanish, nor will the text be understood the same way by its English readers. Others observe that the impact of transplants, which should more accurately described as 'irritants', can be potentially much broader as their reception triggers unexpected transformations in the receiving legal system.[41]

It is nevertheless obvious that outside influences are not only those of foreign legal systems. How should one understand the relationship of a particular legal system or legal regime (and not just of law in general) to non-legal disciplines, such as economics? The traditional answer relies on the distinction between facts and norms. Whereas the latter are a purely legal matter, non-legal expertise might prove necessary to clarify facts, particularly where these are inaccessible to the non-initiated or require careful analysis. There are two main gateways for non-legal expertise to infiltrate legal

---

38 See e.g. Alex Mills, 'The Private History of International Law' (2006) 55 *ICLQ* 1.

39 Pierre Legrand, 'The Impossibility of Legal "Transplants"' (1997) 4 *Maastricht J Eur & Comp Law* 111.

40 Joannis Lianos, 'Lost in translation: towards a theory of economic transplants' (2009) Jean Monnet Working Paper 08/09, NYU School of Law.

41 Gunther Teubner, 'Legal Irritants: Good Faith in British Law or How Unifying Law Ends Up in New Divergences' (1998) 61 *MLR* 11.

practice. The first is through the law of evidence, which will determine the standards under which such expertise might be relied on. The second is policy analysis. Regardless of whether the analysis is performed by legislators, judges or lawyers, non-legal expertise may help clarify how to most effectively and efficiently pursue a certain goal. Economic analysis of law may be said to infiltrate law through such policy analysis. As its most prominent author has argued:

> Economists can usually appeal to a generally accepted goal, such as maximizing the value of output, rather than having to defend the goal. By showing how a change in economic policy or arrangements would advance us toward that goal, they can make a normative statement without having to defend their fundamental premises.[42]

The newer concept of 'economic transplants' provides an alternative view of the relationship between law and economics.[43] The term economic transplant refers to the importation by a legal system of rules, principles and forms of reasoning originating in economics, rather than in the law of a foreign State. As such, the theory of economic transplants obviously draws from that of legal transplants. Both offer an explanation for legal change that refers to outside influences, challenging the idea that such changes are the product of a legal system's internal dynamics. Both work on the functionalist assumption that law can be conceived as a tool, which entails that it can be assessed as good or bad law according to the extent to which it succeeds in fulfilling its assigned goals. What is original about the notion of economic transplants is that the source of those transplants, external to the receiving legal system, is a non-legal discipline. Unlike the theory of legal transplants, which concerns the relationship between legal systems, the concept of economic transplants focuses on the relationship between two different knowledge systems.

The use of the transplant metaphor to describe the relationship of law to economics involves a number of challenging ideas. The first, and perhaps most fundamental one, is that economics is a source not only of empirical statements but also of normative ones, which as such can compete with legal materials and make their way into a legal system. This is of course an idea that runs against a very widespread understanding of the discipline, both among economists and non-economists, as essentially descriptive. It also challenges the distinction between facts and norms on which the traditional law of evidence and policy analysis are based. The second is that economics must be viewed as a tool, which can be measured and assessed according to its practical ability to fulfil social needs, which are at least partly understood to be the same as those of law. This also entails that, like a foreign legal system, economics can reach a further stage of development and prove to do, as a more advanced body of normative knowledge, 'a better job' than law at fulfilling those needs. There is of course no reason to think that, if law happened to overtake economics as the more sophisticated body of knowledge, the process could not work in the opposite direction (i.e. from law into economics). The focus of the economic transplant theory is nevertheless more modest: the specific

---

[42] Richard Posner, *Economic Analysis of Law* 8th edn (New York, Aspen Publishers 2011) 19.

[43] Katja Langenbucher, *Economic Transplants. On Lawmaking for Corporations and Capital Markets* (Cambridge, Cambridge University Press 2017).

transfer of normative ideas from economics to law, and how law accommodates those ideas (or struggles to do so, or fails to do so).[44]

Competition law is perhaps one of the areas that can be profitably analysed through the lens of economic transplants. Crucially, economics is not perceived in this field as limited to providing factual input, the way an engineer provides expert evidence to a judge on the reasons for which a bridge has collapsed, or the way a legislator might take into account scientific predictions about global warming when drafting an environmental protection regulation. Economics is instead commonly seen as an alternative source of norms, which might potentially clash with a legal rationale. Current competition law can thus be seen as agitated by a fundamental tension between the 'lawyer' and the 'economist' view of a certain issue. The prohibition of anti-competitive agreements in EU law is a good example. Even if the prohibition itself is partly the reflection of an economic insight (and thus arguably an economic transplant), EU authorities traditionally took an approach to the interpretation of the relevant provision that was said to be very 'legal', which meant applying it in an all-or-nothing manner and emphasising legal certainty. This approach has been criticised by many, particularly due to its overinclusiveness (i.e. the prohibition of anti-competitive agreements may thus become so broad that it covers also agreements that have no identifiable negative impact on competition). Reacting to these critiques, a so-called 'modern' approach has developed which draws heavily from economics, in particular through its focus on economic efficiency as guiding principle and by gradually replacing traditional categorical rules with a case-by-case assessment of effects. The term 'modernised' can here be read as referring to an economic transplant: the shortcomings of EU competition law have been remedied by borrowing off-the-shelf from the more refined field of economics.[45]

What about the law of insider trading? It certainly fits well with the theory of legal transplants. This is, first of all, because such regulations tend to be viewed in functional terms, which makes the legal transplant interpretation possible. Unlike, say, family law, which is usually seen as expressive of local values or cultural forms rather than in regulatory terms, insider trading regulations are almost exclusively thought of, like other financial and corporate governance regulations, as a tool to guarantee the proper functioning of markets. Indeed, the trading by insiders of material non-public information is to some extent thought to be a 'problem' (a fairness problem, an efficiency problem, a transparency problem, etc.), which therefore needs 'solving'. Law is at least part of that solution. The fact that U.S. law has been the first to address insider trading with a specific set of regulations (doubtless because mass financial trading first developed, and first crashed, in the U.S.), and that many other jurisdictions in the world have followed in its footsteps by imitating the U.S. legislator (generally by prohibiting, under certain conditions, the practice of insider trading), can consequently be seen as

---

[44] For a more general theory of the relationship between different forms of knowledge, see Gunther Teubner, *Constitutional Fragments. Societal Constitutionalism and Globalization* (Oxford, Oxford University Press 2012).

[45] On all these issues, see Richard Whish and David Bailey, *Competition Law* 8th edn (Oxford, Oxford University Press 2015).

an instance of legal transplantation.[46] Or, to put it otherwise, insider trading seems to be a case of legal systems around the world benefiting from innovation by the U.S. legal system (as one kind of innovation that cannot be patented). Conversely, legal diversity in this area can be interpreted either as different jurisdictions experimenting to improve on U.S. regulations, or as responding to local variants of the insider trading problem that call for tweaks of the basic model, or perhaps simply as botched attempts at transplanting the badly-understood American model.

Leaving aside the 'Americanisation' thesis, it is undeniable that insider trading law is subject to considerable outside influences from economics. Can these influences be analysed through the concept of 'economic transplants'? If so, it would mean that law-makers (including legislators, administrators and judges, even if each in their own way) are borrowing from economics, not only as expert support to provide evidence or clarify legally-relevant facts (e.g. to determine the impact on stock price of a certain piece of information), but as a rival normative system. Economics would here be akin to a foreign legal system: as with American law, legal actors may come to import norms from economics because of its perceived superiority on the issue of insider trading. Such norms might take the form of standards, goals, theories, preoccupations, concepts, forms of reasoning, paradigmatic examples, etc.

2. THE *LAFONTA* CASE AND ECONOMIC TRANSPLANTS

Let us now turn, as a case study of economic transplants in the context of judicial decision-making, to the 2015 *Lafonta* decision, where the Court of Justice of the European Union (hereafter 'the CJEU' or 'the Court') was called upon to determine which kind of information was 'precise' enough to qualify as 'inside information', triggering a disclosure obligation under the EU Market Abuse Directives (later replaced by the Market Abuse Regulation). There is abundant evidence to suggest that these pieces of legislation draw heavily from normative insights from economics, in particular through the 'efficient capital market hypothesis'.[47] Can the same be said of the case-law? Economic thinking can be reflected in legislation but fail to influence the judicial interpretations of that legislation. To cite once more the example of competition law, critiques in that field have mostly focused on the allegedly legalistic approach that the Court has historically followed.

The *Lafonta* case is based on a factual scenario that can happen only very exceptionally.[48] Nevertheless, it is often such fringe cases that, paradoxically, allow courts to determine the most fundamental questions. The information in relation to which the disclosure obligation was in dispute concerned the operations leading to the acquisition by Wendel SA of a significant shareholding in the Saint-Gobain group. This piece of information was affected by a very peculiar and perfectly symmetrical form of

---

[46] See generally Stephen M. Bainbridge (ed.), *Research Handbook on Insider Trading* (Cheltenham, Edward Elgar 2013).

[47] See Katja Langenbucher's accompanying commentary.

[48] Lars Klöhn, 'Inside Information Without an Incentive to Trade? What's at Stake in "Lafonta v AMF"' (2015) 10 *Capital Markets LJ* 162.

uncertainty: it was claimed that, if disclosed, the expected market impact of the information could just as probably be an increase of the price of Wendel's shares, as a decrease thereof. Given that it was impossible to determine the direction of the impact on the share price, were Wendel and its chairman of the Board of Directors Mr. Lafonta obliged to disclose this information to outsiders, as claimed by the AMF (the French Financial Markets Authority)?

The empirical and highly complex question of whether the prices of the relevant financial instruments would go up or down or might go either way as claimed by Mr. Lafonta can naturally best be determined by a financial analyst (which we are putting here in the general category of economists). The latter would intervene in his or her capacity as expert fact-finder, as any other expert might be called upon to help determine the more complex facts of a case. This traditional form of cooperation between lawyers and economists is not however the main concern of the economic transplant thesis, as already noted. It is also largely irrelevant in the present case, given in particular that the CJEU only decides on the appropriate interpretation of EU law, depending entirely on domestic judges for factual assessments.

The more pertinent question, from the perspective of economic transplants, is whether the Court's decision can be said to import normative insights from economics, in the same way that the EU legislator could be said to have done when drafting the Market Abuse Directives. The answer to that question seems, as we will see, generally negative. This is apparent in four main features of the decision: the deductive form of reasoning, the standards it relies on, its elaboration of policy objectives and its general sensibility.

Let us look first of all at the Court's approach to the interpretation of what constitutes 'inside information', and in particular the requirement that information be sufficiently 'precise'. The Court's approach can be said to be a textbook example of formalism, i.e. the idea that an abstract legal norm can generate through deduction a more specific subnorm.[49] Indeed, the Court's reasoning is thoroughly and almost entirely deductive, relying on the four methods of interpretation that students of law have been learning for centuries. First, the so-called literal method of interpretation, which relies on the meaning commonly attributed to words (evident here in the arguments based on the 'wording' of Article 1 of Directive 2003/124 and the 'plain and ordinary meaning' of the terms contained therein).[50] Second, the historical method, which focuses on the *ratio legis*, i.e. the meaning intended by the legislator (shown here in the Court's reliance on the Directive's *travaux préparatoires*).[51] Third, the systematic method, according to which the meaning of the provision in question is assumed to be coherent with that of other provisions of the law (referred to in the decision as the 'general scheme of Article 1 of Directive 2003/124').[52] Fourth, the teleological interpretation, on which basis the meaning of a provision can be deduced from the

---

49 Duncan Kennedy, *A Critique of Adjudication {fin de siècle}* (Cambridge MA, Harvard University Press 1997) 105–06.

50 *Lafonta v. AMF*, paras 30–31.

51 Ibid., para 38.

52 Ibid., paras 32–34.

objective that it pursues (identified here as protecting 'the integrity of the EU financial markets' and enhancing 'investor confidence in those markets').[53]

On this basis, the Court concludes that, in Lafonta-type scenarios, the disclosure information is indeed triggered. However, every single one of these methods could of course have yielded the opposite outcome. The wording of Article 1.1, in that it speaks of 'effect' in the singular, could be said to exclude situations such as Lafonta's where the disclosure could lead to multiple and incompatible 'effects'.[54] The legislative history is inconclusive: even if the drafters specifically chose to remove any mention of the direction of the impact of the information, it is fallacious to deduce that the Directive is meant to cover the more specific scenario where the impact is just as likely to be negative as it is to be positive.[55] Etc. But the point here is not to redo the classic critique of formalist reasoning.[56] The point that we wish to underline is that, through its rigorous reliance on traditional methods of interpretation, the Court is projecting a certain image of the law as an autonomous and self-contained knowledge-system. Deductive reasoning leaves very little room for economics (or indeed other forms of non-legal knowledge), since essentially legal tools suffice to decide the case on the basis of the text itself. The Court's formalism is perhaps surprising in the present case, given not only how closely insider trading regulations are tied to economics but also, more specifically, that the Court was asked to decide on a concept that could very reasonably be understood as a matter of degree (given that information can be more or less precise, just how precise should the information be for it to trigger a disclosure obligation?), whereas formalism can only produce black or white answers (the information is either precise or not).

Turning now to the standards employed by the Court, let us examine the following assertion: 'a particular item of information can be used by a reasonable investor as one of the grounds for his investment decision ... , even though it does not make it possible to determine the movement in a given direction of the prices of the financial instruments concerned'. From an economics perspective, whose focus is on 'rationality' rather than reasonableness, this simply makes no sense. A rational investor could not have used the information in possession of Mr. Lafonta, since it did not help determine whether an increase in share price was more likely than a decrease. From a rational investor's perspective, this specific piece of information was, if anything, even less useful than no information at all, since its disclosure would only add to the great sea of useless information that the financial analyst needs to wade through at great expense.[57] The fact that the Court asserts the contrary could therefore be read as a mistake, attributable perhaps to the deficient training of judges.

But was it really simply a mistake? The fact that the Court's decision was backed by the Advocate General and a majority of States that submitted observations should lead us to at least question this possibility. The discrepancy could also be read as the

---

[53] Ibid., paras 21 and 35–36.

[54] Klöhn (n 48) 170.

[55] Ibid.

[56] Felix Cohen, 'Transcendental Nonsense and the Functional Approach' (1935) 35 *Colum L Rev* 809–49.

[57] AG Wathelet's Opinion, para 38.

expression of a different, more lawyerly rationale, one that tends to focus on different kinds of problems, standards and objectives. The key lies in the notion of 'reasonable investor', which should not be read to be equal to 'rational investor'. Who is this reasonable investor? Even if intelligent and possessing of a fair understanding of capital markets, reasonable investors might disagree as to where the wind is heading. In a way, the reasonable investor is anthropologically closer to the judges themselves, and at any rate cuts a more realistic figure than the famed *homo economicus*. If the appropriate standard to interpret the Directive is that of the reasonable investor, it must therefore be read as requiring disclosure of information that could be judged as relevant by at least some such individuals (even if wrongly). This was also the understanding of the Polish government and the Advocate General, who both relied on the following hypothetical:

> the fact that the CEO of an undertaking in the construction industry is retiring and might be replaced by an executive with many years of experience in the field of telecommunications may be information of a precise nature likely to be taken into account by reasonable investors, some of whom will take the view that that replacement will breathe new life into the undertaking whereas others will consider that the recruitment of an executive from outside the industry can only weaken the undertaking.[58]

This leads us to the policy arguments used by the Court. Such arguments could be the natural terrain of infiltration of non-legal expertise, in its traditional fact-finding function. Once one accepts that any given provision seeks to preserve the environment, improve health or develop the economy, it then becomes reasonable to defer to the arguments of environmental scientists, doctors or economists to determine how those goals should best be achieved, and as revealed by their analyses of empirical data. In *Lafonta*, however, this did not happen. Instead, the case might be said to capture a fundamental discrepancy between lawyers and economists in the rationale that they attribute to the Market Abuse Directive. To economists, the Directive protects the market. Insider trading is a source of inefficiency, in that it impairs the ability of market participants to accurately predict future developments and undermines confidence in the publicly available information (hence, indirectly, the economist interpretation of the Directive serves to protect expert economic analysts). If that is indeed the objective of the Directive, then again one must conclude that the *Lafonta* decision was flatly wrong: the non-disclosure of the information possessed by Mr. Lafonta did not make outsiders worse off, since its availability would not have helped a rational investor predict future developments.

The Court, however, seems to reason on a different assumption regarding the Directive's objectives. The decision states:

> if it were accepted that information is to be regarded as precise only if it makes it possible to anticipate the direction of a change in the prices of the instruments concerned, it would follow that the holder of that information could use an uncertainty in that regard as a pretext for refraining from making certain information public and thus profit from that information to the detriment of the other actors on the market.[59]

---

[58] Ibid., para 51.

[59] *Lafonta v. AMF*, para 36.

What is that detriment? If we go back to our previous thoughts on the 'reasonable investor' standard, it is simply the possibility of acting, even if wrongly, on that information. In other words, the Court understands the Directive's in terms of individual deprivation suffered by specific investors, in the vein of the traditional law of obligations, rather than in the more abstract and impersonal terms of market efficiency. Instead of protecting expert analysts, the Court seems to take the side of average investors.

Finally, there is no doubt the case that the *Lafonta* decision is animated by number of preoccupations other than the fulfilment of the Directive's main objective, legal certainty being the Court's primary concern. Mr. Lafonta's interpretation of the Directive, even if backed by economic expertise, would render the application of the provision considerably more complex. As the Advocate General points out, there is reason to be afraid of the

> difficulty, in a very significant number of cases, of assessing ex ante whether information may cause the prices of the financial instruments concerned to rise or to fall, restricting the scope of the concept of information 'of a precise nature' solely to information which makes it possible to anticipate the direction of a change in the prices of those instruments.[60]

To the Court, this difficulty entails two dangers to which it is traditionally sensitive: the risk of unpredictability and the risk of insiders relying on such uncertainty as a 'pretext' to circumvent applicable regulations.[61] Over-inclusive and easy to apply rules are infinitely better to such (legal) pathologies. The reason is not only the lawyer's particular and professional attachment to legal certainty and effective enforcement, which rank highest among the over-arching principles of the legal order. More significantly, and belying the promise to strip away complexity that economics can be said to carry,[62] the Court's position can be read as a candid admission of judicial aversion to economics, the confession by the judges that they feel unable to reliably perform or even adequately oversee such complex economic assessments as the one that Mr. Lafonta was relying on.

What should one make of such fundamental discrepancies between economic theory and legal practice? There is no reason to read *Lafonta* as evidence of the fundamental impossibility for trans-disciplinary borrowings. It is not inevitable that judges remain faithful to legalistic principles or fail to fully master economic concepts and reasoning. Not every tribunal is as formalistic as the CJEU and the latter has proven to be more open to economic influences in other domains, such as competition law.

The decision does showcase, nevertheless, the considerable difficulties of economics to infiltrate judicial reasoning. It is no doubt tempting to attribute the discrepancies to the more legalistic sensibility of the Court's judges. In this regard, *Lafonta* can be read as an effect of legal or judicial acculturation, from which one can draw the broader lesson that economic transplants are subject upon reception to the same kinds of adaptations and inadvertent transformations as legal transplants. The Court's approach is indeed familiar to EU law specialists, who will immediately recognise the decision's

---

60 AG Wathelet's Opinion, para 39.

61 *Lafonta v. AMF*, para 36.

62 Langenbucher (n 43) 76.

argumentative features and blind spots. Take the cases *Ingmar* and *Owusu*, to pick examples that directly concern private international lawyers. In both instances, the Court favoured overinclusive interpretations of the pertinent rules, developed questionably functionalist readings of the applicable regulations, and rejected more nuanced approaches. It did so mainly on the basis of the principles of *effet utile* and of legal certainty. Both cases were also heavily criticised, in particular by 'outsiders' to EU law. There would therefore seem to be a certain pattern to how the Court approaches cases that is broadly characteristic of EU law, and which might be said to call into question one of the promises that economics is said to bring to law: that it may provide, thanks to its objectivity and measurability, a universal language to rise above cultural differences.[63] This promise has clearly failed to materialise in the *Lafonta* case, where the unity of EU law is based not on economics but on the idiosyncratic form of legalism espoused by the CJEU.

Once a certain piece of legislation (such as the Market Abuse Directives) is characterised as based on an economic rationale, any judicial application of that text can be made subject to authoritative critique on the basis of economics. As revealed by some of the reactions to the *Lafonta* decision, such critique will take a much stronger form (the Court was 'wrong', its assertions were 'false', the judges 'misunderstood') than if it came from a purely legal angle (which will focus on the more debatable notions of persuasiveness or coherence). Seeing insider trading regulations through the lens of economics is therefore not only an analytical move, it can also serve, more controversially, to undermine the credibility of the juridical sciences to have a say in the matter. The economic transplant theory might however provide a reply, inasmuch as highlighting the normativity of economics is one of the theory's strong points and most original aspects. By elevating economics to a normative system in competition with legal normativity, the notion of economic transplants paradoxically contributes to undermining the authority of the former discipline. Indeed, when viewed through this lens, the *Lafonta* case serves to illustrate some of the weaker claims of economics, particularly that it is a science of means, rather than a vehicle of infiltration of certain political ends. Rather than through the distinction between means and ends, the judgment is read more appropriately as a clash between the economic standard of 'rationality' and the more legalistic one of 'reasonableness'. Which one is picked will determine not only the meaning of the Market Abuse Directives, but also the 'means' necessary to render the text effective. By foregrounding such fundamental normative choices, the economic transplant theory makes it harder for economics to infiltrate law. It is no longer simply an issue of lawyers misunderstanding non-legal concepts or subjecting them to some kind of deforming legalisation, but one of a fundamental clash of rival forms of expertise.[64]

---

[63] Ibid., 77.

[64] On the politics of expert knowledge, see David W Kennedy, *A World of Struggle. How Power, Law and Expertise Shape Global Political Economy* (Princeton NJ, Princeton University Press 2016).

18. Mestizo international law: *Petrobras* saga

18.1 CASE BACKGROUND

The question raised by The Economist, 'whose oil in Brazil?' shows up Petrobras, a State-controlled Brazilian oil company, to be involved in the regulation of regimes of oil exploitation in Brazil and beyond, including a crucial role in the distribution of the benefits of oil for development. Interestingly, its mestizo identity defines part of its projects and redistributive interventions. Implicated in a series of high-profile corruption scandals and investment disputes, its trajectory can be traced across different scales and processes, varied actors and complex interests.

From a private international law viewpoint, exploring the distributive effects of international adjudication in projects of development based on the exploitation of natural resources might contribute to a more comprehensive view of the role of private law mechanisms, as well as of their interactions with the public ones, in regulating the global economy and distributing resources within it. Along those lines, investigation on the distributive effect of decisions on jurisdiction for the production of scales and boundaries for capital offers a promising path for furthering a discussion on mestizo strategies in reversing hierarchies and redistributing power in a capitalist world-system. The first analysis explores this path.

But it is also intriguing that in the context of investment disputes with Bolivia, Petrobras preferred to resort to diplomatic negotiations as opposed to legally enforceable remedies. Petrobras, as a major economic group, has systematically made its investments under the protection of traditional legal instruments, which allowed it to benefit from contractual remedies and bilateral investment treaties. When Bolivia nationalised its oil and gas sector, instead of having recourse to international arbitral tribunals, the Brazilian government and Petrobras opted for a negotiated solution, based on a plethora of public and private law instruments. Possible explanations must take account of the long history of bilateral relations in the energy sector between Bolivia and Brazil, as envisaged by the second contribution below. Could this, too, be a mestizo contribution to international law, public and private?

18.2 WHOSE OIL IS IT, ANYWAY? PETROBRAS, MESTIZO TRAJECTORIES AND THE POLITICS OF INTERNATIONAL ADJUDICATION

Filipe Antunes Madeira da Silva

1. INTRODUCTION

'Whose Oil in Brazil?' That was the headline of an article published in *The Economist* newspaper, blaming the oil policy of the Workers Party (PT), during the administration of Lula da Silva and Dilma Rousseff, for the losses of the state-controlled oil company Petrobras following a multimillion corruption scandal.[1] The article suggested that one of the many casualties of the scandal had been a misguided industrial policy, which turned the company into an instrument for a development strategy aiming at supporting leading economic sectors and creating national champions. *The Economist* criticised the outcomes of state intervention in Petrobras by partially restoring its monopoly for oil exploitation, and argued that it benefited less the national interest of Brazilians than some managers and leading parties. Beyond discussion over the traditionally liberal and internationalist position explicitly adopted by the newspaper, asking whose oil is it in Brazil connects the functioning of Petrobras with questions of national development and the distribution of the benefits of oil exploitation. The question is indeed a reference to the slogan under which Petrobras had been founded – *o petróleo é nosso* ('the oil is ours') – following a nationalistic campaign in the 1950s to create a state oil company and grant it a monopoly, against reliance on foreign investment. Questions related to the ownership of oil and the distribution of its benefits have thus always informed the role the company has played in Brazilian development and in the reiterated renewal of a promise of economic progress for the country.

The chapter proceeds from a similar question, asking whose oil is it, anyway, in order to observe the role of companies such as Petrobras in the distribution of resources of economic activity in a globalised world. It shows how law defines the conditions for the exploitation of resources in Brazil and the distribution of its benefits amongst interested players at different national and international levels.[2] Disputes for oil have indeed never been purely domestic. Control of Petrobras and the Brazilian oil regime depends upon actors in disparate places, who all have an economic interest in the organisation of the oil industry and attempt to shape it accordingly. Thus legal practices and discourses taking place at different scales can influence national development projects based on the exploitation of natural resources. Following the trajectory of Petrobras, it will be possible to start grasping some of these connections, revealing that such development projects also have a global dimension that should be further examined. The discussion comes in three parts. First, the centrality of Petrobras in the organisation of a national legal regime for the exploitation of oil in Brazil will be presented, with an overview of relevant moments of the company's institutional trajectory and the relationship of the firm with dominant ideas about law and economic development. Second, the international position of Petrobras will be studied, discussing its mestizo condition in the making of global governance and for contesting international hierarchies. Finally, an overview of recent examples of international adjudication involving Petrobras in the United States will be presented as a field for further

[1] 'Whose Oil in Brazil?' *The Economist* (12 February 2015) <.https://www.economist.com/news/americas/21643224-one-many-casualties-petrobras-scandal-misguided-industrial-policy-whose-oil> accessed 9 February 2018.

[2] My perspective on law throughout the article is informed by distributive analysis of law, as discussed in: Helena Alviar Garcia, 'The Unending Quest for Land: The Tale of Broken Constitutional Promises' (2011) 89 *TLR* 1895; Helena Alviar Garcia and Isabel C. Jaramillo Sierra, *Feminismo Y Crítica Jurídica: El Análisis Distributivo Como Alternativa Crítica Al Legalismo Liberal* (Siglo del Hombre Editores, Universidad de Los Andes 2012).

investigation for scholars interested in the role of law in the distribution of economic development resources in a globalised world.

2. PETROBRAS AND THE DISTRIBUTION OF OIL BENEFITS IN BRAZIL

Petrobras ('Petróleo Brasileiro S.A') was created on 3 October 1953 by the enactment of law no. 2.004 so to operate as a fully nationally owned and controlled company, with the State as a majority shareholder.[3] Petrobras' foundation followed at least two decades of hard debate about the best model of oil exploitation for the country, and the role to be played by the State in the development of the oil sector. Positions of actors varied mainly on the extent of private and State participation, and on the presence of foreign capital in exploratory activities. The result was that the company initially enjoyed a full monopoly over all the industrial stages of oil exploitation, except for distribution. At the time Petrobras was created, domestic oil production accounted for only 2.5% of Brazil's oil consumption. The new-born company had no oil reserves to exploit, and no significant technical expertise. However, the government assigned it two main goals: to find domestic oil resources and to develop downstream infrastructure for the refining and distribution of oil products. In time, Petrobras' activities were expected to lower oil imports, thus saving foreign currency, and to supply secure fuel, much needed for Brazil's industrialisation. In order to help the company develop, the government provided very generous fiscal exemptions, protected it from foreign competitors, and assigned earmarked tax resources to its development. Although criticised, this policy allowed Petrobras progressively to develop a solid technical expertise and to become commercially efficient.[4]

The creation of Petrobras and the role it was expected to play in developing oil exploitation in Brazil fits a moment of State intervention in economic development that Law and Development scholars have characterised as the Developmental State.[5] It was based on a notion of development policy roughly between the 1940s and 1970s which focused on the role of the State in managing the economy and transforming traditional societies. At that time, law was seen as an instrument for social and economic change through effective State intervention in the society. State-controlled companies such as Petrobras were directly involved in economic activity, being central for the deployment of a development strategy where private actors were considered either unable, or too connected to foreign interests.

---

[3] Law no. 2.004, 3 October 1953.

[4] In describing the two first moments in the trajectory of Petrobras, I strongly rely on: Adilson Oliveira, 'Brazil's Petrobras: Strategy and Performance' in David G. Victor, David R. Hults and Mark Thurber (eds.), *Oil and Governance: State-Owned Enterprises and the World Energy Supply* (Cambridge, Cambridge University Press 2012).

[5] As described from a critical perspective by: David M. Trubek and Alvaro Santos (eds.), *The New Law and Economic Development: A Critical Appraisal* (Cambridge, Cambridge University Press 2006).

An important shift took place for Petrobras during the 1990s, as a number of neoliberal reforms exposed it to competition, allowing other companies to exploit oil resources in Brazil. Although Petrobras' monopoly was broken, consensus could not be achieved over the initial intent of Fernando Henrique Cardoso's administration to privatise the company. Following the enactment of Law No. 9.478 in 1997, the state kept its monopoly over mineral resources, but opened the market for other companies that could now compete with Petrobras. The government established a new regulatory regime and created the National Petroleum Agency, the role of which was to regulate the auctioning of blocks and to manage the relations between the government and the winning bidders during the production activities. On a different scale, reforms were also meant to bring greater transparency to the management of Petrobras, opening its governance instances to national and foreign investors. The government kept most of the shares and control over the appointment of seven out of nine members of the board of directors. However, some shares of the company entered the Stock Exchange of New York and were sold to private investors.[6]

In this second moment, neoliberal reforms responded to the notion that law should be the foundation for market relations and a limit for State intervention, thereby supplying a framework within which to foster private transactions rather than a direct means for economic intervention.[7] At that moment, the legal consensus shifts towards a notion of the State as a mere regulator of the market. Development relies on economic activity conducted in a liberalised, State-regulated market. Despite these reforms, Petrobras maintained a predominant presence in the market, since it was able to keep its assets. Indeed, about 60 international oil companies entered the market, but they generally preferred to do joint ventures with Petrobras.[8]

A last shift could perhaps be observed with the oil policy of the PT from 2003 to 2015. The discovery of oil reserves in the pre-salt provinces opened the door for new discussion on the organisation of oil production and the distribution of its benefits for national development, and Petrobras was placed again as a central actor for a national industrial policy.[9] The shift entailed two main evolutions: first, the diversification of Petrobras' activities through a series of important investments from the State; second, the support of Brazilian diplomacy to the internationalisation of Petrobras. During Lula's government, the refinery capacities of the company were further developed. Petroquisa, its petrochemical branch sold to investors during the Cardoso reforms, was reintegrated within the company. Major infrastructures were built, like the refinery plant Abreu e Lima[10] which started working in 2014 with up-to-date technology, and

---

6 Oliveira (n 4).

7 Trubek and Santos (n 5).

8 Oliveira (n 4).

9 For describing this last period, I strongly rely on: S Martins de Souza, 'Trajetória desenvolvimentista da Petrobras a partir dos anos 90: Um estudo da empresa estatal como instrumento de política de desenvolvimento' (Bachelor thesis, UFSC 2010).

10 'Refinaria Abreu e Lima: Veja as Principais Operações' (*Petrobras*) <http://www.petrobras.com.br/pt/nossas-atividades/principais-operacoes/refinarias/refinaria-abreu-e-lima.htm> accessed 11 February 2018.

the petrochemical complex of Rio de Janeiro (not yet functioning).[11] The company also started processing biodiesel and ethanol through its Biofuels branch, and commercialising them in Europe. Indeed, the international expansion of the company was the second characteristic of this period. Petrobras started exploring and producing oil in several countries in Latin America and Africa. This internationalisation was supported by an active diplomacy by the Brazilian government, very engaged in south-south cooperation, and by preferential credits from the BNDES.[12] The know-how acquired by the company through the exploitation of the pre-salt reserves was also an important factor that made Petrobras competitive on a global scale for offshore exploration, which led it to conclude contracts in several countries. During the first decade of the 2000s, the value of the company had multiplied, going from US$15.4 billion in 2002 to US$207.9 billion in 2009.[13]

This last moment could be connected to what has been described as a New Developmental State, combining views of the role of law for development from the first and the second moments.[14] Exploring the changing role of State in development and the implications of such changes for the use of law, some Law and Development scholars have suggested that emerging countries might be exploring novel modes of State action to promote growth and equity. The New Developmental State is considered to favour both a strong State and strong market, to employ public-private partnerships, to seek to reduce inequality and to embrace the global economy. New Developmental policies and institutions would therefore require 'policy and rule flexibility, co-ordination among public actors and between them and the private sector, conditions to maximise synergy between public and private actors, and measures to preserve the legitimacy of government intervention'.[15]

3. PETROBRAS AS A MESTIZO INTERVENTION IN INTERNATIONAL LAW

Disputes for the control of Petrobras and the distribution of its resources cannot be properly assessed without taking into account the position of Brazil in an integrated

11 'Complexo Petroquímico do Rio de Janeiro (Comperj)' (*Petrobras*) <http://www.petrobras.com.br/pt/nossas-atividades/principais-operacoes/refinarias/complexo-petroquimico-do-rio-de-janeiro-comperj.htm> accessed 3 October 2018.

12 Isadora Caminha Coutinho, Steffensm Isadora da Silveira and Taís Cristóvão Martins Vieira, 'A atuação da Petrobras na África durante o governo Lula' (2014) 13 *Revista Perspectiva: Reflexões sobre a Temática Internacional* http://seer.ufrgs.br/index.php/Revista Perspectiva/article/view/64856/37437 accessed 9 February 2018.

13 IG Redação, 'Valor de mercado da Petrobras cresce 1250% no governo Lula' *IG* (10 November 2009) <http://economia.ig.com.br/empresas/valor-de-mercado-da-petrobras-cresce-1250-no-governo-lula/n1237573620239.html> accessed 8 February 2018.

14 David M. Trubek et al. (eds), *Law and the New Developmental State: The Brazilian Experience in Latin-American Context* (Cambridge, Cambridge University Press 2013).

15 Ibid., [29].

capitalist world-system.[16] The transformation of the company through different moments of the Brazilian development path points to its centrality in the achievement of economic development and thus in the improvement of the country's relative position in a world characterised by uneven distribution of resources amongst sovereign states. Symbolising the promise of economic development, Petrobras has represented the possibility of a change in the position of Brazil in the international division of labour, in which the country had traditionally occupied an intermediary position between the core and the peripheries. The company was indeed founded with the express objective of offering a 'framework for Brazilian economic independence'.[17] One example shows how, from the moment of its establishment, Petrobras was associated with the Brazilian aspiration to elevate its positioning in the world. Former President Getulio Vargas stressed in his discourse to the nation announcing the decision to create Petrobras that it resulted from a 'nationalistic policy in the economic field'.[18] As much as nationalist policies might be necessary in other fields, he saw effective independence and sovereignty to also require interventions in the economy, in line with developmental ideas prevalent at his time. As such, legal development practices, integrating Petrobras into a specific mode of development thinking at the national level, also represent an intervention beyond national borders, and potentially affecting the relative position of Brazil in the world-system.

An example such as Petrobras is of particular interest in describing how law affects the distribution of power and resources within a capitalist world-system.[19] Petrobras has played a role in projects of redistribution of power and resources, as it organised its national and international operations through a variety of mechanisms and entitlements which influenced market processes at the national level and beyond. Yet, most of the time, international lawyers do not take into account the way corporate actors such as Petrobras participate in global economic governance, and might be advancing particular claims of empowerment for its home State and other associated actors. Similarly, companies such as Petrobras are considered as subjects, but not producers, of regulation. Yet they play a crucial a role in global governance, as they do also within national regimes.[20] Drawing attention, for instance, to the role of Petrobras' foundation in the management of oil resources in the world could usefully complete the usual focus on the political or economic claims of State actors: the latter act at the inter-state level to advance development claims through, for example, the new international

---

[16] Immanuel Wallerstein, *World-Systems Analysis: An Introduction* (Durham NC, Duke University Press 2004).

[17] 'Discurso pronunciado pelo Presidente Getulio Vargas no dia 3 de outubro de 1953, e transmitido pela "Voz do Brasil", da Agência Nacional, em cadeia com todas as emissoras do País' *Biblioteca da Presidência da República* <http://www.biblioteca.presidencia.gov.br/presidencia/ex-presidentes/getulio-vargas/discursos/1953/09.pdf/view> accessed 11 February 2018.

[18] Ibid.

[19] David Kennedy, 'Law and the Political Economy of the World' (2013) 26 *LJIL* 7.

[20] Dan Danielsen, 'Corporate Power and Global Order' in Anne Orford (ed.), *International Law and Its Others* (Cambridge, Cambridge University Press 2006).

economic order and an international law of development.[21] However, thinking of Petrobras as 'a legal institution performing public regulatory functions with public welfare effects not unlike nation-states'[22] might then reveal a number of hidden elements on the role of law in the global political economy of development.

The concept of a mestizo international law offers some insights for connecting the local role of law in national development projects to global governance issues most often associated to international law. The notion was advanced by Arnulf Becker Lorca in his account of the contributions of actors from the peripheries of the world-system to the history of international law.[23] Focusing mostly on semi-peripheral states and their lawyers, the author proposes a decentralised account of the history of international law, more inclusive of the agency of non-European actors. It attempts to take into account the role of local and regional narratives of international law in order to explain its global expansion. By telling a mestizo intellectual history of international law, he pursues a critique on the Eurocentrism of international legal history, condemned for hiding the role of non-European actors in its development through time – and which keeps informing current practices.[24] As he puts it, mestizos were ethnic groups 'with a European father and an indigenous mother … , riddled by questions of identity and belonging'.[25] As such, the notion captures the hybrid nature of European expansion over the globe: international law justified and legitimised expansion and colonisation, but was also appropriated by non-European jurists who saw in it a way to protect and advance their respective interests.[26]

Seeing Petrobras as mestizo project can be useful for connecting its corporate trajectory to issues of global governance and the position of Brazil in a world-system being constantly remodelled. Becker Lorca's focus on semi-peripheries is informed by the notion that semi-peripheries have more margins for resistance in core-periphery relations. As he presents it, 'the semi-periphery specifically describes those states that have acquired some margin of autonomy to insert themselves strategically in the global economy and that aspire to move upwards, but that because of geopolitical or economic reasons still do not amass enough power to become part of the world's core'.[27] That definition fits the Brazilian case: thus Becker Lorca describes the central role of a Brazilian jurist, Ruy Barbosa, in the Hague Conference of 1907, who opposes and

---

21 For a more detailed discussion on the topic, see: Emmanuelle Tourme-Jouannet, *Qu'est-ce qu'une société internationale juste?: Le droit international entre développement et reconnaissance* (Paris, Pédone 2011).

22 Danielsen (n 20) 86.

23 Arnulf Becker Lorca, *Mestizo International Law: A Global Intellectual History 1842–1933* (Cambridge, Cambridge University Press 2014).

24 Martti Koskenniemi, 'Histories of International Law: Dealing with Eurocentrism' (2011) 19 *Rechts Geschichte* 152; Arnulf Becker Lorca, 'Eurocentrism in the History of International Law' in Bardo Fassbender and Anne Peters (eds.), *The Oxford Handbook of the History of International Law* (Oxford, Oxford University Press 2012).

25 Becker Lorca (n 23) 22, citing Leopoldo Zea, *Pensamiento positivista latinoamericano* (Vol. 1, Biblioteca Ayacucho 1980) xiv.

26 Liliana Obregón, 'Between Civilisation and Barbarism: Creole Interventions in International Law' (2006) 27 *Third World Q* 815.

27 Becker Lorca (n 23) 18.

finally defeats the project of a permanent Court of justice, concerned as he was by the respect of the equal sovereignty of smaller states.

Yet, Becker Lorca does not look at mestizo interventions taking place beyond inter-state relations. The role of private actors and private interventions in the shaping of international law or governance is not the focus of his analysis. Nonetheless, the notion of mestizo could be useful if we accept the call for an expanded analysis of international law, going beyond state sovereignty in understanding the creation of hierarchies and distribution of resources in the world.[28] Furthermore, an expanded history of mestizo interventions could take into account the role of other legal structures such as Petrobras in global governance, by investigating the constant interaction of public and private law mechanisms within a variety of processes on different scales. The role of Petrobras in advancing alternative governance models is connected to its operation in a particular international context and facing specific interests, but also to its particularities in the Brazilian scenario. These moves are also linked to processes taking place at a national level, as development choices lead the company towards internationalisation in order to fulfil national development goals.[29] The fascinating case of Petrobras' expropriation in Bolivia and its use of alternative modes of dispute resolution, presented by Michelle Badin and Fabio Morosini in their contribution for this book, provides one example in which the company may be seen as an actor in the reorganisation of dispute resolution at the international level with significant effects on issues of resources management.[30]

4. PETROBRAS AND THE POLITICS OF INTERNATIONAL ADJUDICATION

International adjudication is a field of inquiry which could be further explored in attempts to trace the role of law in the distribution of benefits of oil exploitation at a global scale. Despite its centrality for issues of global governance in its different dimensions and particularly its role in the organisation of the global economy, the field of private international law is generally neglected in global political economy analysis.[31] Seeing Petrobras as a mestizo with a role in global governance might open some possibilities of analysis to further explore the role of conflicts of law and jurisdiction in the distribution of resources associated to oil, as well as the relative positions of actors interested in them in a capitalist world-system. It might indeed offer some clues for providing a more comprehensive view of the role of private international

[28] Martti Koskenniemi, 'Expanding Histories of International Law' (2016) 56 *AJLH* 104; Martii Koskenniemi, 'Empire and International Law: The Real Spanish Contribution' (2011) 61 *University of Toronto Law Journal* 36.

[29] Andrea Goldstein, 'The Emergence of Multilatinas: The Petrobras Experience' [2010] *Universia Business Review* 98.

[30] Fabio Costa Morosini and Michelle Sanchez Badin, 'Petrobras in Bolivia: Is there a rule of law in the "primitive" world?' in this volume.

[31] Horatia Muir-Watt, 'La Fonction Subversive Du Droit Comparé' (2000) 52 (3) *Revue Internationale de Droit Comparé* 503; Horatia Muir-Watt, 'Private International Law beyond the Schism' (2011) 2(3) *TLT* 347.

law in uneven distributions of power and resources in the world, and more particularly of the role of actors in the peripheries and semi-peripheries in legitimising and opposing the formation of such hierarchies. A mestizo private international law might then be seen as a methodology for understanding the private face of development processes based on the exploitation of natural resources, clarifying their conditions of integration within the global economy and the interactions of actors at different scales for their management and distribution.

In the case of Petrobras, a number of recent cases presented before courts in the United States provide the opportunity for asking relevant questions in pursuing a mestizo private international law research agenda. Although the Brazilian Federal Government still controls the majority of shares and voting rights of Petrobras as a majority shareholder, the company is publicly traded with shares being negotiated in the stock exchanges of São Paulo, New York, Buenos Aires and the Latibex in Spain.[32] The company launched in 2010 the largest process of capitalisation of its history – the largest of its type in the world at the time – offering shares at both the São Paulo and New York Stock Exchange, amassing 69.9 billion dollars to its capital with the operation.[33] However, at roughly the same time in 2009, the Brazilian Federal Police launched an investigation on money-laundering practices in several states of Brazil named Operation Car Wash. It was revealed that Petrobras contracts were being used in a corruption scheme by a set of companies, imposing additional expenses in order to benefit political parties, politicians, Petrobras employees, employees of contractors and suppliers amongst others. The results of the investigation were catastrophic for the company, which had to face an important drop in the value of its shares, consolidated by generalised political incertitude in Brazil and the effects of corruption in its assets. The drop in the prices of Petrobras' securities have lead investors all over the world to sue Petrobras before Brazilian and United States courts for providing false and misleading statements on its financial state.

A security class action was certified in 2016 before the Federal Court for the Southern District of New York under the caption Petrobras Securities Litigation, containing claims under the Exchange and the Securities Acts.[34] The class action and other individual actions against Petrobras, its subsidiaries, officers, independent auditors and underwriters was then suspended pending the result of the appeal filed by the defendants before the Court of Appeals for the Second Circuit. The decision was issued on 7 July 2017, remanding the case to the District Court for further proceedings, and clarifying the criteria for membership of a class and for a presumption of 'fraud in the market' necessary to move an Exchange act class action.[35] In January 2018, Petrobras announced the celebration of an agreement in principle to settle the class action, agreeing to pay 2.95 billion dollars to resolve the claims, without recognising any guilt,

[32] Petrobras. Report of the Administration 2016.

[33] 'Exposição Petrobras em 60 momentos' (*Agencia Petrobrás*) <http://exposicao60anos.agenciapetrobras.com.br/decada-2010-momento-52.php> accessed on 9 February 2018.

[34] *In re: Petrobras Securities Litigation* [2016] 312 F.R.D. 354 (S.D.N.Y.).

[35] *In re Petrobras Securities* [2017] 16-1914-cv (United States Court of Appeals for the Second Circuit).

but aiming at eliminating uncertainties, burden and costs associated with litigation.[36] The decision to settle follows several other settlements for individual investor's actions against the company under security legislation.[37]

From the perspective of private international law, one of the main interests of the case is the clarification it provides on the conditions for a class action under the Morrison decision on the extraterritorial reach of US securities legislation, which had limited it to 'transactions in securities listed on domestic exchanges' and 'domestic transactions in other securities'.[38] Applying Morrison's extraterritoriality analysis, District Judge Rakoff considered putative class members had to establish, on an individual basis, that they had acquired their securities in 'domestic transactions'. In response to appellants' argument on the 'ascertainability' of the test in light of concerns over the availability and content of transaction records, the Court of Appeals clarified that a class is ascertainable 'if it is defined using objective criteria that establish a membership with definite boundaries.' In the same decision, it vacated a portion of the certification order in which it considered that the predominance requirement could be satisfied without the need for individual Morrison inquiries regarding the territoriality of transactions in each case. Defining conditions for the securities class action depends, in consequence, upon a criterion of territoriality which favours the regulation of capital markets in US territory over an expansive view of the role of national courts in global economic governance.

However, the choice of territoriality does not deprive international adjudication of its global governance implications. From a mestizo perspective, the asserted neutrality of the decision still affects the economic activity of Petrobras and the projects of global power it represents, precisely by affecting the regulation of capital markets. By defining who is entitled to be a putative class action member, the Morrison territoriality test sets and controls boundaries for capital, regulating its international circulation. Supposedly neutral questions of private law jurisdiction participate in the creation of scales for global governance of capital,[39] with distributive effects on the oil exploitation capacity of Petrobras and its project of emerging as a global leader in the oil sector. Proceeding from the centrality of adjudication for the organisation of the market economy and the distribution of resources of economic development, a mestizo private international law might contribute for a study of the role of law in economic development choices and what it represents in terms of the reproduction of global hierarchies of power.

---

36 'Petrobras Signs Agreement in Principle to Settle Class Action in the U.S.' (*Petrobras*) <http://www.petrobras.com.br/en/news/petrobras-signs-agreement-in-principle-to-settle-class-action-in-the-u-s.htm> accessed 11 February 2018.

37 Petrobras (n 32).

38 *Morrison v. National Australia Bank* [2010] 561 U.S. 247.

39 Mariana Valverde, 'Jurisdiction and Scale: Legal 'Technicalities' as Resources for Theory' (2009) 18 (2) *Soc. Leg. Stud* 139; Sundhya Pahuja, 'Laws of Encounter: A Jurisdictional Account of International Law' (2013) 1(1) *London Rev. Intern't. L.* 63.

18.3 PETROBRAS IN BOLIVIA: IS THERE A RULE OF LAW IN THE 'PRIMITIVE' WORLD?

*Fabio Costa Morosini and Michelle Sanchez Badin**

1. INTRODUCTION

What might lie behind a heterodox approach to legal disputes arising in the struggle for energy resources? Here, the State parties turn to bargained solutions, instead of reaching for remedies available in contracts and in investment treaties, as suggested by the mainstream literature on rule of law of the investment regime.[40] The first part following this introduction (part 2) of this case-note explores the main regulatory instruments put in place between Brazil and Bolivia in relation to the regulation of hydrocarbons, which include documents as diverse (from a normative perspective) as memorandum of understandings, gentlemen's agreements, standard treaties, contracts and exchange of diplomatic letters. Part 3 explores the political momentum in Bolivia that gave rise to a referendum and later the Decree expropriating foreign corporations operating in the country, and introduces the legal remedies available to Brazil and Petrobras. Part 4 explores the aftermath of the case, describing the new contractual arrangements between Petrobras and Yacimientos Petrolíferos Fiscales Bolivianos (YPFB) and theorising on the rule of law format that was employed through public-private negotiated processes. The case is concluded with a word of caution: mainstream explanations of what constitutes winning a case in international law and the legal processes involved therein need to be reconceptualised to include more holistic approaches and alternative legal formats.

---

* The authors would like to thank Marilda Rosado de Sa Ribeiro and Celso Lafer for discussing specific issues concerning this case, and Ricardo Flores Filho and Anna Carolina Cortellini for research assistance. We are also thankful to Bruno Pegorari for editorial assistance. Previous teaching materials on this case, with a different focus, were prepared by André Corrêa and Michelle R. Sanchez Badin at FGV. We thank them and other researchers involved in this research for sharing primary documents unavailable otherwise. Part of these teaching materials is available in Portuguese at <http://ejurparticipativo.direitosp.fgv.br/material-de-ensino>. See also: André R. Correa and Michelle R. Sanchez Badin, 'Regulating property in the natural gas sector in Bolivia: any impact to the development of Bolivia and Brazil?' (Seminario en Latinoamérica de Teoría Constitucional y Política, Buenos Aires, 2008) <http://digitalcommons.law.yale.edu/yls_sela/63/> accessed 23 April 2018. All errors remain ours. We reclaim the term 'primitive' to react to a label that has been used by some scholars in the North to describe Brazil's trade and investment relations with other countries in the Global South, based on our personal academic exchanges in 2015. Since then, we have tried to react to these simplistic characterisations in relation to Brazil and the Global South. See Fabio Morosini and Michelle R. Sanchez Badin (eds), *Reconceptualizing International Investment Law from the Global South* (Cambridge, Cambridge University Press 2017) 326.

[40] For a critical approach on the uses of the rule of law by the World Bank, see Alvaro Santos, 'The World Bank's Use of the Rule of Law Promise' in David Trubek and Alvaro Santos (eds), *The New Law and Economic Development: a Critical Appraisal* (Cambridge, Cambridge University Press 2006).

2. UNVEILING THE PUBLIC-PRIVATE INTERACTION IN THE DESIGN OF BOLIVIA-BRAZIL LEGAL RELATIONS

Official bilateral relations between Brazil and Bolivia date back to 1867, when they signed a Treaty of Friendship Commerce and Navigation to regulate territory boundaries and freedom of navigation.[41],[42] From then on, Brazil and Bolivia signed several other instruments to govern different aspects of what came to be a fruitful bilateral agenda.[43]

It soon became clear that relations between Brazil and Bolivia would centre around hydrocarbons. Bolivia's rich natural endowment in oil and gas could be put into use in Brazil's large consumer market and rapid industrialisation. Thus, Brazil and Bolivia started signing a series of agreements to promote and regulate their oil and gas transactions. In 1938, they signed a treaty on Bolivian outbound oil and its uses, where Brazil committed to perform topographic and geologic studies in Bolivia.[44] In 1958, Brazil and Bolivia signed an agreement concerning technical studies about hydrocarbons with the purpose of improving their transmission from Bolivia to the Brazil.[45] These agreements give the tone of Brazil and Bolivia relations: 1) Brazil's more developed economy and expertise in oil and gas production would assist Bolivia in developing their own sector; 2) such assistance would come at the expense of Brazil benefiting from Bolivia's oil and gas reserves.

In 1988, under the rubric energy integration, the governments of Brazil and Bolivia conducted several negotiations and issued a series of documents – from exchange of diplomatic letters to treaties and contracts. In general lines, they stated Bolivia's commitment to sell hydrocarbons to Brazil and Brazil's commitment to buy Bolivian hydrocarbons.[46] From the perspective of international law, it is worth noting that Petrobras's contracts with YPFB have been, from the start, embedded in bilateral

---

[41] See Roberto C. Albuquerque, 'A Nacionalizacao do Gas e Petroleo na Bolivia a Luz do Direito Internacional' (2006) 101 *RFDUSP Revista da Faculdade de Direito da Universidade de Sao Paulo* 479, 483–84. We avoid using the term nationalisation to describe the situation in Bolivia because by the time the measures that gave rise to this dispute were adopted Bolivia's hydrocarbons already were the property of the country, according to its Constitution.

[42] Treaty of Friendship, Limits, Navigation, Commerce and Extradition [Treaty of Ayacucho] (La Paz, 27 Mar. 1967), the Empire of Brazil and the Republic of Bolivia, entered into force 22 Sep. 1868.

[43] Arbitration Treaty (Petropolis, 25 Jun. 1909), the United States of Brazil and the Republic of Bolivia, entered into force 10 May 1912.

[44] Treaty about Bolivian Outbound Oil and its Uses (Rio de Janeiro, 25 Feb. 1938), the United States of Brazil and the Republic of Bolivia, entered into force 15 Sep. 1938.

[45] Agreement, by Exchange of Reverse Notes, on the Oil Supply of the Brazilian Market [Ata de Robore] (La Paz, 29 Mar. 1958), the United States of Brazil and the Republic of Bolivia, entered into force 29 Mar. 1958.

[46] Agreement, by Exchange of Reverse Notes, Reference to the Joint Permanent Commission for Coordination (Brasília, 17 Jun. 1988), the United States of Brazil and the Republic of Bolivia, entered into force 17 Jun. 1988. The governments of Brazil and Bolivia manifested in their notes the political decision to initiate the energetic integration between both countries.

diplomacy. In 1989, for instance, after Bolivian ENDE signs an energy supply contract with Brazil's ELETROBRAS and ELETROSUL, the Ministries of Foreign Affairs of both countries exchanged correspondence to confirm the contract and its terms, which suggests state engagement beyond their state-owned enterprises.[47] This type of pattern was repeated in 1992 in the supply contract of natural gas between Petrobras and YPFB. In this case, in addition to exchanging diplomatic letters,[48] the governments of Bolivia and Brazil entered into a Treaty of Partial Reach about Trade Promotion between Brazil and Bolivia for the supply of natural gas.[49] This set of documents constitutes a network of public and private instruments complementing each other. And, for some, this has been qualified as a primitive form of legal apparatus in investment relations. We, however, reject the label of primitiveness and suggest that this is an alternative formulation of international law.

In addition to those legal instruments binding Bolivia and Brazil, and Petrobras and YPFB in the hydrocarbon sector, Petrobras had made its investments in Bolivia under the protection of a standard Bilateral Investment Treaty (BIT) signed between Bolivia and The Netherlands. Although Brazilian officials rejected the standard BIT model protection for foreign investments, Petrobras International Braspetro BV, an incorporated subsidiary with headquarters in The Netherlands, was able to benefit from protection under Dutch BITs, including the one signed with Bolivia, in 1992.[50] As a typical 1990 BIT, Petrobras could have recourse to a regime quite protective of its investments in Bolivia. Materially, Petrobras was protected under the standards of treatment available to foreign investors, such as national treatment and fair and equitable treatment. Procedurally, Petrobras was entitled to challenge Bolivian measures before an arbitral tribunal, according to Article 9.6 of the BIT that reads:

> If both Contracting Parties have acceded to the Convention on the Settlement of Investment Disputes between States and Nationals of other States of 18 March 1965, any disputes that may arise from investment between one of the Contracting Parties and a national of the other Contracting Party shall, in accordance with the provisions of that Convention, be submitted for conciliation or arbitration to the international Center for Settlement of Disputes.

In April 1996, under centre-right and Chicago educated President Gonzalo Sanchez de Lozada, Bolivia issued a new hydrocarbon law.[51] This Law assured that Bolivian

---

47 Joint Declaration (Brasília, 29 Nov. 1989), the Federative Republic of Brazil and the Republic of Bolivia.

48 Exchange of letters between Celso Lafer, Ministry of Foreign Affairs of Brazil, and Ronald Mac Lean, Ministry of Foreign Affairs of Bolivia, on the Agreement on the purchase and sale of Bolivian gas to the Federative Republic of Brazil (Santa Cruz de la Sierra, 17 Aug. 1992), the Federative Republic of Brazil and the Republic of Bolivia, entered into force 17 Aug. 1992.

49 Agreement on the purchase and sale of Bolivian gas to the Federative Republic of Brazil. (Santa Cruz de la Sierra, 17 Aug. 1992), the Federative Republic of Brazil and the Republic of Bolivia, entered into force 17 Aug. 1992.

50 In force since 1994 and terminated in 2009.

51 Ley de Hidrocarburos (Bolivia, 30 Apr. 1996).

hydrocarbons, in whatever form, fell under the property of Bolivia and that no concession or contract could change that.[52] However, the Law allowed the State to conduct its hydrocarbon activities in the following manner: 1) Hydrocarbon exploration and commercialisation: conducted by the State through state-owned YPFB, who could undergo risk-sharing contracts with national or foreign corporations; 2) hydrocarbon transport and distribution: could be delegated, by means of administrative concessions, to national or foreign corporations; and 3) hydrocarbon reformulation and industrialisation: could be conducted by national or foreign corporation.

In other words, although the State of Bolivia exercised property over its hydrocarbons, there was ample room for foreign corporations' participation at different stages of oil and gas production. Importantly, under this Law, the exportation of gas as raw material would give Bolivia only 18% of future profits,[53] a fact that would ignite protests from left-wing Bolivians in the decade of the 2000s.

In November 1991, Bolivia and Brazil launched negotiations for the construction of the pipeline connecting Bolivia's gas fields to Brazil – one of the largest infrastructure projects in the history of these countries.[54] And, in February 1993, an agreement between Bolivia and Brazil made specific references to a private agreement to be signed between their state-owned companies, Petrobras and YPFB, and properly described the public-private network of agreements supporting their investments in the gas sector:[55]

> Taking into consideration the Agreement for the Promotion of Trade between the government of the Brazilian Federative Republic and the Republic of Bolivia (for the supply of gas), the preliminary contract for the purchase of gas between Petrobras and YPFB and the Agreement, by exchange of notes, signed in August 17, 1992, in Santa Cruz de La Sierra, the entry into force of the contract, in this date, elevates our bilateral relations at a more complex dimension. In this dimension, we strengthen the mutual knowledge we have acquired through the previous years and the *spirit* of cooperation that moves us to build the future.[56]

---

52 Ibid., art.1.

53 Ibid., art. 18.

54 Letter of Intent in the Agreement on the purchase and sale of Bolivian gas to the Federative Republic of Brazil (Santa Cruz de la Sierra, 10 Aug. 1992), the Federative Republic of Brazil and the Republic of Bolivia, entered into force 17 Aug. 1992. Previous negotiations were undertaken by the parties under the idea of a regional integration in the energy sector, e.g. Agreement, by exchange of Reverse Notes, on the Use of Bolivian Natural Gas in the context of Energy Integration (La Paz, Aug. 2 1988), the Federative Republic of Brazil and the Republic of Bolivia, entered into force Aug. 2 1988; and Agreement, by the Exchange of Reverse Notes, on Energy Integration (Brasilia, 7 Jul. 1989), the Federative Republic of Brazil and the Republic of Bolivia, entered into force 7 Jul. 1989.

55 Agreement, by exchange of reverse notes, on the sale of Bolivian gas to Brazil, regarding the Definitive Agreement between PETROBRÁS and YPFB (Cochabamba, 17 Feb. 1993), the Federative Republic of Brazil and the Republic of Bolivia, entered into force 17 Feb. 1993.

56 Translation by the authors. The Agreement for the Promotion of Trade was signed in the structure of the regional organization named Latin America Integration Association, known as ALADI. See Agreement on the purchase and sale of Bolivian gas to the Federative Republic of Brazil (Santa Cruz de la Sierra, 10 Aug. 1992), the Federative Republic of Brazil and the Republic of Bolivia, entered into force 17 Aug. 1992.

The call for public and private arrangements is a lively part of the narrative in this agreement, much like what happens in the contract for the supply of natural gas, signed in August 1996 between Petrobras and YPFB, whereby the former agrees to buy and the latter agrees to sell for a 20-year period.[57] It is a take or pay contract, and like the public documents signed or exchanged by their sovereigns that make references to the content of contracts, this contract mentions the 1992 Treaty of Partial Reach about Trade Promotion between Brazil and Bolivia for the supply of natural gas, and recalls their mutual interest in energy integration. Such pattern of mutual support between public and private regulations confirms the hybrid feature of these relations that fall somewhere in between the public and private regulatory spheres.

The 1996 contract regulated, *inter alia*, the manner in which the gas was transported from Bolivia to Brazil, including the financing of the Brazil-Bolivia pipeline; the characteristics of the gas and criteria for its measurement; prices established in US dollars; and created a committee to monitor the execution of the contract – composed of three representatives of each Party. In addition, disputes arising from the execution of the contract could be taken to an arbitral tribunal: 'Every dispute, controversies and complaints that may arise from the interpretation or compliance with any clause of this contract … will be submitted exclusively to the American Arbitration Association of New York, under its Rules on International Arbitration.'[58]

Additionally, in 2003, Brazil and Bolivia signed a Memorandum of Understanding on Trade and Investment Promotion.[59] This Memorandum elects a list of topics connected to trade and investment issues, including the financial support for these operations, as part of a single bargain. Moreover, this is a standard format of agreement that Brazil regularly employs to regulate its foreign economic relations.[60] The Memorandum also created an executive working group led by diplomats from both countries, with the occasional participation of other public and private stakeholders.[61] Similar

[57] Contract for the purchase and sale of natural gas (Rio de Janeiro, 16 Aug. 1996), Petrobras SA (a Brazilian mixed economy company created by Law 2004 of October 3, 1953 – President Joel Mendes Renno) and YPFB (a public company of the Bolivian State, represented by its executive president, Arturo Castanos Ichanzo). (On files with authors).

[58] Translation by authors. 'Todas las disputas, controversias y reclamos que podían suscitarse de la interpretación o cumplimiento de cualquiera de las Cláusulas del Contrato … se someterán exclusivamente a la American Arbitration Association de New York, aplicándose su Reglamento sobre Arbitraje Internacional'. See Contract for the purchase and sale of natural gas (Rio de Janeiro, 16 Aug. 1996) Petrobras SA and YPFB, cl 17.2.

[59] Memorandum of Understanding for the Promotion of Trade and Investment (Brasilia, 18 Nov. 2003), the Federative Republic of Brazil and the Republic of Bolivia, entered into force 18 Nov. 2003.

[60] E.g. the Angola case analysed by the authors in Michelle R. Sanchez Badin and, Fabio Morosini 'The Brazilian Approach to South-South Trade and Investment Relations: The Case of Angola' (2015) 43 *Denver Journal of International Law and Policy* 489.

[61] Memorandum of Understanding for the Promotion of Trade and Investment (Brasilia, 18 Nov. 2003), the Federative Republic of Brazil and the Republic of Bolivia, entered into force 18 Nov. 2003, art. 3.

structures have been used in the new Brazilian agreements on cooperation and facilitation of investments.[62]

3. THE (UN)EXPECTED EXPROPRIATION OF HYDROCARBONS IN BOLIVIA

By the beginning of the 2000s, at the domestic level, Bolivia was undergoing political unrest,[63] and the country's property rights over its hydrocarbons, including its governance structure, was at the heart of the debate. Left-wing Bolivians, a coalition of peasants and workers, accused President Sánchez de Lozada of selling Bolivia's resources to powerful countries and started a series of protests to regain property rights and control over hydrocarbons. These protests, which came to be known as the 'Gas War', paralysed the country, generated several deaths and left many injured, and culminated in President Sánchez de Lozada's renouncing and in Mr. Mesa Gisbert, then Vice-President, stepping up.[64]

Attempting to respond to mounting criticism domestically, President Mesa called a binding referendum on Bolivia's energy policy.[65,66] On 18 July 2004, 60.06% of Bolivians voted in favour of the referendum. To contemplate the popular will expressed in the referendum, Bolivia revoked Hydrocarbons Law N. 1.689 and issued a new one,

---

62 Michelle R. Sanchez Badin and Fabio Morosini, 'Navigating between Resistance and Conformity with the International Investment Regime' in Fabio Morosini and Michelle R. Sanchez Badin (eds), *Reconceptualizing International Investment Law from the Global South* (Cambridge, Cambridge University Press 2017).

63 From 2001 to 2006, Bolivia had five presidents in office: (1) Jorge Quiroga Ramirez (2001–02); (2) Gonzalo Sánchez de Lozada (2002–03); (3) Carlos d. Mesa Gisbert (2003–05); (4) Eduardo Rodrígues Veltzé (2005); (5) Evo Morales (2006– …).

64 See Albuquerque (n 41) 479, 490.

65 Referendum Vinculante sobre la Politica Energetica del Pais (Bolívia, May 19, 2004), DS N. 27507. The questions asked were: 1) Are you in favour of revoking Hydrocarbons Law N. 1689, promulgated by Gonzalo Sanchez de Lozada? 2) Are you in favour of the State of Bolivia regaining property rights over all Bolivia's hydrocarbons reserves at the 'well head' (boca de pozo)? 3) Are you in favour of President Carlos Mesa's policy to employ gas as a strategic asset to reach the Pacific Ocean? 4) Are you in favour that Bolivia exports gas under the framework of a national policy that: covers the domestic consumption of gas, promotes gas industrialisation within the national territory, charges taxes on oil companies up to 50% of value of producing oil and gas, and allot the revenues of gas exports and industrialisation mainly to education, health, roads and jobs?

66 It should be noted that the referendum raised criticism from peasants and workers. According to them, the referendum was antidemocratic, because it was not intended to respond to their dissatisfaction, but to create momentum for a new hydrocarbons law that would not substantially differ from the existing one – especially in relation to foreign participation in Bolivia's hydrocarbon industry. See Albuquerque (n 41) 490–91.

Law 3.058 of 17 May 2005.[67] Under the new Law, the State of Bolivia regained property rights over its hydrocarbons at the 'well head,' to be exercised by YPFB.[68,69] In other words, private and foreign corporations were no longer allowed to operate in Bolivia without the participation of YPFB. Importantly, the new law increased the 'government taking' over oil and gas revenues. While in the previous law the government retained only 18% revenues, under the new law the government retains 50%[70] – 18% in royalties and 32% in taxes levied on foreign corporations' profits.[71]

Even if the binding referendum at first sight seemed to contemplate the popular will, it raised strong criticism from peasants and workers – the drivers of this movement, as well as disagreement between President Mesa and Congress. More extreme critics argued that the questions formulated in the referendum were misleading and served only to confirm the status quo, an agenda attributed to the right-wing political elites.[72] Significant sectors of the Bolivian society remained sceptical about real changes brought by the new hydrocarbons law and continued to pressure for raising the royalty rate to 50%. In the light of increased discontent with his government, President Mesa stepped down on 7 July 2005.

In December 2005, Evo Morales took office as the first indigenous President of Bolivia. His political platform was built on resisting US influence in Bolivia, favouring agrarian reforms and regaining complete ownership of the country's natural resources. On 1 May 2006, Morales issued the politically acclaimed Supreme Decree N. 28701, in which the state of Bolivia regained property, possession, and total and absolute control of its hydrocarbons. The main reforms were structured around three axes: 1) the property and exploration of gas; 2) increase in tax revenues and royalty fees; and 3) regaining control of certain activities and acquisition of the shares of foreign companies operating in the gas production business.[73] In this case, specifically, this meant that: 1) Petrobras subsidiaries' production of oil should be rendered to the state-owned company YPFB; 2) YPFB overtook the commercialisation of

---

67 Bolivia's measures were part of a backlash against neoliberal policies experienced in different parts of the world and reaching its peak in 2005. See United Nations Conference on Trade and Development [UNCTAD] World Investment Report (Geneva, 2006) 23.

68 Law N. 3.058 (Bolivia, 17 May 2005) arts 5 and 6.

69 Ibid., art 17.

70 Ibid., art 8.

71 These new rates, however, should be put into perspective: the rates applied go back to Bolivia's practice before 1996. In the 1990s, the country underwent a large privatisation scheme and lowered the royalties retained by Bolivia over its hydrocarbons in order to attract foreign investment following recommendations from the IMF and the World Bank. Seen from this perspective, the measures adopted by Morales are not that extreme. See Stephan Lefebvre and Jeanette Bonifaz, 'Lessons from Bolivia: re-nationalising the hydrocarbon industry' *Open democracy UK* (London, 24 November 2014) <https://www.opendemocracy.net/ourkingdom/stephan-lefebvre-jeanette-bonifaz/lessons-from-bolivia-renationalising-hydrocarbon-indust> accessed 23 April 2018.

72 Albuquerque (n 41) 492–96.

73 In the case of Petrobras, YPFB gained full control of two oil refineries: San Alberto and San Antonio. Petrobras and Brasil acquiesced and agreed on a compensation.

hydrocarbons, defining its conditions, volume and price, both at the internal market as well as for export purposes; 3) new values should be applied to oil and gas revenues: 82% to the state (18% in royalties; 32% in taxes, and 32% for YPFB); and 4) that the stocks of Chaco SA, Andina SA, Transredes SA, Petrobras Bolivia Refinacion SA[74] and Compania Logistica de Hidrocarburos de Bolivia SA were nationalised in order for YPFB to assume control.

The measures taken by Morales produced negative economic effects on foreign corporations operating in Bolivia, including Petrobras, one of the country's largest foreign investor in the hydrocarbons sector. The measures taken by Morales raised several inconsistencies: (1) they conflicted with the Bolivian domestic legal process, including the hydrocarbons law in force at the time; (2) they breached contractual arrangements between foreign investors and YPFB; and (3) they violated certain international investment agreements signed by Bolivia. Under existing rule of law, Petrobras was then left with at least three legal alternatives:

Petrobras could have sued YPFB for breaching their 1996 contractual arrangements and demanded compensation under an AAA arbitration proceedings. (Alternative # 1)

Petrobras could have initiated an Investor-State arbitration against Bolivia, under the 1992 BIT between Bolivia and The Netherlands, asking for compensation to be decided in accordance with arbitration rules of the International Convention on the Settlement of Investment Disputes (ICSID). (Alternative # 2)

Petrobras could make use of the chain of agreements and other documents between Brazil and Bolivia developed under the rubric of regional integration on energy. Under these arrangements, Petrobras could access the Bilateral Working Group and work out a solution with Bolivia. (Alternative # 3)

To the surprise of many, Petrobras opted not to pursue any legal claim against YPFB or Bolivia before an international arbitral tribunal, and, instead, decided to join public-private negotiation under the third alternative described above. In the following section we explore what might explain Petrobras' course of action post-expropriation and its contribution to the theory of international dispute settlement.

---

[74] By the time Bolivia issued the Decree, there were six Petrobras companies in the country: 1) Petrobras Bolivia SA (PEB), in control of production, exploration and commercialisation of hydrocarbons; 2) Petrobras Bolivia Refinacion SA (PBR), in control of refinement, commercialisation and transportation of products, by-products and other hydrocarbons; 3) Petrobras Bolivia Distribuicion SA (PBD), in charge of commercialisation, importation and exportation of hydrocarbons and by-products and industrial and automotive lubricant; 4) Petrobras Bolivia Transportes SA (PBT), owner and operator of the GASAM gas pipeline, between Brazil and Bolivia – GASBOL; 5) PETROGASBOL, in control of engineering, materials purchase and construction of the GASBOL pipeline; and 6) TRANSIERRA, a corporation in which PEB holds shares and is in charge of the operation of the Yacuiba-Rio Grande pipeline (GASYRG). See Marilda Rosado de Sa Ribeiro, 'Sovereignty over Natural Resources Investment Law and Expropriation: the case of Bolivia and Brazil' (2009) 20 *Journal of World Energy Law and Business* 1, 7.

4. TOWARDS AN ALTERNATIVE RULE OF LAW IN INVESTMENT DISPUTE SETTLEMENT?

By the time the expropriation occurred, Brazil was governed by President Lula. From an ideological perspective, Lula was sympathetic to Morales' claim to regain control over Bolivia's natural resources.[75] Following the Decree, dismissing discontentment within Brazil, Lula issued the following statement in his Closing remarks at the XXX Summit of Mercosur States, on 21 July 2006:

> I have already demonstrated my comprehension to Bolivia's decision to nationalize its gas. I have stated in the Brazilian media and to many other aligned Presidents: do not expect me to bring a dispute against Evo Morales and Bolivia. We have reached the maturity to, although diverging and amid adversities, build consensus.[76]

Five months after the Decree expropriating foreign corporations operating in Bolivia, Petrobras was the first foreign company to officially abide to the new regulatory environment and enter into a new contract with YPFB for a new term of 22 years.[77] The first innovation of this contract was to assure YPFB's property rights over its hydrocarbons during all stages of production[78] ('at the well head'), but the contract also

---

[75] In a seminar to celebrate bilateral relations with Bolivia in Sao Paulo, on 5 December 2015, Lula made the following statement prior to issuing the expropriatory decree: 'Evo asked me: how would you react if we were to nationalize Petrobras?' Lula answered: 'The gas is yours, the oil is yours. And that is how we reacted, respecting the sovereign right that Bolivia had over its soil.' (Free translation from the authors). See Rubens Ricupero, *A diplomacia na Construcao do Brasil: 1750-2016* (Rio de Janeiro, Versal Editores 2017) 660.

[76] Translation by authors. Ministerio de Relações Exteriores [MRE] 'Resenha de Pol. Ext. Brasil', (Brasilia 2006) a. 33, n. 99, 2o semestre, 52.

[77] Contrato de Operación entre Yacimientos Petrolíferos Fiscales Bolivianos y Petrobras Energía S.A. Sucursal Bolivia (La Paz, 28 Oct. 2006) (on file with the authors). As stated by UNCTAD: 'In Bolivia, all foreign oil TNCs agreed to convert their production-sharing contracts into operating contracts, and to turn control over sales to YPFB, Bolivia's State-run oil company, as stipulated in the decree for the nationalization of oil and gas resources of May 2006. In addition, the Government reached a deal in 2007 with Petrobras (Brazil) to renationalize the country's only two oil refineries acquired by Petrobras in 1999 as part of a broad privatization programme.' See UNCTAD World Investment Report (Geneva, 2006) 59.

[78] Contrato de Operación entre Yacimientos Petrolíferos Fiscales Bolivianos y Petrobras Energía S.A. Sucursal Bolivia (La Paz, 28 Oct. 2006) (on file with the authors) cl 4.3: 'This Contract does not confer to its Holder [Petrobras] at any moment any property right over oilfields, which will remain at any time under State ownership. Even so, this Contract does not confer to the Holder at any moment property rights over hydrocarbons, which will be property of YPFB.' (Free translation from the authors).

limited Bolivia's risks[79] and responsibilities. Technically, the parties switched from a production-sharing contract to an operation contract (a type of services contract).[80]

The bilateral narrative between Brazil and Bolivia of peaceful relations kept its smooth course following the measures announced by Morales. Examples of such narrative directly connected to the settlement of the case of Petrobras' investments in Bolivia include:

10 May 2006; Joint Statement by Ministry of Minerals and Energy of Brazil and the Ministry of Hydrocarbons and Energy of Bolivia. Making references to Decree 28,701 and to the interest of the parties to deal with the issues bilaterally, a Joint Committee was created composed by representatives of the two ministries, YPFB and Petrobras, in order to discuss the transition and all pending issues concerning the new contract and forms of supply of gas to Brazil. This committee should be assisted by three working groups at the technical level.

17 December 2007; Joint Declaration. 'Brazil-Bolivia: aiming at a strategic partnership.' This document highlights the spirit of partnership and fraternity that permeates their bilateral relations, and put forward an agenda of furthering political integration through UNASUR; integration in the energy and infrastructure sectors; strengthening bilateral trade; technical and educational cooperation, and other areas. It should be noted that in the visit to Bolivia that gave rise to this document, Lula was accompanied by several representatives of the private sector interested in doing business in Bolivia. This could be read as evidence of Brazil's fostering new investments in Bolivia.

17 December 2007; Memorandum of Understanding on Energy between the Ministry of Minerals and Energy of Brazil and the Ministry of Hydrocarbons and Energy of Bolivia. This MoU details the implementation of new projects mentioned in the Joint Declaration (immediately above) – such as new regulations and competent agencies, financing mechanisms, and the involvement of state-owned enterprises. And, as the MoU elected diplomatic negotiations as the dispute settlement mechanism.

Coming back to the question posed in the title of this case, we challenge the notions that turning to contracts and investment treaties' provisions are the sole manner in which to resolve investment disputes. Alternatively, one should consider the combination of different instruments, such as those used in this dispute, as another type of rule of law. There is no doubt that Petrobras investments and the supply of gas to the

[79] See, for example, ibid., cl 4.1, concerning the subject matter of the contract, where Petrobras undertakes the execution of the contract at its own risk, covering all costs – workers, technology, premises, materials and resources necessary for the its execution. YPFB, on the other hand, assumes no risk or responsibility.

[80] About these and other current models of contract in the extractive industry, see UNCTAD World Investment Report (Geneva, 2007) 160. Another regulatory innovation available in the contract and that could work in Bolivia's favour relates to dispute settlement. The new contract states that disputes will be settled according to the arbitration rules of the International Chamber of Commerce, to take place in La Paz, in Spanish and under Bolivian laws. Ibid., cl 22.

Brazilian market were adequately settled under a negotiated process.[81] This settlement was led by a techno-political diplomacy, that included the Presidents of each country in the Joint Declaration, high-level technical diplomacy – the Bolivian Ministry of Hidrocarburos and the Brazilian Ministry of Energy – and representatives of companies directly involved (Petrobras and YPFB).

It could be argued that the choice of instruments used by Brazil and Bolivia, and its oil and gas companies, in this case leads to a 'primitive' type of rule of law, considering that there was a close public-private connection that could make unclear the prevailing interests and the rationality underneath. We, on the other hand, reject this label. This was a very peculiar situation: a context of few players in the market quite dependent on one another. Considering their limited alternatives, the costs of opting for Alternatives 1 and 2 seemed too high. The few players are the ones that jointly share decisions on: 1) policy planning for building the pipeline and the whole supply chain of the gas from Bolivia to Brazil; 2) financing resources to the projects, including the public support from Brazilian public banks; and 3) the connection of their legal arrangements (both public and private). The cost of an 'exit strategy' to BITs and international arbitration[82] in this case could be unbearable.

Finally, it should be noted that the recourse to the techno-diplomatic negotiations was in tune with the macro political decision in Bolivia to withdraw ICSID and to denounce its BITs as the rule of law for inward investment.[83] And, almost ten years later, based on experiences such as this one with Petrobras in Bolivia, Brazil decided to include in its model agreements on cooperation and facilitation of investments an enlarged process of dispute prevention. The nature of this system is again a public-private structure facilitating techno-diplomatic coordination. Should we still read such types of arrangements as a 'primitive' rule of law?

---

[81] As well as other foreign companies, Petrobras froze its investments in Bolivia during 2006. But, by the beginning of 2007, Petrobras already took part in a new bid on a project to export Bolivian natural gas to Argentina. See UNCTAD World Investment Report (Geneva, 2007) 57.

[82] UNCTAD identifies that the recourses to dispute settlement under traditional BITs take place when the situation is perceived by the foreign investors with 'no possibility to continue their investment activities', see UNCTAD World Investment Report (Geneva, 2007) 166. See also Brent Zaup, 'A Neoliberal Nationalization? The Constraints on Natural-Gas-Led Development in Bolivia' (2010) 37 *Latin American Perspectives* 123, about the structures of limited options in the case of Bolivia (and Brazil).

[83] Bolivia had 23 BITs in force, most of them signed during the 1990s. See data and agreements available at UNCTAD investment policy hub: <http://investmentpolicyhub.unctad.org/IIA/CountryBits/24#iiaInnerMenu> accessed 23 Apr. 2018. Bolivia send the notice to withdraw from ICSID on 1 May 2007. This decision came into force only six months later, in November 2007. As to the BITs, for some of them Bolivia waited until their termination date without renewing it; and others were collectively denounced in 2013. It is not easy to assess if there is any BIT still in force in 2017, due to inconsistencies under the main public databases.

19. Legal challenges of data dominance: *Yahoo! v. LICRA* and *Microsoft – Ireland* cases

19.1 CASE BACKGROUND*

Electronic data – everything from e-mails and text messages to Facebook and Instagram posts to Twitter pronouncements to drone warfare data to search algorithms to financial transactions to cloud data storage – travels around the globe with little relationship to physical territory. In addition, all of this data is often in the custody and control of data intermediaries such as Google, Facebook, Twitter, Apple, Microsoft, Amazon, private military contractors, and so on. This has given rise to a cascade of novel legal questions about the appropriate reach of domestic and private international law over issues such as extraterritorially stored data, speech and privacy rights or the emerging right to be forgotten.

Three important consequences flow from this ubiquitous technology-enabled, data-driven global societal activity. First, the territorial allocation of data becomes increasingly arbitrary and substantively unimportant. If I, as a United States citizen based in Maryland, have a Gmail account, and Google, a US corporation, decides to store my archived e-mails in Ireland or France or Indonesia (or indeed to split up the data fragments that make up each e-mail message among data warehouses in all three countries), that decision seems irrelevant to any question of whether I have somehow affiliated myself with any of those communities or governments for purposes of jurisdictional or choice-of-law analysis. Second, because of this deterritorialisation of data, territorially based courts (or law enforcement authorities generally) will sometimes be less able to enforce their decisions because those decisions require cooperation from relevant actors in far-flung communities. Third, as a direct result of the first two problems, governmental and judicial authorities are increasingly relying on multinational corporate data intermediaries to carry out and enforce their orders. It is after all these multinational companies that both have direct control over the data of interest and sufficient global reach to make legal rulings and requests for data effective. This in turn gives private entities an enormous, and increasing, amount of power in determining the rules that apply.

Interestingly, even though scholars first began raising these issues at the dawn of the commercial internet era as far back as 1995, the jurisprudential solutions we see so far are still largely unsatisfying, both conceptually and practically. Indeed, as with many private international law problems that have bedeviled courts and commentators for hundreds of years, there may not be a fully satisfactory solution. Moreover, even if there were a single unifying theory for private international law in the Information Age, it's not at all clear that everyone would agree on what that theory should be. For example, approaches based on the underlying community affiliation of end-users might be more satisfying than those focused solely on the (often-arbitrary) territorial location of data. But community affiliation itself may not always be sufficiently definitive, and such a focus may not address concerns about behaviour in one community affecting people in another. Thus, as legal pluralists have long realised, there may never truly be a stable 'solution' to the reality of legal pluralism. Instead, one might see legal pluralism as an inevitable (and perhaps not

* This case background was written by Paul Schiff Berman.

even an undesirable) result of a world with multiple communities and multiple legal and quasi-legal systems. In such a world, it may be that the best we can do is form provisional compromises that aim to reflect our ever-changing social reality.

Yet, even if there is no single unifying theory that could put an end to legal conflicts, we can still survey the types of cases that are arising and analyse the efforts of courts and others to navigate the problems that arise from the deterritorialisation of information. The observations below aim to do that, providing a series of real-life case studies that any consideration of 21st century private international law must face.

Cases: *Yahoo!, Inc. v. La Ligue Contre Le Racisme*, 169 F. Supp. 2d 1181 (N.D. Cal. 2001); *United States v. Microsoft Corp.*, 584 U.S. ___ (2018)

19.2 *YAHOO! V. LICRA*, PRIVATE INTERNATIONAL LAW, AND THE DETERRITORIALISATION OF DATA

*Paul Schiff Berman***

1. *YAHOO! V. LICRA*

It is perhaps fitting that the most famous legal dispute of the early internet era implicated all three private international law doctrines: jurisdiction, choice of law, and judgment recognition. After all, online interaction has, from the very beginning, destabilised traditional territorially-based conceptions about legally constituted communities and their jurisdictional reach. Even decades later law continues to adapt to this changing social reality.

On 22 May 2000, the Tribunal de Grande Instance de Paris issued a preliminary injunction against Yahoo.com, ordering Yahoo! to take all possible measures to prevent access in France to Yahoo! auction sites that sell Nazi memorabilia or other items that are sympathetic to Nazism or constitute Holocaust denial.[1] Undisputedly, selling such merchandise in France would violate French law, and there would be no jurisdictional dispute had the French officials limited their prosecution to the French end-users who were downloading the illegal materials from Yahoo!'s auction sites. But even in the late 1990s legal authorities were already realising that it is often far more effective to proceed against an intermediary such as Yahoo!, both because the intermediary is usually a larger corporate actor and therefore easier to find and because one legal action can address a broader problem rather than requiring separate enforcement actions against each end-user. In effect, the intermediary becomes the enforcement agent of whatever legal authority issues the order.

** Special thanks to Herb Somers and Samuel Wenzel for helpful research assistance in preparation of this Chapter.

[1] *LICRA v. Yahoo!, Inc* [2000] Tribunal de Grande Instance de Paris [TGI] [High Court of Paris], [22 May 2008], available at <https://perma.cc/738B-V9BM>.

In this case, the intermediary question had two parts, however. Certainly the French court had jurisdictional authority over Yahoo.fr, Yahoo!'s French subsidiary, and Yahoo.fr complied with requests that access to such sites be blocked.[2] What made this action noteworthy was that the suit was brought not only against Yahoo.fr, but against Yahoo.com, an American corporation, and the court sought to enjoin access to non-French websites stored on Yahoo.com's non-French servers.

Of course, one can easily see why the court and the complainants in this action would have taken this additional step. Shutting down access to web pages on Yahoo.fr does no good at all if French citizens can, by entering a slightly different URL in their search box, simply go to Yahoo.com and access those same pages. On the other hand, Yahoo! argued that the French assertion of jurisdiction over Yahoo.com was impermissibly extraterritorial in scope.[3] According to Yahoo!, in order to comply with the injunction it would need to remove the pages from its servers altogether (not just for the French audience), thereby denying such material to non-French citizens, many of whom had the right to access the materials under the laws of their countries. Most importantly, Yahoo! argued that such extraterritorial censoring of American web content would run afoul of the First Amendment of the US Constitution. Thus, Yahoo! and others contended that the French assertion of jurisdiction was an impermissible attempt by France to impose global rules for internet expression. As Greg Wrenn, associate general counsel for Yahoo!'s international division, put it at the time, 'We are not going to acquiesce in the notion that foreign countries have unlimited jurisdiction to regulate the content of US-based sites.'[4]

Yet, it is easy to see that the extraterritoriality charge runs in both directions. If France were *not* able to block the access of French citizens to proscribed material, then the United States would effectively be imposing First Amendment norms on the entire world. And though geographical tracking software might seem to solve the problem by allowing websites to offer different content to different users, such a solution would still require the sites to analyse the laws of all jurisdictions to determine what material to filter for which users.

The arguments in the *Yahoo!* case therefore establish the basic dichotomy that we have subsequently seen repeated in case after case. On the one hand, legal authorities wish to assert jurisdiction anywhere a community is affected by web-based content. This tends to push in the direction of universal jurisdiction, because content uploaded anywhere in the world can potentially cause harmful effects anywhere else in the world. In response, defendants argue for jurisdiction only where content is uploaded or only where their servers are located or only in their home jurisdiction. This theory of jurisdiction tends to result either in arbitrary or easily manipulable jurisdictional principles (such as where a server is located) or a system where actors impacting communities across the globe can only be sued or regulated in their home jurisdiction.

---

2 *LICRA v. Yahoo!, Inc* [2000] Tribunal de Grande Instance de Paris [TGI] [High Court of Paris], [20 Nov 2000], available at <https://perma.cc/ALK9-XM6A>.

3 Ibid.

4 Carl S Kaplan, 'Experts See Online Speech Case as Bellweather' *N.Y. Times* (5 Jan 2001), available at <http://www.nytimes.com/2001/01/05/technology/experts-see-online-speech-case-as-bellwether.html>.

Both of these solutions seem unsatisfying. And finding some other non-web-based territorial nexus to bolster an assertion of jurisdiction can also be problematic. For example, regardless of how one resolves the jurisdictional question in the *Yahoo!* case, it seems clear that where in the world the actual paper share certificate is by which Yahoo! owned Yahoo.fr is irrelevant to the underlying jurisdictional issues at stake.

In the end, Yahoo! 'voluntarily' complied with the French court order,[5] but simultaneously filed suit in United States District Court in the Northern District of California, seeking a declaratory judgment that the French court's orders were not enforceable in the United States pursuant to the First Amendment.[6] Accordingly, what had started as a jurisdictional dispute was transformed into its flip side: a question of recognition of judgments.

Faced with the question of whether or not to enforce the French court's order, the district court started from the assumption that United States law (and United States constitutional norms) must apply. Thus, the court framed the issue for decision solely in US constitutional terms: 'What is at issue here is whether it is consistent with the Constitution and laws of the United States for another nation to regulate speech by a United States resident within the United States on the basis that such speech can be accessed by Internet users in that nation.'[7]

Conceptualised in this way, the district court had little difficulty determining that enforcement of the French court order would violate the First Amendment, concluding both that the French judgment constituted impermissible viewpoint discrimination and that it was unconstitutionally vague. The court therefore concluded that a United States court could not have issued such an order in the first instance without violating constitutional free speech norms.[8] But of course, in a judgment recognition case, that is not the appropriate inquiry. Indeed, in the domestic context the US Constitution's Full Faith and Credit Clause *requires* recognition of judgments that might be completely unavailable or even potentially illegal in the state where recognition is sought.[9] Thus, the real question should have been whether this was the type of judgment that should have been *recognised*, not whether the court could have issued the ruling *as an original matter*.

To its credit, the district court did include a brief discussion of the judgment recognition issue in a section titled 'Comity.'[10] And the court acknowledged that 'United States courts generally recognize foreign judgments and decrees unless enforcement would be prejudicial or contrary to the country's interests.'[11] Yet, after reiterating that the French judgment 'clearly would be inconsistent with the First

---

5 Lisa Guernsey, 'Yahoo to Try Harder to Rid Postings of Hateful Material' *N.Y. Times* (3 Jan 2001), available at <http://www.nytimes.com/2001/01/03/business/technology-yahoo-to-try-harder-to-rid-postings-of-hateful-material.html>.

6 *Yahoo!, Inc. v. La Ligue Contre Le Racisme Et L'Antisémitisme*, 169 F Supp 2d 1181, 1186 (ND Cal 2001), reversed on other grounds, 433 F3d 1199 (9th Cir 2006).

7 Ibid., [1186] (emphasis omitted).

8 Ibid., [1189–90].

9 *Fauntleroy v. Lum*, 210 US 230, 237 (1908) (holding that the judgment of a Missouri court was entitled to full faith and credit in Mississippi even if the Missouri judgment rested on a misapprehension of Mississippi law).

10 *Yahoo!* (n 6) [1192–93].

11 Ibid., [1192].

Amendment if mandated by a court in the United States,'[12] the district court judge concluded that, because the foreign order would unconstitutionally chill speech occurring within US borders, 'the principle of comity is outweighed by the Court's obligation to uphold the First Amendment.'[13]

Thus, while ostensibly addressing principles of judgment recognition, the court ultimately returned to the idea that whenever a judgment would be unconstitutional if issued in the United States, enforcing that judgment also would be unconstitutional, or at least sufficiently contrary to state interests as to overwhelm any principles of comity. By eliding the difference between *issuing* a judgment and *enforcing* a judgment, however, the court neglected to apply in more detail the various principles of judgment recognition or to consider more carefully those circumstances in which US interests might *not* truly be threatened by the application of a foreign norm.

An en banc panel of the Ninth Circuit ultimately reversed, on other grounds, by a 6-5 vote.[14] Three judges in the majority determined that the District Court did not have personal jurisdiction over the French defendants until those defendants actually came to the United States seeking to enforce the French judgment. The other three judges making up the majority also dismissed, but did so on ripeness grounds, similarly concluding that the enforcement issue should not be decided until the French defendants actually sought enforcement. Thus, the Court of Appeals majority never addressed the judgment recognition issues upon which the District Court had relied.

2. MORE RECENT CASES

Lest we think that this case from the early years of the 21st century represents simply the growing pains associated with applying law to a new technology, it is worth considering the following group of more recent cases. Indeed, because more and more of our social identity is now stored remotely by third parties far from our physical location, very little of our data identity actually remains tied to our person anymore. This increasing deterritorialisation of data and identity is resurfacing many of the same conundrums for jurisdiction, choice of law, and judgment recognition that were identified in the early days of the commercial internet.

A. *United States v. Microsoft; In Re Search Warrant No. 16–960–M–01 To Google*[15]

In 2013 US officers conducting a criminal drug investigation served a search warrant on Microsoft Corp. under federal law to seize the e-mails of a Microsoft customer. This is usually a relatively routine process, and as long as the search warrant is valid, then data storage companies such as Microsoft generally comply. And in fact Microsoft did turn over all account information it had that was being stored in the United States.

12 Ibid.

13 Ibid., [1193].

14 *Yahoo!, Inc, v. La Ligue Contre Le Racisme Et L'Antisemitisme*, 433 F3d 1199 (9th Cir 2006).

15 For further discussion of this case, see Jennifer Daskal, 19.3, in this volume.

However, in this case the actual e-mails and their contents were stored overseas in Dublin, Ireland. Microsoft refused to turn over this content, arguing that the federal law pursuant to which the search warrant was issued, the Stored Communications Act, could not be applied extraterritorially.

The US Court of Appeals for the Second Circuit agreed, albeit reluctantly.[16] Applying a presumption against extraterritorial application of US law, the court determined that because Congress had not, in the Stored Communications Act,[17] contemplated cloud-based data storage, it had made no provision for warrants to apply beyond US borders. Significantly, the physical location or the nationality of the underlying *subject* of the investigation was irrelevant. Thus, as interpreted by the Second Circuit, the Stored Communications Act might not permit authorities to obtain a search warrant and seize e-mail records of a US citizen located in the United States who sent e-mails to other US citizens from a computer located in the United States. The only relevant territorial nexus appears to be where the e-mail data happens to be stored. And significantly, this storage decision is entirely within the control of the storage provider, leaving open the possibility of manipulation in order to avoid the law of a particular sovereign.

In contrast, a district court in Pennsylvania subsequently ruled the opposite way on a similar warrant involving Google.[18] Here, the data question was in some ways even more difficult because Google does not store customers' data in one location, such as Ireland. Instead, Google uses an algorithm that divides an individual's user data across data centres and even splinters the data such that an email is not stored as a 'cohesive digital file' but in 'multiple data "shards,"' each in a separate location around the world. Accordingly, even if US law enforcement sought the data through government-to-government treaty, there would be no one government to whom to address the request.

Unlike the Second Circuit, the court in the *Google* case reasoned that, if the Stored Communications Act is meant to protect Fourth Amendment privacy interests, then the relevant question is where the potential invasion of privacy takes place, not where the data is located. And given that Google can move customers' data at will around the globe, the court determined that forcing Google to reterritorialise the data in the United States does not violate any privacy interest. Then, once the data is repatriated the warrant can issue just as it would in any other domestic situation.

In order to resolve this ambiguity, the US Congress in 2018 enacted the CLOUD Act.[19] Under this new statute, United States data and communication companies must provide stored data for United States citizens on any server they own and operate when requested by warrant, regardless of where in the world that data happens to be stored. Thus, the statute sensibly looks at the underlying community affiliation of the *user* rather than the arbitrary territorial location of the *data*. On the other hand, the Act does provide mechanisms for the communications companies or the courts to challenge or

---

16 *United States v. Microsoft*, 829 F3d 197 (2d Cir 2016), certiorari granted, 138 S Ct 356 (2017), vacated and dismissed as moot, 138 S Ct 1186 (2018).

17 18 USC §§ 2701–2712 (2012).

18 In re Search Warrant No 16–960–M–01 to Google, In re Search Warrant No 16-1061-M to Google, 232 F Supp 3d 708 (ED Pa 2017).

19 CLOUD Act, HR 4943 (2018).

reject warrants if they believe the request violates the privacy rights of the foreign country where the data is stored. This caveat still seems to unduly reify the physical location of data even though that physical location may be arbitrary and completely unrelated to the social reality of the person whose data is at issue.

B. *Google Spain Sl v. Agencia Española De Protección De Datos*

As with data, the results of online searches are part of our social identity. And, as with data, searches are fundamentally deterritorialised, linking searchers anywhere in the world with websites also located anywhere in the world. But what if a territorially-based sovereign wants to block certain search results because the sovereign objects in some way to the underlying website that would otherwise be retrieved in the search? In such circumstances, as in the *Yahoo!* case, regulators may focus on the intermediary – here the search company – rather than the offending website, because it is far easier to find the search company and deputise it to leverage the regulation.

In 2014 the European Court of Justice (ECJ) took this approach in a case involving Google.[20] A 1995 European Council data privacy directive[21] had recognised that individuals possess a privacy right in data. As interpreted by the ECJ, such a right allows individuals to object to old reputation-damaging online information about them that is no longer relevant and not of sufficient public concern to continue to be searchable.

Significantly, rather than apply the directive against the website operator, the Court ruled that it was Google, as the search operator, who bore responsibility for ensuring that websites containing this sort of obsolete private information be blocked from search results. Moreover, again as with the *Yahoo!* case, the Court deemed it insufficient only to apply its ruling to google.es, the Spanish subsidiary, instead ruling that google.com must also block offending websites from its search results.

By making Google responsible for enforcing this so-called 'right to be forgotten,' the ECJ effectively deputised Google as a sort of administrative agency. Henceforth, any individual seeking to have a website blocked from Google search must first file a notice with Google. Then, it will be Google's legal team that will apply the ECJ's balancing test to see whether the elements of the right to be forgotten are satisfied and whether there is insufficient countervailing public interest in the information remaining accessible. If the individual disagrees with Google's decision, then that decision can be challenged in court. Given that Google is constantly altering its search algorithms anyway, one can understand why the court would view this as an effective division of labour. Moreover, Google is not jurisdictionally constrained regarding the websites it blocks from its search algorithms, as a government regulator would be if it sought to have a website taken down. Nevertheless, the fact is that a European court has required Google, a US corporation, to perform a quasi-governmental adjudicatory function on a worldwide basis (albeit only at the request of EU citizens).

This case, therefore, not only illustrates issues of jurisdiction, but also the increased importance of intermediaries such as online service providers, social media companies,

---

[20] Case C-131/12 *Google Spain SL v. Agencia Española de Protección de Datos* [13 May 2014], available at <https://perma.cc/2367-44E8>.

[21] Council Directive 95/46, 1995 OJ (L 281) 31 (EC).

search engines, virtual world operators and autonomous vehicle manufacturers. Given that our social lives are often conducted through, or stored with, such intermediary companies, those companies are likely to become the brokers that territorially-based governments use to pursue regulation. And of course as the ubiquitous power those companies wield over data grows, we can expect that they will often be the target of complaints by individuals and governments.

C. *Public Prosecutor v. Yahoo! Inc.; Public Prosecutor v. Skype*

Belgian authorities in 2009, seeking to require Yahoo! to disclose subscriber information about Yahoo! users as part of a fraud investigation, reprised certain arguments made during the French efforts against Yahoo! a decade earlier. And Yahoo! once again argued that the application of the Belgium statute to a company without a physical presence in Belgium was impermissibly extraterritorial.[22] Moreover, Yahoo!'s argument was perhaps even more compelling than in the earlier French case because, although there was a country-specific yahoo.be website, unlike in the French case it does not appear that Yahoo! even had a Belgium subsidiary operating locally.

Nevertheless, the Supreme Court of Belgium rejected Yahoo!'s argument.[23] Significantly, the Court took an extremely broad view both regarding the scope of the statute and Belgian law enforcement authority more generally. First, according to the court, the Belgian law at issue covered 'any operator or service provider that actively directs [its] economic activity to consumers in Belgium,' regardless of whether or not the operator or provider had a physical presence in Belgium.[24] In addition, the Court reasoned that enforcing the law would not require Belgian authorities to act extraterritorially because the statute at issue did not 'require Belgian police officers or magistrates, nor [any] persons acting on their behalf to be physically outside the jurisdiction.'[25] From this perspective, the authorities were simply staying in Belgium asking for data to be provided by Yahoo! Interestingly, whereas the Second Circuit had ruled that US law enforcement authorities could not collect information held abroad because it was akin to travelling beyond their territorial boundaries, the Belgian court emphasised that the Belgian authorities were simply remaining in the jurisdiction receiving data from elsewhere.

Subsequently, a lower court in Belgium has applied the logic of the *Yahoo!* case to assert jurisdiction over Skype in a case where Belgian authorities sought not only subscriber information but the content of communications as well.[26] Skype complied

---

22 *Public Prosecutor v. Yahoo!, Inc, Cours d'Appel* [CA] Hoven van Beroep [HvB] [Court of Appeal] [20 Nov 2013], 2012/CO/1054 Yahoo! Inc (Belg), translated in 11 Digital Evidence and Electronic Signature L Rev 137 (2014).

23 *Public Prosecutor v. Yahoo!, Inc*, Hof van Cassatie [Cass] [Court of Cassation] [Supreme Court of Belgium] [1 Dec 2015], No P.13.2082.N (Belg), translated in 13 Digital Evidence and Electronic Signature L Rev 156 (2016).

24 Ibid., [¶ 8].

25 Ibid., [¶ 6].

26 *Public Prosecutor v. Skype*, Tribunal de Première Instance [Civ] [Tribunal of First Instance], Mechelen, [27 Oct 2016], No ME 20.4.1 105151-12 [¶¶ 1.2–1.5] (Belg), available at <https://perma.cc/C5Z7-EZ9Y>.

with regard to the registration information, but argued that because Skype is a Luxembourg company there was no jurisdiction in Belgium. Instead, according to Skype, any request for communications content must proceed via a mutual legal assistance request of the Luxembourg government.

The Belgian court rejected this argument. The court ruled that, even though Skype was based in Luxembourg, it was 'target[ing] Belgian consumers on the Belgian economic market' by offering services there and was accordingly subject to Belgian jurisdiction.[27] Echoing the Belgian Supreme Court's decision in *Yahoo!*, the court characterised the enforcement action as occurring within Belgium because presumably the requested data would be handed over there, regardless of where that data might have been collected or stored and regardless of whether or not the underlying target of the investigation was a Belgian citizen.

Thus, the two Belgian cases go far beyond what even the US Government argued in the *Microsoft* case because at least with Microsoft the Government clearly had jurisdiction over the intermediary, which was indisputably based in Washington state. In contrast, neither Yahoo! nor Skype had either a physical presence in Belgium or even a subsidiary there. And if the test is merely whether a company 'actively directs economic activity to consumers in Belgium' by offering services to Belgian customers, then jurisdiction may potentially extend to any web page viewed in Belgium regardless of where the content originated. Such a position recalls early internet jurisdiction cases in the United States that asserted jurisdiction over websites wherever they were viewed or viewable, conceptualising a website as a 24-hour-a-day advertisement 'entering' every jurisdiction where the website was accessible.[28]

D. *Google v. Equustek Solutions*

Finally, we turn to a 2017 Canadian Supreme Court decision[29] that in many respects reprises elements of both the *Google Spain* case and the original *Yahoo!* France case with which we began.

In this case, Equustek, a small Canadian technology company, brought a trademark suit in Canada against another company, Datalink, which had been distributing its products. Equustek claimed that Datalink had begun to re-label one of Equustek's products in order to sell the product as its own. Ultimately, Datalink left Canada, and although Equustek was able to secure Canadian court orders enjoining Datalink from continuing to sell Equustek's products on its websites, those orders were ineffectual because Datalink no longer had any presence or assets in Canada and simply ignored the orders.

Thus, we see an inherent difficulty a territorially-based sovereign may face in enforcing its judgment. If the relevant party has insufficient presence in the jurisdiction, there will be limited means of enforcing any order. In such a circumstance, as we have

27 Carly Page, 'Microsoft Forced to Pay eur30k Fine for Refusing to Hand Over Skype Data' *The Inquirer* (16 Nov 2017), available at <https://perma.cc/7GDS-M9BA>.

28 *Inset Systems, Inc v. Instruction Set, Inc*, 937 F Supp 161 (D Conn 1996).

29 *Google Inc v. Equustek Solutions, Inc*, [2017] SCR 34 (Can), available at <https://perma.cc/6JE4-GBSU>.

seen already, a global data intermediary becomes a useful way to leverage power. Accordingly, it is not surprising that the Canadian courts would turn to Google, just as the European Court of Justice did in the 'Right to Be Forgotten' context. As in that case, the courts recognised that if a website exists but can't be found in a Google search the utility of that website will be reduced to almost zero. Following the court order against Datalink and a request from Equustek, Google agreed to de-index some but not all of Datalink's webpages so that they would not be found if they were being searched for on Google's Canadian site, google.ca. However, those same pages could still be found by searching on google.com or other countries' Google search sites. Thus, as with the blocking of Nazi memorabilia only on yahoo.fr, the Canada-specific remedy was insufficient.

Accordingly, Equustek sought a preliminary injunction against Google requiring the company to de-index Datalink's websites through any of its search portals worldwide. Google argued in response that such an injunction would be improperly extraterritorial as it would mean that Canada's judgment would dictate search results around the world.

The Canadian Supreme Court rejected Google's argument. According to the Court,

> [w]here it is necessary to ensure the injunction's effectiveness, a court can grant an injunction enjoining conduct anywhere in the world. The problem in this case is occurring online and globally. The Internet has no borders – its natural habitat is global. The only way to ensure that the interlocutory injunction attained its objective was to have it apply where Google operates – globally.[30]

Accordingly, the Court took a purely functionalist approach. Because there was no other way to make its injunction against Datalink effective, it must require Google, a non-party to the suit, to act as its global enforcement mechanism, just as the ECJ had in the *Google Spain* case.

Significantly, unlike the French *Yahoo!* case, the concerns about chilling free speech in this instance were far less strong because the websites in question were sales sites, and though commercial speech receives First Amendment protection under US Constitutional law, that protection is arguably less stringent.[31] Moreover, if the websites to be de-indexed were in fact infringing trademark, de-indexing them would be unlikely to be the basis for a successful First Amendment claim. And of course because Datalink is not a US corporation, it is not clear they would have valid First Amendment rights to assert in any event. As to Google, it is an open question whether search results count as speech for First Amendment purposes.

Nevertheless, despite the lessened First Amendment concerns at stake, Google took the same path that Yahoo! had 16 years earlier, filing for a declaratory judgment in a US court that the Canadian judgment was unenforceable under US law. This time, however, the US law in question was not the First Amendment, but was section 230 of

---

30 Ibid.

31 *Central Hudson Gas and Elec Corp v. Public Svc Comm'n of New York*, 447 US 557 (1980).

the Communications Decency Act, which generally immunises internet service providers against liability arising from content created by third parties.[32] And, as in the *Yahoo!* case, the District Court granted the declaratory judgment.[33]

The US District Court's declaratory judgment decision is questionable on a number of grounds. First, because no real liability was being imposed on Google, it is possible section 230 would not apply. Moreover, no party was yet seeking to enforce the Canadian court judgment in the United States, arguably rendering Google's suit unripe or requiring dismissal for lack of personal jurisdiction over the defendant Equustek. It was on those grounds, after all, that the Ninth Circuit had ultimately overruled the district court's declaratory judgment order in the *Yahoo!* case. Finally, as noted previously, even if the Canadian Supreme Court order would violate US federal law if the order had been issued by a US court, that does not answer the question of whether it would likewise violate federal law to enforce another court's judgment to the same effect. After all, the judgment recognition decision is based on different considerations from those that are involved in issuing an order in the first instance. This is particularly so given that most of the First Amendment concerns in the *Yahoo!* case were not present in this case.

In the end, although the district court's declaratory judgment order (assuming it stands) seems to create a jurisdictional stalemate, the reality is that Equustek need not ever seek enforcement of the Canadian Supreme Court judgment in the United States anyway because Google presumably wants to continue to do business in Canada as an ongoing commercial enterprise there, and so it is highly likely that Google will ultimately comply with the order, just as Yahoo! did in France. Thus, the declaratory judgment action may be more a public relations ploy than a serious effort to thwart extraterritorial enforcement.

3. THE FUTURE

As difficult as the cases discussed above may be to resolve, if anything the future holds issues that may be tougher still. Similar questions can, and almost certainly will, be raised by automation in vehicles, and by machine-learning based robots and drones for commercial, consumer and military use. These new deployments will likely reshape legal rules regarding product liability, insurance, contract, jurisdiction, criminal law and other areas.

Or possibly not. Ever since the rise of the commercial internet in 1995, legal scholarship regarding online innovation has often divided into two broad camps. On one side were the cyberspace 'unexceptionalists' who argued in various contexts that the online medium did not significantly alter the underlying legal framework and that well-settled principles of law therefore can simply be applied to online interaction.[34]

---

32 47 USC § 230 (2012).

33 *Google v. Equustek Solutions*, No 5:17-cv-04207, 2017 WL 5000834 (ND Cal, 2 Nov 2017).

34 Jack L. Goldsmith, 'The Internet and the Abiding Significance of Territorial Sovereignty' (1998) 5 *Ind J Global Legal Studies* 475; Allan R. Stein, 'The Unexceptional Problem of

On the other, cyberspace 'exceptionalists' argued that the medium itself created radically new problems that required new analytical work to be done.[35]

One core problem with the unexceptionalist position is that it assumes that there actually *are* well-settled principles of law that can simply be applied to new legal settings without alteration. This is a problem because it is the nature of law to change over time. Thus, what is well-settled for one generation (or in one century) is apt to be very different from what is well-settled for the next. Even more importantly, new technologies that alter the culture are precisely the sorts of changes that tend to result in shifts to well-settled legal principles.

For example, in the nineteenth century 'well-settled' US principles of legal jurisdiction and choice of law saw jurisdiction as rooted almost exclusively in the territorial power of the sovereign.[36] Each sovereign was deemed to have jurisdiction, exclusive of all other sovereigns, to bind persons and things present within its territorial boundaries. By the early twentieth century, growth of interstate commerce, transportation, and cross-border corporate activity put pressure on the idea that a state's judicial power extended only to its territorial boundary. In particular, the invention of the automobile and the development of the modern corporation meant that far-away entities could inflict harm within a state without actually being present there at the time of a lawsuit. Not surprisingly, by the end of the twentieth century it had become 'well-settled' in US jurisdiction jurisprudence that a state may at least sometimes assert jurisdiction over a defendant if the effects of the defendant's activities are felt within the state's borders, even if the defendant is not literally present there.[37] Likewise, it had become 'well-settled' that choice-of-law rules could be based on governmental interests or relationships as well as territorial connections.[38] And, of course, these new 'well-settled' rules felt as commonsensical and obvious to most judges, lawyers, and observers as the more territorialist view felt in the nineteenth century.

Now, it seems safe to say that jurisdictional, choice-of-law, and judgment recognition rules are in flux again, at least in part because of online interaction. Indeed, as the cases described in this chapter suggest, the idea of basing jurisdiction on where effects are felt is difficult to apply to online interaction because activity may cause harms in many different locations, anywhere data is stored, used or viewed.

The answers that law will ultimately evolve to address the sorts of problems raised in this chapter are difficult to predict, and scholars and judges will no doubt have differing

---

Jurisdiction in Cyberspace' (1998) 32 *International Lawyer* 1167. Many of these arguments are reprised in Andrew K. Woods, 'Against Data Exceptionalism' (2016) 68 *Stan L Rev* 729.

35 David R. Johnson and David G. Post, 'Law and Borders: The Rise of Law in Cyberspace' (1996) 48 *Stan L Rev* 1367; David G Post, 'Against «Against Cyberanarchy»' (2002) 17 *Berkeley Tech L J* 1365. Many of these arguments are echoed in Jennifer Daskal, 'Borders and Bits' (2018) 71 *Vanderbilt L Rev* 179; Paul Schiff Berman, 'Legal Jurisdiction and the Deterritorialization of Data' (2018) 71 *Vanderbilt L Rev En Banc* 11 (responding to Daskal's article and pointing to continuities with earlier legal scholarship concerning online interaction).

36 *Pennoyer v. Neff*, 95 US 714 (1878).

37 *International Shoe Co v. State of Washington*, 326 US 310 (1945).

38 Restatement (Second) of Conflict of Laws (1971).

approaches to specific questions of jurisdiction, choice of law and judgment recognition regarding online interaction, virtual worlds, data storage, digital currencies, autonomous entities and the like. Suffice to say that however one resolves the issues, 'well-settled' principles of law are unlikely to be determinitive because such principles are themselves always in flux, often precisely because of the pressures placed on such principles by new communications technologies such as the internet and new ways in which social lives become deterritorialised. Thus, in some sense a pure unexceptionalist position is difficult to maintain.

But if unexceptionalists have relied too much on the application of mythical well-settled principles, the exceptionalists have, at times, tended to the opposite extreme, assuming that the rise of online interaction, data storage and the like upend nearly all extant ideas about law and the role of the state. Moreover, as the discussion of digital data makes clear, governments need not only act through the traditional apparatus of lumbering, territorially-limited law enforcers or regulators. Instead, they can commandeer online entities such as search engines or online service providers or social media companies to regulate on the government's behalf, either by turning over data or by building certain regulations into the computer code that dictates online activity itself.

Perhaps then we need to evolve a more cosmopolitan and pluralist vision of private international law. Just as a rigidly territorial conception of jurisdiction eventually gave way in the first part of the 20th century to the idea of jurisdiction based on contacts with a sovereign entity, so too a contacts-based approach may now be yielding to a conception of jurisdiction based on multiple community affiliations. A *cosmopolitan*[39] approach allows us to think of community not as a geographically determined territory circumscribed by fixed boundaries, but as a set of multiple affiliations held simultaneously. In addition, if nation-states are imagined, historically contingent communities defined by admittedly arbitrary geographical boundaries, and if those nation-states – because of transnational flows of information, capital, and people – no longer define unified communities (if they ever did), then there is no conceptual justification for conceiving of nation-states as possessing a monopoly on the assertion of jurisdiction. Instead, any comprehensive theory of jurisdiction must acknowledge that *non-state* communities also assert various claims to jurisdictional authority and articulate alternative norms that are often incorporated into more 'official' legal

[39] By 'cosmopolitan,' I refer to a multivalent perspective that recognises the wide variety of affiliations people feel toward a range of communities, from the most local to the most global. I therefore distinguish cosmopolitanism from a universalist vision (often associated with cosmopolitanism), which sees people solely, or primarily, as members of one world community. Cosmopolitanism, as I use the term, involves an ideal of multiple attachments; it does not necessarily entail the erasure of nonglobal community affiliations. Bruce Robbins, 'Introduction Part I: Actually Existing Cosmopolitanism' in Pheng Cheah and Bruce Robbins (eds), *Cosmopolitics: Thinking and Feeling Beyond the Nation* (Minneapolis, University of Minnesota Press 1998) [1], [3] ('[I]nstead of an ideal of detachment, actually existing cosmopolitanism is a reality of (re)attachment, multiple attachment, or attachment at a distance.').

regimes. This *pluralist*[40] understanding of jurisdiction helps us to see that law is not merely the coercive command of a sovereign power, but a language for imagining alternative future worlds. Moreover, various norm-generating communities (not just the sovereign) are always contesting the shape of such worlds.

Finally, as this survey of cases makes clear, in a world of deterritorialised data, the role of intermediaries as law-makers and law-enforcers has radically increased. When Facebook enforces a Terms of Service agreement, or Twitter is asked (or required) to police hate speech, or Google implements a European Court of Justice ruling, we can call these acts of intermediaries law or not, but a pluralist would argue that it doesn't matter how you define it; the fact is that these actions affect the behaviour of real people in the real world. Indeed, the actions of intermediaries can have more impact than the sometimes empty commands of a sovereign. A pluralist perspective has the advantage of not getting caught up in definitions of law, but instead recognising that the quasi-law created, imposed and/or applied by non-governmental entities should remain within our legal analytical purview, whether we call them law or not.

In any event, it is incumbent on legal scholars today to recognise the new challenges arising in this increasingly data-driven world and to build new cosmopolitan pluralist legal models that may, over time, become simply the way we conceptualise law in the 21st century. After all, law and society are forever like a Mobius strip, each turning into the other, and what seems unsettled and new to us now may become the commonplace assumptions of future generations. Neither law nor society ever stop moving, and so we must push forward to develop new models to respond to new practices in new contexts.

19.3 *MICROSOFT IRELAND* AND CONTENT REGULATION: DATA, TERRITORIALITY, AND THE BEST WAY FORWARD

Jennifer Daskal

1. *MICROSOFT IRELAND*, THE CLOUD ACT, AND ACCESS TO DATA ACROSS BORDERS

On 27 February 2018, the US Supreme Court heard oral arguments in the case of *Microsoft Ireland*. With more than 30 amicus briefs filed – including from members of Congress, the European Commission, the Chamber of Commerce, and dozens of others – the case was one of the most closely watched US Supreme Court showdowns of the year. With good reason. The implications are far-reaching – touching on everything from security, privacy, the future of the internet, democratic accountability and core attributes of sovereignty.

The case dates to December 2013, when the federal government served a warrant on Microsoft, demanding emails associated with a particular email account. Microsoft

[40] For a more detailed application of the insights of legal pluralism to private international law, see Paul Schiff Berman, *Global Legal Pluralism: A Jurisprudence of Law Beyond Borders* (Cambridge, Cambridge University Press 2012).

refused to comply, on the grounds that the data was located in Dublin, Ireland, and thus outside the territorial borders of the United States. According to Microsoft, US law enforcement only has jurisdiction over data physically located in the United States.[41]

The government fought back, arguing that Microsoft, as a Washington-based company, could access the data from within the United States, that the data would be disclosed in the United States, and that this was therefore a territorial – and perfectly permissible – exercise of its authority. The magistrate and district court judges sided with the government. But the Second Circuit reversed, ruling in favour of Microsoft. And the Supreme Court granted certiorari – something it generally does not do in the absence of a split of opinion between different circuit courts. In this case, the Second Circuit was the only circuit to yet speak to the issue; the Supreme Court's decision to take the case highlights its importance.

The case called on the US justices to interpret the Stored Communications Act (SCA), a more than 20-year old statute that both protects the privacy of and regulates the disclosure of stored communications content.[42] The statute, written before there was any such thing as the global Internet, is silent as to its territorial reach. As a result, all parties in the case agreed that it was – as the presumption against extraterritoriality dictates – to be interpreted as if it only applies within the territory of the United States.[43]

But that left open the key question presented by the case: Was this an extraterritorial or territorial application of the statute? More specifically, does the location of the data (Ireland) or the location of the disclosure (the United States) control? Microsoft contended it is the former, while the government asserted the latter. The Court was left with the task of divining the Congressional intent, based on its determination of the statutory 'focus.'[44]

In my view, there wasn't a clear-cut answer to that question. That said, Microsoft faced an uphill battle. Microsoft, after all, argued that the focus is on the security of stored communications; the United States argue it is all about disclosure. But even if Microsoft was right that the focus was on the security of the stored data, Internet service providers and other tech companies move data around all the time without breaching their obligations under the SCA. Any additional erosion of security arguably occurs when the data is handed over to US law enforcement, not simply when it is accessed and moved to the United States.

---

[41] See *Microsoft Corp. v. United States (Microsoft Ireland) (In re Warrant to Search a Certain E–Mail Account Controlled & Maintained by Microsoft Corp.)*, 829 F.3d 197, 200 (2d Cir. 2016), reh'g denied, *Microsoft Corp. v. United States (In re Warrant to Search Certain E-Mail Account Controlled & Maintained by Microsoft Corp.)*, 855 F.3d 53 (2d Cir. 2017) (en banc).

[42] 18 U.S.C. §§ 2701-27123 (2012).

[43] See, e.g., *Morrison v. Nat'l Australia Bank Ltd.*, 561 U.S. 247, 255 (2010) (emphasising the 'longstanding principle of American law that "legislation of Congress, unless a contrary intent appears, is meant to apply only within the territorial ajurisdiction of the United States."') (citations omitted).

[44] See *RJR Nabisco, Inc. v. European Cmty.*, 136 S. Ct. 2090, 2101 (2016); *Morrison v. Nat'l Australia Bank Ltd.*, 561 U.S. at 266–270.

But no matter who who was ultimately right as to how to interpret the then-in place statute, the case highlights the challenges data poses to long-standing assumptions about the link between jurisdiction and territoriality – requiring a reconsideration of why and how territoriality matters and the underlying interests that things like the presumption against extraterritoriality are meant to serve. As Justice Samuel Alito aptly quipped during the oral argument: 'The whole idea of territoriality is strained.'[45]

This, of course, is not the same thing as saying that territoriality is irrelevant. Contrary to the assumptions of the Internet enthusiasts, territoriality matters.[46] The Internet – and the data that underlies it – remains subject to nation-state, and thus territorial-based, control.[47] But the cross-border movement and storage of data carried out by large multinational corporations that manage so much of our digitalised communications, raise questions about what kinds of territorial links matter. As Justice Alito also pointed out: if the target of the investigation 'is not Irish and Ireland played no party in your decision to store the information there and there's nothing that Ireland could do about it if you chose tomorrow to move it someplace else, it is a little difficult … to see what Ireland's interest in this.'[48]

Put another way, the idea that there is an inherent sovereign interest in the 0s and 1s stored on one's soil – and that those interests stop at the nation's borders – is increasingly hard to support. Data, after all, is highly mobile. It is divisible, meaning that a single email account may be broken up so that the bodies of emails are stored in one location and the attachments in another, potentially in a place far from the account owner. The country where the data is stored may not have any connection to the account holder or to the particular crime being investigated. Moreover, the account owner may not even know where his or her data is stored. These are decisions often made by the large multinational companies that manage our data, rather than the individual user.[49] Microsoft's argument that jurisdiction should be tied to data location is, as a result, hard to support.

Legislatures across the globe increasingly recognise this reality, as exemplified by the initiatives of the U.S. Congress,[50] European Commission,[51] and state parties to the

---

45 Transcript., *Microsoft v. United States*, Case 17-2, at 52 (U.S. Feb. 27, 2018), https://www.supremecourt.gov/oral_arguments/argument_transcripts/2017/17-2_j4ek.pdf.

46 See, e.g., John Perry Barlow, 'A Declaration of the Independence of Cyberspace' (8 Feb 1996), online at http://homes.eff.org/°barlow/Declaration-Final.html.

47 See Jennifer Daskal, 'Borders and Bits' (2018) 71 *Vand. L. Rev.* 179; Jack Goldsmith and Tim Wu, *Who Controls The Internet? Illusions Of A Borderless World* (Oxford, Oxford University Press 2006).

48 Transcript., *Microsoft v. United States* at 51.

49 These are all issues I address in much more detail in Jennifer Daskal, 'The Unterritoriality of Data' (2015) 125 *Yale L. J.* 326 and *Borders and Bits* (n 47) 220–32.

50 Clarifying Lawful Overseas Use of Data (CLOUD) Act, Pub. L. No. 115-141, div. V (2018) (enacted) (to be codified in scattered sections of 18 U.S.C.) [hereinafter CLOUD Act].

51 *See Commission Proposal for a Regulation of the European Parliament and of the Council on European Production and Preservation Orders for Electronic Evidence in Criminal Matters*, COM (2018) 225 final (Apr. 17, 2018), https://eur-lex.europa.eu/legal-content/EN/TXT/?qid=1524129181403&uri=COM:2018:225:FIN.

Budapest Convention.[52] Each of these various efforts seeks to decouple access to data from the location of where the data happens to be located. These initiatives also seek to incorporate, to varying degrees, the adoption of baseline substantive and procedural protections governing the access to such data. This is justified for both normative, rights-based reasons, and, from a self-interested, nation-state perspective, as a means of protecting citizens' and residents' data that is intermingled with others.

The CLOUD Act – enacted into law in the US in March 2018 – offers one possible way forward, albeit an imperfect one.[53] Quite remarkably, it had the support of *both* Microsoft and the Department of Justice – the dueling parties in the Microsoft Ireland case.[54] The CLOUD Act clarifies that the warrant authority is decoupled from data location, consistent with the government's position in the *Microsoft Ireland* case. (Microsoft is thus required to turn over the data at issue in the case, absent an alternative, not-yet-raised objection based on conflict of laws.) But the legislation also takes steps to recognise legitimate, countervailing foreign sovereign interests in protecting the foreign government's own citizens' and residents' data. It sets up a statutory mechanism for providers to move to quash a warrant, in certain limited circumstances, if the United States is seeking the data of a foreigner located outside the United States and the request conflicts with foreign law. In such situations, courts are statutorily required to consider a range of factors in deciding whether to enforce the warrant – including the location and nationality of the target, the importance of the evidence to the investigation, and the likelihood that the evidence could be accessed through alternative means that avoid a conflict with foreign law.

The CLOUD Act also explicitly acknowledges the availability of so-called common law comity claims in situations in which such conflicts arise and the statutory provisions do not apply – as it should. After all, as the US government acknowledged at oral argument, even in the absence of the legislation, a win for the government in the *Microsoft Ireland* case would not mean that the United States could simply demand the production of any data without limit, as has been feared by some. If and when a US demand for data creates a conflict of laws – with the United States compelling production and another country prohibiting it – companies can and should raise that concern with the courts. Courts can and should conduct what is known as a comity analysis, weighing the relevant domestic and foreign interests, before deciding whether to enforce the warrant. (Notably, however, no such conflict of laws with Ireland has been asserted in this case.)

In so doing, courts should consider the kinds of factors laid out in the CLOUD Act such as the location and nationality of the target and the possibility of accessing the data through other means that avoid such conflicts. By taking into account these considerations, both courts and the executive branch would minimise the kind of

---

[52] Cybercrime Convention Committee (Y-CY), 'Terms of Reference for the Preparation of a Draft 2d Additional Protocol to the Budapest Convenstion on Cybercrime, 9 June 20178, https://rm.coe.int/terms-of-reference-for-the-preparation-of-a-draft-2nd-additional-proto/168072362b.

[53] See CLOUD Act, supra note 50.

[54] See, e.g., Transcript *Microsoft v. United States*, at 15; Jennifer Daskal, 'New Bill Would Moot Microsoft Ireland – And Much More!' *Just Security* (6 Feb 2018) https://www.justsecurity.org/51886/bill-moot-microsoft-ireland-case-more/.

international discord that cross-border access might otherwise create, while also setting the kind of precedent the United States would and should demand when foreign governments seek US-held data.

The CLOUD Act also addresses the converse problem of foreign governments seeking data that is US-held. Under the same statute at issue in the *Microsoft Ireland* case, US-based providers are prohibited from disclosing stored communications content to foreign governments. This is so even if the foreign government is seeking data about its own citizens and residents in connection with the investigation of local crime. In such situations, the foreign governments must make a request via the US government, employing what is known as the mutual legal assistance process. This is a time-consuming process that ultimately requires multiple reviews by the US Department of Justice and a US attorney to obtain a warrant for the data on behalf of the foreign government based on the US standard of probable cause – and is an increasing source of frustration for foreign governments.[55]

The legislation offers a partial solution. It authorises the US government to enter into bilateral agreements so as to allow foreign governments to directly request communications content from US-based companies in the investigation of serious crime. It thus provides a mechanism for those foreign countries to bypass the mutual legal assistance process when targeting the data of their own citizens and residents, subject to a number of substantive and procedural safeguards. If, however, the target of the investigation is a US citizen or resident, the foreign government still needs to make a diplomatic request for the data and ultimately obtain a US warrant for the data with the assistance of the US government. This reflects the basic premise that while US has a strong basis for applying its standards to the accessing of US citizen and resident data, it has much less justification in insisting on its particular standards when foreign governments seek foreigners' data. Such a demarcation also tracks basic notions of democratic accountability, ensuring that US citizens and residents have a say in the standards that apply to the accessing of their data, while also respecting foreign governments' interests with respect to the accessing of their citizens' and residents' data.

The legislation also sets a number of substantive and procedural protections that foreign governments must meet. To even be eligible for such agreements, the Attorney General must first certify the foreign government as affording 'robust substantive and procedural protections for privacy and civil liberties,' as related to the accessing and use of data. In addition, each disclosure order must meet a list of particularised safeguards: it must be particularised – meaning it must identify a specific person, account, address, personal device or other specific indicator; based on articulable and credible facts; approved or reviewed by a judge, magistrate or other independent authority; lawful

[55] See Jennifer Daskal, 'Law Enforcement Access to Data Across Borders: The Evolving Security and Rights Issues' (2016) 8 *J. Nat'l Security L. and Pol'y* 473; Richard A. Clarke et al., 'Liberty and Security in a Changing World: Report and Recommendations of the President's Review Group on Intelligence and Communications Technologies; (12 Dec. 2013) 227–28 (noting that it takes an average of ten months for the United States to process these MLAT requests); see also Jonah Force Hill, 'Problematic Alternatives: MLAT Reform for the Digital Age' *Harv. Nat'l Security J.* (28 Jan. 2015), http://harvardnsj.org/2015/01/problematic-alternatives-mlat-reform-for-the-digital-age (noting that it often takes months if not years for foreign governments to respond to MLAT requests).

under the foreign country's domestic laws; and cannot be used to infringe freedom of speech. Additional protections and details can and should be written into the executive agreements themselves.

The CLOUD Act thus offers a promising way to address some of the cross-border disputes regarding access to data. It facilitates the ability of governments to access data across borders, based on their legitimate investigatory needs; recognises and respects the legitimate sovereign interest in safeguarding one's citizens' and residents' own data; and establishes baseline substantive and procedural protections in the process.

2. *GOOGLE SPAIN*, THE RIGHT TO BE FORGOTTEN, AND CONTENT REGULATION ACROSS BORDERS

Debates about content regulation raise related, albeit distinct, questions regarding territoriality, jurisdiction and data. The key questions differs, in that they are about controlling content, as opposed to controlling access. But there is a similar underlying set of challenges resulting from the interconnectedness of the Internet, and there are similar debates over whose rules to apply. The issues are exemplified in the case now pending before the European Court of Justice (ECJ) regarding the territorial reach of Europe's right to be forgotten.[56] It is the follow-on case to the 2014 *Google Spain* case, in which the ECJ affirmed the right of individual users to demand that search engines de-index personal information about the user.[57]

As clarified by the ECJ, the right to be forgotten applies with respect to information is 'inadequate, irrelevant or excessive in relation to the purposes of the processing, … not kept up to date, or … kept for longer than is necessary unless … required to be kept for historical, statistical or scientific purposes,' even if true. In such situations, data owners can go to the applicable search engine and demand that the information be delinked. The search engine is required to do so – absent a determination that the data subject is a 'public figure' and there is a countervailing public right to know.[58]

The ECJ placed the initial burden in enforcing the right on search engines.[59] But it left open the key, and still contested, issue as to the territorial scope of the announced

[56] See Conseil d'État (CE) (highest administrative court), 19 July 2017, 399922, (Fr.), http://www.conseil-etat.fr/Decisions-Avis-Publications/Decisions/Selection-des-decisions-faisant-l-objet-d-une-communication-particuliere/CE-19-juillet-2017-GOOGLE-INC.

[57] See Case C-131/12, *Google Spain SL v. Agencia Española de Protección de Datos (AEPD)* (13 May 2014), http://curia.europa.eu/juris/document/document_print.jsf?doclang=EN&text=&pageIndex=0&docid=152065&cid=244711.

[58] Ibid. at ¶¶ 4, 82, 94.

[59] This of course is not the only way to design an implementation system. The court could have, for example, insisted that the data subject had a right to an administrative review of a claimed right to be forgotten. By instead placing the obligation squarely on the search engine, the court gave Google, a private actor, an enormous amount of discretion to make the initial decisions about who constitutes a public figure, what constitutes the countervailing right to know, and how to mediate between these conflicting interests. And while there is the possibility of appeal to a Data Protection Agency, there is no mechanism for a member of the public to

right. How far does the obligation to delink extend? Initially, Google – the search engine of choice for most European users – delinked the information from the European Google search domains (i.e., google.fr, google.de, google.es, etc.) and left it accessible elsewhere, including on google.com. The Article 29 Working Group – made up of Data Protection Officers from across the EU – deemed this insufficient; according to the Article 29 Working Group covered material should be delisted globally in order to adequately protect the right.[60]

In May 2015, the French data protection agency ('CNIL') took up the mantle of the Article 29 Working Group and ordered Google to remove delinked information from all applicable domains, including the .com domain.[61] Google eventually agreed to make covered information inaccessible to anyone accessing the search from the data subject's state of residence, no matter whether the search was conducted from the state-level domain or google.com. But it continued to make the information available to others who accessed Google from outside the EU. And within the EU, the information is still available on google.com if accessed from outside the data subject's home state.

In practice, this means that if a French data subject successfully asserts his or her right to be forgotten, the information in question will not be available to anyone searching the user's name from France – even to those that attempt to search using google.com. It will, however, be accessible to individuals searching from outside Europe, whether using google.com or the default state-level domain, as well as other Europeans that bypass the default settings on their browser and search via google.com.

For the French Data Protection Authority, this doesn't go far enough. The French Data Protection Authority continues to insist that global deindexing is the only way to adequately protect what it deems a fundamental right.

Google, conversely, argues that while it is willing to abide by the requirements of the right to be forgotten in the EU, the EU should not be imposing its particular vision of speech and privacy rights on the rest of the world. As Google's General Counsel, Kent Walker, put it, 'if French law applies globally, how long will it be until other countries – perhaps less open and democratic – start demanding that their laws regulating information likewise have global reach?'[62] Walker warns of a 'global race to the bottom,' ultimately resulting in French citizens being unable to see information that is perfectly lawful to view in France.[63] Google further argues that its current approach is

know about, let alone complain, if Google adheres to the request to delist but does so in an arguably excessive manner.

[60] See Article 29 Data Prot. Working Party, *Guidelines on the Implementation of the Court of Justice of the European Union Judgment on 'Google Spain and Inc v. Agencia Española de Protección de Datos (AEPD) and Mario Costeja González' C-131/12*, at 6 (26 Nov. 2014), http://ec.europa.eu/justice/data-protection/article-29/documentation/opinion-recommendation/files/2014/wp225_en.pdf.

[61] The CNIL is comprised of 17 members, including parliamentarians; members of the French Economic, Social and Environmental Council; representatives of high jurisdictions; and appointed 'qualified public figures.'

[62] Alex Hern, 'Google Takes Right to Be Forgotten Battle to France's Highest Court' *Guardian* (19 May 2016), https://www.theguardian.com/technology/2016/may/19/google-right-to-be-forgotten-fight-france-highest-court (https://perma.cc/A4H3-7C5H).

[63] Ibid.

effective in protecting the applicable right, given that 97% of French users access the search engine via google.fr. While not foolproof, the vast majority of French users would not see the link.[64] As of this writing, the ECJ had not issued its opinion in the case.[65]

This, of course, is not the first time in which France and the United States have clashed over speech rights. The *Yahoo!* case over the sale of Nazi memorabilia – permitted in the United States but prohibited in France – is a precursor of this dispute.[66] Although Yahoo! initially claimed that it could not technically block just French residents' access to the relevant auction site, independent technical experts revealed that in fact it could do so with about 90% accuracy, and it was ordered to do so.[67] That, in fact, was the basic approach Google was attempting to replicate here – creating a differentiated access regime. But the French Data Protection Authority has deemed this insufficient, asserting that individual rights will be insufficiently protected if accessible at all.

Similar disputes are also playing out elsewhere. In a dispute regarding Canada's intellectual property laws, a Canadian court found that a company named Datalink had stolen trade secrets from a company named Equustek and was selling, over the internet, a competing counterfeit product. Datalink fled the jurisdiction and continued to operate from an unknown location. When Equustek requested that Google remove all links to Datalink, it did so – but only for searches stemming from the default Canadian domain,

---

[64] Carol A.F. Umhoefer and Caroline Chance, 'Right to Be Forgotten: The CNIL Rejects Google Inc.'s Appeal Against Cease and Desist Order' *Privacy Matters* (22 Sept 2015), http://blogs.dlapiper.com/privacymatters/right-to-be-forgotten-the-cnil-rejects-google-inc-s-appeal-against-cease-and-desist-order/.

[65] The case has spawned an active debate and commentary. While privacy groups, free speech advocates, and academics support Google, many others disagree. Compare Nani Jansen Reventlow et al., 'A French Court Case Against Google Could Threaten Global Speech Rights' *Wash. Post* (22 Dec. 2016), https://www.washingtonpost.com/news/global-opinions/wp/2016/12/22/a-french-court-case-against-google-could-threaten-global-speech-rights/?utm_term=.8923fa5e5261 (supporting Google to avoid 'a precedent that others will inevitably use to censor search results they don't like'), with Frank Pasquale, 'Reforming the Law of Reputation' (2015) 47 *Loy. U. Chi. L.J.* 515, 517 ('Such removals are a middle ground between info-anarchy and censorship. They neither disappear information from the Internet (it can be found at the original source), nor allow it to dominate the impression of the aggrieved individual.'); see also Farhad Manjoo, '"Right to Be Forgotten" Online Could Spread' *N.Y. Times* (5 Aug. 2015), http://www.nytimes.com/2015/08/06/technology/personaltech/right-to-be-forgotten-online-is-poised-to-spread.html?_r=1 (citing proponents on both sides).

[66] For further discussion of this case, see Paul Schiff Berman, 19.2, in this volume.

[67] See *La Ligue Contre le Racisme et L'Antisésmistisme (L.I.C.R.A.) et L'Union des Étudiants Juifs de France (U.EJ.F.) c. Yahoo! Inc. et Société Yahoo! France* Interim Court Order, Tribunal de grande instance (TGI) (ordinary court of original jurisdiction) Paris, 20 Nov. 2000 (Fr.). Ultimately, however, Yahoo! caved, adopting a new policy that applied across the board (and thus did not require filtering by geography) and would 'no longer allow items that are associated with groups which promote or glorify hatred and violence … [including] Nazi militaria and KKK memorabilia.' Jeff Peline, 'Yahoo to Charge Auction Fees, Ban Hate Materials' *CNET* (29 Mar. 2002), https://www.cnet.com/uk/news/yahoo-to-charge-auction-fees-ban-hate-materials. See also Paul Schiff Berman, 'Global Legal Pluralism' (2007) 80 *S. Cal. L. Rev.* 1155, 1159–60.

google.ca. It left the links available to those searching from google.com or from outside Canada. Equustek then brought an action against Google, seeking a global take down of all the links.

The Canadian Supreme Court sided with Equustek over Google's strong objections. As the Court put it, 'The problem in this case is occurring online and globally. The Internet has no borders – its natural habitat is global. The only way to ensure that the interlocutory injunction attained its objective was to have it apply where Google operates – globally.'[68]

But a US district court has disagreed. In a ruling issued on 2 November 2017, the US district court granted a preliminary injunction in favor of Google's effort to prevent enforcement.[69] The court concluded, by forcing intermediaries to remove links to third party material, the Canadian Supreme Court ruling 'threatens free speech on the global Internet.'[70]

These cases raise important, and still highly contested questions about whose rules govern and who gets to decide. One possible, but particularly unsatisfactory answer, is that offered by the Chinese – for states to increasingly build closed-off Internets with great firewalls. This would allow states to regulate content locally. But it also has huge costs to the free flow of information, to the economic growth potential of the Internet, and global innovation.

Alternatively, states will need to find ways to manage these disputes across borders. The kind of geo-filtering offered by Google and used in a number of other contexts, seems one possible solution, particularly when dealing with governmental efforts to control speech. But in some cases, such filtering may not be sufficiently effective. A person's security is breached whether her stolen card information and social security number is posted on google.us or google.com. Similarly, one might think that privacy interests should be universally protected.

Harmonisation of speech and privacy norms across borders would help, but also is not likely something that can be readily achieved (and might have negative effects of resorting to the lowest common denominator, with a net reduction in speech and privacy rights for many). Absent regulation, states will need to decide which kinds of content regulation are worth pushing on a global basis (and perhaps worth fighting with providers in the process) and which can be sufficiently accommodated on a more local basis. And providers will need to decide when these governmental interests can be effectively accommodated across borders, consistent with providers' own speech and privacy values; in some cases, providers will have to either comply or be forced out of the market. Obviously, this is an easier choice in smaller markets. It's much harder when dealing with, say, the EU.

---

68 Equustek case, Canadian Sup. Court (June 28, 2017) Par. 41, https://scc-csc.lexum.com/scc-csc/scc-csc/en/item/16701/index.do.

69 *Google v. Equustek*, 2017 WL 5000834 (N.D. Ca. Nov. 2, 2017).

70 Ibid. at *5.

3. CONCLUSION

As these examples elucidate, cross-borders flows of data raise new jurisdictional challenges, forcing states to deal with new multinational actors and grapple with competing norms regarding speech and privacy, as well as competing efforts to assert sovereign control. These disputes are messy and complicated and will likely only to grow in the future – calling out for nuanced solutions that respect and reflect differences across borders. Ideally these are solutions that are worked out in legislatures and the kinds of harmonisation processes that occur via bilateral and multilateral agreements between governments. But as these examples elucidate, the political processes will inevitably leave gaps. Solutions will be case-specific, but should seek, to the greatest extent possible, to promote harmonisation, identify and respect the cross-border differences that exist, and promote baseline speech and privacy protections that will inure to the benefit of all.

PART V

GLOBAL MARKET: UNFAMILIAR FOCI OF CONCERN

20. Global contract governance: *Selden v. Airbnb*

20.1 CASE BACKGROUND

This case concerns a racial discrimination suit against Airbnb. The company operates an online marketplace in which people can list, discover and book accommodation around the world. Is Airbnb the contemporary, global equivalent to a hotel; and its hosts to rental agents or hotel employees? Into the limelight with this dispute comes Airbnb's liability for the conduct of its users and the rising importance of alternative dispute resolution in online adhesion contracts.

The claimant, an African American citizen named Gregory Selden, was planning a trip to Philadelphia in March 2015. In order to book accommodation, Selden created a profile on Airbnb by 'signing up with Facebook'. Selden's profile included a photograph of his face and personal information. Shortly afterwards, he made an inquiry about a listing and the host replied that the accommodation was not available. Selden suspected that he was denied access due to his race and created a fictitious Airbnb account using photographs of white men. He then moved to book the same accommodation once more and this time the inquiry was accepted by the host. Selden sought to hold Airbnb responsible under federal civil rights laws for the discriminatory conduct of those who offer accommodation on their website. In May 2016 he filed a putative class action after mobilising social media with the hashtag '#airbnbwhileblack'. Airbnb argued that the issue cannot be brought to court, since Airbnb's Terms of Service stipulates mandatory arbitration for disputes 'arising out of or relating to these Terms…'. However, Selden contested the existence of a conscionable contract and the scope of the arbitration agreement. The Court, therefore, had to analyse three issues: (i) whether Selden agreed to Airbnb's Terms of Service; (ii) whether Airbnb's arbitration agreement encompasses Selden's discrimination claims; (iii) whether Airbnb's arbitration agreement is enforceable.

First, the Court established that 'arbitration is a matter of contract law' and identified Airbnb's Terms of Service agreement as an online adhesion contract. The Court considered that Plaintiff had agreed to the Terms by signing up and using their services. Even though it was acknowledged that consumer's consent can be 'largely passive' in electronic agreements, ignorance is not a defence against knowledge of the precise terms of contract. The Federal Court stated that consumers must be aware that they are entering into contracts by signing up for internet-based services. Second, the Court adopted a broad interpretation of the arbitration agreement and sided with Airbnb ultimately favouring arbitration. The Court recognized that Airbnb's Terms of Service agreement accounted for Selden's claims of unlawful race discrimination. Finally, the Court ruled that federal civil rights claims can be resolved in arbitration.

The Court declared that the arbitration agreement was valid and enforceable, granting Airbnb's Motion to Compel Arbitration.

Case: *Gregory Selden v. Airbnb, Inc.*, No. 16-933, D.D.C.; 2016 U.S. Dist

20.2 DOES A GLOBAL LAW EXIST? A REFLECTION ON *SELDEN V. AIRBNB* CASE AND ITS AFTERMATH

*David Restrepo Amariles and Gregory Lewkowicz**

The question 'does global law exist?' is not a question of fact. It is, first, a polemic formulation of a question of legal theory or epistemology. Similar to questions like 'does social law exist?' or 'does public law exist' that over time have become less controversial, it does not concern the empirical existence of a certain kind of law but the way the law is known, described, observed and understood. This is a disciplinary heuristic; a question of whether it is appropriate to recognise its existence within the legal knowledge of a specialised discipline of which global law is the object[1] and that would be characterised by a particular perspective and method.

Legal history illustrates the extent to which legal science constructs its object by description.[2] It also shows that issues relevant to legal fields and boundaries between disciplines are subject to political quarrels both in the noble and trivial sense of the term.[3] The question of global law is no exception. This contribution will therefore not discuss a question of fact – the existence of a global law as a sort of regime – but a question of opportunity: why global law? Or better yet, the global law for what? The contribution is divided into two parts: the first part provides the theoretical context and grounds that underpin the approach adopted by the authors. The second part substantiates this approach through an in-depth examination of *Selden v. Airbnb*. The study ends with some concluding remarks.

1. THE GLOBAL TURN IN LAW AND THE EMERGENCE OF GLOBAL AND TRANSNATIONAL LAW

Since the 1990s, the social sciences have been experiencing a global shift[4] that extends beyond the vertiginous increase in the study of globalisation in multiple dimensions. It refers instead to the *aggiornamento* of these disciplines, allowing them to be revisited by adopting a global dimension. Beyond its manifestation in a variety of forms, the global shift is characterised by a break from the much criticised 'methodological

* Contribution originally written in French, translated to English by Megan Ma.

1 William Twining and Benoît Frydman, 'A symposium on Global Law, Legal Pluralism and Legal Indicators' (2015) 47 *J L Pluralism and Unofficial L* 1, where William Twining discusses the idea of 'global law' as a field concept.

2 Jan Schröder, *Recht als Wissenschaft: Geschichte der juristischen Methode vom Humanismus bis zur historischen Schule* (1500-1800) (Munich, C.H. Beck Verlag 2001).

3 cf. Frédéric Audren and Ségolène Barbou des Places (eds), *Qu'est-ce qu'une disciplinaire juridique ? Fondations et recomposition des disciplines dans les facultés de droit* (Paris, Lextenso 2018, forthcoming) on the idea of global law as a discipline. In particular refer to the contribution of Benoît Frydman.

4 Alain Caillé and Stéphane Dufoix (eds), *Le tournant global des sciences sociales* (Paris, La Découverte 2013).

nationalism.'[5] That is to say, the tendency to confine society within its territorial limits. The State is perceived through national boundaries, thereby reducing any social phenomenon beyond the State to international relations.

The effect of the aforementioned view, which upsets the habits and even most established methods in other disciplines, concerns the law in a particular way. It maintains a relationship so profound to the state that they have occasionally been conceived as inseparable entities. Therefore, the observation and description of the law from a point of view that is neither domestic nor international is challenging. Yet, the idea is not new; it is the heart of legal pluralism.[6] Nonetheless, the question posed is the idea of observing the law from a global perspective;[7] one that has reappeared intermittently since the end of the 19th century and described as the first globalisation.[8]

In 1928, Japanese jurist Ishizaki observed the formation of global law as a reaction to the silk trade.[9] A few years later, Edouard Lambert noted the emergence of a commercial law with 'the ability to spread freely across the borders of states and nationalities.'[10] In the field of international law, a number of authors, such as Georges Scelle and his reflections on the law of 'a global international community,'[11] have sought to overcome methodological nationalism.[12] The work of the School of Dijon, particularly in the field of international arbitration, *lex mercatoria*,[13] an 'a-national'

[5] The expression 'methodological nationalism' was first coined by sociologist, Herminio Martins, but was not the object of intense debate until the 1990s. cf. Speranta Dumitru, 'Qu'est-ce que le nationalisme méthodologique. Essai de typologie' (2004) 54 *Raisons politiques* 9.

[6] Twining and Frydman (n 1).

[7] For the idea of looking at law from a global perspective, cf. William Twining, 'Institutions of Law from a Global Perspective: Standpoint, Pluralism and Non-State Law' in Maksymilian Del Mar and Zenon Bankowski (eds), *Law as Institutional Normative Order* (Farnham, Ashgate 2009) 21–22.

[8] Suzanne Berger, *Notre première mondialisation. Leçon d'un échec oublié* (Paris, Seuil 2003). The comparisons between contemporary globalisation and globalisation in the 19th century are numerous. cf. notably Jeffry A. Frieden, *Global Capitalism. Its Fall and Rise in the Twentieth Century* (London, Norton 2007); Harold James, *The End of Globalization. Lessons from the Great Depression* (Cambridge MA, Harvard University Press 2002).

[9] Masaichiro Ishizaki, *Le droit corporatif international de la vente des soies. Les contrats-types américains et la codification lyonnaise dans leurs rapports avec les usages des autres places* 3 volumes (Paris, Marcel Giard 1928).

[10] Edouard Lambert, 'Sources du droit comparé ou supranational: Législation uniforme et jurisprudence comparative' in *Recueil d'études sur les sources du droit en l'honneur de François Gény* Volume III (Paris, Sirey 1934).

[11] Georges Scelle, 'La doctrine de Léon Duguit et les fondements du droit des gens' (1932) 83 *Archives de philosophie du droit* 98.

[12] cf. Martti A. Koskenniemi, *The Gentle Civilizer of Nations: The Rise and Fall of International Law 1870–1960* (Cambridge, Cambridge University Press 2004), in particular chapter 4.

[13] Berthold Goldman, 'Le droit des sociétés internationales' (1963) *Journal du droit international* 320.

law,[14] or the works of Philip Jessup on transnational law[15] are all chapters in the genealogy of global law.

Apart from certain specialised fields of law, it was only since the 1990s that the need for the global turn moved beyond methodological nationalism and the sterilising divide between national and international law. The 'intimations of global law,' to quote Professor Neil Walker,[16] have since grown. Far from a fad, it is a form of deepening globalisation that has increasingly heightened the difficult to relegate practices and strategies formerly reserved for a limited range of international actors. The development of global and transnational legal theories, therefore, appear as a doctrinal response to the phenomenon.

Different approaches to global law move across the spectrum of theories and perspectives in jurisprudence. Some scholars such as Raphael Domingo[17] and International Court of Justice judge Cançado Trindade with his thesis on the formation of a new *jus gentium*[18] rely on ancient natural law. A doctrinal movement has also developed seeking to further a constitutionalist reinterpretation of public international law presented as global constitutionalism.[19] Scholars concerned with legal pluralism also elaborate on theories of global law. Different variants exist as reflected in the approaches of Delmas-Marty[20] and Schiff Berman[21] around the idea of ordered pluralism, or that of De Sousa Santos[22] developing a counter-hegemonic view of global law. Scholars of systemic theories such as Gunther Teubner and Andreas Fischer-Lescano seek to understand global law as emanating from sectoral fractures of a global society with a *lex mercatoria*, a *lex sportive*, *lex constructionnis* or *lex electronica.*[23] In New York, Benedict Kingsbury, Nico Krisch and Richard Stewart introduced the notion of Global Administrative Law with great success[24] while in Europe the Brussels School

---

14 Philippe Fouchard, *L'arbitrage commercial international* (Paris, Dalloz 1965).

15 Philip C. Jessup, *Transnational Law* (New Haven CT, Yale University Press 1956).

16 Neil Walker, *Intimations of Global Law* (Cambridge, Cambridge University Press 2015).

17 Rafael Domingo, *The New Global Law* (Cambridge, Cambridge University Press 2010). The author makes the strong claim towards this approach, identifying global law with a 'novum ius totius orbis' (p. 145).

18 Antônio A. Cançado Trindade, *International Law for Humankind: Towards a New Jus Gentium* (Recueil des Cours de l'Académie de Droit International, vol 316, 2006).

19 Anne Peters, Geir Ulfstein and Jan Klabbers, *The Constitutionalization of International Law* (Oxford, Oxford University Press 2009). cf. as well Armin von Bogdandy, 'Constitutionalism in International Law: Comment on a Proposal from Germany' (2006) 47 *HILJ* 223.

20 Mireille Delmas-Marty, *Les forces imaginantes du droit: le pluralisme ordonné* vol 2 (Paris, Seuil 2006). cf. as well Mireille Delmas-Marty, *Trois défis pour un droit mondial* (Paris, Seuil 1998).

21 Paul Schiff Berman, *Global Legal Pluralism: A Jurisprudence of Law Beyond Borders* (Cambridge, Cambridge University Press 2012).

22 Boaventura de Sousa Santos, *Toward a New Legal Common Sense* 2nd edn (Cambridge, CUP 2002).

23 cf. Andreas Fischer-Lescano and Gunther Teubner, 'Regime-Collision: The Vain Search for Legal Unity in the Fragmentation of Global Law' (2004) 25 *MJIL* 999.

24 cf. the seminal article Benedict Kingsbury, Nico Krisch and Richard B. Stewart, 'The Emergence of Global Administrative Law' (2005) 68 *Law & Contemporary Problems* 15. cf.

of Jurisprudence (BSJ) developed a pragmatic approach to global law.[25] This chapter adopts the latter approach.

The works of the BSJ implement a 'micro-legal' approach to law that is based on case studies and the adoption of the perspective of the actors involved; in contrast with the 'macro-legal' approaches that advocate the study of the law through concepts, the index of sources or the legal order. This methodology is particularly favourable for the study of global law and aims to overcome the pitfalls of methodological nationalism through the empirical study of specific cases within certain 'sites' or areas of social life affected by globalisation.[26] As a result, we have identified some important cross-sectional observations.

First, globalisation blurs the formal divide between public international law, that follows a contractual method, and private international law, that relies on rules to distribute jurisdiction and competence between states. The barriers of public international law often occur due to the absence of unanimity amongst states or an unwillingness or inability of implementation. In private international law, the perspective of actors and evolution of material and technical conditions allow for occasional or

---

also Eyal Benvenisti, *The Law of Global Governance* (The Hague Academy of International Law 2014); Sabino Cassese, *Research Handbook on Global Administrative Law* (Cheltenham, Edward Elgar 2016).

[25] For an overview of this work which has served as background for this paper, cf. Benoît Frydman, *Petit manuel pratique de droit global* (Académie Royale de Belgique 2014); Benoît Frydman, Gregory Lewkowicz and Arnaud van Waeyenberge, 'De l'étude à l'enseignement du droit global' in Paul Ancel and Luc Heuschling (eds), *La transnationalisation de l'enseignement du droit* (Brussels, Larcier 2016) 228–40.

[26] cf. notably, on company law and labour law, Ludovic Hennebel and Gregory Lewkowicz, 'La contractualisation des droits de l'homme: de la pratique à la théorie du pluralisme juridique et politique' in Greogory Lewkowicz et Michael Xifaras (eds), *Repenser le contrat* (Paris, Dalloz 2009) 221; Thomas Berns, Benoît Frydman, Pierre-François Docquir, Ludovic Hennebel and Gregory Lewkowicz, *Responsabilités des entreprises et corégulation* (Brussels, Bruylant 2007). On Internet regulation cf. Benoît Frydman and Isabelle Rorive, 'Regulating Internet Content Through Intermediaries in Europe and in the U.S.A.' (2002) 23 *Zeitschrift für Rechtssoziologie* 41; Benoît Frydman, Ludovic Hennebel and Gregory Lewkowicz, 'Co-regulation and the Rule of Law' in Eric Brousseau, Meryem Marzouki and Cécile Méadel (eds), *Governance, Regulations and Powers on the Internet* (Cambridge, Cambridge University Press 2012) 133–50; Caroline Bricteux, 'La contribution de l'ICANN à l'émergence d'un standard global de la liberté d'expression', *Working Paper du Centre Perelman de Philosophie du Droit*, n° 2014/5, 2014. On financial regulation: Bruno Colmant, Etienne de Callataÿ and Xavier Dieux, *Les agences de notation financière: entre marchés et Etats* (Brussels, Larcier 2013). On regulating armed conflict: Gregory Lewkowicz, 'La protection des civils dans les nouvelles configurations conflictuelles: retour au droit des gens ou dépassement du droit international humanitaire' in Jean Marc Sorel and Corneliu-Liviu Popescu (eds), *La protection des personnes vulnérables en temps de conflit armé* (Brussels, Bruylant 2010). On the establishment of a global standard for the definition and dissemination of the rule of law, cf. David Restrepo Amariles, 'The mathematical turn: L'indicateur "Rule of Law" dans la politique du développement de la Banque Mondiale' in Benoît Frydman and Arnaud van Waeyenberge (eds), *Gouverner par les standards et les indicateurs. De Hume aux rankings* (Brussels, Bruylant 2014). On transnational litigation, cf. Benoît Frydman and L. Hennebel, 'Le contentieux transnational des droits de l'homme: une analyse stratégique' (2009) 77 *Revue Trimestrielle des Droits de l'Homme* 73; Benoît Frydman and C. Bricteux (eds), *Les défis du droit global* (Brussels, Bruylant 2018).

systematic circumvention of the domestic legal order by experimenting with connecting factors. Changing global conditions and the availability of forum shopping subvert the logic of private international law, helping to form a global market of domestic rights,[27] and inadvertently creating competition and a race to the bottom.

Second, this race to the bottom does not lead to the systematic destruction of all existing rules. Indeed, actors need rules in order to organise their activities or pursue their interests and values. Since these rules are not given, they will try to create them. At the global level, we observe the proliferation of standards, crafted and implemented directly by actors who venture into normative engineering. These norms are often the result of a collective effort by actors interested in operationalising certain tasks, for example, in standard financial contracts[28] in global institutions.

These rules are eventually a result of a struggle for law. Actors with varied interests seek to influence the regulation of behaviour by attempting to capture or put under pressure the 'points of control',[29] which are those with a capacity or means to shape the behaviour of the actors concerned. These points of control are called upon, sometimes against their own will, to adopt the role of a judge, legislator or law enforcer in response to such requests. Some examples include the empowerment of Internet intermediaries and search engines to control online content, as well as the empowerment of parent companies in a corporate group to enforce corporate social responsibility standards across the entire supply chain. The struggle for regulation, however, does not always lead to the formation of a single global rule. Instead, competing standards materialise, responding from different forms of regulation to a unique global issue. An example is the debate, within the Forest Stewardship Council, between certification systems for sustainable forest management: promoting values of international NGOs and producers in the South; or values defended by the timber sector in Europe (the Pan-European Forest Certification); or the Sustainable Forestry Initiative in the United States.[30]

Third, globalisation not only leads to a change in the scale or geographical reach of rules, but also to a change in their nature. Emerging norms only occasionally borrow from its classic form. Globalisation occurs instead as a breeding ground for the proliferation of instruments that mobilise normativities seemingly foreign to legal rules.

---

[27] cf. cross-section study, Erin A. O'Hara and Larry E. Ribstein, *The Law Market* (Oxford, Oxford University Press 2009).

[28] This is true of the ISDA Master Agreement for the OTC derivatives market. cf. particularly Joanne P. Braithwaite, 'Standard Form Contracts as Transnational Law: Evidence from the Derivatives Markets' (2012) 75 *MLR* 779.

[29] The notion of 'points of control' was first used in the context of the study on Internet regulation. However, it has a broader scope. cf. Jonathan Zittrain, 'Internet Points of Control' (2003) 44 *Boston College Law Review* 653.

[30] cf. Errol Meidinger, 'The Administrative Law of Global Private-Public Regulation: The Case of Forestry' (2006) 17 *European Journal of International Law* 47. cf. also the more recent and critical analysis by Sandra Moog, André Spicer, Steffen Böhm, 'The Politics of Multi-Stakeholder Initiatives: The Crisis of the Forest Stewardship Council' (2014) *J B Ethics*.

Technical standards, indicators, ratings, benchmarks, rankings,[31] codes of conduct,[32] computer programmes and computational protocols[33] are among a few of the numerous normative instruments that have seen exponential growth at the global level, attempting to regulate certain sectors of activity. These instruments do not belong to the usual legal sources. It matters not the form; or to use the analogy by Chaïm Perelman, it is not 'rules in uniform' that are always the most effective.[34] The study of these unidentified legal objects nevertheless constitutes an important aspect in the analysis of global law due to their ability to act as functional equivalents to the rules of law at the global level. That is to say, these instruments work to fulfil what Karl Llewellyn calls 'law-jobs.'[35]

Fourth, these normative instruments are not, as mistakenly perceived, part of a moral, political or ideological project. Like any rule of law, these instruments are at the disposal of all actors. They can be used to promote and defend any cause, albeit some have already capitalised and succeeded with them under a neoliberal agenda. Thus, in the area of corporate social responsibility, trade unions or NGOs do not hesitate to develop and lobby codes of conduct and other control mechanisms to multinational corporations to safeguard the social rights of workers.[36] In the same way, it has been shown that indicators that can be used to defend noble causes and social policies in the framework of practices described as 'statactivism.'[37]

Fifth, for a pragmatic approach, the knowledge of an object is captured by the knowledge of its effects. Moreover, to fully account for these normative instruments, they must be studied by analysing the interactions or potential interaction they establish with each other and with traditional rules and legal institutions. This analysis is also informative of the effectiveness of these instruments when paired in a particular normative fabric; allowing the constitution of real devices that support the definition, implementation and sanction of the norm. As such, we have observed that the Academic Ranking of World Universities, also known as the 'Shanghai Ranking,' is now included in the legislation of several countries on the recognition of foreign

---

[31] On normative techniques and indicators, cf. Benoît Frydman and Arnaud van Waeyenberge (eds), *Gouverner par les standards et les indicateurs. De Hume aux rankings* (Brussels, Bruylant 2014). cf. Kevin Davis, Angelina Fisher, Benedict Kingsbury and Sally Engle Merry (eds), *Governance by Indicators: Global Power through Classification and Rankings* (Oxford, Oxford University Press 2012).

[32] cf. Benoît Frymdan and Gregory Lewkowicz, 'Les codes de conduite: source du droit global ?' in Isabelle Hachez, Yves Cartuyvels, Hugues Dumont, Philippe Gérard, François Ost, Michel van de Kerchove (eds), *Les sources du droit revisitées: normativités concurrentes* (Limal, Anthemis 2012) 179–210.

[33] On the normative effects of computational programs, cf. Kenneth A. Bamberger, 'Technologies of Compliance: Risk and Regulation in a Digital Age' (2010) 88 *TLR* 669.

[34] Chaïm Perelman, 'A propos de la règle de droit. Réflexions de méthode' in Chaïm Perelman (ed.) *La règle de droit* (Brussels, Bruylant 1971).

[35] Karl Llewellyn, 'The Normative, The Legal and The Law-jobs: The Problem of Juristic Method' (1940) 49 *YLJ* 1355.

[36] cf. Berns et al. (n 26).

[37] Isabelle Bruno, Emmanuel Didier and Julien Préveux, *Statactivisme: Comment lutter avec des nombres* (Paris, La Découverte 2014).

university degrees[38] or as part of the rules granting residence permits.[39] The benchmark for the three major financial rating agencies relies on the World Bank's global governance indicators and Transparency International's Corruption Perception Index to establish credit ratings.[40] These ratings are subsequently translated by national legislation and also risk management software used by investors and banking institutions;[41] meaning the denser the normative grid, the stronger the system of global law.

It is nonetheless important to investigate, and even test, the potential interactions between the instruments of global law. Actors will couple and pair instruments accordingly, with varying degrees of success, to achieve their objectives. NGOs, for example, will try to seize French courts on the basis of deceptive marketing practices to sanction a company for failing to ensure compliance of subcontractors in China with its code of conduct,[42] while simultaneously, a corporation providing financial information will seek to rank corporations according to the quality of their corporate social responsibility commitments and performance.[43] In analysing these initiatives, it reveals the dynamics of the subject. Though, a thorough and critical examination of possible combinations of instruments must be completed in order to provide reasonable hypotheses on the probable and desirable evolutions of the matter.

Together, these observations describe an approach to global law. However, they do not reveal the existence of a global legal order that would be superimposed against national, regional or international legal orders. This approach also does not lead to the identification of global norms, in the sense that one could recognise them intuitively, namely, rules whose territorial scope (*ratione loci*) would be the entire world. Instead, global devices ensure or seek to regulate certain behaviours independent of their inclusion in a particular legal order.

---

[38] On 25 April 2012, Government of the Russian Federation, under Resolution 389, granted automatic equivalence to diplomas issued by Universities in the Top 300 of Shanghai and other major international academic rankings.

[39] The Netherlands readily grants residence permits to foreigners holding a Master or Doctorate degree issued by an institution of higher education ranked in the top 150 of the Shanghai ranking. cf. Besluit van de Staatssecretaris van Justitie, 12 December 2008, nr. 2008/30, houdende wijziging van de Vreemdelingencirculaire 2000, *Staatscourant*, nr. 251, 29 December 2008, art. 1.

[40] David Restrepo Amariles, 'Supping with the Devil? Indicators and the Rise of Managerial Rationality in Law' (2017) 13 *IJLC* 465. Also cf. David Restrepo Amariles and Julian McLachlan, 'Legal Indicators in Transnational Law Practice: A Methodological Assessment' (2018) 58 *Jurimetrics* 163.

[41] Gregory Lewkowicz, 'Gouverner les Etats par les indicateurs: le cas des agences de notation de crédit' in Benoît Frydman and Arnaud van Waeyenberge (eds), *Gouverner par les standards et les indicateurs. De Hume aux rankings* (Brussels, Bruylant 2014).

[42] cf. Rémi Barroux, 'Samsung attaqué en justice sur "les conditions de travail indignes" chez ses sous-traitants chinois' *Le Monde* (26 February 2013) <http://www.lemonde.fr/economie/article/2013/02/26/samsung-attaque-en-justice-sur-les-conditions-de-travail-indignes-chez-ses-sous-traitants-chinois_1838865_3234.html> accessed 30 April 2018.

[43] cf. for example the *ESG Ranking* created by the FTSE group in context of developing its FTSE4Good. For a full explanation of the use of metrics in corporate social responsibility: David Restrepo Amariles, Arnaud van Waeyenberge and Lorenzo Colombani, 'Responsabilité sociale des entreprises: Enjeux globaux et technologiques' (2017) 269 *Revue Française de gestion* 161.

The development of digital platforms and the re-intermediation of supply and demand give rise, at the global level, to a pertinent project to examine the formation of global law in accordance with the aforementioned approach. These platforms are indeed powerful points of control that have the capacity to impose and implement specific standards across borders through technology.[44] Actors are not wrong to influence 'platform rights' – an expression used by Orly Lobel[45] – to implement specific standards. This pressure typically stems from a respect for standards of labour law.[46] It may also be relevant to compliance with non-discrimination, as exemplified by Gregory Selden in the *Airbnb* case.

2. *GREGORY SELDEN V. AIRBNB*: A POINT OF DEPARTURE FOR GLOBAL ANTI-DISCRIMINATION LAW ON DIGITAL PLATFORMS

The Airbnb platform is iconic of the 'collaborative economy.'[47] Its tremendous success over the last decade has established it as the leading platform for the short-term rental market. Founded in San Francisco in 2008 by Brian Chesky and Joe Gebbia, it links individuals wishing to rent their homes to those looking for a place to stay in over 34,000 cities and more than 191 countries around the world.[48] As a result, Airbnb is one of the most comprehensive platforms of the collaborative economy both in geographic scope of operation and diversity of its users.

The relationship between supply and demand is dependent on the profiles created online by users. Potential landlords ('hosts') create a profile, detailing their identity and including information on the characteristics of the property they wish to lease. It includes price, availability and conditions for rent. Potential tenants ('travellers'), on

---

44 On the importance of instruments for technological controls in the regulation of the global economy, cf. A. Aneesh, *Virtual Migration: The Programming of Globalization* (Durham NC, Duke University Press 2006). cf. also, Thomas Dietz's thesis on the increasingly significant role of new technologies, in comparison to arbitration, in enforcing compliance with contractual provisions in the software sector. Thomas Dietz, *Global Order Beyond Law: How Information and Communication Technologies Facilitate Relational Contracting in International Trade* (Oxford, Hart Publishing 2014).

45 Orly Lobel, 'The Law of the Platform' (2016) 101 *MLR* 87.

46 cf. the pioneering work of Trebor Scholtz (ed.), *Digital Labor: The Internet as Playground and Factory* (Abingdon, Routledge 2013); Trebor Scholz, *Uberwork and Underpaid. How Workers are Disrupting the Digital Economy* (Cambridge, Polity 2017).

47 For a general overview of 'collaborative economy' platforms and their regulatory framework in the United States, cf. Vanessa Katz, 'Regulating the Sharing Economy' (2015) 30 *Berkeley Technology L J* 1067. For a critical analysis on the collaborative nature of these platforms, cf. Brad Tuttle, 'Can We Stop Pretending the Sharing Economy Is All About Sharing?' *TIME* (30 June 2014) <http://time.com/money/2933937/sharing-economy-airbnb-uber-monkeyparking/> accessed 30 April 2018.

48 For information on the scope of Airbnb's activities, cf. <https://fr.airbnb.be/about/about-us> accessed 30 April 2018.

the other hand, also create a profile with details of their identity.[49] These profiles contain personal information such as a photo, first and last names, home address, and a personalised self-description. Airbnb remotely confirms the validity of this information, particularly through means of document verification and publication on its website. When a reservation is confirmed, further information is made available to the parties including the address of the property, and the telephone numbers of the host and traveller. They can also choose to communicate using a platform-specific email service.[50]

In addition to information about the parties' identities, the platform offers users access to past assessments of guests and travellers. The Airbnb site therefore disseminates ratings given by previous tenants to the host and his property. These reviews crucially comment on the accuracy of the property description, cleanliness, location, conditions of accommodation, the quality of communication with the host, as well as the price-quality ratio.[51] According to Airbnb, 'the number of stars displayed at the top of a listing page is an aggregate of the primary scores guests have given for that listing … A host needs to receive star ratings from at least 3 guests before their aggregate score appears.'[52] Hosts can also access the ratings assigned to travellers by previous hosts. This grading system as well as its public display on the site aim to reduce the asymmetry of information between users of the platform or, in the words of Airbnb, to 'help build trust and cultivate a transparent community marketplace.'[53] Unlike the traditional hotel market, the Airbnb platform operates on a 'peer-to-peer' mechanism. As a result, users' trust is not based on the brand reputation nor the regulatory obligation imposed on hotel services. Instead, Airbnb's business model is entirely based on building trust between its players.[54]

The case initiated by Gregory Selden is revealing of the regulatory model described in the first half of the paper. Gregory Selden, an African-American citizen, planned to spend a weekend in the city of Philadelphia in March 2015. He decided to create a profile on Airbnb, including his photograph and proceeded to contact a landlord. The landlord subsequently responded by noting that housing was no longer available.[55] Selden then created a second profile, under a pseudonym and used a photograph of a white man instead. He proceeded to contact the same host with the exact same request.

---

49 cf. Terms and condition of Airbnb, available at <https://fr.airbnb.be/host/homes?from_nav=1.> accessed 30 April 2018.

50 Ibid.

51 For further information on Airbnb's ratings system, cf. <https://www.airbnb.fr/help/article/1257/how-do-star-ratings-work> accessed 30 April 2018.

52 Ibid.

53 The manner in which Airbnb claims to establish a relationship of trust between guests and travellers, cf. <https://www.airbnb.fr/help/article/4/how-does-airbnb-help-build-trust-between-hosts-and-guests> accessed 30 April 2018.

54 This trust is not only generated through mechanisms of transparency and ratings implemented by the platform, Airbnb also offers insurance guarantees and a payment system through an escrow account model.

55 *Gregory Selden et al v. Airbnb Inc*, Case n 16-cv-933 (CRC), US District Court for the District of Columbia.

In contrast, Selden's request was accepted.[56] As a result, Selden concluded that he was a victim of discrimination, noting that the only difference between the two requests made to the same was the profile of the traveller and his racial identity. Selden then shared his 'experience' on social media with the hashtag '#airbnbwhileblack.' The message posted online quickly went viral.[57]

Yet, Gregory Selden's public denunciation stems from a wider context concerning the presence of discrimination on the Airbnb platform. Benjamin G. Edelman and Michael Luca, two researchers at Harvard University, had previously documented such concerns in their work. They published two empirical studies on the subject in 2014 and 2015,[58] but unfortunately did not receive significant media coverage. What set ablaze and propelled the issue of discrimination on the Airbnb platform was rather the interview in April 2016 with Ms. Quirtina Crittenden, an African-American consultant that also claimed to have fallen victim to discrimination. Subsequently, she had re-launched the discussion and hashtag '#airbnbwhileblack.'[59] As a result, Selden's original denunciation became emblematic, widely disseminated in the international press on the issue of discrimination on digital platforms. The case became global.

A. The Fight Against Discrimination on Digital Platforms: Limits of the Domestic Approach

In addition to public denunciation, Selden decided to bring a class action lawsuit against Airbnb on 17 May 2016 to US courts for racial discrimination. While he remained the only plaintiff, he brought the claim on behalf of other African-American citizens who have been subjected to comparable treatment on the grounds of US federal law on discriminatory practices.[60] He argued before the District Court for the District of Columbia that Airbnb had violated (1) Title II of the Civil Rights Act of 1964 (42 USC §2000a), condemning racial discrimination in public places; (2) the Civil Rights Act of 1866 (42 USC §1981), prohibiting racial discrimination in the making and enforcing of contracts; and (3) the Fair Housing Act (42 USC §3604), prohibiting racial discrimination in the sale or rental of housing.[61] Airbnb denied liability and instead, further requested the Court to refer the case to arbitration.[62] According to Airbnb,

---

56 Ibid.

57 Elaine Glusac, 'As Airbnb Grows, So Do Claims of Discrimination' *N.Y. Times* (26 June 2016) <http://www.nytimes.com/2016/06/26/travel/airbnb-discrimination-lawsuit.html.> accessed 30 April 2018.

58 cf. Benjamin Edelman and Michael Luca, 'Digital Discrimination: The Case of Airbnb.com' (2014) *Harvard Business School NOM Unit Working Paper*, n°14-054. Both authors published their work in December 2015; cf. also the now published working versions: Benjamin Edelman, Michael Luca and Dan Svirsky, 'Racial Discrimination in the Sharing Economy: Evidence from a Field Experiment' (2017) 9 *American Economic Journal: Applied Economics* 1.

59 Leigh Gallagher, *Airbnb Story: Comment trois jeunes ont disrupté un secteur, gagné des millions … et créé la polémique* (Paris, Dunod 2018).

60 *Gregory Selden et al v. Airbnb Inc*, 16-cv-933, 2016 WL 6476934 (D.D.C. 1 November 2016).

61 Ibid.

62 Ibid.

Selden had signed and agreed to the 'Terms of Services', that any dispute relevant to the contract will be brought before an arbitral tribunal. Airbnb also stated that, in accordance with the terms of these conditions, no civil proceedings requiring the presence of a jury, including class actions, can be brought.[63]

The general conditions under Article 19.4 contain an arbitration clause, the terms of which are as follows:

> *19.4 Agreement to Arbitrate*. You and Airbnb mutually agree that any dispute, claim or controversy arising out of or relating to these Terms or the breach, termination, enforcement or interpretation thereof, or to the use of the Airbnb Platform, the Host Services, or the Collective Content (collectively, 'Disputes') will be settled by binding arbitration (the 'Arbitration Agreement'). If there is a dispute about whether this Arbitration Agreement can be enforced or applies to our Dispute, you and Airbnb agree that the arbitrator will decide that issue.

Selden argued that he was not bound by the provision for arbitration since he was not fully informed of its implications. Alternatively, he contended that the arbitration clause does not apply to cases of discrimination and was considered unconscionable.[64]

Ultimately, the District Court for the District of Columbia upheld Airbnb's arguments, ordering the stay of legal proceedings and referral to arbitration. The reasoning of the Court rests on three key arguments. First, the Court states that the plaintiff had consented to Airbnb's general terms and conditions, and thereby to the arbitration agreement. Second, the Court confirms that arbitration is permissible for matters relevant to racial discrimination. Finally, the Court indicated that there is no reason to doubt the validity of the arbitration agreement. This decision was confirmed on appeal.[65] On 2 October 2017, the Supreme Court of the United States dismissed the petition for writ of certiorari. To date, Selden has not commenced any proceedings before an arbitral tribunal.[66]

The decision rendered in the *Selden* case remain controversial. In any event, it illustrates the limits of access to state justice for consumers who are victims of violations of fundamental rights. This phenomenon is particularly aggravated in the digital economy where consumers are systematically confronted with adhesion contracts that, by definition, must be accepted in order to benefit from the services offered. In this context, arbitration is undoubtedly one of the more remarkable means used by global digital platforms to reduce the role of domestic rights in their activities; and to establish and promote standardised legal practices at the international level. In this way, digital platforms can choose the applicable law for their contracts, but also dispute resolution mechanisms most favourable to them. As a result, we observe the emergence of a global law of digital platforms based on relatively uniform contracts offered to all co-contractors regardless of domicile, location, or where services are procured.

---

[63] Ibid.

[64] Ibid.

[65] *Gregory Selden et al v. Airbnb Inc*, 16-cv-933, 2016 WL 7373776 (D.D.C. 19 December 2016).

[66] *Gregory Selden et al v. Airbnb Inc*, 16-cv-933, 681 Fed.Appx (D.C. Cir, 2 February 2017).

B. Class Actions and Dispute Arbitration in Consumer Protection: A Comparative Perspective

The option to resort to class actions or to arbitration for disputes in consumer protection varies significantly in the United States and for Member States in the European Union. These differences illustrate how states seek to regulate economic activities, but also how to influence the activities of multinational corporations beyond their own jurisdictions.

Class actions in the United States are governed by Rule 23 of the Federal Rules of Civil Procedure (FRCP). The 1960s and 1970s, during the era of mass consumption in the United States, saw the proliferation of this type of procedure, playing a significant role in consumer protection and antitrust laws. An important characteristic of the spirit of American civil procedure is its class system. It is based on an opt-out format: class members are presumed to belong to it based on the established criteria unless they have explicitly decided to leave.

Rule 23 of the FRCP outlines four criteria in order to initiate a class action:

The class is so numerous that joinder of all member is impracticable;
There are questions of law or fact common to the class;
The claims or defences of the representative parties are typical of the claims or defences of the class; and
The representative parties will fairly and adequately protect the interests of the class.

From an economic perspective, these provisions aim to sanction harmful economic conduct at the macroeconomic level, while the cost of litigation would be far too great for potential individual gains. As a result, litigation acts as a form of sectoral or macroeconomic regulation. The effect of class actions is not limited to possible sanctions. Companies' anticipation of the high cost of class actions should, in principle, deter from practices that may be contrary to market rules.

On the other hand, European states have traditionally allocated the responsibility of ensuring against harmful market behaviour to the public administration rather than the actors themselves. Nevertheless, a number of procedural mechanisms have been adopted to increase the efficiency of litigation.[67] Although there is no harmonised mechanism at the European level, the Member States of the European Union (EU) have developed their own procedural tools, such as the French collection action,[68] to safeguard the effectiveness of laws on consumer protection.

---

[67] European Parliament and Council Regulation (EC) No 805/2004 of 21 April 2004 creating a European Enforcement Order for uncontested claims [2004] OJ L 143/15; European Parliament and Council Regulation (EC) No1896/2006 of 12 December 2006 creating a European Order for payment procedure [2006] OJ L 399/1; European Parliament and Council Regulation (EC) No 861/2007 of 11 July 2007 establishing a European Small Claims Procedure [2007] OJ L 199/1.

[68] Journal Officiel de la République Française n°0065, Loi n° 2014-344, 17 March 2014 on consumer protection [2014].

Parallel to class actions, class arbitration has also developed in the United States.[69] The idea piques the interest of jurists, since procedurally they combine the most public form of litigation with the most private mode of dispute resolution. The class arbitration is thus 'regarded as a mythical beast: half litigation, half arbitration and rarely seen.'[70] Yet, it is simply a class action proceeding conducted not before a state or federal court, but before an arbitral tribunal.[71] Although arbitration clauses have exponentially grown in the recent decades, owed in part to policy relieving congestion in courts, class arbitration remains relatively few.

The development of arbitration, against the backdrop of decongesting American courts, has become one of the primary methods of dispute resolution in the field of consumer protection. Surprisingly, arbitration has proven to circumvent class actions in two ways. First, a large number of contracts, such as Airbnb's terms and conditions, opt for arbitration as a method of resolving disputes rather than the typical courts. More importantly, the arbitration clause attaches a waiver on class actions. The combined effect of these provisions privileges arbitration rather than class action litigation before ordinary courts. This widely adopted contractual strategy, as a result, disaggregates plaintiffs and discourages them from raising claims.

In the EU, the privatisation of consumer disputes has taken a very different path with the adoption of the Alternative Dispute Resolution (ADR) Directive on Consumer Protection[72] and Regulation of ADR online[73] in 2013. It remains unthinkable in European law to adopt arbitration clauses under the aforementioned American model, particularly given the restraints set by the Directive on unfair terms in consumer contracts.[74]

C. How are Consumers Protected Today? *United States v. Europe*

In the United States, the notion of 'unconscionable' clauses, or 'abusive' clauses, remains an important means to protect consumers. The Californian state courts have particularly advanced case law on the protection of consumer rights, finding themselves

---

69 Ramona L. Lampley, 'Is Arbitration under Attack?: Exploring the Recent Judicial Skepticism of the Class Arbitration Waiver and Innovative Solutions to the Unsettled Legal Landscape' (2009) 18 *Cornell J L and Public Policy* 477; Richard Nagareda, 'Aggregation and its Discontents: Class Settlement Pressure, Class-Wide Arbitration, and CAFA' (2006) 106 *CLR* 1872; Neal Troum, 'The Problem With Class Arbitration' (2014) *Vermont L. Rev* 419; Gary Born and Claudio Salas, 'The United States Supreme Court and Class Arbitration: A Tragedy of Errors' (2012) 21 *J Dispute Resolution* 21.

70 Kelly Thompson Cochran and Eric J. Mogilnicki, 'Current Issues in Consumer Arbitration' (2005) 60 *Business Lawyer* 791.

71 cf. Matteo M. Winkler, 'Arbitrage et droit de la consommation dans une perspective transatlantique: la Cour Suprême des Etats-Unis (ne) montre (pas) la bonne voie' (2016) *Revue de droit des affaires internationales* 519.

72 European Parliament and Council Directive 2013/11/EU of 21 May 2013 on alternative dispute resolution for consumer disputes [2013] OJ L 165/63.

73 European Parliament and Council Regulation (EU) No 524/2013 of 21 May 2013 on online dispute resolution for consumer disputes [2013] OJ L 165/1.

74 Council Directive (ECC) 93/13 of 5 April 1993 on unfair terms in consumer contracts [1993] OJ L 95/29.

at odds with the Supreme Court of the United States. In contrast to the concepts of 'duress' or 'fraud', unfair terms are defined as 'no man in his senses and not under any circumstances.'[75] The formation of the contract cannot result from oppression or undue influence resulting from unequal bargaining power.[76]

Regulation against the abusive nature of waiver clauses for class actions typically arise at the state level, particularly in California. The difference of opinion between state courts and the US Supreme Court is important, to the extent that state and federal law are applied simultaneously. The contractual aspects of a dispute are subject to state law, though contractual clauses in most states follow the Uniform Commercial Code, while litigation relevant to arbitration is regulated by federal law, the Federal Arbitration Act (FAA).

The State of California has enacted the Consumers Legal Remedies Act (CLRA) with the goal of (a) protecting consumers from misleading and unfair and deceptive commercial practices; (b) and implementing cost-effective and efficient procedures to guarantee the effectiveness of the instituted protections.[77] In particular, Section 1751 of the CLRA states 'any waiver by a consumer of the provisions of this title is contrary to public policy and shall be unenforceable and void' and section 1770 (a) (19) prohibits the act of 'an unconscionable provision in the contract.'

In *Discover Bank v. Superior Court*,[78] the divergence in opinion between California state law and US federal law was particularly pronounced. The California Supreme Court ruled that class action waivers in consumer contracts are considered unconscionable. On the other hand, the federal courts assert party autonomy by declaring the validity of arbitration clauses prohibiting class actions. The result, in effect, set aside the entire public policy on consumer protection which, in the United States, is recognised as a specific contractual field separate from other types of contracts. California attempted to isolate consumer contracts as distinct but was overruled by federal courts, citing that the FAA takes precedence over any qualification of clauses contended under unfair terms.

Stolt-Nielsen S.A. v. AnimalFeeds Int'l Corp. (*Stolt-Nielsen*) is illustrative of the decline in class arbitration. The Court stated in *Stolt-Nielsen* that a party cannot be compelled to submit class arbitration under the FAA except 'if there is a contractual basis to conclude that parties have so agreed.'[79] Consequently, absent explicit agreement, recourse to class arbitration must be rejected. The nuance is important should one consider the effects on the general economy of the procedure. Which companies would then decide to include, against its own interest, an explicit agreement to submit to class arbitration? It may not also decide against including any such clause, definitively avoiding any class action. The consequence of this decision suggests that class arbitration is virtually impossible in the face of digital platforms. Additionally, few

---

[75] Restatement (Second) of Contracts § 208 cmt. B (1981).

[76] *Armendariz v. Foundation Health Psychcare Servs*, Inc 24 C 4th 83 (2000).

[77] Article 1760 of the California Civil Code, Consumers Legal Remedies Act (1970).

[78] *Discover Bank v. Superior Court*, 36 Cal 4th 148, 113 P.3d 1100 (2005).

[79] *Stolt-Nielsen SA v. AnimalFeeds Int'l Corp*, 559 US 662, 683, 130 S. Ct 1758, 1774 (2010). The original texts signals that 'a party may not be compelled under the FAA to submit to class arbitration unless there is a contractual basis for concluding that the party agreed to do so.'

consumers would be interested in raising a claim in cases where the risks or procedural costs are significant and potential gains are low. Moreover, *American Express Co. v. Italian Colors Restaurant* further buried class arbitration by stating that class arbitration waivers are valid where the cost of the procedure exceeds the potential gains of the petition.[80]

The US Supreme Court goes a step further with *AT&T Mobility v. Concepcion*, in which the Court reverses the opinions of the federal courts. The Court rejected in its majority opinion, written by then Justice Scalia, that a state court could invalidate a clause prohibiting class arbitration to which the parties had agreed by distinguishing consumer contracts from other types of contracts; that the FAA preempts state law that poses an obstacle to the accomplishment of FAA objectives. In *DirectTV, Inc. v. Imburgia*, the US Supreme Court ended the debate by noting that the federal law on arbitration prevails over the applicable law of the contract, thereby allowing class arbitration waivers.[81]

The EU's position strikes as a stark contrast to the one observed in the United States. Directive 93/13/EEC acts as an equivalent to the unconscionability doctrine. This Directive applies to contracts of adhesion[82] between consumers and professionals, aiming to provide a common guidance on the rights of domestic contracts. Prior to its entry into force, most domestic laws did have consumer protection, but the lack of uniformity created distortion in competition and worked against the common market. As a form of harmonisation and deepening of the common market, the Directive defines the consumer as a physical person acting in a non-commercial or professional context. It also defines the unfairness of clauses in consumer contracts as the existence of a significant imbalance of power that acts to the detriment of the consumer.[83] This Directive became one of the first steps towards harmonisation in EU contract law.[84]

The application of this standard of protection suggests that clauses renouncing class arbitration are not viable in the European legislative environment. The appendix to the Directive states under point (q) that clauses with the purpose 'to remove or impede the exercise of legal actions or remedies, particularly in obligating the consumer to refer exclusively to arbitration not covered in legal provisions through the imposition of a burden of proof which, under the applicable law, should normally return to another

---

80 *American Express Co v Italian Colors Restaurant*, 133 S. Ct. 3204 (2013).

81 *DirectTV, Inc v Imburgia*, at II, 2, 136. S. Ct 463 (2015).

82 Article 3 of the Council Directive (ECC) 93/13 (n 74).

83 Please note that significant imbalance here should not equated with the French doctrine of significant imbalance in contract law. For further information on the latter, cf. David Restrepo Amariles, Matteo Winkler and Eva Mouail, 'The French Doctrine of Significant Imbalance: Implications for International Contracts' (2018) *JBL* 148. The Annex of the Directive 93/13/CEE (n 74) cites some of examples of unfair clauses and includes among them the following: '1. (q) excluding or hindering the consumer's right to take legal action or exercise any other legal remedy, particularly by requiring the consumer to take disputes exclusively to arbitration not covered by legal provisions, unduly restricting the evidence available to him or imposing on him a burden of proof which, according to the applicable law, should lie with another party to the contract'.

84 Ewoud Hondius, 'EC Directive on Unfair Terms in Consumer Contracts: Towards a European Law of Contract' (1994) *J Contract L* 34.

party to the contract.' While the annex is only descriptive and non-exhaustive, thereby mere guidance for Member States, it nevertheless is persuasive before a court given its underlying doctrine to promote the effective realisation of economic integration.[85] This interpretation parallels a recommendation in its recitals:

> most consumer disputes, by their nature, are characterized by a disproportion between the economic value at stake and the cost of its judicial settlement; whereas the difficulties that court procedures may involve may, notably in the case of cross-border conflicts, discourage consumers from exercising their rights in practice.[86]

Finally, it should be noted that instruments of European constitutional law, of European and international law, include the enunciation of the right to just and fair trial, and effective remedy. Therefore, if the costs of arbitration were allocated to the consumer and not exclusively to the corporation, the financial capacity of many consumers would inhibit raising the claim. In this scenario, or in any that demonstrate consumers are deprived of a remedy, they would be contrary to fundamental rights, particularly under Article 6 of the European Convention on Human Rights and Article 47 of the EU Charter of Fundamental Rights.

In Airbnb, the general terms and conditions offer an award of the costs of arbitration to the consumer. Airbnb's general terms and conditions should therefore be assessed against consumer protection and a right to an effective remedy. The ability of this type of clause to prevent the implementation of public policies aimed at protecting consumers, such as insolvency proceedings, is especially questionable. Article 19.11 of Airbnb's general conditions states:

> *19.11 No Class Actions or Representative Proceedings*. You and Airbnb acknowledge and agree that we are each waiving the right to participate as a plaintiff or class member in any purported class action lawsuit, class-wide arbitration, private attorney-general action, or any other representative proceeding as to all Disputes. Further, unless you and Airbnb both otherwise agree in writing, the arbitrator may not consolidate more than one party's claims and may not otherwise preside over any form of any class or representative proceeding.[87]

D. From American Arbitration to Global Non-Discrimination Policy

The failure of civil procedure in US courts and the recognition of the validity of arbitration clauses in *Gregory Selden v. Airbnb* is however not the end. The effects of non-discrimination extend beyond the US legal order. *Selden* highlighted both the incapacity to hold platforms of the digital economy accountable for the discriminatory behaviour of users and the inability of such platforms to remedy online discrimination.[88] *Selden* will thus become the crucial impetus behind the development of

[85] CJCE, 31 March 1971, *Commission v. Council*, AETR case, Aff. 22/70, rec. 1971, p. 263.

[86] Recommendation by the Commission on March 30, 1998 on the principles applicable to the bodies responsible for extrajudicial resolution on consumer disputes.

[87] Airbnb, Terms of Service <https://www.airbnb.fr/terms> accessed 30 April 2018.

[88] cf. Sarah Whitten, 'Airbnb Sued for Allegedly Ignoring Racial Discrimination on Its Site' *CNBC* (10 May 2016) <https://www.cnbc.com/2016/05/20/airbnb-sued-for-allegedly-ignoring-racial-discrimination-on-its-site.html> accessed 30 April 2018; Hope King, 'Airbnb Sued for

regulatory tools Airbnb will use to defend its reputation. More importantly, it offers alternative regulatory strategies that states can implement to ensure consumer protection against collaborative platforms in the digital economy.

Beyond issues of consumer arbitration in the United States and Europe, Airbnb was forced to manage the problem of discriminatory behavior exhibited by users of the platform in order to protect its reputation. In this sense, Airbnb took the traditional route on developing a global policy for corporate social responsibility.

While proceedings before the District Court of the District of Columbia were underway, Airbnb decided to solicit the help of Laura W. Murphy, a known activist invested in defending civil liberties and fundamental rights, and former director of the Legislative Office in the American Civil Liberties Union. In her report, *Airbnb's Work to Fight Discrimination and Build Inclusion*,[89] Murphy makes eight recommendations aimed to formalise mechanisms to avoid or respond to discriminatory user behaviour: (1) creating a commitment to a non-disclosure policy; (2) developing a system to implement and enforce rules provided for by this policy; (3) an 'open door' system that guarantees housing to persons who are discriminated against; (4) anti-discrimination training programmes; (5) establishing the 'instant booking' service to allow travellers to book accommodation immediately and without prior approval of the host; (6) elevating the importance of previous user ratings; (7) establishing a team of engineers dedicated to remedying online discrimination; and (8) promotion of diversity among employees at Airbnb.[90]

As a follow-up to the report, Airbnb launched, in December 2016, its general non-discrimination policy, modifying its existing general conditions. Interestingly, two distinct sets of rules emerged dependent on the location of the host's accommodation: whether the property was in a Member State in the European Union or the United States, or another part of the world. For housing within the European Union and the United States, the policy strictly prohibits guests from denying travellers or engaging in discriminatory online or offline behaviour based on skin colour, nationality, religion or sexual orientation. It also prohibits discrimination against gender unless the host is sharing accommodation with the traveller or because of a real or perceived disability.[91]

Discrimination' *CNN* (18 May 2016), available on <http://money.cnn.com/2016/05/18/technology/airbnb-lawsuit-discrimination/> accessed 30 April 2018; Katie Benner, 'Airbnb Vows to Fight Racism, but Its Users Can't Sue to Prompt Fairness' *New York Times* (19 June 2016) <https://www.nytimes.com/2016/06/20/technology/airbnb-vows-to-fight-racism-but-its-users-cant-sue-to-prompt-fairness.html> accessed 30 April 2018; Katie Benner, 'Federal Judge Blocks Racial Discrimination Suit Against Air' *New York Times* (1 November 2016) <https://www.nytimes.com/2016/11/02/technology/federal-judge-blocks-racial-discrimination-suit-against-airbnb.html> accessed 30 April 2018.

[89] Laura W. Murphy, 'Airbnb's Work to Fight Discrimination and Build Inclusion – A Report Submitted to Airbnb' (8 September 2016) <https://blog.atairbnb.com/wp-content/uploads/2016/09/REPORT_Airbnbs-Work-to-Fight-Discrimination-and-Build-Inclusion.pdf?3c10be> accessed 30 April 2018.

[90] Ibid., 19–25.

[91] Airbnb, *Nondiscrimination Policy* available at <https://www.airbnb.fr/terms/nondiscrimination_policy> accessed 30 April 2018.

For all accommodation outside of the United States and the European Union, Airbnb noted that the laws of some states may 'allow or even require people to make accommodation distinctions based on, for example, marital status, national origin, gender or sexual orientation, in violation of our general nondiscrimination philosophy.'[92] As a result, Airbnb requires hosts to communicate these restrictions on their online profiles clearly and accurately to all potential travellers, allowing Airbnb to confirm the need for such restrictions. This gesture reflects Airbnb's role as a global point of control, overcoming constraints imposed by the domestic law of states. Thus, Airbnb indicates in its non-discrimination policy: if a particular listing contains language contrary to this nondiscrimination policy, the host will be asked to remove the language and affirm his or her understanding and intent to comply with this policy and its underlying principles. Airbnb may also, in its discretion, take steps up to and including suspending the host from the Airbnb platform. If the host improperly rejects guests on the basis of protected class, or uses language demonstrating that his or her actions were motivated by factors prohibited by this policy, Airbnb will take steps to enforce this policy, up to and including suspending the host from the platform.[93] Airbnb has also modified the design of the platform to decrease the opportunities for discriminatory behaviors by users.[94]

In the state of California, Airbnb's role as a point of control in the fight against discrimination has been institutionalised in the form of a settlement agreement[95] between Airbnb and the Department of Fair Employment and Housing of the State of California (DFEH). Following allegations of discrimination on the platform, Airbnb agreed to prepare a biannual report on complaints of discrimination from users of the platform as well as progress on the implementation of its nondiscrimination policy.[96] This report is sent to Airbnb's General Counsel and presented at least once a year to the Chief Executive Officer. In addition to accessing the report, DFEH can also perform technical tests on platform hosts located in California that have had at least three accounts of discrimination.[97] It is precisely within the context of this agreement that the first Airbnb host was sanctioned in April 2017 for racial discrimination, receiving a fine of US$5000 and the obligation to undergo antidiscrimination training.[98]

---

92 Ibid.

93 Ibid.

94 cf. A.R. Shariq Mohammed, 'Designing for Racial Impartiality: The Impact of Relocating Host Photos on the Airbnb Website', *Job Market Paper* available at <https://static1.squarespace.com/static/59dc19e003596ed02a2348e3/t/59f123a0f9a61ef6a799a1fb/1508975527058/2017_10_25_Airbnb.pdf> accessed 30 September 2018.

95 *Department of Fair Employment and Housing of the State of California v. Airbnb* (Voluntary Agreement), Case n. 574743-231889 et 574743-231634 (19 April 2017).

96 Ibid., §25.

97 Ibid., §38.

98 Olivia Solon, 'Airbnb host who canceled reservation using racist comment must pay $5,000' *The Guardian* (13 July 2017) <https://www.theguardian.com/technology/2017/jul/13/airbnb-california-racist-comment-penalty-asian-american> accessed 30 April 2018.

E. Conclusion: Regulation by Ratings – Towards Co-regulation?

In the context of the digital economy, there are signs of an emerging model of co-regulation, that is to say, *de facto* collaboration between public authorities and digital platforms. In addition to the agreement between Californian authorities and Airbnb as signs of this evolution, the European Commission appears to also be leaning towards this model. Increasing reliance on the use of information collected by the platforms, particularly from consumer ratings, aims to reduce the asymmetry of information, dissuade harmful behaviour of market players, and limit public regulation. The European Commission noted:

> rating and reputational systems or other mechanisms to discourage harmful behavior by market participants may in some cases reduce risks for consumers stemming from information asymmetries. This can contribute to higher quality services and potentially reduce the need for certain elements of regulation, provided adequate trust can be placed in the quality of the reviews and ratings.[99]

Only time will tell if and how far the system of co-regulation will take shape. It appears that digital platforms are becoming new participants in the field of global lawmakers. While they do not have the legitimacy to legislate, they have the power to set global standards. They have above all the technologies to enforce them in a digital environment where regulation by design and technology-driven compliance are gaining prominence. Airbnb is an exemplar of global law device formation discussed in the first half of the article. Facing inefficient domestic remedies for discrimination, vested stakeholders instead applied pressure directly to Airbnb. As a result, Airbnb has been the sole actor capable of regulating the behaviour of its users at the global level. In response to injunctions from a vast number of actors, Airbnb set up a global code of conduct on non-discrimination. The platform also established itself as an auditor and enforcing agent of its policy, working concurrently with public authorities. While it is up to readers to determine the most suitable name for a set of standards applicable in 191 countries and 35,000 cities, the expression 'global law' seems to be a worthy candidate.

---

[99] European Commission, A European Agenda for the Collaborative Economy, *Communication from the Commission to the European Parliament, the Council, the European Economic and Social Committee and the Committee of the Regions.* 2.6.2016 COM (2016) 356 final (2 June 2016).

21. Free movement of corporations: *Centros Ltd. v. Erhvervs-og Selskabsstyrelsen*

21.1 CASE BACKGROUND

One of the challenges European law has had to face in recent years involves the harmonisation of company law. Practised by a significant number of Member States, the 'real seat theory' prevented the growth of an internal market for corporate charters analogous to the one which thrives (albeit under the dominance of Delaware) in the United States. According to this theory, company executives do not have the liberty to freely choose a charter – laws governing the constitution and internal management of the corporate entity – other than that of the place of its seat (defined as the centre of corporate decision-making, at least as far as it appears as such to third parties). In practice, this meant that a company with a seat in France cannot choose to incorporate in Germany. Doing so would be seen as invalid in both countries; either for noncompliance to French formal and substantive requirements for incorporation, or for not having its corporate seat in Germany. By contrast, when a country practises the 'theory of incorporation', companies are free to create their own rules, or corporate charter, regardless of the place of its seat. Under this system, companies are much more mobile: they may transfer their headquarters from one place to any other practising the same criterion (it takes two to tango!), without having to re-incorporate under that country's laws. Certain Member States applied the 'theory of incorporation' as opposed to the 'real seat theory.'

The change came in 1999, in the name of free movement. In *Centros*, the Court of Justice held that the companies incorporated in one Member State enjoyed the freedom to set up a branch in another Member State; that regardless of the place of incorporation, a Member State was free to conduct its operations in another Member State without having to comply with the legal requirements demanded by the 'real seat theory.'

The facts of the *Centros* case are as follows. Centros Ltd was a private limited company registered in England and Wales on 18 May 1992 and owned by two Danish nationals, Mr. and Mrs. Bryde, who both resided in Denmark. Since English law does not impose any requirements for minimum share capital on limited liability corporations, Mr. and Mrs. Bryde had not made a payment on the share capital of Centros. At the time, Centros' share capital cost £100 per share. However, in accordance with English law, the registered office of Centros was situated in the United Kingdom, at the home of a friend of Mr. Bryde. In 1992, Mrs. Bryde requested Erhvervs-og Selskabsstyrelsen, the Danish Trade and Companies Board, to register a branch of Centros in Denmark. The Board refused registration on the grounds that Centros, which did not trade in the United Kingdom, was in fact seeking to establish in Denmark, as its place of principal establishment and not simply a branch. It considered that Centros tried to circumvent the national rules concerning the payment of the minimum capital fixed at DKK 200 000. Centros brought an action before the Danish Courts, which upheld the decision of the Board. Upon appeal, it argued that since the company was lawfully formed in the United Kingdom, it was entitled to set up a branch in Denmark, pursuant to Articles 52 and 58 of the EC Treaty. The Court stayed proceedings and referred this issue to the ECJ, which held that by reason of furthering the integration of the internal market and for free movement across the market, Centros should be permitted to set up a branch in Denmark.

Centros was the first in an initial trilogy *Centros – Uberseering – Inspire Art* (followed since by many others) of rulings by the ECJ that changed the landscape of European company law, affecting a number of aspects to relevant private international rules.

Case: C-127/97 *Centros Ltd v. Erhvervs-og Selskabsstyrelsen* [1999] ECR

21.2 FREEDOM OF ESTABLISHMENT: ONE STEP CLOSER TO MAKING A EUROPEAN DELAWARE POSSIBLE?

*Jeremy Heymann**

Although *Centros* constituted a textbook case, it has nonetheless provided European Law with one of its landmark judgments, at least as far as company law is concerned.[1] All it took was for two Danish nationals to travel to the United Kingdom in order to establish, in extremely favourable conditions,[2] a company, before being notified of the refusal by the Danish authorities to register, in Denmark, a branch of the company which they were directing and managing.

Triggering a shift towards the liberalisation of cross-border corporate activities, this judgment constitutes the starting point of a proactive case-law at the level of the European Court of Justice. The Court has indeed consistently attempted to limit the prerogatives of Member States in the field of company law, thereby implementing what is now referred to as 'the mobility' of companies.[3] Ultimately, this case was less about mobility than a matter of recognising the legal existence of a given company – unless the term 'mobility' refers to the mobility of company founders, the enhancement of

---

* Contribution originally written in French, translated to English by Louis Hill.

[1] The literature concerning this case is too abundant to be entirely mentioned here. See, *inter alia*: Michel Menjucq, 'Liberté d'établissement et fraude en droit communautaire' (1999) *Recueil Dalloz* 550; Paul Krüger Andersen and Karsten Engsig Sorensen, 'Free Movement of Companies from a Nordic Perspective' (1999) 6 *MJ* 47; Jean-Pierre Deguée, '"Forum shopping", usage ou abus de la liberté d'établissement' (2000) *Rev. prat. soc.* 51; Richard M. Buxbaum, 'Back to the Future? From "Centros" to the "Überlagerungstheorie"' in *Festschrift für Otto Sandrock zum 70. Geburtstag* (Frankfurt, Verl. Recht und Wirtschaft 2000); Eddy Wymeersch, 'Centros: A Landmark Decision in European Company Law' in Theodor Baums, Klaus J. Hopt and Norbert Horn (eds.), *Corporations, Capital Markets and Business in the Law, Liber Amicorum Richard M. Buxbaum* (Alphen aan den Rijn, Kluwer Law International 2000); Werner F. Ebke, 'Centros – Some Realities and Some Mysteries' (2000) 48 *Am. J. Comp. L.* 623; Wulf-Henning Roth, '"Centros": Viel Lärm um Nichts?' (2000) *ZGR* 311; Tito Ballarino, 'From Centros to Überseering. EC Right of Establishment and the Conflict of Laws' (2002) 4 *Yearbook of Private International Law* 203.

[2] It is worth mentioning that British company law did not provide any minimal capital requirement for the constitution of a limited responsibility company in the United Kingdom. In this case, Centros' registered capital represented £100, divided in two shares. Comparatively, the Danish legislation on the matter required the constitution of a registered capital equating 200.000 Danish Krones (approximatively 25.000 Euros).

[3] See the precursory work of Michel Menjucq, *La mobilité des sociétés dans l'espace européen* (Paris, LGDJ 1997).

which has bolstered, over the years, law shopping and thereby also vivifying the underlying competition between the legislation of each Member State.[4]

The *Centros* case constituted the starting point of a three-fold case-law saga concerning the exercise of freedom of establishment by foreign companies, lawfully registered in a country other than the one in which they intend to carry out business.[5] In that respect, this case was crucial in the process of unveiling a change in the configuration of markets, the implementation and consequences of which remained uncontemplated by a large proportion of Member States. The internal market (formerly the European common market), henceforth allows companies – once they are lawfully incorporated in a given Member State – to carry out cross-border activities in the Member State of their choice, through the constitution of entities without legal personality (agencies or branches), and without taking into account any constraints other than those imposed by the Member State in which these companies are incorporated. In other words, the *lex societatis* is no longer automatically binding for the founders of a corporate entity.[6] Thus, in *Centros* the two Danish nationals mentioned above were, as they admitted, attempting to circumvent the minimum capital threshold established by Danish company law, which was perceived as being burdensome (paragraph 18).

By considering the situation outlined above as a purely domestic one, the Danish authorities were in fact endorsing an approach that belonged to the old world, in which the market for corporate charters and its cross-border environment were not fully integrated. That is why the Danish authorities did not succeed in their claims (1).

Nevertheless, by reserving two hypotheses of fraudulent conduct and abuse of freedom of establishment, the Court of Justice intended to provide defence mechanisms to Member States, especially in respect of private 'U-Turn' strategies.[7] Yet, it appears that these supposedly enforceable exceptions are stripped of any real effectivity (2).

In the end, although this judgment deserves to be characterised as a landmark case of the ECJ's case-law,[8] it seems that its importance lies solely in the fact that it participated in unveiling a specific problem; that of the irresolvable nature of diagonal conflicts – unless the European Union and its Member States are willing to tackle the issue (3).

---

[4] See Thomas Mastrullo, *Le droit international des sociétés dans l'espace régional européen* (Paris, PUAM 2009) 356 ff.

[5] In addition to *Centros*, see Case C-208/00 *Überseering v. Nordic Construction Company Baumanagement GmbH* [2002] ECR I-9919; Case C-167/01, *Kamer van Koophandel en Fabrieken voor Amsterdam v. Inspire Art* [2003] ECR I-10155.

[6] Needless to say that the least burdensome legislation on the matter will generally enjoy large support from entrepreneurs.

[7] The expression refers to the process by which a person injects a cross-border element in a corporate operation for the sole purpose of benefiting from the right of freedom of movement granted by European Law, and circumvent, as a result, a given domestic law (Anne Looijestijn-Clearie, 'Centros Ltd – A Complete U-Turn in the Right of Establishment for Companies?' (2000) 49 *ICLQ* 621, 638).

[8] Louis d'Avout, 'CJCE, 9 mars 1999, *Centros Ltd*' in Michaël Karpenschif and Cyril Nourissat (eds), *Les grands arrêts de la jurisprudence de l'Union européenne* 3rd edn (Paris, PUF 2016) 299.

1. FREEDOM OF ESTABLISHMENT AND PURELY DOMESTIC SITUATIONS

The argumentation held by the Danish government before the European Court of Justice appeared, in principle, unquestionable: the situations governed by article 49 (formerly article 52 of the EEC Treaty) of the Treaty on the Functioning of the European Union (hereinafter 'TFEU') were not applicable to this case since the contentious situation was a purely domestic or internal one. The founders of the company were Danish nationals who had formed the company for the sole purpose of carrying out business in Denmark. Furthermore, the Danish government claimed that 'in such circumstances the formation by nationals of one Member State of a company in another Member State does not amount to a relevant external element in the light of Community law and, in particular, freedom of establishment' (paragraph 16).

Consequently, the Danish government apprehended the legal existence of Centros as a mere factual consideration among others, denying any relevance to the fact that English law provided legal personality to the company. Undoubtedly, it was conceded that the company had never carried out any business in the United Kingdom. However, the legal personality of Centros could not be ignored on the sole grounds that its founders were Danish citizens!

Admittedly, by virtue of article 49 of the TFEU according to which 'restrictions on the freedom of establishment of nationals of a Member State in the territory of another Member State shall be prohibited', the restrictions imposed by the Danish authorities on its own citizens appeared to be outside the scope of application of such a provision. The ambiguity of the provision according to which '[s]uch prohibition shall also apply to restrictions on the setting-up of agencies, branches or subsidiaries by nationals of any Member States established in the territory of any Member State', supported the government's claims, in the sense that it gave credit to the idea that EU Law was not applicable to requests formulated by nationals establishing a corporate branch in their own country of origin.

Such a rationale could not be endorsed by the ECJ, since article 54 of the TFEU (formerly article 58 of the TEEC) clearly states that

> [c]ompanies or firms formed in accordance with the law of a Member State and having their registered office, central administration or principal place of business within the Union shall, for the purposes of this Chapter [Chapter on the Freedom of establishment], be *treated* in the same way *as natural persons who are nationals of Member States.*[9]

By treating natural and legal persons alike, this provision removes any ambiguity as to the meaning of the provisions established by Article 49 of the TFEU: the legal entities formed in accordance with the law of a Member State and on its territory are nationals of that State, regardless of the nationality of their founders and directors. In other words, a plain reading of these provisions supported the thesis, also endorsed by the Advocate General La Pergola in his opinion, according to which 'the newly formed

[9] Emphasis added.

company may set up its principal – and indeed its secondary – establishment *wherever it wishes* within the Community'.[10]

Freedom of establishment therefore implies the right for the founders of a company to choose freely the law governing the company that they intend to form. Besides, this choice of law will equally apply to the secondary establishments that the company might subsequently set up on the territory of other Member States (as the given establishments will merely consist in the setting up of an agency or a branch). Consequently, this case embodied, in the field of company law, the mutual trust that Member States owe to each other, thereby forcing each State to recognise companies as the legislative product of other States – the legal personality of companies flowing directly from the law – as is the case concerning manufactured goods[11] since the well-known decision *Cassis de Dijon*.

In *Centros* the Court of Justice relied on its opinion in *Segers*,[12] by recalling 'that a situation in which a company formed in accordance with the law of a Member State in which it has its registered office desires to set up a branch in another Member State falls within the scope of Community law' and that it is 'immaterial' to examine the goals that the company is attempting to achieve through such an establishment in the second Member State, even when this very purpose consists in carrying out, in this second Member State, 'its main, or indeed entire, business' (paragraph 17).

In the eyes of the Court, freedom of establishment is, therefore, based on the assumption that all Member States must grant free access to their market, not only to the nationals of another Member State who intend to form a company on their territory – as is required by article 49 of the TFEU, paragraph 2 – but also to the companies, formed in another Member State, that wish to conduct business on their territory, notably by establishing an agency or a branch in these States. The only condition that appears to be imposed by the Court of Justice is that such an establishment be 'real' and that business is, as a result, effectively conducted in that State.

Implicitly thereby, the European Court of Justice is providing a margin of discretion to the Member States when regulating the establishment of 'mail box companies' on their territory. Consequently, it favours, *volens nolens*, those Member States that have instituted formal criteria of registration, and, where the voluntary establishment of a company and its incorporation in that country leads to the applicability of the law of that Member State.

Since it was constitutive of an unlawful restriction, one might wonder whether the Danish authorities' refusal to proceed with the registration of the company's branch, could, nevertheless, be justified by virtue of overriding reasons of general interest. More generally, was any attempt from the Danish government to defend itself against such U-Turn tactics, bound to fail?

---

[10] Case C-212/97 *Centros Ltd v. Erhvervs* [1999] ECR I-1459, Opinion of AG La Pergola, para 20. The text is also underlined in the Opinion.

[11] Case C-120/78 *Rewe Zentral AG v. Bundesmonopolverwaltung für Branntwein* [1979] ECR 1979-00649, cited by AG La Pergola in his opinion; Also mentioned by L. d'Avout (n 8) para 60-9.

[12] Case C-79/85 *D.H.M Segers v. Bestuur van de Bedrijfsvereniging voor Bank – en Verzekeringswezen, Groothandel en Vrije Beroepen* [1986] ECR 1986-02375.

2. FREEDOM OF ESTABLISHMENT AND THE EXCEPTION OF FRAUD

Was the legal device conceived by the plaintiffs constitutive of a fraud on the law?[13] The Danish authorities were convinced that this was, in fact, the case. They argued that the claims formulated by the plaintiffs, to the extent that they invoked the relevant Treaty provisions, constituted an 'abuse of the freedom of establishment' (Paragraph 23).

The Court of Justice began by conceding that, in accordance with its case-law on the matter, the parties may not 'improperly or fraudulently [take] advantage of provisions of Community Law', and that each Member State 'is entitled to take measures designed to prevent certain of its nationals from attempting, under cover of the rights created by the Treaty, improperly to circumvent their national legislation' (paragraph 24). In doing so, the Court simply appealed to a well-established principle, first stated in *Van Binsbergen* (concerning the provision of services) and *Knoors* (concerning freedom of establishment).[14]

The Court subsequently reminded the parties that the Danish rules which the parties were attempting to circumvent constituted rules governing the incorporation and establishment of companies rather than the carrying out of particular professional activities. Since the principle of freedom of establishment was designed to permit companies to conduct business in another Member State than their country of origin, by means of the constitution of an agency or a corporate branch in the Member States in question (paragraph 26), the Court was well founded in stating that '[t]he right to form a company in accordance with the law of a Member State and to set up branches in other Member States is inherent in the exercise, in a single market, of the freedom of establishment guaranteed by the Treaty' (paragraph 27). As a result, the Court of Justice judged that the legal montage designed by the plaintiffs could not, 'in itself, constitute an abuse of the right of establishment' (paragraph 27).

Nonetheless, one last issue was to be addressed by the Court; that of the (un)justified character of the Danish refusal to register the branch of the English company.

To succeed in their claims, the Danish authorities argued that the goal pursued by Denmark through the enactment of the contentious provisions, namely the protection of creditors – whether public or private – was sufficient to justify the existence of the minimal capital requirement imposed upon limited companies seeking registration in that Member State. Besides, the Danish authorities claimed that such a restriction constituted the least burdensome means of satisfying the aforementioned objective.

Yet, this defence failed to convince the Court of Justice. More precisely, as the Court applied the double proportionality and necessity test to the facts of the case, as

[13] B. Audit, *La fraude à la loi* (Paris, Dalloz 1974) paras 110–20.

[14] Case C-33-74 *Van Binsbergen v. Bestuur van de Bedrijfvereniging voor de Metaalnijverheid* [1974] ECR 1974-01299, para 13; Case C-115/78 *J. Knoors v. Staatssecretaris van Economische Zaken* [1979] ECR 1979-00399, para 25.

established by its case-law,[15] it came to the conclusion that the minimum capital requirement in question did not, in fact, ensure the protection of creditors, insofar as the Danish authorities would actually have accepted to register the company, had it effectively been conducting business in the United Kingdom (paragraph 35). The protection of local creditors, which allegedly underpinned the enactment of the contentious provisions, was furthermore already ensured by European Law, and notably by two European directives.[16] According to the Court, the pursuit of such an objective did not entail, in itself, the imposition of a minimum capital requirement for companies seeking registration in Denmark (paragraph 36).

Although the Court of Justice was not compelled to go beyond that reasoning, it took great care in stating that in spite of the impossibility for a Member State to refuse to register a branch or agency of a company formed in accordance with the Law of another Member State, the first Member State can, however, as stated in paragraph 38, take

> any appropriate measure for preventing or penalising fraud, either in relation to the company itself, if need be in cooperation with the Member State in which it was formed, or in relation to its members, where it has been established that they are in fact attempting, by means of the formation of the company, to evade their obligations towards private or public creditors established on the territory of a Member State concerned.

The Court thus established, to the benefit of Member States, a fraud exception in the field of company law. Yet, since the Court refused to qualify the behaviour of the two Danish persons in *Centros* as being fraudulent, one might wonder what exactly is meant by 'fraud'!

Admittedly, the Court mentioned the prospect of inter-state cooperation so as to provide meaningful content to the concept of 'fraud'. However, as highlighted by the Court's subsequent case-law, as long as each Member State is free to establish the criteria for making a company subject to its law, this avenue appears to be somewhat hypothetical.

In any event, it would seem clear that, by empowering Member States to oppose an exception of fraud, the Court intended to establish a legal framework that allows for a wide margin of appreciation on this point. Under this reading, the Member States wishing to make use of such an exception are therefore permitted to take 'any appropriate measure for preventing or penalising fraud' (paragraph 38, see above). However, a subsequent case, *Inspire Art*,[17] proved crucial in testing the width of the framework established four years earlier. Despite its apparently extensive scope, it turned out to be an extremely restrictive one.

---

[15] Case C-19/92 *Dieter Kraus v. Land Baden-Württemberg* [1993] ECR 1993 I-01663, para 32; Case C-55/94 *Reinhard Gebhard v. Consiglio dell'Ordine degli Avvocati e Procuratori di Milano* [1995] ECR 1995 I-04165, para 37.

[16] Fourth Council Directive (EEC) 78/660 on the annual accounts of certain types of companies [1978] OJ L222/11; Eleventh Council Directive (EEC) 89/666/EEC concerning disclosure requirements in respect of branches opened in a Member State by certain types of company governed by the law of another State [1989] OJ L395/36.

[17] Supra, footnote 5.

Inspire Art Ltd, a private limited liability company formed in accordance with the law of the United Kingdom and established on its territory, was directed by a sole administrator, residing in The Hague. As it took the view that the activities conducted by the company – through its branch – were solely carried out in the Netherlands, the Chamber of Commerce of Amsterdam required the company, apprehended as a sham foreign company, to add to its registration in the commercial register, a statement formally revealing its true nature; that of being a pseudo foreign company.[18] Such a requirement entailed the additional obligations not only to conform to the capital requirements imposed by Dutch law, but also to produce and publish annual reports.

The measures taken by the Dutch authorities appeared to be appropriate and proportionate, and thus in accordance with the legal framework established by the European Court of Justice in *Centros* – given that the legal existence of the company, which was governed by the laws of the United Kingdom, was actually recognised by the Dutch authorities, and its branch succeeded in being registered on the territory of this Member State. Yet, the Court adopted a different view. It judged that the application of Dutch law – comprising overriding mandatory provisions[19] – constituted an impediment to freedom of establishment and that no reason relating to a local conception of the public interest on this point could provide sufficient justification.[20]

Consequently, the European Court of Justice gave a judgment that can be presented as *Centros*' fraternal twin. What separates *Inspire Art* from the *Centros* case, besides its date of birth, is the fact that the Dutch authorities, unlike their Danish counterparts, fully acknowledged the legal personality of the company, which was formed in accordance with the law of the United Kingdom. They simply attempted to impose on the Company's branch a number of Danish mandatory legal provisions on the grounds that such a company was not conducting any activity in the Member State in which it was formed. In this context, a semantic shift can also be pinpointed, as the Court solely referred to the notion of 'abuse'[21] and did not mention the term 'fraud'.

Whether such a semantic shift could enhance the Member States' ability to combat U-Turn tactics remains highly debatable. This is even more so as the Court does not indicate a suitable way for Member States to take defensive measures in such a case. The message that the Court is sending is clear: competition between the legal systems

---

[18] This obligation was stipulated by a Law enacted on the 17 December 1997, which entered into force on the 1 January 1998 (*Staatsblad* 1997, n° 697). See Levinus Timmerman, 'Das niederländische Gesellschaftsrecht im Umbruch' in *Festschrift für Marcus Lutter zum 70. Geburtstag* (Cologne, Otto Schmidt 2000) 173, 184–85.

[19] Comparable to the *Überlagerungstheorie* formulated by Otto Sandrock ('Ein Amerikanisches Lehrstück für das Kollisionsrecht der Kapitalgesellschaften' [1978] *RabelsZ* 227), and the *maatschappelijke prioriteit* doctrine formulated by Paul Vlas ('The Fight Against Pseudo Foreign Corporations in the Netherlands' in Katharina Boele-Woelki (ed.), *Comparability and Evaluation. Essays on Comparative Law, Private International Law, and International Commercial Arbitration, in Honour of Dimitra Kokkini-Iatridou* (Leiden, Martinus Nijhoff Publishers 1994)).

[20] Case C-167/01 *Kamer van Koophandel en Fabrieken voor Amsterdam v. Inspire Art* [2003] ECR I-10155, paras 105–42.

[21] Ibid., para 105.

of Member States implied, in the field of company law,[22] by the very existence of a European internal market, cannot be regulated by means of State intervention (on the fallacious pretext that such intervention would – or could – prevent market distortion).[23] In other words, regulation of competition between Member States falls to the internal market alone.

Comparing the American and European approaches to the regulation of U-Turn tactics constitutes an enlightening exercise. While the criteria of incorporation and the *internal affairs* doctrine have been virtually canonised[24] in the United States, the States' efforts to combat U-Turns, through the establishment of unilateral corrective rules[25] – which can be compared to the aim pursued by the Dutch authorities in *Inspire Art* – have been, reluctantly but surely, materialised with the 'blessing' of the United States Supreme Court.[26]

This comparative development conveys that the solution adopted in *Inspire Art* could well have been different. This is all the more so that the criterion of incorporation is not the only connecting factor to be applied within the internal market by Member States. Consequently, a situation of diagonal conflict[27] has come into existence.

3. FREEDOM OF ESTABLISHMENT AND DIAGONAL CONFLICT

A proper understanding of the notion of 'diagonal conflict', as revealed by the *Centros* case and its fraternal twin, the *Inspire Art* case, cannot be fully grasped without apprehending these cases as being part of a wider framework; that of the relations between primary European law and domestic company law.

As mentioned above,[28] it follows from the provisions of Article 54 TFEU, that a 'company' – within the meaning of the second paragraph of the provision – might benefit from freedom of establishment, granted by Article 49 TFEU, every time its

---

22 See Horatia Muir Watt, 'Aspects économiques du droit international privé' (2004) 307 *RCADI* 25, at para 13 ff, and at para 42 ff; Mastrullo (n 4) para 858 ff, and 907 ff; Luis de Lima Pinheiro, 'Competition between Legal Systems in the European Union and Private International Law' (2008) *IPRax* 206, 210–12.

23 See Horatia Muir Watt, 'De la liberté d'établissement des succursales' (2004) *Rev. crit. DIP* 151, 182.

24 P. John Kosyris, 'Some Observations on State Regulation of Multistate Takeovers: Controlling Choice of Law Through the Commerce Clause' (1989) 14 *Del. J. Corp. L.* 499, 515.

25 *Cal. Corp. Code*, § 2115 (West, 1977, and Supp. 1989); *N.Y. Bus. Corp. Law*, § 1320 (McKinney, 1986).

26 See Muir Watt (n 23) 151, 182; *Edgar v. MITE Corp.* (1982) 457 U.S. 624; *CTS Corp. v. Dynamics Corp. of America* (1987) 481 U.S. 69, 90: '[the] free market system depends at its core upon the fact that a corporation – *except in the rarest situations* – is organized under, and governed by, the law of a single jurisdiction, traditionally the corporate law of the State of its incorporation'. The words were also underlined in the text of origin.

27 Jeremy Heymann, *Le droit international privé à l'épreuve du fédéralisme européen* (Paris, Economica 2010), at para 141 ff, and especially at para 175 ff. See also 'The Relationship between EU Law and Private International Law Revisited: Of Diagonal Conflicts and the Means to Resolve Them' (2011) 13 *Yearbook of Private International Law* 557, at para 16 ff.

28 Supra (n 4).

connection with the European Union has been established. Naturally, establishing such a connection will require applying one of the three connecting criteria provided by the first paragraph of Article 54 TFEU (by localising, on the territory of a Member State, the registered office of the company, its central administration, or its principal place of business).

Placed on an equal footing with each other, these criteria can be applied interchangeably by a given Member State in order to entrench a company in that very State and transform the company into a subject of its laws, following the same logic as the one that prevails when dealing with the nationality of natural persons.[29] Consequently, the only companies to benefit from the provisions related to freedom of establishment are those which have been formed in accordance with the law of a given Member State – as a result of the application of the aforementioned criteria – since,

> in the absence of a uniform Community law definition of the companies which may enjoy the right of establishment on the basis of a single connecting factor determining the national law applicable to a company, the question whether article 4[9 TFEU] applies to a company which seeks to rely on the fundamental freedom enshrined in that article … is *a preliminary matter which … can only be resolved by the applicable national law*.[30]

Furthermore, endorsing one connecting factor at the expense of other criteria does not constitute a neutral choice, and largely mirrors the broad interests that a State may attempt to protect and defend in the field of corporate law. The European Court of Justice's case-law in corporate matters conveys the adoption of an approach which promotes exclusively the registered office as connecting factor, despite the fact that Article 54 TFEU does not explicitly do so. A diagonal conflict thus appeared, as a result of the clash between the aims pursued by Member States and the European Union, since the said States, fully competent when choosing between competing connecting factors, were effectively deprived, on the basis of freedom of establishment, of the possibility of drawing the legal consequences which such a choice of criteria entailed. In addition, in the two cases dealt with above, *Centros* and *Inspire Art*, this conflict was two-fold, as the States, which were fully competent to combat fraud and legal abuses, were also placed in a situation where it became impossible for them to actually exercise these prerogatives, since freedom of establishment – as interpreted by the Court of Justice – precluded them from doing so.

In other words, these cases shed light on the existence of a *power* struggle, which raises the question of the distribution and *articulation* of EU and national competences: both actors enjoy a set of competing prerogatives. Such a clash of competences is, in itself, insoluble, as no view can claim the higher ground in asserting the superiority of

---

[29] For a comprehensive comparative analysis of the connecting process through which a company is subjected to the Law of a given Member State to benefit from freedom of establishment, and the grant of the nationality of a Member State to physical persons wishing to enjoy EU citizenship, See Jeremy Heymann, 'De la mobilité des sociétés dans l'Union. Réflexions sur le *droit* d'établissement' in *Mélanges en l'honneur du Professeur Bernard Audit. Les relations privées internationales* (Paris, LGDJ 2014) 425, 435–38.

[30] Case C-210/06 *Cartesio Oktató és Szolgáltató bt* [2008] ECR 2008 I-09641, para 109. Emphasis added.

one competence over the others, for all of these are equally legitimate. Yet, by defending freedom of establishment at the expense of the exercise, by the Member States, of their established right to combat fraud and abuses in corporate matters, the Court of Justice gave priority to a competence – its own – at the expense of another – enjoyed by Member States. Besides, the Court favoured, in a quasi-exclusive manner, the registered office (or incorporation) as connecting factor, although the TFEU provides the possibility for Member States to prefer other criteria, and thus, to adopt another system of private international company law.[31]

A suitable way of dissolving the conflict may lie in the establishment by the Court of a legal framework, in which the personal rights of economic actors and the constitutional rights of Member States are justly balanced, as is the case in the United States owing to the intervention of the Supreme Court.[32] But, to do so, it must be acknowledged that the Court of Justice is becoming a Constitutional Court, in charge of balancing the competing interests pursued simultaneously, and conflictingly, not only by natural and legal persons, but also by the European Union and its Member States. This may be the price to pay to ensure the effectiveness of the federal principle governing the functioning of the European Union – or indeed, its very survival.[33]

21.3 ECONOMIC INTEGRATION, CORPORATE PLANNING AND CORPORATE NATIONALITY AT THE CROSSROADS

Régis Bismuth[*]

The *Centros* case concerns, primarily, the relationship between, on the one hand, the freedom of establishment recognised in Articles 49 and 54 of the Treaty on the Functioning of the European Union (TFEU), and, on the other hand, the private international law issue of the law applicable to the internal affairs and the status of corporations. Understanding the interactions between these two sets of rules and, in particular, the extent to which the former has affected the latter, requires a brief reminder of the two main models of determination of applicable law adopted by the Member States.[34] Some (United Kingdom, Ireland, Denmark, etc.) follow the incorporation theory, according to which the applicable law is that of the State in which the corporation was constituted. Others (Germany, Austria, France, Belgium, etc.) have

---

31 Germany drew the consequences of such case-law by enacting a statutory provision (*Gesetz zur Modernisierung des GmbH-Rechts und zur Bekämpfung von Missbrauchen*) dropping the requirement, previously imposed to limited companies formed in Germany to establish their real seat on its territory.

32 Supra, n 10 and n 26.

33 Heymann (n 27).

* Contribution originally written in French, translated into English by Camille Fromentin.

34 Marc-Phillippe Weller and Chris Thomale, 'Companies' in Jürgen Basedow, Giesela Rühl, Franco Ferrari and Pedro de Miguel Asensio (eds), *Encyclopedia of Private International Law* (Cheltenham, Edward Elgar 2017) 405; Andra Cotiga, *Le droit européen des sociétés – Compétition entre les systèmes juridiques dans l'Union européenne* (Brussels, Larcier 2013) 151.

adopted the real seat theory, according to which the applicable law is that of the State on whose territory the real seat is located (or 'workforce').

These two theories are grounded on significantly different conceptions. The real seat theory is based on an 'objective and realistic' connecting link of the corporation and has an institutional dimension in the sense that it seeks to make the applicable law coincide with the legal system and the economy of the State in which the company is integrated. That of incorporation leaves the determination of the *lex societatis* to the free choice of the founders. It reflects a contractual conception where party autonomy prevails.

The real seat theory is likely to hinder the international mobility of corporations. A corporation willing to transfer its headquarters abroad while retaining its social form may face a refusal from the authorities of the State of incorporation (or 'State of origin'). Also, the legal existence of a corporation that establishes its headquarters abroad may be denied by the authorities of the host State on the ground that the separation between the head office (located in the State of origin) and the actual headquarters (located in the 'host State') constitutes a manoeuver designed to circumvent the application of the *lex societatis* (that is, the law of the host State'). A cross-border transfer may therefore require the creation of a new corporation in the host State (operation referred to as 'reincorporation') or the respect of certain mandatory rules (for example minimum capital requirement) by a company seen to be 'pseudo-foreign'. It is in the light of these elements that the *Centros* case and its progeny can be understood.

The construction of the internal market has revolved around four freedoms of movement (goods, services, capital and people). Free movement of persons (designated 'right of establishment') benefits to 'nationals' of the Member States (Article 49 TFEU), including 'companies established in accordance with the law of a Member State' that 'are assimilated … to the natural persons who are nationals of the Member States' (Article 54 TFEU). Companies willing to transfer their real seat from one Member State to another but facing obstacles raised both by the State of origin (requiring a dissolution prior to the transfer) and the host State (requiring reincorporation or the respect of certain mandatory rules) have invoked the right of establishment. This has generated two types of disputes. One concerns the compatibility with the right of establishment of the restrictions imposed by the State of origin on the 'emigration' of the real seat (*Daily Mail*[35] and *Cartesio*[36] cases in particular), the other the restrictions imposed by the host State of the 'immigration' of the actual seat (business constituting the trilogy *Centros*,[37] *Überseering*[38] and *Inspire Art*[39]).

[35] Case 81/87 *The Queen v. H. M. Treasury and Commissioners of Inland Revenue, ex parte Daily Mail and General Trust plc.* [1988] ECR I-5505.

[36] Case C-210/06 *Cartesio Oktató és Szolgáltató bt* [2008] ECR I-9641.

[37] Case C-212/97 *Centros Ltd v. Erhvervs- og Selskabsstyrelsen* [1999] ECR I-1459.

[38] Case C-208/00 *Überseering BV v. Nordic Construction Company Baumanagement GmbH (NCC)* [2002] ECR I-9919.

[39] Case C-167/01 *Kamer van Koophandel en Fabrieken voor Amsterdam v. Inspire Art Ltd* [2003] ECR I-10155.

The Court of Justice drew a distinction between the two situations.[40] On the one hand, in a logic somewhat reminiscent of that of *Cassis de Dijon*,[41] it has censored the restrictions imposed by the host States on the basis of freedom of establishment (reincorporation, capital requirement, non-recognition of legal personality, imposition of specific rules of directors' liability). On the other hand, it has nonetheless refused to recognise an infringement of freedom of establishment in emigration situations. In the *Cartesio* case, the Court stressed that 'companies are creatures of national law and exist only by virtue of the national legislation which determines its incorporation and functioning'[42] and emphasised that it is thus the province of national law to define 'the connecting factor required of a company if it is to be regarded as incorporated under the law of that Member State'.[43] Consequently, the law of the State of origin has the possibility of no longer recognising as its own a company willing to transfer its seat to another Member State, 'thereby breaking the connecting factor required under the national law of the Member State of incorporation'.[44]

This case law has produced an asymmetrical situation. In emigration cases, freedom of establishment does not generally restrict the right of the State of origin to control the transfer of the real seat. In immigration cases, the freedom of establishment compels the receiving State to recognise the foreign company willing to transfer its seat without being able to impose the requirements stemming from the mandatory rules of its company law, except for 'imperative requirements in the general interest' which have not been successfully invoked in *Centros*, *Überseering* and *Inspire Art*. The freedom of establishment has thus significantly affected the possibility for host States to apply the real seat theory in order to manage the personal status of foreign companies.

The *Centros* judgment has a quasi-iconic dimension in the narrative of EU law[45] and the European discourse on company law.[46] Beyond its EU law or private international law aspects relevant to the mobility of companies, alternative readings of the *Centros* judgment are available. Indeed, this case, both in respect of its outcome and as a symbol, is particularly rich and can be viewed from the perspective of other disciplines.

---

40 On those aspects, see Cotiga (n 34) 175; Otto Sandrock and Jean J. du Plessis, 'The Impact of European Developments on German Codetermination and German Corporate Law' in Jean J. du Plessis, Bernhard Großfeld, Claus Luttermann, Ingo Saenger, Otto Sandrock and Matthias Casper (eds) *German Corporate Governance in International and European Context* 2nd edn (New York, Springer 2012) 204.

41 Andrew Johnston, *EC Regulation of Corporate Governance* (Cambridge, Cambridge University Press 2009) 146. The author refers in particular to '(t)he extension of Cassis to companies' (p. 152).

42 *Cartesio* (n 36) [104].

43 Ibid., [110].

44 Ibid.

45 See in particular, Martin Gelter, '*Centros*, the Freedom of Establishment for Companies and the Court's Accidental Vision for Corporate Law' in Fernanda Nicola and Bill Davies (eds), *EU Law Stories – Contextual and Critical Histories of European Jurisprudence* (Cambridge, Cambridge University Press 2017) 309.

46 Ibid., 332–34. The author shows that it is following the *Centros* case that certain reviews concerning European or comparative company law were created (*European Business Organization Law Review* created in 2001, *European Company and Financial Law Review* and *European Company Law* both created in 2004, etc.).

Three such perspectives can be explored. The first consists in evaluating what the *Centros* case can teach us about the different models of economic integration (1), the second relates to the (social) functions of company law from the point of view of host States' interests (2) and the last is related to current debates concerning the nationality of corporations in public international law (3).

1. THE 'ECONOMIC INTEGRATION' PERSPECTIVE

As they concern the relations between liberalisation and regulation, the *Centros* case and its progeny involve issues of economic integration, particularly those relating to the distinction between two different models of integration, positive and negative.

Economic integration aims at creating a space of economic free movement and implies the removal of barriers to trade. It is not surprising therefore that different integration processes are based on similar disciplines (e.g. the principle of non-discrimination) even while they fall under distinct legal frameworks. This is, to a certain extent, the case of EU law and WTO law, that can be studied from a comparative perspective.[47] However, these two instruments are distinguished by the fact that WTO law is part of a negative integration process (removal of barriers to trade), whereas EU law is broadly part of a positive integration dynamic (removal of barriers to trade coupled with the implementation of common policies and regulatory harmonisation through supranational instruments).[48] The first one relies on a dissociation between the spaces of liberalisation and regulation, while the second works to make the two coincide. However, not all national regulations are subject to harmonisation initiatives and there are pockets of negative integration in the European context. This is the case with certain aspects of company law; *Centros* can be understood from this perspective.

By controlling national restrictive measures on matters not harmonised in EU law with regard to European economic freedoms (in this case, the refusal by the Danish authorities to register the branch of a company incorporated under UK law in order to circumvent the Danish national minimum capital requirements), the *Centros* judgment is part of a logic of 'negative integration'.[49] What is striking about this decision, however, is that the intra-European dimension of the situation (the establishment of a British company in Denmark) is not the result of a genuine economic flow between these two areas but rather the sole result of the Danish founders' wish to benefit from the foreign system of company law, considered to be the most advantageous. In essence, the only flow that can be observed between the two Member States is that of

[47] See, Sanford E. Gaines, Birgitte Egelund Olsen and Karsten Engsig Sørensen (eds), *Liberalising Trade in the EU and the WTO – A Legal Comparison* (Cambridge, Cambridge University Press 2012).

[48] Federico Ortino, *Basic Legal Instruments for the Liberalisation of Trade – A Comparative Analysis of EC and WTO Law* (Oxford, Hart 2004) 16.

[49] Christian Joerges 'Sur la légitimité d'européaniser le droit privé – Plaidoyer pour une approche procédurale' (2004) 2 *Revue Internationale de Droit Economique* 142; Johnston (n 41) 152.

British company law! As such, the Court has not only made it possible 'to transform a purely internal situation into an intra-Community situation',[50] but has also, in a way, permitted the free circulation of company law in the European internal market as an extension of the freedom of establishment. The Court has indeed clearly assumed this form of *law shopping*, emphasising that it is possible for any European national to choose to form a company 'in the Member State whose rules of company law seem to him the least restrictive'.[51] Therefore, by refusing to subject the benefit of the more advantageous regulatory regime to a real economic flow within the internal market, and by disregarding the intention of the persons concerned to circumvent the rules of the host State, the Court thus introduced direct competition between national systems of company law.

This competition manifested itself in the years following the *Centros – Überseering – Inspire Art* trilogy through the expansion of a pan-European incorporation market, in which the British limited liability company was particularly popular. It was the case in Germany, where new intermediaries were created in charge of completing the incorporation formalities.[52]

This has generated a debate about the risk that this competition would generate a regulatory race to the bottom and dismantle the protections of corporate law for the sole benefit of shareholders or other stakeholders.[53] It should be noted that these ECJ decisions have triggered reforms to simplify the law of limited liability companies in many Member States willing to ensure the competitiveness of their company law, such as Germany, France, Spain or the Netherlands – noting that, in the latter case, the reform explicitly mentioned the case-law of the Court.[54]

These developments make it possible to return to the considerations relating to the models of economic integration. This case law has generated what some people refer to as a 'defensive regulatory competition'[55] through which several Member States have sought to align certain aspects of their limited liability company law on the UK model. The position of the Court, through its interpretation of the right of establishment, thus favoured a process of convergence of national laws, in other words a form of positive (albeit imposed or coerced) integration in an area where Member States had until now refused to harmonise domestic regulations.

---

50 Horatia Muir Watt 'Aspects économiques du droit international privé (Réflexions sur l'impact de la globalisation économique sur les fondements des conflits de lois et de juridictions)' (2004) 307 *Recueil Des Cours* 108.

51 *Centros* (n 37) [27].

52 Marco Becht, Luca Enriques and Veronika Korom '*Centros* and the Cost of Branching' (2009) 9 *Journal of Corporate Law Studies* 171; Gelter (n 45) 326; Martin Höpner and Armin Schäfer 'A New Phase of European Integration: Organised Capitalisms in Post-Ricardian Europe' (2010) 33 *West European Politics* 360.

53 Gelter (n 45) 327. See also *infra* s 2.

54 Ibid., 328–29.

55 Ibid., 328; Johnston (n 41) 183.

2. THE (SOCIAL) FUNCTIONS OF CORPORATE LAW FOR THE HOST STATE

The Court's approach in *Centros* and subsequent cases is to require the host State to justify any restriction on the freedom of establishment resulting from additional requirements imposed on foreign companies. Such restrictions may be compatible with the freedoms of movement since, as the Court indicates, they respect four conditions: 'they must be applied in a non-discriminatory manner; they must be justified by imperative requirements in the general interest; they must be suitable for securing the attainment of the objective which they pursue; and they must not go beyond what is necessary in order to attain it'.[56] The Court has thus controlled the means employed by host States to ensure the achievement of certain objectives and the protection of certain interests through the rules of company law. This liberal jurisprudence appears to be rather strict for States and moreover short-sighted if one tries to place it in a more general framework of the functions of corporate law.

In the context of the *Centros* case, the rules at stake related to the constitution and the release of a minimum capital for limited liability companies, minimum that had been circumvented since Danish law required a minimum of approximately 20,000 euros, while the incorporation process in the UK for the same type of company was only about £100. The Danish authorities emphasised that these minimum capital requirements had the objective of protecting both public creditors (who cannot secure those debts by means of guarantees) and private creditors against a risk of fraudulent bankruptcy resulting facilitated by inadequate capitalisation.[57]

The Court rejected these arguments expeditiously. In particular, it pointed out that the minimum capital requirements are clearly not aimed at protecting the creditors, because if the UK company had had a real activity in the State of origin, the Danish branch would have nonetheless been registered. In this respect, a foreign company having a real activity in the State of origin could not be treated more favourably than a company that was incorporated abroad for the sole purpose of circumventing national rules relating to minimal capital! It further indicated that the protection of creditors is ultimately guaranteed insofar that they are informed that their debtor is a foreign law company.[58] In *Inspire Art*, the Court reiterated that the information concerning the foreign origin of the company was sufficient for the protection of creditors, noting, in passing, that it did not need 'to consider whether the rules on minimum share capital constitute in themselves an appropriate protection measure'.[59]

The requirements of company law are nonetheless not confined to the interests of creditors alone, and the *Überseering* case provided an opportunity for the German Government to emphasise that the real seat theory is also necessary for the protection of minority shareholders and employees.[60] Germany was particularly worried about the future of its co-management system allowing employees to be represented in the organs

[56] *Centros* (n 37) [34].
[57] Ibid., [32].
[58] Ibid., [35–36].
[59] *Inspire Art* (n 39) [135].
[60] *Überseering* (n 38) [88–89].

of certain types of companies.[61] If the Court has considered, in a very cautious way, that 'it is not inconceivable that overriding requirements relating to the general interest, such as the protection of the interests of … employees … may, in certain circumstances and subject to certain conditions, justify restrictions on freedom of establishment',[62] it nevertheless pointed out that the German measures aimed at pseudo-foreign companies (in this case, the deprivation of a local forum) amounted to 'an outright negation of the freedom of establishment'.[63]

Beyond the question of the proportionality of the national measures implemented by the host State in order to sanction the breach of mandatory national requirements (necessity of reincorporation, non-recognition of the legal personality of the foreign company, etc.), this case-law leads implicitly to an assessment of the merits of the corporate structures on aspects that it would be unthinkable to question on other grounds. Indeed, it is hardly conceivable to challenge minimum capital requirements or co-management rules on the basis of freedom to conduct a business by asserting that they constitute an unnecessary obstacle to the conduct of an economic activity in a given national system. However, these very same requirements do not withstand the logic of the freedom of establishment, which can thus be seen ultimately to be very invasive.[64]

The *Centros* ruling and those that have followed it have more fundamentally opened the breach of a disembodied or off-shore company law by enabling the unravelling of certain models of capitalism (for example Rhenish capitalism) that are also the result of a historical process.[65] It is also not excluded that this case-law will lead Member States to ensure that the requirements of company law censored under the freedom of establishment (minimum capital requirement or joint and several liability of the directors in *Inspire Art*) following an *ex ante* logic, are later reconstituted in another form according to an individualized *ex post* approach. This would be the case for instance through insolvency law proceedings, or through the standards relevant to the lifting of the corporate veil, in order to engage the liability of the shareholders in the event of insolvency of an underfunded company.[66]

The Court's analysis also raises other questions. By holding that the rules on minimum capital are not necessary for the protection of creditors because they are informed that the company is foreign,[67] the Court identifies, to be sure, a less restrictive measure available to the host State, but such a measure is based on a very different conception of the creditors' protection policy.

A minimum capital requirement can be considered as a discipline intended to preserve the interests of professional and non-professional co-contractors, as well as those of persons incurring the tort liability of the company. Relying solely on the

---

61 Ibid., [89].

62 Ibid., [92].

63 Ibid., [93].

64 Meanwhile underlying that there exists a debate on the real questioning of the German co-management system on the basis of the freedom of establishment. On those issues, see Sandrock and du Plessis, *supra* note 40.

65 Höpner and Schäfer (n 52) 344.

66 Gelter (n 45) 335.

67 *Centros* (n 37) [35]; *Inspire Art* (n 39) [135].

information provided to creditors, the Court assumes that they all have similar capacities to analyse the risk to which they are exposed – and in the same breath, it also ignores cases of tort liability. This approach runs counter to the more 'paternalistic' creditors' protection mechanisms of continental Europe that assume the limited rationality of certain vulnerable actors.[68] To a certain extent, the *Centros* doctrine also implicitly acknowledges the primacy of private autonomy in contractual matters, the very concept that is at the heart of the theory of incorporation in respect of the determination of the law applicable to companies.

3. THE ISSUE OF THE NATIONALITY OF CORPORATIONS IN PUBLIC INTERNATIONAL LAW

In its approach to the nationality of corporations and the effectiveness of their connection to a given State, the *Centros* case echoes several well-known problems of public international law, which also offers an interesting angle to read the position taken by the ECJ.

In an approach similar to the *Centros* case, it may be useful to determine the nationality of a company in order to know whether it enjoys specific rights or protections, for example in order to identify the State entitled to exercise diplomatic protection or the conventional regime granting certain protections to foreign investments. With regard to diplomatic protection, the *Barcelona Traction* decision of the International Court of Justice considered that the criteria of incorporation and head office 'have been confirmed by long practice and by numerous international instruments'.[69] These criteria are generally those used in international investment agreements, which refer essentially to the criterion of incorporation[70] and very rarely to that of the seat alone.[71] It is worth emphasising that, in the case of connection through the criterion of incorporation, there is no requirement in customary international law to establish the existence of an effective link between the company and the State of incorporation,[72] whereas this is required for natural persons.[73]

---

68 Gelter (n 45) 335.

69 *Barcelona Traction, Light and Power Company, Limited (Belgium v. Spain) (New Application: 1962)*, Judgment of 5 February 1970, ICJ Reports 3 [70].

70 For example, the Energy Charter Treaty indicates that an investor can be 'a company or other organization organized in accordance with the law applicable in that Contracting Party' (article 1(7)(a)(2)).

71 For the sole criteria of the seat, see article I(4) of the Italian model of bilateral treaty indicating that an investor can be a 'legal person of a Contracting Party', and this 'shall mean any entity having its head office in the territory of one of the Contracting Parties and recognized by it' (UNCTAD, *International Investment Instruments: A Compendium – vol. XII* (2003) 296).

72 As regards companies, the ICJ has refused to transpose, by analogy with natural persons, the criterion of the effective link from the *Nottebohm* case. It had nevertheless, in the *Barcelona* Traction case, recognised that 'Barcelona Traction's links with Canada are … manifold' (n 69 [70–71]).

73 While the nationality of natural persons most often results from factual elements (birth or ancestry), it can also proceed, for example in the context of a naturalisation, from a choice of the

The wide recognition of the criterion of incorporation therefore offers several opportunities for investors. The formation of companies in States with an investment agreement allows the granting of certain economic rights and freedoms (for example admission and treatment of investments) and certain procedural safeguards, such as investor/State dispute settlement mechanisms (for example the Convention on the Settlement of Investment Disputes (ICSID)). These opportunities are amplified when they are combined with the freedom of establishment under EU law, since a company incorporated in a Member State can benefit from the mobility deriving from the *Centros* case-law, even when it is owned by nationals of a third State.[74]

This phenomenon of treaty shopping then gave rise to several cases in which the respondent State (the host State of the investment) challenged the investor's right to be placed under the protection of the treaty, given the lack of effective link between the investor and the State of incorporation (the State of origin of the investment).[75] In general, the case-law distinguishes the situation of 'legitimate corporate planning'[76] from cases of abuse in which the applicant has specifically manoeuvered in order to resort to arbitration as a mode of dispute resolution. In fact, the courts have held that 'it is not uncommon practice and … not illegal to locate one's operation in a jurisdiction and to provide for a proper regulatory and legal environment, for examples, of taxation or the substantive law of the jurisdiction, including the availability of a BIT'.[77] However, a corporate restructuring will be considered an abuse if it was exclusively motivated by the desire to benefit from the procedural safeguards of the investment regime.[78] This is particularly the case when it is proved that the restructuring was carried out after the dispute had arisen or when it was foreseeable.[79]

---

person concerned, taking the form of an internal administrative act. This link of nationality is enforceable against other States in the context of an action for diplomatic protection only if it is based on an 'individual's genuine connection with the State' and is 'the exact juridical expression of a social fact' (*Nottebohm (Liechtenstein v. Guatemala)*, Judgment of 6 April 1955, ICJ Reports 4, 23–24). The nationality of companies as well as ships, aircraft and space objects also depend on such a voluntary choice of shareholders or owners and is based on an internal administrative act of incorporation or registration. However, this connection is not conditional on the existence of an effective link, thus restricting neither mailbox companies nor flags of convenience.

74 Case C-299/02 *Commission v. Netherlands* [2004] ECR I-9761. See also, from Anna De Luca 'The Legal Framework for Foreign Investments in the EU: The EU Internal Market Freedoms, the Destiny of Member States' BITs, and Future European Agreements on Protection of Foreign Investments' in Leon E. Trakman and Nicola W. Ranieri (eds) *Regionalism in International Investment Law* (Oxford, Oxford University Press 2013) 129.

75 See Jorun Baumgartner, *Treaty Shopping in International Investment Law* (Oxford, Oxford University Press 2016) 202.

76 *Mobil Corporation et al. v. Venezuela*, ICSID Case No. ARB/07/27, Decision on Jurisdiction, 10 June 2010 [191].

77 *Aguas del Tunarie v. Bolivia*, ICSID Case No. ARB/02/3, Decision on Respondent's Objections to Jurisdiction, 21 October 2005 [330(d)].

78 *Philip Morris Asia Limited v. Australia*, PCA Case No. 2012-12, Award on Jurisdiction and Admissibility, 17 December 2015 [584].

79 Ibid., [566].

Beyond such a case of abuse, arbitral case-law, in the wake of customary international law, shows little interest in the links that unite the investor to the State of origin. By retaining a very formal reading of the treaties that use the criterion of incorporation, tribunals have held that there is no abuse when the incorporated company in the State of origin is a 'letterbox company',[80] or even in so-called 'round-tripping' situations when the company is almost exclusively controlled by nationals of the host State. In this configuration, internationality is purely formal, and is distinctly reminiscent of the situation encountered in the *Centros* case.

It is only through an evolution of treaty practice that States have worked to better regulate this situation and to avoid that the benefit of the treaties extends to economic operators who do not have an effective link with one of the parties. Beyond the now frequent 'denial of benefits' clause,[81] some of the more recent treaties contain much more restrictive definitions of the investor. This is the case of the CETA, concluded between the EU and its Member States on the one hand, and Canada on the other hand. This instrument indicates that an investor can be 'an enterprise that is constituted or organised under the laws of that Party and has substantial business activities in the territory of that Party'.[82] To some extent an anti-*Centros* formula, one could say, or a moment of normative reflux, designed to neutralise the effects of an overly formal reading of the theory of incorporation.

80 Baumgartner (n 75) 108.

81 See for example article 1113(2) of NAFTA indicating that a party may refuse to grant the benefits of the treaty to 'an investor of another Party that is an enterprise of such Party … if investors of a non-Party own or control the enterprise and the enterprise has no substantial business activities in the territory of the Party under whose law it is constituted or organized'.

82 CETA, Article 8.1.

22. Financial markets: *Banco Santander v. Transport Companies*

22.1 CASE BACKGROUND

This judgment handed down by the English High Court concerned the validity of nine derivative transactions, in the first affair ever having been litigated under the rules of the 2015 Financial List. Significantly from the point of view of private international law, the debate turned on what makes a contract international, as opposed to domestic, under Article 3(3) of the Rome Convention 1980 (now Regulation Rome I). According to this provision,

> Where all other elements relevant to the situation at the time of the choice are located in a country other than the country whose law has been chosen, the choice of the parties shall not prejudice the application of provisions of the law of that other country which cannot be derogated from by agreement.

In this case, both the claimant Banco Santander Totta and the defendants, Companhia de Carris de Ferro de Lisboa SA, Sociedade Transportes Coletivos do Porto SA, Metropolitano de Lisboa and Metro do Porto SA, were from Portugal.

The defendants were public sector transport companies running the metro, bus and tram in Lisbon and Porto. They engaged in a number of long-interest rate swaps with Banco Santander between 2005 and 2007. These swaps took place under ISDA Master Agreements, subject to English law and their national jurisdiction. The swaps were very risky given their long life-span and the volatility of interest rates. Importantly, while Banco Santander pledged to pay a floating rate, the Transport Companies were fixed rate payers; though, should certain market conditions be met, a 'spread' would be added to the fixed rate. Initially, the swaps provided a positive cash flow for the defendants. However, owed to a consortium of factors, the spread was triggered and subsequently led to a substantial increase in the interest rates payable by the Transport Companies under the swaps. In 2013, they ceased the payments. Banco Santander brought an action against the Transport Companies seeking a declaration that the defendants' obligations under the respective swaps were valid and binding, and that they were liable for the payments owed in addition to further damages. Among the Transport Companies' three different defences, their second argument invoked Article 3(3) of the Rome Convention in an attempt to displace English law governing the Master Agreements. They argued that all elements relevant to the situation at the time of the choice of law were connected with Portugal only, which meant that Portuguese (domestic) mandatory laws were to be applied to the swaps. Under the Portuguese law, the swaps were void for being unlawful 'games of chance'. Moreover, by raising the 'change of circumstances' defence under Portuguese law, they claimed to be entitled to terminate the swaps in any event.

In March 2016, the English High Court held that Article 3(3) could not be used to displace English law governing the contract in favour of Portuguese law because all the elements relevant to the situation at the time of the choice were not connected with Portugal exclusively. It therefore confirmed that the 'snowball' swaps concluded between the parties under ISDA Master Agreements valued at 1.3 billion euro were legal and binding. The appeal was dismissed.

Case: *Banco Santander Totta S.A. v. Companhia de Carris de Ferro de Lisboa S.A. and others* [2016] EWHC 465 (Comm)

22.2 BALANCING BETWEEN DOMESTIC AND INTERNATIONAL CONTRACTS IN THE POST-CRISIS GLOBAL FINANCIAL MARKETS

Catalina Avasilencei

On 4 March 2016, the Financial List of the High Court issued a decision on interest rate swaps based on ISDA documentation,[1] confirming a market-based, economic approach to the question of what makes a financial contract international: 'swaps were anchored in a market that is necessarily international in its operation' (n°409 (6) (ii)).[2] Subsequently, the Court of Appeal confirmed on 13 December 2016[3] the rejection of the application of Article 3(3) of the Rome Convention concerning (domestic) mandatory provisions in this case, and consequently the characterisation of the relevant derivatives as domestic contracts was also rejected. The same occurred in the *Dexia* case on 15 June 2017.[4]

Although a relatively young sector of international commerce, the derivatives market is living proof of the globalisation of finance, which now sets itself objectively as 'structure of the reality'[5] relevant to the legal characterisation of international contracts. This relationship deserves a multilateral analysis due to its impact on the epistemology of private international law and international commercial law. The *Santander* case endorses a mutual relationship: while the international character of contracts nourished the globalisation of finance, through a feedback effect the latter transforms the former, and even absorbs it. In this case, the Transport Companies challenged the international character of the swaps with the purpose of rendering applicable the mandatory provisions of the Portuguese law. In purely domestic contracts, such provisions may not be derogated from by exercising party autonomy, as the parties did by using the ISDA contractual documentation. However, first the object of proof had to be defined: according to the English court, it was not concerned to determine the applicable law to the contract (n°394), but whether all elements relevant to the situation are connected with Portugal (n°396). The answer is negative based on the international operation of the market for derivatives concluded off-exchange (over-the-counter or OTC). As legal instrument, the contractual standard of the International Swaps and Derivatives Association (ISDA) reifies the functioning of such market. Therefore, the OTC derivatives market seems to simultaneously absorb and export the international character of contracts which have created it and continue to supply it. While in the *Santander* case the legal reasoning is embedded in the specific facts related to the swaps, the subsequent confirmations of its outcome by the Court of Appeal enable a conceptual reading: as long as a financial contract corresponds to a market which is intrinsically

1 See commentary in French by Georges Affaki, (May–June 2016) *Banque&Droit* 48.

2 The numbers refer to the paragraphs of the decision.

3 *Banco Santander Totta SA v. Companhia de Carris de Ferro de Lisboa SA and others* [2016] EWCA Civ 1267.

4 *Dexia Crediop SpA v. Comune di Prato* [2017] EWCA Civ 428, reversing [2015] EWHC 1746 (Comm).

5 Chaïm Perelman and Lucie Olbrechts-Tyteca, *Traité de l'argumentation* 6th edn (Brussels, Éditions de l'Université de Bruxelles 2008) 351.

international, or even global, its characterisation as domestic contract is excluded. Such representation highlights the shadow character of finance, as well as the self-referential dynamics between legal characterisation and the economic facticity.[6] In this respect, the financial market is subject to two competing representations: on one hand, there is an economic decentralised picture, and on the other there is a legal national-based perception which stems from the setup of state financial regulations. Before the 2008 global financial crisis, the former has been supported by an exclusively *ut singuli*, private law approach,[7] prevailing in the absence of state intervention with respect to derivatives. Moreover, the stakes with respect to the international character of the contract have become relevant to the parties after the instatement of the financial crisis. Consequently, the derivatives contract-market expanded in the shadow of systemic risk concerns. This contribution begins by making the observation that the ISDA documentation is a financial innovation which, in order to be effective, relies on limiting the party autonomy with respect to choice of law (1). Furthermore, the analysis follows the dynamics of the global derivatives market to its drivers, namely a market sociology which is embedded in the contractual architecture (2). Finally, an alternative representation for party autonomy is proposed, which could be relevant for managing the post-crisis globalisation: in the absence of a necessary connecting factor between the contract and the law chosen by the parties, the exercise of party autonomy in the context of the ISDA documentation serves not only the globalisation process through aggregation, but also a selective denationalisation of finance (3).

1. A FINANCIAL INNOVATION IN SEARCH OF LEGAL CERTAINTY

Swaps belong to the 'first generation' of derivatives which also includes options and futures, used since the 1970s and the 1980s.[8] Before the financial crisis, such contracts, although pertaining to an over-the-counter market, were regarded as simple contracts.[9] If post-crisis EU law has imposed transparency and clearing through central counterparty requirements,[10] the legal operation of derivatives carries the trademark of the private sector. Created in 1985, ISDA has made the standardisation of derivatives one of its goals.

---

[6] For a detailed analysis of the matter in terms of 'co-production' (Science and Technology Studies) see Catalina Avasilencei, *De la sécurité des rapports financiers dénationalisés. Exercice épistémologique sur la normativité juridique et scientifique* (PhD Paris 1 2017, dir. by H. Muir Watt).

[7] On the contract 'envisaged by law at singular' while it is the 'legal model of the market' see Horatia Muir Watt, 'L'émergence du réseau et le droit international privé' in *Mélanges en l'honneur du Professeur Bernard Audit* (Paris, LGDJ 2014) 533, no7.

[8] Hubert de Vauplane and Jean-Pierre Bornet, *Droit des marchés financiers* 3rd edn (Paris, Litec 2001) 629.

[9] See Thierry Bonneau and France Drummond, *Droit des marchés financiers* 3rd edn (Paris, Economica 2010) 1048.

[10] European Parliament and Council Regulation (EU) 648/2012 on OTC derivatives, central counterparties and trade repositories OJ L 201/1.

In 1987 the first contracts were proposed, and in 1992 the first Master Agreement, with two versions, the Local Currency-Single Jurisdiction and the Multicurrency-Cross Border, was issued. These two versions seem to have been intended to distinguish between domestic and international contracts, however practitioners remarked that the Multicurrency-Cross Border version could also be used for domestic contracts,[11] having the advantage of being more flexible, especially on a long term basis.[12] The 2002 Master Agreement no longer has these two versions.[13] In the *Santander* case, the swaps had been concluded on the basis of the Multicurrency-Cross Border version of the 1992 Master Agreement (n°399). The English court considered this aspect relevant to the parties' situation, and not connected to Portugal (n°409(iii)). Although it is not self-sufficient and needs to be corroborated in order to prove the objective international character of the contract (n°399), such formal element presumes *prima facie* the international nature of the contract. So does the presence of the choice of law clause, almost inherent to the use of the ISDA standard contract.

The architecture of ISDA contracts, deemed as codification of the market practice,[14] grants the parties a limited freedom to adapt the contractual clauses. With respect to choice of law and choice of court clauses, only English and New York jurisdiction and law may be designated,[15] although arbitration clauses are also used.[16] For this reason, the subjective international character of contract is to be found in the quasi-totality of legal relations based on the ISDA documentation.[17]

Positive law has endorsed a concept of party autonomy answering to legal certainty objectives: parties must be allowed to have their contractual relationship governed by the law which they consider suitable in this respect. Even though there is no requirement that parties' choice be reasonable, the designation of the law of each of

---

[11] ISDA Master Agreement (*Practical Law Glossary*) <https://content.next.westlaw.com/Document/I54ea9fc41c9a11e38578f7ccc38dcbee/View/FullText.html?originationContext=document&transitionType=DocumentItem&contextData=(sc.DocLink)&firstPage=true&bhcp=1>, accessed 30 November 2017.

[12] Field Fisher Waterhouse, 'Commentary on the ISDA Master Agreements' (February 2008) <http://www.fieldfisher.com/media/1979379/Commentary-ISDA-master-agreements.pdf> accessed 30 November 2017.

[13] Ibid.

[14] See Annelise Riles, *Collateral Knowledge. Legal reasoning in the global financial markets* (Chicago IL, University of Chicago Press 2011) 31, observing that the definitions of contractual terms are proposed as 'unified understanding of the market as a global whole'.

[15] ISDA response to UK consultation regarding revision of Brussels I Regulation (11 February 2011) <https://www.isda.org/2011/02/11/isda-response-to-the-uk-consultation-on-the-opt-in-to-the-revised-eu-brussels-1-regulation-on-jurisdiction-recognition-and-enforcement-of-judgments-in-civil-and-commercial-matters> accessed 30 November 2017.

[16] 2013 ISDA Arbitration Guide <https://www.isda.org/a/6JDDE/isda-arbitration-guide-final-09-09-13.pdf> accessed 30 November 2017.

[17] Except in cases where all the elements relevant to the situation are located in the state the courts and law of which have been designated, that is UK or New York, hypothesis that seems also excluded now. Data with respect to the Local Currency-Single Jurisdiction version would be useful, although its impact seems limited ('virtually all cross-border transactions under an ISDA Master Agreement are governed either by the 1992 ISDA Master Agreement (Multicurrency – Cross Border) or by the 2002 ISDA Master Agreement') – see ISDA response … , supra n 15).

the two important financial centres appears as such. However, it is not state financial regulation that renders these legal orders suitable to govern exclusively the ISDA contracts. As all financial innovation often based on simple contractual mechanisms,[18] the effectiveness of ISDA contracts relies on the flexibility of the applicable law of obligations, excluding mandatory provisions – due to protective or public policy considerations – thereof. It is therefore relevant that historically one may find the *lex mercatoria* principles incorporated to the Anglo-American private law.[19] The *pacta sunt servanda* principle serves in this respect to achieve a *de facto* regulation of the derivatives market by the ISDA contractual normativity. Accordingly, as already noted in the legal doctrine, such normativity does not actually need to claim autonomy from state legal orders.[20] The effectiveness of the ISDA documentation travels globally under the umbrella of two legal orders, which furthermore grants ISDA normativity an epistemological immunity regarding the emancipation-from-the-state critique. In order to advance the debate, the question ought to be reformulated in terms of the privileged, even exclusive relationship that ISDA normativity enjoys in relation to certain states, while all other states have theoretically the potential to govern such contracts based on objective proximity. In this respect, it seems impossible to separate the development of a financial centre from the politics protecting the market interest and the export of financial innovation, phenomenon known as legislative externality.[21] Sociological and historical reading levels need to be addressed in order to render visible the relationship between market globalisation as change in economic and legal behaviour and the underlying process of contractual standardisation.

2. THE GLOBAL DYNAMICS OF THE CONTRACT-MARKET ARCHITECTURE

It has been remarked that ‘if one may consider that all market relies on contracts, contrariwise not all contracts spread according to market rationale’.[22] The growth of

---

[18] Alain Couret, ‘Innovation financière et règle de droit’ (1990) *Dalloz* 135.

[19] Francis M. Burdick, ‘What Is the Law Merchant?’ (1902) *Columbia Law Review* 470, 482: ‘an extensive amalgamation of the rules of the law merchant with those of the common law. These two bodies of rules no longer stand apart, as they did three centuries ago. Each has been modified by the other and, to a great extent, has lost its separate identity’.

[20] Gilles Cuniberti, ‘The Merchant Who Would Not Be King. Unreasoned Fears about Private Lawmaking’, in Horatia Muir Watt and Diego P. Fernández Arroyo (eds), *Private International Law and Global Governance* (Oxford, Oxford University Press 2014) 141, 155.

[21] Bram van der Eem, ‘Financial Stability as a Global Public Good and Private International Law as Instrument for its Transnational Governance – Some Basic Thoughts’, in Muir Watt and Fernández Arroyo (n 20) 293, 296, fn 15.

[22] Hugues Bouthinon-Dumas, ‘L’appréhension du marché par le droit’, in Guy Bensimon (ed), *Histoire des représentations du marché* (Paris, Michel Houdiard 2005) 755, 756: ‘si l’on peut considérer que tout marché repose sur des contrats, en revanche, tous les contrats ne se déploient pas selon une logique de marché’.

OTC derivatives at the beginning of the 21st century[23] corresponds to a market rationale which is inseparable from the contractual architecture set up in this respect, cause and effect of the contractual standardisation in the financial sector.[24] While financial innovation carries the seed of its own market, the ISDA contractual architecture is simultaneously the cell and the regulatory organ of such market, norm and process with respect to its creation.

The economic stake in concluding derivatives lies in the possibility for economic agents to manage the risks related to their activity. In the *Santander* case, through the conclusion of the interest rate swaps, the Transport Companies had been able to reduce their costs before the financial crisis (n°142). However, the snowball effect of the relevant clauses multiplied losses under the swaps once the crisis occurred. Banco Santander had transferred its risk through the conclusion of back-to-back swaps, made possible by the use of the ISDA documentation. This economic risk was therefore hedged, however the counterparty risk subsisted (n°154). The structuring shows that although ISDA documentation grants access to an international market of counterparties willing to contract on the financial risk, which is being transferred on a bilateral basis, such dispersion does not eliminate, and may even enhance the systemic financial risk. In this respect, it has been underlined that 'the proliferation of all new products would almost always be able to provide the necessary counterparties and, in doing so, transfer the risks without the (overall) assurance that the systemic risk generated is not greater than the sum of the specific risks insured'.[25] The English court apprehends the intrinsic relationship between the global nature of the derivatives market – substantially different from overlapping national markets – and the contractual architecture, as if it were an objective economic reality. The elements relevant to the situation which are not connected with Portugal are identified amongst the built-in characteristics of the global rationale pertaining to the ISDA contractual architecture (n°411): the right of the local bank to assign its rights and obligations to any other subsidiary of Santander Spain, the practical necessity for a relationship with the group, as well as the hedging through the back-to-back swaps by interposing a Portuguese party but ultimately concluded with Santander Spain. All these factors amount to a sociological dimension of the derivatives market, reified in the ISDA contractual architecture itself. Consequently, the specificity

---

[23] See BIS statistics <https://www.bis.org/statistics/about_derivatives_stats.htm?m=6%7C32%7C639> accessed 30 November 2017. On the growth of the OTC market which contrasted with the stagnation of derivatives traded on exchanges see BIS Press Release (13 November 2000) <http://www.bis.org/publ/otc_hy0011.pdf> accessed 30 November 2017.

[24] Katharina Pistor, 'A legal theory of finance' (2013) *Journal of Comparative Economics* 315, 318: 'Over-the-counter (OTC) derivatives had been known for quite a while before a global market in these instruments arose. For this to occur, contractual practices had to be standardized to ensure scalability and investors needed reasonable assurance that these instruments would withstand legal scrutiny by regulators and courts in countries where they were issued, held and traded'.

[25] Henri Bourguinat, *Finance internationale* 4th edn (Paris, PUF 1999) 118 citing Henri Bourguinat, *Les vestiges de la finance internationale* (1987), 139: 'la prolifération de tous les nouveaux produits serait à même de fournir presque toujours les contreparties nécessaires et, ce faisant, de transférer les risques sans pour autant que l'on soit assuré (globalement) que le risque systémique généré ne soit supérieur à la somme des risques particuliers assurés'.

of ISDA normativity lies in its meta-normative epistemology, acting as reading grid for the economic reality relevant to the legal characterisation.[26] This level of analysis corresponds to the one depicted by Annelise Riles in the anthropological study of the derivatives market, which highlights the mobilisation of 'knowledge practices'[27] consisting in a series of 'institutions, actors, doctrines, ideas, material documents'.[28]

The epistemology of private international law naturally builds on a sociology which articulates, in older terms, the 'interests of international commerce'. The 'osmosis'[29] between the globalisation of finance and the international character of the contract echoes the adoption of an economic perspective by the French courts a century before, in order to extend the relevant criteria for international contracts.[30] The history of private international law offers more than one example in this respect: in the cases *Mardelé* and *Dambricourt*,[31] the validity of the choice of court clause is derived from the representation of the interests of international commerce as being at stake. In these cases, the choice of English law and courts was based on the parties having adopted a contractual standard conceived under English law (the conditions of the London Corn Trade Association). It is therefore possible to reach the conclusion that the legal characterisation of international contracts is prone to import reading grids through contractual standardisation (pre-established). However, the phenomenon remains invisible. The shield with respect to the existence of a meta-normativity linked to the representation of the economic reality is an epistemological barrier[32] regarding alternative models which may co-exist and gain legal relevance.

3. PARTY AUTONOMY FACING FINANCIAL DENATIONALISATION

The rising of the nation-state challenged the 'natural' self-regulatory condition of financial markets,[33] which suffered a process of legal nationalisation through the rules of access to market and market regulation. However, the economic agents are not

---

[26] On several illustrations of meta-normativity see our dissertation, supra n 6.

[27] Riles (n 14) 34.

[28] Ibid.

[29] This epistemological perspective is borrowed from Denys Simon who refers to 'l'invocabilité par osmose' – see (June 2016) *Europe*, commentary no186.

[30] See *Pelissier du Besset*, French Court of Cassation, Civil Chamber [Cass. Civ.], 17 May 1927, (1928) *Dalloz* 1.25, conclusions by Matter, note by Capitant. On the rejection of this criterion for the international character of contract see Vincent Heuzé, 'La notion de contrat en droit international privé' (1995–98) *Travaux du Comité Français de Droit International Privé* 319, 340 (Debates) cited by Philippe Leboulanger, 'La notion d' "intérêts" du commerce international' (2005) *Revue de l'arbitrage* 487, 496.

[31] *Mardelé* [Cass. Civ.] 19 February 1930, and *Dambricourt* [Cass. Civ.] 27 January 1931, (1931) *Revue Critique de Droit International Privé* 514, (1933) Sirey I.41 note by Niboyet.

[32] On the closeted epistemology of private international law see Horatia Muir Watt, 'Private International Law Beyond the Schism' (2011) *Transnational Legal Theory* 347.

[33] On the self-regulatory origin of financial markets see Claire Sieuzac, *Contribution à l'étude de la* lex mercatoria *financière* (PhD Paris 1 2006) 22.

necessarily confined, and in this respect party autonomy functions as rule of access to the international market. For this reason, private international law determines not only the legal regime of the parties' rights and obligations, relevant to enforcement, but also the attributes of economic markets. Picturing the concurrent private law jurisdiction of states as slowing down the international commerce may be considered a theoretical issue when confronted with the globalisation of the OTC derivatives market. The existence of closed-ended choice of court and choice of law clauses (granting only few options) in the ISDA documentation eliminates, *de facto*, the possibility of jurisdictions other than those eligible for designation, to co-regulate not only contracts, but also markets potentially relevant to their economy, other than through legal capacity provisions.[34] This latter possibility, although it may regulate access to market, appears as an all-or-nothing option. Moreover, legal capacity restrictions for economic agents other than public entities may negatively impact the economic activity.

While exercising party autonomy does not render, *per se*, legal relations international, its functioning in the context of the ISDA standard contract makes visible the dynamics of the globalisation of finance. The globalisation process co-occurs with a denationalisation of finance though the absence, if not the impossibility, of legally relevant domestic contracts in the financial sector.

A pluralism of representations is desirable, and litigation regarding the ISDA documentation before English courts, inevitable during the crisis, has a transparency function[35] regarding custom in the financial sector, the evolving codification of which is ensured by the ISDA. Dispute resolution creates the context for a genuine debate regarding the stakes of the globalisation of finance, both in court and in the legal doctrine.

Irrespective of the courts acting as co-regulators, including *de facto*, of the OTC derivatives market, they are confronted, as 'juridical touchdown points'[36] for this market, with the substantial stakes of a rather old debate, which needs to be articulated. The financial crisis brings up 'moral hazard' as the concept suitable for reflection, due to the fact that the term 'abuse of right' already carries the limits of a legal regime. On one hand, neither subjective rights nor the market can exist without the legal certainty corresponding to the principle *pacta sunt servanda*. In the *Santander* case this pragmatic requirement renders unacceptable the abandoned solution (n°411).[37] The reasoning supports the view that the methodological function of the party autonomy principle[38] is accompanied by a practical function corresponding to the effectiveness of

---

[34] Portuguese law is applied to the *ultra vires* issue regarding the capacity of the Transport Companies to execute the swaps.

[35] Highlighting the transparency and instructive functions of litigation before English courts, see Joanne P. Braithwaite, 'OTC derivatives, the courts and regulatory reform' (2012) *Capital Markets Law Journal* 364.

[36] Robert Wai, 'Transnational Liftoff and Juridical Touchdown: The Regulatory Function of Private International Law in an Era of Globalization' (2001–02) *Colum. J. Transnat'l L.* 209, 265.

[37] 'In short, these were not purely domestic contracts. Any other conclusion, the court believes, would undermine legal certainty'.

[38] Horatia Muir Watt, '"Party Autonomy" in International Contracts: from the Makings of a Myth to the Requirements of Global Governance' (2010) *ERCL* 1, 5.

international contracts.[39] On the other hand, the contractual structuring in the *Santander* case highlights the moral hazard related to the unlimited transfer of the financial risk made possible by the contractual architecture, censured exceptionally in the context of the financial crisis.[40] In addition, the comprehensive character of the ISDA contractual architecture has considerably diminished the overall need for judicial review, aspect subject to continuous evolution, as proved by the establishment of the Credit Derivatives Determinations Committees.[41]

A position of the Court of Justice would be useful, however the opportunity was missed when Portuguese courts withdrew the request for a preliminary ruling regarding international jurisdiction.[42] Furthermore, the restrictive interpretation of Article 3(3) was considered established by English courts based on the *Unamar*[43] case regarding overriding mandatory provisions and on the position of English legal doctrine (n°374). However, a case before the Court of Justice may still be envisaged with respect to the interpretation of Article 3(4) of Rome I Regulation, in order to clarify whether globalisation is able to exclude an 'European OTC interest rate derivatives market' (n°365(7)) from having legal relevance. Although the legal provision in this respect was not applicable in the *Santander* case, it may determine to what extent the globalisation of finance may be apprehended through systemic requirements of the European Union legal order, which, post-Brexit, loses the courts co-regulating the OTC derivatives market.

22.3 CHOICE OF LAW IN DOMESTIC CONTRACTS: TOWARDS A RIGHT TO ACCESS FOREIGN FINANCIAL MARKETS?

Gilles Cuniberti[*]

The scope of party autonomy has traditionally been limited, in private international law, to relations connected to several States. The exclusion of the power to choose the applicable law in domestic contracts is conventionally perceived as a mechanism aiming to prohibit parties from escaping the mandatory rules of their legal order of origin. This question might require to be revisited in the event that the parties to a domestic contract seek to benefit from economic advantages resulting from their participation in a market which its promoters have placed under the aegis of a few legal

39 *American Trading* [Cass. Civ.] 5 December 1910, (1911) *Revue de Droit International Privé* 395. For a unilateralist position see Pierre Gothot, 'La méthode unilatéraliste face au droit international privé des contrats' (1975–77) *Travaux du Comité Français de Droit International Privé* 201, 207.

40 See Cuniberti (n 20) 155.

41 See the analysis of Mathias Audit, 'Les dérivés de crédit à l'ombre du contrat sans loi' (2014–16) *Travaux du Comité Français de Droit International Privé* 81.

42 Case C-136/16 *Sociedade Metropolitana de Desenvolvimento* closed on 10 March 2017.

43 Case C-184/12 *Unamar.*

* Contribution originally written in French, translated to English by Agathe Daney de Marcillac.

orders.[44] Since such markets cannot be usefully developed in other legal orders, the benefits they provide are subordinated to the subscription of contracts subject to the law of the legal orders governing these markets.[45] The most striking example is the financial derivatives market, dominated by the New York-based International Swaps and Derivatives Association (ISDA). Participation in the ISDA derivative contracts exchange platform requires subscribing to model contracts (ISDA Master Agreements) that provide for the application of New York law or English law. If two Portuguese banks wish to benefit from the financial advantages of participating in such financial markets, they have little choice but to sign contracts subject to one of these national laws.

It is therefore unsurprising that the rule limiting party autonomy in domestic contracts has been examined on several occasions in recent years by English courts in financial matters, in particular in the context of derivatives markets. In a first *Dexia* case, a bank and a municipality, both Italian, had wished to participate in the SWAPS market under the auspices of the ISDA. The parties had therefore concluded contracts that were connected to Italy only (where both parties were domiciled, and where contracts were concluded and performed), but were nevertheless subject to English law. The English High Court classically held that, since the contract had no connection with any State other than Italy, the choice of English law could not lead to the exclusion of mandatory rules of Italian law.[46] The opposite solution was reached in the *Santander* case,[47] clearly raising the question of the special status to be accorded to financial markets.

1. THE ORIGIN OF THE DISTINCTION BETWEEN DOMESTIC AND INTERNATIONAL CONTRACTS

The necessity to distinguish between domestic and international contracts originates in the peculiarity of the choice of law rule in contractual matters. It provides, in principle, for the application of the law chosen by the parties. It therefore uses a subjective connecting factor, the choice made by the parties. Traditionally, choice of law rules in other fields of the law have used objective connecting factors: nationality of the parties in matters of personal status, place of the damage in torts, place of the relevant asset in property matters, etc … The essential consequence of using an objective connecting factor is that it becomes unnecessary to limit the operation of the rule to international disputes. If the rule is applied in domestic litigation, it will systematically indicate the

---

44 On the impact of market globalisation on private international law, see generally H. Muir Watt, 'Globalisation des marchés et économie politique du droit international privé' (2003) *Archives de philosophie du droit* 243.

45 The limitation of the number of legal orders under which such markets can develop is tied to costs. See G. Cuniberti, 'Three Theories of Lex Mercatoria' (2014) 52 *Columbia J. Transnational L.* 369.

46 *Dexia Crediop SpA v. Comune di Prato* [2015] EWHC 1746 (Comm).

47 Both in first instance and on appeal, allowing the judgment to become a precedent on the basis of which the Court of Appeal had to allow the appeal in the *Dexia* case: [2017] EWCA Civ 428.

law of the State with ties to the dispute, including the link identified as the connecting factor by the choice of law rule. If the dispute is international, it will be necessary to apply the choice of law rule that could designate a foreign law if the connecting factor points to a foreign country. In the end, however, the question holds no practical consequence.[48]

It is quite different if the connecting factor is subjective, since it may lead to the application of a foreign law not only in an international dispute, but also in a domestic case.[49] It is sufficient, in the latter case, that the parties choose a foreign law to govern a contract that would not otherwise have any connection with any foreign country. This consequence has traditionally been considered unacceptable. First and foremost, the application of a foreign law renders inapplicable the mandatory rules of the State that has the only ties to the contract and the dispute. However, the very definition of a mandatory rule is that it is binding on the parties, who are not free to derogate from it,[50] in particular by stipulating clauses that would contradict it. If the parties were allowed to stipulate the application of a foreign law, they would be indirectly given the power to circumvent the implementation of mandatory rules of the only State concerned with the contract and the transaction, and to replace them with those of the law chosen by the parties. This power is recognised in international matters because an international contract is by definition linked to several legal orders (for example the States where the parties are domiciled). In the absence of a truly international law of contracts, it is necessary to choose the law of a single State to govern the contract,[51] and thus to exclude the application of all other laws along with their mandatory rules.[52] Therefore, why not allow parties to choose: the result will be the same, and parties will have chosen the application of the law that they prefer. This argument is particularly convincing when the parties' choice is limited to those laws that are related to the contract, which is the traditional rule in American private international law.[53] The power to choose the applicable law then amounts to giving the parties the ability to choose the mandatory rules of one of the laws connected to the contract, and which may therefore have been designated through an objective factor. The argument becomes much weaker when the conflict of laws rule gives the parties unlimited power to choose the law applicable to their international contract, which is the rule in European private international law.[54] The parties could then choose a law that has no connection to the

---

48 M.E. Ancel, P. Deumier and M. Laazouzi, *Droit des contrats internationaux* (Paris, Sirey 2017) No. 12.

49 P. Mayer, 'Réflexions sur la notion de contrat international', *Mélanges Tercier* (Zurich, Schulthess 2008) 873.

50 See French Civil Code, Article 6: 'Statutes relating to public policy and morals may not be derogated from by private agreements.'

51 It would not be acceptable to apply cumulatively the mandatory rules of all States interested in the relationship.

52 The only exception is the most fundamental among them which may be deemed 'overriding mandatory provisions' and shall be applied regardless of the law chosen by the parties. See Rome I Regulation, art 9.

53 Restatement Second on the Conflict of Laws, 1971, § 187.

54 Rome I Regulation, art 3, § 1.

contract for the sole purpose of avoiding the application of mandatory rules that could be common to all laws related to the contract.

It is therefore essential to regulate the choice of a foreign law in the framework of domestic contracts. In this regard, two rules are conceivable. The first is to simply prohibit choice of law clauses in domestic contracts.[55] Any choice of law clause inserted into such contracts would be invalid. The second is to allow choice of law clauses, while severely limiting their effect. This is the solution enshrined in European private international law,[56] in contractual matters,[57] and in several other areas where party autonomy has been recognised.[58] The choice of law clause is valid, but it does not allow the parties to derogate from the mandatory rules of the State with which the contract has all the relevant connections. The choice of law clause has the effect of derogating only from the default rules in that State, which parties are by definition free to replace by any contractual stipulation of their choice and which may therefore be the provisions of a foreign law.

In the *Santander* case, the relevant contracts were connected to only one single legal order, Portugal. Both contracting parties were Portuguese legal persons and the contracts were to be performed in Portugal. It therefore seemed clear that the contracts had to be regarded as domestic and the choice made by the parties in favour of English law should have been made subject to the application of Portuguese mandatory rules. Thus, as already pointed out, a few months earlier, another judge of the same English High Court had ruled, in the *Dexia* case, that comparable transactions between Italian parties and to be performed in Italy were indeed domestic contracts.[59] Though domestic, these contracts had been concluded with the goal of participating in an international financial market. Could they therefore really be considered domestic contracts? This raised the fundamental issue of the concept of a domestic contract.

2. THE CONCEPT OF A DOMESTIC CONTRACT

The concept of a domestic contract within the meaning of article 3(3) of the Rome I Regulation is difficult to define. In fact, it is well known that the drafters of the Rome Convention deliberately chose not to positively define the concept due to the complexity of the issues it raises.

One can first of all question the value of certain connections which, while being objective, may not appear relevant in the context of certain legal relations. The classic example is the nationality of natural persons, which is of unclear relevance in the context of commercial transactions.[60]

---

55 This is the rule under the American Uniform Commercial Code: see § 1-105.

56 The same solution was taken up by a large number of non-European legislations, such as the Quebec Civil Code (art 3111) and the Russian Civil Code (art 1210 §5).

57 Rome Convention, and later Rome I Regulation, art 3, § 3.

58 See Rome II Regulation, art 14, § 3 (torts).

59 *Dexia Crediop SpA v. Comune di Prato* [2015] EWHC 1746 (Comm).

60 Mayer (n 49); Ancel, Deumier and Laazouzi (n 48) No. 14.

Then comes the question of a possible evolution in time of connections of the relevant contracts with foreign legal orders. In the *Santander* case, such a development was conceivable, since the contracts included clauses allowing the substitution of a contracting party. English courts saw in this clause an essential factor in favour of the characterisation of the contract as international on the ground that the performance of such contracts lasted, on average, for 14 years and that it was therefore highly possible that one of the parties would in the end not be Portuguese. There is no doubt that the domestic or international character of a contract can evolve over time and that a substitution of parties can embody such an evolution. It appears, however, that the drafters of the Rome Convention were aware of the difficulty and resolved it clearly by specifying the date at which the nature of the contract should be assessed: at the moment when the choice of law is made. The European legislator had therefore specifically anticipated that evolutions of the internationality of the contract should remain without any impact on the operation of Article 3(3).

Third, it is necessary to consider whether the domestic nature of the contract should be appreciated exclusively in light of the sole contract at issue, or whether the context in which it may have been concluded is pertinent. The Rome I Regulation appears to have clearly opted for a broad conception of internationality, referring not to the localisation of the contract, but to that of the 'situation'. The word, doubtless chosen in full awareness by the drafters, therefore invites, if need be, the collection of elements other than those exclusively concerned with the contract, to determine its domestic or international nature. The most obvious example seems to be that of a domestic contract with ties to an international contract[61] or concluded in the framework of an international operation.[62] The party who has gained a contract in a foreign State could thus subcontract part of his services to a contractor based in his State of origin: the subcontract could thus present ties to a single country but be linked to an international contract and would fit in an international operation. In this respect, an interesting comparison can be drawn with the economic conception of internationality enshrined in French arbitration law, which considers arbitration as international if 'international trade interests are at stake'.[63] It would be appropriate to align the definitions of internationality used in these different contexts, so as to prevent a domestic contract within the meaning of European private international law from being subject to an arbitration clause and a foreign law.

It is precisely on this basis that the English courts were able in the *Santander* case to establish the existence, if not of a contract, at least of an international situation. This conclusion, however, is reached by putting forward two propositions, which are both unconvincing.

The first issue was whether the purpose of focusing on the situation (as opposed to the contract) was to identify connections between the situation and a second State, or

---

61 F. Ragno, in F. Ferrari (ed.) *Rome I Regulation – Pocket Commentary* (Paris, Sellier 2015) Art. 3 No. 53. *Adde* Mayer (n 49).

62 L. Collins of Mapesbury (ed.), *Dicey, Morris & Collins on the Conflict of Laws* (London, Sweet & Maxwell 2012) No. 32-087; *Caterpillar Financial Services v. SNC Passion* [2004] EWHC 569.

63 French Civil Procedure Code, art. 1504.

whether the situation could be characterised as international without any connection with another State. The *Santander* court accepted this second view, and held it was enough that the situation be international although there was no connection between either the contract or the situation with any other State. The first view had been accepted by the *Dexia* court, which had ruled that the distinction between the contract and the situation could matter only if the situation was connected to another State, but that it was not the case where two local entities were using an international model contract for the purpose of concluding an international contract.

Secondly, the *Santander* court established the internationality of the situation in which the contract is inserted by reference to the standard contracts used by the parties. They had indeed wanted to use the 'Multicurrency-Cross Border' version of the ISDA Master Agreement instead of a local version of the same standard contract ('Local Currency-Single Jurisdiction'). From the traditional perspective, the argument is unpersuasive. It allows the parties to create an international situation merely by using certain clauses. The purpose of the limitation introduced in Article 3(3) is precisely to prevent parties from internationalising their agreement at their sole will.

An alternative approach would be to see the extension of the notion of internationality as an acknowledgement of the transnational nature of derivatives markets and related transactions. It is argued that this would reveal the transnational character of finance[64] and the real nature of credit derivatives, which would be modern versions of lawless contracts ('*contrat sans loi*').[65] This innovative thesis stumbles, however, on an undeniable reality: international finance prefers the application of State laws. ISDA Master Agreements provide for the application of English law or New York law. A complete detachment from national legal orders would have been possible by combining arbitral clauses with choice of law clauses providing for the application of *lex mercatoria*, but it is well known that common lawyers have never been convinced of the benefits of this theory. One should not be deceived: the question at the heart of the *Santander* and *Dexia* cases is much more prosaically that of the promotion of the economic interests of the City of London as a financial centre, and that of English lawyers.[66]

Finally, submitting to the relevant model contract could be perceived as a necessary condition for accessing to a market. The question should then be asked: does access to an international market justify derogating from the limits of Article 3(3), or redefining the notion of international situation?

---

64 See above the contribution by Catalina Avasilencei.

65 See M. Audit, 'Les dérivés de crédit à l'ombre du contrat sans loi' (2014–16) *Travaux du Comité Français de Droit International Privé* 8.

66 In this regard, it is noteworthy that the architect of the *Santander* decision, Judge Blair, had participated in the drafting of ISDA's Master Agreements as a financial law specialist. The *Santander* case was the occasion to provide after-sales services.

3. MARKET ACCESS FOR DOMESTIC ACTORS

Should the purpose pursued by the parties to these financial contracts justify an exception to the prohibition to choose a foreign law in a domestic contract? Several arguments can be advanced in this direction.

It would first be conceivable to appeal to the foundation of the rule in an attempt to limit its scope. By allowing freedom of choice while restricting exclusively its effects to the application of mandatory rules, Article 3(3) of the Rome I Regulation is often explained by reference to the concept of evasion of law ('*fraude à la loi*').[67] It could therefore be argued that the implementation of this provision would require the demonstration of fraudulent intent. In other words, the party wishing to disregard the application of foreign law should demonstrate that the purpose of the choice of law was to circumvent the application of mandatory rules of domestic law. Conversely, in the absence of such an intention, the application of local mandatory provisions should be abandoned, and the chosen foreign law applied in its entirety. In the event of parties wishing to participate in a financial market such as credit derivatives, it could be convincingly argued that the aim pursued was not to avoid local laws but simply to participate in the market and benefit from its economic advantages. The argument was put forward by the creditor party in the *Santander* case. It was rejected on the grounds that the wording of Article 3(3) makes no reference to fraudulent intent and that confirming this theory would undoubtedly add to the provision a condition it does not contain.

In truth, it is probably illusory to look to the general doctrines of private international law for justifying an exception specific to markets, or to financial markets. If a legal regime could possibly seek to advance specific solutions in this regard, it would logically be substantive economic law, and more specifically the principles governing financial markets. The question must be asked both from the point of view of market-regulating organisations and from that of its potential users.

In an intra-European context, the essential principles of market law are the fundamental freedoms recognised by European Union law. These freedoms could be the basis for ISDA's claim to offer its services freely to domestic operators based in the Union. Specifically, the local mandatory rules preventing subscription of ISDA Master Agreements could be analysed as a restriction on the UK-based financial operator's freedom to provide services.[68] Moreover, the fact that the application of these standards is based on an EU law norm (Article 3(3) of the Rome I Regulation) could in no way immunise them. The Court of Justice has already applied, in a series of well-known judgments,[69] the principles of freedom to provide services to control the implementation of local mandatory rules whose implementation was otherwise grounded in

67 In this regard, see Ragno (n 61) Art. 3, No. 54.

68 Until Brexit takes effect thereby rendering the UK fully sovereign and depriving all its operators of the benefits of the freedoms of the European Internal Market.

69 See Case C-376/96 *Criminal proceedings against Jean-Claude Arblade and Arblade & Fils SARL and Bernard Leloup, Serge Leloup and Sofrage SARL*, ECLI:EU:C:1999:575; Case C-165/98, *Procédure pénale contre André Mazzoleni et Inter Surveillance Assistance SARL, civilement responsable, en présence de Eric Guillaume et autres*, ECLI:EU:C:2001:162.

classical private international law doctrines and recognised by EU legal instruments (overriding mandatory provisions). It follows from these decisions that local mandatory rules may constitute restrictions to the freedom to provide services of an operator established in a Member State, and that these may only be justified by overriding reasons of public interest, such as the protection of workers. It would be important, therefore, to determine whether the mandatory rules of Italian law (in the *Dexia* case) or of Portuguese law (in the *Santander* case) could meet such a test.

From the opposite perspective of the parties wishing to participate in a financial market requiring the conclusion of contracts subject to a foreign law, the freedoms of movement could establish a right of access to the market for internal operators in the Member States. The Court of Justice has indeed consistently ruled that the freedom to provide services equally benefits service providers and recipients.[70] Local mandatory rules could therefore be considered as restrictions on the right of local operators to access the services offered by ISDA, which should consequently be disregarded unless they could be justified by overriding reasons of public interest.

70 See for example Cases C-403/08 and C-429/08, *Football Association Premier League and Others v. QC Leisure and Others and Karen Murphy v. Media Protection Services Ltd*, ECLI:EU:C:2011:631.

23. Global labour market: *Laval*

23.1 CASE BACKGROUND

The European Union protects, on one hand, freedom of movement and establishment; and on the other hand, the right to take industrial action. The interaction between these two principles becomes highly sensitive in situations where the purpose of collective action by workers is to limit the free movement of the employer. Such is the case in the context of the cross-border posting of workers needed to carry out a service in another Member State. This difficult issue arose in 2007 between the company, Laval, and the Swedish Workers' Union Byggnads. The dispute led to a ruling by the ECJ and a subsequent decision of the European Committee of Social Rights.

Laval un Partneri Ltd was a Latvian construction company that won a public tender offer for construction work on a school near Stockholm. Laval then proceeded to post Latvian workers to Sweden in accordance with the 96/71/EC Posting of Workers Directive ('Directive'). It was estimated that Latvian workers earned 40% less than Swedish workers. The Swedish Building Workers' Union demanded Laval to sign a collective agreement that would align the conditions applicable for Latvian workers to applicable Swedish standards enforced in the industry. As Laval refused to sign the agreement, the Swedish Workers Union, joined by the Swedish Electricians Union, initiated a strike against Laval and barricaded Laval's construction site. The strike had caused its Swedish subsidiary, Baltic Bygg, to declare bankruptcy, forcibly sending all of its workers back to Latvia. Laval then filed an action before the Swedish Labour Court for a declaration that the blockade was in breach of the Directive and for compensation for damages suffered.

The Directive defines a set of mandatory rules applicable to posted workers. While the workers from another Member State are employed by the sending company, they are only entitled to a set of core rights applicable to workers in the host Member State. These include, for example, maximum work periods and minimum rest periods, minimum rates of pay, health, safety and hygiene at work or equal treatment between men and women. The purpose of this provision is to ensure minimum protection of workers rather than fair competition between the two Member States. The difficulty here, however, was that unlike most EU countries, there is no legislation concerning salaries in Sweden; pay deals for each industry are bargained for collectively.

The ECJ held that there was no minimum pay by Swedish law on which the foreign workers' pay could be aligned, and that the Swedish Unions could not force Laval into a collective agreement. Relying on the *Viking* judgment delivered only one week prior to Laval – a similar case in which workers' rights clashed with freedom of establishment – the Court confirmed that collective action constitutes a fundamental right, thereby an integral part of the general principles of European law. Nevertheless, it ruled that such a right must be reconciled with other rights protected under the Treaty, including the right to post workers to another Member State within the framework of the transnational provision of services. Consequently, the collective action by the Swedish Unions constituted a restriction on the freedom to provide services.

In the aftermath of the *Laval* case, Sweden adopted a new legislation known as *Lex Laval*, restricting certain rights of trade unions. In response, the Swedish Trade Union Confederation and Swedish Confederation of Professional Employees brought a collective complaint before the European Committee of Social Rights. In 2013, the Committee unanimously accepted the complaint, asserting that the free movement of services, including the right to post workers to another Member State, could not be treated as having a greater value than core labour rights, such as the right of collective action; a fundamentally opposite conclusion as the decision rendered in *Laval*.

Case: *Laval un Partneri Ltd v. Svenska Byggnadsarbetareförbundet*, Application No. 341/05, Council of Europe: European Court of Human Rights, 18 December 2007

23.2 EUROPEAN LABOUR MARKET: POSTED WORKERS DIRECTIVE AND THE SOCIAL IMPLICATIONS OF THE MOVEMENT OF LABOUR

Uglješa Grušić

1. INTRODUCTION

Much can be, and has been, said about *Laval*.[1] Yet one thing that can hardly be said about this case is that it concerned the *global* labour market. *Laval* was a European affair. Nevertheless, this rich case tells us a lot about the economic and social constitution of the European Union (EU), the world's most deeply integrated regional economic organisation, and the role of law in shaping that constitution. *Laval* also prompts us to think more generally about the social implications of the global movement of labour, goods, services and capital.

This chapter starts by describing the European context of *Laval* and arguing that the factors which gave rise to this case do not exist on the global plane. It then addresses the specific mode of reasoning mandated by EU law which largely determined the outcome of *Laval*. This indicates one of the social pitfalls of economic integration driven by law which ought to be taken into account in the creation and development of any economic and political union of states. Next, the chapter describes the role of private international law in the clash of the economic and social spheres of the EU. The final section mentions some other key challenges facing regional and global labour markets.

2. *LAVAL*: A EUROPEAN AFFAIR

Laval cannot be discussed in isolation from its sister case, *Viking*.[2] These cases concerned two situations where the economic and social spheres of the EU clash with particular force.

---

[1] Case C-341/05 *Laval un Partneri Ltd v. Svenska Byggnadsarbetareförbundet, Svenska Byggnadsarbetareförbundets avdelning 1, Byggettan and Svenska Elektrikerförbundet* [2007] ECR I-11767.

[2] Case C-438/05 *International Transport Workers' Federation and Finnish Seamen's Union v. Viking Line ABP and OÜ Viking Line Eesti* [2007] ECR I-10779.

In *Laval*, a Latvian company by the name of Laval posted its Latvian workers to Sweden to perform a construction contract that its Swedish affiliate had won there. After Laval refused to negotiate and enter into collective agreements with local trade unions and to pay Swedish wages to its Latvian workers, the unions organised a blockade of all Laval's construction sites in Sweden. This forced Laval to withdraw from Sweden and to file for bankruptcy of its Swedish affiliate. Laval then brought proceedings in Sweden seeking remedies for the violation of its freedom to provide services.

In *Viking*, a Finnish company by the name of Viking owned a ferry registered in Finland, plying its trade between Finland and Estonia. It decided to re-register the vessel in Estonia in order to benefit from lower labour costs in that country. The International Transport Workers' Federation (ITF) has a policy of combatting the use of flags of convenience. It called on its members to boycott Viking. Viking then commenced proceedings in England against the ITF and its affiliate, the Finnish Seamen's Union, seeking an injunction to stop the boycott. The claim was based on the violation of Viking's freedom of establishment.

Primary EU law guarantees economic operators the freedoms of establishment and to provide services.[3] The European Court of Justice (ECJ) held that these freedoms have a horizontal direct effect against trade unions.[4] Since an industrial action aimed at forcing a service provider from one Member State to comply with the employment standards of another Member State or an establishment to abandon its plan to move from one Member State to another is liable to make the exercise of the fundamental economic freedoms 'less attractive, or more difficult',[5] it represents a restriction of those freedoms. In order to be lawful, the industrial action has to be non-discriminatory, justified and proportionate.

Although in both cases the ECJ recognised that the right to take collective action is a fundamental right forming an integral part of the general principles of EU law,[6] it subordinated this right to the fundamental economic freedoms. In *Laval*, the imposition of Swedish collectively agreed employment standards and the running wage on out-of-state service providers was not in accordance with the then extant version of the Posted Workers Directive (PWD).[7] The PWD seeks to coordinate the laws of the Member States with regard to employment standards that are applicable to service

---

[3] Consolidated Version of the Treaty on the Functioning of the EU [2016] OJ C59/47, arts 49 (freedom of establishment) and 56 (freedom to provide services).

[4] *Laval* (n 1) [98]; *Viking* (n 2) [55].

[5] *Laval* (n 1) [99]. Similarly, *Viking* (n 2) [72].

[6] *Laval* (n 1) [91]; *Viking* (n 2) [44].

[7] Directive 96/71/EC of the European Parliament and of the Council of 16 December 1996 concerning the posting of workers in the framework of the provision of services [1997] OJ L18/1. This directive has been amended by Directive (EU) 2018/957 of the European Parliament and of the Council of 28 June 2018 amending Directive 96/71/EC concerning the posting of workers in the framework of the provision of services [2018] OJ L 173/16, which is mentioned below in text accompanying nn 22–24.

providers from a Member State that post workers within the EU.[8] It lays down a 'nucleus of mandatory rules for minimum protection' that have to be observed by out-of-state service providers in the host Member State.[9] Since the Swedish collectively agreed employment standards in question and the running wage were not part of this 'nucleus', their enforcement against an out-of-state service provider by means of industrial action could not be justified.[10] In *Viking*, the ECJ noted that the right to take collective action for the protection of workers was a legitimate interest which, in principle, justified the restriction of the fundamental economic freedoms,[11] but then added that a collective action could be justified only where the jobs or conditions of employment of the trade union members were jeopardised or under serious threat.[12] The ECJ further noted that a collective action would not be proportionate unless the unions had exhausted other means at their disposal less restrictive of the freedom of establishment.[13] *Laval* and *Viking* have had a chilling effect on industrial action in Europe.

The factors that gave rise to *Laval* and *Viking* do not exist on the global plane. Primary EU law guarantees the freedoms of establishment and to provide services. It has long been established that the freedom to provide services entails the right of a service provider established in one Member State to move freely with all its workers whom it lawfully employs in that country to other Member States for the purpose of providing services there and that the imposition of the host Member State employment standards, which represents a burden on out-of-state service providers, is a restriction of the free movement of services that has to be non-discriminatory, justified and proportionate in order to be lawful.[14] *Laval* and *Viking* controversially extend this case law to circumstances where the fundamental economic freedoms are restricted not by public authorities, but by trade unions. The World Trade Organization has done much to liberalise the trade in services by virtue of the General Agreement on Trade in Services. But the global opening up of the trade in services is not nearly as

---

8 Ibid., Recital 13.

9 Ibid., Art 3 contains a list of employment standards that either must or may be imposed on out-of-state service providers.

10 *Laval* (n 1) [106]–[111].

11 *Viking* (n 2) [77].

12 Ibid., [81].

13 Ibid., [87].

14 Case C-113/89 *Rush Portuguesa Ld^a v. Office national d'immigration* [1990] ECR I-1417; Case C-43/93 *Raymond Vander Elst v. Office des Migrations Internationales* [1994] ECR I-3803; Joined Cases C-49/98, C-50/98, C-52/98 to C-54/98 and C-68/98 to C-71/98 *Finalarte Sociedade de Construção Civil Ld^a (C-49/98), Portugaia Construções Ld^a (C-70/98) and Engil Sociedade de Construção Civil SA (C-71/98) v. Urlaubs- und Lohnausgleichskasse der Bauwirtschaft and Urlaubs- und Lohnausgleichskasse der Bauwirtschaft v. Amilcar Oliveira Rocha (C-50/98), Tudor Stone Ltd (C-52/98), Tecnamb-Tecnologia do Ambiante Ld^a (C-53/98), Turiprata Construções Civil Ld^a (C-54/98), Duarte dos Santos Sousa (C-68/98) and Santos & Kewitz Construções Ld^a (C-69/98)* [2001] ECR I-7831.

comprehensive and deep as the free movement of services within the EU.[15] This is why *Laval* tells us a lot about the EU's economic and social constitution, but little, if anything, directly about the global labour market.

3. THE MODE OF LEGAL REASONING IN *LAVAL*: PITTING SOCIAL RIGHTS AGAINST FUNDAMENTAL ECONOMIC FREEDOMS

Almost anyone who has written about *Laval* and *Viking* agrees that these two cases contributed to the erosion of social rights within the EU. The ECJ decisions have indeed undermined the employment standards and systems of industrial relations of countries like Sweden and Finland.

Sweden, for example, is a country that traditionally relies on trade unions for the setting, monitoring and enforcement of the level of wages and other employment standards.[16] Interestingly, sectoral collective agreements in Sweden do not, in principle, regulate wages. Instead, the level of wages is generally left to be negotiated on a case-by-case basis at the level of each workplace. If an employer refuses to negotiate the level of wages, unions will force it to do so by means of primary and secondary industrial action. When implementing the PWD, Sweden introduced legislation laying down many employment standards to be observed by out-of-state service providers as the nucleus of mandatory rules for minimum protection. But with respect to the minimum wage, Sweden decided to rely on the suitability and effectiveness of its traditional system of industrial relations. The PWD seeks to accommodate the interest of countries like Sweden by providing that Member States that have neither legislatively set employment standards nor a system for declaring collective agreements or arbitration awards to be of universal application may, 'if they so decide', impose, on a basis of equality of treatment, employment standards set by 'collective agreements or arbitration awards which are generally applicable to all similar undertakings in the geographical area and in the profession or industry concerned' and/or 'collective agreements which have been concluded by the most representative employers' and labour organisations at national level and which are applied throughout national territory'.[17] By deciding not to introduce legislation laying down the minimum wage and not to impose generally applicable collectively set employment standards, Sweden

[15] A. Mattoo and A. Carzaniga (eds), *Moving People to Deliver Services* (World Bank and OUP, 2003) ix: 'One area has, however, reaped only limited benefits from this climate of openness: the supply of services through the "temporary movement of individual service suppliers" (mode 4). The Uruguay Round negotiations on mode 4 served primarily to facilitate exploratory business visits and the movement of high-level personnel within multinational corporations. Developing countries were disappointed by the limited commitments in their area of comparative advantage and are now seeking greater openness.'

[16] M. Rönnmar, 'Free Movement of Services versus National Labour Law and Industrial Relations Systems: Understanding the *Laval* Case from a Swedish and Nordic Perspective' (2007–2008) 10 *CYELS* 493.

[17] PWD, art 3(8), second subparagraph.

had created a situation where the attempts of Swedish unions to force out-of-state service providers to negotiate the level of wages by means of industrial action led to the violation of the service providers' freedom to provide services.

The outcome in *Laval* was largely determined by the specific mode of reasoning mandated by EU law. *Laval* concerned a clash of a fundamental economic freedom guaranteed by primary EU law and the right to take collective action. The ECJ in both *Laval* and *Viking* recognised the right to take collective action as a fundamental right forming an integral part of the general principles of EU law.[18] One should be forgiven for thinking that the recognition of the right to take collective action as a fundamental social right should have led the Court to balance this right on more or less equal terms with the fundamental economic freedoms. This is, however, not something that the ECJ did or indeed could have done. The moment the Court approached *Laval* and *Viking* with the premise that these two cases concerned the economic operators' fundamental economic freedoms and decided that these freedoms had a horizontal direct effect against trade unions, which was a rather controversial decision, the outcome of these cases was by and large determined. The actions of the unions in question became prima facie violations of the economic operators' fundamental economic freedoms. The industrial action in *Laval* stood little chance of being regarded as justified because the attempt of the unions to force the out-of-state service provider to negotiate the level of wages was not in accordance with the PWD. The industrial action in *Viking* similarly stood little chance of being regarded as proportionate because the (threat of) infliction of as much economic harm as possible on the employer is in the very nature of industrial action. This is why *Laval* and *Viking* were seen as representing one step forward for the recognition of social rights as fundamental rights, but two steps back in terms of their enjoyment within the EU.[19]

Let us imagine for a moment that the ECJ had started off with a different premise in *Laval* and *Viking*, namely that these two cases were primarily about the trade unions' right to take collective action and that any restriction of that right had to be non-discriminatory, justified and proportionate to be lawful. Had the Court adopted this approach, it would have probably found the restriction of the unions' right to take collective action by the fundamental economic freedoms to be justified. But it is questionable whether the total subordination of the right to take collective action to the fundamental economic freedoms would have been proportionate. Had the ECJ adopted this approach, it would have probably had to strike a different balance between the interests of the internal market and the interests of Member States like Sweden in protecting their employment standards and systems of industrial relations. That the outcome of *Laval* and *Viking* was largely determined by the mode of reasoning mandated by EU law is clear if one compares these two cases with the 2013 decision of the European Committee of Social Rights.[20] Here, the Committee started off with the

---

[18] *Laval* (n 1) [91]; *Viking* (n 2) [44].

[19] A. C. L. Davies, 'One Step Forward, Two Steps Back? The *Viking* and *Laval* Cases in the ECJ' (2008) 37 *ILJ* 126.

[20] *Swedish Trade Union Confederation (LO) and Swedish Confederation of Professional Employees (TCO) v. Sweden*, Decision on admissibility and the merits, Complaint No 85/2012, Complaint No 85/2012, 3 July 2013.

premise that the Lex Laval adopted by Sweden in the aftermath of the *Laval* case restricted the social rights of the complainant Swedish trade unions. Since the fundamental economic freedoms '[could] not be treated, *from the point of view of the system of values, principles and fundamental rights embodied in the [European Social] Charter*, as having a greater *a priori value* than core labour rights,'[21] the Committee came to the opposite conclusion to that of the ECJ.

It is this disbalance in the economic and social constitution of the EU that has been at the heart of debates since *Laval* and *Viking*. An important part of the European Pillar of Social Rights proclaimed at the Social Summit for Fair Jobs and Growth held in November 2017,[22] whose ambition was to remedy the incompleteness of the EU's economic and social constitution, was a revision of the PWD. A directive amending the PWD was adopted in June 2018.[23] The main objectives of the revision of the PWD are to implement the principle that the same work at the same place should be remunerated in the same manner and to ensure a level playing field between posting and local companies in the host Member State.[24]

Laval, *Viking* and the 2013 decision of the European Committee of Social Rights are of further interest for showing that the view on the balance to be struck between the economic and social spheres of the EU depends on one's standpoint. The criticism of *Laval* and *Viking* has primarily come from scholars from the core Western and Northern European Member States. The revision of the PWD has also primarily found support in these countries.[25] This is understandable because it is in these countries that the unfettered fundamental economic freedoms put employment standards and systems of industrial relations under considerable strain. But *Laval* and *Viking* look different when viewed from the perspective of Eastern European Member States.[26] Since 2004, the EU has been considerably enlarged by the accession of 13, mostly former communist, countries. The level of wages and other employment standards in these countries were, and still largely is, considerably lower than in the rest of the EU. Cheap labour is the comparative advantage of these countries. The ability of service providers from these countries to move freely with all their workers to other Member States for the purpose of providing services there and to undercut local competition by virtue of lower labour costs could be seen as part of the EU-wide social contract. Looked at from this perspective, the decisions in *Laval* and *Viking* at least partly balance out the socially

---

21 Ibid., [122] (emphasis added).

22 European Commission, 'Social Summit for Fair Jobs and Growth: Strengthening the EU's Social Dimension' (Press Release, Brussels, 16 November 2017).

23 Directive (EU) 2018/957 of the European Parliament and of the Council of 28 June 2018 amending Directive 96/71/EC concerning the posting of workers in the framework of the provision of services [2018] OJ L 173/16.

24 European Commission, 'Proposal for a Directive of the European Parliament and of the Council amending Directive 96/71/EC of the European Parliament and of the Council of 16 December 1996 concerning the posting of workers in the framework of the provision of services' COM(2016) 128 final.

25 Ibid., 4: 'Austria, Belgium, France, Germany, Luxembourg, the Netherlands and Sweden have claimed support for a modernisation of the Posting of Workers Directive'.

26 Ibid., 5: 'Bulgaria, Czech Republic, Estonia, Hungary, Lithuania, Latvia, Poland, Slovakia and Romania … have argued that a review of the 1996 Directive is premature'.

negative effects in Eastern European Member States of the free movement of goods and services into (eg diminished production capacity and 'goods dumping') and capital out of these countries.[27] The revision of the PWD will have the effect of depriving Eastern European Member States of their comparative advantage.

4. THE ROLE OF PRIVATE INTERNATIONAL LAW IN THE CLASH OF THE ECONOMIC AND SOCIAL SPHERES OF THE EU

This section addresses the role that private international law plays in this clash of the economic and social spheres of the EU. There are two aspects of this role. First, the rules of private international law form part of the relevant legal framework. Second, private international law has a role to play in the enforcement of this legal framework.

Pursuant to the Rome I Regulation on the law applicable to contractual obligations,[28] employment contracts are governed by the law of the country of the habitual place of work.[29] Absent a habitual place of work, the employment contract is governed by the law of the country of the engaging place of business.[30] Exceptionally, if another country is more closely connected with the employment contract, the law of that country will govern.[31] Even if the parties have chosen the applicable law, the employee cannot be deprived of the protection afforded to him by the law of the country designated as applicable by the objective connecting factors.[32] These provisions lay down a kind of a country-of-origin rule. Employment contracts are essentially governed by the law of the country of the *employee's origin*. The law applicable to the employment contract is stable. It does not change when the employee is temporarily posted abroad.[33]

Pursuant to the Brussels I Regulation on jurisdiction and the recognition and enforcement of judgments in civil and commercial matters,[34] the employee has the choice of suing the employer in several courts, most importantly in the courts of the employer's domicile,[35] in the courts for the habitual place of work[36] or, in the absence of a habitual place of work, in the courts of the engaging place of business.[37] The

---

[27] D Kukovec, 'Whose Social Europe?' (Harvard Institute for Global Law and Policy Working Paper Series 2011/#3) <www.harvardiglp.org/category/allresources/working-papers/> accessed 16 April 2018.

[28] Regulation (EC) No 593/2008 of the European Parliament and of the Council of 17 June 2008 on the law applicable to contractual obligations (Rome I) [2008] OJ L177/6.

[29] Ibid., art 8(2).

[30] Ibid., art 8(3).

[31] Ibid., art 8(4).

[32] Ibid., art 8(1).

[33] Ibid., art 8(2), second sentence and Recital 36.

[34] Regulation (EU) No 1215/2012 of the European Parliament and of the Council of 12 December 2012 on jurisdiction and the recognition and enforcement of judgments in civil and commercial matters [2012] OJ L351/1.

[35] Ibid., art 21(1)(a).

[36] Ibid., art 21(1)(b)(i).

[37] Ibid., art 21(1)(b)(ii).

employee, on the other hand, may, in principle, be sued only in the courts of his domicile.[38] A choice-of-court agreement is effective only if it is entered into after the dispute has arisen[39] or if it increases the number of courts available to the claimant employee.[40] A temporary posting abroad neither deprives the courts competent under the Brussels I Regulation of their jurisdiction nor confers jurisdiction on the courts of the country where the employee is temporarily posted.

The Rome I and Brussels I Regulations complement the provisions of primary EU law on the freedom to provide services. Whenever an out-of-state service provider posts its workers to the host Member State, the rules of the two Regulations support its freedom to provide services. The service provider is guaranteed that the law governing the employment contracts it has with its workers and the courts having jurisdiction over disputes concerning those contracts will not change with the temporary posting of workers abroad. It is only by means of the PWD that posted workers are able to invoke the nucleus of mandatory rules for minimum protection in force in the host Member State[41] and are granted the right to access the courts in that country in order to enforce those mandatory rules.[42]

Ever since the adoption of the PWD, one of the main problems concerning this instrument has been its enforcement.[43] Generally speaking, there are three basic ways of monitoring the compliance with, and enforcing, the nucleus of mandatory rules for minimum protection to which posted workers are entitled in the host Member State. These are public monitoring and enforcement by public authorities, primarily labour inspectorates and immigration authorities, collective monitoring and enforcement by trade unions and private monitoring and enforcement by posted workers themselves. The recently adopted Posted Workers Enforcement Directive (PWED)[44] seeks to remedy the deficiencies in the mechanisms for the enforcement, in particular public enforcement, of the PWD. Private international law plays an important role with respect to the collective and private enforcement of the PWD and of the legal framework surrounding the posting of workers more generally.

With respect to the collective enforcement of the legal framework surrounding the posting of workers, the role of private international law is best illustrated by *Viking*, where a Finnish service provider commenced proceedings in England against the International Transport Workers' Federation and its Finnish affiliate. One may wonder why an essentially Finnish industrial dispute concerning a company from Finland which owned a ferry registered in Finland, plying its trade between Finland and

---

38 Ibid., art 22(1).

39 Ibid., art 23(1).

40 Ibid., art 23(2).

41 PWD, Recital 13 and art 3.

42 Ibid., art 6.

43 See generally U. Grušić, *The European Private International Law of Employment* (Cambridge, Cambridge University Press 2015) 273 et seq.

44 Directive 2014/67/EU of the European Parliament and of the Council of 15 May 2014 on the enforcement of Directive 96/71/EC concerning the posting of workers in the framework of the provision of services and amending Regulation (EU) No 1024/2012 on administrative cooperation through the Internal Market Information System ('the IMI Regulation') [2014] OJ L159/11.

Estonia, and which wanted to re-register the vessel in Estonia, ended up in the English courts? The reason lies in private international law. The ITF, which had its domicile in England, called for the boycott of the Finnish company. The High Court assumed jurisdiction over the ITF on the basis of the general jurisdictional rule in what is now Article 4(1) of the Brussels I Regulation. Jurisdiction over the Finnish union was assumed on the basis of the rule of jurisdiction over co-defendants in what is now Article 8(1) of the Regulation. The real reason why the proceedings were commenced in England was the fact that an injunction to stop industrial action can be obtained relatively easily in this country.[45] Private international law therefore played an effective role in enforcing the fundamental economic freedoms.[46]

With respect to private enforcement, the role of private international law is potentially more beneficial for the interests of posted workers. The rules of jurisdiction of the Brussels I Regulation allow posted workers to commence proceedings to enforce their rights in the courts of their employer's domicile and in the courts for the habitual place of work/engaging place of business. The rules of jurisdiction of the PWD allow posted workers to commence proceedings in the host Member State. This range of jurisdictional options facilitates the private enforcement of the Directive. With respect to the applicable law, the PWD allows posted workers to invoke the nucleus of mandatory rules for minimum protection in force in the host Member State, but only before the courts of that country. There is nothing in the PWD, the PWED or the Rome I Regulation[47] that would allow posted workers to invoke the nucleus of mandatory rules for minimum protection in force in the host Member State before the courts of their employer's domicile or the courts for the habitual place of work/engaging place of business. This is one of the aspects where the PWD and the PWED require improvement with the aim of further facilitating the private enforcement of the Directive.[48]

The role of private international law in the clash of the economic and social spheres of the EU shows that this legal discipline has a prominent public dimension. The rules of private international law complement and reinforce the provisions of primary EU law on the fundamental economic freedoms, thus contributing to the shaping of the economic and social constitution of the EU. Private international law is also being used as an instrument by actors who participate in the transnational European labour market for the achievement of their goals. In *Viking*, for example, the jurisdictional rules of the Brussels I Regulation were used by the claimant economic operator in order to dislocate the resolution of an essentially Finnish industrial dispute to England with the aim of obtaining a powerful English injunction. The instrumentalisation and politisation of private international law in cases like *Viking* is so obvious that in a later case of this kind the English courts held that the claimant could not rely on the jurisdictional rules

---

45 *American Cyanamid Co (No 1) v. Ethicon Ltd* [1975] AC 396 (HL).

46 For a more detailed presentation of this argument, see U. Grušić, 'The Right to Strike versus Fundamental Economic Freedoms in the English Courts, Again: Hiding Behind The "Public Law Taboo" in Private International Law' (2013) 9 *JPIL* 413, 426–29.

47 Art 9(3) Rome I lays down very strict conditions for giving effect to the overriding mandatory provisions of third countries.

48 For a more detailed presentation of this argument, see Grušić (n 43) 295–98.

of the Brussels I Regulation to dislocate the resolution of an essentially Spanish industrial dispute to England because the dispute was found not to have been a 'civil and commercial', but a public law matter.[49] Although the correctness of this decision is questionable,[50] this case is a reminder of the public dimension of private international law in this area.

5. LESSONS FOR THE GLOBAL LABOUR MARKET

While *Laval* tells us a lot about the economic and social constitution of the EU and about the role of law in shaping that constitution, it tells us little, if anything, directly about the global labour market. Nevertheless, *Laval* prompts us to think more widely about the social implications of the global movement of labour, goods, services and capital.

If the World Trade Organization ever achieves the opening up of the trade in services at the global level that would be as comprehensive and deep as the free movement of services that exists within the EU,[51] *Laval* would usefully illustrate some of the problems that any such free trade regime would have to address. For the same reason *Laval* is of potential importance to every other regional economic organisation.

But *Laval* has nothing to say about some of the more pressing problems that the global labour market is confronted with and the role of law in creating and resolving such problems, as the following two examples show.

The first example is the link between technology and non-standard work. This problem can be illustrated by the *Uber* case, recently decided by the English Employment Appeal Tribunal.[52] Uber is an international transport network which operates in many cities throughout the world through a smartphone app. A crucial element of Uber's business model is relatively low labour costs which are achieved, among other things, by shifting many business risks onto Uber drivers. Uber tries to achieve this by means of a complex transnational contractual network. The mentioned *Uber* case reveals that Uber, as it operates in the UK, is comprised of a Dutch company, which holds the legal rights to the app, and two UK companies which hold relevant licences to operate private hire vehicles in London and beyond. The passenger is said to enter into several different contractual relationships each time he or she uses the app, one with one of the UK companies for the provision of booking services (governed by English law), one with the Dutch company for the use of the app (governed by Dutch law) and one with the driver for the provision of transportation services (governed by English law). The driver is said to enter into a contractual relationship with the passenger (governed by English law) and the Dutch company (governed by Dutch law), although he or she has a much closer effective relationship with one of the UK companies. One of the purposes of this complex transnational

---

49 *British Airways Plc v. Sindicato Espanol de Pilotos de Lineas Aeras* [2013] EWHC 1657 (Comm), [2013] ILPr 45.

50 See Grušić (n 46).

51 See Mattoo and Carzaniga (eds) (n 15).

52 *Uber BV v. Aslam* [2018] ICR 453 (EAT).

contractual network, which relies on 'fictions, twisted language and even brand new terminology',[53] is to present Uber drivers as self-employed workers not entitled to the protection of employment legislation and to dislocate the resolution of any dispute between Uber drivers and Uber to international arbitration. The phenomenon of 'Uberisation', which is brought about by the rise of platform capitalism and shared economy worldwide, presents significant challenges for the global labour market, the most important of which is how to adequately respond to the consequent rise of non-standard work.

The second example is the use of complex corporate structures and supply chains to procure cheap labour in developing countries. In capital-intensive industries, such as extraction and chemical industries, it is not uncommon for a parent company from a developed country to carry on its activities abroad, typically in a developing country, through a local subsidiary. In many other industries, for example IT and fashion, the traditional, vertically-integrated firm is increasingly giving way to flexible forms of business organisation. Members of the modern economic enterprise are often not connected by bonds of ownership, but are independent firms bound together through long-term cooperative contractual and quasi-contractual relations or informal alliances. In such modern economic enterprises, it is not uncommon for a dominant member of the contractual business network located in a developed country to procure goods and services from other network members located in developing countries. There are many reports of workers of subsidiaries and network members located in developing countries working for low wages and poor conditions, often the result of downward spirals triggered by regulatory competition.[54] There are several reasons, including the doctrines of separate legal personality and limited liability, regulatory failures in developing countries and the territorially-limited jurisdictions of public authorities, why such wrongs are often not remedied and any legal responsibility does not extend beyond the local firm directly employing the workers in question.

6. CONCLUSION

Laval is a rich case that tells us a lot about the economic and social constitution of the EU and the role of law in shaping that constitution. But because of its European context, *Laval* tells us little, if anything, directly about the global labour market. *Laval* offers important lessons for any international economic organisation that may wish to implement the free movement of services that exists within the EU, but the prospect of this happening is currently remote. Otherwise, *Laval* is of little, or no, relevance for the more pressing problems that the global labour market is confronted with, e.g. the 'Uberisation' brought about by the rise of platform capitalism and shared economy and labour abuses within transnational corporations and transnational contractual business networks, and the role of law in creating and resolving such problems.

---

53 [2017] IRLR 4 [87] (ET) (footnotes omitted).

54 Many examples are reported on the Business and Human Rights Resource Centre website: <https://www.business-humanrights.org> accessed 16 April 2018.

23.3 THE AFTERMATH OF THE *LAVAL* AFFAIR: SWEDISH *LEX LAVAL* BEFORE THE EUROPEAN COMMITTEE OF SOCIAL RIGHTS

*Etienne Pataut**

1. INTRODUCTION

Essentially thought for and through the economics prism, the spectacular trade liberalisation of globalisation has nonetheless had a fundamental impact on the social organisation of States.[55] This impact is often perceived as essentially negative. Globalisation is the cause of a true downward spiral in the field of social rights; it allows for competition to exist between national social systems through the collapse of economic borders, enabling operators to organise production chains beyond borders and thus exerts a strong pressure on labour costs. This effect is even more vigorous as labour law rules, and, more broadly, the organisation of labour markets, have remained strictly national. The contrast between the internationalisation of capital and the strict maintenance of labour frameworks within national boundaries is striking.

Of course, such a situation has led to counter-reactions, the first of which are institutional. In this respect, the most accomplished structure is the European Union. By the twofold way of coordination and harmonisation, the EU is attempting to fulfil the mission it has set for itself: to become a 'social market economy', aiming at 'full employment and social progress' (Article 3 Treaty on the European Union (TEU)). Its achievements are certainly not inconsiderable. However, they remain largely insufficient to counterbalance the strong asymmetry that continues to prevail between economic and social concerns. The same could be said regarding other institutional initiatives, whether global like the ILO, or regional such as NAFTA, whose social role, although not insignificant, is not likely to be an effective counterweight either.[56]

Other responses involve the development of new standards for protagonists themselves, independently of any institutional framework. In this respect, the development of corporate social responsibility, no matter how slow and difficult, is undeniably a major step forward.[57] By developing standards that aim to overcome the double compartmentalisation of legal personalities and legal orders, corporate social responsibility is undoubtedly a path to the development of adapted social standards in the globalised context which is now that of corporations. In addition, the gradually increasing share of international framework agreements in this context, albeit still

* Contribution originally written in French, translated to English by Alice Lorrain.

[55] On the whole question, see M.-A. Moreau, *Normes sociales, droit du travail et mondialisation* (Paris, Dalloz 2006).

[56] On the ILO and its progressive marginalisation, even though the original project aimed at the reconstruction of a global economic system in which labour would have its place, see A. Supiot, *L'esprit de Philadelphie* (Paris, Seuil 2010).

[57] For a recent synthesis, see R. de Quénaudon and K. Martin-Chenut (dir.), *La RSE saisie par le droit – Perspectives internes et internationales* (Paris, Pedone 2016).

relatively modest, indicates that a path towards a transnational social dialogue, even if narrow, is not completely closed.[58]

Mixing institutional considerations and specific norms intended for protagonists, the development of fundamental labour rights is also part of the response to a globalisation that cannot be solely economic. The abundance of standards in this area is spectacular.[59] It is well known that the International Labour Organization, ever since the 1998 Declaration, has largely steered its action in favour of the development of these specific standards.[60] At the regional level, the 1994 North American Agreement on Labour (NAALC) complements the North American Free Trade Agreement (NAFTA) and lays down a number of fundamental rights inspired by the ILO Declaration, while expanding those rights already proclaimed.[61] For its part, the constitutive agreement of Mercosur is completed by a Social Declaration of 1998.[62] The effectiveness of these agreements remains disputed, but they do establish the reality of the progressive propagation of fundamental social rights.

But it is in Europe especially that fundamental social rights are diffused most effectively, through two essential instruments: the Charter of Fundamental Rights of the European Union and the European Social Charter. The first is distinctive for its substantial social chapter, which is likely to have a major influence on the EU as a whole.[63] The second has been adopted by the Council of Europe and is exclusively devoted to social issues. Far less famous than the European Convention on Human Rights, the European Social Charter has nonetheless gradually acquired a certain importance, to the point that we can now attempt to see it as a real 'social constitution for Europe'.[64]

These last two texts are distinctive in that they are backed by an institutional dispute settlement system: the Court of Justice of the European Union in the first case, and the European Committee of Social Rights in the other.

This myriad of fundamental norms and jurisdictional and para-jurisdictional forums inevitably generates confusion. However, it also testifies to the gradual emergence of new modes of dispute resolution, still largely under construction, compelling new methods of articulation of legal standards and legal orders.

---

[58] A. van Hoek and F. Hendrickx, 'International private law aspects and dispute settlement related to transnational company agreements' 20 October 2009, available at: ec.europa.eu/social/BlobServlet?docId=4815&langId=en (last accessed 10 December 2017).

[59] On the whole, see I. Daugareilh (dir.), *Mondialisation, Travail et Droits Fondamentaux* (Bruxelles-Paris, Bruylant-LGDJ 2005).

[60] F. Maupain, 'L'OIT, la justice sociale et la mondialisation' (1999) 278 *Rec. Cours* 201.

[61] L. Compa, 'L'ALENA et les droits fondamentaux des travailleurs des pays partenaires' in Daugareilh (n 59) 83.

[62] G. von Potobsky, 'La déclaration sociale du Mercosur' in Daugareilh (n 59) 99.

[63] L. He, Droits sociaux fondamentaux et droit de l'Union européenne, Typed thesis, Paris 1, 2017.

[64] O. de Schutter, *La Charte sociale européenne: une constitution sociale pour l'Europe* (Brussels, Bruylant 2010).

The 3 July 2013 decision of the European Committee of Social Rights is emblematic in this respect.[65] Taken by an authority whose fame and legitimacy are still largely to be established, devoid of the binding authority of a real international judicial decision and adopted in response to another decision which illustrated the limits of the fundamental rights of workers in a global economic context, the *LO and TCO v. Sweden* case is a most vivid illustration of the practical difficulties in protecting workers in a globalised world.

Now let us see this for ourselves.

2. FROM THE *LAVAL* CASE TO THE *LEX LAVAL*

The remote starting point of this procedure is the famous *Laval* judgment of the Court of Justice of the European Union.[66] This decision is specific to the EU, in that it can only be understood within the tightly woven network of economic liberties peculiar to the construction of Europe. In this sense, it does not concern the global labour market (which is the focus of this chapter). It is nonetheless a particularly striking occurrence of the difficulties such a market raises, even if this is only in a local context. The mobility of labour is indeed at stake here, as well as the difficult confrontation between an economic sphere that bypasses borders and a social sphere firmly rooted within them.

The response of the Court of Justice to the refusal of a Latvian employer who had posted workers to a construction site to accept a Swedish collective agreement and the subsequent blockade of the construction site, is well known. The Court of Justice found that the employer was a victim of excessive interference with the freedom of movement. It considered, in its usual course of reasoning, that an obstacle to free movement of services was indeed established; that it could admittedly be justified by a fundamental right to collective action, which it sanctioned in passing; but that such justification entailed that a requirement of proportionality be met, which it was not in this case. The posting directive was of no assistance:[67] being a collective agreement that was applicable only to its signatories, it could not benefit from the mandatory application mechanism provided for by the directive.

This summary does not do justice to the nuances and complexity of the case, but it shows how its stakes resided in the clash between the liberalisation of trade – here free movement of services – and its social consequences. Most importantly, it explains that following this decision, Sweden adopted a law, significantly called the '*lex Laval*',

---

[65] CEDS, 3 July 2013, Confédération générale du travail de Suède (LO) et Confédération générale des cadres, fonctionnaires et employés (TCO) c. Suède, n°85/2012. On this decision, see, in French, K. Chatzilaou, 'La réponse du Comité européen des droits sociaux aux arrêts Viking et Laval' (2014) *RDT* 160 and N. Moizard, 'Le droit d'action collective en droit de l'Union après la décision LO et TCO c. Suède du Comité européen des droits sociaux' (2015) *RTDH* 603.

[66] CJEU, *Laval*, aff. C-341/05 of 18 December 2007. For more details regarding this decision, see contribution by U. Grusic, The Laval Case, *supra*, p. 473.

[67] Directive 96/71 of 16 December 1996 concerning the posting of workers in the framework of the provision of services, *OJEC*, n° L. 18 of 21 January 1997, p. 1.

whose purpose was precisely to restrict collective actions of employees aimed at the conclusion of collective agreements.

In practice, this law doubly limited the right to collective action against a company employing posted workers. Firstly, actions could only take place in a number of areas, essentially corresponding to the field of the posting directive; secondly, actions could have no other purpose than to require the employer to comply with minimum requirements, in particular with regard to remuneration, to the exclusion of more demanding claims.

The law thus constituted a restriction to the freedom of collective action of employees, which is nevertheless undeniably a fundamental right. This is evident in the European Union: beyond the *Laval* case, the Charter of Rights makes the right to collective action a fundamental right. In fact, the Charter explicitly recognises the right of workers 'in cases of conflicts of interest, to take collective action to defend their interests, including strike action' (Article 28).

But it is not alone in this. This right to collective action is also enshrined in other fundamental rights instruments, notably in the European Social Charter, which protects in Article 6§4 'the right of workers and employers to collective action in cases of conflicts of interest, including the right to strike'.[68]

It is on the basis of the provisions of this Charter that the Swedish *lex Laval* was challenged.

3. THE RESPONSE OF THE EUROPEAN COMMITTEE OF SOCIAL RIGHTS

The European Social Charter includes a para-jurisdictional mechanism, in the form of an appeal to an expert panel, the European Committee of Social Rights. Its decisions have neither the binding force nor (for now) the prestige of the decisions of the European Court of Human Rights or, *a fortiori*, of the Court of Justice of the European Union. Nevertheless, they are an essential source for the interpretation of fundamental social rights.

Having activated the collective redress mechanism provided for in the Charter, some Swedish unions challenged the *lex Laval*'s compliance with the Charter and, in particular, with Article 6§4. The Committee ruled in favour of the trade unions, in interesting terms that highlight the difficulties that may, in the future, characterise relations between the European Union and the Council of Europe in the social field. Three points are significant. The first two relate to the European Union in general, the third to the non-conformity of a national law with the Charter.

The first point is about the absence of a presumption of conformity of EU law with the Charter. It is well known that the European Court of Human Rights held in the famous *Bosphorus* case[69] that the compatibility of European legislation with the

---

[68] For a more systematic analysis of article 6, see part. F. Dorssemont, 'Article 6: The Right to Bargain Collectively: A Matrix for Industrial Relations' in N. Bruun et al., *The European Social Charter and Employment Relation* (Oxford, Hart Publishing 2017).

[69] CEDH, 30 June 2005, *Bosphorus Airlines c. Irlande*, req. n° 45036/98.

European Convention on Human Rights could be presumed. Taking note of the still minor place given to fundamental social rights in the Union, the Committee adopts here the opposite position, in stinging terms worthy of attention. It considers that (Nb. 74): 'Neither the current status of social rights in the EU legal order nor the substance of EU legislation and the process by which it is generated would justify a general presumption of conformity of legal acts and rules of the EU with the European Social Charter'.

Although the Committee also declares itself ready to change its position were the situation to evolve, it could hardly be clearer about the relative circumspection, if not suspicion, with which it contemplates EU law in social matters.

This is mostly due to the subordination in the EU legal order of social concerns to economic ones, which is the second point. The Committee here takes the exact opposite stance to the Court of Justice's in the *Laval* case. The latter, bound by its precedents and the mighty legal construction of the freedom of movement, started from the principle of freedom of movement to assess thereafter whether an obstacle to it could be justified. In doing so, the Court prioritised economic requirements (freedom of movement) over social requirements (protection of fundamental rights of workers) by instituting a relationship of principle to exception. Yet this was not logically necessary, as the Committee decision very clearly shows. In fact, if one started reasoning from fundamental social law instead of freedom of movement, the reasoning would reverse. Thus, as stated by the Committee at number 121:

> Legal rules relating to the exercise of economic freedoms established by State Parties either directly through national law or indirectly through EU law should be interpreted in such a way as not to impose disproportionate restrictions upon the exercise of labour rights as set forth by, further to the Charter, national laws, EU law, and other international binding standards.

The burden of proof is reversed: it is for freedom of movement not to affect disproportionately the initial principle of workers' rights. The contradiction between these two sets of reasoning can, of course, be explained by the source of the interpreted norm: the EC Treaty in one case, the European Social Charter in the other. In this sense, this contradiction also illustrates the 'theory of legal constraints', which shows how much interpretation of the law is indissolubly linked to the configuration of legal systems and to the way protagonists think of it.[70] Nevertheless, by proposing the exactly opposite analysis, the European Committee of Social Rights offers argumentative resources to construct an alternative reading to that of the Court, and potentially relevant to the EU system. Beyond the failed attempt of the *Monti II* proposal, which sought to establish equal treatment of freedom of movement and the right to collective action,[71] the integration of the EU Charter of Fundamental Rights into primary law has enshrined a strict legal equality between fundamental rights and freedom of movement.

---

[70] M. Troper, V. Champeil-Desplats and C. Grzegorczyk (dir.), *Théorie des contraintes juridiques* (Paris, LGDJ 2005).

[71] European Commission, Proposal for a council regulation on the exercise of the right to take collective action within the context of the freedom of establishment and the freedom to provide services, of 21.3.2012, COM(2012) 130 final.

Nothing but the historical precedence of the freedom of movement now imposes the hierarchy sanctioned in the *Laval* case. The European Committee of Social Rights here proposes an alternative route which could easily be taken by the European Union.

The third point tackles substantive issues. The incompatibility of Swedish law with the protected rights is clear. After recalling the importance of the rights to collective bargaining and to collective action (Nb. 109), the Committee notes that 'this statutory framework imposes substantial limitations on the ability of Swedish trade unions to make use of collective action in establishing binding collective agreements on other matters and/or to reach agreements at a higher level' (Nb. 112). It is therefore constitutive of a 'disproportionate restriction on the free enjoyment of the right of trade unions to engage in collective action' (Nb. 123).

Thus the opposition is radical and Swedish law, framed as a simple application of the *Laval* jurisprudence and of the posting directive, is irrevocably condemned.

One should however be under no illusion about the immediate effectiveness of this ruling. If the *lex Laval* was indeed eventually repealed, it was only in April 2017, as the result of political changeover and not out of willingness to comply with the committee.[72] The fact remains, however, that the discussion in front of the European Committee of Social Rights clearly showcased a possible alternative discourse to a narrative that is all too often seen as reasonable or logically necessary. There is no logical necessity in the position of the Court of Justice, only a vision of the hierarchy of norms that can evolve.

The *LO and TCO v. Sweden* ruling, more than an isolated decision, should be viewed within a more general debate on the evolution of the interplay of various standards in Europe and beyond, and on the emergence of a global jurisprudence of fundamental rights.

4. FITTING DIVERSE STANDARDS

The *Laval* debate arose out of a very technical issue: the posting of salaried workers, which is itself part of the larger debate on the law applicable to employment contracts in international situations.

In general, the model of labour mobility that underlies the conflict of law rules in labour law (Regulation 593/2008, Rome 1) is that of the long-term (if not definitive) integration of the workers in their host community. It is labour immigration that is first at issue. Such integration implies the application of the law of the place of performance of the work, which will determine both the legal regime of the employment contract and, in the field of social security (Regulation 883/2004), that of social benefits. The innumerable advantages to the application of that law are well established. The fundamental requirements of a State's social cohesion entail that labour rules of that State are applicable to all workers in that territory and explain that these rules are very

[72] Michaela Danielsson and Anna-Karin Gustafsson, 'Sweden: the repeal of Lex Laval' *Eurowork* (14 July 2017) available at: https://www.eurofound.europa.eu/observatories/eurwork/articles/sweden-the-repeal-of-lex-laval.

frequently mandatory. The predominance of the State of performance of work therefore justifies the applicability of its rules, in terms of labour law and of social protection.

But this scheme becomes blurred when employees are intrinsically mobile and thus have connections with several states. Workers employed in international transports, for instance, or, above all, posted workers, are attached to several legal orders at once, all of which, one way or another, may have an interest in imposing the application of their own rules. In the context of freedom of movement, this question fits within the issue of the competition between social systems, facilitated by labour mobility, which causes concerns, as showcased in France with the irruption into public debate of the alien and nauseating representation of the Polish plumber.

The private international law question at stake remains fairly classical: it consists, in the face of a legal situation extending over different locations, in weighing the various connecting factors to find the most relevant one in order to designate the applicable law. But the relative neutrality of this technique is insufficient. The answer must consider both the substantial objectives of the European Union – ensuring free movement of workers – and the social concerns of States. Beyond the localisation process itself, the difficulty is to find an equilibrium between opposing impulses: of the EU to enforce the free movement requirements, of States to uphold the fundamental principles of their social systems, and of individuals to benefit from the most advantageous rules. The extreme difficulty of reconciling these interests explains the scholarly attention paid to the question of the posting of salaried workers.

The search for this equilibrium led to the adoption of Directive 96/71 which, after decisions of the Court of Justice to that effect, enabled the host State to compel application of its laws as mandatory provisions in several specific cases, instead of the normally applicable law of the place of habitual performance.[73] The 1996 directive has had the practical advantage of putting an end to a major debate on the possibility of imposing application of the host State's rules, when in principle the home State laws applied; by providing a list of the specific cases concerned, it also put an end to a vast theoretical debate on the identification of these mandatory provisions.

But this answer was insufficient, as the *Laval* case showed. Beyond the applicability of collective agreements, which were at issue in the case, the real question was about the respect of the fundamental requirements of the host State's social relations system. The peculiarity of conventional labour relations in Sweden and the existence of a proactive model, alternative to the legicentric model at the heart of the 1996 directive, showed how inadequate this approach was. The question is not so much that of the mandatory provisions but whether to allow the social institutions of the host State to play the role which is theirs. In this respect, strictly regulating the possibility for trade unions to take collective action to improve working conditions, as required by the *Laval* case and the *lex Laval*, was a clear illustration of the pernicious influence on social systems of a too abruptly designed model of articulation of norms. More broadly,

---

[73] Article 8§2 of the Rome 2 Regulation, which designates the law of the place of performance as applicable to the employment contract, adds that 'The country where the work is habitually carried out shall not be deemed to have changed if he is temporarily employed in another country'.

the debate showed how much the question is not merely the difficulty of the articulation of norms. There are, beyond coordination, substantial aims to preserve.

The European Union is now moving forward in this direction. The European Commission's proposal for the revision of the posting directive made on 8 March 2016[74] aims precisely to question the logic of pure articulation of standards, by introducing substantive considerations relating to equal treatment, particularly regarding remuneration. This solution goes directly against the *lex Laval*, which in terms of posted workers prohibited unions from claiming anything other than minimum wage through collective action.

The use of modes of articulation based on the reality of social relations in the country in question, not on an abstract view of the conflict rule, is a model to monitor closely. There is here, in our view, a more general sense of the evolution of private international labour law, by the progressive integration of substantive considerations into rules of the conflict of laws.

5. A GLOBAL CASE LAW OF FUNDAMENTAL RIGHTS?

The decisions of the Court of Justice and of the European Committee of Social Rights are mostly about the legal order of the European Union. They can only be understood within the framework enshrining free movement and, more broadly, the economic integration specific to the European institutional structure. In this respect, these decisions are but a milestone in a broader discussion that has gained momentum in the context of the economic crisis that has been rattling Europe since 2008.

The austerity measures implemented in many countries have led to such social regression that they inevitably offend fundamental rights. In this respect, there is again a striking contrast between the Court of Justice and the European Committee of Social Rights. The former sheltered behind the competence argument to justify extremely cautious – if not cowardly – solutions, which did not fail to disappoint. Several judgments held that determination between austerity measures and the protection of social rights was not within the scope of EU law.[75] This general statement is hardly convincing, especially as regards the Charter. The Court was not in any way asked to comment on the principle or the nature of the austerity measures themselves, but rather to compare some of their social provisions with the Charter. Those consequences undeniably fall within the scope of application of EU law, by virtue of Article 153

---

[74] Proposal for a directive amending Directive 96/71/EC of the European Parliament and the Council of 16 December 1996 concerning the posting of workers in the framework of the provision of services, COM(2016) 128 final; proposal then discussed within the Council (General Orientation 24 October 2017, 13612/17), then Parliament (Draft legislative Resolution of Parliament of 19 October 2017 (2016/0070(COD)).

[75] v. ECJ, 27 December 2012, aff. C-370/12, *Pringle*; more specifically on fundamental social rights see the cases relating to Portugal: ECJ, 7 March 2013, aff. C-128/12, *Sindicato dos Bancarios do Norte*; ECJ, 26 June 2014, aff. C-264/12 *Sindicato Nacional dos Profissionais de Seguros e Afins*; ECJ, 21 October 2014, C-665/13, *Sindicato Nacional dos Profissionais de Seguros e Afins*.

TFEU and extensive related secondary law. The competence argument, therefore, seems barely convincing.[76]

The solution must, above all, be contrasted with the audacity of the European Committee of Social Rights, which ruled that the austerity measures imposed on Greece were contrary to the requirements of the Charter.[77] The particularly strong words of the Committee, deeming that the economic crisis could not justify the violation of fundamental social rights, are a striking contrast to the cautious technicality of the Court of Justice.

The generality of the Committee's words makes it possible to go beyond the European framework alone. The condemnation of the subordination of fundamental social rights requirements and the strong reaffirmation of their primacy, including against central economic freedoms, are part of the broader framework of development of international standards on fundamental social rights and arenas in which to invoke them. The multiplication of fundamental social rights has gradually led to the emergence of new para-jurisdictional actors, who will perhaps play their full role tomorrow. The OECD, the ILO and the Council of Europe are all opening today, with varying success, collective redress mechanisms allowing protagonists themselves, and in particular the unions, to challenge national rules and practices.[78]

In this respect, the 'case law' of the European Committee of Social Rights contributes to the creation of a 'global case law of fundamental rights' in the sense of a process generating a stock of potential solutions, rendered in deterritorialised frameworks, and from which national or international judges could draw.[79]

This gradual affirmation of fundamental human rights in labour thus shows that the creation of a global labour market does not inevitably lead to a weakening of the protection of workers. The path will of course be very long, but it is certainly one worth taking. This is also one of the lessons of the *LO and TCO v. Sweden* decision.

---

76 F. Martucci, 'La Cour de justice face à la politique économique et monétaire : du droit avant toute chose, du droit pour seule chose' (2013) *RTDE* 267.

77 ECSR, 23 May 2012, Fédération générale des employés des compagnies publiques d'électricité (GENOP-DEI) et Confédération des syndicats des fonctionnaires publics (ADEDY) c. Grèce, n° 65/2011 et n° 66/2011. On these decisions, see part. J.-P. Marguénaud and J. Mouly, 'Le comité européen des droits sociaux face au principe de non-régression en temps de crise économique' (2013) *Droit social* 339; C. Deliyanni-Dimitrakou, 'La Charte sociale européenne et les mesures d'austérité grecques: à propos des décisions nos 65 et 66/2012 du Comité européen des droits sociaux fondamentaux' (2013) *Rev. Dr. Trav* 457.

78 I. Daugareilh, 'Les modes de règlement para juridictionnels des différends relatives aux droits sociaux dans les organisations internationales' in M. A. Moreau et al. (dir.), *Justice et mondialisation* (Paris, Dalloz 2010) 235.

79 E. Carpano, 'Réflexions sur l'idée d'une jurisprudence globale des droits fondamentaux', in *Mélanges en l'honneur du Professeur Dominique Turpin, Etat du droit, état des droits* (Paris, LGDJ 2017) 507.

PART VI

PERSONHOOD: CHANGING IDENTITIES

24. Surrogacy issues: *Mennesson v. France*

24.1 CASE BACKGROUND

In a complex world with interjurisdictional mobility, surrogate motherhood and assisted reproductive technologies, what is parenthood? Two recent judgments by the European Court of Human Rights (ECtHR) demonstrate that it is possible to consider parenthood as a concept 'under construction'; that the balance of interests at stake is proven a challenging task for courts.

In *Mennesson v. France*, a married French couple engaged in an international surrogacy agreement with a woman from California in the United States; where such agreements are recognised by law. The embryos were formed from a donated egg and sperm from Mr. Mennesson. Following an *in vitro* fertilisation procedure, the surrogate became pregnant with twins. A Californian court had issued an order declaring that the Mennessons shall be recognized as the genetic father and legal mother once the children were born. The Californian birth certificate mentioned the couple as the mother, respectively the father, without any reference to the surrogate mother. Upon returning to France, French authorities refused to grant legal recognition to the parent-child relationship that had been legally established in the United States. The refusal of a French birth certificate was made on the grounds of public policy since surrogacy arrangements are not recognised by French law (vid. Cour de Cassation, 6 April 2011, n. 10-19.053). How compatible is this decision with the right to respect for private and family life, as articulated in Article 8 of the European Convention on Human Rights (ECHR)? The case resultantly went before the ECtHR. The Court held that the refusal to issue a birth certificate put the children in a position of legal uncertainty, thereby constituting as a violation of the right to respect for their private life. It was assessed that French authorities created a restriction on the children's ability to establish their identity in law, particularly as they are biologically related to one of the parents. Therefore, the ECtHR took into consideration the best interest of the children and ruled that they could not be deprived of parenthood. It is noteworthy that there are other similar cases on the matter, such as *Labassee v. France.*

Paradiso and Campanelli v. Italy is also a case involving the non-recognition of foreign birth certificates of children born out of surrogacy. However, the child had no genetic link to the intended parents. In addition to birth registration and surrogacy issues, *Paradiso* furthers the narrative with an added element of complexity: parental care. Not only was the child no longer allowed to live with the intended parents, but the measures taken by the Italian authorities were questionable. The Italian couple had brought the child from Russia and attempted to register the birth. However, inconsistencies and false information were found. In May 2011, the Italian couple was charged with 'misrepresentation of civil status' and violation of the adoption. The child had been transferred to a foster institution, with no contact with the applicants and no formal identity. In 2013, the child received a new birth certificate indicating that he had been born to unknown parents.

As outlined in Article 8 of the ECHR, the Italian couple filed a claim against the Italian authorities for the violation of their and the child's right to respect for private and family life before the ECtHR. It considered the importance of balancing Italy's public policy considerations against best interests of the child. Ultimately, the ECtHR concluded that there was *de facto* existence of family life between the couple and the child; and that the Italian authorities had violated the applicants' rights under the ECHR by forcibly removing the child. The case was overturned by the Grand

Chamber in January 2017, thereby allowing a wide margin of appreciation to the national authorities on the issue.

Main cases: *Mennesson v. France*, Application No. 65192/11, Council of Europe: European Court of Human Rights, 26 June 2014; *Paradiso and Campanelli v. Italy*, Council of Europe: European Court of Human Rights, Application No. 25358/12, 27 January 2015;

Other similar cases: *Laborie v. France* (No. 44024/13), *Foulon v. France* (No. 9063/14), and *Bouvet v. France* (No. 10410/14)

24.2 SURROGACY IN THE CONTEXT OF PRIVATE INTERNATIONAL LAW? CROSS-BORDER EFFECTS OF INTERNATIONAL REPRODUCTIVE AGREEMENTS

Kellen Trilha

The *Mennesson* and *Paradiso Campanelli* cases have two elements in common: one factual and one concerning private international law techniques. As for the facts, both touch the difficult issue of the global regulation of reproductive technologies – and more particularly, the access to surrogacy. The discrepancies dividing national legal systems in this area make it possible for individuals who cannot have children to move to a State where they could have access to techniques otherwise forbidden in their home countries (at least as far as they have the material resources to do so). The differences opposing States in the matter of reproductive rights have no North/South, East/West divide – as both cases illustrate, there is an opposition within the occidental world in itself, and this opposition is presented as a fundamental one. States prohibiting access to surrogacy and disregarding the international effects of surrogacies realised abroad do so in the name of fundamental values, such as the dignity of the human being. When those issues reach the European Court of Human Rights, we see the culmination of this opposition, where a transnational court has to settle a conflict among fundamental policies: those of the State and those safeguarded by the Convention itself.

The common points from the perspective of Private International Law techniques concern the role public policy exception plays in the recognition of filiation links resulting from surrogacy agreements. In both situations, public policy has been put forward as the ultimate obstacle against the recognition of birth certificates linking a couple to a child born from a surrogate. In one case, this refusal of recognition did not prevent the family from living together in France. In the other, however, it led to the removal of the child from the couple's domicile in Italy. Both manifestations illustrate possible reactions of States facing cross-border effects of international reproductive agreements. A purely domestic approach on the issue prevents a comprehensive treatment of these complex situations, as the following points will illustrate.

1. THE CONTEXT: COMMERCIAL SURROGACY AS AN UNREGULATED TRANSNATIONAL ACTIVITY

States have very different views on whether surrogacy should be permitted and, if so, how to best regulate it. Some completely prohibit it; others allow surrogacy only on an altruistic basis, while some States permit commercial surrogacy under more or less liberal conditions.[1] This discrepancy opens the way for law shopping in a matter very deeply entrenched within individual lives and aspirations, such as the possibility of having a child. Sterile or same-sex couples who cannot have children naturally struggle with this reality while longing for an offspring of their own. As a result, those among these individuals who have the economic conditions to do so might be tempted of going abroad in order to require the services of a surrogate mother, even if the practice is prohibited in their home State. Before the Indian government issued a circular limiting the access to commercial surrogacy to Indian couples only, up to 50% of babies born from surrogacy in the country were destined to foreign couples.[2] In spite of the national dimension of surrogacy regulation, it is hence impossible to disregard its current practice as a transnational phenomenon working on its own basis. While in States such as India the whole process remains local (local surrogates, local laboratories for fertilisation and local clinics for pregnancy controls and birth), in other cases intended parents can have access to agencies intermediating their contact with a surrogate in a third country, while the laboratory fertilisation may take place in a third State.[3] In these situations, should the surrogacy agreement be seen as an *in vitro* fertilisation under the law of a State and a surrogacy under the laws of another or as a whole, complex transaction? The professionalisation of an industry specifically oriented towards foreign customers makes it more attractive for aspiring parents, and its results, more certain. More approachable and with less unpredictable results, international surrogacy is thus an activity destined to increase.

If international surrogacy can be seen as a sector of activity on its own, it also raises policy concerns that are proper to it. Indeed, if States do not deem necessary to regulate a local practice that remains isolated, they may face a rise in the number of surrogacy arrangements realised for foreign intended parents. In this case, how to properly protect women against overexploitation? How to make sure that surrogates are acting according to their will, instead of the will of their husbands or fathers? Is it possible to

---

1 For a presentation and an analysis of the different surrogacy regimes in place around the globe, see Katarina Trimmings and Paul Beaumont, *International Surrogacy Arrangements: Legal regulation at the international level* (Oxford, Hart Publishing 2013).

2 Kishwar Desai, 'India's surrogate mothers are risking their lives. They urgently need protection' *The Guardian* (5 June 2012) <http://www.guardian.co.uk/commentisfree/2012/jun/05/india-surrogates-impoverished-die> accessed 29 April 2018.

3 These different solutions for international surrogacy can be quickly verified through a search for surrogacy solutions in any web search engine. Any results will be preceded by a series of sponsored advertisements for clinics and agencies offering reproductive services, sometimes with prices and detailed solutions. These advertisements are of course accessible through the web, even from a country where surrogacy is prohibited. It shows the proximity that actually exists between aspiring parents and offers for reproductive services, in spite of a State's efforts to impose obstacles to it.

dissociate the will to be a surrogate from the desperate economic situation in which these women live in some countries? In this case, should a State allow women to increase their incomes by offering themselves as surrogates or should it prohibit the practice in order to safeguard their human dignity?

Besides the protection of women, international surrogacy also raises specific issues concerning the fate of children born through the practice. In the most dramatic cases, States face the problem of children abandoned by the intended parents – because of a divorce[4] or because of a handicap discovered at birth.[5] Once the intended parents return to their home States, the State of birth is left alone with the issue of protecting a child that might not even be a national. How then to increase the responsibility of intended parents for children born on their behalf?

Moreover, surrogacy agreements are open to anyone, without any preliminary control on who intended parents are, and whether they are fit to raise a child. In this sense, surrogacy can be a venue for those who, for any reasons, failed to satisfy the conditions imposed by their home States to adopt a child. These requirements have been established on the very purpose of protecting children from abuse and exploitation, and one can wonder whether children born from surrogacy are fully protected against such risks.[6]

Finally, and more directly connected to the cases that are here at stake, the intended parents' home State can refuse to recognise the filiation link established abroad with the child born through surrogacy. Without recognition children risk, firstly, lacking the necessary documents to leave the country of birth with the intended parents. In States that do not confer citizenship based upon *ius soli*, these children are not citizens of the country of birth, and cannot have a passport.[7] Further, if the local consulate agrees to provide the child with the necessary documents,[8] the State of origin of the intended

---

[4] In 2008 Manji Yamada, born from a surrogate on behalf of a Japanese couple, was abandoned by the intended mother after 'matrimonial discords': *Baby Manji Yamada vs. Union of India* [2008] Supreme Court of India (writ petition n. 379 of 2008). The grandmother petitioned for an extension of her expiring visa and the concession of travel documents for baby Manji, after Japanese authorities refused to issue a passport certifying the child's filiation and citizenship.

[5] Baby Gammy, born in 2013 in Thailand from a surrogate mother, has been abandoned by his intended parents, an Australian couple. The boy had Down syndrome, and the couple went back to Australia with only his tween sister, Pipah: Sascha Callaghan and Ainsley Newson, 'Surrogacy, Motherhood and baby Gammy' (2014) 766 *BioNews* <http://www.bionews.org.uk/page_444683.asp> accessed 27 April 2018. The surrogate kept Gammy and also claimed the custody of Pipah. This latter has finally been rejected by the Australian judges: *Farnell & Anor and Chanbua* [2016] FCWA 17.

[6] In baby Gammy's case (supra n 5), the intended father had been previously convicted for sexual assault. This was one of the reasons put forward by the surrogate to claim the custody of baby Pipah to the Australian judges.

[7] This issue became broadly discussed since the baby Manji case (supra n 4).

[8] The delivery of citizenship certificates to children born abroad from a surrogate is guaranteed in France since the *circulaire Taubira*, enacted in 2013 (NOR: JUSC1301528C): Jean-René Binet, 'Circulaire Taubira – ne pas se plaindre des conséquences dont on chérit les causes' (2012) 7 *JCP (G)* 161; Nicolas Mathey, 'Circulaire Taubira – entre illusions et contradictions' (2012) 7 *JCP (G)* 162.

parents might then refuse to recognise any civil effects to the birth certificate issued by the State of birth. This is the context in which the situations concerning the families Mennesson and Paradiso Campanelli evolved until they arrived in front of the European Court of Human Rights.

2. THE BLIND SPOTS IN THE REGULATION OF INTERNATIONAL SURROGACY AGREEMENTS

Blind spots are areas that fall outside an observer's eyesight, because occulted by a screen or in a point that cannot be seen without the help of a reflection. In cross-border cases, blind spots denote situations that cannot be fully considered by decision makers because of the fragmented legal framework in which they evolve. By focusing on an aspect of the situation, decision makers fail to assess the entirety of the issue at stake. All interests and rights are not equally taken into account, leading to a decision that while accomplishing a normative goal harms conflicting interests that are also affected by the outcome.[9]

Decisions rendered in international surrogacy cases, such as *Mennesson* and *Paradiso Campanelli*, offer an example of blind spots in the governance of cross-border situations. While pursuing a clear normative goal – fighting against a practice that would harm the dignity of a human being according to the principles of the forum – these decisions negatively affect the interests of children born through surrogacy. *In abstracto*, the public policy exception prevents a result incompatible with the forum's legal organisation. Concretely, however, decision makers often justified their decisions by presenting it as a deterrent preventing other intended parents to take the same road. In practice, it is unable to discourage these individuals, while not granting any improvement in the protection of women providing surrogacy services abroad.

Blind spots can hardly be prevented by an isolated approach on a complex issue such as international surrogacy. As a driver parking a car needs the help of mirrors in order to avoid colliding with objects concealed from eyesight in a blind spot, legal systems shall cooperate in order to contemplate and address the different aspects of a complex cross-border practice. However, despite recent efforts, the discrepancy among national policies on surrogacy makes an international convention on the matter hardly negotiable.[10] Although reaching a common ground on the national regulation of surrogacy does not seem feasible (or even auspicious), an international agreement on the matter could at least prevent issues that are proper to the discontinuity of the child's civil status through national borders – thus addressing problems related to its treatment in Private International Law.

In the absence of such a common instrument, it is up to States to, unilaterally, adopt perspectives that bring to light elements eclipsed in blind spots, by fully considering, for example, the fate of the child and the protection of this latter's rights under

[9] On the blind spots proper to complex cross-border situations, see Kellen Trilha Schappo, *Les angles morts d'un monde juridiquement hétérogène* (thesis IEP Paris, 2016).

[10] See the project at the Hague Conference on Private International Law: <https://www.hcch.net/en/projects/legislative-projects/parentage-surrogacy> accessed 29 April 2018.

international conventions (such as the ECHR). Or, on the other sense, by imposing conditions on the access to surrogacy that are proper to set aside the requests of parents whose link with the child would not be subsequently recognised.[11]

Overall, the result of isolated national policies as they are illustrated by the cases *Mennesson* and *Paradiso Campanelli* is to burden the child, instead of the intended parents, with the heaviest concrete effects of these normative choices. The negative impact of a refusal of recognition on the families' lives can amount to a violation of article 8 of the European Convention on Human Rights. By denouncing this violation in front of the Strasbourg Court, intended parents force States to assume a different perspective on the policy conflict underneath the regulation of international surrogacy agreements. The blind spots that remain outside the appreciation of fragmented national policies may be finally assessed by a supranational court observing the situation from a different standpoint – the respect of individual rights even in hard cross-border cases like the ones at stake.

3. THE FRAMEWORK RESULTING FROM THE ECHR DECISIONS

The participation of the European Court of Human Rights in this framework could, to a certain extent, attenuate side effects imposed by public policy decisions on the child's wellbeing. However, limited as it is to the scope of the Court's functions, this result is only partial. The legal framework resulting from both ECHR decisions presented here, while affording more protection to the child, also creates artificial distinctions among policies that can (and cannot) be adopted by those States willing to prevent their citizens from entering international surrogacy agreements.

A. The Obligation for States to Recognise the Civil Status Resulting from the Foreign Birth Certificate

The Strasbourg Court's decision in the *Mennesson* case clearly assesses the lack of conformity to the Convention of a decision refusing, on public policy grounds, to recognise the filiation link between a couple and a child born from a surrogate. Following this decision, France adapted its own position on the matter, admitting to give some effects to foreign birth certificates even if they have been issued at the end of a surrogacy process.

Notwithstanding this opening, the changes this new solution brings are only partial. Without a clear specification made by the European Court of Human Rights, French judges limited themselves to modify their orientation as far as the conformity with the *Mennesson* judgment was ensured. In that case, the Court stressed that the infringement of article 8 at stake was not the one claimed by the intended parents on their own behalf, but rather the one concerning the rights of the child. More specifically, denying recognition to a filiation link enacted in a birth certificate that actually reflects a

[11] Policy adopted by India before entirely closing the access to surrogacy to foreign intended parents.

biological truth would violate the child's right to have their identity recognised and preserved.

By providing a strict interpretation of this decision, French Courts in the subsequent cases involving international surrogacy limited themselves to recognise the link between the child and the genetic father. The intended mother, who did not give birth to the child, could not be recognised as such. This solution certainly changed the lives of children born from surrogacy for the better. If before *Mennesson* their connection with the intended parents had to be constantly demonstrated through a foreign birth certificate – what made bureaucratic acts such as registering at school or having access to health insurance much more difficult – after the decision the link with at least one of the intended parents can be immediately demonstrated by a national document. Moreover, civil claims relating to succession and maintenance can now be invoked against the father. Nonetheless, these rights were not extended to the mother. The possibility for the child of having access to maintenance or taking part to a succession is hence arbitrarily cut in half. For the intended mother (whose rights are not safeguarded by the ECHR Convention, as stated by the Strasbourg Court), the main risk consists in being deprived from any contacts with the child in case of divorce.[12] Moreover, children who are not genetically linked to the intended father seem to fall outside this opening.

B. The Possibility to Disregard Links that are not Genetically Established

The violation of article 8 is limited, as far as it concerns the ECHR case law, to the lack of recognition of filiation links that reflect a genetic truth. In *Mennesson*, it resulted in only recognising the link between children born from surrogacy and their genetic father. In *Paradiso Campanelli*, the absence of genetic link prevented the recognition of any family ties between the intended parents and the child – and this latter's removal from the couple's custody.

It appears clearly from the arguments put forward by the Italian authorities during the national proceedings of the *Paradiso Campanelli* case that the main reason behind the denial of recognition was their intent to sanction these parents for having had recourse to a surrogate in another country. The motivation would hardly have changed if the father were in fact genetically related to the child – since the national proceedings preceded the *Mennesson* decision, Italian courts were not yet bound to recognise the genetic link. As in the French *Menesson* proceedings, the main purpose was to avoid any effects created by a situation that so bluntly violated the forum's public policy.

However, differently from the *Mennesson* case, the Italian authorities did not limit themselves to denying recognition to the Russian birth certificate at stake. They went as far as removing the child, who had been for eight months under the custody of the intended parents, and entrusting him to a foster house. The couple seized the European Court of Human Rights against the Italian decisions, but it was already too late to have the child back. A first decision recognised that the removal of the child was not proportionate to the policy goals pursued by the Italian State. Nonetheless, after Italy

---

[12] French law allows however the intended mother to adopt the child: [2017] Cass. civ. 1re n° 824, 825, 826 and 827.

referred the case to the Grand Chamber, a second decision was aligned to the more strict approach focusing on the genetic link between father and child.

First of all, the decision of the Italian authorities (removing the child from the custody of the Paradiso Campanelli couple) had an impact in the characterisation of a family life in the sense of article 8. Distinguishing the case from *Wagner*, the Court considered the length of coexistence insufficient to constitute a *de facto* family life. As a result, the applicability of the text could only depend on the existence of a genetic link, as it had been the case in *Mennesson*. Since in *Paradiso Campanelli* such a connection had not been established, the couple was not entitled to raise the violation of the child's rights protected under article 8. Furthermore, following what had already been stated in *Mennesson*, the intended parents could neither invoke a violation of their own rights, since they deliberately chose to evade national law. The decisions decried by the claimants could hence not be the object of a control of conformity with the ECHR provision safeguarding their right to a family life.

It is unclear whether the Strasbourg Court would have identified a violation of the child's rights if the question could have been raised. In the *Mennesson* case, the fact for the child to live with the intended parents as a family, without however being recognised as such, weighted on the Court's decision. Denying any legal legitimacy to a family situation that existed *de facto* harmed thus the child's right to have their identity preserved. However, as already highlighted, the length of cohabitation between the child and the Paradiso Campanelli family has not been considered enough by the Strasbourg Court to characterise a *de facto* family life. Pursuing this reasoning, one could assume that the child could neither identify himself as being part of this household (an identity feeling that could hence not be built due to the decisions taken by the Italian authorities, separating the child from the intended parents).

On the other hand, the experience of having been removed from the family at eight months, entrusted to a foster house and not receiving a new name or a new family until the age of three might certainly have had an impact on the child's life. If his identity right in the sense of identifying himself as the child of the Paradiso Campanelli might have remained unharmed because of their short common life, State decisions affected the possibility for this child of simply having *any* identity. Or simply having any family life. These issues put forward the most problematic aspect in the governance of international surrogacy agreements: how to fully safeguard the child's rights amidst State decisions of scarce effectiveness in accomplishing unclear policy goals.

4. INTERNATIONAL SURROGACY IN PRACTICE AFTER THE DECISIONS OF THE ECHR

The States concerned by the decisions rendered by the Strasbourg court had to adapt their local practices in order to comply with article 8 of the Convention. However, this adaptation was limited to the only extension of the *Mennesson* decision: the recognition of a filiation bound certified by a genetic link. We shall now evaluate whether national practices can achieve their goals while providing for minimum protection for the children, and whether these solutions have evolved in the past years.

A. Discouraging Intended Parents from Hiring Surrogacy Services Abroad?

If States freely recognised family status obtained through surrogacy, aspiring parents might feel tempted to take this path, with the certainty that their project would be successful. States refusing recognition present this hypothesis as a main justification for their decisions. By doing so, they refuse to take part in an activity that goes against their most fundamental principles – above all the respect of the human dignity of a woman whose activity could be assimilated, to a certain extent, to the commercialisation of her own body.

The practical developments of the prohibition fail, however, to attain this goal. It is unclear whether the risk of denial of recognition might have an influence on the decision of aspiring parents planning to pursue their family project in another State. In a case such as *Mennesson*, where it was still possible for the intended parents to live with the children as a family, one could even question whether the concrete result fulfils this aim. Indeed, intended parents can have their family project realised, even without legal homologation. The sanction admitted in *Paradiso Campanelli* could, on the contrary, be more deterrent, but it remains limited to cases in which there is no genetic link between the intended father and the child (or a cohabitation insufficiently long to characterise a *de facto* family life). Having access to a professional and trustworthy surrogacy provider, in order to avoid mistakes as the ones claimed to be at the origin of the absence of genetic link between the intended father and the child in *Paradiso Campanelli*, would limit this risk. Moreover, a recent French decision was clear in assessing that authorities should limit themselves to recognise what is stated in foreign documents, without proceeding to new genetic tests.[13]

Negotiating a surrogacy contract and spending months in another country until the child is ready to travel is a consistent material obstacle. If intended parents accept to go through this process, they might not be discouraged by bureaucratic complications that may arise once they are back in their State of origin, as far as they can stay with their children. Once aspiring parents continue to go abroad in order to have access to surrogacy, how is the refusal of recognition helping to protect vulnerable surrogates?

B. If the Refusal of Recognition does not Efficiently Prevent the Conclusion of Surrogacy Agreements, how could International Surrogacy be Better Governed?

A strict refusal of recognition as an answer to the regulatory issues underlying international surrogacy fails to capture the essence of international surrogacy as a global phenomenon distinct from national practices taken separately. Marketing through internet and efficient means of transportation and communication make surrogacy available for individuals from all parts of the globe, without targeting a sole category (nationals; foreigners unable to hire a surrogate in their State of origin; nationals or residents of States where surrogacy is prohibited and its effects cannot be recognised). The possibility of having a direct link with surrogacy providers in other States enables individuals to simply compare the different offers available. Aspiring

[13] [2017] Cass. civ. 1re (supra).

parents taking part in international surrogacy agreements might in this sense even reside in a State where surrogacy is admitted, but prohibitively expensive for their personal means. The development of commercial surrogacy in other States, with an international offer and competitive prices, allows these individuals to achieve their family project.

However, the different range of costs and offers also hinders how differently surrogacy is framed from a State to another. In some States, it is not only tolerated, but is also the object of a detailed regulation – surrogates' rights are hence more safeguarded. Surrogacy regulation ensures the protection of the surrogate's consent (to abandon the child or to proceed to a selective abortion, for example), while providing for limits protecting their health (such as on the number of embryos that can be implanted). These differences do not create a divide between Eastern and Western States, but are rather transversal.[14] They might hence not be directly linked to the overall cost of the service. However, the fact that surrogates can perceive much less in some countries can raise questions regarding the different conditions under which these women provide their services.

By treating all surrogacy practices identically – by sanctioning all of them under the same public policy exception – States ignore these differences. The material treatment provided to each surrogate under these contracts becomes then irrelevant. It is true that the policy goal of preventing surrogacy as being a practice contrary to fundamental rights can only be satisfied by this solution. However, as pointed out above, this policy goal remains essentially abstract. As far as decisions refusing recognition are not sufficient to discourage aspiring parents, the policy remains unfulfilled. On the other hand, the protection of surrogates could still be pursued, to a certain extent, by guiding aspiring parents not to choose a destination based on the cost of surrogacy, but rather on the basis of good practices adopted locally.

Such a model of conditional recognition could, with difficulty, be achieved through national techniques of private international law. Without being able to review foreign policies on surrogacy, a State is left with little less than accepting its effects (for the sake of the children) or on the contrary opposing the public policy exception. It can nonetheless inspire and motivate international cooperation on the matter.[15] Following

---

[14] In California, a surrogate refused to terminate the pregnancy for one of the triplets she was expecting after all three embryos implanted successfully developed. She was however bound to accept the abortion according to the surrogacy agreement, and the intended father could be entitled to reparation of the expenses resulting from this refusal and the birth of the third child. She challenged the constitutionality of California surrogacy laws on the grounds that it violated her (and the newborn's) due process and equal protection rights. After losing in front of Californian courts, she sought to submit the question to the Supreme Court, which denied certiorari (order available at: <https://www.supremecourt.gov/orders/courtorders/100217zor_o7 jp.pdf> accessed 29 April 2018). She was unsuccessful in claiming the custody of the third child for herself and in challenging the qualities of the intended father (a deaf and mute postal worker of 51 years old living with his parents) to properly raise the children. This case illustrates the fact that issues surrounding a proper regulation of surrogacy are not limited to South-Eastern States, but can also be found within the United States.

[15] As the project organised within the Hague Conference on Private International Law, cf. supra n 10.

the sophisticated framework developed for international adoptions, international surrogacies might also benefit from conditions regarding their validity (i.e. minimum requirements for the protection of the surrogates and the aptitude of intended parents). These would provide a safer basis for surrogacy agreements, while ensuring the continuity of their effects and by such providing legal certainty for the parties.

24.3 A CASE FOR HARMONISATION OF PRIVATE INTERNATIONAL LAW? JUGGLING BETWEEN SURROGACY, INTERESTS OF A CHILD AND PARENTHOOD

Dagmar Coester-Waltjen

1. INTRODUCTION

The decisions[16] of the ECtHR focus on the result of the cases for the children, the 'parents' and the legal order of the Member State concerned. This correlates with the function and the mission of the Strasbourg Court. However, national courts will have to deal with private international law issues first, when striving for a result that conforms or at least does not violate the ECHR.

The very important questions – concerning the applicable law and the issue of public policy – might arise in different legal frameworks and within these frameworks in various factual constellations. There might be a decision of a foreign court confirming or establishing the intended parents as legal parents of the child born to a surrogate – like in the *Mennesson* case. Instead of a foreign court a foreign public authority might have decided on these matters, or simply issued a birth certificate – like in *Paradiso and Campanelli*. Or, there might be no official statement of any evidentiary value at all.

As the case may be, in all these legal frameworks the factual situation may differ: both of the intended parents might be the genetic parents of the child born to a surrogate (very often called 'full surrogacy'). Or, the intended father has a genetic link to the child, but not the intended other parent – as in *Mennesson* (often called 'partial surrogacy'). Or, as in *Paradiso and Campanelli* there is no genetic or biological link of the intended parents to the child whatsoever (often equated to child trafficking), but only a short or long *de facto* relationship. Each of these situations in combination with the respective legal framework will be looked at shortly in the following part.

2. FOREIGN COURT DECISION

Many legal systems – as well as the Brussels Regulations – distinguish between the effects of a legal situation established or certified by the decision of a foreign court or comparable authority on the one side and the situation without such a decree on the

---

[16] *Mennesson v. France* App no. 65192/11 (ECtHR 26 June 2014); *Paradiso et Campanelli v. Italy* App no. 25358/12 (ECtHR 24 Jan 2017).

other. In general, a court decision attracts greater respect and is subject (only) to special rules on recognition (with or without a certain procedure to be required).

The rules of the European Regulations on recognition of foreign judgments are not applicable in matters of establishment of parenthood. The international regime of the CIEC (Commission Internationale de l'Etat Civil) provides only for registration of the civil status, but does not deal with the legal tie between the persons concerned. Due to the lack of any other international convention on these subject matters, it is up to the national law to decide under what circumstances the legal situation created or affirmed by a foreign court decree will be recognised.

The grounds for non-recognition are very often reduced to incorrect or missing service, violation of the right to be heard, irreconcilability with local or earlier foreign judgements, lack of jurisdiction and violation of public policy.[17] In some legal systems, however, the courts may refuse to recognise a foreign judgment, if the foreign court applied another law than that applicable to the case according to the private international rules of the recognising court.[18] In the latter situation the determination of the applicable law might cause additional problems. In the other legal systems the main issue of discussion will be whether the recognition of the decision of a foreign court might violate public policy. Other reasons for refusal of recognition have very little practical relevance in cases of surrogacy. The arguments for and against the permissiveness of surrogacy arrangements and the problems involved are discussed thoroughly in the preceding article of Kellen Trilha. Those are the issues which the courts will have to deal with when it comes to the interests of the national legal order. There is no need to repeat this discussion. However, if there is a foreign court decision, the public policy shield generally is less strong (*ordre public attenué*), because of the respect for the foreign court.

In the *Mennesson* case[19] the ECtHR emphasised the paramount consideration which has to be given to the 'interest of the child to live with his or her family'. This aspect has to prevail over general concerns of the legal order of the recognising state.

'Family life' in this case was established not only by a *de facto* relationship, but also by a genetic link of the intended father to the children. Thus, where there is a genetic link of one of the intended parents and the child, other concerns of the state – like the enforcement of its prohibition of surrogacy and the prevention of future intending parents to take part in a surrogacy arrangement – have to give way.

Although the ECtHR did not expressly limit its arguments to situations where there is a genetic link to at least one of the intended parents and did not restrict its decision to the position of the genetic parent, French courts seem to have waived their public

---

17 Comp. Dutch Civil Code Art. 10.100; English FLA 1986 sec. 44 seq.; Austrian Non-contentious Elements Law § 91a; German Law on Family Proceedings § 108; Swiss PIL Art. 70; Swedish PIL §§ 7,8; in the United States some states require in addition reciprocity, David Currie, Herma Hill Kay, Larry Kramer and Hermit Roosevelt, *Conflict of Laws* 9th edn (Eagan MN, West Academic Publishing 2013) 896 seq.

18 See for example, Italian PIL, Art. 65; expressly abstaining from such a ground for non-recognition: Dutch Civil Code Art. 10.100.

19 *Mennesson v. France* App no. 65192/11 (ECtHR 26 June 2014).

policy concerns only in these special situations and only with regard to the genetic parent,[20] referring the non-genetic intended parent to adoption proceedings.[21]

Following *Mennesson* the German Supreme Court took a more generous approach. The Court recognised a Californian court decree ordering that not only the genetic intended father, but also his civil partner, be registered as legal parent of the respective child(ren). In the eyes of the German court respecting the paramount interests of the child(ren), the Californian court decree did not violate German public policy although surrogacy is prohibited in Germany. But the German Court also stressed that there was a genetic link of the child(ren) to one of the intended parents. The Court left open whether this genetic link was decisive. It might be added that there had been a long and intensive *de facto* relationship of the child(ren) with both intended parents.

In a very similar case the Swiss Supreme Court,[22] however, refused to recognise the other intended parent as legal parent. Only with regard to the genetic father the Californian decision was recognised – following the restricted view of *Mennesson* taken by the French courts.

The emphasis the ECtHR (and the other courts) so far put on the genetic link might indicate that in a case where both intended parents are genetic parents of the child (full surrogacy) the right of the child to live with its parents and to be identified as the child of these parents has to prevail, at least when the child is living with these parents and has been given to them by the surrogate deliberately without any coercion.[23] This indeed was the result reached by the Austrian Constitutional Court even before *Mennesson.*[24] Whether there might be situations in which, despite genetic links and *de facto* relationship between the child and the intended parents public policy concerns may justify non-recognition remains to be seen. It seems that these would have to be very strong issues, for example relating to the individual surrogate, but not only general and abstract interests of the national legal order.

The issue of public policy becomes more complicated if there is no genetic link to either intended parent – as was the case in *Paradiso and Campanelli.*[25] In such situation the Swiss Supreme Court – in conformity with the ECtHR decision – denied recognition of the foreign court decree completely.[26] The main argument of the Swiss Supreme Court was that the intended parents had not only circumvented the Swiss prohibition of surrogacy, but also the provisions and proceedings for adoption. Such cases have some similarity with child trafficking, even though the intended parent may prove that all arrangements had been made before the child was conceived.[27]

---

20 Cass Civ. 1re 3 July 2015.

21 Cass Civ. 1re 5 July 2017.

22 BGE 141 III 312, 325.

23 Erwin Bernat, 'Leihmutterschaftstourismus und seine Folgen' (2015) 24 *Annual Review of Law and Ethics* 3, 12.

24 VfGH Dec. 14, 2011, B13/11, (2012) *RdM*, 104 (note Erwin Bernat).

25 *Paradiso et Campanelli v. Italy* App no. 25358/12 (ECtHR 24 Jan. 2017). This case is mentioned here because of the complete want of any genetic link to the intended parents, although it did not involve the recognition of a foreign judgment. Therefore the position of the Italian court will not be dealt with here.

26 BGE 141 III 328, 344.

27 Konrad Duden, note 64 (2017) *FamRZ* 444, 445.

Despite the similarity with child trafficking the decisive factor in the course of consideration in these situations will be – or at least should be – whether a *de facto* parent-child-relationship exists and whether it is necessary to accept the legal situation established by the foreign decree in order to avoid a situation in which the child would to be deprived of his or her family life altogether. The *Paradiso and Campanelli* decision indicates (only very reluctantly) that a long *de facto* relationship might require protection. This seems to be still a very controversial issue. Some judges of the ECtHR stated that a *de facto* relationship on its own – i.e. absent marriage, registration or a genetic link – does not constitute 'family life' within the meaning of the Convention.[28] Aside from this the majority of the judges held that a *de facto* relationship of the child to its intended parents for a time of eight months definitely did not amount to a tie deserving the protection of the Convention,[29] although eight months is a very long and important time for a newborn. Only the dissenting minority (of five judges) wanted to protect this relationship.[30]

Thus, it seems that under the ECHR national legislators and courts have a great margin of appreciation when it comes to the recognition of foreign decisions establishing parenthood of persons who have no genetic link to the child. This means that there is a great uncertainty for the fate of the child and the intended parents in these cases.

3. ACTS OF FOREIGN PUBLIC AUTHORITIES

Although the rules on recognition of foreign decrees may also apply to declaratory decisions of courts[31] as well as to decisions of public authorities, which function like courts in other jurisdictions,[32] not all acts of foreign public authorities are treated in this way. In many legal systems birth certificates and entries in birth registries as such do not have the same 'dignity' as court decisions, because they do not amount to a judicial decision on the legal tie between the child and the parents. In some cases it may be difficult to draw a line, if the foreign public authority did not only rubberstamp the information given, but had some authority to evaluate the factual and legal situation.[33] There may be legal regimes which give almost the same weight to legal documents issued by a public authority as to court decisions, but in many legal systems the acceptance of the legal situation documented in a foreign country according to foreign law depends on the question whether the law applicable under the private international law rules of the recognising state has been applied, or – at least – would

---

28 *Paradiso et Campanelli v. Italy* App no. 25358/12 (ECtHR 24 Jan 2017), joint concurring opinion of Judges De Gaetano, Pinto De Albuquerque, Wojtyczek and Dedov.

29 *Paradiso et Campanelli v. Italy* App no. 25358/12 (ECtHR 24 Jan 2017), no. 140 seq.

30 *Paradiso et Campanelli v. Italy* App no. 25358/12 (ECtHR 24 Jan 2017), diss. opinion of Judges Lazarova Trajkovska, Bianku, Laffranque, Lemmens and Grozev.

31 BGHZ 203, 350.

32 For example, divorces by a Norwegian Fylkesman or adoptions by a Notary Public in Guatemala.

33 Compare the case decided by the Court of Appeal Celle of 22 May 2017 – 17 W 8/16, 70 StAZ 2017, 343, crit. note Christian Gomille (2017) 70 *StaZ* 321; Hans Prütting, Tobias Helms and Wolfgang Hau, *FamFG* 4th edn (Cologne, Otto Schmidt 2018) § 108 no. 8.

lead to the same result. Thus, the acceptance of birth certificates and entries in registries depends solely on the private international law issues, even before the question of public policy concerns might be raised.

4. DETERMINATION OF THE APPLICABLE LAW

Private international law rules in matters of parenthood differ considerably. These differences in determining the applicable law and in establishing parenthood may produce limping relationships. This means that the legal parent-child relation may exist in the legal system of state A, but may be non-existent in the legal system of state B. Even worse, it can happen that such different approaches cause blind spots: for example state A where the surrogate lives and has delivered the child may apply its own law. According to that law the intended parents are the legal parents of the child. All legal links of the child to the surrogate, her husband, and – as the case may be – to the woman whose egg cells have been fertilised may be cut.

On the other hand, under the law of state B where the intended parents now live with the child, the private international law rules may differ and parenthood might be established only according to the law of B, because this is the law of the nationality (or domicile or habitual residence) of the intended parents and/or of the habitual residence of the child. The affiliation rules of state B, however, may not allow intended parents to become legal parents just by their intention. These rules may designate as mother always and only the person who gave birth to the child. Thus, from the point of view of the law of state B, the surrogate is the legal parent. In this situation the child may end up without having any parent at all.[34] The case of *Paradiso and Campanelli* is a deterrent example.

To a certain extent the harsh result might be softened in those cases in which the sperm of the intended father has been used for fertilisation and – in addition – he has the possibility to acknowledge paternity of this child. The latter might not be possible in cases where the surrogate is married, because according to the law of state B (including state B's conflict rules) the surrogate's husband might be the legal father and this legal tie might hinder any further acknowledgement of the child. In such cases, the child will have no chance (except by being adopted) to establish a legal link to the intended father, although he might be in fact the genetic father of the child.

Even if the legal relation of the child to the father can be rectified by an acknowledgement of paternity by the father, the position of the child with regard to the intended mother remains problematic. Outside adoption the applicable law may not provide for a legal relationship with any other woman than the birth mother. Thus, despite the possible genetic link between the child and the intended mother – and even if there is a long-lasting *de facto* relationship between mother and child – the private international law rules deprive the child of its family life with its mother. It appears that this result would amount to a violation of the child's right to live with its family and to be identified as a child of its family – as the Strasbourg Court found fault with in *Mennesson*.

---

[34] Christian Gomille (2017) 70 *StAZ* 323, 326.

The special problems in these situations result from the divergences of the private international law approaches, even before the question of public policy concerns can be raised. Rectification of the legal situation seems very difficult. National courts and decision-makers will not arrive at discussing of public policy objections. They simply apply their own law applicable according to their own private international law rules. Thus, a better adaptation of public policy considerations to the needs of the child will be of no help.

5. FUTURE SOLUTIONS?

To hope for a unified or harmonised approach of the national legislations to the permissiveness of surrogacy seems to be unrealistic in the next future, because the views on the subject matter are far too divergent. The same applies to efforts of harmonising affiliation rules which will remain in the realm of the national legal systems and will remain different from state to state.

However, it might be worthwhile to try to harmonise at least the private international law rules in the area of affiliation. If, for example, the applicable law for establishment of parenthood would be the law of the habitual residence of the child at the time of its birth (preceded by a pregnancy in that state), the blind spot demonstrated above, would not appear. The law governing the determination of parenthood would be the same from the point of view of state A as from the point of view of state B. As surrogates nearly always will live in those states which allow the intended parents to become legal parents, the law of that state (A) would be applied by the courts, registries and other authorities in state A and also in state B allowing the intended parents to become parents of the child, thus respecting the rights of the child to family life.

A new decision of the CJEU concerning the determination of the habitual residence of a child for the purposes of the Brussels IIbis Regulation (and the Hague Abduction Convention) might be a good guideline.[35] The CJEU stressed that habitual residence is a factual concept, and the intention of a change alone cannot influence the determination of the habitual residence at the present time. Therefore, if the law of the place of birth of the child would be applied unanimously no conflicting legal situation would arise and the laws of place of birth would prevail.

Of course, there might be still the issue of public policy objections, when, for example, state B is applying the law of state A. But this objection allows the weighing of interests in each case under consideration. Due respect could be given to the interests of the child according to the standards of the ECtHR.

Another solution, which can ensure greater certainty of the results of all cases, would be a model of conditional recognition, as Kellen Trilha has proposed in her preceding contribution. Such a model could be applied for the recognition of foreign decisions. But it could also have significance for the acceptance of legal situations documented or solely originated in another legal system. However, there is still a long way to go.

---

[35] Case C – 111/17 *OL v PQ* (CJEU, 8 June 2017) ECLI:EU:2017:436.

25. Blind spots (persons and family): *Blood*

25.1 CASE BACKGROUND

The *Blood* case concerns access to health care and health services, in relation to assisted reproductive technology. It raises ethical and legal questions around the right to bodily integrity, the right to family life and the right to health within the framework of the European Union. Mrs. Diane Blood married her husband, Stephen, in 1991, according to the rites of the Anglican Church. In 1994, Mrs. Blood and her husband commenced plans to start a family. Soon after, Mr. Blood contracted meningitis. In March 1995, while her husband was in a comatose state, Mrs. Blood asked the doctors to take samples of Mr. Blood's sperm. After his death, Mrs. Blood commenced a legal battle to use these samples, entrusted in the care of the Infertility Research Trust (IRT), so as to bear her late husband's child.

The Human Fertilisation and Embryology Act 1990 prohibited the storage or use of gametes without the clear written consent of the gamete provider. In the case at hand, Mr. Blood had never signed this document. As a result, the authorities (HFEA) could not allow Mrs. Blood to undergo assisted reproductive treatment in the United Kingdom. The question, therefore, was whether the HFEA would authorise the release of the sperm abroad for treatment in another EU country. Mrs. Blood requested that the sperm be exported to Belgium, where she could obtain treatment under Belgian law. Nevertheless, the authorization was not granted. In response, Mrs. Blood filed an application for judicial review. The application was dismissed on 17 October 1996, but the judge gave leave for appeal.

The Court of Appeal held that although the HFEA's decision regarding the statutory interpretation was correct – that treatment in the United Kingdom could not take place without Mr. Blood's written consent – the authority did not properly consider the importance of European law and its fundamental freedoms in reaching its decision to refuse the export of the sperm. The Court recognized that Mrs. Blood had the right to be treated in Belgium unless there were reasonable public policy concerns for disallowing treatment. The Court concluded that the HFEA had therefore failed to exercise its discretion correctly.

Case: *R. v. Human Fertilisation and Embryology Authority, ex parte Blood* [1997] 2 All ER 687, Court of Appeal, Lord Woolf

25.2 WHEN LAW FALLS BEHIND FAIRNESS CONSIDERATIONS: JUDGES' DUBIOUS APPLICATION OF INTERNATIONAL PROVISIONS

*Elsa Supiot**

When presented to a French jurist, the *Blood* case is likely to bring to mind the 2016 *Gomez* decision given by the Conseil d'Etat.[1] Mrs. Gomez, of Spanish nationality, lived in France with her Italian husband. He suffered from an illness for which treatment was likely to affect his fertility. He benefited therefore from the provisions of the Public Health Code (CSP) that allowed the conservation of gametes in such a case. As a result, his sperm was taken and stored for future in vitro fertilization processes. The couple even made arrangements for a posthumous artificial insemination in Spain, if necessary. However, the rapid deterioration of the husband's health did not allow to follow through with the plan. He eventually had passed away on 9 July 2015, without having benefited from an IVF in France and without a second semen sample to carry out the process in Spain. Following his death, his widow moved back to Spain with her family and requested for the transfer of her husband's gametes. However, such a transfer was explicitly prohibited under French law.[2] The regulatory agency in charge (the Bio-medical Agency) as well as the first instance judges denied the request. That latter decision was overturned by the Conseil d'Etat which expressed that the provisions of the Public Health Code in contention were to comply with Article 8 of the European Convention on Human Rights (ECHR). With consideration of the particular facts of the case, the agency's refusal constituted, for the judges, a disproportionate infringement of Mrs. Gomez's right to private life.

In the *Gomez* decision, as in the *Blood* case, the domestic judges applied supra-national texts in order to temporarily exclude the application of domestic law. Interestingly, the domestic provisions neither lacked clarity nor ambiguity. The application of supranational norms was made out of consideration for the particular circumstances of each cases. Therefore, this seems to indicate, that the law only operates on a case-by-case basis rather than on ongoing evaluation of the conformity of

---

* Contribution originally written in French, translated to English by Megan Ma.

[1] CE, 31 May 2016, n°396848, au Lebon; *RTD civ.* 2016.600, obs. Jean Hauser; ibid., 578, note Pascale Deumier; *AJDA* 2016.1092; ibid., 1398, chron. Louis Dutheillet de Lamothe and Guillaume Odinet; D.2016.1470, obs. Marie-Christine de Montecler; ibid., 1472, note Henri Fulchiron; ibid., 1477, note Bernard Haftel; *AJ fam.* 2016.439, obs. Caroline Siffrein-Blanc; ibid., 360, obs. Amélie Dionisi-Peyrusse; *RFDA* 2016.740, concl. Aurélie Bretonneau; ibid., 754, note Pierre Delvolvé ; *Gaz. Pal.* 2016, n°24, note Mustapha Afroukh, n°27, p. 16, note Patrice Le Maigat et n°28, p. 29, note Mattias Guyomar; *JCP* 2016.864, note Jean-Philippe Vauthier et François Vialla; *Dr. Adm.* 2016. Repère 7, obs. Jean-Henri Stahl; *Dr. Fam.* Sept. 2016. Etude 15, Jean-René Binet et Comm. 178, note Richard Vessaud.

[2] Public Health Code (CSP) article L.2141-2: 'The objective of medically assisted procreation is to remedy infertility or to avoid the transmission to the child or a member of the couple a disease of particular gravity. The pathological character of infertility must be medically diagnosed. The husband and wife forming the couple must be alive … insemination or the transfer of embryos from a deceased member of the couple is prohibited.'

a law to a superior norm.[3] Moreover, this reasoning appears without much consideration of its potential legal consequences. Thus, (1) in mobilising a supranational norm as an argument of equity, the (2) judges did not dwell on the legal consequences of their subjective case-based analysis.

1. SUPRANATIONAL NORMS AS AN ARGUMENT OF EQUITY

In discussion of the *Gomez* case, it was suggested that the Conseil d'Etat acted like the good judge Magnaud, for whom 'the judge can and should interpret with humanity the inflexible prescriptions of the law'.[4] The commonality between the two cases resides in the judges' desire to grant relief to an individual situation, perceived as particularly unjust. Moreover, reason is opposed to the otherwise applicable legal prescriptions through the mobilization of a supranational norm: European law in the *Blood* case, ECHR for Mrs. Gomez. The specific circumvention of domestic law (A) will lead us towards a broader critique on the recourse to supranational norms (B).

A. Circumventing National Requirements

In *Blood* as in *Gomez*, the dispute concerned the feasibility of transferring sperm samples abroad for *post mortem* insemination. However, the basis of the two claims were notably different. The HFE Act 1990, applicable to Mrs. Blood's case, did not prohibit *post mortem* insemination, but imposes the donor's written consent, which was missing. The only evidence of a consent available was Mrs. Blood's statement that her husband had explicitly expressed his hopes of resorting, if necessary, to *post mortem* insemination in order to have a child together. It was understood that they were trying to have a child at the time of his death and that under their religious views, marriage involved procreation.[5] Nonetheless, this evidence did not satisfy the legal requirements for consent. The judicially created right of gametes' transfer, on the grounds of free provision of services, therefore squarely circumvented this requirement.

On the contrary, in *Gomez*, consent was not the issue. The spouse had personally and formally consented to the sperm retrieval. Rather, it was the prohibition against *post*

---

[3] On this point, see François Chénedé, 'Contre-révolution tranquille à la Cour de cassation?' (2016) *D* 796.

[4] Delvolvé (n 1).

[5] Katrina Bills, 'The Ethics and Legality of Posthumous Conception' (2005) 9 *S. Cross U. L. Rev.* 1–18; Carson Strong, 'Gamete Retrieval after Death or Irreversible Unconsciousness: What counts as Informed Consent?' (2006) 15(2) *Camb. Q. Healthc. Ethics* 161–71; Derek Morgan and Robert G. Lee, 'In the Name of the Father? Ex parte Blood: Dealing with Novelty and Anomaly' (1997) 60 *Modern Law Review* 840; Tamara K. Hervey, 'Buy Baby: The European Union and Regulation of Human Reproduction' (1998) 18 *Oxford Journal of Legal Studies* 207; Jacqueline Flauss-Diem, 'Insémination post mortem: droit anglais et droit communautaire' in *Liber Amicorum M.-T. Meulders-Klein* (Brussels, Bruylant 1998) 217.

mortem insemination that the widow had attempted to get around by invoking her right to private life.[6]

Interestingly, the choice to enforce international norms by each court invites a comparison. The freedom to provide services is listed under Articles 56 and 57 of the Lisbon Treaty (or Articles 49 and 50 of the Treaty on European Union).[7] In order to give effect to the free provision of services, English judges had considered that medically assisted procreation was a service,[8] to which the transfer of gametes constituted an accessory.[9] By recognising that the legal requirement of consent was not fulfilled but by insisting that the *Blood* case would not constitute a precedent to be used to override domestic regulation, the Court of Appeal tailored the law to Mrs. Blood's wishes, striking down the decision of the HFEA for not having reasoned according to the rules laid down by European law. Thereby it temporarily set aside the application of English law in light of the particularism of the case.

By contrast, the Conseil d'Etat emphasises from the outset the French ban on *post mortem* insemination and the transfer of gametes for such insemination. Nonetheless, it then stated that the French ban was 'not incompatible with the provisions of the ECHR and in particular, Article 8 … this prohibition is within the margin of appreciation given to States … and does not, in itself, disproportionately affect the right to respect for private and family life, as guaranteed by the provision of Article 8.'[10] The Conseil d'Etat then proceeded with a proportionality test[11] in order to determine whether, under the specific circumstances of the case, the French ban was or not disproportionately interfering with Mrs. Gomez's right to privacy. The Court took notice of the husband's consent for the insemination prior to his death, and observed that Mrs Gomez would ultimately relocate back to her home country where such insemination was permitted. The lower court found no fraudulent intent here and the Conseil d'Etat considered that the rejection of her claim was a disproportionate infringement of her right and ordered the gametes transfer to Spain.

---

6 As *post mortem* insemination is prohibited under French law, finding consent was not necessary. Nevertheless, the Conseil d'Etat took careful note that Mr. Gomez' intention to allow such insemination was established by the facts.

7 As stated by the terms of the articles, 'the restrictions on the freedom to provide services within the Union are prohibited with respect to nationals of Member States who are established in a Member State other than that of their own to whom the services are to be delivered, provided that they are considered as services normally provided for remuneration and are not governed by provisions on the free movement of goods, capital, and persons.'

8 The judges reference the *Grogan* decision (CJCE, 4 October 1991, C-159/90), stating that as long as a medical act is considered a service, it will be confirmed as such in subsequent decisions. See particularly, *Kohll*, CJCE, 28 April 1998, C-158/96.

9 *Schindler*, CJCE, 24 March 1994, C-275/92: Rec. CJCE, I, p. 1039.

10 Supra n 8.

11 Supra n 9.

Like *Blood*, the decision was intended as an exception and without prejudice to the state of French positive law.[12] In reality, it had opened a door to a subjective assessment and a case-by-case approach to legal restrictions. Thus, it might allow for example, a widow, who at the time of her husband's death was pregnant, had lost the child she was carrying and request the transfer of sperm samples so as to proceed with artificial insemination abroad. The administrative court in Rennes, after careful examination of the facts, decided in favor of the widow, without giving any consideration that this could nevertheless constitute a fraud under French law.[13]

Arguably here, the decisions, while seemingly grounded in the law, are in fact a poor attempt to conceal a judgment in equity.

B. Dubious Grounds

In *Blood*, the English judges sought to demonstrate that *post mortem* insemination was a service, within the realm of the free provision of services, and that the transfer of gametes a simple accessory of this service. In doing so, the court sidestepped several issues: (1) can the gametes be characterised as a good?; (2) how about the mandatory requirements of general interest in the balance?[14] The need for the donor's written consent is a clear example of such a requirement. While English laws governing medically assisted procreation are one of the most permissive,[15] the existing requirement of consent is largely shared across Europe and notably in Belgium, the importing country in the *Blood* case.[16] Therefore, beyond the critique of the case itself, the evolution of comparative law in Europe suggests reasons to challenge the judges' decision. Moreover, the 2004/23/EC Directive of the European Parliament and Council

---

[12] By a similar line of reasoning before the judge, but concerning a past situation and not future, see Civ. 1re, 4 December 2013, n° 12-26.066, Bull, I, n° 234, D. 2014. 179, obs. C. de la Cour, note François Chénedé; ibid., 153, perspective of Hughes Fulchiron; ibid., 1342, obs. Jean-Jacques Lemouland and Daniel Vigneau; *AJ fam.* 2014. 124, obs. Sylvain Thouret; ibid., 2013. 663, perspective of François Chénedé; *RTD civ.* 2014. 88, obs. Jean Hauser; ibid., 307, obs. Jean-Pierre Marguénaud; ibid. 2015. 596, note Jean Hauser; *Dr. fam.* 2014. 1, note Jean-René Binet; *JCP* 2014.I.93, note Marie Lamarche et 2016, suppl. 1-2, January 2016, note Denys de Béchillon; similarly in, Civ. 1re, 10 June 2015, n° 14-20.790, unpublished to Bull., *D.* 2015. 2365, note Hughes Fulchiron; ibid., 2016. 857, obs. Frédérique Granet-Lambrechts; *RTD civ.* 2015. 596, obs. Jean Hauser; ibid., 825, obs. Jean-Pierre Marguénaud.

[13] Jean-René Binet, 'Insémination post mortem: d'une injustice à l'autre' (2016) 12 *Dr. fam.* comm. 267; on the fraud of the law, see David Sindres, 'Le tourisme procréatif et le droit international privé' (2015) 2 *Journal de droit international (Clunet)* doctr. 4.

[14] Jean-Sylvestre Bergé, 'Le droit communautaire dévoyé – Le cas Blood' (2000) 7 *JCP G* doct. 206; 'Tourisme procreative et droit communautaire européen des échanges: le cas Blood' in M.T. Meulders-Klein et al. (eds), *The Family and Human Rights* (Alphen aan den Rijn, Kluwer Law International 2002) 599–605.

[15] Margaret Brazier, 'Regulating the Reproduction Business?' (1999) *Medical Law Review* 1663.

[16] The requirement of consent relative to sperm retrieval follows the principle on the inviolability of human persons ('*noli me tangere*'), that is to say the fundamental right to have one's bodily integrity preserved. Consent is therefore an expression of an individual's will, respected as a subject and not an object.

of 31 March 2004 establishing quality and safety standards for donation, procurement, control, processing, preservation, storage and distribution of human tissues and cells, provides under Article 13(1) that 'the procurement of human tissues or cells shall be authorized only after all mandatory consent or authorization requirements in force in the Member State concerned have been met.'

Could the *Blood* case have been decided in the same way under Article 8 of the ECHR? Since the Human Rights Act was not in force until 1998,[17] Mrs. Blood could not rely on this argument to obtain the transfer of her deceased husband's sperm samples. It was, however, unlikely that the right to privacy could be used to circumvent donor's consent in the case of medically assisted procreation. Consent for the use of gametes for procreation, not to be confused with consent for the collection of gametes,[18] has since been protected by the European Court of Human Rights (ECtHR) under the 'right to respect the decision to become or not become parents.'[19]

As seen above, the issue of consent was not problematic in *Gomez*. But here, the application of Article 8 of the ECHR raises different concerns regarding both method and substance. With regard to the method, the Conseil d'Etat deviates from the proportionality test in order to make a decision that runs *contra legem*: it acknowledges the legislative ban, but then considers its application disproportionate in this specific incidence.[20] The hierarchy of interests as orchestrated by the law was therefore freely rearranged by the court, who considered here that there was excessive interference with the disadvantaged interest. One might argue that it arrogates prescriptive power,[21] introducing a case-law approach, while renouncing its traditional function of unifying the law. In other words, if 'the law is the same for all, proportionality is specific to each case.'[22] This allows the Conseil d'Etat to implicitly apply *in fine* provisions of foreign law, under the rules of private international law.[23]

On the merits, the mere possibility of invoking Article 8 ECHR has been questioned. The ECtHR retains a broad interpretation of 'private life', but is careful in determining such issues as the right to become genetic parents. The Court equally defines its limits by specifying for example that 'by guaranteeing the right to respect for family life,

[17] Diane Blood, 'Human Rights: A Personal Comment' (2002) 7 *Jud. Rev.* 146–47.

[18] The consent given by a person in his lifetime to the retrieval of his gametes for preservation does not automatically make way for his consent on the use of these gametes for procreation after his death.

[19] Consider the *Evans* case: both retrieval and *in vitro* fertilization were authorised by the couple for the birth of their child, despite the wife's sterility following her surgical treatment for cancer. The couple had since separated and the husband withdrew his consent, preventing the wife from following through with the process. The ECtHR considered that the 'right to respect the decision to become or not become parents' covered by the right to respect for private life imposed respecting the will of the man not have a child with his former companion. *Evans v. United Kingdom* App. n° 6339/05 (ECHR, Grand Chamber, 10 April 2007), (2007) *D* 1202, obs. Christelle Delaporte-Carré; ibid., 2008. 1435, obs. Jean-Christophe Galloux et Hélène Gaumont-Prat; *RDSS* 2007. 810, note Diane Roman; *RTD civ.* 2007. 295, obs. Jean-Pierre Marguénaud; ibid., 545, obs. Jean Hauser.

[20] Delvolvé (n 1); Chénedé (n 3).

[21] Chénedé (n 3); Delvolvé (n 1).

[22] Chénedé (n 3).

[23] Delvolvé (n 1).

Article 8 presupposes the existence of a family.'[24] This means that a desire for a family, as opposed to the existence of one, is not protected by the Convention.[25] However, despite its savvy arguments, the Conseil d'Etat did not clarify which aspects of the right to privacy were applicable to the young widow, given that she did not suffer from infertility.

Could the Conseil d'Etat had reasoned on other grounds than the ECHR, such as European Union law and its right to free movement? Subject to the criticism addressed to the decision in *Blood*, such reasoning would have indubitably been possible.[26] It would have had the merit of being (1) within the legitimate remit of judicial power; (2) characterised as the provision of services (here, for medically assisted procreation in the transfer of gametes); and (3) applicable to many analogous situations. On the other hand, recourse to this solution should be left to other test cases, such as the transfer of gametes or embryos for surrogacy in a permissive country within the European Union (such as Greece, the United Kingdom or Portugal), without modification to legitimate modes of judicial reasoning – here, a case-based approach.

2. THE UNCERTAIN IMPLICATIONS OF CASE-BASED REASONING

While the *Blood* and *Gomez* decisions are considered exceptions, the use of supranational norms as standards of fairness have raised strong criticism on the 'deviation' of supranational norms for individualistic ends. Thus, in *Blood* as in *Gomez*, 'a personal case subtracts from the law, an individual claim prevails over the general will, the subjective right of one outweighs the objective right of all',[27] creating uncertainty as to the subsequent implications of this casuistic approach. Reasoning by reference to French law, the circumvention of the rules relevant to *post mortem* insemination are based on (A) the establishment of parentage; and (B) the possible transposition of the resulting legal regime to surrogacy.

---

24 *Marckx v. Belgique*, n°6833/74 (ECHR, 13 June 1979).

25 *Paradiso and Campanelli v. Italy*, n°25358/12, (ECHR, 24 January 2017) where the Grand Chamber recalls that the Convention 'does not accommodate any right to become a parent and that the general interest outweighs the desire for parenthood'; Hughes Fulchiron, 'Contrôle de proportionnalité ou décision en équité' (2016) *D.*1472.

26 However, according to the Minister of Health, 'on the basis of Article 4 of Directive 2004/23/EC and to ensure a high degree of protection of public health, only germinal tissues of gametes can be imported or exported at the quality and safety standards obtained in accordance with the principles under Articles 16 to 16-8 of the Civil Code (voluntary and unpaid donations, anonymity of the recipient and donor) and the principles of the Public Health Code relevant to medically assisted procreation.' Report of the President of the Republic relative to the ordonnance no. 2008-480 of 22 May 2008 on gamete donation and medically assisted procreation through Directive 2004/23/CE of the European Parliament and Council of 31 March 2004, JO 23 May 2008, texte n°30.

27 Delvolvé (n 1).

A. The Consequences of Reasoning on Parentage

In Belgium, Mrs. Blood had given birth to two children, but only her own status as parent was known, the deceased father being indicated as 'unknown'. Mrs. Blood returned to courts and in 2003 obtained no less than a modification of English substantive law relating to the recognition of *post mortem* parentage. By contrast to the thus obtained change in the United Kingdom, French law remains unclear.

To begin with, since the ban on *post mortem* insemination remains a matter of public policy, it could equally justify the refusal to establish parentage with regard to the father.[28] Indeed, if conception is inseparable from parentage – a position that was retained by the Cour de Cassation notably on surrogacy[29] – then a *post mortem* insemination should equally exclude establishing the father's parentality in respect of the child. On this point, the ECtHR clarified that Article 8 'implies that everyone has the power to determine the substance of his or her identity, including his or her parentage', meaning that the child born out of surrogacy must necessarily be granted the right to establish his or her parentage with respect to his or her biological parents.[30] Applied to *post mortem* insemination, the decision should thereby lead to the recognition of the parental status of the deceased father.

It remains that French law neither determines a particular form of establishing parentage for children born out of *post mortem* insemination, nor does it expressly prohibit it. However the rules under Section 310-1 of the Civil Code on establishing parentage do not necessarily allow for such a recognition. Since the child was conceived after the father's death, the husband's presumption of paternity would not be applicable. This presumption is indeed rejected for children born 300 days after the end of the marriage (in this case, through death). Raising a claim on the grounds of effective possession of status, as defined in Articles 311-1 and following of the Civil Code, is a possibility if the father dies when the mother is already pregnant. Fatherhood's possession of status usually requires the proof of facts such as announcements or statements made to relatives, preparations for the birth of the child, presence at prenatal examinations, etc. However, such facts are difficult to establish within the framework of *post mortem* insemination.[31] Moreover, Article 316 of the Civil Code on prenatal recognition requires that the father present documents relating to the 'date and place of birth, the sex and first names of the child, or any information relevant to the birth.'[32] But pregnancy following *post mortem* artificial insemination cannot satisfy these conditions. Therefore, the establishment of parentage would probably be granted by courts. The mother, on behalf of her child, would need to file a claim for the establishment of paternity on the basis of Article 327 of the Civil Code. The evidence

---

[28] Sindres (n 13).

[29] Ibid.

[30] *Labassée v. France*, n°65941/11 (ECHR, 26 June 2014) pt 78; *Mennesson v. France*, n°65192/11 (ECHR, 26 June 2014), pt 99; *Mandet v. France*, n°30955/12 (ECHR, 14 January 2016).

[31] Though perhaps not impossible if the father had explicitly consented to insemination and was actively involved in the birth project prior to his death.

[32] Article 62 of the Civil Code.

could then take any form,[33] given however that the use of *post mortem* genetic material as evidence remains prohibited in France (except in cases of express agreement of the person in his lifetime).[34]

Once parentage is established, the question of succession arises. Article 725 of the Civil Code requires that in order to be eligible for inheritance, a person must be living at the time of the succession, or at least already conceived and born viable. There is also a buffer period of ten years, suspended during the youth of the potential heir. Should the heir be a child born from *post mortem* insemination, two situations must be distinguished. If *in vitro* fertilisation occurred around the time of the death of the father, it would be possible to say that the child was 'conceived' at the time the succession was opened, but that the pregnancy itself was delayed.[35] But should only a sperm sample have been taken at the time of death, fertilisation and the conception of the child would necessarily occur after death.

In both cases, however, if the father is French, French nationality would be conferred to the child. In accordance with Article 18 of the Civil Code, 'the child is French if one of the parents is French.' This suggests that the child's French nationality has European citizenship since the European Court of Justice (ECJ) states 'Article 20 of the TFEU confers that every person holding the nationality of a Member State shall be a citizen of the Union.'[36] The child's citizenship will allow the mother, should she be a national of a third country, a right to stay as asserted by the ECJ.[37]

B. Analogising the Line of Reasoning to Surrogacy

The question of establishing parentality for fathers of children born out of *post mortem* insemination is not purely symbolic, as we have just seen. More importantly, applying the reasoning used in *post mortem* insemination cases may open a new line of argumentation on the French ban on surrogacy. Indeed, just as Article L.2141-2 of the Public Health Code prevents insemination or the transfer of embryos of the deceased to one of the members of the couple, Article 16-7 of the Civil Code states that 'any contract relevant to procreation or the management of it on behalf of others is void.' These two texts taken together reinforce the firm prohibition against medically assisted

---

[33] The traceability of the samples may allow the mother to establish the identity of the parent.

[34] Article 16-11 of the Civil Code. The ECtHR has condemned France for this article, stating that it is in violation of Article 8 of the ECHR, *Pascaud v. France*, n° 19535/08 (ECHR 16 June 2011). However, the conseil constitutionnel considered the text in accordance with the principle on the right to privacy protected by the Constitution. Décision n° 2011-173 QPC du 30 September 2011.

[35] The sample can be retrieved within 36 hours after death. Eric Favereau, 'Prélever el sperme d'un mort' *Libération* (Paris, 28 April 2014).

[36] *Lassal*, aff. C-162/09, (ECJ, 7 October 2010).

[37] See in particular *Zambrano* aff. C-34/09, (ECJ, Grand Chamber, 8 March 2011); *Rendon Marin c/ Administracion del Estado* aff. C-165/14, (ECJ, Grand Chamber, 13 September 2016); *Secretary of State for the Home Department c/ CS*, aff. C-304/14, (ECJ, Grand Chamber, 13 September 2016).

procreation. One might say that like the ban on surrogacy, the prohibition of *post mortem* insemination is not inconsistent with Article 8 of the ECHR.[38]

Following the reasoning of the Conseil d'Etat in *Gomez*, it is clear that it is up to the judges to ascertain whether the specific facts of the case would make the ban on surrogacy interfere disproportionately with the right to privacy; there is no incompatibility *per se*. Imagine then facts parallel to those of *Gomez*, or in the decision by the administrative judges in Rennes (cited above), where a heterosexual couple proceeded to conserve the wife's oocytes or embryos so that the husband, possibly of Greek nationality, could carry forth the parental project following the death of his wife; or the same husband might perhaps wish to use *in vitro* fertilisation following the brutal death of his wife in the course of her pregnancy. Tragic circumstances, similar to the cases studied, raise the question of whether a man would be allowed to obtain the transfer of the embryos or oocytes to a foreign country in order to pursue the parental project with the help of surrogacy.

Ultimately, the cases of *Blood* and *Gomez* carry an interesting message: 'Insemination post mortem is prohibited … unless the judge decides exceptionally in your favour.' This outcome does not serve the interests of equality, predictability or legibility of the law.

25.3 WHEN LAW FALLS BEHIND THE SCIENTIFIC DEVELOPMENT: RETHINKING THE MEANING OF CONSENT AND PARENTHOOD

Michael Wells-Greco

Law and society have always attached a distinct significance to a person's status, and 'parentage' confers status on both the adult(s) and on the child. Every legal system assigns parents to children because each legal system attaches legal consequences to the status of being a parent or child of a certain person. These legal consequences are very diverse. For example, in nationality law, the child may obtain the nationality of his or her parents; in terms of private law, children may be entitled to inherit from their parents or have access to social benefits. In each of these cases, it must be determined who is (are) the legal parent(s) of the child.

The last 40 years[39] have seen the creation, and the subsequent ready availability in some States, of human reproductive technology. This evolution in family forms and in science has given rise to a number of legal developments across States, including the law on parentage. However, difficulties have arisen because these developments have not been globally uniform. States' approaches to issues such as paternity (dis)establishment (in light of DNA testing), human reproductive technology, and same-sex families

[38] ECHR, 26 June 2014 (n 30); 24 January 2017, *Paradiso et Campanelli v. Italy* (n 25).

[39] The first birth of a child conceived by IVF and embryo transfer occurred on 25 July 1978 in the United Kingdom. The first reported gestational surrogacy in the world occurred in 1984 (Wulf Utian et al, 'Successful Pregnancy After an In-vitro Fertilization-Embryo Transfer from an Infertile Woman to a Surrogate' (1985) 313 *NEMJ* 1351).

and parenting and, the focus of this discussion, posthumous conception,[40] have varied greatly, depending on the State's cultural, political and social environment. Technological advances have altered the balance of individual and social interests in deciding the use of a dead person's gametes[41] and the legal consequences of that use for any child who is born. As a result, there is, as yet, no international consensus how to establish and contest legal parentage in these circumstances.[42]

These scientific developments coupled with the possibility of reproductive travel[43] have brought with them not only fraught ethical[44] dilemmas but also challenging legal questions. Should a sperm or egg donor be a legal parent? How does the law regard a mother who gives birth to a child who is genetically unrelated to her? And, of relevance here, can gametes be used after death? And, if so, what impact, if any, is there on the law of parentage? What rights do posthumously conceived children have – or should they have? How can their interests be protected? Questions about the scope of reproductive freedom, the limits of consent, and the value of genetic material as property are all relevant.

The landmark case of *R v. Human Fertilisation and Embryology Authority, ex parte Blood*[45] required the English Courts to give such consideration to the posthumous use of sperm and Diane Blood helped to effect a change in the law to allow posthumous fathers to be listed on birth certificates when the consent to the use of the sperm for the purposes of conception is effective. The subsequent case law in England (and

---

[40] Reports suggest that the first posthumous conception occurred in 1977, the first posthumous sperm retrieval was in 1980, and the first child born after posthumous sperm retrieval was in *R v. Human Fertilisation and Embryology Authority, ex parte Blood* [1997] 2 All ER 687. Egg retrieval and preservation is even more recent. See Maya Sabatello, 'Posthumously Conceived Children: An International and Human Rights Perspective' (2014) 27 *J. L. & Health* 29.

[41] Gametes (sperm, eggs and embryos) and reproductive tissues are special, inasmuch as they can lead to conception – in other words, to the creation of an individual whose genetic complement is partially derived from the gamete donor. This genetic connection between individuals is of potential medical, emotional and legal significance.

[42] Given these national differences, the Permanent Bureau of the Hague Conference on Private International Law has been working specifically on the private international law issues surrounding the status of children, including issues arising from ISAs (the Parentage/Surrogacy Project) since 2010. The Parentage/Surrogacy Project focuses on the issue of cross-border recognition of parent-child relationship statuses, including ISAs.

[43] Guido Pennings, 'Legal Harmonization and Reproductive Tourism in Europe' (2004) 19(12) *Human Reproduction* 2689–94.

[44] For a global discussion of the challenges, see Pamela Ferguson and Graeme Laurie, *Inspiring a Medico-Legal Revolution: Essays in Honour of Sheila McLean* (Abingdon, Routledge 2015).

[45] [1997] 2 All ER 687. The question before the court was not whether the removal of gametes had been lawful but whether the decision taken by the Human Fertilisation and Embryology Authority to refuse to make a Direction permitting export to Belgium was a lawful one. The Court of Appeal was principally required to consider the guarantees concerning free movement within the then European Community for the provision of medical services.

elsewhere)[46] demonstrates that the Court of Appeal was overoptimistic in 1997 when it observed that *ex parte Blood* raised issues 'which should never arise again'.[47]

My concern here is not to examine the points of law which were directly at stake in the case, but to identify some wider themes which have relevance beyond the case itself and examine them from a predominantly (though not exclusively) legal perspective. In particular, the discussion considers: (1) the importance of gamete donors and gamete recipients alike consenting to fertility treatment involving them or their bodily material and the potential (future) challenges and (2) the implications of posthumous conception and public policy considerations.

1. POSTHUMOUS CONCEPTION AND LEGAL PARENTHOOD

States' approaches to the establishment and contestation of legal parentage, particularly in the context of children born by means of assisted reproductive technology ('ART'), vary significantly.[48] Posthumous conception is permitted in, for example, the UK, the Netherlands and Greece, and subject to specific conditions; soon to be permitted in Ireland,[49] but prohibited in, for example, Switzerland and Italy.

In those States which permit posthumous conception, consideration has had to be given to the legal framework for such conception and the impact on birth registration and the law of parentage.[50] However, where children are connected with more than one State or move cross-border, the application of different rules on jurisdiction, applicable law and the international circulation of foreign public documents (i.e., birth certificates,

---

46 The *ex parte Blood* decision has also had an impact beyond the UK. For example, in France (see CE, 31 May 2016, n°396848), in Australia (see *RE H, AE (No 3)* [2013] SASC 196), in Japan (see Takamatsu High Court, Judgment of 16 July 2004 1748), in the USA (see *Re Martin B.*, 841 N.Y.S.2d 207 (Sur. Ct. 2007)).

47 [1999] Fam. 151, 178; *Evans v. Amicus Healthcare Ltd and others* [2004] 3 All ER 1025; *L v. Human Fertilisation and Embryology Authority & Secretary of State for Health* [2008] EWHC 2149.

48 As concluded by the research undertaken by the Permanent Bureau. See also Michael Wells-Greco, *The status of children arising from inter-country surrogacy arrangements* (The Hague, Eleven Publishing 2015); Paul Beaumont and Katarina Trimmings, 'Recent jurisprudence of the European Court of Human Rights in the area of cross-border surrogacy: is there still a need for global regulation of surrogacy?', Working Paper No 2015/2.

49 If the Assisted Human Reproduction Bill 2017 is passed. The law will also permit gametes and embryos to be used for posthumous fertility treatment by the patient's surviving partner, if the applicable consents are in place. See <http://health.gov.ie/blog/publications/general-scheme-of-the-assisted-human-reproduction-bill-2017/>.

50 It does suggest some sort of continuation of the traditional family structure of a husband and wife, unmarried heterosexual couples, and potentially more recently a same-sex couple, even if one party to the relationship is no longer alive. While national law commonly treats children born within a certain accepted time period after the father's death (generally, around 300 days from the father's death) as any other child who is born into the relationship, posthumous conception can extend the timeframe for a longer period, and potentially, indefinitely. See Kees Saarloos, '*European private international law on legal parenting? Thoughts on a European instrument implementing the principle of mutual recognition in legal parenting* (Dissertation, Maastricht University 2010).

civil status documents) and judicial decisions (i.e., rules on recognition) has led to situations of uncertain and 'limping' legal parentage.

In the UK, the legal framework of posthumous conception has resulted in the following positions. If a woman's stored eggs or embryos are used to conceive a child (for example through surrogacy)[51] after she has died, she is not treated as the legal mother.[52] In line with the general law on parenthood, the woman who carries the child is treated as the mother. If a man's sperm or embryos created by his sperm are used to conceive a child after he has died, the position is a little more complex. In the UK, the Human Fertilisation and Embryology Act of 2008 ('the 2008 Act', which amended the 1990 Act[53]) allows for posthumous conception when the deceased provided sperm and consented in writing (and, importantly, he did not withdraw the consent)[54] for the use of his sperm by a specific woman after his death, and for his being named as the father on the birth certificate of any resulting child.[55]

When the laws on parenthood were first passed in 1990, however, they made clear that any man who conceived posthumously would not be treated as the legal father. The reason for this was to prevent practical difficulties; for example, a man's estate could not be wound up if there remained a possibility that he could conceive a child in the future who might have a claim to a share of the estate. In 2003, it was recognised that men should be treated in law as the father of a child where the child has resulted from certain fertility treatment undertaken after the man's death.[56] The law was amended to allow a father conceiving posthumously to be named on his child's birth certificate. The 2008 Act introduced[57] parallel provisions for same-sex partners where a surviving partner conceives after her partner's death (after 6 April 2009).[58]

---

51 See Michael Wells-Greco, 'Inter-Country surrogacy and public policy: Lessons from the European Court of Human Rights' (2014/2015) 16 *Yearbook on Private International Law*; Wells-Greco (n 48).

52 Section 47 HFEA 2008.

53 For a history of the development of the UK's legislation, see Julie McCandless and Sally Sheldon, 'The Human Fertilisation and Embryology Act (2008) and the tenacity of the sexual family form' (2010) 73(2) *Mod. Law Rev* 175–207.

54 The HFEA's General Code of Practice is available at https://www.hfea.gov.uk/code-of-practice/5.

55 Section 39(1) and (3) HFEA 2008.

56 Human Fertilisation and Embryology (Deceased Fathers) Act 2003.

57 A number of further changes of interest are not discussed here. Notably, the new law also includes an extension of the rights of children conceived via gamete donation to information regarding the circumstances of their conception. See Christine Jones, 'The Identification of "Parents" and "Siblings": New Possibilities Under the Reformed Human Fertilisation and Embryology Act' in Julie Wallbank, Shazia Choudhry and Jonathan Herring (eds), *Rights, Gender and Family Law* (London, Routledge Cavendish 2009) ch 10.

58 A deceased non-birth mother is treated as a parent for all legal purposes where the birth mother is already pregnant when she dies. A deceased non-birth mother can be named on the birth certificate as a parent (but is not a parent for any other purpose) if an embryo was created with donor sperm before she died, and then transferred to her partner after her death (Section 46 HFEA 2008).

This has left a rather complex set of rules on legal parenthood in posthumous conception cases.[59] If a man dies when his wife or partner is pregnant, he is treated as the father for all legal purposes, including property rights and succession. This applies both where he is the genetic father and in certain circumstances where donor sperm has been used.[60] If a woman is inseminated with her husband or partner's sperm after his death, or if embryos are transferred to her after his death that are either created with his sperm or created with donor sperm before he died, he can be named on the birth certificate if his wife or partner makes a special written election within 42 days of the birth. However, he is not the legal father for any purpose other than naming him on the birth certificate.[61] If a woman is inseminated with donor sperm after her husband or partner's death, or if embryos are transferred to her that were created with donor sperm after his death, the man is not the father for any purpose and cannot be named on the birth certificate. Where a woman in a civil partnership or same-sex marriage is seeking treatment using donor sperm, or embryos created using donor sperm, the woman's civil partner or wife will be treated as the legal parent of any resulting child unless, at the time of placing the embryo or sperm and eggs in the woman, or of her insemination a judicial separation or separation order was in force, or that the civil partner or wife did not consent to the placing in her of the sperm and eggs, or embryos, or to the insemination.

If a child is conceived posthumously and legal parentage is not established[62] then the child will not have legal parent-child relationship with significant resulting legal consequences[63] for that child as well as questions relating to the social construction of kinship and status.

2. THE NEED FOR CONSENT

What is clear from the UK's legislative approach is that it is very important that *consent* to posthumous storage and use of eggs, sperm or embryos is given carefully and with sufficient detail, since the consent will be relied on after it is too late to clarify someone's intentions. The need for *consent* has been subject to judicial consideration following *ex parte Blood*.

In *L v. Human Fertilisation & Embryology Authority & Secretary of State for Health*[64] the Court of Appeal held that the UK's Human Fertilisation and Embryology Authority's ('HFEA') absolute requirement of effective consent for use of continued storage and use of sperm is compatible with the right to respect for private and family life under Article 8 of the European Convention on Human Rights (ECHR).[65]

---

[59] Section 39 HFEA 2008.

[60] See sections 39–40 HFEA 2008, respectively. Note the separate provisions here for posthumous genetic fatherhood and posthumous non-genetic fatherhood.

[61] Section 39(1)d) HFEA 2008.

[62] For example, because the UK's statutory conditions are not satisfied.

[63] For example, citizenship, inheritance rights and access to social benefits.

[64] [2008] EWHC 2149 (Fam).

[65] (1950) ETS 5. Article 8 ECHR: Right to respect for private and family life.

The claimant wished to undergo fertility treatment services using her deceased husband's sperm in order to have the chance of a full genetic sibling for her daughter. On 26 June 2007 the claimant's husband died in hospital unexpectedly after an appendectomy. Shortly after his death the claimant made an urgent out-of-hours application to retrieve and preserve his sperm, which was granted. The hospital was notified of that application, but HFEA was not. The sperm was transferred to a clinic where it continued to be stored. The claimant then sought declaratory relief so that the sperm could lawfully continue to be stored and then used either in the UK or exported for storage and use in a clinic abroad. The claimant also applied to the HFEA for permission to transfer the sperm abroad. The HFEA adjourned the application for export pending the court's ruling as to the lawfulness of the storage of the sperm.

The claimant argued, among other submissions, that the absolute requirement of effective consent under the 1990 Act was incompatible with Article 8 ECHR. The Court dismissed the claimant's application. Mr. Justice Charles commented that 'at the heart of the competition between the rights of those involved is the issue of autonomy and choice'.[66] The Court held that the absolute and bright line rules relating to effective consent for storage for use (and that subsequent use) in the UK as they relate to a dead person were within the State's margin of appreciation.[67] In relation to storage for use and such subsequent use outside the UK, the Court regarded the position as less clear, given the discretion conferred on the HFEA to authorise the import or export of gametes subject to such conditions as the HFEA thinks fit.

Mr. Justice Charles rejected the claimant's argument that the overall effect of the Court of Appeal's decision in *ex parte Blood* was that the UK legislation rendered the export of gametes without effective consent to storage impossible or impracticable. Rather, *ex parte Blood* referred to a power exercisable by the HFEA to consider and grant a special direction that permits storage and export of gametes prior to them being retrieved. Absent such a special direction, storage without consent was not permitted.

3. PERIOD OF STORAGE

The need for *consent* for the period of storage of gametes has also been subject to judicial consideration. In *Jefferies v. BMI Healthcare Ltd and another*[68] the key issue before the court was whether the deceased had validly varied his consent to storage from a period of ten years to a period of two years. The claimant, Samantha Jefferies, and her husband Clive were just about to commence their third cycle of IVF when Clive unexpectedly passed away from a subarachnoid brain haemorrhage. When Samantha and Clive first started IVF treatment, they had been asked to sign a number of consent forms by the clinic, including the HFEA's prescribed consent forms (the 'WT and MT forms'). The WT and MT forms contain provision for a person to consent to storage of embryos, or gametes, for a period of up to ten years. Samantha and Clive filled out the forms at home and agreed to store their embryos for a period of ten years.

66 At para 94.

67 Applying *Evans v. UK* App No 6339/05 (ECHR, 10 April 2007).

68 [2016] EWHC 2493 (Fam).

At the time, the clinic's policy was to offer storage for an initial period of two years, to reflect the period of NHS-funded storage. Clive's MT form was amended to say that he agreed to a two-year period, however the amendment was not signed, contrary to the statutory requirements.

Samantha wanted to be able to store the embryos for longer than two years. Clive had given written consent to the use of the embryos in Samantha's treatment after his death, so there was no issue about their posthumous use. However, the clinic was told by the HFEA that it could not store the embryos for longer than two years without a declaration from the Court that this would be lawful. Any consent to storage and any variation of that consent must be in writing and signed by the person giving it. The Court found that the form as originally signed by Clive at home, consenting to a ten-year storage period, was a valid consent for the purposes of the 1990 Act. The amendment made to the MT form had not been signed (all other amendments to the form had been initialled by Clive) meaning that there had been no valid variation to the form.

The significance of the judgment for the claimant cannot be overstated. She is now able to pursue her wish to become a mother to her husband's child. Fortunately, her case was, in the end, reasonably straightforward from a legal perspective because it was clear that the requirement for consent to be in writing and signed had not been fulfilled. However, the case exposes some uncertainties in the statutory requirements. For example, a future case may require the Court to answer the question of whether amendments to written consents must also be informed and what is meant by an informed consent in this context (that is whether a person should be offered counselling and given such information as is proper before the written consent is withdrawn or amended).

At some stage the Court will also have to consider the relationship between the consent requirements in the 2008 Act and Article 8 ECHR. There is every reason to believe that Article 8 ECHR should read down the requirements of the 2008 Act where a clinic had not given the claimant's deceased partner the opportunity to consent to the storage of his or her gametes or for the full statutory storage period.[69]

4. POSTHUMOUS CONCEPTION AND SURROGACY

As illustrated above, the most common scenario for a posthumous conception is that the partner of the deceased, generally his widow or girlfriend, seeks to use his frozen gametes herself, intending to fertilise the egg and carry the pregnancy to term. However, other scenarios[70] are arising, including surrogacy. In February 2016, Mr. and Mrs. M were granted permission to appeal the decision of Mr. Justice Ouseley in which

---

69 See *Warren v. Care Fertility (Northampton) Ltd* [2014] EWHC 602 (Fam), [2014] 2 FLR 1284 [117–126].

70 DPA, 'Israeli Woman Becomes Mother Two Years After Dying of Cancer' *Haaretz* (Israel, 14 June 2011), <http://www.haaretz.com/print-edition/news/israeli-woman-becomesmother-two-years-after-dying-of-cancer-1.367523> accessed 16 April 2018; M. Leidig, 'Russian Woman May Lose Grandson Conceived from Dead Son's Frozen Sperm' (2006) 332 *BMJ* 627.

he held that the Statutory Approvals Committee (the 'Committee') of the HFEA was entitled to decline Mr. and Mrs. M's application to export the eggs of their deceased daughter, AM, to a fertility centre in the United States of America.[71] The couple had claimed that AM had consented to the posthumous use of her eggs and anonymous sperm to allow Mrs. M to become a surrogate mother and grandmother simultaneously.

AM had been diagnosed with cancer at the age of 21 and had died six years later in 2011. Throughout the greater part of that time, she had been in hospital. In 2008, three years before her death, AM had been counselled and given relevant information before she signed a consent form, which had been provided by the Hammersmith IVF Clinic, to permit her eggs to be harvested and stored after her death.[72] However, AM was not offered the relevant form in which to state how she wanted her eggs to be used in the event of her death. Her failure to complete this form meant that her eggs could not be used posthumously by her mother to conceive a child in the UK.

One way to overcome AM's lack of written consent was for Mr. and Mrs. M to apply to the HFEA to export AM's eggs to the US, fertilise them with anonymous sperm and for any resultant embryos to be implanted in Mrs. M. When such an application is made, the HFEA via the Committee, may waive the written consent requirement. However, in doing so, it must not evade the purposes of the Act in which great importance is attached to consent. Therefore, the Committee had to consider whether there was sufficient evidence that of AM had consented to her mother acting as a surrogate after AM's death. It concluded that AM had not been given the relevant information relating to posthumous conception and that she had not made her intentions clear in any way which could be regarded as an effective consent.

Mr. and Mrs. M sought judicial review of the Committee's Decision.[73] They submitted that the Committee had disregarded the greater part of Mrs. M's evidence of AM's verbal wishes. It had also erroneously considered that AM could not have consented to Mrs. M becoming a surrogate mother and a grandmother unless she had received information about all the necessary steps for that to be achieved.

Lady Justice Arden gave the Court's unanimous decision and considered three factors to be of relevance in allowing Mr. and Mrs. M's appeal:[74] (i) the Committee had misstated that there was no evidence of AM's consent to the use of her eggs by her mother to become pregnant after AM's death; (ii) the Committee had failed to explain why AM, in order to give an effective consent, needed to have received all the information relevant to each of the steps which her mother would have to take to give birth to AM's posthumous child; and (iii) the Committee had not revealed what information the 1990 Act required AM to have been given for her consent to be effective.

Lady Justice Arden accepted that the requirement of relevant information for those seeking fertility treatment was fundamental to the policy behind the 2008 Act.[75] It not

---

71 *R (M and MM) v. HFEA* [2015] EWHC 1706.

72 See Section 12 and Schedule 3 to the HFEA 1990.

73 *R (on the application of IM and another) v. Human Fertilisation and Embryology Authority* [2016] EWCA Civ 611, [2016] All ER (D) 06.

74 Ibid., paras 63 to 84.

75 At para 2.

only ensured regulatory certainty but it also respected the autonomy of patients. However, there was no abstract concept of relevant information laid down in the Act. It merely requires 'such relevant information as is proper' to be given.[76] Such information would vary according to the circumstances of the case including the type of treatment and the nature of the person seeking it.

Following the Court of Appeal's judgment, the Committee has 'in the exceptional and unique circumstances of this case', granted Special Directions for centre 0078 (IVF Hammersmith) to export three eggs to New York.[77] Nevertheless, further interesting questions remain to be considered. Mrs. M may fail to become pregnant; only three eggs were placed in storage and Mrs. M is over the age of 60. The status of a child conceived in this way would be problematic under UK law. Mr. and Mrs. M would not be eligible, on the face of the Act, to apply for a parental order for the child under section 54 of the HFEA 2008[78] as neither of their gametes would have been used to procreate the child.[79]

The decision draws attention to the complexity and ethical implications of a posthumous surrogacy arrangement. Given the likelihood that this situation will arise again in future, the decision may lead the HFEA to overhaul its procedures and determine what information should be provided by licensed clinics in the UK for patients who require storage of their gametes. It must also stress the need for patients to clarify their wishes in writing about the future use of stored gametes.

---

[76] Schedule 3 specifies the requirements for effective consent from the provider of the gametes for the storage and subsequent use of the gametes, including, para 1, which provides: 'A consent under this Schedule must be in writing and, in this Schedule, "effective consent" means a consent under this Schedule which has not been withdrawn,' and para 3, which provides; '(1) Before a person gives consent under this Schedule— (a) he must be given a suitable opportunity to receive proper counselling about the implications of taking the proposed steps, and (b) he must be provided with such relevant information as is proper.' He must also be informed of the effect of para 4 of Sch 3, namely, informed that he can vary or withdraw his consent.

[77] See Centre 0078 (IVF Hammersmith) – application for Special Directions to export gametes to New York Fertility Services, New York, USA Friday, 5 August 2016 available at <https://ifqlive.blob.core.windows.net/inspectiondocuments/6096.pdf>. See also <http://www.telegraph.co.uk/news/2016/09/09/uk-woman-allowed-to-export-dead-daughters-eggs-to-us-for-treatme/> and <http://www.bbc.co.uk/news/health-37320466> accessed 16 April 2018.

[78] Section 54(1) provides: 'On an application made by two people ("the applicants"), the court may make an order providing for a child to be treated in law as the child of the applicants if— (a) the child has been carried by a woman who is not one of the applicants, as a result of the placing in her of an embryo or sperm and eggs or her artificial insemination, (b) the gametes of at least one of the applicants were used to bring about the creation of the embryo …'

[79] An adoption order might be a possibility although Theis J's concerns which she expressed in *B v. C (Surrogacy: Adoption)* [2015] EWFC 17, [2015] 1 FLR 1392 would have to be considered.

5. IMPLICATIONS

The issues raised in this paper touch upon difficult questions of public policy. It is an area in which there will be differences of opinion (nationally, regionally, internationally) about the proper balances to be struck, for example, between regulating the conduct of adults and their reproductive choices and ensuring protection for the rights or best interests of the born child. Nevertheless, a number of themes can be identified.

These cases illustrate the importance of gamete donors and gamete recipients alike consenting to fertility treatment involving them or their bodily material and that when the decision to freeze gametes is made, all possible uses of those gametes are considered, discussed and recorded. Sometimes these matters will need to be considered quite quickly and at times of emotional distress, but what is clear is that it is important to think through the implications to ensure that they are stored and used as the gamete provider intends. IVF providers in the UK have a duty to ensure, as far as possible, that patients (whether they may be resident) are notified of the possibilities and options available to them.

These decisions also establish that issues of consent should be looked at in context, and not just in relation to what the clinic paperwork says. Ultimately, this approach may make UK law more difficult to apply, but at the same time, it maintains the UK law's fundamental principle of consent to storage and to use of gametes: that a gamete provider has the right to decide what happens to his or her sperm or eggs. At the same time, given the significant implications for the resulting child, posthumous conception is not a mere matter of privacy but also of public interest.[80] The history of the law relating to posthumous conception and procedure in the UK appears to be steering away from best interests of the child considerations, elevating instead the interests of the prospective parent(s). For some, this approach is inconsistent application of law and policy. For others, a focus on the reproductive interests of prospective parent(s) is proportionate and legitimate. It remains to be seen – from a global perspective – whether other legal systems will adopt the same or similar standards.

[80] Including children's perspectives either through research with posthumously conceived children themselves if they are already sufficiently old is essential. I endorse Maya Sabatello's conclusion for the need for further research, supra n 40 [66].

26. Cultural identities: *Wagner v. Luxembourg*

26.1 CASE BACKGROUND

The *Wagner* case stemmed from the non-recognition by Luxembourg of the adoption, in Peru, of a Peruvian child by a Luxembourg national. In November 1996, the Family Court of the province of Huamanga had pronounced the adoption in accordance with the legal conditions for full adoption in Peru, so that the child lost her family ties with her original family and acquired the status of daughter of the adopting parent, Ms. Wagner. Once in Luxembourg, Ms. Wagner, relying on the pre-existent judicial practice, expected the foreign adoption to be registered. However, that practice had been abolished and Ms. Wagner had to make an application before the District Court in order to obtain the enforcement (*exequatur*) of the foreign judgment. The enforcement would allow the child to acquire Luxembourgish nationality, and thereby European Union citizenship, and be granted definitive permission to remain in the country.

In 1998, the Court dismissed the application for enforcement, based on the Luxembourg rules on the conflict of laws, which provide that the conditions for adoption are governed by the national law of the adoptive parent. According to Luxembourg's Civil Code, an application for full adoption could only be made by a married couple. Ms. Wagner contested that the Court was dealing with an application for enforcement and not an application to adopt; and that the real issue consisted in the rights of the child adopted following the Peruvian judgment. However, the District Court held that it was for the legislator to assess the interests of children and that the Peruvian adoption had been delivered contrary to the Luxembourg law. The foreign judgment, therefore, could not be enforced. The case went to the Court of Appeal, which, however, confirmed the decision of the District Court, without examining the complaint that the lower Court should have examined the case under Article 8 of the European Convention on Human Rights (the Convention). By 2001, the Court of Cassation had also dismissed the appeal, stating that the Court of Appeal made a correct application of the law.

On the basis of Articles 6, 8 and 14 of the Convention, Ms. Wagner and the child made an application to the European Court of Human Rights. The complaint consisted in the breach of their right to a fair trial, to respect for their family life and of discriminatory treatment, owing to the non-recognition in Luxembourg of the Peruvian judgement. The Court found that the Luxembourg courts had violated Article 6 by not examining the complaint raised under Article 8, directly applicable in Luxembourg. Regarding Article 8, the Court recognised that the Contracting States enjoy a wide margin of appreciation on the matter and that it was not the Court's task to determine the most appropriate policy for regulating the adoption of the children. In the case at hand, the Court limited itself to review, under the Convention, the decisions that Luxembourg authorities have taken in the exercise of their power of appreciation. In this sense, the Court considered, mindful of the paramountcy of the best interests of the child, that Luxembourg's decision refusing enforcement failed to take account of the social reality of the situation. The Court held that the child was deprived of legal protection, leading to obstacles for her integration into the adoptive family. This interference was not 'necessary' in the sense of Article 8, paragraph 2. The Court concluded that Luxembourg courts could not refuse to recognise the family ties that pre-existed *de facto* between Ms. Wagner and the adopted child. Moreover, in the light of Article 14, the refusal was also disproportionate, and an unjustified discrimination both in respect of the child (compared with other adopted children in Luxembourg), and of the adoptive mother. The

Court found, therefore, that, in addition to the violation of Article 6, there has been a violation of Article 8, and Article 8 read together with Article 14, of the Convention.

Main Cases: *Wagner and J.M.W.L v. Luxembourg*, Application no 76240/01, Council of Europe: European Court of Human Rights, 28 June 2007

26.2 ENSURING CONTINUITY OF PERSONAL STATUS AND FAMILY RELATIONS ACROSS BORDERS: THE INTERACTION BETWEEN PRIVATE INTERNATIONAL LAW AND HUMAN RIGHTS

Hans van Loon

1. PRIVATE INTERNATIONAL LAW, THE RIGHT TO FREEDOM OF MOVEMENT, AND THE PROTECTION OF PRIVATE AND FAMILY LIFE

Wagner was, and remains, a wake-up call for private international law (PIL) concerning personal status and family relations, much as *Marckx* was 40 years ago for domestic family law.[1] Like *Marckx* regarding internal law, *Wagner* is a reminder that PIL, in the daily practice of courts and administrations, operates not in isolation but in a broader context of law, including human rights law – in Europe above all the European Convention on Human Rights (ECHR).

Previously, the Court of Justice of the European Union (CJEU) had already ruled that national PIL rules on family names are subject to the principle of freedom of movement of persons (article 21(1) TFEU).[2] But the CJEU's jurisprudence has a crucial limitation: the right to freedom of movement applies to EU citizens only, the attribution, denial or revocation of citizenship remaining essentially within the reserved domain of EU Member States.[3] Yet, many grievances of *non*-EU nationals, based on human rights principles, are precisely related to this right to freedom of movement. Indeed, a major complaint in *Wagner* concerning the refusal of exequatur was that it deprived the Peruvian child of the advantages of Luxembourg and thereby EU citizenship, including the right to free movement (paragraph 156). The limitation of the right of free movement to EU nationals limits the potential of the CJEU's jurisprudence

1 *Marckx v. Belgium* App no 688/74 (ECtHR, 13 June 1979).

2 Case C-148/02, *Garcia Avello* (CJEU 2 October 2003); followed by Cases C-353/06, *Grunkin Paul* (CJEU 14 October 2008), and C-208/09 *Sayn-Wittgenstein* (CJEU 22 December 2010). Cf. also, in respect of the freedom of establishment of companies, Case C-208/00, *Überseering* (CJEU 5 November 2002).

3 See further infra, s 4.

based on article 21 (1) TFEU[4] to liberalise PIL more generally, i.e. with equal extension to nationals of third countries.

By contrast, PIL and international human rights law meet at a deeper level. The ECHR is a first step for 'the collective enforcement of certain of the rights stated in the Universal Declaration' of Human Rights (UDHR),[5] which according to its Preamble is based on the 'recognition [that] the inherent dignity and the equal and inalienable rights of all members of the human family is the foundation of freedom, justice and peace in the world'. Following the enumeration of rights, article 28 UDHR declares: 'Everyone is entitled to a social and international order in which the rights and freedoms set forth in this Declaration can be fully realized'. Obviously, this provision does not establish a justiciable and enforceable right for individuals.[6] But applied to our contemporary world, in which large numbers of people face multiple and complex cross-border legal issues, including in their personal and family lives, it implies a duty for States to work towards a global legal architecture in which people should be able to navigate through the diversity of legal orders and systems without being unduly frustrated in the exercise of their fundamental rights – thus avoiding situations such as in *Wagner*. In the fulfilment of this best efforts obligation, both human rights law and PIL – together with related fields of law, in particular migration, refugee, and nationality law – have their role to play.

The beginnings of an awareness of this necessary interaction between human rights law and PIL, and indeed migration law, are visible in recent global instruments. While the drafters of the UDHR and the ECHR did not yet give particular attention to human rights in cross-border circumstances, the 1989 UN Convention on the Rights of the Child (UNCRC) – referred to in *Wagner* paragraph 120 – explicitly identifies various transnational situations carrying enhanced risks for children. In several of its provisions the UNCRC calls on States to cooperate to resolve the resulting legal issues, including by acceding to other existing international instruments or by concluding new ones.[7] In response to this call, several Hague multilateral treaties on PIL – the 1980 Child Abduction Convention, 1993 Adoption Convention, 1996 Child Protection Convention

---

4 On the possible extension of the CJEU's case law to other aspects of personal status, and to elements of personal status constituted in third States, see P. Lagarde, 'La reconnaissance mode d'emploi', in *Vers de nouveaux équilibres entre ordres juridiques Liber Amicorum H. Gaudemet-Tallon* (Paris, Dalloz 2008) 481–501, 488–90. Thus far, however, such extensions have not manifested itself in the Court's case law on art 21 (1) TFEU. In case C-673/16, *Coman*, (CJEU, Grand Chamber, 5 June 2018), the CJEU ruled that this provision precludes a Member State to recognise 'for the sole purpose of granting a derived right of residence to a third-country national' the marriage of that national to a Union citizen of the same sex lawfully concluded in another Member State. This judgment could be a first step towards recognition of other effects of such marriages, e.g. in the field of social security and, indeed, under civil law.

5 Cf., e.g., *Soering v. UK* App 14038/88 (ECtHR, 7 July 1989), para 87, in which the Court stressed this 'special character [of the ECHR] as a treaty for the collective enforcement of human rights and fundamental freedoms' in support of its judgment enlarging the scope of Contracting States' responsibility for breaches of the Convention in relation to its dealings with third States.

6 Cf. A. Eide et al. (eds.), *The Universal Declaration of Human Rights: A Commentary* (Oslo, Aschehoug 1992) 433.

7 See, e.g., arts 11 (2), 21 (e), and 27 (4).

and 2007 Child and Family Support Convention and its Protocol on applicable law – support the objectives of the UNCRC.

At the time of the relevant facts in *Wagner*, the 1993 Hague Adoption Convention had been ratified by Peru, but not yet by Luxembourg. As a result, its safeguards and procedures were not applicable.[8] There had been no determination by the receiving State 'that the child is or will be authorised to enter and reside permanently in that State' – an integral part of the Convention's safeguards[9] – nor an agreement of *both* States at the administrative level 'that the adoption may proceed'.[10] Failing the certified observance of the Convention's mandatory requirements, the obligation for both States directly involved, and for *all* other States parties to the Convention, to recognise the adoption by operation of law, did not apply.

As noticed in the context of the revived interest of the notion of 'acquired rights',[11] the 1993 Convention establishes, albeit in a limited field, a powerful framework to ensure continuity of personal status and family relations across borders.[12] This framework being of no avail in *Wagner*, however, it was the ECHR which had to come to rescue. The ECtHR had already recognised the principle of legal security, and respect for legitimate expectations in internal circumstances.[13] In cross-border situations it had applied article 8, and occasionally article 6, to lend support to the effective operation of the 1980 Hague Child Abduction Convention.[14] Since article 8, protecting the right to respect for 'private and family life', envisages the notion of family as a *living unit*, it naturally also applies to cross-border situations.[15] Moreover, article 8 'must be interpreted in the light of the [UNCRC]' (paragraph 120), which in respect of children's rights makes it a norm of global extent.

---

[8] Cf. *Wagner*, paras 38–39, and see the references in paras 65 and 134, which, however, apparently concern a case that arose *after* the 1993 Convention had entered into force for Peru and Luxembourg.

[9] Art. 5 c); art. 17 d).

[10] Art. 17 c).

[11] See E. Pataut, 'Le renouveau de la théorie des droits acquis' in *Travaux du Comité français de droit international privé, Années 2006-2008* (Paris, Pedone 2009) 71–114, 88.

[12] In simplified form the 1996 Child Protection Convention (art 33), and in its footsteps, EU Regulation 2201/2003 (Brussels II a) (art 56), also establish a consultation procedure to ensure that cross-border placements of children in a foster family or institutional care, or provisions of care by kafala, take place without frictions and such a way that the child's right to enter and reside in the receiving State – at least for the time of the placement in that State – is guaranteed.

[13] Cf P. Kinsch, 'Droits de l'homme, droits fondamentaux et droit international privé' (2007) 318 *Recueil des cours* 8–331, 252.

[14] In a series of judgments, starting with *Ignaccolo-Zenide v. Romania*, App no 31679/96 (ECtHR, 25 January 2000), the ECtHR held that art. 8 establishes positive obligations for ECHR States both in respect of the removal and retention of children and access rights. More recently, the Court's case law regarding the relationship between the ECHR and the Hague Child Abduction Convention has been less consistent, cf., e.g. *Neulinger and Shuruk v. Switzerland* App no 41615/07 (ECtHR 6 July 2010) and *X v. Latvia* App No 27853/09 (ECtHR 26 November 2013).

[15] And so its protection extends to family situations existing in non-European situations, unless this conflicts with fundamental values of ECHR States parties. The 'effet atténué de l'ordre public international' is thus inherent to respect for private and family life, cf. Kinsch (n 13) 247 *et seq.*

2. *WAGNER*'S CRITICISM OF THE PROCEEDINGS AND DECISIONS AT THE NATIONAL LEVEL

Ensuring respect of article 8, also in transnational settings, is primarily the task of national authorities. Indeed, the applicants' primary complaint in *Wagner* was that the Luxembourg courts had paid no heed to their argument based on article 8, and on article 8 read together with article 14, that the Peruvian full adoption was entitled to enforcement. By ignoring this claim based on the Convention itself, they argued, the national authorities had violated their right to a fair trial, also protected by the Convention. The ECtHR agreed, and found that article 6 had been violated.

What *should* the Luxembourg courts have done? Two years after *Wagner*, the Luxembourg Court of Appeal, in a different case, ruled that the *substantive rule* of Luxembourg law prohibiting full adoption by a single person violated articles 8 and 14, and therefore should be left unapplied.[16] *Wagner*, however, does not go that far. Certainly, the Court found that from a comparative perspective the Luxembourg prohibition of full adoption by a single person was rather exceptional among ECHR States parties. But it did not condemn the rule itself, nor did it revisit its established case law that article 8 does not grant a right to adopt (paragraphs 121–22). Moreover, the Court found that subjecting by way of precaution – to protect the child against abuse – the recognition of a foreign adoption of a child to a conflict of laws test per se was 'not unreasonable' (paragraphs 126 and 42). What was *not* acceptable, however, and not 'necessary' within the meaning of article 8 (2) – taking into account the best interests of the child (paragraph 133) – was the strict application of this test, and thereby of the substantive Luxembourg rule, in the 'social reality of the situation' (paragraph 132).

The refusal of exequatur could have been avoided if the courts had decided not to apply the Luxembourg substantive rule to the case at hand. They could have done so either by applying articles 8 and 14 directly against the rule, or by setting it aside through the international public policy exception, considering that the values and norms protected by this exception transcend national borders and include rights protected by the ECHR.[17] That is exactly what follows from another adoption case (but there concerning an adult), decided by the Court in 2011, *Negrepontis-Giannis v. Greece.*[18] There the Court rejected the ruling by the Greek Supreme Court that Greek international public policy opposed the recognition of a full adoption pronounced in the United States of America. Transplanted to the facts in *Wagner*: the Luxembourg courts could have granted the enforcement of the Peruvian adoption by eliminating the

---

[16] Cour d'appel, 16 December 2009, Journal des Tribunaux Luxembourg (J.T.L.) 2010, 73.

[17] Cf. para 131 in fine. Traditionally, the international public policy exception is applied to set aside the application of a foreign law or judgment, to protect the fundamental norms or values of the forum; but once those fundamental values include transnational norms, there is no reason why the exception should not also be used to set aside the application of an internal law of the forum which, in the concrete case, disregards such transnational fundamental norms.

[18] App no 56759/08 (ECtHR 3 May 2011). See P. Kinsch 'La non-conformité du jugement étranger à l'ordre public international mise au diapason de la Convention européenne des droits de l'homme' (2011) *Rev. crit. DIP* 817–23.

blockade raised by the mechanical application of Luxembourg's PIL through its international public policy exception.

It is tempting to read more into *Wagner*, in particular in the expression 'social reality of the situation', than it says. But one should not overlook the Court's detailed analysis of the context: the importance it attaches to the legal status validly obtained through the Peruvian judgment, to the preexisting practice whereby Peruvian judgments pronouncing full adoption by single women were recognised by operation of law in Luxembourg without the need for an exequatur, to the fact that Ms. Wagner relied in good faith on that established practice, only to be trapped by the unexpected sudden change thereof, and, as a result – and this was obviously a major concern of the Court – the legal vacuum in which the child found herself following the completion of the adoption – a full adoption of an abandoned child – despite a prolonged effective family life with her adoptive mother and her children.

Also, against the background sketched by the judgment, there is no ground for the view that *Wagner* has 'immense potential for party autonomy' since the 'fact that the "legal status" was ever established de facto was due to the will of the applicant, intent on adopting.'[19] It appears from the judgment that Peru was the *only* country with which Luxembourg had an *established practice* allowing single parents to adopt, on which Ms. Wagner could legitimately rely, and that it was the sudden closure of this established channel, at the expense foremost of the child, that the Court counted against the conduct of the Luxembourg authorities.

3. SUBSEQUENT CASE LAW OF THE EUROPEAN COURT OF HUMAN RIGHTS

The overall conclusion from the Court's case law in *Wagner* and subsequent judgments is rather that while the Court clearly pursues a policy aimed at ensuring continuity of personal status and family relations acquired abroad, this is balanced with the need to respect well-founded concerns of ECHR States parties. *Well-founded* concerns: the mechanical application of PIL rules simply ignoring, as in *Wagner*, or not responding to, serious complaints[20] will not do. The margin of appreciation of the States 'will vary according to the circumstances, the subject matter and the context'.[21] It will be larger if concerns are shared with many other States parties, and smaller if such concerns are of diminishing importance, shared with a dwindling number of States, as in *Wagner*. And, again as in *Wagner*, when children are involved, their best interests and rights will weigh heavily in the balance.

---

[19] M. Wells-Greco, *The status of children arising from inter-country surrogacy arrangements, the past, the present, the future* (The Hague, Eleven International Publishing 2016) 376. Unrestricted party autonomy in this field obviously would put children's rights at risk; such an interpretation would be inconsistent with the major concern of the judgment to protect the rights of the adopted child.

[20] As, e.g., in *Henry Kismoun v. France*, App no 32265/10 (ECtHR 5 December 2013), paras 35–36.

[21] *Mennesson v. France* App no 65192/11 (ECtHR 26 June 2014), para 77.

The cases of *Mennesson v. France* and *Labassee v. France*[22] – although they leave many questions open – illustrate this delicate balancing process. On the one hand, the Court ruled that respect for the children's private life entails an obligation for France to recognise the parent-child relationships established by the US courts. On the other, however, the Court respected France's 'wish to deter its nationals from going abroad to take advantage of methods of assisted reproduction that are prohibited on its own territory'.[23] Therefore, France was not obliged to respect the family life established between the parents and the children under article 8.

A similar balancing act appears in the Court's approach to the recognition of foreign same-sex marriages. In the recent case of *Orlandi and others v. Italy*,[24] the Court found that, since Italy, following the Court's judgment in *Oliari and others v. Italy*,[25] had made it possible for same-sex couples to engage in a legal partnership, with more or less the same legal effects as marriage, Italy was not under an obligation to register a foreign same-sex marriage *as a marriage*, since the foreign marriage could have effect within the Italian legal order in the form of a legal partnership.

The ECtHR's case law also shows that the interaction between PIL and human rights law is not a one way street. In *Harroudj v. France*[26] the French courts had denied an application for the full adoption of an abandoned Algerian child born in Algeria, by a French woman who had been granted the right to take the child into her legal care by way of *kafala* and authorised by the Algerian court to leave the country and settle in France. Algerian law prohibits adoption, and *kafala* does not create a legal parent-child relationship between the child and the caretaker (*kafil*). The French courts based their refusal to grant the adoption on the French choice of law rule which does not allow the adoption of a child if his or her national law prohibits adoption, unless the child's habitual residence is in France and the child was born in France.[27]

In contrast to *Wagner*, the ECtHR found no violation of article 8 ECHR in this case. It reasoned that the legal distinction between *kafala* and adoption was recognised by the UNCRC,[28] the 1993 Hague Adoption Convention[29] and the 1996 Hague Child Protection Convention.[30] Moreover, the child could still acquire inheritance rights under a will, and, after having been raised for five years in foster care, acquire French nationality and *then* be adopted by her *kafil*. The Court concluded that the French

22 App no 65941/11 (ECtHR 26 June 2014).

23 *Mennesson*, paras 62, 99; *Labassee*, paras 54, 78.

24 App no 26431/12; 26742/12; 44057/12 and 60088/12 (ECtHR 14 December 2017).

25 App no 18766/11 and 36030/11 (ECtHR 21 July 2015), in which the Court held that, although States were free, under arts. 8, 12 and 14, to restrict access to marriage to different-sex couples, nevertheless in the absence of a prevailing community interest against which to balance the applicants' momentous interests, Italy had a positive obligation to ensure them a specific legal framework providing for the recognition and protection of their same-sex unions.

26 App no 43631/09 (ECtHR 4 October 2012).

27 Art. 370-3 (2) Code civil.

28 Art. 20 (3).

29 The 1993 Convention is limited to 'adoptions which create a permanent-child relationship', art. 2 (2).

30 The 1996 Convention makes specific reference to *kafala* in its arts. 3 and 33.

authorities, therefore, 'applying the international conventions that govern such measures ha[ve] put in place a flexible arrangement to accommodate the law of the child's State of origin and the national law'.

> [b]y gradually obviating the prohibition of adoption … seek[ing] to encourage the integration of children of foreign origin without cutting them off immediately from the rules of their country of origin, [they have] shown respect for cultural pluralism and ha[ve] struck a fair balance between the public interest and the right of the applicant [the kafil].[31]

The case shows that PIL may *inform* the human rights norm, here article 8, so that it will be applied with due regard to a person's cultural identity and its evolution over time.[32]

4. SOME CONCLUSIONS AND PERSPECTIVES

Where the ECtHR finds that the application of a PIL rule conflicts with a human right guaranteed by the ECHR, the Court does not prescribe a new PIL rule or methodology.[33] Yet, the ECHR as a regional pillar of the 'social and international order' which the UDHR holds as a promise, and which nowadays increasingly includes transnational situations, *does* encourage a *reorientation* of PIL.

Traditionally, PIL takes its perspective *from within* the domestic legal order, its mission being to find solutions for legal issues with an *'élément d'extranéité'*. Nowadays, this anchoring within the domestic legal order needs to be mirrored by an anchoring in the wider, regional and emerging global legal order. The mere volume and complexity of cross-border legal issues require a plural anchoring.

The current revival of the discussion on acquired rights and the debate on the 'recognition method' (or 'methods'), seeking – in various degrees – to make room for a broader though not unlimited recognition of foreign decisions and, especially, *ex lege* legal situations, have the merit of assisting in opening up PIL systems to such a wider orientation. Yet, recognition is a *'mode d'emploi'*,[34] it needs refinement as a technique and is not a panacea. Defining precise conditions for its application is necessary, to avoid unpredictable corrective intervention through the back-door, e.g. by public

---

[31] Para 51. The Court also considered that no separate issue arose under art. 14 ECHR (para 55).

[32] Cultural identity encompasses individual, group and national identity, which, as they evolve during a person's life time, may reinforce but also contradict each other, see L. Gannagé, 'Les méthodes du droit international privé à l'épreuve des conflits de cultures' (2013) 357 *Recueil des Cours* Nos 12 et seq. Cf. also S. Bollée and E. Pataut (eds.), *L'identité 'l'épreuve de la mondialisation* (Paris, LGDJ 2016).

[33] No more than the CJEU when it finds that a certain national PIL rule conflicts with the basic EU freedoms.

[34] Cf. supra n 4.

policy.[35] Other techniques, such as alternative choice of law rules,[36] retain their value. In short, it is not just the technique that counts, but most of all the message, the need for PIL to anchor itself not just in the forum but also in the wider world.

But there is more. *Wagner*, *Harroudj* and other ECHR cases show that the interaction between PIL and human rights, article 8 in particular, with its impact on a person's *civil* rights, may, in turn, interact with his or her status under *public* law. An important effect of *Wagner* was that the child could obtain the nationality of Luxembourg, and thereby EU citizenship. Likewise, in *Harroudj* the child's residence status would be secured by her obtaining French citizenship in the near future, which in turn would make her adoption possible. Access to French citizenship for the child was also an important consideration in *Menesson* and *Labassee*. Although the ECHR, in contrast to the UDHR (article 15), does not establish a right to citizenship, nevertheless, since nationality is a core element of a person's identity, its attribution, denial or revocation may come under the scrutiny of article 8, as part of the protection of private and family life.[37] Similarly, although the ECHR does not guarantee per se the right of an alien to enter and reside in a State party, immigration policies are not outside its ambit.[38] A key question in *Chbihi Loudoudi v. Belgium*[39] was the precarious residence status of a Moroccan child entrusted to a Belgian couple under a *kafala* arrangement. The Court narrowly held, four to three, that the refusal by the Belgian authorities to grant the child a permanent residence status did not violate article 8.

A comprehensive, empirically grounded, view of the PIL of personal status and family relations in our world on the move, therefore, should include the full breadth of its interaction with human rights law, the law of citizenship, migration law and refugee law. Coordination of these different fields, as well as cooperation between the responsible authorities in each field, is very much needed.[40] Global efforts are now

---

35 Cf., generally, on the conditions for recognition (proximity, public policy, fraud, legitimate expectations of the parties), P. Lagarde, 'Introduction au thème de la reconnaissance des situations: rappel des points les plus discutés' in E. Tourme Jouannet et al. (eds.), *Droit international et reconnaissance* (Paris, LGDJ 2016) 293–99.

36 A classic example is the 1961 Hague Convention on the Form of Testamentary Dispositions, which, by offering a wide range of potentially applicable laws, effectively almost eliminates the risk of formal invalidity for wills in international situations. See H. van Loon, 'La méthode de la reconnaissance et les conventions de droit international privé de La Haye' in P. Lagarde (ed.) *La Reconnaissance des situations en droit international privé* (Paris, 2013) 121–129.

37 For an extensive discussion of '[t]he right to citizenship in the context of European human rights law', see the dissenting opinion of Judge Pinto de Albuquerque, in *Ramadan v. Malta*, App no 76136/12 (ECtHR 21 June 2016), arguing that 'State citizenship belongs to the core someone's identity, which is protected by Article 8 of the Convention' (para 24).

38 See *Abdulaziz, Cabales and Balkandali v. the United Kingdom*, App no 9214/80; 9473/81 (ECtHR, 28 May 1985) (violation of art. 8 read together with art. 14).

39 App no 52265/10 (ECtHR, 16 March 2015).

40 Cf. for the many issues from an EU perspective, the studies by S. Corneloup (ed.) for the JURI Committee, *Private International Law in a Context of Increasing International Mobility: Challenges and Potential* (2017), and S. Corneloup and J. Verhellen (eds.), *Children On the move: A Private International Law Perspective* (2017).

underway, in the broader context of the 2030 UN Agenda for Sustainable Development,[41] focusing in particular on migration and refugee law, to ensure 'safe, orderly and regular' migration and enhance protection of refugees.[42] They should be an encouragement for PIL to consider its possible contribution to these efforts, and to realise its full potential to ensure continuity of personal status and family relations across borders in the regional as well as the global context.[43]

26.3 'FOREIGN SITUATIONS' AND CONFLICT OF LAWS: THINKING OUTSIDE-THE-BOX APPROACH TO PRIVATE INTERNATIONAL LAW

*David Sindres**

The *Wagner* case occupies, within private international law case law, a unique position: it indeed represents, for numerous authors, an important phase in the renewal of methods in this area of law.

These methods were typically dependent on the source of the rights claimed before the competent forum.[44] When these rights have already been affirmed by a foreign judgment and when the parties, or one of them, seek their benefit, the seized judge has recourse to the method of recognition in order to determine whether the rights created abroad can equally be granted to the parties in the host legal order. If, on the other hand, the parties do not benefit from a foreign judgment to support their claims, the method of recognition makes way for a conflict of law analysis, which will allow for the determination of the applicable law to the legal questions submitted to the court.

This alternative is not, ordinarily, ever questioned in the presence of rights acquired in the foreign state: if these rights have their roots in a foreign judgment, the method of recognition applies, whilst in the absence of such a decision, the conflict of law rules regain dominance. At most, the conflict of laws method makes certain adjustments to take into account the fact that some rights have been legitimately acquired abroad, without fraud. Thus, in this situation the international public policy exception is in principle mitigated.[45] When it comes to '*renvoi*', it can, even if it is not its primary

---

[41] General Assembly Res A/70/1 of 25 September 2015, 'Transforming our world: the 2030 Agenda for Sustainable Development', para 29.

[42] General Assembly Res A/71/1 of 19 September 2016, New York Declaration for Refugees and Migrants, which sets out steps towards the achievement of a "Global compact on refugees" and a "Global compact for the safe, orderly and regular migration" by 2018.

[43] Cf. S. Corneloup, 'Can Private International Law Contribute to Global Migration Governance' in H. Muir Watt and D. Fernández Arroyo (eds.), *Private International Law and Global Governance* (Oxford, Oxford University Press 2014) 3012–317; H. van Loon, 'The Global Horizon of Private International Law' (2016) 380 *Recueil des cours* 9–108, 77–82.

* Contribution originally written in French, translated to English by David Woodcock.

[44] See in this regard, P. Mayer, *La distinction entre règles et décisions et le droit international privé* (Paris, Dalloz 1973).

[45] See, Civ. 28 February 1860, *Bulkley*; Civ. 17 April 1953, *Rivière*.

function, be put into effect to favour the respect of vested rights. This is reflected by the famous 'Bronze Rock' with which Raape confronted the opponents of *renvoi*:[46] in this example, the acceptance by the German Court of a *renvoi au deuxième degré* resulted in the application of Russian law, which allowed the union of two Swiss nationals in Russia, whereas in the absence of *renvoi*, the German judge would have applied Swiss Law, under which the marriage was null and void.[47]

In France at least, only a few months before the *Wagner* case, the distinction between the methods of recognition and conflict of laws seemed to have gained clarity: by deciding, in the *Cornelissen* case,[48] that the enforcement judge did not have to verify that the law applied by the foreign judge was that which was designated by the French conflict of laws rule, the French Supreme Court (Cour de cassation) in effect removed the conflict of laws reasoning from the process of recognition of foreign judgments.

Henceforth excluded in France by the *Cornelissen* case, the verification by the enforcement judge of the law applied by the foreign court was further weakened by the *Wagner* decision. Here, the non-observance by the foreign judge of the law designated by the Luxembourg conflict of laws rule had led to the refusal by the Luxembourg court to enforce a Peruvian judgment granting a full adoption. Such a refusal was however deemed by the European Court of human rights to be interfering disproportionately with the family life of the plaintiffs, as well as being discriminatory.

Beyond the question of the verification of the applicable law at the enforcement stage, the *Wagner* case contains a crucial questioning of the role of the conflict of laws rule in regard to situations constituted abroad. It emerges that recourse to this rule risks hindering a recognition that is otherwise imposed on fundamental rights grounds.

If it appears, at first glance, to conform to a settled line of reasoning as set out by the *Cornelissen* case, the *Wagner* case could, on reflection, be invested with a whole other purport: far from confirming the distinction between the method specific to the conflict of laws and the method of recognition, this case may symbolise on the contrary the passing of this distinction.

Consequently, therefore, the *Wagner* decision requires us to think about the extension of the recognition method to situations constituted abroad (1) and to the problems that such an extension would bring about (2).

1. THE EXTENSION OF THE RECOGNITION METHOD TO SITUATIONS CONSTITUTED ABROAD

The analysis developed by the *Wagner* case for the purpose of refusing the enforcement of a foreign judgment could, without difficulty, be transposed to situations created abroad in the absence of any judgment.

---

46 L. Raape, 'The legal relationship between parents and children as a starting point for explaining old and new fundamental problems in international private law' (1934) IV(50) *RCADI* 405 and esp. 413.

47 On this example, see infra.

48 Civ. 1re 20 February 2007, Cornelissen.

More than just the existence of a Peruvian adoption, the recogntion of which was refused by the Luxembourg court, it is indeed the 'social reality of the situation' (point 132) that proved decisive for the European judges. Thus, they based the application of Article 8, which guarantees the right to the respect of family life, on the fact that 'the plaintiff behaves in all respects as the mother of the minor since 1996, so that "family bonds" exist *de facto* between them' (point 117).

The decision adopted by the Court in Strasbourg would therefore have probably been similar in the absence of a foreign judgment: faced with a simple factual situation, amounting to a family life in respect to Article 8, a national court would have incurred a condemnation if it had, on the basis of the law designated by its own conflictual rule, refused the recognition.

Therefore, beyond an ad hoc condemnation of the verification of the applicable law at the enforcement stage, the *Wagner* case also seems to question the very legitimacy of the conflict of laws rule in the presence of a factual situation already constituted abroad: if indeed the implementation of this conflictual method leads to ignoring fundamental rights that the parties may invoke in this situation, it must be set aside in order to preserve those rights. It is therefore necessary to identify the factual situations that justify an eviction of conflict of law rules.

Even though the *Wagner* case was about the recognition of a foreign judgment, it could, from this point of view, illustrate one of the situations highlighted by many scholars: the 'crystallisation' of a factual situation through the passage of time.[49] Thus, since 1996, the adopting parent had acted as the mother of the minor, which in turn gave rise to a family life between the two protagonists.

The passage of time is not however the only form of possible 'crystallisation': a situation can also be constituted abroad thanks to the non-decisional intervention of a public servant, in the course of a civil marriage for instance.[50] This intervention can indeed create in the mind of the parties a belief in the validity of the situation there created.

The crystallisation concept, popular with scholars, might appear *prima facie* as a mere reformulation of the vested rights doctrine. However, it is of particular interest insofar as it also underlines the process through which rights may be acquired within the international sphere.

Yet, in a context where the duty of States to respect these rights is always more compelling, under the combined burden of fundamental rights and Europeans freedoms,[51] the conflict of laws method seems doomed to an inevitable decline, which neither the mitigating effect of public policy nor the use of *renvoi* will be enough to curb.

---

[49] See in this regard, P. Mayer, 'Les méthodes de la reconnaissance en droit international privé' in *Mélanges en l'honneur by P. Lagarde* (Paris, Dalloz 2005) 547 and esp no 30, 563.

[50] Mayer, ibid., no 29, 562.

[51] See in this regard, in the field of family name: CJCE, 14 October 2008, *Grunkin-Paul*, aff. C-353/06; CJUE, 22 December 2010, *Sayn-Wittgenstein*, C-208/09; ECHR 5 December 2013, n°32265/10, *Henry Kismoun v. France*; CJUE, 2 June 2016, *Bogendorff von Wolffersdorff*, aff. C-438/14; CJUE, 8 June 2017, *Freitag*, aff. C-541/15. See also, in the field of marriage, ECHR, 14 December 2017, *Orlandi and others v. Italy*, n°26431/12.

The mitigated effect of public policy is, in this regard, only applicable on the condition that the law designated by the conflict of laws rule validates the rights acquired abroad: it is therefore of no help where this law does not acknowledge the existence of these rights. With regard to *renvoi*, it can sometimes be employed with a view to protecting vested rights, but it was not designed for this reason. Its use can thus easily lead to the application of a law which also denies the recognition of these rights.

Concerned with avoiding this outcome, and in order to better protect the rights acquired abroad, certain scholars have suggested that the conflict of laws rule should be set aside in favour of a new method, the so-called recognition of foreign situations.[52] The underlying thesis is rather simple: it is indeed based upon the extension to factual situations, which would typically fall within the conflict of laws method, of the type of reasoning which presides over the recognition of foreign judgments.

Thus, the recognition of factual situations that occurred abroad would be permitted whenever the conditions ordinarily applied to verify the legality of foreign judgments are met.

The situation shall therefore have been created free of fraud, in a legal order having a connection with the situation. Furthermore, its recognition should not harm the international public policy of the forum.[53]

Contrary however to foreign judgments, which result in, according to the expression used by the European Court of Human Rights in the *Wagner* case, 'a *legal status* legitimately created abroad' (point 133), the situations formed abroad remain merely factual. On their own, they do not therefore give rise to any legal right. It is necessary, as already highlighted by Savigny,[54] to identify the law from which the rights derive.

Since the recognition method advocates the eviction of the conflict of laws method, the law from which the rights derive cannot be chosen through the latter method. Thus,

---

52 See amongst the abundant literature, P. Lagarde, 'Développements futurs du droit international privé dans une Europe en voie d'unification : quelques conjectures' (2004) *RabelsZ* 225; from the same author, 'La reconnaissance mode d'emploi' in *Mélanges in honour of Hélène Gaudemet-Tallon* (Paris, Dalloz 2008) 481 et seq.; 'La méthode de la reconnaissance est-elle l'avenir du droit international privé' (2015) 371 *RCADI* 19 et seq.; Mayer (n 49); H. Muir Watt, 'Quelques remarques sur la théorie anglo-américaine des droits acquis' (1986) *Rev. crit. DIP* 425 et seq.; H. Muir Watt and G. Goldstein, 'La méthode de la reconnaissance à la lueur de la Convention de Munich du 5 septembre 2007 sur la reconnaissance des partenariats enregistrés', JDI n°4, October 2010, doctr. 12; E. Pataut, 'Le renouveau de la théorie des droits acquis' (2006–08) *Trav. Com. fr. DIP* 71 et seq.; S. Bollée, 'L'extension du domaine de la reconnaissance unilatérale' (2007) *Rev. crit. DIP* 307 et seq.; C. Pamboukis, 'La renaissance-métamorphose de la méthode de la reconnaissance' (2008) *Rev. crit. DIP* 513; *La reconnaissance des situations en droit international privé*, sous. la dir. de P. Lagarde (Paris, Pedone 2013); P. Mayer and V. Heuzé, *Droit international privé* 11th edn (Paris, LGDJ 2014) esp. no115; D. Bureau and H. Muir Watt, *Droit international privé*, T.1, 3rd edn (Paris, PUF 2014) esp. no581 et seq.; L. d'Avout, 'La reconnaissance dans le champ des conflits de lois' (2014–16) *Trav. com. fr. DIP* 215 et seq. Aj. In German doctrine, the references cited by P. Lagarde, *La reconnaissance mode d'emploi*, ibid, esp. note 4.

53 One will recognise here the regularity conditions of foreign judgments as determined by the Cornelissen case.

54 F-C von Savigny, *Traité de droit romain* 2nd edn (Tome VIII, 1860, Paris, Librairie Firmin Didot Frères, Fils et Cie, Réimpr. 2002, éd. Panthéon-Assas), esp. §361, 131.

according to some scholars, the law must be chosen through the rules of private international law in place in the legal order in which the situation has crystallised.[55] This solution is for instance set out by the Hague Convention of 14 March 1978 on the Celebration and Recognition of the validity of marriages, in force in the Netherlands, in Luxembourg and in Australia. This Convention stipulates at Article 9, paragraph 1, that 'A marriage validly entered into under the law of the State of celebration or which subsequently becomes valid under that law shall be considered as such in all Contracting States, subject to the provisions of this Chapter'. The 'law of the State of celebration' designates here the private international law of that State.[56]

Thus described, the method of recognition of situations is hailed by many as the adequate tool to protect vested rights. At the most, there are differences of opinion as to the subsidiary nature of the method: whilst part of the scholarship in this point recommends confining its use to situations where the conflict of laws rule would not allow for the recognition of the rights acquired abroad,[57] the other part wants this method to replace the other from the outset.[58]

The fact remains though that despite the considerable interest that this method has sparked among scholars and the important role that it has been given by some key decisions, such as *Wagner*, the method of recognition has not, for the time being, gained further momentum in positive law.[59]

Although it is difficult to decipher the reasons for this failure, there are undoubtedly reasons not to complain about it.[60]

---

[55] See in particular, P. Lagarde 'Développements futurs du droit international privé dans une Europe en voie d'unification : quelques conjectures' (n 52) esp. 233; P. Mayer, 'Le phénomène de la coordination des ordres juridiques étatiques en droit privé' (2007) *RCADI*, t.327, esp. no 339; Mayer and Heuzé (n 52) n°115; Bollée (n 52) esp. 326–27. A very similar idea had already been developed by Droz, through his distinction between the forum of the judgment and the forum of the reasoning (see 'Regards sur le droit international privé comparé – cours général de droit international privé' (1991) IV *RCADI* 9 and 351 et seq.). The taking into account of private international law rules of the legal order which, according to the forum, has the closest connections with the matter, knows other illustrations outside of the recognition of situations method. In succession matter, this is set out by article 91, paragraph 1 of the Swiss federal law on private international law and by §260 of the Second Restatement of Conflict of Laws. In France, this approach is illustrated by the famous *Machet* (Rabat, 24 October 1950) and *Banque Ottomane* (Paris, 19 March 1965) cases.

[56] See in this respect, Mayer (n 49) 559.

[57] See in this regard, Mayer (n 49) no45, 571; d'Avout (n 52) no19, 231.

[58] See for example, Bollée (n 52) no19, 331 and no33, 349.

[59] On this point, see, d'Avout (n 52) no1, 215. S. Bollée, 'Les conditions de la reconnaissance, notamment à la lumière des conventions internationales' in *La reconnaissance des situations en droit international privé* (n 52) 113.

[60] For another critical analysis of the recognition method, see Y. Lequette, 'De la "proximité" au "fait accompli"' in *Mélanges in honour of Professor Pierre Mayer* (Paris, LGDJ 2015) 481 et seq.; see also, from the same author, *Les mutation du droit international privé : vers un changement de paradigme ? Cours général de droit international privé*, RCADI 2017, t. 387, esp. no 353 et seq. p. 559 et seq.

2. THE PITFALLS OF THE METHOD OF RECOGNITION OF SITUATIONS

Because the recognition method presupposes taking into account the private international law rules of the legal order in which the situation has crystallised, it turns out to be particularly complex from the outset. This method is not unlike the *renvoi* system, but it goes further in requiring the Court to adopt the entire private international law reasoning of the foreign forum and not only its conflict of laws rule. Thus, in this respect, the method evokes the 'double *renvoi*'[61] scenario, which is arguably obsolete elsewhere.

Highly complex, the approach can moreover misfire: indeed, nothing guarantees that the law designated by the private international law rules of the legal order in which the situation has crystallised is the law to which the parties spontaneously thought they were submitted. The parties' expectations are, indeed, usually based on the domestic law of the legal order in which the situation was created, as was the case in *Wagner*, where the adopting parent expected to benefit from the conditions of adoption found in Peruvian substantive law. Thus, where the parties have fixed their domicile and lived for several years in a country where the law recognises the legitimacy of the situation in which they are involved, it is generally this law that they naturally rely upon in order to assert their rights. Yet in numerous situations, the rules of private international law in the legal order in which the situation occurred leads to the designation of the law of a third-State, whose application will ruin the parties' expectations.

Other tried and tested methods could however, in numerous situations, lead to better outcomes with less complexity. One of these methods consists for the forum in complementing its conflict of laws rule with subsidiary connecting factors, designating the domestic law of the legal order in which the situation has crystallised – i.e. the law of the country in which the adoption of the child took place, the place where the marriage was celebrated or the country in which the spouses elected their domicile, etc … These subsidiary connecting factors would only enter in effect in the case where the primary connecting option would lead to the selection of a law denying the parties the rights that they thought they had acquired. One may recognise here the method of 'substantive conflict of laws rules' (*règles de conflit de lois à 'coloration matérielle'*) whose purpose may precisely be to facilitate a given result.

Another solution could involve, if the aim is to avoid a problematic detour by the private international law rules of the legal order in which the situation has crystallised, to look within the recognition rule itself in order to find the source of the rights which this rule is simultaneously designed to recognise. The introduction of a substantive dimension within the recognition rule itself could notably, where applicable, rely on the European Convention on Human Rights. The latter, as the *Wagner* case clearly showed, leads to discover fundamental rights in merely factual situations: thus it is sufficient,

61 On this mechanism, also named '*foreign court theory*' or theory of '*renvoi intégral*', see Ph.Francescakis, *La théorie du renvoi et les conflits de systèmes en droit international privé* (Paris, Sirey 1957) esp. no106; adde H. Muir Watt 'Quelques remarques sur la théorie anglo-américaine des droits acquis' esp. no17 et seq.; H. Batiffol and P. Lagarde, *Droit international privé*, T.1, 8th edn (Paris, LGDJ 1993) esp. no309.

for the right to a family life to be protected under Article 8, that the parties had *de facto* established familial ties between themselves. The simple implementation of the ECHR provisions in the context of the recognition method would lead to recognition of the rights acquired abroad without the bother of a detour by the private international law rules of the legal order in which the situation has crystallised.

Beyond these technical points, the recognition method poses even more serious difficulties, in comparison with the classical conflict of laws method. In this regard, the conflict of laws rule achieves a fair balance between the point of view of the forum and the expectations of the parties, the former not being sacrificed for the latter. If indeed, the forum accepts to take into account the expectations of the parties when it comes to the applicable law, rather than imposing its own system of substantive rules, it is only because it deems these expectations to be legitimate, that is to say consistent with its conception of 'conflictual justice' as embodied in its conflict of laws rule. Moreover, the objectives sought by the forum through its conflict of law rules are very diverse, and are not limited to the respect of vested rights or to the pursuit of international harmony of solutions.[62] For instance, in matters of personal status, the choices of the forum in the field of conflict of laws are sometimes guided by a willingness to preserve the continuity and stability of the status of the people involved. These choices can equally be explained by its commitment to the principles of the inalienability of civil status and the integrity of the human body.

Hence, the primary purpose of the conflict of laws method is neither to comply with the wishes of the parties, nor to recognise at all costs the rights which they believe to have acquired abroad. By contrast, if States were to adopt the method of recognition, they would renounce any primacy of their own conflict of laws rules, and of sacrifice their own conception of conflictual justice in order to meet private parties' expectations. Indeed, instead of giving precedence to their own point of view, the States would embrace the stance of the legal order where the situation was created. Moreover, they would do so solely to increase the chances of international recognition of the claimed rights.

Decided by the forum in the sole interest of the parties, or one of them, this submission to the point of view of a foreign legal order involves an obvious risk: it can indeed lead to the prevalence of a law whose application no way aligns with the values of the forum.

The problem is already familiar in the *renvoi* scenario, as evidenced by the symbolic example of the 'Bronze Rock': in order to validate the marriage celebrated in Russia between an uncle and his niece, both Swiss nationals, the German forum should have, in line with the *renvoi* system, submitted the substantive legal issues relating to the validity of the marriage to the Russian law of the place of celebration. The latter was thus supposed to replace the national law of the parties, as designated by the connecting German factor, which considered that the disputed marriage was void on grounds of incest.

Such a renouncement by a court to assert its own approach to private international law justice is questionable. In the 'Bronze Rock' example, this led the seized court to submit the personal status of the parties to the law of the country where their marriage

62 See in this regard, Mayer (n 55) no156 and 157, 172 et seq.

was celebrated rather than to their national law, for the purpose of maintaining the validity of an incestuous marriage. Yet, while the application of the parties' personal law meets the expectations of stability and continuity in respect of civil status and limits the influence of the will of the parties in an area that is refractory to the principle of autonomy, the application of the law of the place of celebration provides the parties with excessive freedom. It allows them to choose this place with the intention of circumventing the legal system with the strongest connections to the dispute,[63] and this arguably verges on fraud.

Already apparent in the *renvoi* framework, this type of abdication by the forum is even more clear-cut under the auspices of the recognition method. Whilst, indeed, *renvoi* does not signify the abandonment of the conflict of laws rule of the forum, but a type of coordination between this rule and the foreign conflict of law rules that it is deemed to select,[64] the recognition method leaves no room for the conflict rule of the forum. As already shown, this rule depends on taking account of the private international law of the legal order in which the situation has crystallised, and this is not the system that is identified through the conflict of laws rule of the forum.

Not only does the recognition method expose the court to the risk of trading away its own rules of private international law for others, which do not correspond in any way to its approach to justice in private international law relationships, but it can also lead it to grant a blank cheque to private parties. Indeed, these parties benefit from a great deal of flexibility in the choice of the legal order in which they intend to create the situation of which they will later seek the recognition This is particularly the case where the situation arose from the non-decisional intervention of a public officer exercising international jurisdiction too widely:[65] the parties have an incentive to go before that public officer to acquire rights, even though they have no meaningful connection there. And if this legal order moreover adopts permissive rules of private international law, whether substantive,[66] or consisting in the autonomy principle, the parties' task will be made a lot easier still.

The potential combination of the recognition method and the autonomy principle, which continues to win over new swathes of private law, can, in this regard, only cause concern: the attitude of submission on the part of State legal orders, that endeavour to recognise the rights defined by the parties themselves thanks to the autonomy principle, at the cost of renouncing their own private international law rules, results in a policy of

63 This was certainly not the case in the example of the Bronze Rock, Raape taking care to specify that the spouses were domiciled in Russia at the time of their marriage. The problem could however have been raised if the couple had gone to Russia to celebrate their marriage.

64 See in this regard, H. Batiffol, *Aspects philosophiques du droit international privé* (Paris, Dalloz 1956, 2002 edition, presented by Y. Lequette) esp. no142, 315; aj. Francescakis (n 61) no97, 101.

65 In this respect, we can cite the French rules governing the jurisdiction of civil status officers in matters of same-sex marriage, as set out at Article 74, 165 and 171-9 of the Civil Code.

66 See for example Article 202, paragraph 2 of the Civil Code, where it states 'Two persons of the same sex may enter into marriage when, for at least one of them, either his personal law or the law of the State on the territory of which he is domiciled or has his residence permits such marriage'.

fait accompli.[67] Within the States who are parties to the ECHR, this policy could thrive with all the more ease, as this Convention requires the Courts to erect simple facts to the rank of human rights. The right to a private and family life, which is at the heart of the *Wagner* case, is an excellent example of this phenomenon.

There are, of course, limits to the recognition of situations, drawn from fraud and international public policy, which can even be combined in cases of fraud to the intensity of public policy ('*fraude à l'intensité de l'ordre public*'). While such limits are sometimes invoked in the context of recognition,[68] they are however of little weight when set against fundamental rights. Thus, the typical weakening of international public policy when these rights have been acquired abroad is even more pressing when these rights become human rights. Long applied to international public policy, this mitigation tends today to extend to the exception of fraud, which is bypassed when the denial of recognition to which it would lead conflicts with fundamental rights. In this regard, the condemnations imposed on France in relation to surrogate motherhood should be borne in mind. France's refusal, first based on the international public policy exception[69] and then on fraud,[70] to allow surrogacy conventions concluded and performed abroad to have effect in France, was indeed considered by the European Court of Human Rights to be a violation of the right of the child to have a private life, which implies the right for this child to establish a legal relationship with his biological parent.[71] Yet the *Wagner* case already included the premises of the reasoning which, seven years later, was to lead the European Court to impose on France a partial recognition of surrogacy, notwithstanding the fraud of the sponsoring parent(s). Amongst the reasons for which the judges in Strasbourg decided, in the *Wagner* case, to condemn the refusal of recognition of the Peruvian judgment, was, already, the 'the superior interest of the child' (point 133), which mandated, as in the case of surrogacy, to extract the child from the 'judicial vacuum' (point 155) in which the denial of recognition of the foreign judgment had left it. The child was not, in any way, 'to be reproached facts that were not attributable to it' (point 158).

The area of surrogate motherhood reveals the dangers that the recognition of situations carries with it as a method. This method can indeed lead the forum to ignore not only its own approach to private international law justice, but also certain fundamental values, whose importance is such that they are otherwise at the heart of the forum's international public policy. Such renunciation is all the more damaging that it occurs in situations where these values are intentionally circumvented by the parties.

Both scholars and courts suggest a way to revive the international public policy exception, and to thus oppose the recognition of situations which occurred in violation of certain of its crucial principles. This would require having recourse to the exception of proximity, and more specifically to one of its variants, named by certain scholars the

[67] See in this regard Y. Lequette (n 60).

[68] See for example, CJEU, 22 December 2010, *Sayn-Wittgenstein* (n 51) pt 95.

[69] Civ. 1re 6 April 2011, no10-19.053, *Mennesson* and no 09-17.130, *Labassée*.

[70] Civ. 1re 13 September 2013, no12-30138 and no12-18315.

[71] ECHR 26 June 2014, no65192/11, *Mennesson v. France* and n°65941/11, *Labassée v. France*; ECHR 21 July 2016, n°9063/14 and 10410/14, *Foulon and Bouvet v. France*; ECHR 19 January 2017, n°44024/13, *Laborie v. France*.

'public policy of the personal status'.[72] From this standpoint, it would be necessary to trigger the international public policy exception when the parties involved are nationals of the forum State. For instance, the French Cour de cassation recently opposed, after a reasoning along the lines of the method of recognition, the transcription on French consular records, of a polygamous marriage celebrated in Algeria between a French man and an Algerian woman 'in light of the violation of international public policy caused by a marriage of a French national abroad without the prior dissolution of his previous marriage'.[73] However, the introduction of such a difference in treatment between French citizens and foreigners, in respect of the values which are at the core of French society, is cause for concern: it paves the way for an asymmetrical recognition process, which is not unlike the discriminations condemned by the Court in Strasbourg. The renewal of methods initiated by the *Wagner* case would thus have a paradoxical outcome: the initial discrimination condemned by this decision would give rise to another, embodied by the public policy of proximity.

72 Mayer and Heuzé (n 52) no216.

73 Civ. 1re 19 October 2016, no 15-50.098.

27. Privatisation of international migration flows: Manus Island class action

27.1 CASE BACKGROUND

Kamasaee v. Commonwealth & Ors, also known as the Manus Island class action, is the largest settlement in the field of human rights in Australian legal history. The settlement marks a potentially important step for the recognition and application of migrants' rights in the present context, where States go out of their way to avoid responsibilities towards refugees and asylum seekers. It arose out of the allegations of false imprisonments of refugees held at the Manus Island Regional Processing Centre between 21 November 2012 and 12 May 2016. The decision of the Supreme Court of Victoria to approve the settlement for compensation reached between the plaintiffs and the Australian Government in June 2017 came more than a year after the Supreme Court of Papua New Guinea had ruled that the centre was illegal and unconstitutional.

In December 2014, Majid Karami Kamasaee, an Iranian refugee, brought an action against the Commonwealth of Australia and two other defendants for the failure to take reasonable care of people held at Manus Island Regional Processing Centre. He claimed damages for himself and almost 2,000 asylum seekers for the consequences arising out of their transfer from Australia and subsequent confinement in the centre located in the Los Negros Island in Papua New Guinea. According to Mr Kamasaee's claim, the asylum seekers detained in the centre suffered physical and psychological injuries as a result of the Government's negligence. Later on, a second claim for false imprisonment was also added. The claimants argued that the conditions in the centre were far below equivalent Australian standards in terms of hygiene, security and access to basic necessities.

After numerous mediations and legal negotiations, the parties reached a settlement for $70 million plus costs. The Government's decision to settle instead of going to trial was criticised by a number of human rights and refugees' rights groups, who claimed that the Government was avoiding scrutiny over the degrading conditions suffered by the refugees while in detention.

In terms of private international law, the case opens a Pandora's box. States attempt increasingly to contract out of their responsibilities with respect to the reception, regulation, and management of migrant populations: privatisation and externalisation are two such methods. In the middle of the so-called 'European refugee crisis', the case takes on symbolic significance.

Case: Manus Island class action, *Kamasaee v. Commonwealth & Ors* (S CI 2014 06770)

27.2 THE MANAGEMENT OF INTERNATIONAL MIGRATIONS BY CONTRACT: MANUS ISLAND GROUP ACTION

*Sabine Corneloup**

The class action brought by asylum seekers from the Manus Island Detention Center in Papua New Guinea[1] is emblematic of the major trends affecting the rights of foreigners at the global level today. Our times are experiencing unprecedented migration flows, caused by the inequality of wealth between countries and the large number of conflicts in the world. According to the UNHCR, 65.6 million people around the world were forced to flee their homes by the end of 2016, including 22.5 million refugees.[2] Most Western countries react by seeking to limit or even prevent the access of migrants to their territory. However, as the UN Special Rapporteur on the human rights of migrants recently recalled, migration as such is a natural phenomenon of human existence and the current collective response to limit this mobility is actually part of the problem and not of the solution.[3] This policy of closing the borders is accompanied by a policy of confinement of migrants, which has led to the proliferation of all kinds of camps: refugee camps, transit camps, camps for the displaced, labor camps, detention centres etc.[4] On the side of the States of destination, two preoccupations dominate: to hinder the entry of migrants on their territory and to remove from the territory those whose entry could not be prevented. Thus, while the European Union organises with its neighboring countries the maintenance of refugees at the gates of Europe (Turkey, Lebanon, Jordan and Libya in particular) and while the United States of Donald Trump plan to build a wall along the border with Mexico, Australia has set up offshore detention centers for asylum seekers, notably in the Republic of Nauru and on the island of Manus in Papua New Guinea.[5] Immigration law thus joins, in its own way, the current debate on extraterritoriality.[6]

---

* Contribution originally written in French, translated to English by Jerome Nicolai.

[1] Written submissions before the Supreme Court of Victoria can be accessed at <http://www.supremecourt.vic.gov.au/home/law+and+practice/class+actions/manus+island+detention+centre+class+action>.

[2] <http://www.unhcr.org/figures-at-a-glance.html>.

[3] François Crépeau, 'We Need a Long-term Strategy for Human Migration' *Refugees Deeply* (June 2017) <https://www.newsdeeply.com/refugees/community/2017/06/08/u-n-rapporteur-we-need-a-long-term-strategy-for-human-migration>.

[4] Michel Agier (ed.), *Un monde de camps* (Paris, La Découverte 2014).

[5] On the migration policy of Australia, see, in particular, Yves Pascouau, 'An Australian "model" for the EU's migration crisis?' *European Policy Center* (2 June 2017) <http://www.epc.eu/pub_details.php?pub_id=7726&cat_id=4>; Sasha Lowes, 'The Legality of Extraterritorial Processing of Asylum Claims: the Judgment of the High Court of Australia in the "Malaysian Solution" Case' (2012) 12 *Human Rights Law Review* 168; Kazimierz Bem, Nina Field, Nic Maclellan, Sarah Meyer and Tony Morris, 'A price too high: the cost of Australia's approach to asylum seekers' (2007) <http://www.ajustaustralia.com/resources/53c93e62aebb725295fc6c95f0b19604_a%20price%20too%20high%20-%20email.pdf>; Susan Kneebone, 'The Pacific Plan: The Provision of "Effective Protection"?' (2006) 18 *International Journal of Refugee Law* 696.

[6] See, in particular, Thomas Gammeltoft-Hansen, *Access to Asylum. International Refugee Law and the Globalisation of Migration Control* (Cambridge, Cambridge University Press 2011) 100; Ruben Zaiotti (ed.), *Externalizing Migration Management: Europe, North America and the*

In this global context, the management of migration flows is increasingly comprehended by hitherto unknown legal techniques. The most important – and arguably the most unsettling for the very foundations of the law in this area – is the use of contract[7] (understood in a broad sense encompassing private and public law as well as international agreements). Contract is indeed becoming a privileged mode of governance of international migration. While immigration law, like all matters marked by sovereignty, is traditionally characterised by the unilateral action of States, today we are witnessing a complex phenomenon of contractualisation, which implies that conflicting interests and rationalities become a subject of negotiations between contracting parties. This phenomenon reflects the emergence of a growing global migration market. There are, first of all, an increasing number of agreements that are concluded between States. These agreements, which can take various forms, allow Western States to organise the outsourcing of the management of migration flows in third States. Then, there are more and more contracts that States enter into with private companies for the provision of various services. These contracts reflect a privatisation of the management of migratory flows. Finally, with the Manus Island case comes a third variety of contractualisation: agreements that the State concludes with migrants for the settlement of disputes arising in the context of the management of migratory flows.

One of the consequences of this phenomenon of contractualisation is manifest in respect of the distinction between public and private law, which is strongly questioned, as is already the case in other areas of law.[8] Private law reasoning, based on contractual and civil liability, is emerging in immigration law and contributing thereby to a partial privatisation of this area of the law. Notably, they introduce the question of the conflict of laws in the area traditionally marked by the 'public law taboo'.[9] At the same time, they raise a multitude of new issues, particularly regarding the responsibility for the violation of human rights.

The originality of the Manus Island case lies in the fact that it covers the three types of contracting mentioned above at the same time. Thus, Australia has concluded agreements with Papua New Guinea for the reception of asylum seekers wishing to join Australia (1); it has also concluded contracts with various service providers, including security and medical services, to operate the detention centers in Papua New Guinea (2); and finally, it has reached an amicable settlement agreement with the migrants held on Manus Island in order to put an end to the class action brought by them before the Australian courts (3).

Spread of 'remote Control' Practices (Abingdon, Routledge 2016); Madeline Garlick, 'The EU Discussions on Extraterritorial Processing: Solution or Conundrum?' (2006) 18 *International Journal of Refugee Law* 601; Jennifer Hyndman and Alison Mountz, 'Another Brick in the Wall? Neo-Refoulement and the Externalization of Asylum by Australia and Europe' (2008) 43 *Government and Opposition* 249.

[7] See on this phenomenon more generally, Claire Cutler and Thomas Dietz (eds), *The Politics of Private Transnational Governance by Contract* (Abingdon, Routledge 2017).

[8] See Horatia Muir Watt (ed.), *Private International Law and Public Law* 2 vols (Cheltenham, Edward Elgar 2015), compiling the most significant publications on the subject.

[9] That is, by the traditional principle of the inapplicability of a foreign public law, thus rendering the conflict of laws impossible in public law.

1. CONTRACTING BETWEEN STATES (THE OUTSOURCING OF MIGRATORY FLOWS MANAGEMENT)

Inter-State agreements on the management of international migration have developed in all regions of the world. In Europe, for example, the European Union concluded a migration agreement with Turkey in March 2016 in order to drastically reduce the number of asylum seekers.[10] This agreement combines various measures, such as the return to Turkey of irregular migrants, the resettlement of refugees from Turkey to Europe, financial and logistical support granted by the EU to Turkey, and the liberalisation of the visa regime for Turkish nationals.[11]

In the same way, in order to outsource the reception of migrants, Australia has developed since 2001 a strategy called the Pacific Solution, on the model of the Caribbean strategy of the United States. For its implementation, it builds on the Bali Process, which is a regional forum for inter-State dialogue and cooperation aimed at combating the smuggling of migrants, trafficking of persons, and related transnational crimes.[12] It is in this context that it concluded the Memorandum of Understanding with Papua New Guinea, which allowed Australia to transfer asylum seekers to Manus Island, in return for financial support and various measures relating to development policy (health, education, law, etc.).[13] These transfers concern people who arrived irregularly by sea in Australia or who were intercepted at sea while trying to reach Australia irregularly. The examination of asylum applications is entrusted to the Papua authorities and in case of granting of refugee status, Papua New Guinea must allow migrants to settle in its territory. The role of the Australian authorities is limited to a brief review of health, safety and identity before proceeding with the transfer.

Such interstate agreements raise many new legal issues. From the point of view of the Papuanian legal order, first of all, the agreement has given rise to rather incongruous constitutional questions, particularly with regard to the legality of the detention of migrants.[14] National laws generally provide for the possibility of administrative detention only in the event of irregular entry into the national territory, whereas under the agreement with Australia, entry into Papua New Guinea was not only regular, but was even imposed on migrants against their will by the national authorities, although it was not provided for by Papua's legislation. In the absence of

---

[10] See, in particular, the reports of the European Commission on the progress made in the implementation of the EU-Turkey declaration: Fifth Report of 2 March 2017, COM(2017) 204 final.

[11] We can also mention the example of the treaties concluded between France and the United Kingdom: Treaty of Touquet concluded on 4 February 2003, organising cooperation between the two States for the migration management on both sides of the Channel, JORF, 13 February 2004, p. 2949; Treaty of Sandhurst concluded with the aim of reinforcing the cooperation on 18 January 2018, JORF, 13 April 2018, text no 11.

[12] http://www.baliprocess.net.

[13] See the Memorandum of understanding between Papua New Guinea and Australia relating to the transfer to, and assessment and settlement in, Papua New Guinea of certain persons, and related issues, 6 August 2013.

[14] Supreme Court of Papua New Guinea, 26 April 2016, SCA. No. 84 OF 2013 declaring the detention of migrants on the island of Manus contrary to the constitution.

a legal basis, the detention was arbitrary and had to trigger the responsibility of the State, with the particularity, however, in this case, that the migrants had made the choice to engage the responsibility of Australia, and not that of Papua New Guinea (see below, under section 3).

In addition, certain agreements, such as the Franco-British Treaty of Le Touquet,[15] institute extra-territorial State action.[16] For instance, this treaty allows the UK authorities to carry out checks on French territory, which may lead to the detention of a migrant under the conditions and in accordance with the terms of British legislation. Here again, it raises the question of the responsibility of the State, not only that of the United Kingdom but also that of France, especially when a violation of human rights has been committed by the British officials on French territory. A similar question also arises in connection with the European policy of externalising asylum in the event that an infringement on the fundamental rights of an asylum seeker would be committed by the Turkish authorities in Turkey but under the umbrella of the agreement concluded with the European Union. Can Member States be held accountable, for example in the context of an appeal brought by a migrant to the European Court of Human Rights? No Member State is directly responsible for the infringement. However, they all have a responsibility in choosing the partner country and in defining the terms of the agreement. Total irresponsibility would not be justified. For Australia, the issue of international State liability is probably not exactly the same, since it is not bound by a constitutional regime for the protection of human rights, nor by a regional convention comparable to the ECHR.[17]

Moreover, the agreements thus concluded between States also raise the question of their binding force and, where appropriate, of the means of constraint available when a State does not honor its commitments. For example, as part of the Manus and Nauru detention centre dismantling programme, Australia reached an agreement with the United States in November 2016 for the relocation to the United States of several hundred refugees detained in Australian offshore centres. The agreement, whose content was kept confidential, was concluded by the Obama administration and it is not entirely clear today how far it will be implemented by the Trump administration.[18]

All these issues emerge today because the fate of migrants is comprehended, more and more often, through a contractual approach, whereby the States negotiate – bargain – between them the international distribution of migratory flows. This policy reminds us more of a quota system for export/import of goods than a legal regime for the protection of vulnerable people.

---

15 See supra, n 11.

16 See also the rise of the 'hotspots' instituted by the States of destination in transit States, where asylum applications are registered and examined, in order to separate economic migrants from political refugees.

17 See Pascouau (n 5).

18 See, for instance, Nayla Rush, 'U.S.-Australia Refugee Resettlement Deal Is Underway' *Center for Immigration Studies* (10 June 2017) <https://cis.org/sites/cis.org/files/rush-australia-refugee.pdf>.

2. CONTRACTING WITH PRIVATE COMPANIES (PRIVATISATION OF MIGRATORY FLOWS MANAGEMENT)

States not only contract with each other, but also with private companies, which leads to the privatisation of a growing share of the management of migratory flows thus entrusted to operators pursuing an exclusively lucrative goal.[19] While immigration control is traditionally part of the sovereign functions of the State, considered as inalienable, new forms of public management have emerged under the influence of a neoliberal model of governance, which even affect activities previously perceived as sovereign. In their quest for greater economic efficiency, governments are increasingly using the services of private companies. This affects, for example, the management of visa applications, the transportation of migrants, border surveillance, or as in the case of Manus Island, the management of administrative detention centres, which may include security and monitoring of migrants, medical services, catering, etc.[20] Businesses, in turn, often resort to subcontracting to perform contracts.

While not all States today accept the same degree of privatisation, a general trend towards increasing private sector involvement can nevertheless be observed globally. This privatisation and the multiplication of private actors – often involved in complex contractual schemes – bring about profound changes in legal methods. Part of the State's obligations, particularly with regard to the international protection of refugees and fundamental rights, is backed by contractual obligations, such as the obligation to ensure that any migrant who requires it is presented to the health services provider present in the detention centre.[21] In other words, the implementation of major principles, such as the prohibition of inhuman and degrading treatment, ultimately depends on the quality of the contractual arrangement and on its implementation by employees of commercial enterprises.

From the point of view of private international law, this paves the way for reasoning in terms of conflicts of laws and international jurisdiction of domestic courts since the situations frequently include a foreign element (multinational companies operating on

---

[19] See, in particular, with many other references, Thomas Gammeltoft-Hansen and Ninna Nyberg-Sørensen (eds), *The Migration Industry and the Commercialization of International Migration* (Abingdon, Routledge 2013); Sabine Corneloup, 'Les contrats internationaux de l'Administration dans le domaine de la gestion de l'immigration: un nouveau champ à explorer', in *Mélanges P. Mayer* (Paris, LGDJ 2015) 173; GISTI, 'Le business de la migration' *Plein droit* (June 2014); see also the special issue on the migration industry which was published online on 14 July 2017 by the *Journal of Ethnic and Migration Studies*, <http://www.tandfonline.com>.

[20] This can include involvement in decision-making processes, for example as experts in modern border surveillance technologies using drones or radars (see Martin Lemberg-Pedersen, 'Private security companies and the European borderscapes', in Thomas Gammeltoft-Hansen and Ninna Nyberg-Sørensen (n 19) 152), or involvement in regional forums for dialogue and cooperation aimed at defining the policy to combat human trafficking and modern slavery (see the recent initiative to involve the private sector in the Bali process <http://www.bali process.net>).

[21] Such a clause is notably included in the contract between the Commonwealth of Australia and G4S Australia ofin 2013.

different continents, performance of contracts abroad, etc.). Different levels of relationships must then be distinguished, each of which is likely to obey a different legal regime: the relationship between the State and the co-contracting firm, the relationship between the company and its subcontractors, the relationship between the State and the subcontractors, the relationship between the State and the migrants, as well as the relationship between each company and the migrants. Contracts may be governed by different laws and the dispute settlement system may also be subject to special features from one contract to another.

From the point of view of migrants, this privatisation may lead to a problematic dilution of responsibility when human rights abuses are committed, as was the case on Manus Island. The State is no longer directly responsible as the direct instigator of such violations, but, rather, its responsibility exists in connection with the control it exercises over private enterprises,[22] whereas the latter are not 'debtors' of human rights in horizontal relations.[23] Moreover, because of the multiplicity of operators, the responsibilities are shared on the basis of differentiated legal regimes, between the State, the main contractor and the various subcontractors involved.

The extraordinary legal complexity of the situation is completely out of step with the state of vulnerability that characterises asylum seekers, especially when they are detained and suffer violations of their rights. As individual action on their part can often seem illusory, the development of class actions, like that of the Manus Island inmates, is likely to shape the future of immigration law, at least in countries that have class actions.[24] From this point of view also, the litigation in the area of immigration law is joining a more general trend that can already be observed in other sectors of contemporary transnational litigation.

3. CONTRACTING WITH MIGRANTS (THE CONSEQUENCES OF MIGRATION MANAGEMENT)

When custodial measures are put in place, it is not uncommon for the rights of migrants to be insufficiently guaranteed and to be damaged. An action for compensation can be envisaged, without it being necessary to wait for a situation as extreme as that on Manus Island, where riots had caused a death and many serious injuries, where migrants were deprived of access to medical care, where accommodation, food and

[22] In certain national laws, the surveillance and control activities exercised by the administration trigger the responsibility of the State only in case of gross negligence. See in French law, Jean-François Auby, 'Contrôle administratif: responsabilité à l'occasion de l'exercice du contrôle' (2017) *Répertoire Dalloz de la responsabilité de la puissance publique*. See also Corneloup (n 19) 180; and more generally, Fabrizio Marrella, 'Protection internationale des droits de l'homme et activités des sociétés transnationales' (2017) 385 *Collected Courses of the Hague Academy of International Law* 33, 105.

[23] See Marrella, ibid., 188.

[24] For an illustration before the European Court of Human Rights, see the application introduced in 2016 by 51 asylum seekers forcibly held in a hotspot in Greece: *Allaa Kaak ao v. Greece*, App no 34215/16. The applicants are represented by a lawyer from the French association for the defence of migrants GISTI.

security conditions were notoriously inadequate, etc. The legal regime of such an action varies according to the State (application of the common law, or of a special regime of administrative responsibility), the defendant (public or private entity, local company or foreign multinational), and the place of occurrence of the relevant facts. As part of the Manus Island class action, the international and private law perspective was particularly apparent: the action was brought before an Australian court for facts that had occurred exclusively abroad. It was directed against the Australian State and against various private service providers, in the apparent absence of a specific public law regime.

If the exercise of jurisdiction by the Australian court may not raise an eyebrow, given the action against the Australian State and various Australian companies, it might be more surprising, however, that, on the issue of the applicable law, there was no real debate: all the parties agreed on the principle of the *lex loci delicti* and, consequently, on the application of the Papuan law.[25] It was simply stated by one of the co-defendants that this did not prohibit the interpretation of Papua's substantive law in the light of the contractual clauses, in particular to determine the standard of conduct required and therefore the possible existence of a breach on the part of the service provider. This confirms the paramount importance of the contractual framework for immigration law today. From a methodological point of view, this approach, which consists in interpreting the applicable law in the light of the contract, reminds us of the method of taking foreign law into account as a matter of fact, well known in private international law. It would also allow to take into account certain requirements of Australian law to which the contracts referred to and which undeniably governed the activity of the Australian State as well as part of the activity of private providers.[26] The absence of a debate on the applicable law confirms, in fact, what has already been observed in other types of liability actions against multinationals. For example, in the proceedings relating to Shell's activities in Nigeria, the issue for the victims was to establish the jurisdiction of the courts of the country of the multinational's headquarters, while the application of Nigerian tort law was not really problematic in itself.[27] There is thus a certain 'fungibility' of private tort laws.[28] In terms of private international law methods, this leads to a very clear shift of the centre of gravity from the conflict of laws to international jurisdiction. The stakes at play on the determination of the forum are

25 In this field, important differences persist today between the legal systems, since we cannot imagine that the French State could see its responsibility towards migrants triggered on the basis of Turkish law for facts that would have taken place in a detention centre for asylum seekers in Turkey.

26 See, within the framework of the European Union, art. 17 of Regulation 864/2007 'Rome II', which however only envisages the rules of safety and behavior of the place of 'the event giving rise to the liability'. It does not seem possible to consider, for all the defendants, that this place was in this case in Australia.

27 See, in particular, the actions brought by Nigerian farmers before the Dutch courts: Court of Appeal of The Hague, 17 December 2015, *Dooh v. Shell* (ECLI:NL:GHDHA:2015:3586); *Shell v. Akpan* (ECLI:NL:GHDHA:2015:3587); *Oguru-Efanga v. Shell* (ECLI:NL:GHDHA: 2015:3588).

28 Subject, of course, to the cases where the local law of responsibility is manifestly insufficient. See Horatia Muir Watt, 'Globalization and Private International Law', in *Encyclopedia of Private International Law* (Cheltenham, Edward Elgar 2017).

paramount indeed – especially in the absence of independence of local justice or to guarantee the admissibility of class actions, an institution that many countries in the world do not accept, or admit only under very restrictive conditions. Moreover the issue of the competent forum is also paramount in view of the fact that amicable dispute settlement occupies a different role in various national legal cultures.

And it is here that appears the third variety of contractualisation in the area of immigration law. The class action of the Manus Island inmates was settled by an amicable agreement. To our knowledge, this is the first time, globally, that a group of migrants collectively receive damages in the context of an amicable settlement for the conditions of detention. Australia has thus contracted out all stages of the right of asylum. The role of the State court is therefore reduced, but nonetheless still existent, since the settlement was approved by the Supreme Court of Victoria. Such complete contractualisation would not be possible everywhere in the world. In countries such as France, State responsibility is subject to a derogatory public-law regime, in which mediation and amicable settlement are not practised – even if they are not completely inconceivable. The idea of an amicable solution appears in Europe so far mainly through the policy of regularisation of the status of individual migrants, which is implemented by the States in a discretionary way.[29] However, an amicable settlement with private providers would be possible, provided that migrants have sufficient bargaining power. However, this would imply modes of collective action that are currently unavailable.

At the time of writing, the outcome of this Australian case is still subject to some uncertainties, particularly as to the practical feasibility of fair compensation for all members of the group, some of whom have returned to their countries of origin, while others cannot be found or have died in the meantime. However, there is little doubt that the contractualisation of the management of international migration is not ready to stop. This global organisation of migratory flows through networks of contracts is accompanied by a withdrawal of public sovereignty, in particular the States of destination of migrants. Through the combined effect of externalisation and privatisation of the management of migratory flows, migrants leave the public field of vision in the States of destination. However, to allow democratic control and ensure the principle of accountability, it is now fundamental that this transnational governance by contract be integrated into the field of vision of the national laws of the States of destination. In our example, the class action made this possible, thereby reminding Australia of its obligations vis-à-vis the migrants it receives.

[29] See also the Grand Chamber decision *S.J. v. Belgium* App no 70055/10 (ECHR, 19 March 2015), where the Court notes that a 'friendly settlement' was concluded between the Belgian Government and the applicant, whose asylum application had been rejected by the Belgian authorities and who had seized the ECHR. In order to avoid a conviction under the ECHR, Belgium finally granted the applicant a residence permit of unlimited duration. Such regularizations, or waivers by the State to enforce a return decision in order to avoid a conviction for violation of the ECHR are not rare (see also *Khan v. Germany* App no 38030/12, ECHR, 21 September 2016), but it is nevertheless a form of 'friendly settlement' quite different from that concluded by Australia in the commented case.

27.3 CLASS ACTIONS IN THE CURRENT MIGRATION CONTEXT IN EUROPE: WITH OR WITHOUT PRIVATE INTERNATIONAL LAW?

Jinske Verhellen

The class action on behalf of refugees detained at Australia's offshore asylum seeker detention centre on Manus Island,[30] offers an opportunity for an exploratory reflection on group actions in the current migration context in Europe.

Group actions or group proceedings, in very different forms and models, are provided for in many countries. This contribution will not elaborate on group or class actions as such.[31] It will only explore whether specific problems ('injuries') in the field of migration law and at the crossroads between migration law and private international law could lead to group proceedings, in this instance the group being refugees and migrants with similar interests/injuries.

Mostly large (transnational) corporations are the targets of tort based collective proceedings: consumer cases, insurance, product liability or medical cases. In recent years, we have witnessed more and more 'collective vindication of the public interest',[32] as in environmental claims[33] or human rights suits. The Manus Island class action is an apt illustration of the last one.

In Europe, group proceedings to obtain remedy in the name of refugees and migrants are still scarce. In addition to the fact that group actions are 'procedurally' not always possible, a stumbling block for these actions is the lack of (public) sympathy for the group concerned.[34] In Europe we are indeed witnessing a foreigner-unfriendly climate. Nonetheless, or perhaps especially therefore, it is challenging to reflect on proceedings whereby certain organisations act on behalf of a similarly situated group of refugees or migrants in cases where the claims raise common factual and legal questions.

In this short contribution I would like to draw attention to a real – still pending – case in the Netherlands and to present (or draft) a purely hypothetical case: the former

---

30 See <https://www.supremecourt.vic.gov.au/law-and-practice/class-actions/manus-island-detention-centre-class-action>.

31 This is left to experts in the field: see for instance, Deborah R. Hensler, Christopher Hodges and Ianika Tzankova (eds.), *Class Actions in Context. How Culture, Economics and Politics Shape Collective Litigation* (Cheltenham, Edward Elgar 2016); Antonio Gidi, 'The class Action Code: A Model for Civil Law Countries' (2005) 23 *Arizona Journal of International and Comparative Law* 37 and <https://ssrn.com/abstract=930439>; Duncan Fairgrieve and Eva Lein (eds.), *Extraterritoriality and Collective Redress* (Oxford, Oxford University Press 2012) (with several contributions on class action from a private international law perspective); Ismaël Omarjee and Laurence Sinopoli (dir.), *Les actions en justice au-delà de l'intérêt personnel* (Paris, Dalloz 2014).

32 Horatia Muir Watt, 'Brussels I and Aggregate Litigation or the Case for Redesigning the Common Judicial Area in Order to Respond to Changing Dynamics, Functions and Structures in Contemporary Adjudication and Litigation' (2010) *IPRax* 111, 113.

33 Hans van Loon, 'The Global Horizon of Private International Law' (2016) 380 *Recueil des Cours* 82.

34 On societal responses to mass injury victims, see Deborah R. Hensler, 'Class actions in context', in Hensler, Hodges and Tzankova (n 31) 391.

is the Dutch group action for the relocation of asylum seekers from Greece to the Netherlands, the latter is a tentative case in the field of personal status and the lack of documentary evidence with regard to the age of unaccompanied migrant children. The first one illustrates the potential for group actions before civil courts in Europe in the field of asylum and migration law; the second one explores this potential for one concrete 'mass injury' at the crossroads between migration law and private international law.

1. RELOCATION OF ASYLUM SEEKERS FROM CAMPS IN GREECE TO THE NETHERLANDS

In 2017 in the Netherlands, a Foundation called 'We gaan ze halen'[35] took the Dutch State to court, arguing that the Netherlands has taken too few asylum seekers from Greece under the terms of the EU relocation and resettlement deal of 2015.[36]

Two decisions of the European Council were at stake: the Council Decision 2015/1523 of 14 September 2015[37] and the Council Decision 2015/1601 of 22 September 2015[38] establishing provisional measures in the area of international protection for the benefit of Italy and Greece. 'The provisional measures are intended to relieve the significant asylum pressure on Italy and on Greece, in particular by relocating a significant number of applicants in clear need of international protection who will have arrived in the territory of Italy or Greece' following the date on which these Decisions became applicable.[39] Both Council Decisions provide for the relocation of a certain number of applicants from Italy and Greece to other Member States (40,000[40] and 120,000[41]).

The Dutch Foundation was of the opinion that the Netherlands wasn't doing enough and started preliminary relief proceedings against the State, more specifically against the Dutch Ministry of Security and Justice. The claim was dismissed in the first instance.[42] However, the court accepted that a group action was possible. The Dutch State had argued that the claim was inadmissible because the interests defended by the Foundation do not lend themselves for 'collective bundling'. In this dispute, the Foundation acted as a statutory stakeholder for refugees in Greece, Italy and Turkey who qualify for relocation or resettlement. The Dutch Civil Code sets forth the

35 'We will fetch them'.

36 Commission (EU) 'A European Agenda on Migration' COM (2015) 240 final, 13 May 2015 and its implementation packages, see <https://ec.europa.eu/home-affairs/what-we-do/policies/european-agenda-migration/background-information_en> accessed 18 January 2018.

37 Council Decision (EU) 2015/1523 on establishing provisional measures in the area of international protection for the benefit of Italy and of Greece [2015] OJ L239/146.

38 Council Decision (EU) 2015/1601 on establishing provisional measures in the area of international protection for the benefit of Italy and Greece [2015] OJ L248/80.

39 Ibid., consid 26.

40 Council Decision 2015/1523 (n 37) art 4.

41 Council Decision 2015/1601 (n 38) art 4.

42 *Stichting We Gaan Ze Halen v. de Staat der Nederlanden* (24 March 2017) ECLI:NL:RB-DHA:2017:2809 <www.rechtspraak.nl>

conditions under which a foundation can institute legal proceedings with the aim to prevent the interests of other people. One of the preconditions for such a collective action is that it must be about similar interests,[43] which entails that the interests must lend themselves for bundling. The court was – contrary to the State – of the opinion that this precondition had been met. According to the court there is no question of divergent interests: 'The Foundation advocates for those refugees in the above mentioned countries with an interest of housing in the Netherlands.'[44] The State rightly pointed out that the refugees in this case did not constitute a clearly defined group, however, the Dutch law does not lay down such a requirement. The court ruled that 'even far-reaching group actions like general interest actions are allowed, whereby an individualization of the people whose interests are at stake is in any way not possible'.[45] In the field of migration law, the conclusion of the court is challenging: a group action can be lodged even if the group of people whose interests are at stake, cannot be clearly defined.

The Foundation lodged an appeal against this decision. The decision of the Hague Court of Appeal[46] also is instructive from the perspective of group proceedings in the field of asylum and migration law.

The Court makes it very clear that the question how the State shapes its migration policy is primarily a political question that requires political consideration. In making that assessment, the State has a wide policy freedom.

> The margin for the civil judge to take action within that policy freedom by ordering the State to actively achieve that a fixed number of asylum seekers comes to the Netherlands, is therefore limited. This could only be different when there exist provisions of European Union law or (other) international or legal provisions by which the State is bound and that introduce enforceable rights for third parties. The question if the State in the light of such provisions still has policy freedom depends on the content of those provisions and the obligations that derive from it for the State.[47]

Subsequently, the Hague Court focuses on the question of the direct effect of the abovementioned Council Decisions. A provision of a decision addressed to a Member State could be invoked by a citizen against that Member State, when the said provision imposes on the Member State an unconditional and sufficiently clear and precise obligation. According to the Court, the amount of asylum seekers mentioned in the two Council Decisions is based on 'an expectation' with regard to the influx of asylum seekers. The Court considers that

> the fact that the numbers recorded in the Decisions (i) are based on the influx of asylum seekers in the past, even though they predominately have an effect on asylum seekers who reach Italy and Greece after the entry into force of the Decisions and (ii) primarily aim at

[43] Art 3:305a Civil Code.

[44] *Stichting We Gaan Ze Halen* (n 42) [4.3] (own translation from Dutch).

[45] Ibid., [4.3] (own translation from Dutch).

[46] *Stichting We Gaan Ze Halen v. de Staat der Nederlanden* (20 June 2017) ECLI:NL:GHDHA:2017:1664 <www.rechtspraak.nl>.

[47] Ibid., [7] (own translation from Dutch).

> relieving Italy and Greece, constitutes an important indication that the therein recorded numbers do not create an absolute obligation upon Member States irrespective of the actual influx.[48]

Instead, the Court continues, they impose on Member States an obligation depending on the actual number of the registered asylum seekers eligible for relocation. Hence, it is obvious that when the predictions on which the numbers were based fail to come true, the actual number of asylum seekers who need to be relocated will also be modified. According to the Court the numbers in the Council Decisions are 'estimations and not well-defined obligations'.[49] Therefore, it cannot be concluded that the Decisions impose an unconditional and a sufficiently clear and precise obligation on the State. The Court concludes that the Decisions do not have direct effect making it impossible for the Foundation to enforce the compliance of the Decisions in the present interim proceedings.[50]

Even in the absence of tangible results, this Dutch case is not without any importance within the current migration context in Europe. First, it shows the potential for 'general interest actions' in the field of asylum and migration law, at least in The Netherlands. Second, the following interesting passage in the decision of the Hague Court of Appeal reveals that Dutch civil courts do not exclude their role in this field: 'it is not impossible that under circumstances there would be room for actions by the civil judge, when with a certain obviousness it would be established that the State would not comply with its obligations or would obviously fail in some other way.'[51]

So far, we mainly witnessed 'migration group actions' outside of Europe: in Argentina,[52] Australia, the United States,[53] etc. All these group or class actions challenged government behaviour in a variety of asylum and migration law settings: in the Manus Island case the degrading detention conditions and false imprisonment of refugees; in the US the practice to deny refugees the right to seek protection in the US[54] or the laws that block refugees seeking resettlement to the US.[55]

Within this challenging context of migration group proceedings the interactions between private international law and migration law should not remain out of sight. Indeed, mass injuries at the crossroads between migration law and private international law can be identified. In the next point, I will make an exploratory attempt to devise the

---

48 Ibid., [12] (own translation from Dutch).

49 Ibid., [16] (own translation from Dutch).

50 Ibid., [17] (own translation from Dutch).

51 Ibid., [20] (own translation from Dutch).

52 Lila García, 'Argentina's Migration Law: Changes Challenging the Human Right to Migrate' (11 September 2017) <https://www.law.ox.ac.uk/research-subject-groups/centre-criminology/centreborder-criminologies/blog/2017/09/argentinas> accessed 9 January 2018.

53 Jill E. Family, 'Threats to the Future of Immigration Class Action' (2008) 27 *Washington University Journal of Law and Policy* 71.

54 See e.g. the class action lawsuit that challenges the practice of turning away asylum seekers at US Southern border <https://ccrjustice.org/home/what-we-do/our-cases/al-otro-lado>, accessed 9 January 2018.

55 National Immigration Law Center 'Groups File Class Action Challenge to Trump Administration's Latest Refugee Ban' (13 November 2017) <https://www.nilc.org/2017/11/13/class-action-challenges-latest-refugee-ban> accessed 9 January 2018.

outlines of a possible group action at this crossroads, more specifically one that relates to the denial of protection to unaccompanied migrant children.

2. UNACCOMPANIED MIGRANT CHILDREN: TOWARDS A HARMONISED PRESUMPTION OF MINORITY?

One of the legal problems encountered by refugees and migrants (both in transit and at their arrival in Europe) is the absence of (authentic) documentary evidence, and thus the inadequate cross-border portability of their personal status (age, parental status, marital status, etc.). This short contribution will only focus on one specific group, the unaccompanied migrant children, and on one specific problem, the lack of documentary evidence with regard to their age.[56]

The number of children that migrate unaccompanied and separated from their parents has been increasing worldwide.[57] In a recent Joint General Comment, the Committee on the Rights of the Child and the Committee on the Protection of the Rights of all Migrant Workers stress that States should ensure that 'anyone claiming to be a child is treated as such, promptly referred to child protection authorities and other relevant services, and appointed a guardian if unaccompanied or separated'.[58]

However fine-sounding this recommendation may be, 'claiming to be a child' suffices by no means. The protection of unaccompanied migrant children depends on the proof of their age.[59] A guardian, for instance, will only be appointed if minority is demonstrated; age often is a deciding factor in the access to education and healthcare, in the success of an asylum application, etc. It is particularly here that a private international law hurdle arises: age is often not known or cannot be evidenced because birth certificates do not exist or have never been issued in the country of birth, children have lost their birth certificates or foreign personal status documents are (considered to

---

[56] For more topics, see Jinske Verhellen, 'Cross-Border Portability of Refugees' Personal Status' (2018) *Journal of Refugee Studies* <https://doi.org/10.1093/jrs/fex026>; Jinske Verhellen, 'La portabilité transfrontalière du statut personnel des réfugiés' (2017) *Rev.crit.DIP* 173.

[57] See <http://www.ohchr.org/EN/HRBodies/CRC/Pages/CMWCRCContextofInternational Migration.aspx>. For Europe, see information issued by Eurostat, 'Almost 90 000 unaccompanied minors among asylum seekers registered in the EU in 2015' (Press release) (2 May 2016) <http://ec.europa.eu/eurostat/documents/2995521/7244677/3-02052016-AP-EN.pdf> accessed 18 January 2018. For child migration from Central America to the United States, see the excellent work of the novelist and essayist Valeria Luiselli, *Tell Me How It Ends. An Essay in Forty Questions* (Minneapolis MN, Coffee House Press 2017).

[58] Joint general comment No. 3 of the Committee on the Protection of the Rights of All Migrant Workers and Members of Their Families and of the Committee on the Rights of the Child on the Human Rights of Children in the Context of International Migration (2017) <http://www.ohchr.org/EN/HRBodies/CRC/Pages/CMWCRCContextofInternationalMigration.aspx> accessed 18 January 2018.

[59] See also, UNHCR and UNICEF 'The Way Forward to Strengthened Policies and Practices for Unaccompanied and Separated Children in Europe' (Report) (10 July 2017) 9–12.

be) unreliable.[60] Migration authorities 'routinely suspect children in these circumstances of saying they are younger than they are to receive more lenient treatment'.[61] Without proof of their minority, those children often do not stand a chance. They can be considered as victims of 'mass injury' if no legal solutions are provided for.

In several European countries alternative methods to prove minority exist. It is, nonetheless, very striking to ascertain how different the national age assessment methods and procedures are.[62] In some countries, minority is presumed until the contrary is proven.[63] In other countries, migration and other authorities easily rely on medical examinations.[64] In other countries, emphasis is put on a more pedagogical and cultural approach before turning to medical testing, such as interviewing the child in the presence of a cultural mediator, experienced staff of youth welfare offices, etc.[65] These differences 'have resulted in discordant decisions on the age of the individuals and disruptions in the provision of care and protection' to unaccompanied migrant children.[66]

In the study 'Children on the Move: A Private International Law Perspective' for the European Parliament, several private international law scholars recommended that uniformity of age assessment procedures within the European Union is an urgent matter.[67] Recently, UNHCR and UNICEF also called (again) for harmonised age assessment across Europe.[68] To this day, we are still far from this uniformity. Moreover, different EU Regulations and Directives even reflect this lack of consistency. On the one hand, there is the approach of presumption of minority which can be found in

---

[60] In some countries, for instance, in order to obtain a birth certificate parents have to wait until the authorities come to their village, which occurs for instance twice a year. As a result, birth certificates from those countries only have January or June as birth months, which may lead to suspicion of fraud and to the discussion whether a person is still a minor or not. Similar problems can occur when children come from countries that use another era (for instance the Persian calendar).

[61] See <https://www.crin.org/en/home/what-we-do/policy/childrens-rights-and-refugee-crisis/problem/rights-not-charity> accessed 18 January 2018.

[62] Sabine Corneloup, Bettina Heiderhoff, Costanza Honorati, Fabienne Jault-Seseke, Thalia Kruger, Caroline Rupp, Hans van Loon and Jinske Verhellen, 'Private International Law in a Context of Increasing International Mobility: Challenges and Potential' (Study) (June 2017) 14–18 <http://www.europarl.europa.eu/committees/en/juri/events-workshops.html?id=20170607WKS00621> accessed 18 January 2018. See also UNHCR and UNICEF (n 59) 9.

[63] See for instance Article 388 of the French Civil Code, as amended in 2016.

[64] Under the Belgian Guardianship Law, the Federal Guardianship Service within the Federal Public Service Justice, which is responsible for designating guardians for unaccompanied minors, decides whether or not a person has attained the age of majority. If the Guardianship Service or the asylum and migration authorities have reasonable doubts as to the age of the person concerned, the Guardianship Service immediately orders a medical (skeletal and dental age) examination by a doctor.

[65] As is the case in Germany and Italy, see Corneloup et al. (n 62) 16–18.

[66] UNHCR and UNICEF (n 59) 9.

[67] Sabine Corneloup, Bettina Heiderhoff, Costanza Honorati, Fabienne Jault-Seseke, Thalia Kruger, Caroline Rupp, Hans van Loon and Jinske Verhellen, 'Children on the Move: A Private International Law Perspective' (Study) (June 2017) 38 <http://www.europarl.europa.eu/committees/en/juri/events-workshops.html?id=20170607WKS00621> accessed 18 January 2018.

[68] UNHCR and UNICEF (n 59) 9–12.

Article 13.2 of the Anti-Trafficking Directive 2011/36/EU.[69] On the other hand, instruments within the framework of the Common European Asylum System (CEAS) (over)value medical examinations, for instance Article 25.5 of the Asylum Procedures Directive 2013/32[70] and Article 24.1 of the Commission's Proposal of 13 June 2016 replacing this Directive with a Regulation.[71]

It would be an important, even essential step forward to follow the same approach in all EU instruments and across Europe. Taking into account the ongoing controversy over the use of medical procedures for age assessment,[72] a harmonised approach should include a systematic use of giving the benefit of the doubt.[73] The Committee on the Rights of the Child and the Committee on the Protection of the Rights of all Migrant Workers recently cautioned

> against age determination methods based on, inter alia, bone analysis, that are flawed and inaccurate with wide margins of error. States should refrain from using these methods. The Committees remind States that age determination processes should be a measure of last resort and be carried out in a prompt, child-friendly, gender sensitive, culturally appropriate and multi-disciplinary manner, and be conducted by child protection officials or officials with

---

69 'Member States shall ensure that, where the age of a person subject to trafficking in human beings is uncertain and there are reasons to believe that the person is a child, that person is presumed to be a child in order to receive immediate access to assistance, support and protection' Council and European Parliament Directive (EU) 2011/36 on preventing and combating trafficking in human beings and protecting its victims, and replacing Council Framework Decision 2002/629/JHA [2011] OJ L 101/1.

70 'Member States may use medical examinations to determine the age of unaccompanied minors within the framework of the examination of an application for international protection where, following general statements or other relevant indications, Member States have doubts concerning the applicant's age. If, thereafter, Member States are still in doubt concerning the applicant's age, they shall assume that the applicant is a minor.' Council and European Parliament Directive (EU) 2013/32 on common procedures for granting and withdrawing international protection (recast) [2013] OJ L 180/60.

71 Article 24.1 confirms the same order: first medical examinations and where 'the result of the medical examination is not conclusive, or includes an age-range below 18 years, Member States shall assume that the applicant is a minor.' It should be noted that the proposed Article 24.1 also refers to psychosocial assessments. See Commission (EU), 'Proposal for a Regulation of the European Parliament and of the Council establishing a common procedure for international protection in the Union and repealing Directive 2013/32/EU' COM (2016) 467 final, 13 July 2017.

72 See amongst others, Pieter J.J. Sauer, Alf Nicholson and David Neubauer 'Age determination in asylum seekers: physicians should not be implicated' (2016) 175 (3) *European Journal of Pediatrics* 299; Vivien Feltz, 'Age assessment for unaccompanied minors. When European countries deny children their childhood' (28 August 2015) 17, https://www.google.com/search?q=Vivien+Feltz%2C+%E2%80%98Age+assessment+for+unaccompanied+minors.+When+European+countries+deny+children+their+childhood%E2%80%99%2C+28+August+2015%2C+17&ie=utf-8&oe=utf-8&client=firefox-b; Katja Fournier, 'L'estimation de l'âge des MENA en question: problématique, analyse et recommendations' (September 2017) 7 <http://www.liguedh.be/les-documents-des-commissions-thematiques/2909-lestimation-de-lage-des-mena-en-question-problematique-analyse-et-recommandations> accessed 18 January 2018.

73 UNHCR and UNICEF (n 59) 9.

> sufficient and relevant expertise and training. The benefit of the doubt should always be given to the individual being assessed.[74]

As the Anti-Trafficking Directive is stronger and more child-centred and as there is no guarantee that article 25.5 and the future 24.1 of the above-mentioned CEAS instruments will be applied in a uniform manner in all Member States,[75] the approach of presumption of minority is to be supported. This is, of course, a political decision to be taken by the European legislator. A group action before a civil court (in the Netherlands?) could transcend this political and legislative context of opposing interests (children as victims of trafficking versus children as migrants) and challenge the lack of uniformity in order to ensure unaccompanied migrant children a better access to justice and adequate civil protection. Refugee and migrant children are first and foremost children. They cannot be deprived of their rights due to the differences in age assessment methods across Europe.

One could raise the question whether a group action is the 'procedurally' correct way forward. Indeed, in cases where there is a (reasonable) doubt regarding the age of a person, individual litigation before civil courts is possible. And private international law rules on international jurisdiction and applicable law are there: age assessment falls within the scope of civil protection of children and thus within the scope of application of the 1996 Hague Child Protection Convention.[76] However, thinking – be it completely out of the box – in terms of a more collective approach should not be ruled out. Even without a fully-developed procedural framework for collective proceedings (both at the EU and national level), this specific group with a well-defined common interest must be given a voice. When children arrive in Europe without proper documentation in support of their stated age, they are in an extremely vulnerable position. So, instead of keeping a migration-policy driven focus on age determination, a way forward might be 'to move away from the chronological age of the individual and instead to consider the

---

[74] Joint general comment of the Committee on the Protection of the Rights of All Migrant Workers and Members of Their Families and of the Committee on the Rights of the Child on the Human Rights of Children in the Context of International Migration (2017) <http://www.ohchr.org/EN/HRBodies/CRC/Pages/CMWCRCContextofInternationalMigration.aspx> accessed 18 January 2018.

[75] Article 24.6 of the Commission's proposal replacing the Asylum Procedures Directive with a Regulation stipulates that a Member State 'shall recognise age assessment decisions taken by other Member States on the basis of a medical examination carried out in accordance with this Article and based on methods which are recognised under its national law'. At first sight, this proposal sounds attractive. It is indeed of crucial importance that the results of an age determination in a Member State are accepted by other authorities, both within that Member State and in all other Member States. But again, methods of age assessment procedures are left to national law with the risk of (major) differences and this Commission's proposal still illustrates an over-reliance on the use of medical age assessments.

[76] Article 3d of the Hague Convention on Jurisdiction, Applicable Law, Recognition, Enforcement and Co-operation in Respect of Parental Responsibility and Measures for the Protection of Children (19 October 1996) refers to measures that relate to the designation and functions of any person or body having charge of the child's person or property, representing or assisting the child. For the text of the Convention <https://www.hcch.net/en/instruments/conventions>.

need for support'.[77] The need for support and protection is a human right. According to Article 22 of the 1989 Convention on the Rights of the Child, States have to take appropriate measures to ensure that a child who is seeking asylum or who is considered a refugee shall, whether unaccompanied or accompanied by his or her parents or by any other person, receive appropriate protection and assistance. Whether there is proof or no proof of age, 'children are human *beings* and therefore entitled to all human rights. Children do not need to be *given* rights, they *have* them'.[78] If majority cannot be confirmed with absolute certainty because there are no birth certificates or only copies or fraudulent documents, anyone claiming to be a child should be treated as such.[79] Advancing towards a presumption of minority as a necessary precondition for exercising fundamental rights – a presumption which may always be rebutted in the child's best interest – can be defined as a clear and precise obligation on the Member States. Organizations such as Defence for Children International[80] or the European NGO-network 'Separated Children in Europe Programme' (SCEP)[81] should explore whether, how and where it is possible to act on behalf of a number of unaccompanied migrant children and to bring a group case to the civil court … even if only to challenge the status quo.[82]

---

77 Sauer, Nicholson and Neubauer (n 72) 299.

78 Eugeen Verhellen, 'The Convention on the Rights of the Child' in Wouter Vandenhole, Ellen Desmet, Didier Reynaert and Sara Lembrechts (eds.), *Routledge International Handbook of Children's Rights Studies* (Abingdon, Routledge 2015) 46.

79 The following decision of the Austrian Constitutional Court could be a source of inspiration: Verfassungsgerichtshof (7 March 2012) U1558/11 <http://www.asylumlawdatabase.eu/en/case-law/austria-constitutional-court-7-march-2012-u155811> accessed 18 January 2018. In this case a young man, claiming to be 17 years old, applied for asylum in Austria after entering Europe via Italy. His asylum claim was rejected on grounds of the Dublin Regulation and an expulsion order to Italy was issued. The Austrian Federal Asylum Office did not accept the copy of the applicant's birth certificate and thus the documentary proof that he was a minor. The Constitutional Court ruled that the majority age had not been confirmed with absolute certainty and the applicant should therefore have been treated as a minor. The fact that only a copy of the birth certificate was submitted was not a sufficient base to doubt its authenticity.

80 See <https://defenceforchildren.org>.

81 At a SCEP meeting in the Netherlands (January 2017) one of the main topics of discussion was the age assessment practices of countries. 'From the meeting it became clear that the rights of separated children continue to be under threat. Major concerns were raised about the fact that some countries do not apply accurate criteria in assessing the age of a child and allow unqualified individuals to conduct the assessments. As a result, many separated children lose their rights to proper housing, a guardian and school. Some are even kept in detention under the suspicion of being adults.' <http://www.scepnetwork.org/p/1/217/mo8-cgltxt=*age%20assessment*/scep-network-meeting-in-the-netherlands> accessed 18 January 2018.

82 Or as Hensler puts it: 'By providing mechanisms for mobilizing the less powerful in a society, collective litigation procedures have the potential to disrupt the power structure.', see Hensler (n 34) 401.

3. A REFLECTION IN PROGRESS

The Manus Island case initiated this modest exploratory reflection on group proceedings to obtain remedy in the name of refugees and migrants. It is not the most obvious group action subject-matter. This process of reflection on group actions in the field of migration law and at the crossroads between migration law and private international law will continue. Group actions could challenge migration practices which would not be possible in individual hearings.[83] After all, there are many challenges in the current migration context. Proof of age is just one of the many private international law issues relating to the recognition of facts and documents concerning migrants' and refugees' personal status. Let's hope that private international law does not remain on the sideline. Cross-border portability of personal status is at the heart of our discipline and of crucial importance in a migration context.

---

[83] Family (n 53) 75.

Index